Introduction to Health Care Management

Second Edition

Edited by

Sharon B. Buchbinder, RN, PhD
President
American Hospital Management Group Corporation
MASA Healthcare Co.
Owings Mills, MD

Nancy H. Shanks, PhD
Professor
Department of Health Professions
Health Care Management Program
Metropolitan State College of Denver
Denver, CO

JONES & BARTLETT
LEARNING

World Headquarters

Jones & Bartlett Learning	Jones & Bartlett Learning	Jones & Bartlett Learning
5 Wall Street	Canada	International
Burlington, MA 01803	6339 Ormindale Way	Barb House, Barb Mews
978-443-5000	Mississauga, Ontario L5V 1J2	London W6 7PA
info@jblearning.com	Canada	United Kingdom
www.jblearning.com		

Jones & Bartlett Learning books and products are available through most bookstores and online booksellers. To contact Jones & Bartlett Learning directly, call 800-832-0034, fax 978-443-8000, or visit our website, www.jblearning.com.

Substantial discounts on bulk quantities of Jones & Bartlett Learning publications are available to corporations, professional associations, and other qualified organizations. For details and specific discount information, contact the special sales department at Jones & Bartlett Learning via the above contact information or send an email to specialsales@jblearning.com.

Production Credits
Publisher: Michael Brown
Associate Editor: Maro Gartside
Editorial Assistant: Teresa Reilly
Production Manager: Tracey McCrea
Senior Marketing Manager: Sophie Fleck
Manufacturing and Inventory Control Supervisor: Amy Bacus
Composition: Cenveo Publisher Services
Cover Design: Scott Moden
Cover Image: © Yegor Korzh/ShutterStock, Inc.
Printing and Binding: Malloy, Inc.
Cover Printing: Malloy, Inc.

Library of Congress Cataloging-in-Publication Data
Introduction to health care management / [edited by] Sharon Buchbinder, Nancy Shanks. -- 2nd ed.
　　p. ; cm.
　Includes bibliographical references and index.
　ISBN-13: 978-0-7637-9086-8 (pbk.)
　ISBN-10: 0-7637-9086-9 (pbk.)
　1. Health services administration. I. Buchbinder, Sharon Bell. II. Shanks, Nancy H.
　[DNLM: 1. Health Services Administration. 2. Efficiency, Organizational. 3. Health Care Costs.
4. Leadership. 5. Organizational Case Studies. W 84.1]
　RA971.I58 2012
　362.1—dc23
　　　　　　　　　　　　　2011013461

6048
Printed in the United States of America
15 14 13 12　　　10 9 8 7 6 5 4 3

We dedicate this book to our loving husbands,
Dale Buchbinder and Rick Shanks—
Who coached, collaborated, and coerced us to
"FINISH THE SECOND EDITION!"

Contents

FOREWORD. xv
PREFACE. xvii
ACKNOWLEDGMENTS xxi
ABOUT THE EDITORS. xxiii
CONTRIBUTORS xxv

CHAPTER 1   **An Overview of Healthcare Management**. 1
*Jon M. Thompson, Sharon B. Buchbinder, and
Nancy H. Shanks*

Introduction. 1
The Need for Managers and Their Perspectives 2
Management: Definition, Functions, and Competencies 4
Management Positions: The Control in
the Organizational Hierarchy. 6
Focus of Management: Self, Unit/Team, and Organization 8
Role of the Manager in Talent Management 9
Role of the Manager in Ensuring High Performance 10
Role of the Manager in Succession Planning 12
Role of the Manager in Healthcare Policy 13
Chapter Summary 13

CHAPTER 2   **Leadership** 17
Louis Rubino

Leadership vs. Management 17
Followership. 19
History of Leadership in the United States. 20
Contemporary Models 22

Leadership Styles 26

Leadership Competencies 27

Leadership Protocols 27

Governance 29

Barriers and Challenges 31

Ethical Responsibility 32

Leaders Looking to the Future 33

CHAPTER 3   **Management and Motivation** **39**
Nancy H. Shanks and Amy Dore

Introduction 39

Motivated vs. Engaged—Are the Terms the Same? 40

Motivation—The Concept 40

Why Motivation Matters 41

History of Motivation 42

Theories of Motivation 43

A Bit More about Incentives and Rewards 47

Misconceptions about Motivation and Employee Satisfaction 48

Motivational Strategies 50

Motivating Across Generations 51

Conclusion 52

CHAPTER 4   **Organizational Behavior and Management Thinking** **57**
Sheila K. McGinnis

Introduction 57

The Field of Organizational Behavior 58

Organizational Behavior's Contribution to Management 58

Key Topics in Organizational Behavior 59

Organizational Behavior Issues in Health Organizations 59

How Thinking Influences Organizational Behavior 60

Managing and Learning 69

How to Work with Thinking 70

Conclusions 73

CHAPTER 5 **Strategic Planning** 77
Susan Judd Casciani

Introduction. 77

Purpose and Importance of Strategic Planning. 78

The Planning Process. 78

SWOT Analysis 80

Strategy Identification and Selection 86

Rollout and Implementation 88

Outcomes Monitoring and Control 89

Strategy Execution 90

Strategic Planning and Execution: The Role of
the Healthcare Manager 92

Conclusion. 92

CHAPTER 6 **Healthcare Marketing.** 95
Ruth Chavez and Nancy Sayre

Introduction. 95

What Is Marketing? 96

A Brief History of Marketing in Health Care 98

The Strategic Marketing Process 100

Understanding Marketing Management. 102

Healthcare Buyer Behavior. 105

Marketing Mix 107

Marketing Plan. 108

Ethics and Social Responsibility 108

Conclusion. 108

CHAPTER 7 **Quality Improvement Basics** 113
Eric S. Williams, Grant T. Savage, and Dennis G. Stambaugh

Introduction. 113

Defining Quality in Health Care 114

Why Is Quality Important? 115

Key Leaders in Quality Improvement. 117

Baldrige Award Criteria: A Strategic Framework for
Quality Improvement.................................. 118
Common Elements of Quality Improvement 120
Two Approaches to Quality Improvement 122
Quality Improvement Tools............................. 125
Conclusion... 129

CHAPTER 8   **Information Technology** 133
            Tressa Springmann
            Introduction.. 133
            Information Systems Used by Managers.................... 134
            The Electronic Medical Record (EMR) 136
            The Challenges to Clinical System Adoption 139
            The Future of Healthcare Information Technology (HIT):
            The Vision of an Integrated U.S. Healthcare System 141
            The Impact of Information Technology on
            the Healthcare Manager............................... 142
            Conclusion... 143

CHAPTER 9   **Financing Health Care and Health Insurance** 147
            Nancy H. Shanks
            Introduction.. 147
            Introduction to Health Insurance....................... 150
            Brief History of Health Insurance 150
            Characteristics of Health Insurance 152
            Private Health Insurance Coverage....................... 155
            The Evolution of Social Insurance 159
            Major "Players" in the Social Insurance Arena 162
            Statistics on Health Insurance Coverage and Costs............ 173
            Those Not Covered—The Uninsured 175
            Conclusion... 178

CHAPTER 10   Managing Costs and Revenues **183**
Kevin D. Zeiler

Introduction 184
What Is Financial Management and Why Is It Important? 184
Tax Status of Healthcare Organizations 185
Financial Governance and Responsibility Structure 186
Managing Reimbursements from Third-Party Payers 188
Controlling Costs and Cost Accounting 194
Setting Charges 196
Managing Working Capital 197
Managing Accounts Receivable 199
Managing Materials and Inventory 200
Managing Budgets 203
Conclusion 206

CHAPTER 11   Managing Healthcare Professionals **211**
Sharon B. Buchbinder and Dale Buchbinder

Introduction 211
Physicians 212
Registered Nurses 224
Licensed Practical Nurses/Licensed Vocational Nurses 232
Nursing and Psychiatric Aides 232
Home Health Aides 234
Midlevel Practitioners 234
Allied Health Professionals 237
Conclusion 239

CHAPTER 12   The Strategic Management of Human Resources **249**
Jon M. Thompson

Introduction 249
Environmental Forces Affecting Human
Resources Management 251

Understanding Employees as Drivers of
Organizational Performance............................254

Key Functions of Human Resources Management............255

Workforce Planning/Recruitment 256

Employee Retention.................................264

Conclusion..281

CHAPTER 13 Teamwork 287
Sharon B. Buchbinder and Jon M. Thompson

Introduction.......................................287

What Is a Team? 288

The Challenge of Teamwork in
Healthcare Organizations.............................290

The Benefits of Effective Healthcare Teams 292

The Costs of Teamwork..............................294

Real-World Problems and Teamwork 297

Who's on the Team? 298

Emotions and Teamwork.............................300

Team Communication...............................302

Methods of Managing Teams of
Healthcare Professionals.............................303

Conclusion..306

CHAPTER 14 Addressing Health Disparities: Cultural Proficiency 313
Nancy Sayre and Ruth Chavez

Introduction.......................................313

Changing U.S. Demographics and Patient Populations 317

Addressing Health Disparities by Fostering Cultural
Competence in Healthcare Organizations 318

Best Practices 321

Addressing Health Disparities by Enhancing Public Policy 327

Conclusion..328

CHAPTER 15 **Ethics and Law** 333
Kevin D. Zeiler

Introduction 333

Legal Concepts 335

Tort Law 338

Malpractice 339

Contract Law 340

Ethical Concepts 341

Patient and Provider Rights and Responsibilities 343

Legal/Ethical Concerns in Managed Care 345

Biomedical Concerns 346

Beginning- and End-of-Life Care 347

Conclusion 347

CHAPTER 16 **Fraud and Abuse** 351
Kevin D. Zeiler

Introduction 351

What Is Fraud and Abuse? 352

History 352

The Social Security Act and the Criminal-Disclosure Provision ... 354

The Emergency Medical Treatment and Active Labor Act 355

Antitrust Issues 357

Physician Self-Referral/Anti-Kickback/Safe Harbor Laws 358

Management Responsibility for Compliance and
Internal Controls 361

Corporate Compliance Programs 361

Conclusion 363

CHAPTER 17 **Healthcare Management Case Studies and Guidelines** 367
Sharon B. Buchbinder, Donna M. Cox, and Susan Judd Casciani

Introduction 367

Case Study Analysis 368

Case Study Write-Up 370

Team Structure and Process for Completion 372

CASE STUDIES* 375

Oops Is Not an Option—Case for Chapter 16 375

Building a Better MIS-Trap—Case for Chapter 8 377

The Case of the Complacent Employee—Case
for Chapter 12 379

The Brawler—Case for Chapters 11 and 12 382

End Days—Case for Chapter 15 384

I Love You…Forever—Case for Chapters 12 and 11 386

Managing Healthcare Professionals—Mini-Case
Studies for Chapter 11 388

Problems with the Pre-Admission Call Center—Case for
Chapters 13 and 10 390

Such a Nice Young Man—Case for Chapters 11 and 12 392

Sundowner or Victim?—Case for Chapter 15 394

All Children's Pediatrics: Changing with the Times—
Case for Chapter 6 396

High Employee Turnover at Hillcrest Memorial Hospital—
Case for Chapter 3 399

Set Up for Failure?—Case for Chapter 3 401

Negotiation in Action—Case for Chapter 10* 403

The Merger of Two Competing Hospitals—Case for
Chapters 5, 2, and 12 406

Sexual Harassment at the Diabetes Clinic—Case for
Chapters 12 and 15* 412

Prelude to a Medical Error—Case for
Chapters 4 and 7 416

The Finance Department at Roseville Community
Hospital—Case for Chapters 4 and 10 418

Madison Community Hospital Addresses Infection Control
Prevention—Case for Chapter 7* 419

Seaside Convalescent Care Center—Case
for Chapters 13 and 3 422

Staffing at River Oaks Community Hospital: Measure Twice,
Cut Once—Case for Chapter 12*. 424

Heritage Valley Medical Center: Are Your Managers Culturally
Competent?—Case for Chapters 14 and 13 430

Emotional Intelligence in Labor and Delivery—
Case for Chapters 2 and 13 434

Are We Culturally Aware or Not?—Case for
Chapters 14 and 5 436

A Nightmare Job Interview—Case for
Chapter 12. 438

A Small Healthcare Clinic Confronts Health Insurance
Problems—Case for Chapter 9. 441

Choosing a Successor—Case for
Chapters 1 and 2 444

The New Toy at City Medical Center—Case for
Chapters 11 and 13 449

The "Easy" Software Upgrade at Delmar Ortho—Case for
Chapters 8 and 13 451

Recruitment Challenge for the Middle Manager—
Case for Chapter 12 454

Humor Strategies in Healthcare Management Education—
Case for Chapter 14 455

Medication Errors Reporting at Community
Memorial Hospital—Case for Chapter 7 459

Dr. Nugget's Medical Practice—Case
for Chapter 15 465

Fraud and Abuse—Help Me, the Feds
Are Coming!—Case for Chapter 16 468

Managing Costs and Revenues at Happy Town
Neurology—Case for Chapter 10* 471

INDEX. 475

*Instructors: Please note that an instructor's guide is available online for these cases.

Foreword

Undergraduate healthcare management education is now recognized as a significant component of the healthcare delivery matrix. The evolution of undergraduate healthcare management education has been pushed for a disparate number of reasons in the dynamic healthcare field. One of the primary factors has been the recognition by leaders and administrators of healthcare delivery that a need exists for entry-level managers who have the basic business and healthcare educational knowledge, skills, and competencies to fill a variety of roles. These entry-level positions are found in almost all healthcare delivery settings, including hospitals, long-term care facilities, medical group practices, governmental agencies, home healthcare agencies, and insurance institutions—just to name a few. Undergraduate programs across the United States have seen their enrollments increase significantly in response to this recognition. The parallel recognition by potential students that healthcare management provides an almost unequaled opportunity for employment has also been instrumental in this growth.

The growth and development has been encouraging, but not absent of challenges. Over the past decade, we have struggled with program development, curriculum issues, certification ambiguities, and meaningful outcome measures. Fortunately, we have turned the corner on most of these and are seeing great progress in achieving excellence in our programs. The one remaining and often discussed impediment to achieving greater excellence is the lack of an array of textbooks that fit undergraduate curricula and missions. In my role as chair of the Undergraduate Program Committee of the Association of University Programs in Health Administration (AUPHA), I have significant contact with many of the undergraduate program directors and faculty. The one recurrent theme that I hear from them is that there is a lack of well-written and crafted textbooks suitable for undergraduate education. The majority of the textbooks written in the field have until recently been geared toward graduate education. Instructors in undergraduate programs have been forced to try to adapt these texts to an audience for which they were not intended.

As enrollment in the undergraduate programs has increased, an obvious market has developed for appropriate textbooks. Some progress has been made in this direction, but there still exists a void in many subject areas. Arguably, one of the most important texts sought by educators in this field was a comprehensive introduction to the areas of healthcare management education. The first edition of this textbook satisfied this need by providing an excellent treatment of most key areas. This second edition provides an even better overview by introducing new items and allowing the reader to be kept abreast of the most current developments in the field.

A necessary ingredient for the successful production of a textbook that has exceptional value is that the authors and editors possess a true understanding of all facets of undergraduate healthcare management education. Sharon Buchbinder and Nancy Shanks have developed mastery of this process because of their total immersion in it. Both exemplify the "boots on the ground" approach as they have been involved in administering undergraduate programs, teaching in them, and serving AUPHA in a great variety of capacities.

The measure of an excellent textbook is whether it has created a union of content, insights, experience, and a genuine understanding of the target audience. This text accomplishes these goals and, because of its scope of topics, has great utility beyond its targeted audience. The range of topics covered affords the reader the opportunity to become aware of the most significant concepts that are part of healthcare management. At its core, healthcare delivery is the consummate service profession. Almost all that we do must be done through and with people. The ability to have the skills to guide and motivate people is therefore instrumental to success. This text provides an excellent blueprint for learning these skills.

If you are reading this text, in all probability you are either a healthcare management student or a healthcare administrator. In either case, you are to be congratulated for your choice of career. The healthcare management profession is a noble endeavor that is crucial to the effective delivery of health care. As such, it serves a true linchpin role in our society's quest for health and happiness. From a practical perspective, you have chosen well in terms of career longevity. In this latter context, you will need resources to keep you current in what is transpiring in the field. Drs. Buchbinder and Shanks have put together an excellent example of one of these needed resources. Use it well, and enjoy your careers.

Peter G. Fitzpatrick, EdD, RPh
Professor/Department Head
Health Care Management
School of Business
Clayton State University
Morrow, GA

Preface

The second edition of *Introduction to Health Care Management* is driven by our desire to have an excellent textbook that continues to meet the needs of the healthcare management field, healthcare management educators, and the students enrolled in healthcare management programs around the world. The inspiration for the first edition of this book came over a good cup of coffee and a deep-seated unhappiness with the texts available in 2004. This edition builds on the strengths of the first edition and is based an ongoing conversation with end users—instructors and students—from all types of higher education institutions and all types of delivery modalities. Whether your institution is a traditional "bricks and mortar" school or a fully online one, this book and its ancillary materials are formatted for your ease of use and adoption.

For this edition, many of the same master teachers and researchers with expertise in each topic revised and updated their chapters. Several new contributors stepped forward and wrote completely new chapters for this text because we listened to you, our readers and users. With a track record of more than three years in the field, we learned exactly what did or did not work in the classrooms and online, so we further enhanced and refined our student- and professor-friendly textbook. We are grateful to all our authors for their insightful, well-written chapters and our abundant, realistic case studies.

As before, this textbook will be useful to a wide variety of students and programs. Undergraduate students in healthcare management, nursing, public health, and allied health programs will find the writing to be engaging. In addition, students in graduate programs in discipline-specific areas, such as business administration, nursing, pharmacy, occupational therapy, public administration, and public health will find the materials both theory-based and readily applicable to real-world settings. With more than three decades of experience in higher education, we know first and foremost that teaching and learning are *not* solo sports, but a team effort—a *contact* sport. There must be a give-and-take between the students and the instructors for deep learning to take place. This text uses active learning methods to achieve this goal. Along with lively writing and contents critical for a foundation in healthcare management, this second edition continues to provide realistic information that can be applied immediately to the real world of healthcare management. In addition to revised and updated chapters from the first edition, there are learning objectives, discussion questions, and case studies included in each chapter, with additional instructors' resources online and Instructor's Guides for the more advanced case studies. PowerPoint slides and test items are included for each chapter. A sample syllabus is also provided. Specifically, the second edition contains:

- A new first chapter that provides the reader with an overview of the profession of healthcare management and discusses the major functions, roles, responsibilities, and competencies for healthcare managers.
- A new chapter on healthcare marketing that speaks to the growing significance of consumer-driven health care, the boom of the Internet on all frontiers, the increased demand for personalized services, and the need for the healthcare manager to understand the principles of strategic marketing.
- A new chapter on information technology written by a practicing Chief Information Officer to address the current state of information technology in health care and the impact the acceleration of its implementation has had on healthcare managers.
- A new chapter on addressing health disparities, cultural proficiency, and the impact of a diverse population on the management of a culturally competent healthcare organization.
- A significantly revised chapter on fraud and abuse with a focus on the beginnings of fraud and abuse prevention programs and a look at the investigative processes used to uncover fraud and abuse, as well as the responsibilities of employees of healthcare organizations.
- An extensively revised case study guide, with new and improved rubrics for evaluation of student performance, enabling professors at every level of experience to hit the ground running on that first day of classes.
- Thirty-five case studies, twenty of which are new to this edition, that cover a wide variety of settings and an assortment of healthcare management topics. At the end of each chapter in the text, at least one specific case study is identified and linked to the content of that chapter. Many chapters have multiple cases. Plus, there are now four completely online case studies that do not appear in the text.

Never underestimate the power of a good cup of joe. We hope you enjoy this book as much as we enjoyed revising it. May your classroom and online discussions be filled with active learning experiences, may your teaching be filled with good humor and fun, and may your coffee cup always be full.

Sharon B. Buchbinder, RN, PhD
American Hospital Management Group Corporation

Nancy H. Shanks, PhD
Metropolitan State College of Denver

Acknowledgments

This second edition is the result of a six-year process that involved the majority of the leaders in excellence in undergraduate healthcare management education. We continue to be deeply grateful to the Association of University Programs in Health Administration (AUPHA) faculty, members, and staff for all the support, both in time and expertise, in developing the proposal for this textbook and for providing us with excellent feedback at every step of the way.

More than 30 authors have made this contributed text a one-of-a-kind book. Not only are our authors expert teachers and practitioners in their disciplines and research niches, they are also practiced teachers and mentors. As we read each chapter and case study, we could hear the voices of each author. It has been a privilege and honor to work with each and every one of them: Maron Boohaker, Dale Buchbinder, Susan Casciani, Ruth Chavez, Donna Cox, Amy Dore, Daniel Fahey, Mary Anne Franklin, Brenda Freshman, Barry Gomberg, Kenneth Johnson, Dale Mapes, Audrey McDow, Sheila McGinnis, Karen Mithamo, Michael Moran, Wayne Nelson, Dawn Oetjen, Woody Richardson, Velma Roberts, Lou Rubino, Grant Savage, Nancy Sayre, W. Carole Shepherd, Windsor Sherrill, Donna Slovensky, Tressa Springmann, Dennis Stambaugh, Jon Thompson, Rosalind Trieber, Eric Williams, and Kevin Zeiler.

And, finally, and never too often, we thank our husbands, Dale Buchbinder and Rick Shanks, who listened to long telephone conversations about the book's revisions, trailed us to meetings and dinners, and served us wine with our whines. We love you and could not have done this without you.

About the Editors

Sharon B. Buchbinder, RN, PhD, was professor and chair of the Department of Health Science at Towson University and is now president of the American Hospital Management Group Corporation, MASA Healthcare Co, a healthcare management education and healthcare delivery organization based in Owings Mills, MD. For more than three decades, Dr. Buchbinder has worked in many aspects of health care as a clinician, researcher, association executive, and academic. With a PhD in public health from the University of Illinois School of Public Health, she brings this blend of real-world experience and theoretical constructs to undergraduate and graduate face-to-face and online classrooms, where she is constantly reminded of how important good teaching really is. She is past chair of the Board of the Association of University Programs in Health Administration (AUPHA) and coauthor of the Bugbee-Falk Award-winning *Career Opportunities in Health Care Management: Perspectives from the Field.*

    Nancy H. Shanks, PhD, has extensive experience in the healthcare field. For 12 years, she worked as a health services researcher and health policy analyst and later served as the executive director of a grant-making, fund-raising foundation that was associated with a large multihospital system in Denver. During the last 15 years, Dr. Shanks has been a healthcare administration educator at Metropolitan State College of Denver, where she has taught a variety of undergraduate courses in health services management, organization, research, human resources management, strategic management, and law. She is currently a professor in the Health Care Management Program after having served as chair of the Department of Health Professions for seven years. Dr. Shanks's research interests have focused on health policy issues, such as providing access to health care for the uninsured.

Contributors

Maron Joseph Boohaker, MPH
Compliance Audit Manager
HealthSouth Corporation
Birmingham, AL

Dale Buchbinder, MD, FACS
Chairman, Department of Surgery and
    Clinical Professor of Surgery
The University of Maryland Medical School
Good Samaritan Hospital
Baltimore, MD

Susan Judd Casciani, MSHA, MBA, FACHE
Clinical Assistant Professor and
    Coordinator, Health Care Management Program
Department of Health Science
Towson University
Towson, MD

Ruth Chavez, PhD, MBA
Assistant Professor
Department of Marketing
Metropolitan State College of Denver
Denver, CO

Donna M. Cox, PhD
Professor and Director
Alcohol Tobacco and Other Drugs Prevention Center
Department of Health Science
Towson University
Towson, MD

Amy Dore, DHA
Assistant Professor, Health Care Management Program
Department of Health Professions
Metropolitan State College of Denver
Denver, CO

Daniel F. Fahey, PhD
Associate Professor
Health Science Department
California State University, San Bernardino
San Bernardino, CA

Mary Anne Franklin, EdD, MSA, LNFA
Professor Emerita
Taos, NM

Brenda Freshman, PhD
Assistant Professor
Health Administration Program
California State University, Long Beach
Long Beach, CA

Barry G. Gomberg, JD
Executive Director of Equal Opportunity/Affirmative Action Office
Weber State University
Ogden, UT

Kenneth L. Johnson, PhD, CHES
Interim Dean
Dumke College of Health Professions
Weber State University
Ogden, UT

Dale Mapes, MSA
Vice President of Human Resources and Support Services
Portneuf Regional Medical Center
Pocatello, ID

Audrey McDow
Former Student
Department of Health Care Administration
Idaho State University
Pocatello, ID

Sheila K. McGinnis, PhD
Alexandria, VA

Karin Mithamo
Former Graduate Student
Department of Business
Idaho State University
Pocatello, ID

Michael Moran, MS, MSHA
Adjunct Faculty, Health Care Management Program
Department of Health Professions
Metropolitan State College of Denver
Denver, CO

H. Wayne Nelson, PhD
Professor
Department of Health Science
Towson University
Towson, MD

Dawn M. Oetjen, PhD
Professor and Graduate Program Director
Health Services Administration Program
Department of Health Management and Informatics
University of Central Florida
Orlando, FL

Woody D. Richardson, PhD
Instructor
Department of Management and Information Systems
College of Business
Mississippi State University
Mississippi State, MS

Velma Roberts, PhD
Associate Professor
Healthcare Management Division
School of Allied Health Sciences
Florida A & M University
Tallahassee, FL

Louis Rubino, PhD, FACHE
Professor/ Director, Health Administration Program
Interim Director, Institute for Community
Health and Wellbeing at CSUN
California State University, Northridge
Northridge, CA

Grant T. Savage, PhD
Professor of Management
Management, Information Systems &
    Quantitative Methods Department
University of Alabama at Birmingham
Birmingham, AL

Nancy K. Sayre, PA, MHS
Assistant Department Chair, Coordinator Health Care Management
    Program and Visiting Assistant Professor
Department of Health Professions
Metropolitan State College of Denver
Denver, CO

W. Carole Shepherd, MS
Part-Time Faculty
Department of Health Sciences
Health Administration Program
California State University, Northridge
Northridge, CA

Windsor Westbrook Sherrill, PhD
Associate Professor
Public Health Sciences
Clemson University
Clemson, SC

Donna J. Slovensky, PhD, RHIA, FAHIMA
Associate Dean for Student and Academic Affairs
School of Health Professions
University of Alabama at Birmingham
Birmingham, AL

Tressa Springmann, MS, CPHIMS
Vice President and Chief Information Officer
The Greater Baltimore Medical Center
Baltimore, MD

Dennis G. Stambaugh
Chief Quality Officer
University of Missouri Health System
Columbia, MO

Jon M. Thompson, PhD
Professor and Director, Health Services Administration Program
Department of Health Sciences
James Madison University
Harrisonburg, VA

Rosalind Trieber, MS, CHES
Trieber Associates, Inc.
Owings Mills, MD

Eric S. Williams, PhD
Professor of Health Care Management
Minnie Miles Research Professor
University of Alabama
Tuscaloosa, AL

Kevin D. Zeiler, JD, MBA, EMT-P
Assistant Professor, Health Care Management Program
Department of Health Professions
Metropolitan State College of Denver
Denver, CO

CHAPTER 1

An Overview of Healthcare Management

Jon M. Thompson, Sharon B. Buchbinder, and Nancy H. Shanks

LEARNING OBJECTIVES

By the end of this chapter, the student will be able to:

- Define healthcare management and the role of the healthcare manager;
- Differentiate between the functions, roles, and responsibilities of healthcare managers; and
- Compare and contrast the key competencies of healthcare managers.

INTRODUCTION

Any introductory text in healthcare management must clearly define the profession of healthcare management and discuss the major functions, roles, responsibilities, and competencies for healthcare managers. These topics are the focus of this chapter. Healthcare management is a growing profession with increasing opportunities in both direct care and non–direct care settings. As defined by Buchbinder and Thompson (2010, pp. 33–34), direct care settings are "those organizations that provide care directly to a patient, resident or client who seeks services from the organization." Non–direct care settings are not directly involved in providing care to persons needing health services, but rather support the care of individuals through products and services made available to direct care settings.

The Bureau of Labor Statistics (BLS) indicates that healthcare management is one of the fastest growing occupations, due to the expansion and diversification of the healthcare industry (Bureau of Labor Statistics, 2010). The BLS projects that employment of medical and health services managers is expected to grow 16% from 2008 to 2018, faster than the average for all occupations.

These managers are expected to be needed in inpatient and outpatient care facilities, with the greatest growth in managerial positions occurring in outpatient centers, clinics, and physician practices. Hospitals, too, will experience a large number of managerial jobs because of the hospital sector's large size. Moreover, these estimates do not reflect the significant growth in managerial positions in non–direct care settings, such as consulting firms, pharmaceutical companies, associations, and medical equipment companies. These non–direct care settings provide significant assistance to direct care organizations, and since the number of direct care managerial positions is expected to increase significantly, it is expected that growth will also occur in managerial positions in non–direct care settings.

Healthcare management is the profession that provides leadership and direction to organizations that deliver personal health services, and to divisions, departments, units, or services within those organizations. Healthcare management provides significant rewards and personal satisfaction for those who want to make a difference in the lives of others. This chapter gives a comprehensive overview of healthcare management as a profession. Understanding the roles, responsibilities, and functions carried out by healthcare managers is important for those individuals considering the field to make informed decisions about the "fit." This chapter provides a discussion of key management roles, responsibilities, and functions, as well as management positions at different levels within healthcare organizations. In addition, descriptions of supervisory level, mid-level, and senior management positions within different organizations are provided.

THE NEED FOR MANAGERS AND THEIR PERSPECTIVES

Healthcare organizations are complex and dynamic. The nature of organizations requires that managers provide leadership, as well as the supervision and coordination of employees. Organizations were created to achieve goals that were beyond the capacity of any single individual. In healthcare organizations, the scope and complexity of tasks carried out in provision of services are so great that individual staff operating on their own couldn't get the job done. Moreover, the necessary tasks in producing services in healthcare organizations require the coordination of many highly specialized disciplines that must work together seamlessly. Managers are needed to make certain that organizational tasks are carried out in the best way possible to achieve organizational goals and that appropriate resources, including financial and human resources, are adequate to support the organization.

Healthcare managers are appointed to positions of authority, where they shape the organization by making important decisions. Such decisions relate, for example, to recruitment and development of staff, acquisition of technology, service additions and reductions, and allocation and spending of financial resources. Decisions made by healthcare managers not only focus on ensuring that the patient receives the most appropriate, timely, and effective services possible, but also address achievement of performance targets that are desired by the manager. Ultimately, decisions made by an individual manager affect the organization's overall performance.

Managers must consider two domains as they carry out various tasks and make decisions (Thompson, 2007). These domains are termed external and internal domains (see Table 1-1). The external domain refers to the influences, resources, and activities that exist outside the boundary of the organization but that significantly affect the organization. These factors include community needs, population characteristics, and reimbursement from commercial insurers, as well as government plans such as the Children's Health Insurance Plans (CHIP), Medicare, and Medicaid. The internal domain refers to those areas of focus that managers need to address on a daily basis, such as ensuring the appropriate number and types of staff, financial performance, and quality of care. These internal areas reflect the operation of the organization where the manager has the most control. Keeping the dual perspective requires significant balance on the part of management and significant effort in order to make good decisions.

TABLE 1-1 Domains of Health Services Administration

External	Internal
Community demographics/need	Staffing
Licensure	Budgeting
Accreditation	Quality services
Regulations	Patient satisfaction
Stakeholder demands	Physician relations
Competitors	Financial performance
Medicare and Medicaid	Technology acquisition
Managed care organizations/insurers	New service development

Source: Thompson, 2007.

MANAGEMENT: DEFINITION, FUNCTIONS, AND COMPETENCIES

As discussed earlier, management is needed to support and coordinate the services that are provided within healthcare organizations. Management has been defined as the process, comprised of social and technical functions and activities, occurring within organizations for the purpose of accomplishing predetermined objectives through humans and other resources (Longest, Rakich, & Darr, 2000). Implicit in the definition is that managers work through and with other people, carrying out technical and interpersonal activities, in order to achieve desired objectives of the organization. Others have stated that a manager is anyone in the organization who supports and is responsible for the work performance of one or more other persons (Lombardi & Schermerhorn, 2007).

While most beginning students of healthcare management tend to focus on the role of the senior manager or lead administrator of an organization, it should be realized that management occurs through many others who may not have "manager" in their position title. Examples of some of these managerial positions in healthcare organizations include supervisor, coordinator, and director, among others (see Table 1-2). These levels of managerial control are discussed in more detail in the next section.

TABLE 1-2 Managerial Positions, by Organizational Setting

Organizational Setting	Examples of Managerial Positions
Physician practice	Practice Manager
	Director of Medical Records
	Supervisor, Billing Office
Nursing home	Administrator
	Manager, Business Office
	Director, Food Services
	Admissions Coordinator
	Supervisor, Environmental Services
Hospital	Chief Executive Officer
	Vice President, Marketing
	Clinical Nurse Manager
	Director, Revenue Management
	Supervisor, Maintenance

Managers implement six management functions as they carry out the process of management (Longest et al., 2000):

Planning: This function requires the manager to set a direction and determine what needs to be accomplished. It means setting priorities and determining performance targets.

Organizing: This management function refers to the overall design of the organization or the specific division, unit, or service for which the manager is responsible. Furthermore, it means designating reporting relationships and intentional patterns of interaction. Determining positions, teamwork assignments, and distribution of authority and responsibility are critical components of this function.

Staffing: This function refers to acquiring and retaining human resources. It also refers to developing and maintaining the workforce through various strategies and tactics.

Controlling: This function refers to monitoring staff activities and performance and taking the appropriate actions for corrective action to increase performance.

Directing: The focus in this function is on initiating action in the organization through effective leadership and motivation of, and communication with, subordinates.

Decision making: This function is critical to all of the aforementioned management functions and means making effective decisions based on consideration of benefits and the drawbacks of alternatives.

In order to effectively carry out these functions, the manager needs to possess several key competencies. Katz (1974) identified several key competencies of the effective manager, including conceptual, technical, and interpersonal skills. The term competency refers to a state in which an individual has the requisite or adequate ability or qualities to perform certain functions (Ross, Wenzel, & Mitlyng, 2002). These are defined as follows:

Conceptual skills are those skills that involve the ability to critically analyze and solve complex problems. Examples: a manager conducts an analysis of the best way to provide a service or determines a strategy to reduce patient complaints regarding food service.

Technical skills are those skills that reflect expertise or ability to perform a specific work task. Examples: a manager develops and implements a new incentive compensation program for staff or designs and implements modifications to a computer-based staffing model.

Interpersonal skills are those skills that enable a manager to communicate with and work well with other individuals, regardless of whether they are peers, supervisors, or subordinates. Examples: a manager counsels an employee whose performance is below expectation or communicates to subordinates the desired performance level for a service for the next fiscal year.

MANAGEMENT POSITIONS: THE CONTROL IN THE ORGANIZATIONAL HIERARCHY

Management positions within healthcare organizations are not confined to the top level; because of the size and complexity of many healthcare organizations, management positions are found throughout the organization. Management positions exist at the lower, middle, and upper levels; the upper level is referred to as senior management. The hierarchy of management means that authority, or power, is delegated downward in the organization and that lower-level managers have less authority than higher-level managers, whose scope of responsibility is much greater. For example, a vice president of Patient Care Services in a hospital may be in charge of several different functional areas, such as nursing, diagnostic imaging services, and laboratory services; in contrast, a director of Medical Records—a lower-level position—has responsibility only for the function of patient medical records. Furthermore, a supervisor within the Environmental Services department may have responsibility for only a small housekeeping staff, whose work is critical but confined to a defined area of the organization. Some managerial positions, such as those discussed previously, are line managerial positions because the manager supervises other employees; other managerial positions are staff managerial positions because they carry out work and advise their bosses, but they do not routinely supervise others. Managerial positions also vary in terms of required expertise or experience; some positions require extensive knowledge of many substantive areas and significant working experience, and other positions are more appropriate for entry-level managers who have limited or no experience.

The most common organizational structure for healthcare organizations is a functional organizational structure whose key characteristic is a pyramid-shaped hierarchy, which defines the functions carried out and the key management positions assigned to those functions (see Figure 1-1). The size and complexity of the specific health services organization will dictate the particular structure. For example, larger organizations—such as large community hospitals, hospital systems, and academic medical centers—will likely have deep vertical structures reflecting varying levels of administrative control for the organization. This structure is necessary due to the large scope of services provided and the corresponding vast array of administrative and support services that are needed to enable the delivery of clinical services. Other characteristics associated with this functional structure include a strict chain of command and line of reporting, which ensure that communication and assignment and evaluation of tasks are carried out in a linear command and control environment. This structure offers key advantages, such as specific divisions of labor and clear lines of reporting and accountability.

Other administrative structures have been adopted by healthcare organizations, usually in combination with a functional structure. These include matrix, or team-based, models

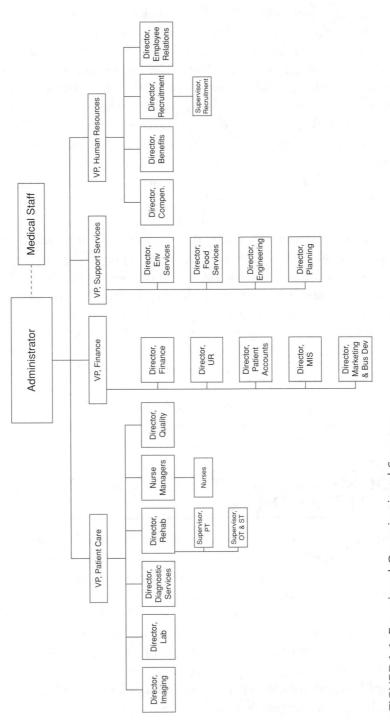

FIGURE 1-1 Functional Organizational Structure

and service line management models. The matrix model recognizes that a strict functional structure may limit the organization's flexibility to carry out the work, and that the expertise of other disciplines is needed on a continuous basis. An example of the matrix method is when functional staff, such as nursing and rehabilitation personnel, are assigned to a specific program such as geriatrics, and they report for programmatic purposes to the program director of the geriatrics department. Another example is when clinical staff and administrative staff are assigned to a team investigating new services that is headed by a marketing or business development manager. In both of these examples, management would lead staff who traditionally are not under their direct administrative control. Advantages of this structure include improved lateral communication and coordination of services, as well as pooled knowledge.

In service line management, a manager is appointed to head a specific clinical service line and has responsibility and accountability for staffing, resource acquisition, budget, and financial control associated with the array of services provided under that service line. Typical examples of service lines include cardiology, oncology (cancer), women's services, physical rehabilitation, and behavioral health (mental health). Service lines can be established within a single organization or may cut across affiliated organizations, such as within a hospital system where services are provided at several different affiliated facilities (Boblitz & Thompson, 2005). Some facilities have found that the service line management model for selected clinical services has resulted in many benefits, such as lower costs, higher quality of care, and greater patient satisfaction compared to other management models (Duffy & Lemieux, 1995). The service line management model is usually implemented within an organization in conjunction with a functional structure, as the organization may choose to give special emphasis and additional resources to one or a few services lines.

FOCUS OF MANAGEMENT: SELF, UNIT/TEAM, AND ORGANIZATION

Effective healthcare management involves exercising professional judgment and skills and carrying out the aforementioned managerial functions at three levels: **self, unit/team, and organization wide**. First and foremost, the individual manager must be able to effectively manage himself or herself. This means managing time, information, space, and materials; being responsive and following through with peers, supervisors, and clients; maintaining a positive attitude and high motivation; and keeping a current understanding of management techniques and substantive issues of healthcare management. Managing yourself also means developing and applying appropriate technical, interpersonal, and conceptual skills and competencies and being comfortable with them, in order to be able to effectively move to the next level—that of supervising others.

The second focus of management is the **unit/team work level**. The expertise of the manager at this level involves managing others in terms of effectively completing the work. Regardless of whether you are a senior manager, mid-level manager, or supervisor, you will be "supervising" others as expected in your assigned role. This responsibility includes assigning work tasks, review and modification of assignments, monitoring and review of individual performance, and carrying out the management functions described earlier to ensure excellent delivery of services. This focal area is where the actual work gets done. Performance reflects the interaction of the manager and the employee, and it is incumbent on the manager to do what is needed to shape the performance of individual employees. The focus of management at this echelon recognizes the task interdependencies among staff and the close coordination that is needed to ensure that work gets completed efficiently and effectively.

The third management focus is at the **organizational level**. This focal area reflects the fact that managers must work together as part of the larger organization to ensure organization-wide performance and organizational viability. In other words, the success of the organization depends upon the success of its individual parts, and effective collaboration is needed to ensure that this occurs. The range of clinical and nonclinical activities that occur within a healthcare organization requires that managers who head individual units work closely with other unit managers to provide services. Sharing of information, collaboration, and communication are essential for success. The hierarchy looks to the contribution of each supervised unit as it pertains to the whole. Individual managers' contributions to the overall performance of the organization—in terms of various performance measures such as cost, quality, satisfaction, and access—are important and measured.

ROLE OF THE MANAGER IN TALENT MANAGEMENT

In order to effectively master the focal areas of management and carry out the required management functions, management must have the requisite number and types of highly motivated employees. From a strategic perspective, healthcare organizations compete for labor, and it is commonly accepted today that high-performing healthcare organizations are dependent upon individual human performance, as discussed further in Chapter 12. Many observers have advocated for healthcare organizations to view their employees as strategic assets who can create a competitive advantage (Becker, Huselid, & Ulrich, 2001). Therefore, human resources management has been replaced in many healthcare organizations with "talent management." The focus has shifted to securing and retaining the talent needed to do the job in the best way, rather than simply fill a role (Huselid, Beatty, & Becker, 2005). As a result, managers are now focusing on effectively managing talent and workforce issues because of the link to organizational performance (Griffith, 2009).

Beyond recruitment, managers are concerned about developing and retaining those staff who are excellent performers. Many healthcare organizations are creating high-involvement organizations that identify and meet employee needs through their jobs and the larger organizational work setting (Becker et al., 2001). There are several strategies used by managers to develop and maintain excellent performers. These include formal methods such as offering training programs; providing leadership development programs; identifying employee needs and measuring employee satisfaction through engagement surveys; providing continuing education, especially for clinical and technical fields; and enabling job enrichment. In addition, managers use informal methods such as conducting periodic employee reviews, soliciting employee feedback, conducting rounds and employee huddles, offering employee suggestion programs, and other methods of managing employee relations and engagement. These topics are explored in more detail in a later chapter in this book.

ROLE OF THE MANAGER IN ENSURING HIGH PERFORMANCE

At the end of the day, the role of the manager is to ensure that the unit, service, division, or organization he or she leads achieves high performance. What exactly is meant by high performance? To understand performance, one has to appreciate the value of setting and meeting goals and objectives for the unit/service and organization as a whole, in terms of the work that is being carried out. Goals and objectives are desired end points for activity and reflect strategic and operational directions for the organization. They are specific, measurable, meaningful, and time oriented. Goals and objectives for individual units should reflect the overarching needs and expectations of the organization as a whole because, as the reader will recall, all entities are working together to achieve high levels of overall organizational performance. Studer (2003) views the organization as needing to be results oriented, with identified pillars of excellence as a framework for the specific goals of the organization. These pillars are: people (employees, patients, and physicians), service, quality, finance, and growth. Griffith (2000) refers to high performing organizations as being championship organizations—that is, they expect to perform well on different yet meaningful measures of performance. Griffith further defines the "championship processes" and the need to develop performance measures in each: governance and strategic management; clinical quality, including customer satisfaction; clinical organization (caregivers); financial planning; planning and marketing; information services; human resources; and plant and supplies. For each championship process, the organization should establish measures of desired performance that will guide the organization. Examples of measures include medication errors, surgical complications, patient satisfaction, staff turnover rates, employee satisfaction, market share, profit margin, and revenue growth, among others. In turn, respective divisions, units, and services will set targets and carry out activities to address key performance processes. The manager's job, ultimately, is to ensure that these targets are met by carrying out the previously discussed management functions. A control process for managers has been advanced by Ginter, Swayne, and Duncan (2002) that describes five key steps in the performance management process: set objectives, measure performance, compare performance with objectives, determine reasons for deviation, and take corrective action. Management's job is to ensure that performance is maintained or, if below expectations, is improved.

Stakeholders, including insurers, state and federal governments, and consumer advocacy groups, are expecting, and in many cases demanding, acceptable levels of performance in healthcare organizations. These groups want to make sure that services are provided in a safe, convenient, low-cost, and high-quality environment. For example, The Joint Commission (formerly JCAHO) has set minimum standards for healthcare facilities operations that ensure quality, the National Committee for Quality Assurance (NCQA) has set standards for measuring performance of health plans, and the Centers for Medicare and Medicaid Services (CMS) has established a website that compares hospital performance along a number of critical dimensions. In addition, CMS has provided incentives to healthcare organizations by paying for performance on measures of clinical care and not paying for care resulting from "**never events**," i.e., shocking health outcomes that should never occur in a healthcare setting such as wrong site surgery (e.g., the wrong leg) or hospital-acquired infections (Agency for Healthcare Research and Quality, n.d.). Health insurers also have implemented pay-for-performance programs for healthcare organizations based on various quality and customer service measures.

In addition to meeting the reporting requirements of the aforementioned organizations, many healthcare organizations today use varying methods of measuring and reporting the performance measurement process. Common methods include developing and using dashboards or balanced scorecards that allow for a quick interpretation on the performance across a number of key measures (Curtright, Stolp-Smith, & Edell, 2000; Pieper, 2005). Senior administration uses these methods to measure and communicate performance on the total organization to the governing board and other critical constituents. Other managers use these methods at the division, unit, or service level to profile its performance. In turn, these measures are also used to evaluate managers' performance and are considered in decisions by the manager's boss regarding compensation adjustments, promotions, increased or reduced responsibility, training and development, and, if necessary, termination or reassignment.

ROLE OF THE MANAGER IN SUCCESSION PLANNING

Due to the competitive nature of healthcare organizations and the need for highly motivated and skilled employees, managers are faced with the challenge of succession planning for their organizations. Succession planning refers to the concept of taking actions to ensure that staff can move up in management roles within the organization, in order to replace those managers who retire or move to other opportunities in other organizations. Succession planning has most recently been emphasized at the senior level of organizations, in part due to the large number of retirements that are anticipated from baby boomer chief executive officers (CEOs) (Burt, 2005). In order to continue the emphasis on high performance within healthcare organizations, CEOs and other senior managers are interested in finding and nurturing leadership talent within their organizations who can assume the responsibility and carry forward the important work of these organizations.

Healthcare organizations are currently engaged in several practices to address leadership succession needs. First, mentoring programs for junior management that senior management participate in have been advocated as a good way to prepare future healthcare leaders (Rollins, 2003). Mentoring studies show that mentors view their efforts as helpful to the organization (Finley, Ivanitskaya, & Kennedy, 2007). Some observers suggest that having many mentors is essential to capturing the necessary scope of expertise, experience, interest, and contacts to maximize professional growth (Broscio & Sherer, 2003). Mentoring middle-level managers for success as they transition to their current positions is also helpful in preparing those managers for future executive leadership roles (Kubica, 2008).

A second method of succession planning is through formal leadership development programs. These programs are intended to identify management potential throughout an organization by targeting specific skill sets of individuals and assessing their match to specific jobs, such as vice president or chief operating officer (COO). One way to implement this is through talent reviews, which, when done annually, help create a pool of existing staff who may be excellent candidates for further leadership development and skill strengthening through the establishment of development plans. Formal programs that are being established by many healthcare organizations focus on high potential people (Burt, 2005). McAlearney (2010) reports that about 50% of hospital systems nationwide have an executive-level leadership development program. However, many healthcare organizations have developed programs that address leadership development at all levels of the organization, not just the executive level, and require that all managers participate in these programs in order to strengthen their managerial and leadership skills to contribute to organizational performance.

ROLE OF THE MANAGER IN HEALTHCARE POLICY

As noted earlier in this chapter, managers must consider both their external and internal domains as they carry out management functions and tasks. One of the critical areas for managing the external world is to be knowledgeable about health policy matters under consideration at the state and federal levels that affect health services organizations and healthcare delivery. This is particularly true for senior-level managers. This is necessary in order to influence policy in positive ways that will help the organization and limit any adverse impacts. Staying current with healthcare policy discussions, participating in deliberations of health policy, and providing input where possible will allow healthcare management voices to be heard. Because health care is such a popular yet controversial topic in the United States today, continuing changes in healthcare delivery are likely to emanate from the legislative and policy processes at the state and federal levels. For example, the Patient Protection and Affordable Care Act, signed into law in 2010 as a major healthcare reform initiative, has significant implications for healthcare organizations in terms of patient volumes and reimbursement for previously uninsured patients. Other recent federal policy changes include cuts in Medicare reimbursement and increases in reporting requirements. State legislative changes across the country affect reimbursement under Medicaid and the Children's Health Insurance Program, licensure of facilities and staff, certificate of need rules for capital expenditures and facility and service expansions, and state requirements on mandated health benefits and modified reimbursements for insured individuals that affect services offered by healthcare organizations.

In order to understand and influence health policy, managers must strive to keep their knowledge current. This can be accomplished through targeted personal learning, networking with colleagues within and outside of their organizations, and through participating in professional associations, such as the American College of Healthcare Executives and the Medical Group Management Association. These organizations, and many others, monitor health policy discussions and advocate for their associations' interests at the state and federal levels. Knowledge gained through these efforts can be helpful in shaping health policy in accordance with the desires of healthcare managers.

CHAPTER SUMMARY

The profession of healthcare management is challenging yet rewarding, and it requires that persons in managerial positions at all levels of the organization possess sound conceptual, technical, and interpersonal skills in order to carry out the required managerial functions of planning, organizing, staffing, directing, controlling, and decision making. In addition, managers must maintain a dual perspective where they understand the external and internal domains of their organization and the need for development at the self, unit/team, and organization levels. Opportunities exist for managerial talent at all levels of a healthcare organization, including supervisory, middle-management, and senior-management levels. The role of manager is critical to ensuring a high level of organizational performance, and managers are also instrumental in talent recruitment and retention, succession planning, and shaping health policy.

Note: This chapter was originally published as "Understanding Health Care Management" in *Career Opportunities in Healthcare Management: Perspectives from the Field*, by Sharon B. Buchbinder and Jon M. Thompson, and an adapted version of this chapter is reprinted here with permission of the publisher.

DISCUSSION QUESTIONS

1. Define *healthcare management* and *healthcare managers*.

2. Describe the functions carried out by healthcare managers, and give an example of a task in each function.

3. Explain why interpersonal skills are important in healthcare management.

4. Compare and contrast three models of organizational design.

5. Why is the healthcare manager's role in ensuring high performance so critical? Explain.

Cases in Chapter 17 that are related to this chapter include:

- Choosing a Successor—see p. 444

Additional cases, role-play scenarios, video links, websites, and other information sources are also available in the online Instructor's Materials.

REFERENCES

Agency for Healthcare Research and Quality (AHRQ). (n.d.). Never events. Retrieved from http://www.psnet.ahrq.gov/primer.aspx?primerID=3

Becker, B. E., Huselid, M. A., & Ulrich, D. (2001). *The HR scorecard: Linking people, strategy, and performance*. Boston, MA: Harvard Business School Press.

Boblitz, M., & Thompson, J. M. (2005, October). Assessing the feasibility of developing centers of excellence: Six initial steps. *Healthcare Financial Management, 59,* 72–84.

Broscio, M., & Scherer, J. (2003). Building job security: Strategies for becoming a highly valued contributor. *Journal of Healthcare Management, 48,* 147–151.

Buchbinder, S. B., & Thompson, J. M. (2010). *Career opportunities in health care management: Perspectives from the field.* Sudbury, MA: Jones & Bartlett.

Bureau of Labor Statistics. (2010). *Occupational outlook handbook 2010–11 edition.* Retrieved from www.bls.gov/oco/ocos014.htm

Burt, T. (2005). Leadership development as a corporate strategy: Using talent reviews to improve senior management. *Healthcare Executive, 20,* 14–18.

Curtright, J. W., Stolp-Smith, S. C., & Edell, E. S. (2000). Strategic management: Development of a performance measurement system at the Mayo Clinic. *Journal of Healthcare Management, 45,* 58–68.

Duffy, J. R., & Lemieux, K. G. (1995, Fall). A cardiac service line approach to patient-centered care. *Nursing Administration Quarterly, 20,* 12–23.

Finley, F. R., Ivanitskaya, L. V., & Kennedy, M. H. (2007). Mentoring junior healthcare administrators: A description of mentoring practices in 127 U.S. hospitals. *Journal of Healthcare Management, 52,* 260–270.

Ginter, P. M., Swayne, L. E., & Duncan, W. J. (2002). *Strategic management of healthcare organizations* (4th ed.). Malden, MA: Blackwell.

Griffith, J. R. (2000). Championship management for healthcare organizations. *Journal of Healthcare Management, 45,* 17–31.

Griffith, J. R. (2009). Finding the frontier of hospital management. *Journal of Healthcare Management, 54*(1), 57–73.

Huselid, M. A., Beatty, R. W., & Becker, B. E. (2005, December). "A players" or "A" positions? The strategic logic of workforce management. *Harvard Business Review, 83,* 100–117.

Katz, R. L. (1974). Skills of an effective administrator. *Harvard Business Review, 52,* 90–102.

Kubica, A. J. (2008). Transitioning middle managers. *Healthcare Executive, 23,* 58–60.

Lombardi, D. M., & Schermerhorn, J. R. (2007). *Healthcare management.* Hoboken, NJ: John Wiley.

Longest, B. B., Rakich, J. S., & Darr, K. (2000). *Managing health services organizations and systems.* Baltimore, MD: Health Professions Press.

McAlearney, A. S. (2010). Executive leadership development in U.S. health systems. *Journal of Healthcare Management, 55*(3), 206–224.

Pieper, S. K. (2005). Reading the right signals: How to strategically manage with scorecards. *Healthcare Executive, 20,* 9–14.

Rollins, G. (2003). Succession planning: Laying the foundation for smooth transitions and effective leaders. *Healthcare Executive, 18,* 14–18.

Ross, A., Wenzel, F. J., & Mitlyng, J. W. (2002). *Leadership for the future: Core competencies in health care.* Chicago, IL: Health Administration Press/AUPHA Press.

Studer, Q. (2003). *Hardwiring excellence.* Gulf Breeze, FL: Fire Starter.

Thompson, J. M. (2007). Health services administration. In S. Chisolm (Ed.), *The health professions: Trends and opportunities in U.S. health care* (pp. 357–372). Sudbury, MA: Jones & Bartlett.

Leadership
Louis Rubino

LEARNING OBJECTIVES

By the end of this chapter, the student will be able to:

- Distinguish between leadership and management;
- Define followership and why it's as important as leadership;
- Summarize the history of leadership in the United States from the 1920s to current times;
- Compare contemporary models of leadership;
- Describe leadership domains and competencies;
- Compare leadership styles;
- Summarize old and new governance trends;
- Discuss how culture plays a role in leadership; and
- Provide a rationale for why healthcare leaders have a greater need for ethical behavior.

LEADERSHIP VS. MANAGEMENT

In any business setting, there must be **leaders** as well as **managers**. But are these the same people? Not necessarily. There are leaders who are good managers and there are managers who are good leaders, but usually neither case is the norm. In health care, this is especially important to recognize because of the need for both. Health care is unique in that it is a service industry that depends on a large number of highly trained personnel as well as trade workers. Whatever the setting, be it a hospital, a long-term care facility, an ambulatory care center, a medical device company, an insurance company, or some other healthcare sector, leaders as well as managers are needed to keep the organization moving in a forward direction and, at the same time, maintain current operations. This is done by leading and managing its people.

Leaders usually take a focus that is more **external**, whereas the focus of managers is more **internal**. Even though they need to be sure their healthcare facility is operating properly, leaders tend to spend the majority of their time communicating and aligning with outside groups that can benefit their organizations (partners, community, vendors) or influence them (government, public agencies, media). See Figure 2-1. There is crossover between leaders and managers across the various areas, though a distinction remains for certain duties and responsibilities.

Usually the top person in the organization (e.g., Chief Executive Officer, Administrator, Director) has full and ultimate accountability. There are several managers reporting to this person, all of whom have various **functional responsibilities** (e.g., Chief Nursing Officer, Physician Director, Chief Information Officer). These managers can certainly

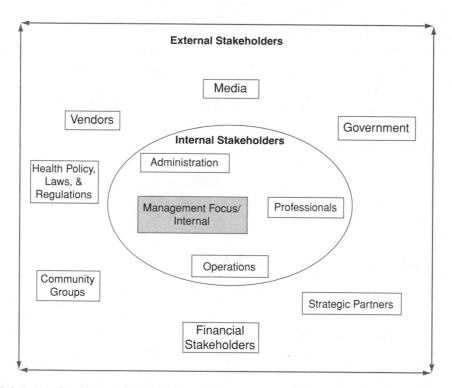

FIGURE 2-1 Leadership and Management Focus

Note: Arrows represent continual interactions between all elements of the model.

be leaders in their own areas, but their focus will be more internal within the organization's operations.

Leaders have a particular set of competencies that require more forward thinking than those of managers. Leaders need to set a direction for the organization. They need to be able to motivate their employees, as well as other stakeholders, so that the business continues to exist and, hopefully, thrive in periods of change. No industry is as dynamic as health care, with rapid change occurring due to the complexity of the system and government regulations. Leaders are needed to keep the entity on course and to maneuver around obstacles, like a captain commanding his ship at sea. Managers must tend to the business at hand and make sure the staff is following proper procedures. They need a different set of competencies. See Table 2-1.

FOLLOWERSHIP

For every leader, there must be followers. Leaders must have someone they can lead in order to accomplish what they set out to do. Not everyone can or should be a leader. Leaders should have certain recognizable traits that will help them take charge, while followers must have a willingness to be led as well as the ability to do the task requested. True leaders inspire commitment from dedicated people.

Atchison (2003) wrote about this process in his book *Followership*. He describes followership as complementary to leadership and recommends that it be recognized as a necessary component for an effective leader. A self-absorbed administrator will not make a good leader. A true leader will recognize the importance of getting respect, not simply compliance, from the people who follow. It is one thing to have people do what you say, but to have someone want to do it is another thing. The leader who understands this is on the way to greatness and will create a much more meaningful work environment.

TABLE 2-1 Leadership vs. Management Competencies

Leadership Competencies	Management Competencies
Setting direction or mission	Staffing personnel
Motivating stakeholders	Controlling resources
Being an effective spokesperson	Supervising the service provided
Determining strategies for the future	Overseeing adherence to regulations
Transforming the organization	Counseling employees

As Atchison says, "An executive title without followers has an illusion of power. These titled executives create a workplace without a soul."

HISTORY OF LEADERSHIP IN THE UNITED STATES

Leaders have been around since the beginning of man. We think of the strongest male becoming the leader of a caveman clan. In Plato's time, the Greeks began to talk about the concept of leadership and acknowledged the political system as critical for leaders to emerge in a society. In Germany during the late 19th century, Sigmund Freud described leadership as unconscious exhibited behavior; later, Max Weber identified how leadership is present in a bureaucracy through assigned roles. Formal leadership studies in the United States, though, have only been around for the last 100 years (Sibbet, 1997).

We can look at the decades spanning the 20th century to see how leadership theories evolved, placing their center of attention on certain key components at different times (Northouse, 2010). These emphases often matched or were adapted from the changes occurring in society.

With the industrialization of the United States in the 1920s, productivity was of paramount importance. Scientific management was introduced, and researchers tried to determine which characteristics were identified with the most effective leaders based on their units having high productivity. The **Great Man Theory** was developed out of the idea that certain traits determined good leadership. The traits that were recognized as necessary for effective leaders were ones that were already inherent in the person, such as being male, being tall, being strong, and even being Caucasian. Even the idea that "you either got it or you don't" was supported by this theory, the notion being that a good leader had charisma. Behaviors were not considered important in determining what made a good leader. This theory discouraged anyone who did not have the specified traits from aspiring to a leadership position.

Fortunately, after two decades, businesses realized that leadership could be enhanced through certain conscious acts, and researchers began to study which behaviors would produce better results. Resources were in short supply due to World War II, and leaders were needed who could truly produce good results. This was the beginning of the **Style Approach to Leadership**. Rather than looking at only the characteristics of the leader, researchers started to recognize the importance of two types of behaviors in successful leadership: completing tasks and creating good relationships. This theory states that leaders have differing degrees of concern over each of these behaviors, and the best leaders would be fully attentive to both.

In the 1960s, American society had a renewed emphasis on helping all of its people and began a series of social programs that still remain today. The two that impact health care directly, by providing essential services, are Medicare for the elderly (age 65 and over) and the disabled and Medicaid for the indigent population. The **Situational Approach to Leadership** then came into prominence and supported this national concern. This set of theories focused on the leader changing his or her behavior in certain situations in order to meet the needs of subordinates. This would imply a very fluid leadership process whereby one can adapt one's actions to an employee's needs at any given time.

Not much later, researchers believed that perhaps leaders should not have to change how they behaved in a work setting, but instead the appropriate leaders should be selected from the very beginning. This is the **Contingency Theory of Leadership** and was very popular in the 1970s. Under this theory, the focus was on both the leader's style as well as the situation in which the leader worked, thus building upon the two earlier theories. This approach was further developed by what is known as the **Path–Goal Theory of Leadership**. This theory still placed its attention on the leader's style and the work situation (subordinate characteristics and work task structure) but also recognized the importance of setting goals for employees. The leader was expected to remove any obstacles in order to provide the support necessary for them to achieve those goals.

In the later 1970s, the United States was coming out of the Vietnam War, in which many of its citizens did not think the country should have been involved. More concern was expressed over relationships as the society became more psychologically attuned to how people felt. The **Leader–Member Exchange Theory** evolved over the concern that leadership was being defined by the leader, the follower, and the context. This new way of looking at leadership focused on the interactions that occur between the leaders and the followers. This theory claimed that leaders could be more effective if they developed better relationships with their subordinates through high-quality exchanges.

After Vietnam and a series of weak political leaders, Americans were looking for people to take charge who could really make a difference. Charismatic leaders came back into vogue, as demonstrated by the support shown to President Ronald Reagan, an actor turned politician. Unlike the Great Man Theory earlier in the century, this time the leader had to have certain skills to transform the organization through inspirational motivational efforts. Leadership was not centered upon transactional processes that tied rewards or corrective actions to performance. Rather, the **transformational leader** could significantly change an organization through its people by raising their consciousness, empowering them, and then providing the nurturing needed as they produced the results desired.

In the late 1980s, the United States started to look more globally for ways to have better production. Total Quality Management became a popular concept and arose from researchers studying Japanese principles of managing production lines. In the healthcare setting, this was embraced through a process still used today called Continuous Quality Improvement or Performance Improvement. In the decade to follow, leaders assigned subordinates to a series of work groups in order to focus on a particular area of production. Attention was placed on developing the team for higher level functioning and on how a leader could create a work environment that could improve the performance of the team. Individual team members were expendable, and the team entity was all important.

CONTEMPORARY MODELS

We have entered the 21st century with some of the greatest leadership challenges ever in the healthcare field. Critical personnel shortages, limited resources, and increased governmental regulations provide an environment that yearns for leaders who are attentive to the organization and its people, yet can still address the big picture. Several of today's leadership models relate well to the dynamism of the healthcare field and are presented here. Looking at these models, there seems to be a consistent pattern of self-aware leaders who are concerned for their employees and understand the importance of meaningful work. As we entered the 2000s, the **Self-Actualized Leadership Theory**, taking the term from Maslow's top level in his **Hierarchy of Needs** (Maslow, 1943), defines this type of leader. Today requires leaders to use **Adaptive Leadership** to create flexible organizations able to meet the relentless succession of challenges faced (Heifetz, Grashow, & Linsky, 2009). Plus, today's astute healthcare leaders recognize the importance of considering the global environment, as health care wrestles with international issues that impact us locally, such as outsourcing services, medical tourism, and over-the-border drug purchases. See Table 2-2.

Emotional Intelligence (EI)

Emotional Intelligence (EI) is a concept made famous by Daniel Goleman in the late 1990s. It suggests that there are certain skills (**intrapersonal and interpersonal**) that a person needs to be well adjusted in today's world. These skills include **self-awareness** (having a deep understanding of one's emotions, strengths, weaknesses, needs, and drives), **self-regulation** (a propensity for reflection, an ability to adapt to changes, the power to say no to impulsive urges), **motivation** (being driven to achieve, being passionate about one's profession, enjoying challenges), **empathy** (thoughtfully considering others' feelings when interacting), and **social skills** (moving people in the direction you desire by your ability to interact effectively) (Freshman & Rubino, 2002).

Since September 11, 2001, leaders have needed to be more understanding of their subordinates' world outside of the work environment. EI, when applied to leadership, suggests

TABLE 2-2 Leadership Theories in the United States

Period of Time	Leadership Theory	Leadership Focus
1920s and 1930s	Great Man	Having certain inherent traits
1940s and 1950s	Style Approach	Task completion and developing relationships
1960s	Situational Approach	Needs of the subordinates
Early 1970s	Contingency and Path–Goal	Both style and situation
Late 1970s	Leader–Member Exchange	Interactions between leader and subordinate
1980s	Transformational Approach	Raise consciousness and empower followers
1990s	Team Leadership	Team performance and development
2000s	Self-Actualized Leadership	Introspection and concern for meaningfulness
2010s	Adaptive Leadership	Build capacity to thrive in a new reality
2010s	Global Leader	Recognizing the impact of globalization for their industry

a more caring, confident, enthusiastic boss who can establish good relations with workers. Researchers have shown that EI can distinguish outstanding leaders and strong organizational performance (Goleman, 1998). For health care as an industry and for healthcare managers, this seems like a good fit. See Table 2-3.

Authentic Leadership

The central focus of **authentic leadership** is that people will want to naturally associate with someone who is following their internal compass of true purpose (George &

TABLE 2-3 Emotional Intelligence's Application to Healthcare Leadership

EI Dimension	Definition	Leadership Application
Self-Awareness	A deep understanding of one's emotions and drives	Knowing if your values are congruent with the organization's
Self-Regulation	Adaptability to changes and control over impulses	Considering ethics of giving bribes to doctors
Motivation	Ability to enjoy challenges and being passionate toward work	Being optimistic even when census is low
Empathy	Social awareness skill, putting yourself in another's shoes	Setting a patient-centered vision for the organization
Social Skills	Supportive communication skills, abilities to influence and inspire	Having an excellent rapport with the board

Sims, 2007). Leaders who follow this model are ones who know their authentic selves, define their values and leadership principles, understand what motivates them, build a strong support team, and stay grounded by integrating all aspects of their lives. Authentic leaders have attributes such as confidence, hope, optimism, resilience, high levels of integrity, and positive values (Brown & Gardner, 2007). Assessments given to leaders in a variety of international locations have provided the evidence-based knowledge that there is a correlation between authentic leadership and positive outcomes based on supervisor-rated performance (Walumbwa , Avolio, Gardner, Wernsing, & Peterson, 2008).

Inspirational Leadership

This model's focus is on leaders who **inspire by giving people what they need**. This can be very different from what they want. Inspirational leaders are not perfect and in fact expose their weaknesses so people can relate to them better. As with emotional intelligence, empathy is recognized as important. Inspirational leadership supports the concept known as "tough empathy," which is the quality of leaders caring passionately about their employees and their work yet being prudent in what they provide in the way of support. Inspirational leaders will rely on intuition to act and use their uniqueness (e.g., expertise, personality, or even something as simple as a greeting) as a way to distinguish themselves in the leadership role (Goffee & Jones, 2000).

Diversity Leadership

Our new global society forces healthcare leaders to address matters of diversity, whether with their patient base or with their employees. This commitment to diversity is necessary for today's leader to be successful. The environment must be assessed so that goals can be set that embrace the concept of diversity in matters such as employee hiring and promotional practices, patient communication, and governing board composition, to name a few. Strategies have to be developed that will make diversity work for the organization. The leader who recognizes the importance of diversity and designs its acceptance into the organizational culture will be most successful (Warden, 1999). Healthcare leaders are called to be role models for **cultural competency** (see Chapter 14 for more on this important topic) and to be able to attract, mentor, and coach those of different, as well as similar, backgrounds (Dolan, 2009).

Servant Leadership

Many people view health care as a very special type of work. Individuals usually work in this setting because they want to help people. **Servant leadership** applies this concept to top administration's ability to lead, acknowledging that a healthcare leader is largely motivated by a desire to serve others. This leadership model breaks down the typical organizational hierarchy and professes the belief of building a community within an organization in which everyone contributes to the greater whole. A servant leader is highly collaborative and gives credit to others generously. This leader is sensitive to what motivates others and empowers all to win with shared goals and vision. Servant leaders use personal trust and respect to build bridges and use persuasion rather than positional authority to foster cooperation. This model works especially well in a not-for-profit setting, since it continues the mission of fulfilling the community's needs rather than the organization's (Swearingen & Liberman, 2004).

Spirituality Leadership

Recently, the United States has experienced some very serious misrepresentations and misreporting by major healthcare companies, as reported by U.S. governmental agencies (e.g., HealthSouth, Tenet, and Paracelsus Healthcare). Trying to claim a renewed sense of confidence in the system, a model of leadership has emerged that focuses on spirituality. This **spiritual focus** does not imply a certain set of religious beliefs but emphasizes ethics, values, relationship skills, and the promotion of balance between work and self (Wolf, 2004). The goal under this model is to define our own uniqueness as human beings and to appreciate our spiritual depth. In this way, leaders can deepen their understanding and at the same time be more productive. These leaders have a positive impact on their workers and create a working environment that supports all individuals in finding meaning in what they do (see Table 2-4). They practice five common behaviors of effective leaders as described by Kouzes and Posner (1995): (1) Challenge the process, (2) Inspire a shared vision, (3) Enable others to act, (4) Model the way, and (5) Encourage the heart, thus taking leadership to a new level (Strack & Fottler, 2002).

TABLE 2-4 Spirituality Leadership's Application

Behavior	Definition	Leadership Application
Challenge the process	Always striving to do better	Change management
Inspire a shared vision	Collective sense of purpose	Strategic orientation
Enable others to act	Meeting needs of followers to get results	Gaining trust and confidence to achieve goals
Model the way	Setting a personal example	Coaching to motivate
Encourage the heart	Developing others to find meaning in work	Encouraging personal development of followers

LEADERSHIP STYLES

Models give us a broad understanding of someone's leadership philosophy. Styles demonstrate a particular type of leadership behavior that is consistently used. Various authors have attempted to explain different leadership styles (McConnell, 2003; Northouse, 2009; Studer, 2008). Some styles are more appropriate to use with certain healthcare workers, depending on their education, training, competence, motivation, experience, and personal needs. The environment must also be considered when deciding which style is the best fit.

In a **coercive leadership style** power is used inappropriately to get a desired response from a follower. This very directive format should probably not be used unless the leader is dealing with a very problematic subordinate or is in an emergency situation and needs immediate action. In healthcare settings over longer periods of time, three other leadership styles could be used more effectively: **participative, pacesetting, and coaching**.

Many healthcare workers are highly trained, specialized individuals who know much more about their area of expertise than their supervisor. Take the generally trained chief operating officer of a hospital who has several department managers (e.g., Radiology, Health Information Systems, Engineering) reporting to him or her. These managers will respond better and be more productive if the leader is **participative** in his or her style. Asking these managers for their input and giving them a voice in making decisions will let them know they are respected and valued.

In a **pacesetting style**, a leader sets high performance standards for his or her followers. This is very effective when the employees are self-motivated and highly competent—e.g., research scientists or intensive care nurses. A **coaching style** is recommended for the very top personnel in an organization. With this style, the leader focuses on the personal development of his or her followers rather than the work tasks. This should be reserved for followers the leader can trust and those who have proven their competence. See Table 2-5.

TABLE 2-5 Leadership Styles for Healthcare Personnel

Style	Definition	Application
Coercive	Demanding and power based	Problematic employees
Participative	Soliciting input and allowing decision making	Most followers
Pacesetting	Setting high performance standards	Highly competent
Coaching	Focus on personal development	Top level

LEADERSHIP COMPETENCIES

A leader needs certain **skills, knowledge, and abilities** to be successful. These are called **competencies**. The pressures of the healthcare industry have initiated the examination of a set of core competencies for a leader who works in a healthcare setting (Dye & Garman, 2006; Shewchuk, O'Connor, & Fine, 2005). Criticism has been directed at educational institutions for not producing administrators who can begin managing effectively right out of school. Educational programs in health administration are working with the national coalition groups (e.g., Health Leadership Alliance, National Center for Healthcare Leadership, and American College of Healthcare Executives) and healthcare administrative practitioners to come up with agreed upon competencies. Once identified, the programs can attempt to have their students learn how to develop these traits and behaviors.

Some of the competencies are technical—for example, having analytical skills, having a full understanding of the law, and being able to market and write. Some of the competencies are behavioral—for example, decisiveness, being entrepreneurial, and an ability to achieve a good work/life balance. As people move up in organizations, their behavioral competencies are a greater determinant of their success as leaders than their technical competencies (Hutton & Moulton, 2004). Another way to examine leadership competencies is under four main groupings or domains. The **Functional and Technical Domain** is necessary but not sufficient for a competent leader. Three other domains provide competencies that are behavioral and relate both to the individual (**Self-Development and Self-Understanding**) and to other people (**Interpersonal**). A fourth set of competencies falls under the heading **Organizational** and has a broader perspective. See Table 2-6 for a full listing of the leadership competencies under the four domains.

LEADERSHIP PROTOCOLS

Healthcare administrators are expected to act a certain way. Leaders are **role models** for their organizations' employees, and they need to be aware that their actions are being watched at all times. Sometimes people at the top of an organization get caught up in what they are doing and do not realize the message they are sending throughout the workplace by their inappropriate behavior. Specific ways of serving in the role of a healthcare leader can be demonstrated and can provide the exemplary model needed to send the correct message to employees. These appropriate ways in which a leader acts are called **protocols**.

There is no shortage of information on what protocols should be followed by today's healthcare leader. Each year, researchers, teachers of health administration, practicing

---

TABLE 2-6 Leadership Domains and Competencies

Domain: Functional and Technical
Competencies:

Knowledge of business/business acumen

Strategic vision

Decision making and decision quality

Managerial ethics and values

Problem solving

Change management/dealing with ambiguity

Systems thinking

Governance

Domain: Self-Development and Self-Understanding
Competencies:

Self-awareness and self-confidence

Self-regulation and personal responsibility

Honesty and integrity

Lifelong learning

Motivation/drive to achieve

Empathy and compassion

Flexibility

Perseverance

Work/life balance

Domain: Interpersonal
Competencies:

Communication

Motivating

Empowerment of subordinates

Management of group process

Conflict management and resolution

Negotiation

Formal presentations

Social interaction

Domain: Organizational
Competencies:

Organizational design

Team building

Priority setting

Political savvy

Managing and measuring performance

Developing others

Human resources

Community and external resources

Managing culture/diversity

Source: Hilberman, Diana (Ed.), The 2004 ACHE-AUPHA Pedagogy Enhancement Work Group. June, 2005.

administrators, and consultants write books filled with their suggestions on how to be a great leader (for some recent examples, see Dye, 2010; Ledlow & Coppola, 2011; and Rath and Conchie, 2008). There are some key ways a person serving in a leadership role should act. These are described here and summarized in Table 2-7.

Professionalism is essential to good leadership. This can be manifested not only in the way people act but also in their mannerisms and their dress. A leader who comes to work in sloppy attire or exhibits obnoxious behavior will not gain respect from followers. **Trust and respect** are very important for a leader to acquire. Trust and respect must be a two-way exchange if a leader is to get followers to respond. Employees who do not trust their leader will consistently question certain aspects of their job. If they do not have respect for the leader, they will not care about doing a good job. This could lead to low productivity and bad service.

TABLE 2-7 Key Leadership Protocols

1. Professionalism
2. Reciprocal trust and respect
3. Confident, optimistic, and passionate
4. Being visible
5. Open communicator
6. Risk taker/entrepreneur
7. Admitting fault

Even a leader's mood can affect workers. A boss who is **confident, optimistic, and passionate** about his or her work can instill the same qualities in the workers. Such enthusiasm is almost always infectious and is passed on to others within the organization. The same can be said of a leader who is weak, negative, and obviously unenthusiastic about his or her work—these poor qualities can be acquired by others.

Leaders must be very **visible** throughout the organization. Having a presence can assure workers that the top people are "at the helm" and give a sense of stability and confidence in the business. Quint Studer (2009), founder and CEO of Studer Group, states how "**rounding**" can help leaders meet certain standard goals: making sure that the staff know they are cared about, know what is going on (what is working well, who should be recognized, which systems need to work better, which tools and equipment need attention), and know that proper follow-up actions are taking place. Leaders must be **open communicators**. Holding back information that could have been shared with followers will cause ill feelings and a concern that other important matters are not being disclosed. Leaders also need to take **calculated risks**. They should be cautious, but not overly so, or they might lose an opportunity for the organization. And finally, leaders in today's world need to recognize that they are **not perfect**. Sometimes there will be errors in what is said or done. These must be acknowledged so they can be put aside and the leader can move on to more pressing current issues.

GOVERNANCE

Individuals are not the only ones to consider in leadership roles. There can be a group of people who collectively assume the responsibility for strategic oversight of a healthcare organization. The term **governance** describes this important function. Governing bodies can be organized in a variety of forms. In a hospital, this top accountable body is called a board of trustees in a not-for-profit setting and a board of directors in a proprietary, or for-profit, setting. Since many physician offices, long-term care facilities, and other healthcare entities are set up as professional corporations, these organizations would also have a board of directors.

Governing boards are facing heightened scrutiny due to the failure of many large corporations in the last decade. The U.S. government recognizes the importance of a group of people who oversee corporate operations and give assurances for the fair and honest functioning of the business. **Sarbanes-Oxley** is a federal law enacted in 2002 that set new or enhanced standards for proprietary companies that are publicly traded. Financial records must be appropriately audited and signed off by top leaders. Operations need to be discussed more openly so as to remove any possibility of cover-up, fraud, or self-interest. Each governing board member has fiduciary responsibility to forgo his or her own personal interests and to make all decisions concerning the entity for the good of the organization. Many believe the not-for-profits should have the same requirements and are applying pressure for them to fall under similar **rules of transparency**.

Although healthcare boards are becoming smaller in size, they recognize the importance of the **composition** of their members. A selection of people from within the organization (e.g., system leaders, the management staff, physicians) should be balanced with outside members from the community (see Table 2-8). The trend is to appoint members who have certain expertise to assist the board in carrying out its duties. Also, having governing board members who do not have ties to the healthcare operations will reduce the possibility of conflicts of interests. Board meetings have gone from ones in which a large volume of information is presented for a "rubber stamp" to meetings that are well prepared, purposeful, and focused on truly important issues. A **self-assessment** should be taken at least annually and any identified problem areas (including particular board members) addressed. This way, the governing board can review where it stands in its ability to give

TABLE 2-8 Healthcare Governance Trends

Function	Old Way	New Trend
Size of board	Large (10 to 20 people)	Smaller (6 to 12 people)
Membership	Many members from within the organization	More balance of members within and outside the organization
Conflicts of interest	Some present, not disclosed	Must be disclosed but prefer none
Meetings	Voluminous detailed information presented	Strategic information and trends presented
Evaluations	If done, not taken too seriously	Taken seriously to identify issues and correct
Leadership	Fiduciary and strategic responsibilities	Generative source

fair, open, and honest strategic oversight (Gautam, 2005). A new way of looking at governance goes beyond fiduciary and strategic responsibility, whereby the board serves as the generative source of leadership, espousing the meaning for the organization's healthcare delivery (Chait, Ryan, & Taylor, 2005).

BARRIERS AND CHALLENGES

Health care is one of the most dynamic industries in the world. The only constant is change. Healthcare leaders are confronted with many situations that must be dealt with as they lead their organizations. Some can be considered barriers that, if not managed properly, will stymie the capacity to lead. Certain other areas are challenges that must be addressed if the leader is to be successful. A few of the more critical ones in today's healthcare world are presented here. See Table 2-9.

Due to the complex healthcare system in the United States, many **regulations and laws** are in place that sometimes can inhibit innovative and creative business practices. Leaders must ensure that the strategies developed for their entity comply with the current laws, or else they jeopardize its long-term survivability. Leaders are expected to sometimes think "outside the box," i.e., go beyond the usual responses to a situation, to provide new ideas for the development of their business, but this can be challenging when many constraints must be considered. Some examples are the government's antitrust requirements, which can affect developing partners; federal moratoriums on certain services, which can affect growing the business; and safe harbor requirements, which can affect physician relations. These and other laws and regulations can affect a healthcare leader's ability to lead.

The healthcare industry is unique. Major players in the arena, **physicians**, are not always easily controlled by the medical organizations where they work (e.g., hospitals, insurance companies, long-term care facilities). Yet this very influential group of stakeholders has substantial input over the volume of patients that a healthcare facility receives. This necessitates that the healthcare leader find ways to include doctors in the process of setting a

---

TABLE 2-9 Key Healthcare Leadership Barriers and Challenges

1. Laws and regulations (Barrier)
2. Physicians (Challenge)
3. New technology (Barrier)
4. Culture of safety (Challenge)
5. Resource limitation (Barrier)
6. Economy (Challenge)

---

direction, monitoring the quality of care, and fulfilling other administrative functions. The wise healthcare leader will include physicians early on in any planning process. Doctors are usually busy with their own patients and practices, but if they are not looked to for their expertise and advice on certain important matters in the facilities where they work, then they will become disengaged. This could cause essential functions to be overlooked. It could also cause physicians to alter the referral patterns for their patients. Everybody would much rather work at a place where their opinions are requested and respected.

Technology is a costly requirement in any work setting. Information systems management and new medical equipment are especially expensive for the modern healthcare facility or practice due to the rapidly changing data collection requirements and medical advances in the field. Healthcare leaders must assess the capabilities of their entities for new technology and determine if their systems and equipment are a barrier to making future progress. Healthcare leaders cannot be successful if their organizations have antiquated systems and out-of-date support devices in today's high-tech world. Computer hardware and clinical software must be integrated to provide the quality and cost information needed for an efficient medical organization. Electronic medical records, wireless devices, and computerized order entry systems, as well as advanced medical equipment and new pharmaceuticals, will be items the leader must have in place in order to lead his or her healthcare organization into the 21st century.

Safety concerns have traditionally been a management responsibility. However, safety has become such an important issue in today's healthcare world that leaders must be involved in its oversight. A top-down direction must be given throughout the organization that mistakes will not be tolerated. Coordinated efforts must shift from following up on errors to preventing their recurrence to developing systems and mechanisms to prevent them from ever occurring. The Joint Commission has leadership standards for all sectors, calling for the leaders in the healthcare entity to accept the responsibility for fostering a culture of safety. The focus of attention is on the performance of **systems and processes** instead of the individual, although reckless behavior and blatant disregard for safety are not tolerated (The Joint Commission, 2010).

ETHICAL RESPONSIBILITY

Ethics are principles determining behavior and conduct appropriate to a certain setting. It is a matter of doing right vs. wrong. Ethics are especially important for healthcare leadership and require two areas of focus. One area is **biomedical ethics** and the actions a leader needs to consider as he or she relates to a patient. Another is **managerial ethics**. This involves business practices and doing things for the right reasons. A leader must ensure an environment in which good ethical behavior is followed.

TABLE 2-10 American College of Healthcare Executives Code of Ethics

Responsible Area	Sample Guidelines
To the profession	Comply with laws Avoid any conflicts of interest Respect confidences
To the patients or others served	Prevent discrimination Safeguard patient confidentiality Have process to evaluate quality of care
To the organization	Proper resource allocation Improve standards of management Prevent fraud and abuse within
To the employees	Allow free expression Ensure a safe workplace environment Follow nondiscrimination policies
To the community and society	Work to meet the needs of the community Provide appropriate access to services Advocate for healthy society
To report violations of the code	Healthcare executive–supplier interactions Decisions near the end of life Impaired healthcare executives

The **American College of Healthcare Executives (ACHE)** does an excellent job in educating its professional membership as to the ethical responsibilities of healthcare leaders (American College of Healthcare Executives, 2009). Ethical responsibilities apply to several different constituencies: to the profession itself, to the patients and others served, to the organization, to the employees, and to the community and society at large (see Table 2-10). A healthcare leader who is concerned about an ethical workplace will not only model the appropriate behavior but will also have zero tolerance for any deviation by a member of the organization. A Code of Ethics gives specific guidelines to be followed by individual members. An Integrity Agreement would address a commitment to follow ethical behavior by the organization.

LEADERS LOOKING TO THE FUTURE

Some people believe that leaders are born and that one cannot be taught how to be a good leader. The growing trend, however, is that leaders can, in fact, be taught skills and behaviors that will help them to lead an organization effectively (Parks, 2005). In health care, many clinicians who do well at their jobs are promoted to supervisory positions. Yet they do not have the management training that would help them in their new roles. For example, physicians, laboratory technologists, physical therapists, and nurses are often pushed into management positions with no administrative training. We are doing a disservice to these clinicians and setting them up for failure.

Fortunately, this common occurrence has been recognized, and many new programs have sprouted to address this need. Universities have developed **executive programs** to attract medical personnel into a fast-track curriculum to attempt to give them the essential skills they need to be successful. Some schools have developed majors in healthcare leadership, and some healthcare systems have started internal leadership training programs. This trend will continue into the future, since healthcare services are expected to grow due to the aging population, and thus there will be a need for more people to be in charge. In addition, leaders should continually be updated as to the qualities that make a good leader in the current environment, and therefore, professional development, provided through internal or external programs, should be encouraged. The **Baldrige National Quality Program** recognizes in its most recent criteria for performance excellence the need for senior leaders to create a sustainable environment for their organizations through the continual development of future leaders by enhancing their personal leadership skills (Baldrige National Quality Program, 2009). Yet Garman and Dye (2009) caution us to distinguish **leader development** from **leadership development**. They call for the need to bind leadership development activities into a collective network of leaders who are linked to organizational level goals rather than each leader's individual performance. Further understanding of the difference can be explained through decision making. A leader collaborating with his or her superior would be considered leader development, but in leadership development, the process would be team based.

Each of the different sectors in health care has a professional association that will support many aspects of its particular career path. These groups provide ongoing educational efforts to help their members lead their organizations. Another benefit for leaders is that these groups provide up-to-date information about their particular field. **Professional associations** are a good way to network with people in similar roles, a highly desirable process for healthcare leaders. Also, ethnic professional associations link healthcare leaders from representative minority groups as they attempt to increase diversity in the healthcare profession and improve health status, economic opportunities, and educational advancement for their communities. Most of these various professional groups have student chapters, and early involvement in these organizations is highly recommended for any future healthcare leader. Table 2-11 lists some of these associations.

To prepare an organization for the future, its leader needs to be looking out for opportunities to partner with other entities. Health care in the United States is fragmented, and to be successful, different services need to be aligned and networks need to be created that will allow patients to flow easily through the continuum of care. It is the astute leader who can determine who are the best partners and negotiate a way to have a win–win situation.

TABLE 2-11 Professional Associations

Name	Acronym	Targeted Career	Website
American College of Healthcare Executives	ACHE	Health administrators	www.ache.org
Healthcare Financial Management Association	HFMA	Healthcare chief financial officers	www.hfma.org
Association for University Programs in Health Administration	AUPHA	Health administration education Program directors	www.aupha.org
Medical Group Management Association	MGMA	Medical groups administrators	www.mgma.org
American College of Health Care Administrators	ACHCA	Long-term care administrators	www.achca.org
American Academy of Nursing	AAN	Nurse leaders	www.aannet.org
American College of Physician Executives	ACPE	Physician leaders	www.acpe.org
National Association of Health Services Executives	NAHSE	Black healthcare leaders	www.nahse.org
National Forum for Latino Healthcare Executives	NFLHE	Latino healthcare leaders	www.nflhe.org
Asian Health Care Leaders Association	AHCLA	Asian healthcare leaders	www.asianhealthcareleaders.org

Of course, these efforts to develop partnerships must be in line with the organization's mission and vision, or the strategic direction will have to be reexamined.

A leader who is concerned about the future will stay on top of things in the healthcare industry. Reading newspapers, industry journals, and Web reports, as well as attending industry conferences, helps to keep leaders in the know and allow them to determine how changes in the field could impact their organization. Leaders who remain current will be better positioned to act proactively and to provide the best chance for their organizations to seize a fresh opportunity.

The healthcare leader who is concerned about the future, as well as today's business, must continuously reassess how he or she fits in the organization. Nothing could be worse than a disenchanted person trying to lead a group of followers without the motivation and enthusiasm needed by great leaders. A leader should consider his or her own **succession planning** so that the organization is not left at any time without a person to lead. Truly unselfish leaders think about their commitment to their followers and do their best to ensure that consistent formidable leadership will be in place in the event of their departure.

This final act will allow adequate time for a smooth transition and ensure the passage of accountability so that the followers can realign themselves with the new leader.

Finally, the recently enacted **Patient Protection and Affordable Care Act** may not yet provide us full healthcare reform, but it will dramatically alter the way health insurance is administered. A call is made for a new breed of leaders at every level to tame the chaos associated with this dynamic industry (Lee, 2010). These will certainly be challenging times for healthcare leaders, and some of the key elements identified for success will be perspective, adaptability, and finding their inner passion as a personal driving force (Sukin, 2009). There is no doubt there will be opportunities for leaders in all disciplines to make a difference for their organizations and their communities as we enter this exciting new phase of American healthcare delivery.

DISCUSSION QUESTIONS

1. What is the difference between leadership and management?

2. Are leaders born, or are they trained? How has the history of leadership in the United States evolved to reflect this question?

3. List and describe the contemporary models of leadership. What distinguishes them from past models?

4. What are the leadership domains and competencies? Can you be a good leader and not have all the competencies listed in this model?

5. Why do healthcare leaders have a higher need for ethical behavior than might be expected in other settings?

6. Do healthcare leaders have a responsibility to be culturally competent? Why or why not?

7. Why is emotional intelligence important for healthcare managers? Identify three ways someone who is new to the field can assess and develop his or her EI quotient.

Cases in Chapter 17 that are related to this chapter include:

- Choosing a Successor—see p. 444
- Emotional Intelligence in Labor and Delivery—see p. 434
- The Merger of Two Competing Hospitals—see p. 406

Additional cases, role-play scenarios, video links, websites, and other information sources are also available in the online Instructor's Materials.

REFERENCES

American College of Healthcare Executives. (2009). *Annual report and reference guide.*

Atchison, T. A. (2003). *Followership: A practical guide to aligning leaders and followers.* Chicago, IL: Health Administration Press.

Baldrige National Quality Program. (2009). *2009–2010 Health care criteria for performance excellence.* Retrieved from http://www.baldrige.nist.gov/PDF_files/2009_2010_HealthCare_Criteria.pdf

Brown, J. A., & Gardner, W. L. (2007). Effective modeling of authentic leadership. *Academic Exchange Quarterly, 11*(2), 56–60.

Chait, R., Ryan, W., & Taylor, B. (2005). *Governance as leadership.* Hoboken, NJ: Wiley.

Dolan, T. C. (2009). Cultural competency and diversity. *Healthcare Executive, 24*(6), 6.

Dye, C. F. (2010). *Leadership in healthcare: Essential values and skills* (2nd ed.). Chicago, IL: Health Administration Press.

Dye, C. F., & Garman, A. N. (2006). *Exceptional leadership: 16 critical competencies for healthcare executives.* Chicago, IL: Health Administration Press.

Freshman, B., & Rubino, L. (2002). Emotional intelligence: A core competency for health care administrators. *The Health Care Manager, 20,* 1–9.

Garman, A., & Dye, C. (2009). *The healthcare c-suite: Leadership development at the top.* Chicago, IL: Health Administration Press.

Gautam, K. (2005). Transforming hospital board meetings: Guidelines for comprehensive change. *Hospital Topics: Research and Perspectives on Healthcare, 83*(3), 25–31.

George, B., & Sims, P. (2007). *True north: Discover your authentic leadership.* San Francisco, CA: Jossey-Bass.

Goffee, R., & Jones, G. (2000, September). Why should anyone be led by you? *Harvard Business Review,* 62–70.

Goleman, D. (1998, December). What makes a leader? *Harvard Business Review,* 93–102.

Heifetz, R., Grashow, A., & Linsky, M. (2009, July–August). Leadership in a (permanent) crisis. *Harvard Business Review.* Retrieved from http://hbr.org/2009/07/leadership-in-a-permanent-crisis/ar/1

Hilberman, D. (Ed.). (2005, June). *Final report: Pedagogy enhancement project on leadership skills for healthcare management.* The 2004 ACHE-AUPHA Pedagogy Enhancement Work Group. Association of University Programs in Health Administration.

Hutton, D., & Moulton, S. (2004). Behavioral competencies for health care leaders. *Best of H&HN OnLine.* American Hospital Association, 15–18.

The Joint Commission. (2010). *Hospital accreditation standards.* Oakbrook Terrace, IL: Author.

Kouzes, J. M., & Posner, B. Z. (1995). *The leadership challenge: How to keep getting extraordinary things done in organizations.* San Francisco, CA: Jossey-Bass.

Ledlow, G. R., & Coppola, M. N. (2011). *Leadership for health professionals.* Sudbury, MA: Jones & Bartlett.

Lee, T. H. (2010, April). Turning doctors into leaders. *Harvard Business Review, 88*(4), 50–58.

Maslow, A. H. (1943). A theory of human motivation. *Psychological Review, 50,* 370–396.

McConnell, C. (2003). Accepting leadership responsibility: Preparing yourself to lead honestly, humanely, and effectively. *The Health Care Manager, 22*(4), 361–374.

Northouse, P. (2009). *Introduction to leadership concepts and practice.* Thousand Oaks, CA: Sage.

Northouse, P. (2010). *Leadership: Theory and practice* (5th ed.). Thousand Oaks, CA: Sage.

Parks, S. (2005). *Leadership can be taught: A bold approach for a complex world.* Boston, MA: Harvard Business School Press.

Rath, T., & Conchie, B. (2008). *Strengths-based leadership: Great leaders, teams, and why people follow.* New York, NY: Gallup Press.

Shewchuk, R., O'Connor, S., & Fine, D. (2005). Building an understanding of the competencies needed for health administration practice. *Journal of Healthcare Management, 50*(1), 32–47.

Sibbet, D. (1997, September/October). 75 years of management ideas and practice 1922–1997. *Harvard Business Review Supplement.*

Strack, G., & Fottler, M. (2002). Spirituality and effective leadership in healthcare: Is there a connection? *Frontiers of Health Services Management, 18*(4), 3–18.

Studer, Q. (2008). *Results that last: Hardwiring behaviors that will take your company to the top.* Hoboken, NJ: Wiley.

Studer, Q. (2009). *Straight A leadership: Alignment, action, accountability.* Gulf Breeze, FL: Fire Starter Publishing.

Sukin, D. (2009). Leadership in challenging times: It starts with passion. *Frontiers of Health Services Management, 26*(2), 3–8.

Swearingen, S., & Liberman, A. (2004). Nursing leadership: Serving those who serve others. *The Health Care Manager, 23*(2), 100–109.

Walumbwa, F., Avolio, B., Gardner, W., Wernsing, T., & Peterson, S. (2008). Authentic leadership: Development and validation of a theory-based measure. *Journal of Management, 34*(1), 89–126.

Warden, G. (1999). Leadership diversity. *Journal of Healthcare Management, 44*(6), 421–422.

Wolf, E. (2004). Spiritual leadership: A new model. *Healthcare Executive, 19*(2), 22–25.

Additional Websites to Explore

National Center for Healthcare Leadership:	www.nchl.org
Health Leadership Council:	www.hlc.org
National Public Health Leadership Institute:	www.phli.org
World Health Organization Leadership Service:	www.who.int/health_leadership
Health Leaders Media:	www.healthleaders.com
Institute for Diversity of Health Management:	www.diversityconnection.org
Healthcare Leadership Alliance Competency Directory:	www.healthcareleadershipalliance.org/
Coach John Wooden's Pyramid of Success:	www.coachwooden.com

CHAPTER 3

Management and Motivation

Nancy H. Shanks and Amy Dore

LEARNING OBJECTIVES

By the end of this chapter, the student will be able to:

- Frame the context for understanding the concept of motivation, particularly who and what motivates employees;
- Distinguish the concept of engagement and its relationship to motivation;
- Offer insights into reasons why motivation is important;
- Recognize historic fundamentals of motivation;
- Provide an overview of the different theories of motivation;
- Identify extrinsic and intrinsic factors that impact motivation;
- Assess misconceptions about motivation;
- Analyze issues relating to motivating across generations; and
- Suggest strategies to enhance employee motivation.

INTRODUCTION

Managers are continually challenged to motivate a workforce to do two things. The first is to motivate employees to work toward helping the organization achieve its goals. The second is to motivate employees to work toward achieving their own personal goals.

Meeting the needs and achieving the goals of both the employer and the employee is often difficult for managers in all types of organizations. In health care, however, this is often more difficult, in part as a result of the complexity of healthcare organizations, but also as a function of the wide array of employees who are employed by or work collaboratively with healthcare providers in delivering and paying for care. The types of workers run the gamut from highly trained and highly skilled technical and clinical staff members, e.g., physicians and nurses, to relatively unskilled workers (see Chapter 11 for more on this topic). To be successful, healthcare managers need to be able to manage and motivate this wide array of employees.

MOTIVATED VS. ENGAGED—ARE THE TERMS THE SAME?

Oftentimes when you read about motivation, the term *engaged* appears within the same context. In order to be motivated, employees must be engaged—and in order to be engaged, they must be motivated. Over "the past decade, Gallup interviewed more than 1.2 million employees at more than 800 hospitals" (2010). The purpose of the research conducted was to understand what engaged healthcare employees look like. Results showed that engaged healthcare employees:

- Are more productive
- Are more focused on patient care and treatment
- Are safer
- Are loyal to their employers
- Model positive pro-organizational behaviors
- Contribute to greater profitability for a provider than a disengaged employer

Disengaged employees bring morale down and impact the organization's bottom line. According to Gallup, within the U.S. workforce, more than $300 billion is lost in productivity alone in disengaged employees. Top-performing organizations recognize that employee engagement requires motivation and is the driving force behind organizational performance and outcomes (Gallup, 2010; Manion, 2009).

MOTIVATION—THE CONCEPT

According to Webster's New Collegiate Dictionary, a **motive** is "something (a need or desire) that causes a person to act." **Motivate**, in turn, means "to provide with a motive," and **motivation** is defined as "the act or process of motivating." Thus, motivation is the act or process of providing a motive that causes a person to take some action. In most cases, motivation comes from some need that leads to behavior that results in some type of reward when the need is fulfilled. This definition raises a couple of basic questions.

What Are Rewards?

Rewards can take two forms. They can be either **intrinsic/internal rewards** or **extrinsic/ external** ones. **Intrinsic rewards** are derived from within the individual. For a healthcare employee, this could mean taking pride and feeling good about a job well done (e.g., providing excellent patient care). **Extrinsic rewards** pertain to those reinforcements that are given by another person, such as a healthcare organization giving bonuses to teams of workers when quality and patient satisfaction are demonstrated to be exceptional.

Who Motivates Employees?

While rewards may serve as incentives and those who bestow rewards may seek to use them as motivators, the real motivation to act comes from within the individual. Managers do exert a significant amount of influence over employees, but they do not have the power to force a person to act. They can work to provide various types of **incentives** in an effort to influence an employee in any number of ways, such as by changing job descriptions, rearranging work schedules, improving working conditions, reconfiguring teams, and a host of other activities, as will be discussed later in this chapter. While these may have an impact on an employee's level of motivation and willingness to act, when all is said and done, it is the employee's decision to take action or not. In discussing management and motivation, it is important to continually remember the roles of both managers and employees in the process of motivation.

Is Everybody Motivated?

As managers, we often assume that employees are motivated or will respond to inducements from managers. While this is perhaps a logical and rational approach from the manager's perspective, it is critical to understand that this is not always the case. The majority of employees do, in fact, want to do a good job and are motivated by any number of factors, however, others may not share that same drive or high level of motivation. Those people may merely be putting in time and may be more motivated by other things, such as family, school, hobbies, or other interests. Keeping this in mind is useful in helping healthcare managers understand employee behaviors that seem to be counterproductive.

WHY MOTIVATION MATTERS

Healthcare organizations face pressure externally and internally. Externally, the healthcare system must confront challenges such as the aging population, economic downturns, reductions in reimbursements, increases in market competition, increases in the cost of providing care, and healthcare reform. Internally, our healthcare system faces pressure stemming from challenges such as shortages of certain types of healthcare workers, increasing accreditation requirements, dealing with limited resources, increasing responsibilities connected with providing quality care, and ensuring patient safety. These pressures can lead to employees who feel burned out, frustrated, and overworked. As healthcare employees are continually being asked to increase their responsibilities with fewer resources, managers must create a work environment in which employees are engaged, happy at their job, inspired, and motivated.

People spend approximately one-third of their lives at work, and managers need to recognize that the workplace is one of the most important aspects of a person's identity. In situations where people are not free to work at their maximum effectiveness and their self-esteem is constantly under attack, stress occurs, morale diminishes, illness prevails, and absenteeism goes up (Scott & Jaffe, 1991). As noted above, motivated employees are fully engaged in their work and contribute at a much higher level than their counterparts who see their work as simply a job. Additional reasons why motivation matters include:

- Employees who are motivated feel invested in the organization, are happier, work harder, are more productive, and typically stay longer with an organization (Levoy, 2007, p. 70).
- Managers who understand employees' job-related needs experience a higher level of motivated behavior from their employees (Levoy, 2007, p. 113).
- All behavior is needs oriented. Even irrational behavior stems from a motivator of some sort. Once a need is satisfied, its impact as a motivator lessens. This basic foundational understanding of motivation is essential to successful motivation and management of employees (Levoy, 2007, p. 118).
- A motivated and engaged workforce experiences better outcomes and provides an organization with a competitive edge to successfully compete and be viewed as a dominant force in the market.

HISTORY OF MOTIVATION

There is a plethora of research on the topic of motivation, particularly motivation in the workplace. The concepts of management and motivation often coincide when an organization is striving toward a goal. In order to fully understand the concept of motivation, a manager must understand its significance. Motivation is not a new concept. Approximately 2,500 years ago, Athens rose to unparalleled political and economic power and allowed the citizenry to become active in civic governance. Through an engaged and participative citizenry, the Athenian people helped produce the first great Greek empire, which allowed for better commerce and trade, increased wealth of its citizens, and a culture that spawned historically known philosophers, artists, and academics. To achieve this type of success, organizations must recognize the full power of their employees and motivate them to reach for the common good of the organization (Manville & Ober, 2003).

Fast forward to more recent times, and we can continue to identify the historical significance of motivation. In 1890, empirical psychologist William James identified aspects of motivation and its relationship with **intrinsically motivated behavior**. In 1943, psychologist Clark Hull published his now famous **drive theory**. Hull believed all behaviors to be connected to "four primary drives: hunger, thirst, sex, and the avoidance of pain." According to this view, all drives provide the energy for behavior (Deci & Ryan, 1985). Research into human behavior started being recognized in the workplace in the 1940s. Researchers recognized that people are motivated by several types of varying needs, not only in the workplace but also in their personal lives (Sperry, 2003). Workplace motivational theories continue to evolve, as is shown in the discussion concerning theories of motivation.

THEORIES OF MOTIVATION

Psychologists have studied human motivation extensively and have derived a variety of theories about what motivates people. This section briefly highlights the motivational theories that are widely known in the field of management. These include theories that focus on motivation being a function of (1) employee **needs** of various types, (2) **extrinsic factors**, and (3) **intrinsic factors**. Each set of theories is discussed below.

Needs-Based Theories of Motivation
Maslow's Hierarchy of Needs

Maslow (1954) postulated a "**hierarchy of needs**" that progresses from the lowest, subsistence-level needs to the highest level of self-awareness and actualization. Once each level has been met, the theory is that an individual will be motivated by and strive to progress to satisfy the next higher level of need. The five levels in Maslow's hierarchy are:

- **Physiological needs**—including food, water, sexual drive, and other subsistence-related needs;
- **Safety needs**—including shelter, a safe home environment, employment, a healthy and safe work environment, access to health care, money, and other basic necessities;
- **Belonging needs**—including the desire for social contact and interaction, friendship, affection, and various types of support;
- **Esteem needs**—including status, recognition, and positive regard; and
- **Self-actualization needs**—including the desire for achievement, personal growth and development, and autonomy.

The movement from one level to the next was termed "**satisfaction progression**" by Maslow, and it was assumed that over time individuals were motivated to continually progress upward through these levels. While useful from a theoretical perspective, most individuals do not view their needs in this way, making this approach to motivation a bit unrealistic.

Alderfer's ERG Theory

The three components identified by Alderfer (1972) in his **ERG theory** drew upon Maslow's theory but also suggested that individuals were motivated to move forward and backward through the levels in terms of motivators. He reduced Maslow's levels from five to the following three:

- **Existence**—which related to Maslow's first two needs, thus combining the physiological and safety needs into one level;
- **Relatedness**—which addressed the belonging needs; and
- **Growth**—which pertained to the last two needs, thereby combining esteem and self-actualization.

Alderfer also added his **frustration–regression principle**, which postulated that individuals would move in and out of the various levels, depending upon the extent to which their needs were being met. This approach is deemed by students of management to be more logical and similar to many individuals' worldviews.

Herzberg's Two-Factor Theory

Herzberg (2003) further modified Maslow's needs theory and consolidated down to two areas of needs that motivated employees. These were termed:

- **Hygienes**—These were characterized as lower-level motivators and included, for example, "company policy and administration, supervision, interpersonal relationships, working conditions, salary, status, and security" (p. 5).
- **Motivators**—These emphasized higher-level factors and focused on aspects of work, such as "achievement, recognition for achievement, the work itself, responsibility, and growth or advancement" (p. 5).

Herzberg's is an easily understood approach that suggests that individuals have desires beyond the hygienes and that motivators are very important to them.

McClelland's Acquired Needs Theory

The idea here is that needs are acquired throughout life. That is, needs are not innate but are learned or developed as a result of one's life experiences (McClelland, 1985). This theory focuses on three types of needs:

- **Need for achievement**—which emphasizes the desires for success, for mastering tasks, and for attaining goals;
- **Need for affiliation**—which focuses on the desire for relationships and associations with others; and

- **Need for power**—which relates to the desires for responsibility for, control of, and authority over others.

All four of these theories approach needs from a somewhat different perspective and are helpful in understanding employee motivation on the basis of needs. However, other theories of motivation also have been posited and require consideration.

Extrinsic Factor Theories of Motivation

Another approach to understanding motivation focuses on external factors and their role in understanding employee motivation. The best known of these follow.

Reinforcement Theory

B. F. Skinner (1953) studied human behavior and proposed that individuals are motivated when their behaviors are reinforced. His theory is comprised of four types of reinforcement. The first two are associated with achieving desirable behaviors, while the last two address undesirable behaviors:

- **Positive reinforcement**—relates to taking action that rewards positive behaviors;
- **Avoidance learning**—occurs when actions are taken to reward behaviors that avoid undesirable or negative behaviors. This is sometimes referred to as **negative reinforcement**;
- **Punishment**—includes actions designed to reduce undesirable behaviors by creating negative consequences for the individual; and
- **Extinction**—represents the removal of positive rewards for undesirable behaviors. Likewise, if the rewards for *desirable* behaviors cease, those actions can be impacted as well.

The primary criticism of the reinforcement approach is that it fails to account for employees' abilities to think critically and reason, both of which are important aspects of human motivation. While reinforcement theory may be applicable in animals, it doesn't account for the higher level of cognition that occurs in humans.

Intrinsic Factor Theories of Motivation

Theories that are based on **intrinsic or endogenous factors** focus on internal thought processes and perceptions about motivation. Several of these are highlighted below:

- **Adams' Equity Theory**—which proposes that individuals are motivated when they perceive that they are treated equitably in comparison to others within the organization (Adams, 1963);

- **Vroom's Expectancy Theory**—which addresses the expectations of individuals and hypothesizes that they are motivated by performance and the expected outcomes of their own behaviors (Vroom, 1964); and
- **Locke's Goal-Setting Theory**—which hypothesizes that by establishing goals individuals are motivated to take action to achieve those goals (Locke & Latham, 1990).

While each of these theories deals with a particular aspect of motivation, it seems unrealistic to address them in isolation, since these factors often do come into play in and are important to employee motivation at one time or another.

Management Theories of Motivation

Other approaches to motivation are driven by aspects of management, such as productivity, human resources, and other considerations. Most notable in this regard are the following:

- **Scientific Management Theory**—Frederick Taylor's ideas, put into practice by the Gilbreths in the film *Cheaper by the Dozen*, focused on studying job processes, determining the most efficient means of performing them, and in turn rewarding employees for their productivity and hard work. This theory assumes that people are motivated and able to continually work harder and more efficiently and that employee pay should be based on the amount and quality of the work performed. Over time, this approach is limited by the capacity of employees to continue to increase the quantity of work produced without sacrificing the quality.
- **McGregor's Theory X and Theory Y**—This approach again draws upon the work of Herzberg and develops a human resources management approach to motivation. This theory first classifies managers into one of two groups. **Theory X** managers view employees as unmotivated and disliking work. Under the Theory X approach, the manager's role is to focus on the hygienes and to control and direct employees; it assumes that employees are mainly concerned about safety. In contrast, **Theory Y** managers focus on Herzberg's motivators and work to assist employees in achieving these higher levels. In assessing this theory, researchers have found that approaching motivation from this either/or perspective is short-sighted.
- **Ouchi's Theory Z**—This theory is rooted in the idea that employees who are involved in and committed to an organization will be motivated to increase productivity. Based on the Japanese approach to management and motivation, **Theory Z** managers provide rewards, such as long-term employment, promotion from within, participatory management, and other techniques to engage and motivate employees (Ouchi, 1981). In fact, Theory Z can be considered an early form of engagement theory.

While all of these theories are helpful in understanding management and motivation from a conceptual perspective, it is important to recognize that most managers draw upon a combination of needs, extrinsic factors, and intrinsic factors in an effort to help motivate employees, to help employees meet their own personal needs and goals, and ultimately to engage employees in and to achieve effectiveness and balance within the organization. Managers typically take into account most of the aspects upon which these theories focus. That is, expectations, goal setting, performance, feedback, equity, satisfaction, commitment, and other characteristics are considered in the process of motivating employees.

A BIT MORE ABOUT INCENTIVES AND REWARDS

Throughout this chapter, we have discussed what motivates employees. As the previous discussion indicates, motivation for employees results from a combination of incentives that take the form of extrinsic and intrinsic rewards. These topics warrant a bit more discussion.

Extrinsic Rewards

There are a host of external things that managers can provide that may serve as incentives for employees to become more engaged in an organization and increase their productivity. These include:

- **Money**—in the form of pay, bonuses, stock options, etc.
- **Benefits**—also in many different forms, including health, dental, and vision insurance; vacation days; sick leave; retirement accounts; etc. Increasingly benefits are offered under some form of cafeteria plan, allowing employees flexibility in what can be selected and in the management of their own benefit package. Providing employees choices in benefits can itself be a motivating factor.
- **Flexible schedules.**
- **Job responsibilities and duties.**
- **Promotions.**
- **Changes in status**—conveyed either by changes in job titles or in new and different job responsibilities.
- **Supervision of others.**
- **Praise and feedback.**
- **A good boss.**
- **A strong leader.**
- **Other inspirational people.**
- **A nurturing organizational culture.**

As this list demonstrates, extrinsic rewards are all tangible types of rewards. Intrinsic rewards stand in marked contrast to these.

Intrinsic Rewards

Intrinsic rewards are internal to the individual and are in many ways less tangible. In fact, they are highly subjective in that they represent how the individual perceives and feels about work and its value. Five types of **intrinsic rewards** that have been summarized by Manion (2005) include:

- **Healthy relationships**—in which employees are able to develop a sense of connection with others in the workplace.
- **Meaningful work**—where employees feel that they make a difference in people's lives. This is typically a motivator for people to enter and stay employed in the healthcare industry. This type of work is viewed as that in which the meaningful tasks outweigh the meaningless. This reinforces the mantra Herzberg first espoused in 1968 and revisited in a 2003 issue of the *Harvard Business Review*, in which he stated: "Forget praise. Forget punishment. Forget cash. You need to make their jobs more interesting." As paperwork in health care has increased, managers need to be aware that such tasks detract from the meaningfulness quotient.
- **Competence**—where employees are encouraged to develop skills that enable them to perform at or above standards, preferably the latter.
- **Choice**—where employees are encouraged to participate in the organization in various ways, such as by expressing their views and opinions, sharing in decision making, and finding other ways to facilitate participatory approaches to problem solving, goal setting, and the like.
- **Progress**—where managers find ways to hold employees accountable, facilitate their ability to make headway toward completing their assigned tasks, and celebrate when progress is made toward completing important milestones within a project.

Intrinsic rewards, coupled with extrinsic ones, lead to high personal satisfaction and serve as motivators for most employees.

MISCONCEPTIONS ABOUT MOTIVATION AND EMPLOYEE SATISFACTION

Managers tend to have many misconceptions about motivation. As healthcare managers, it is important to assess and understand such misconceptions in an effort to become more effective managers and to not perpetuate myths about motivation. For example, research indicates that managers typically make incorrect assumptions about what motivates their employees. Morse (2003) states that "managers are not as good at judging employee motivation as they think they are. In fact, people from all walks of life seem to consistently misunderstand what drives employee motivation." The following is an enumeration of many of these misconceptions.

- **Although I'm not motivated by extrinsic rewards, others are.** This idea is discussed by Morse (2003) in his review of Chip Heath's study of intrinsic and extrinsic rewards. The conclusion is that an "extrinsic incentive bias" exists and is, in fact, widespread among managers and employees. That is, individuals assume that others are driven more by extrinsic rewards than intrinsic ones. This has been shown to be a false assumption.

- **All motivation is intrinsic.** Managers need to remember that typically a combination of factors motivates employees, not just one type of extrinsic or intrinsic reward (Manion, 2005, p. 283).

- **Some people just are not motivated.** Everyone is motivated by something; the problem for managers is that "that something" may not be directed toward the job. This creates challenges for managers who must try to redirect the employees' energies toward job-related behaviors (Manion, 2005, p. 283).

- **People are motivated by money.** Compensation motivates only to a point; that is, when compensation isn't high enough or is considered to be inequitable, it's a de-motivator. In contrast, when it is too high, it also seems to be a de-motivator, what Atchison (2003) calls the "**golden handcuffs,**" and results in individual performance being tempered to protect the higher compensation level. Santamour states that "Eighty-nine percent of managers believe that for their employees it is all about the money, but there is no research to support that" (2009b, p. 10). Generally, employees tend to rank pay as less important than other motivators. This is supported by the 1999 Hay Group study, in which 500,000 employees ranked fair pay and benefits as the least important of 10 motivating factors that keep them committed to staying with their companies. The bottom line from Atchison's perspective is that "as soon as money is predictable, it is an entitlement, not a motivator" (2003, p. 21).

- **Motivation is manipulation.** Manipulation carries negative implications; in contrast, motivation is positive and benefits both management and the employee (Manion, 2005).

- **One-size-fits-all reward and recognition programs motivate staff.** People, being people, are different, act in different ways, and are motivated by different things. Tailoring rewards and recognition is viewed as a way to focus on and understand the individual and his/her unique qualities (Atchison, 2003, p. 21).

- **Motivational people are born, not made.** Studies show that people aren't born to motivate. In fact, Manion states, "anyone can become an effective motivator. It simply takes an understanding of the theories and basic principles" (Manion, 2005, p. 284), as well as the desire to develop these skills.
- **There is one kind of employee satisfaction.** Atchison (2003) discusses the pros and cons of "egocentric and other-centered satisfaction" and suggests that in the short run, employees respond to specific rewards that they receive personally, but in the longer run, they respond to quality performance of the team and the organization. Thus, they migrate from being self-centered to being other-centered in terms of job satisfaction—from a "me" to a "we" mentality.

MOTIVATIONAL STRATEGIES

The literature provides an array of strategies for managers to use in seeking to help motivate and engage individuals. Some of these seem very obvious, while others represent the "tried-and-true" approaches to management. Still others represent innovations. No matter, they are worth enumerating here.

- **Expect the best.** People live up to the expectations they and others have of them. As stated best by Henry Ford: "Whether you think you can or you think you can't, you're right!" (Manion, 2005).
- **Reward the desired behavior.** Make sure that rewards are not given for undesirable behaviors and be sure to use many different types of rewards to achieve the desired outcomes (Manion, 2005). Do something special to recognize desired behavior; examples suggested by Studer (2003) include sending a thank you note to an employee's home or using a "WOW card." The latter is a simple card that can be filled out and sent to an employee, explaining that "Today you 'WOWed' me when you _____." Fill in the blank with an explanation of what that special something was.
- **Create a "FUN (Focused, Unpredictable, and Novel) approach."** Atchison (2003, p. 21) suggests using money for a variety of creative employee rewards, such as giving $50 gift certificates to a shopping center in recognition of employees' exceeding expected patient outcomes.
- **Reward employees in ways that enhance performance and motivate them.** Don't waste money on traditional types of recognition. Though these are viewed as being nice, they don't motivate (Atchison, 2003). Money is better spent on true rewards for specific types of performance and outcomes.
- **Tailor rewards.** As mentioned in the previous section, Atchison (2003) steers managers away from standard types of rewards, such as giving the obligatory Thanksgiving

turkey—unless the employees look forward to those turkeys. Instead, he recommends finding more creative ways to spend the organization's money and reward employees.

- **Focus on revitalizing employees.** Research shows that, when employees are working on overloaded circuits, motivation is diminished and productivity declines. This is particularly true in healthcare organizations. Hallowell (2005) suggests that managers can help to motivate employees by encouraging them to eat right, exercise regularly, take "real" vacations, get organized, and slow down.

- **Find creative ways to obtain information and recognize excellence in employees.** Studer (2003) suggests asking for feedback on service excellence when doing patient satisfaction surveys and hospital discharge phone calls. With data and information from these sources, recognition can be provided to individual employees, thereby motivating them to continue providing excellent customer service. This also communicates to the entire organization the importance of and commitment to a patient-centered and service-oriented culture.

- **Get subordinates to take responsibility for their own motivation.** This can be achieved by managers taking steps to deal with problem employees, to understand employees' needs, to determine what motivates their employees, to engage employees in the problem-solving process, and to really work hard at resolving, rather than ignoring, difficult employee problems (Nicholson, 2003).

- **Play to employees' strengths, promote high performance, and focus on how they learn.** This requires managers to know what their employees' strengths and weaknesses are, to find out what will be required to get specific employees to perform, and to understand how to capitalize on the ways those employees learn as an alternative method of encouraging and motivating them (Buckingham, 2005).

- **Give employees "three compliments for every criticism."** Studer states: "I thought I heard that compliments and criticism were supposed to be balanced. But the truth is, if you give a staff member one compliment and one criticism, it equals a negative relationship. If you give a staff member two compliments to one criticism, it will equal a neutral relationship. If you give a staff three compliments to one criticism, it will equal a positive relationship" (2003, p. 232).

MOTIVATING ACROSS GENERATIONS

The United States has experienced a labor force shortage in the area of health professions over the last decade. By the year 2020, a nationwide shortage is projected of approximately 100,000 physicians, 1 million nurses, and 250,000 public health professionals (Health Resources and Services Administration, n.d.). This shortage, along with the aging baby boomer population, means an intense focus is vital in order for healthcare organizations to successfully function over the next few decades. Total employment is estimated by the U.S. Bureau of Labor Statistics (BLS) to increase by 15.3 million, or 10.1%, during the period of 2008–2018. These projections include a changing labor force, specifically one that is older as well as more racially and ethnically diverse. More than 50% of new jobs are projected to be in professional and service-providing occupations (BLS, 2009).

Healthcare managers need to embrace the challenges, opportunities, and new strategies when managing such a diverse labor force (American Hospital Association, 2010). This will require managers to evaluate their current management styles, especially when considering actively engaging and motivating a labor force across multiple generations. According to the American Hospital Association's (AHA) 2010 study, *Workforce 2015: Strategy Trumps Shortage,* social trends over the last several decades have been dominated by the values, preferences, and experiences of the **baby boomer generation**, which includes those born between 1946 and 1964. However, the baby boomers are only one of four generations that comprise today's labor force. Members of the four main generations include **the traditionalists, the baby boomers, Generation X, and the Millennials**. Each of these generations has unique characteristics and expectations and is motivated in different ways. Table 3-1 illustrates generational differences among workplace characteristics and motivational preferences.

What appeals to one generation more than likely will not appeal to another generation. Motivational techniques such as rewards and incentives vary widely across generations. One generation might prefer recognition based on proof of their time-tested work ethic, while another generation might expect instant gratification stemming from what they consider a job well done. Different standards of motivation are required for each generation. In order for healthcare organizations to be successful in the future, the workplace needs to be one of coexistence of all generations, even when their workplace characteristics and motivational preferences are drastically different. This is the first time in the history of the United States that employees face working side by side with four different generations (Hammill, 2005). Managers play a key role in how the four generations will work together and what it takes to engage employees to be motivated workers.

CONCLUSION

Motivation of employees is a tricky business. Managers often do not understand the concepts, principles, and myths about motivation well enough to put them in practice. Greater awareness and better understanding of motivation will result in better management. Managers can improve their success rate by providing extrinsic rewards that will help their employees to be intrinsically motivated to become top performers. Successful managers also are able to recognize the differences when managing across varying generations.

TABLE 3-1 Generation Characteristics and Motivational Preferences

Generation	Traditionalist	Baby Boomers	Generation X	Millennials
Born:	Before 1945	1946–1964	1965–1978	1979–present
Cohort size	27 million	76 million	60 million	88 million
Workplace characteristics	Respectful of authority	Individuality	Self-reliant	Image conscious
	Value duty and sacrifice	Driven by goals for success	Highly educated	Need constant feedback and reinforcement
	Value accountability and practical experience	Measure work ethic in hours worked and financial rewards	Questioning	Idealist
			Risk-averse	
			Most loyal employees	Team-oriented
	Strong work ethic with emphasis on timeliness and productivity	Believe in teamwork	Want open communication	Want open communication
	Strong interpersonal skills	Emphasize relationship building	Respect production over tenure	Search for an individual who will help them achieve their goals
	Value academic credentials	Expect loyalty from coworkers	Value control of their time	Search for ways to shed stress
	Accept limited resources	Career equals identity	Invest loyalty in a person, not in an organization	Racial and ethnic identification of reduced importance
	Loyal to employer and expect loyalty in return	A democratic approach		Organized and prefer structure
Motivational preferences	Loyalty	Work for managers who treat them as equals	Genuine and informal managers	Value instant gratification
	Hierarchical structure		Training and growth opportunities	Collaborative and positive interactions
	Status	Assurance that they are making a difference	Flexibility	Achievement-oriented
	Rewards based on promotion and job tenure	Work-life balance	Work deadlines, but with freedom and flexibility on how to reach those deadlines	Coaching and support focused
	Recognition of hard work and work ethic		Results-oriented	Personal fulfillment in job

Source: Adapted from American Hospital Association, 2010.

DISCUSSION QUESTIONS

1. Motivation is not a new concept, so why is motivation important? Is it more important that an employee is motivated or engaged?

2. Compare and contrast needs-based theories of motivation. Which offers the most value to healthcare managers?

3. Discuss any limitations of the management approaches to motivation.

4. Which types of rewards are more important: intrinsic or extrinsic?

5. Does the importance of different types of rewards change over time as one progresses through one's career?

6. Which myth of motivation is the most important? Are there other myths that you can identify?

7. What motivational strategy would you apply with an employee who you think is capable of doing the work but is underperforming?

8. What motivational strategy would you apply with a highly effective employee whom you want to keep performing at a very high level?

9. Which generation resonates best with you? In your opinion, which generation do you feel would be the most difficult to manage or motivate? Why?

10. Grace Jones is a four-decade Billing department employee in Happy Hollow Hospital. A recent graduate of Whassamatter U, Lindsey Flohan is a new hire in the Billing department. Grace has been assigned to train Lindsey to do her new job. Using the generational framework provided above, what conflicts can you anticipate between Grace and Lindsey?

Cases in Chapter 17 that are related to management and motivation (or related to this chapter) include:

- High Employee Turnover at Hillcrest Memorial Hospital—see p. 399
- Set Up for Failure?—see p. 401
- Seaside Convalescent Care Center—see p. 422

Additional cases, role-play scenarios, video links, websites, and other information sources are also available in the online Instructor's Materials.

REFERENCES

Adams, J. S. (1963, November). Towards an understanding of inequity. *Journal of Abnormal and Social Psychology, 67*(5), 422–436.

Alderfer, C. P. (1972). *Existence, relatedness and growth: Human needs in organizational settings.* New York, NY: Free Press.

American Hospital Association (AHA). (2010, January). *Workforce 2015: Strategy trumps shortage.* Retrieved from http://www.healthcareworkforce.org

Atchison, T. A. (2003). Exposing the myths of employee satisfaction. *Healthcare Executive, 17*(3), 20.

Buckingham, M. (2005). What great managers do. *Harvard Business Review, 3*(3), 70–79.

Bureau of Labor Statistics (BLS). (2009, December). *Employment projections: 2008–2018.* Retrieved from http://www.bls.gov/news.release/ecopro.toc.htm

Deci, E., & Ryan, R. (1985). *Intrinsic motivation and self-determination in human behavior.* New York, NY: Plenum Press.

Gallup, Inc. (2010). *Employee engagement.* Retrieved from http://www.gallup.com

Hallowell, E. M. (2005). Overloaded circuits: Why smart people underperform. *Harvard Business Review, 83*(1), 54–62.

Hammill, G. (2005). Mixing and managing four generations of employees. *FDU Magazine Online.* Retrieved from http://www.fdu.edu/newspubs/magazine/05ws/generations.htm

Health Resources and Services Administration (HRSA). (n.d.). *Health workforce studies.* Retrieved from http://bhpr.hrsa.gov/healthworkforce/default.htm

Herzberg, F. (2003). One more time: How do you motivate employees? *Harvard Business Review, 81*(1), 86–96.

Levoy, B. (2007). *222 secrets of hiring, managing, and retaining great employees in healthcare practices.* Sudbury, MA: Jones & Bartlett.

Locke, E. A., & Latham, G. P. (1990). *A theory of goal setting and task performance.* Englewood Cliffs, NJ: Prentice Hall.

Manion, J. (2005). *From management to leadership.* San Francisco, CA: Jossey-Bass.

Manion, J. (2009). *The engaged workforce: proven strategies to build a positive health care workplace.* Chicago, IL: Health Forum, Inc.

Manville, B., & Ober, J. (2003). Beyond empowerment: Building a company of citizens. *Harvard Business Review, 81*(1), 48–53.

Maslow, A. H. (1954). *Motivation and personality.* New York, NY: Harper & Row.

McClelland, D. C. (1985). *Human motivation.* Glenview, IL: Scott, Foresman.

Morse, G. (2003). Why we misread motives. *Harvard Business Review, 81*(1), 18.

Nicholson, N. (2003). How to motivate your problem people. *Harvard Business Review, 81*(1), 57–65.

Ouchi, W. G. (1981). *Theory Z.* Reading, MA: Addison-Wesley.

Santamour, B. (2009). Inspired staff can see you through hard times. *Hospitals & Health Networks, 83*(3), 10.

Scott, C., & Jaffe, D. (1991). *Empowerment: A practical guide for success.* Los Altos, CA: Crisp.

Skinner, B. F. (1953). *Science and human behavior.* New York, NY: Macmillan.

Sperry, L. (2003). *Becoming an effective health care manager.* Baltimore, MD: Health Professions Press.

Studer, Q. (2003). *Hardwiring excellence.* Gulf Stream, FL: Fire Starter Publishing.

Vroom, V. H. (1964). *Work and motivation.* New York, NY: Wiley.

Organizational Behavior and Management Thinking

Sheila K. McGinnis

LEARNING OBJECTIVES

By the end of this chapter, the student will be able to:

- Define organizational behavior;
- Identify and discuss 10 challenges of healthcare management;
- Define what is meant by cognition (or thinking) as it relates to behavior in organizations;
- Describe how perception and thinking influence behavior in the workplace;
- Describe the role of thinking in communication and problem solving in the workplace;
- Explain the role of thinking in organization change and learning; and
- Recommend and provide rationales for three ways a manager can use knowledge of thinking processes to improve communication between individuals and within groups and organizations.

INTRODUCTION

Healthcare managers, like managers in other industries, are responsible for effectively using the material, financial, information, and human resources of their organizations to deliver services. As you can see from the topics presented in this textbook, the manager's role requires a wide range of both technical and interpersonal skills. Leadership (Chapter 2), motivation (Chapter 3), managing healthcare professionals (Chapter 11), and teamwork

(Chapter 13) are some of the most important interpersonal skills of a manager that are examined at length in other chapters of this text. The purpose of this chapter is to provide a sample of how knowledge of **human cognition (or thinking and reasoning)** offers valuable insights about **organizational behavior** to help future health managers understand human behavior at work. While this chapter will not make you an expert on organizational behavior or managerial thinking, it will help you appreciate how the science of organizational behavior and management thinking can be used to work with others in a way that leads to beneficial outcomes for both people and organizations.

The chapter begins with a brief background on the field of organizational behavior, describes several organizational behavior applications for health administration, and then offers an extended discussion and illustration of how the healthcare manager can use managerial thinking and organizational behavior to achieve important organization goals.

THE FIELD OF ORGANIZATIONAL BEHAVIOR

Organizational behavior is a broad area of management that studies how people act in organizations. Managers can use theories and knowledge of organizational behavior to improve management practices for effectively working with and influencing employees to attain organization goals. The field of organizational behavior has evolved from the scientific study of management during the industrial era to administrative theories of the manager's role, principles of bureaucracy, and human relations studies of employees' needs (Scott, 1992). Organizational behavior is an **interdisciplinary field** that draws on the ideas and research of many disciplines concerned with human behavior and interaction. These include psychology, social psychology, industrial psychology, sociology, communications, and anthropology (Robbins, 2003). In this chapter, we will highlight ideas from cognitive psychology (the science of human thinking) and their application to organizational behavior.

ORGANIZATIONAL BEHAVIOR'S CONTRIBUTION TO MANAGEMENT

The most successful organizations make the best use of their employees' talents and energies (Heil, Bennis, & Stephens, 2000; Huselid, 1995). Firms that effectively manage employees hold an advantage over their competitors. Pfeffer (1998) estimates that organizations can reap a 40% gain by managing people in ways that build commitment, involvement, learning, and organizational competence.

Because employees are key to an organization's success, how well the manager interacts and works with a variety of individuals is key to a manager's success. A manager who is skilled in organizational behavior will be able to work effectively with employees and colleagues across the organization, assisting and influencing them to support and achieve organization goals.

KEY TOPICS IN ORGANIZATIONAL BEHAVIOR

Organizational behavior is a broad field comprised of many subject areas. Work behaviors are typically examined at different levels—**individual behavior, group behavior, and collective behavior across the organization**—with different issues salient at each level. Studying individual behavior helps managers understand how perceptions, attitudes, and personality influence work behavior, motivation, and other important work outcomes like satisfaction, commitment, and learning. Examining interactions in the group setting provides insight into the challenges of leadership, teamwork, communication, decision making, power, and conflict. Studying **organization-wide behavior** (sometimes referred to as organization theory) helps explain how organizations structure work and power relationships, how they use systems for decision making and control, how organization culture affects behavior, how organizations learn, and how they adapt to changing competitive, economic, social, and political conditions.

ORGANIZATIONAL BEHAVIOR ISSUES IN HEALTH ORGANIZATIONS

Organizational behavior, whether in a healthcare organization or another type of organization, is concerned with behavior that occurs under the conditions posed by an organizational situation. While a specific organization setting may create unique challenges or certain sets of problems, the behaviors of interest are similar to those of individuals, groups, and often organizations in other settings or industries (Weick, 1969). Thus, healthcare organizational behavior does not create unique management issues so much as certain issues are more prevalent in health care and occur along with other challenges (Shortell & Kaluzny, 2000).

Many of these challenges directly or indirectly affect what is expected of healthcare workers and how they behave in healthcare organizations. Health organizations are staffed with a highly professional workforce and impose exacting requirements on how work is organized and accomplished. The complex work of health care has a high risk of serious or deadly error, which necessitates highly reliable systems of practice at all organization levels. Complex technical and medical systems demand sophisticated technical expertise, which requires a highly educated, efficient, and well-coordinated workforce. Professional workers, especially physicians, work with a great deal of autonomy and control over the technical and clinical aspects of care delivery. As a result, healthcare managers are responsible for facilitating the delivery of highly complex medical services that must be carefully coordinated by autonomous professionals over whom the manager has little direct authority—all within an industry system that is facing extreme financial and policy challenges.

Squeezed by rising costs and declining reimbursements, many health organizations struggle to survive financially. In the face of increased competition and consumer demands, the health delivery system is changing rapidly to create new services and adopt new technologies, often by forming new partnerships. The chronic health conditions that characterize an aging population demand more outpatient care, which dramatically changes the nature of care delivery. Concern over patient safety and quality of care demands workers skilled in clinical information management, Total Quality Management techniques, and evidence-based practice; yet labor shortages abound and are predicted to increase.

The work of health care is carried out against the backdrop of these demands. Yet every day, the healthcare manager facilitates and orchestrates the collective accomplishment of organizational goals with an eye toward helping employees and colleagues successfully negotiate the complexities presented by the nature of healthcare work and the healthcare industry. To do this, the managers must be sure they themselves and those with whom they work continually find ways to effectively work together in a demanding industry. Organizational behavior skills help managers do this.

HOW THINKING INFLUENCES ORGANIZATIONAL BEHAVIOR

The Effect of Thinking on Behavior

Organization science explanations of human behavior increasingly draw upon human thinking, especially **cognition and the creation of meaning**. In the cognitive framework, behavior is inextricably tied to thinking and reasoning. We cannot understand behavior without understanding the thoughts, assumptions, and perceived attributes of a situation that precede behavior and its consequences.

Cognition refers to the mental processes involved in thinking, including attending to information, processing information, and ordering information to create meaning that is the basis for acting, learning, and other human activities. Cognitive science has taught us that information processing capacities and mental processes shape and govern one's perceptions, language, and ultimately one's behaviors. A focus on thinking highlights the importance of perceptions, assumptions, and social cues. It points out biases in information processing and creating common meaning during communication. Finally, thinking sets the stage for individual and organizational learning. The human capacity to adapt is rooted in learning new ways of thinking and acting, which depend upon how we perceive the facts of a situation and act upon them. Contrary to the idea that organizations can be well-oiled machines that respond perfectly to every management command, studies of thinking teach managers that humans have a limited capacity to process information. We learn that humans simplify and take shortcuts, that individuals' actions are largely determined by how they perceive the world, and that humans engage in an ongoing construction of their world by using stored information structures to guide perception and interpretation of events and information (Fiske & Taylor, 1984).

At its simplest, the role of thinking in management action can be depicted as shown in Table 4-1. Cognition highlights how individual and collective thinking processes intervene and influence actions taken in response to a situation.

As mentioned earlier, organizational behavior looks at individual, group, and organization-wide behaviors. Similarly, cognition and thinking also play out at the individual, group, and organization-wide levels. You probably have observed individual perceptions and biases and learning. Cognitive science shows that organizations as **collectives of individuals** can also be viewed as perceiving, thinking, and learning—though collective processes operate differently than individual processes.

In short, the lessons of cognition suggest that the workplace is perceptually complex and ambiguous. Thus, one of management's foremost tasks is to create common understanding among organization members. Understanding ways others think and applying these principles, especially to **group and collective understanding**, is a challenging skill for managers to master. While thinking has long been implicit in understanding organizational behavior, its importance grows in a knowledge economy that is driven by information (Huff, Huff, & Barr, 2000; Spender, 1998). The effective healthcare manager works with organization members to make sense of their interactions and experiences and agree upon meaning so they can work together, make decisions, and take action. The sections below describe some cognitive principles commonly present in human interaction that often complicate organizational processes, and then discuss ways a manager can work to create shared understanding that facilitates organizational effectiveness.

TABLE 4-1 Role of Thinking in Organizational Behavior

Situation or Task	→	Thinking	→	Behavior and Action
Interpersonal relations		Perceptions and intentions		Reactions and decisions
Workplace cues		Beliefs and biases		Work tasks
Problem solving		Cognition principles		Learning
Industry environment		Knowledge		Business practices

Perception and Thinking

Human understanding and the resulting organizational behavior are largely based upon how a person perceives and thinks about a situation (Elsbach, Barr, & Hargadon, 2005; Fiske & Taylor, 1984). **Perceptions** matter because how a person makes sense of a situation affects his or her attitudes, attributions, and behaviors. The **process of perceiving** involves noticing, selecting, and organizing information in order to respond. Information is naturally lost or distorted in this complex process, so the knowledge upon which a person's action is based may be incomplete or inaccurate. However, the actor assumes his or her knowledge is complete, and thus may act upon deficient information.

Theory X and Theory Y—The Role of Assumptions

As noted in Chapter 3, an early organization psychologist, Douglas McGregor, described two very different ways of managing, termed Theory X and Theory Y, which were the basis for an early approach to managing employee motivation. The two different approaches were based on very different underlying assumptions about human nature (McGregor, 1967). McGregor observed that early industrial management techniques were based on negative beliefs that employees naturally dislike work and tend to avoid responsibility, so they must be compelled to perform (termed "**Theory X**"). He espoused a view based instead on positive beliefs that employees are naturally motivated and committed and that managers can fully tap employee talents by fostering employee growth, responsibility, and development of their potential (termed "**Theory Y**"). A growing body of research supports the merits of an intrinsically motivating (i.e., Theory Y) approach to engaging employees. So managers must assess how well their own assumptions and behaviors and their organization's policies and practices promote employee growth, development, engagement, and contribution (Heil et al., 2000).

It is instructive to this discussion of management thinking to realize that, as explained in Chapter 3, McGregor's Theory X and Theory Y do not accurately describe motivated employee behavior. Instead, X and Y more accurately describe a **manager's assumptions** and highlight the role of the **manager's beliefs** about employees as a key determinant of how a manager behaves. The real lesson from McGregor is that effective managers must "examine their deepest held beliefs about people and the nature of work" (Heil et al., 2000, p. 15). Arguably the first step to managerial success begins with knowledge of one's own ways of seeing the world—that is, learning to recognize your personal beliefs and experiences that shape your approach to managing.

Beyond the assumptions underlying Theory X and Theory Y, experts have identified predictable **habits of the mind** based on the power of our perceptions and patterns of thinking. Those with particular relevance for managers and organizations include **perceptions, cognitive biases, expectancies, expectancy theory, attribution theory, schemas, framing, mental models, and sensemaking**. Collectively, these principles demonstrate the power of thought, showing that how people view a situation has a strong effect on how they respond to and act upon that situation. They remind managers that much of organizational behavior is about each person's **"inner game,"** which is often not known by the individuals themselves nor revealed during interpersonal interactions. Thus, a valuable skill for managers is to elicit thoughts in a way that organization members can work with them and reduce differences in understanding.

Perception

People vary greatly in what they notice and what draws their focused attention. Their attention processes will be influenced and filtered by their assumptions, values, knowledge, goals, past experiences, and other personal differences. As a result, they will only take in part of the information they are presented with and subsequently act upon partial information. In addition, the partial information that is taken in is subject to other mental processes that can create further distortions.

Scholars have found that physician perceptions have important implications for healthcare quality and patient health outcomes. Researchers studying patient–physician communication have found that perceptions influence a variety of patient–physician interactions and subsequent outcomes (Street, Gordon, & Haidet, 2007; Hall, Epstein, DeCiantis, & McNeil, 1993). For example, liking or disliking a patient may affect the quality of the physician–patient relationship and the patient's ultimate health outcome. Studies show healthier patients and male patients were liked better (i.e., perceived more positively) by physicians than sicker patients and female patients (Hall, Horgan, Stein, & Roter, 2002). In addition, most patients accurately perceived physicians' like or dislike for them. Physicians' positive perceptions of their patients are further associated with important behaviors such as providing and eliciting information, longer visits with patients, and positive support and expectations. These physician behaviors help build trust, respect, and rapport that can improve medical diagnosis, care management, and treatment compliance. As a result, physicians' positive perceptions of patients are associated with higher patient satisfaction with care and better patient health (Hall et al., 2002).

Cognitive Biases

As we have learned previously, our human capacity to effectively process information is limited. So individuals compensate with judgment shortcuts (called **heuristics**) that simplify the decision process but create systematic biases affecting their judgments (Bazerman, 1998). These shortcuts make the complex processes of perceiving and judging vulnerable to the influence of assumptions and prior experiences that are readily recalled. A perceiver may notice and select only a subset of the information to which he is exposed because he is more apt to notice familiar cues or to arrange cues into meaningful groups based on his **preconceptions** and what he has learned from his own prior experiences and the experiences of others. For example, a mother can identify her child's cry in a noisy room, while a stargazer finds it easier to locate a constellation when she knows the pattern to expect. Similarly, a physician who does not expect to see an exotic condition like hanta virus may fail to diagnose the problem because she is not attuned to the possibility.

Studies consistently document more than a dozen common biases, or systematic errors of perception and judgment, that, used inappropriately, diminish the quality of thinking by limiting the amount and richness of information processing. Croskerry (2002) has identified 30 **heuristics and biases or cognitive dispositions** that can lead to error in emergency medicine. According to Das and Teng (1999), the four main categories of cognitive biases are: (1) use of prior beliefs and assumptions that constricts one's capacity to absorb more information or prompts use of preselected outcomes that narrow the range of options considered; (2) oversimplifying the problem definition or possible solutions, or relying on intuition in a way that again limits the range of outcomes considered; (3) flawed assessments of the likelihood of occurrence; and (4) overestimating one's capacity to influence events (Korte, 2003).

The cognitive simplifications provided by judgment heuristics and biases do help streamline information processing. However, heuristics and biases are problematic when used inappropriately. Clearly, human thinking and decision processes are seldom ideal, even at critical points in delivering health care. Managers and clinicians identify several strategies to reduce the effects of bias, including bias awareness and training, considering multiple alternatives, decision protocols, evidence-based medicine, use of cognitive aids, and decision support systems (Croskerry, 2003). Managers who are aware of biases (including their own) can reduce bias and error through thoughtful reflection, open discussion, and appropriate use of information to significantly improve organizational decisions and actions (Bazerman, 1998).

TEXTBOX 4-1. THE ATYPICAL HEART ATTACK

Dr. Pat Croskerry examined an apparently healthy forest ranger experiencing chest pain and failed to recognize coronary artery disease. The ranger appeared so healthy—athletic, fit, and trim without the typical warning signs that precede a heart attack—that Croskerry failed to consider possible heart disease. The next day, the ranger was admitted and successfully treated for acute myocardial infarction. Croskerry realized he had made the cognitive mistake of **representiveness error**. That is, perceiving that the ranger fit a very healthy stereotype (called a **prototype**), Croskerry's thinking was guided by this prototype, and he overlooked the true cause of the ranger's symptoms. Croskerry went on to research and teach medical students about cognitive error.

Source: Groopman, 2007.

Expectancy

Perceptual expectations can create a situation in which "believing is seeing." That is, prior knowledge or experience tends to make us perceive what we expect to perceive. **Expectations or beliefs** ("my boss won't like my idea") or **situational cues** ("organic chemistry is a difficult course") influence how we tend to act in certain situations and events (Bandura, 1977). In addition to individual expectations, expectations can also arise from social interactions between people. At an extreme, expectations about another's behavior can create a "self-fulfilling prophecy." For example, classroom teachers who expect students to perform a certain way may verbally and nonverbally transmit their expectations to students in a way that increases the likelihood that the expected effect will occur. A nurse who believes a dementia patient is aggressive may try to overcontrol the patient and increase the patient's agitation and resistance. Similarly, a manager who believes that a certain employee has an "attitude problem" may treat that person in a way that elicits the very behavior that is objectionable.

Expectancy Theory

The effect of expectancies is very robust and also appears in the expectancy theory of individual work motivation (see Chapter 3). This is a cognitive theory of outcome expectancy in which an employee's motivation to put forth effort on the job depends on the expectations that the individual will be able to perform a task and that successful performance will result in valued outcomes (Vroom, 1964). The manager who recognizes the role that employee and managerial expectations play in motivation can strengthen motivation by providing appropriate encouragement and assistance to help an employee succeed at a task, by identifying the employee's desired outcomes and rewarding appropriately, and by clearly conveying organizational goals and the manager's own performance expectations.

Attribution Theory

To attribute is to make an inference, or to explain what causes something. According to **attribution theory**, people naturally seek to explain the likely cause of another's behavior. Regardless of their accuracy, our perceptions will influence what we presume to be the cause of another's behavior. In general, the presumed cause of observed behavior will be attributed to either a person's disposition and personality or to the situation in which the behavior occurs. Fundamental attribution error is a cognitive bias in which an observer makes incorrect causal attributions. In fundamental attribution error, the observer erroneously attributes an actor's behavior to the actor's internal disposition, rather than the external circumstances. For instance, if a stranger cuts in line ahead of you at the movies, you may conclude that the action is intentional and decide the person is rude, even though it may have occurred because the entrance signs were not clear to the person who cut in line.

In health care, physicians who label a patient with a negative stereotype (e.g., smokers, obese, alcoholics, homeless) risk erroneously attributing their health concerns to risky behavior the patients brought upon themselves (Groopman, 2007). As a result, they may distance themselves from the patient, miss important information, and provide poor-quality care.

Managers are susceptible to fundamental attribution error when judging employee performance, blaming an employee for poor performance that may actually be caused by circumstances beyond the employee's control. For example, attribution error occurs when a manager decides an employee who performs a task poorly is lazy or incompetent, rather than recognizing that the employee needs training, clear incentives, or improved work equipment. To avoid making an erroneous performance attribution requires the manager to fully understand both how the work context affects employee performance and how the employee perceives the work context and how it is affecting performance.

Schemas

Schemas are cornerstones of cognitive simplification. Schemas are mental representations of one's general knowledge and expectations about a concept, including the concept's attributes and relations among those attributes (Fiske & Taylor, 1984). Schemas direct how we perceive, classify, store, and act upon information received. They organize what we know and guide how we use our knowledge. In short, they help people make sense of the world. According to Fiske and Taylor (1984), people develop schemas for many different concepts and situations. **Person schemas** characterize a certain person's traits and actions (Dad will loan me his car if I mow the lawn); **role schemas** define appropriate behaviors and expectations for a social category (grandmothers bake cookies, professors should grade fairly); and **event schemas** dictate one's expected "scripts" for how certain events should unfold (taking final exams, interviewing for a job, conducting a performance evaluation). In health organizations, members may hold schemas about strategies to attract and retain nurses, the patient's role in deciding about treatment, or how to work with other healthcare organizations in the local market.

Thinking is an individual process. While an organization does not think, its capacity to take collective action depends upon the degree to which organization members share a common view or shared way of thinking about a situation. Organizational schemas are viewed as a form of organizational thinking. Shared schemas can support organizational goals and initiatives that are consistent with the schemas and hinder goals and initiatives that do conflict with existing schemas. For example, when introducing a patient safety initiative, managers need to legitimatize key elements of the new schema (i.e., the safety initiative, its purpose, how it works, how it changes daily work, etc.) and reduce barriers posed by the old schema (e.g., individuals are to blame for medical errors, it is not okay to challenge authority or question clinical experts, the work of independent units is more important than the work of the entire system).

Managers increasingly recognize the need to foster **collective thinking and common understanding** needed to execute organization-wide action. **Interpretative schemas**—commonly known as frames—are one way managers shape collective understanding. **Frames** guide our interpretation of information by focusing our attention on certain elements and organizing our understanding of the social world (Goffman, 1974). Frames act as filters by structuring how we see things. Frames make it easier to handle complex information, yet can restrict our capacity to understand something in a new way. How managers frame or present important ideas and major changes to the organization can influence how the idea or change is interpreted and how well it is accepted.

To summarize, all schemas are thought structures that affect how we process information. They function as powerful mental devices that simplify information processing about people and situations. Because schemas are cognitive simplifications, they can also be incomplete, inaccurate, and difficult to change. If schemas are ignored, they may cause distortions that prevent bringing organization members to shared understanding of their work and its contribution to common goals. The skillful manager will learn to elicit others' schemas and thought patterns, validate the elements that fit organization goals, and find ways to address the elements that conflict with organization goals.

TEXTBOX 4-2. REFRAMING ALZHEIMER'S DISEASE WITH A NEW INTERPRETIVE SCHEMA

Dr. Peter Whitehouse, a leading expert on Alzheimer's disease (AD), says it is time to reframe our understanding of cognitive decline in the elderly. Over time, the medical community, the media, and society have framed dementia and cognitive impairment as a disease, which is accompanied by a stereotypical set of symptoms and a stigmatizing label. After many years treating patients and researching cognitive decline, Whitehouse concluded that the scientific case for the disease of Alzheimer's is weak and diagnosis is imprecise. AD cannot be clearly distinguished from normal brain aging or other dementias with any certainty. Furthermore, the stereotyping and stigmatizing that accompany the diagnosis of AD can harm patients and create barriers to constructively meeting their needs. Whitehouse advocates that individuals and society reframe age-related cognitive decline as normal brain aging. Changing the frame means changing our view from disease to aging, from curing to caring, from disability to changing ability, and from hopeless to hopeful.

Source: Whitehouse, 2008.

Mental Models

Recent efforts to understand how organizations change and learn has led to the study of "mental models" in organizations. **Mental models** are "mind-sets" (Pfeffer, 2005, p. 125), or "deeply held internal images of how the world works" (Senge, 1990, p. 174). While expectancies and schemas are concerned with how we receive and store information, mental models are concerned with how we use that information in reasoning. Mental models are similar to expectancies and schemas in that they are abstract representations of reality that define expectations and interpretations. They are a guide to reasoning, and they can also restrict how people think and act. Managers can change and improve organizations by discovering, sharing, challenging, and changing the schemas and mental models that guide how organization members think.

For example, a new long-term care center manager finds the facility's occupancy rate is too low, and the staff is convinced the center's location is undesirable. When the manager does a market analysis, he learns that client decisions are more influenced by available services rather than location. The staff's mental model that location drives client choice of facility was incorrect. When they revised their mental model to address range of services, the center's occupancy rate improved.

Sensemaking in Organizations

Perception and thinking are mainly concerned with human ability to accurately process information and how well one's understanding corresponds to the information stimuli. A related problem is how people individually and collectively comprehend the meaning of ambiguous information or situations that are subject to several plausible interpretations. **Ambiguous information** is unclear and equivocal in that it has multiple meanings and is open to several interpretations (Weick, 1995). Individuals frequently encounter ambiguous situations in organizations. Ambiguity becomes increasingly problematic as more individuals are involved, making it hard to find a common meaning on which to base action.

In today's challenging business climate, managers carefully plan and promote change initiatives such as improving patient satisfaction or increasing employee retention. While increased patient safety is a top health industry priority, it can be very difficult for an organization to establish common attitudes and expectations that support patient safety. In a recent survey of safety climate in 92 hospitals, nearly 20,000 employees rated the presence of key factors known to diminish safety and reliability. These factors included things such as engagement of senior managers in safety, existence of safety norms on units, witnessing or involvement in providing unsafe care, and fear of being blamed, to name but a few. A large number of responses (17%) show that employees perceived a lack of safety attitudes and behaviors in their hospital and that frontline employees perceived more weakness in the safety climate than supervisors and managers (Singer, Falwell, Gaba, & Baker, 2008).

Sharing common perceptions about safety is clearly important to ensure employees understand and agree upon what a complex and ambiguous concept like patient safety really means and how to act upon it. However, the patient safety study shows that fostering desired perceptions and behaviors organization-wide is difficult. The term "**sensemaking**" refers to the process by which organizations arrive at a **shared interpretation** of what a complex and ambiguous situation means (Weick, 1995). While sensemaking begins with the cognitive and interpretive processes of individuals, engaging multiple people (as in a patient safety initiative) makes it a social process that also depends upon communication, interpersonal dynamics, and the give and take of dialogue and negotiation. Studies of perception and thinking call attention to mental habits that alter information processing in a way that shapes and distorts our understanding. Sensemaking focuses on how organization members select information and communicate about alternative interpretations to arrive at an understanding that defines an ambiguous situation and guides subsequent actions. Sensemaking is thus a fundamental component of many core organizational behaviors and processes, including communication, problem solving and decision making, coordination, conflict, and change.

According to Weick, Sutcliff, and Obstfeld (2005), sensemaking has some important lessons for the manager. First, through the process of **determining what is important** in a situation, we define our environment and thus create our own opportunities and constraints—an organizational parallel to the self-fulfilling prophecy. For example, in health care, long-established norms foster blaming individuals for medical errors, which leads to covering up mistakes. This constrains the organization's ability to learn from errors and strengthen patient safety. Second, **meaning is made retrospectively**, in that the meaningful pattern we call understanding often emerges in hindsight as we process events with others. When healthcare workers feel safe discussing past safety problems, they can see how their own actions help or hinder patient safety and jointly create new safety norms. Third, **sensemaking organizes information** to create a plausible (if not necessarily accurate) understanding of a situation that is sufficient for organizational action and learning. As suggested by the patient safety survey above, organization members may nominally agree on the importance of patient safety, and their actual experience of patient safety may differ greatly, yet they are able to work toward the goal of patient safety.

Proponents of sensemaking argue that when all organization members share a clear, common understanding of an ambiguous situation, they can work together more effectively. Managers must keep in mind that reasoned analyses, deliberative decisions, and careful planning and implementation are not sufficient to achieve shared meaning. Managers must also address individual perceptions and collective sensemaking.

MANAGING AND LEARNING

As we have seen, perception and thinking among individuals are complex processes. Knowledge of biases, fundamental attribution error, mental models, and sensemaking won't fix every situation encountered in an organization. However, these ideas point out that how people comprehend a situation can be very different from the actual facts of the situation and will vary across individuals. The adage that "perception is reality" applies to organizations, and thinking and sensemaking principles can help the manager work with perceived realities. Cognition demonstrates that what one believes about a person or a situation, even if incomplete or inaccurate, will determine how one responds to that person or situation. The manager who is blind to assumptions and perceptions, both her own and others', will be working from an incomplete and inaccurate knowledge base.

A critical management task is to remedy the limits of human and organizational thinking and create common understanding among organization members, which is largely accomplished through conversation and discussion. The process of sharing assumptions and perceived realities makes them available to others, encourages individuals to refashion their own mental constructs, and promotes elaboration of common mental frameworks. In short, learning occurs and knowledge is created in the process of discussing and revising individual and organizational mental models (Easterby-Smith, Crossan, & Nicolini, 2000). In a knowledge economy, organizations with a superior ability to learn and adapt are expected to create new knowledge, master new behaviors, innovate, continually improve their work processes, outperform their competitors, and adapt to competitive pressures. The manager who can work with perceptions and mental models contributes to making a learning organization.

Current methods to foster learning and knowledge development in organizations often target ways to expand shared understanding, to improve shared mental models, and to engage in collective sensemaking. For example, Peter Senge (1990) outlines a set of five essential practices or "disciplines" that characterize the learning organization. These disciplines include **systems thinking**, or the ability to discern the pattern of connections between elements of a system, and a **drive for individual proficiency** that leads to personal mastery. Senge's last three disciplines help address the innate cognitive limits of individuals and groups. They are **surfacing and challenging mental models**, **creating a common identity with a shared vision of the future**, and **team learning** that uses dialogue to remove assumptions and create shared meaning.

HOW TO WORK WITH THINKING

Thinking and Sensemaking in Communication and Problem Solving

The bottom line of the organization and learning literature is that, instead of assuming meaning is clear, effective managers examine and test mental models and assumptions about the organizational world in order to increase shared understanding among members. Bias is inherent to human thinking, yet a manager can reduce bias through skillful collective communication and problem solving. One of the simplest ways to accomplish this is by sharing mental representations and beliefs with others through questioning, discussion, and debate (Heil et al., 2000). Thus, communication and problem-solving skills are paramount to successfully working with thinking in organizations. However, as the ideas in this chapter suggest, successful communication and problem solving are less about following step-by-step procedures and more about creating clear, common meaning.

TEXTBOX 4-3. THE WRONG DIAGNOSIS—A LESSON FOR MANAGERS?

In *How Doctors Think*, Dr. Jerome Groopman (2007) examines physician thinking and medical reasoning, summarizing the extensive research on this subject. Experts estimate that 10–15% of all medical diagnoses are wrong and are learning that physician reasoning is a more likely culprit than lack of knowledge or technical error. Groopman explains that "cognitive traps" skew doctors' clinical reasoning and reinforce the negative effects of biases, heuristics, and intuition.

Managers face a parallel situation when facing a problem and making a decision on how to solve it. The act of medical diagnosis is similar to problem identification in management. Identifying and solving organizational problems is a process much different from clinical diagnosis and treatment. However, organizational problem solving is probably subject to even greater cognitive distortion because management information is more ambiguous. When solving problems, the skilled manager will beware of "gut feelings," question assumptions, search for best evidence and gaps in knowledge, and be open to many ideas and alternatives.

Source: Groopman, 2007.

Communication

Communication is "the creation or exchange of understanding between sender(s) and receiver(s)" (Shortell & Kaluzny, 2000, p. 224). Communication is one of the manager's most powerful tools and most important responsibilities because it can be used to create a shared, common focus. While communicating sounds easy, it is really much more than exchanging words and messages—it is about exchanging meaning. Experts identify many barriers to communication. Communication failure may occur if the sender does not clearly convey the purpose or message or provides too much information. The receiver may not correctly comprehend the message, may resist the message content or distort its meaning, or may not view the sender as credible. The communication setting also creates barriers, which can include relaying messages through an organizational chain of command, role or status differences between sender and receiver, or simply the logistical challenges of available time and media.

Some of the most potent communication barriers are the thoughts and perceptions of the sender and receiver. Successful communication only occurs when we overcome the myriad assumptions, biases, and preconceptions brought to the conversation to achieve shared meaning. Shared understanding is the ultimate test of communication success (Shortell & Kaluzny, 2000).

Problem Solving

Perhaps the most important work of a manager is to ensure that organizational problems are solved. A problem exists when the current and the desired state of things differ, and the manager solves the problem by finding a way to reach the desired state. Every day,

---

TEXTBOX 4-4. ACTION INQUIRY: A FRAMEWORK FOR CHECKING ASSUMPTIONS

Torbert's (2004) Action Inquiry approach to organizational research fosters a type of dialogue that is an antidote to the assumptions and beliefs that limit thinking and learning and serves to build shared understanding. Torbert's framework consists of four "forms of speech," or four steps to follow in the course of a conversation. Using these steps or forms of speech promotes awareness of self and awareness of others in a way that tests perceptions and assumptions. All four parts of speech are to be used sequentially during a conversation to steadily question (or inquire) how well practices (or action) support desired results:

Framing: State the purpose and objectives for the current discussion, including any assumptions that need testing, to reveal the speaker's intentions and seek a common purpose.

Advocating: State an opinion, perception, or feeling at an abstract level.

Illustrating: Relate an anecdote or give an example that highlights the direction the speaker advocates.

Inquiring and listening: Ask questions of listeners to learn their views and experiences regarding the speaker's explanation of the situation (as expressed by the speaker's prior framing, advocacy, and illustration statements).

Repeated questioning or inquiry using Torbert's four forms of speech will heighten awareness of the manager's own perspectives and practices and the perspectives and practices of other organization members. The purpose of this form of dialogue is to directly address assumptions and perceptions. The result is to increase personal and organizational effectiveness because this type of inquiry elicits and discusses people's understandings in a way that increases the parties' common understanding. Through the process of action inquiry, organization members can better create a common or collective viewpoint that provides a framework for collective organizational action.

Source: Torbert, 2004.

healthcare organizations face problems related to treatment plans for patients, improving patient safety and quality of care, meeting patients' needs and expectations, determining the best mix of services to offer, and attracting and retaining the best workers. The successful manager is able to handle complex, ambiguous problems that are not clearly defined and for which opinions vary on the nature of the problem and possible solutions. This does not mean that the manager always knows exactly what to do. Rather it means that the manager finds a way to engage others in finding an appropriate solution.

Problem solving involves two main phases, **problem identification** and problem solution, with various tasks occurring in each phase (Daft, 1992; Schein, 1988; Whetten & Cameron, 1998). The first phase involves recognizing and identifying the problem and its causes, setting goals, and generating options. The second phase involves assessing options and choosing, implementing, and evaluating the chosen solution. While these problem-solving steps appear to be logical, actual problem solving and decision making in organizations often vary from this ideal process. Problem solving can be difficult because managers may have incomplete information or may be unable to process all of the information related to the problem, goals and priorities may be unclear or in dispute, and results of alternatives may be uncertain.

CONCLUSIONS

This chapter offers a brief overview of organizational behavior in health care. It highlights how perceptions, thinking, mental models, and other thinking patterns play out in organizational life. The study of thinking processes indicates that human and organizational behavior is best understood as driven by people's perceptions of their world, rather than assuming they clearly comprehend all the facts of a complex world. The implication for managers is that fundamental organizational activities like communication, problem solving, and decision making depend less on following a certain procedure and more on the manager's efforts to bring employees together in defining a shared understanding that supports a focus on collective action. As mentioned earlier, one of the best ways to address distortions and differences in thinking is by sharing mental models and understandings with others through questioning, discussion, and debate.

DISCUSSION QUESTIONS

1. Describe an incident from a past job where you would like to better understand how the organizational setting influenced employee behavior. What was the situation, and what happened? If you had been the manager in that situation, what would you have needed to understand to handle that situation?

2. Give examples of incidents from your past jobs where perceptions and cognition (or thinking) may have had a strong influence on employee behavior. What was the situation, who was involved, and how did they act? Describe the thinking patterns you observed.

3. Discuss the role of thinking in promoting organizational change and learning. In what ways could you, as a manager, use thinking to improve learning and bring about change?

4. Discuss the role of thinking processes in organizational communication and problem solving. In what ways could you, as a manager, use thinking to improve communication and problem solving?

5. Think of a recent situation in which you participated where it would have been helpful to address underlying assumptions. Describe the situation, who was involved, their roles, what they were trying to accomplish, and what actually happened. What did you observe that leads you to believe assumptions played a role in this situation? What could you have done differently to change the situation? What will you do or say differently in similar situations in the future?

Cases in Chapter 17 that are related this chapter include:

- Prelude to a Medical Error—see p. 416
- The Finance Department at Roseville Community Hospital—see p. 418

Additional cases, role-play scenarios, video links, websites, and other information sources are also available in the online Instructor's Materials.

REFERENCES

Bandura, A. (1977). Self-efficacy: Toward a unifying theory of behavioral change. *Psychological Review, 84*, 191–215.

Bazerman, M. (1998). *Judgment in managerial decision-making* (4th ed.). New York, NY: Wiley.

Croskerry, P. (2002). Achieving quality in clinical decision making: Cognitive strategies and detection of bias. *Academic Emergency Medicine, 9*, 1184–1204.

Croskerry, P. (2003). The importance of cognitive errors in diagnosis and strategies to minimize them. *Academic Medicine, 78*, 775–780.

Daft, R. L. (1992). *Organization theory and design.* St. Paul, MN: West.

Das T. K., & Teng, B. S. (1999). Cognitive biases and strategic decision processes: An integrative perspective. *Journal of Management Studies, 36*(6), 757–778.

Easterby-Smith, M., Crossan, M., & Nicolini, D. (2000). Organizational learning: Debates past, present and future. *Journal of Management Studies, 37*(6), 783–795.

Elsbach, K. D., Barr, P. S., & Hargadon, A. B. (2005). Identifying situated cognition in organizations. *Organization science, 16*(4), 422–433.

Fiske, S. T., & Taylor, S. E. (1984). *Social cognition.* New York, NY: Random House.

Goffman, E. (1974). *Frame analysis: An essay on the organization of experience.* London, UK: Harper and Row.

Groopman, J. (2007). *How doctors think.* Boston, MA: Houghton Mifflin.

Hall, J. A., Epstein, A. M., DeCiantis, M. L., & McNeil, B. J. (1993). Physicians' liking for their patients: More evidence for the role of affect in medical care. *Health Psychology, 12*, 140–146.

Hall, J. A., Horgan, T. G., Stein, T. S., & Roter, D. L. (2002). Liking in the physician–patient relationship. *Patient Education and Counseling, 48*, 69–77.

Heil, G., Bennis, W., & Stephens, D. C. (2000). *Douglas McGregor, revisited.* New York, NY: Wiley.

Huff, A. S., Huff, J. O., & Barr, P. S. (2000). *When firms change direction.* New York, NY: Oxford University Press.

Huselid, M. A. (1995). The impact of human resources management practices on turnover, productivity, and corporate financial performance. *Academy of Management Journal, 38*, 645.

Korte, R. E. (2003). Biases in decision making and implications for human resource development. *Advances in Developing Human Resources, 5*(4), 440–457.

McGregor, D. (1967). *The professional manager.* New York, NY: McGraw-Hill.

Pfeffer, J. (1998). *The human equation.* Boston, MA: Harvard Business School Press.

Pfeffer, J. (2005). Changing mental models: HR's most important task. *Human Resource Management, 44*, 123–128.

Robbins, S. P. (2003). *Essentials of organizational behavior.* Upper Saddle River, NJ: Prentice Hall.

Schein, E. H. (1988). *Process consultation.* Reading, MA: Addison-Wesley.

Scott, W. R. (1992). *Organizations: Rational, natural, and open systems* (3rd ed.). Englewood Cliffs, NJ: Prentice Hall.

Senge, P. M. (1990). *The fifth discipline.* New York, NY: Currency-Doubleday.

Shortell, S. M., & Kaluzny, A. D. (2000). *Health care management* (4th ed.). New York, NY: Thomson Learning.

Singer, S. J., Falwell, A., Gaba, D. M., & Baker, L. C. (2008). Patient safety climate in US hospitals. *Medical Care, 46*, 1149–1156.

Spender, J.-C. (1998). The dynamics of individual and organizational knowledge. In C. Eden & J.-C. Spender (Eds.), *Managerial and organizational cognition.* London, UK: Sage.

Street, R. L., Gordon, H., & Haidet, P. (2007). Physicians' communication and perceptions of patients: Is it how they look, how they talk, or is it just the doctor? *Social Science & Medicine, 65*, 586–598.

Torbert, B., & Associates. (2004). *Action inquiry.* San Francisco, CA: Berrett-Kohler.

Vroom, V. (1964). *Work and motivation.* New York, NY: Wiley.

Weick, K. E. (1969). *The social psychology of organizing.* Reading, MA: Addison-Wesley.

Weick, K. E. (1995). *Sensemaking in organizations.* Thousand Oaks, CA: Sage.

Weick, K. E., Sutcliff, K. M., & Obstfeld, D. (2005). Organizing and the process of sensemaking. *Organization Science, 16*(4), 409–420.

Whetten, D. A., & Cameron, K. S. (1998). *Developing management skills.* Reading, MA: Addison-Wesley.

Whitehouse, P. (2008). *The myth of Alzheimer's.* New York, NY: St. Martin's Press.

Strategic Planning
Susan Judd Casciani

LEARNING OBJECTIVES

By the end of this chapter, the student will be able to:

- Describe strategic planning and the strategic planning process;
- Discuss the importance of strategic planning as a dynamic process;
- Identify healthcare market powers and trends, and understand their potential impact on health services;
- Conduct a SWOT analysis;
- Identify methods to monitor and control strategy execution; and
- Identify the role of the manager in the strategic planning process.

INTRODUCTION

Every organization needs to be successful over the long term in order to survive; a critical factor leading to that success lies in how well an organization can plan for the future and tap market opportunities. **Strategic planning** is the process of identifying a desired future state for an organization and a means to achieve it. Through an ongoing analysis of the organization's operating environment, matched against its own internal capabilities, an organization's leadership is able to identify strategies that will drive the organization from its present condition to that desired future state.

Strategic planning in health care has had a relatively short history. As recently as the 1970s, strategic planning in the healthcare industry mainly consisted of planning for new buildings and funding expanding services in response to population growth. With the introduction of the federal Prospective Payment System (PPS) in the 1980s, the field of healthcare strategic planning received a transforming jolt as organizations scrambled to compete in an increasingly demanding environment. The turbulent managed care era of the 1980s and 1990s only served to further fuel the growth of the field as the cost of health care continually rose faster than the gross domestic product (GDP) and competition among providers intensified. Today, hospitals and other healthcare organizations have come to embrace strategic planning as a valuable tool to evaluate alternative paths and help them prepare for the future. Healthcare managers at all levels need to understand the purpose of strategic planning, its benefits and challenges, the key factors for its success, and their vital role in the process.

PURPOSE AND IMPORTANCE OF STRATEGIC PLANNING

In any organization's operating environment, there are market forces, both controllable and uncontrollable, that will undoubtedly influence the future success of that organization. Only by identifying these forces and planning for ways to adapt to them can an organization achieve the greatest success. At the extreme, completely ignoring these forces can most certainly lead to organizational death. Although no one can predict the future, one can systematically think about it; the purpose of strategic planning is to identify market forces and how they may affect the organization and to determine an appropriate strategic direction for the organization to take that will counteract those forces and/or tap their potential.

Furthermore, strategic planning serves to focus the organization and also its resource allocation. At any given point in time, there are multiple and often competing initiatives and projects to be undertaken in an organization. By understanding the organization's operating environment and identifying a strategy to reach a desired future state, resources can be allocated appropriately and effectively.

THE PLANNING PROCESS

The **strategic planning process** consists mainly of two interrelated activities: the development of the strategic plan and execution of the organization's strategy. The development of the plan is most often done with a multiyear time horizon (3 or 5 or 10 years, for example) and updated annually. Strategy execution, on the other hand, is done on a continuous basis and is the critical factor in management of the organization's strategic intentions, optimally providing continual feedback for the development of any future plans.

Although strategic planning is a dynamic and not a linear process, Figure 5-1 attempts to depict a logical progression of the steps undertaken to develop a strategic plan. As shown

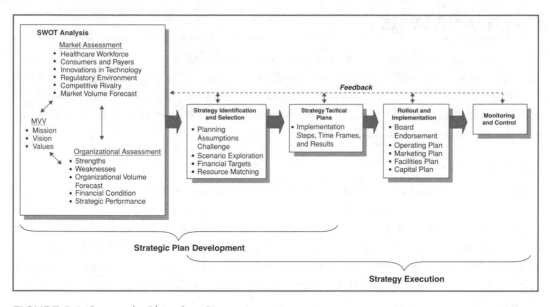

FIGURE 5-1 Strategic Planning Process

in Figure 5-1, the **SWOT (Strengths, Weaknesses, Opportunities, Threats) Analysis** provides a foundation for strategy development. This analysis serves two important functions: to gather a snapshot of how the organization is currently interacting with the market in comparison to the internal capabilities and intended strategic direction of the organization, and to identify market opportunities and threats that the organization may want to address in future strategic efforts.

Through analysis of the SWOT, strategy identification can begin. In this stage, the organization's leadership team uses the information provided in the SWOT analysis to identify specific strategies that may be worthy of pursuit either to grow the organization or to protect current areas of strength. Once these strategies have been identified, they must be narrowed down to a manageable number through selection and prioritization, and tactical implementation plans must be created. With the strategic plan completed, operating, marketing, and other supporting plans are developed. Control and monitoring of the plan follows and is most effectively done on an ongoing basis throughout the year. We will look at each of these stages of strategic planning in more detail; however, it is important to again keep in mind that strategic planning is not a linear process. The feedback loop depicted in Figure 5-1 attempts to show the critical nature of planning as an ongoing, dynamic process.

SWOT ANALYSIS

The initial planning phase is often referred to as a **SWOT analysis**, as it aims to identify the internal strengths and weaknesses of an organization, along with external market opportunities and threats. It includes three distinct but intricately related components: the **market assessment**; the statement of the **mission, vision, and values** of the organization; and the **organizational assessment**.

Market Assessment

The development of the **market assessment** may be the most complex and time-consuming section of the strategic plan in that, in this component, virtually *all* aspects of the market must be examined to determine whether they represent opportunities or threats for the organization and to determine their future implications for the organization. Any of a number of market assessment models can be utilized for this analysis, but one of the most common is the **Five Forces Model** developed by Harvard University professor Michael Porter (1998). In this model, Porter identifies five market or industry forces that, when combined, determine the attractiveness of competing in a particular market. For health care, this model can be adapted to analyze the interactions between the **power of the healthcare workforce, the power of consumers and payers, innovations in technology, the regulatory environment, and competitive rivalry,** as depicted in Figure 5-2.

Power of the Healthcare Workforce

The **power of the healthcare workforce** can have significant strategic implications for any healthcare organization, as the workforce is composed of the front line of caregivers

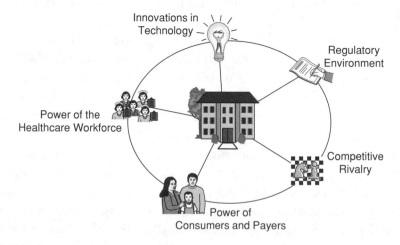

FIGURE 5-2 Market Assessment Model

in providing services. In the SWOT analysis, an organization should look at the availability of all subsets of healthcare providers that are critical to its success. As an example, if obstetrics is a major clinical program of the organization, the organization should closely consider the future anticipated supply and demand of obstetricians (OBs) in its market. Currently, with the significant increases in malpractice insurance targeted at obstetricians across the country, many OBs have elected to discontinue delivering babies and focus solely on gynecology, while others have opted to retire early. This has dramatically reduced the supply of obstetricians in many areas of the country and forced some hospitals to hire their affiliated obstetrical staff in an effort to cover their malpractice insurance premiums and keep them practicing. Other hospitals have developed "laborists"—OBs who are hired solely to work in the hospital and deliver babies. These moves are examples of strategies that could be adopted by organizations to either maintain or grow their obstetrical services and are in response to market trends.

Another example of the power of the healthcare workforce is the potential ramifications of the current nursing and radiology personnel shortages. With a shortage of personnel, wage and hiring expenses increase, jeopardizing the ability to offer those specific services. A nursing shortage may affect a hospital's ability to add beds to meet growing demand for services. A shortage of radiology technicians may affect an organization's opportunity to offer new state-of-the-art technologies. The influence and availability of these and other healthcare personnel (and the organization's dependency on them) must be considered when developing future strategies.

Power of Consumers and Payers

At the other end of the spectrum, as the ultimate purchasers of health care, the power of consumers is becoming a more significant market force—and one that has required a dramatic shift in the way the industry offers services. Today's consumers are demanding more and more from their healthcare providers on all levels (e.g., physicians, payers, hospitals), both in terms of the availability of specific service offerings and in the delivery of those services. Historically, healthcare organizations viewed physicians as the primary customers; without them, the organization could not provide services. However, in today's world, the *patient* is becoming the central focus of customer service. The potential impact of this shift to a **patient-centric model** needs to be considered when developing future strategies.

Consumers can influence the healthcare market in other ways as well. Different communities have different healthcare needs—one community may need increased access to primary care channels, while another may need better health education and screenings. By identifying specific **community needs**, healthcare organizations can better target their services and potential growth opportunities. The best way to do this is to understand the consumer.

In concert with consumers is the **power of payers**. Some markets have multiple payers of various sizes and strengths, while others have one or two major payers that dictate market payments. In either case, a healthcare organization that relies on these payers must stay abreast of their needs and demands and how each may affect future operations and strategies. A good example of this is a market with one or two powerful payers that prefer a "late adopter" stance for new medical technologies. In other words, they prefer not to pay for new technologies until the technologies have been proven either medically effective or financially efficient or both. This would be a significant threat to an organization that strives for a competitive advantage by being first to market with the adoption of new medical technologies. Alternately, the power of payers may also create opportunities for an organization. An example would be the general preference of payers for less costly outpatient services. Healthcare organizations that specialize in these types of service offerings (e.g., ambulatory surgery centers, diagnostic/ imaging centers) have capitalized on this payer influence in many areas of the country.

Innovations in Technology

Another market force to be considered is **innovations in technology**. These innovations may represent the threat of substitute products, as new technologies often replace standard operations and services. A good example of this is the introduction of **Picture Archive Communication Systems (PACS)**. This filmless imaging system significantly reduces the need for storage space for films and readers and the staff to maintain those areas and allows for remote electronic accessing of files, ultimately requiring a potentially smaller number of physicians necessary to interpret the images. Innovations in technology may also reduce the need for other types of clinical staff, as in the case of some surgical innovations (e.g., minimally invasive surgery, robotic technologies, drug advancements, etc.), and/or they may significantly increase the requirement of financial resources, as in the case of new radiology equipment (e.g., a new CT scanner, new fluoroscopy equipment, MRI, etc.). As these and other new technologies become available, their potential impact on operations and systems needs to be considered in strategy development.

The Regulatory Environment

As a market force, the **regulatory environment**—on all levels, federal, state, and local—needs to be monitored for its effects on strategy development as well. Congress continually enacts influential legislation, such as the 1986 Emergency Medical Treatment and Active Labor Act (EMTALA), the 1996 Health Insurance Portability and Accountability Act (HIPAA), and the current focus on mandatory error reporting and physician self-referrals, that has significant and rippling effects on all participants in the healthcare industry. Furthermore, the **Centers for Medicare and Medicaid Services (CMS)** take the lead in changes in healthcare payment formulas that are frequently followed by payers at local levels. Other far-reaching issues such as liability reform and quality of care measures may be dealt with on local, state, and federal levels as well. All of these actions can influence a particular healthcare organization's strategy and need to be monitored and analyzed for their potential impacts.

Competitive Rivalry

Competitive rivalry, the last market force to be considered, is probably given the most significant attention in most organizations' strategy development. Whether an organization operates in a near monopoly or an oligopoly, strategically savvy organizations always track their competitors' moves and suspected intentions. Although it is highly unlikely that you will gain access to the actual strategy of your competitors, much information on their strategic intent can be gleaned from their market activities. Information on their service volumes, market share, and news coverage and press releases should be monitored. Ongoing discussions with your own physicians, staff, and suppliers will likely also yield valuable competitive intelligence. Compiling this information together to see a larger picture often leads to an indication of competitors' strategies. Once their strategic intent has been identified, market opportunities for and threats against your own organization can be further addressed.

Mission, Vision, Values

The information gleaned regarding the interaction of these five forces (healthcare workforce, consumers and payers, innovations in technology, regulatory environment, and competitive rivalry) in the market is matched against the organization's **Mission, Vision, and Value (MVV)** statements. As the driving purpose of the organization, the MVVs are reviewed as part of the strategic planning process to ensure they continue to be aligned with the organization's future market environment and to help identify future desired strategic directions. The **mission** of any organization is its enduring statement of purpose. It aims to identify what the organization does, whom it serves, and how it does it. For example, Radiologix, a radiology services company, "strives to be the premier provider of diagnostic imaging services through high-quality service to patients, referring physicians and mutually beneficial relationships with radiologists who provide expert interpretations of diagnostic images" (http://www.radiologix.com). On the other hand, a **vision** statement strives to identify a specific future state of the organization, usually an inspiring goal for many years down the road. The vision of the American Hospital Association is "of a society of healthy communities, where all individuals reach their highest potential for health" (http://www.aha.org). The **values** statement should help define the organization's culture—what characteristics it wants employees to convey to customers. An example of one such value from Duke University Health System in North Carolina is: "We earn the trust our patients place in us by involving them in their health care planning and treatment and by exceeding their service expectations" (http://www.dukehealth.org/AboutDuke/Mission/mission_statement).

Although the mission statement is generally the most enduring of the three, each of these statements may be altered over time to adapt to the environment. As an example, the increasing influence of **consumerism** in health care drove many an organization to revise its vision and value statements to become more **customer service focused**, which in turn (hopefully) helped to change the organization's culture. Reaffirming and/or adjusting these three statements in relation to market activity is a critical step in determining the desired future state of the organization.

Organizational Assessment

Now that we have an idea of what our market looks like and understand our desired intent from our (reaffirmed) MVV, it's time to take a hard, honest look at our own organization. In conducting an internal assessment, an organization turns the analytical lens inward to examine the areas in which it has strengths and weaknesses, as well as how it may build or sustain a competitive advantage in the market. Like the market assessment, the **organizational assessment** has both quantitative as well as qualitative components. The quantitative section of the internal assessment consists mainly of the organizational volume forecast and an assessment of the financial condition. The qualitative section focuses on past strategic performance and leadership's interpretation of the organization's core capabilities (or lack thereof). Each of these components is discussed further.

Organizational Volume Forecast

The **volume forecast** is initiated by identifying the organization's service area—usually a zip code–defined area where 70–80% of its patients are drawn from—and determining the population use rates for applicable service lines (e.g., cardiology, orthopedics, home care visits, CT scans, etc.). These data are usually collected for several historical time periods (e.g., the previous three years) and can then be forecasted out several more time periods simply by using a mathematical trend formula, resulting in a **baseline scenario**. Historical market share information is then applied to each service line, therein highlighting some of an organization's strengths and weaknesses. By holding its **market share growth** trends constant, an organization can formulate a preliminary idea of how well it would fare if it were to stay its current course (and if its competitors do as well). Examining the forecast from the perspective of market share, contribution margin, and/or medical staff depth will also yield service lines of strength that may need to be protected and service lines that could be developed further.

Financial Condition

As with the volume forecast, several years' worth of **key financial indicators** should be analyzed to highlight additional strengths and weaknesses of the organization. These may include indicators such as operating margin, net income, gross and net revenues, bond ratings, fund-raising, key financial ratios, payer mix, pricing, and/or rate-setting arrangements. The organization's historical performance against budget is also helpful to analyze and should yield further insight into strengths and weaknesses. Any financial forecasts that are available should also be included, as well as any routine or planned capital spending and/or facility improvement plans. It is critical to tie the financial reserves and needs of the organization to the strategic planning process to ensure the resulting strategies can and will be funded appropriately. Tying the financial information to the volume forecast also serves to provide budget targets for the upcoming year(s).

Strategic Performance

It is important to remember that strategic planning is a dynamic rather than linear process and, as such, there should optimally be no distinct beginning or end. Thus, a review of the organization's past **strategic performance** should be included as part of future strategy development. This review can be as simple as an assessment of whether past strategies accomplished their intended goals or as multifaceted as an ad hoc leadership meeting to discuss roadblocks that led to failure or factors that drove success. Either way, this review can and should provide valuable information for future strategy development and implementation.

Organizational Core Capabilities

In addition to the more quantitative strengths and weaknesses that can be outlined through the volume forecast and financial condition review, there are subjective strengths and weaknesses that need to be identified for strategy development as well. Identifying these capabilities can be quite challenging, as planners usually have to rely on surveys of and/or interviews with the leadership of the organization to gather this information. This can be both time-consuming and value laden, but this information will be critical input for the plan's overall success. With that said, Table 5-1 highlights some common methods of collecting this information and the benefits and limitations of each.

TABLE 5-1 Data Collection Methods

	Pros	Cons
Interviews	■ opportunity to clarify responses ■ encourages free thinking ■ can ensure representative sample	■ time-consuming ■ potential for interviewer bias ■ open answers difficult to analyze
Focus Groups	■ opportunity to clarify responses ■ allows for relatively large sample ■ can be economically efficient	■ potential for groupthink ■ open answers difficult to analyze
Surveys	■ effective way to obtain large sample ■ standardized answers allow for easier analysis ■ no interviewer bias	■ can be expensive ■ lag time for responses ■ potential for low response rate

The key to gathering the most value from the leadership input is to challenge leaders (e.g., executives, physicians, managers, etc.) to think within a strategic context, as opposed to the operational mode they are involved in on a day-to-day basis. Merely asking leaders to identify an organization's weaknesses, for example, can result in responses such as poor parking or a lack of marketing, whereas framing the question to identify challenges to the organization in growing service volumes may better yield answers such as an aging medical staff, lack of capacity, etc. It is important to incorporate these identified strengths and weaknesses into the organizational assessment for further discussion.

STRATEGY IDENTIFICATION AND SELECTION

Throughout the development of the SWOT, the building blocks for strategy identification begin to emerge. If the organization is at the start of the development of a multiyear plan, it will usually conduct a rather thorough SWOT analysis. However, if the organization has an identified long-term strategic direction, the SWOT may selectively analyze only those areas that are relevant to the identified strategic direction. For example, if the organization has resolved to grow defined service lines, the analysis may focus more specifically on those areas of the market. Alternately, if the direction is diversification, the analysis may focus more on areas related to the organization's current strengths, whether they are related to service line or internal capability. Regardless of the depth of the SWOT, it serves as input for the next step in the process, strategy identification and selection.

Scenario Development

Strategy identification usually begins with the baseline scenario developed for the volume forecast. However, at this point, it is important to apply planning assumptions to the scenario and not simply accept the baseline. For example, will the organization plan to hold market share constant for a particular service, or will the organization hope to grow that market? Alternatively, the organization may decide to discontinue a specific service, perhaps due to predicted declining reimbursement or lack of physicians. By applying different planning assumptions, many different scenarios may result.

It is also critical that the information and data gathered in the market assessment, including the competitor assessment, be incorporated into this forecast in the form of further planning assumptions. For example, are there new technologies on the horizon that will affect service volumes? Or is there a dearth of providers that may counteract predicted increasing utilization of a particular service for a period of time? Desired financial targets also need to be incorporated here.

Overlaying these planning assumptions onto the baseline scenario can result in any number of future scenarios by adjusting their relative impacts. This is where strategic planning really becomes an art vs. a science, and it is often difficult to quantitatively determine the extent to which market forces may affect future market volumes. Because of this, the underlying planning assumptions should be debated extensively. To this end, there are several companies that provide assistance and/or models for quantifying market forces; a sampling of these companies is provided as additional resources at the end of this chapter.

From this scenario analysis, several potential strategic directions for the organization may emerge. The strategic direction is the goal that the organization desires to accomplish within the planning time frame. Generally, as each scenario may have different probabilities for success and may require different levels of resource investment, the specific scenario (and strategic direction) that will ultimately be chosen will often depend on an organization's tolerance for risk.

Outcomes

Once a strategic direction is chosen, specific desired outcomes should be targeted and strategies to accomplish this identified. As an example, if an organization concludes it will differentiate itself through its orthopedic services (strategic direction), the desired outcome may be to lead the market in orthopedic service volumes within two years. To accomplish this, the organization may identify strategies to increase its surgeon base, add rehabilitation services, or develop a center-of-excellence program. A strategy is a carefully designed plan to accomplish the desired outcomes.

Even the largest and most fiscally sound organization cannot successfully implement all the strategies it can conceive of, nor should it try to. A successful strategic plan is focused and, just as importantly, executable; too many strategies may render the plan ineffective simply because there is too much to do. **Strategy is all about making choices**. A clear and focused strategy will guide decision making, prioritize resource allocation, and keep the organization on its desired course; in choosing which strategies to pursue, an organization is also choosing which strategies *not* to pursue. At this stage in the planning process, the organization's leadership must determine its ability to successfully execute the strategies it has identified.

Factors to consider in making this determination are highlighted in Table 5-2 and include, for example, the degree to which the strategy has the ability to help the

TABLE 5-2 Successful Strategies

Successful Strategies

- Are focused on the desired future state
- Align internal capabilities with market opportunities and threats
- Provide or sustain a competitive advantage for the organization
- Are funded and resourced long term

TABLE 5-3 Tactical Plan Template

Goal	Key Actions	Target Completion Date	Resources Required	Dependencies	Revenue Projection	Success Metric

organization meet its financial targets. Alternatively, does the organization have the financial resources to fund the strategy appropriately in terms of operating and capital expense? Additionally, does the organization have the internal capabilities to successfully execute the strategy—does it have, or can it acquire, the necessary human resources? Is the strategy transformational enough to bring about the desired change? Equally important, is there a champion to take ownership of the strategy's success? By going through the exercise of matching potential strategies to financial and other targets, and matching implementation requirements to resource availability, strategy selection is accomplished.

Strategy Tactical Plans

The final step in the actual development of the strategic plan is the creation of specific **tactical plans** for each strategy, which are necessary for translating the plan into action. Tactical plans answer the who, what, when, where, and how questions of strategy implementation. Table 5-3 shows an example of a basic template for a tactical plan that, when completed, will help drive implementation of the strategy.

ROLLOUT AND IMPLEMENTATION

With the development of the tactical plans, the strategic plan is complete. The plan is then presented to the board of directors for approval and endorsement and is then rolled out across the organization. **Rollout of the plan** has two main steps: first, the plan is **communicated at all levels of the organization**; only by communicating the strategy to all necessary stakeholders can an organization gain the support necessary for successful execution of the strategy. Second, **supporting plans such as the financial and budgeting,**

FIGURE 5-3 Supporting Plans

operating, marketing, capital, and master facilities plans are developed or updated with their intent and strategies developed in the strategic plan. Having all of the organization's supporting plans tied to the strategic plan is a critical factor in reinforcing its strategic direction. Figure 5-3 depicts some of the supporting plans that may be drawn from the strategic plan.

OUTCOMES MONITORING AND CONTROL

Monitoring and control of the strategic plan is most often accomplished through the use of an organizational dashboard, or scorecard. A dashboard is a visual reference used to monitor an organization's performance against targets over time. Its simplistic design should allow for quick assessment of areas that may need adjustment, similar to an automobile dashboard. Dashboards can depict strategic, operational, and/or financial outcome indicators, depending on the organization's needs, but care must be taken to highlight a *manageable* number of indicators, or the dashboard will lose its functionality. Figure 5-4 depicts an example of a dashboard, although templates abound in the industry.

Depending on the organization's needs and on the types of indicators management identifies, the dashboard should be monitored regularly (e.g., monthly or quarterly). At a minimum, as soon as an indicator highlights a variance from the desired target, managers must address the variance with tactics that correct or alter the results. Optimally, the dashboard should serve to facilitate ongoing management discussion regarding execution of the strategy. To help best ensure success of the strategic plan, dashboard indicators are aligned with operational plans and their associated identified goals.

ABC Health Care, Inc.

People		Actual	Budget	
	Employee Satisfaction			
	Vacancy Rate			
	RN			
	Total			
	Turnover			
	RN			
	Total			

Service		Actual	Budget	
	Patient Satisfaction			
	Inpatient			
	ED			
	Ambulatory			

Growth				
	Admissions			
	Births			
	Surgeries			
	ED Visits			

Quality		Actual	Budget	
	CMS/JCAHO			
	Heart Failure			
	Pneumonia			
	AMI			
	Medication Errors			
	E - I			
	G - I			
	Central Line Infections			
	MICU			
	SICU			

Financial				
	Operating Margin			
	Days Cash on Hand			
	Current Ratio			

FIGURE 5-4   Dashboard

STRATEGY EXECUTION

Although the development of the actual strategic plan occurs in a logical progression, other than perhaps the creation of the SWOT, every stage of the plan's development should really be viewed as part of its execution. **Strategy execution** is crucial for organizational success and cannot be overstated in terms of importance; unfortunately, this is often an element of strategic planning that many organizations overlook. With the flurry of activity and intensity that usually surrounds the development of the strategic plan itself, there can be a collective sigh of relief following board approval of the plan, and leadership may be relieved to be able to return to their "real work" and the day-to-day operations. Yet successful organizations know that execution is much more important than the plan.

Barriers

Execution, however, isn't easy, and there are many roadblocks on the path to success. For example, it has been said that "**culture eats strategy for lunch,**" and even that may be an understatement. If an organization's stakeholders are not ready for the strategy, it will not be executed by even the most tenacious of leaders. With the heightened influence of consumerism, many healthcare organizations attempted strategies early on to shift the organization from a physician-centric to a more patient-centric focus, aiming to gain a competitive advantage on this emerging market trend. However, many of these organizations were faced with a strong undercurrent of resistance from an internal culture that was not prepared for this new paradigm, and the strategy failed. This example demonstrates the need for strategy execution to start early in the planning process, enabling the organization to either better prepare itself for implementation of the strategy or table the strategy until the organization is ready to implement it successfully.

Other barriers to successful strategy execution include a lack of focus of the strategy. Often, during the plan development phase, leadership will inevitably develop more strategies than it can successfully execute. If this list is not pared down to a reasonable number, or if the few strategies that are planned do not align appropriately, execution attempts will be futile. Additionally, as mentioned earlier, if the strategies are not appropriately funded and resourced, they cannot be executed, or if they result in competing priorities, the organization will likely be unsuccessful. All of these barriers can be overcome, however, in part by focusing on execution at the earliest stages of strategy development.

Strategy execution is also most successful with a combination of strong leadership and organizational buy-in. Although leadership will need to have flexibility to adjust strategies as market conditions and internal developments warrant, they must also have the consistency over time to stay the course. Too often, strategies have failed because the organization has fallen to temptation of new priorities, or they simply fail to resource the strategy over multiple years or time periods. Strategy is not a quick fix or immediate turnaround, and strong leadership is needed to maintain a long-term focus. In addition, organizational buy-in at all levels is critical. As demonstrated earlier in the example regarding culture, strategy cannot be implemented solely in the top layers of an organization. All stakeholders must be aware of and buy in to the desired future state and the path that leads them there in order to ensure the momentum necessary to achieve results. Optimally, a successfully conducted strategic planning process will generate "strategy champions" at all levels of the organization.

Participants

All organizations generally involve key leadership in the strategic planning process, but the extent to which other stakeholders are involved varies considerably. There is no one best answer as to who should be involved in the planning process and how, because each organization and culture is different, but one caveat generally holds true: the more stakeholders that are aware of and own the strategy, the greater the chance of success. That said, the strategic planning process should involve representatives from the board of trustees, upper and middle management, the medical staff, general staff, and community leaders as much as possible to the extent appropriate throughout the process. When the plan is completed, it should be communicated to all stakeholders as discussed earlier.

STRATEGIC PLANNING AND EXECUTION: THE ROLE OF THE HEALTHCARE MANAGER

A good portion of this chapter has been dedicated to discussion of the content of the strategic plan, and with good reason: healthcare managers need to understand the types of information and intelligence gathered and analyzed for plan development, and how that information is interpreted and acted upon. However, it has often been said that the plan is worthless but planning is priceless; the value of strategic planning lies not in the plan itself, but in the planning process. Properly conducted, the strategic planning process will challenge management to robustly confront the facts of its market and the organization, to persistently test planning assumptions, and to continually refine the organization's execution skills.

Healthcare managers at all levels have the responsibility to continually monitor their environment—both internal and external—and assess and act upon the possible implications of any trends or events that are of note. They have the responsibility to understand their local market on an ongoing basis and to know their organization's strategic direction and intent. They are responsible for identifying ways to support the organization's strategy and for ensuring that their subordinates have the knowledge and understanding of the strategy in order to do the same. Strategic planning may be driven by the planning or business development function of an organization, but it is the responsibility of leadership at all levels to help execute and manage the organization's strategy. Strategic plans may also be developed for departments and other levels within the organization and may be helpful to the manager in achieving the department's goals as well.

CONCLUSION

Effective strategic planning is a critical element in the success of today's healthcare organizations. Through understanding its competitive and other market environments, an organization can best identify a desired future state and a means to achieve it, but as discussed, the true value of strategic planning lies in the process, and less in the resulting plan. In a recent study, Begun and Kaissi (2005) investigated the perceived value of strategic planning to leaders in 20 healthcare organizations. Consistent with the information presented in this chapter, the authors found that leadership stressed the dynamic vs. static nature of planning and the importance of execution of the strategic plan. Strategic planning will likely continue to be a valued function in healthcare organizations in the future, and management at all levels needs to understand the process, and its purpose and their critical role in development and execution of the successful strategy.

DISCUSSION QUESTIONS

1. What are some of the healthcare market trends you can identify in your market? How might they affect your job as a manager, and how would you react to/prepare for them?

2. In what ways can you, as a manager, contribute to the management and execution of your organization's strategy?

3. Discuss how strategic planning is a dynamic, vs. linear, process. Why is this important?

4. Summarize the purpose of the SWOT analysis and how it is best used in the planning process.

5. Describe resources you could use as a manager to stay current in your field/area.

Cases in Chapter 17 that are related to this chapter include:

- The Merger of Two Competing Hospitals—see p. 406
- Are We Culturally Aware or Not?—see p. 436

Additional cases, role-play scenarios, video links, websites, and other information sources are also available in the online Instructor's Materials.

REFERENCES

Begun, J., & Kaissi, A. (2005). An exploratory study of healthcare strategic planning in two metropolitan areas. *Journal of Healthcare Management, 50*(4), 264–274.

Porter, M. (1998). *On competition.* Boston, MA: Harvard Business School Press.

Additional Readings

Bossidy, L., & Charan, R. (2004). Execution: The discipline of getting things done. *AFP Exchange, 24*(1), 26–30.

Brandenburger, A., & Nalebuff, B. (1995). The right game: Use game theory to shape strategy. *Harvard Business Review, 73*(4), 57–71.

Collins, J. (2001). *Good to great: Why some companies make the leap . . . and others don't.* New York, NY: Harper Business.

Ginter, P., Swayne, L., & Duncan, W. J. (2002). *Strategic management of healthcare organizations* (4th ed.). Malden, MA: Blackwell.

Jennings, M. (Ed.). (2000). *Health care strategy for uncertain times.* San Francisco, CA: Jossey-Bass/AHA Press Series.

Kaplan, R., & Norton, D. (1996). *The balanced scorecard: Translating strategy into action.* Boston, MA: Harvard Business School Press.

Kaplan, R., & Norton, D. (2005). The balanced scorecard: Measures that drive performance. *Harvard Business Review, 83*(7), 172.

Prahalad, C. K., & Ramaswamy, V. (2004). *The future of competition: Co-creating unique value with customers.* Boston, MA: Harvard Business School Press.

Senge, P., Kleiner, A., Roberts, C., Ross, R. B., Roth, G., & Smith, B. J. (1994). *The fifth discipline fieldbook: Strategies and tools for building a learning organization.* New York, NY: Doubleday.

Zuckerman, A. (2005). Creating competitive advantage: Product development. *Healthcare Financial Management, 59*(6), 110–113.

Additional Resources

Sg2 Health Care Intelligence:	www.sg2.com
Thomson Reuters:	http://thomsonreuters.com/products_services/healthcare/
Data Bay Resources:	www.databayresources.com
The Advisory Board Company:	www.advisoryboardcompany.com

CHAPTER 6

Healthcare Marketing
Ruth Chavez and Nancy Sayre

LEARNING OBJECTIVES

By the end of this chapter, the student will be able to:

- Define marketing and the progression of becoming a market-oriented organization;
- Explain the important role of strategic marketing in today's healthcare environment;
- Distinguish between traditional and social marketing approaches;
- Explain the major functions that are part of the marketing management process;
- Discuss several important marketing terms, including market segmentation, target marketing, marketing mix elements, and relationship marketing;
- Define consumer behavior and the decision making process as it relates to healthcare offerings; and
- Describe how healthcare managers can integrate ethics and social responsibility into marketing strategy.

INTRODUCTION

Today's practicing healthcare managers are being challenged to operate in increasingly complex, interdependent, and dynamic markets. These same managers must understand essential principles and practices of marketing in order to support the firm's broader strategic goals and objectives, as identified in the previous chapter. **Strategic healthcare marketing** consists of the kinds of activities the firm uses to satisfy customer needs; the approaches managers pursue to create, communicate, and deliver value in selected markets; and the means of capturing value in return (Kotler, Shalowitz, &

Stevens, 2008). A **customer** is the purchaser of products, services, and ideas (Pride & Ferrill, 2009). All marketing activities should focus on the customer. In this sense, the role of healthcare marketing must be understood as the process of creating long-term, mutually beneficial relationships between the organization and well-defined target customers. However, as discussed later in detail, the purchaser of products, services, or ideas may not necessarily be the ultimate healthcare consumer. Nonetheless, optimal integrated marketing practice will take into consideration the various roles in the healthcare decision-making process.

To quote Peter Drucker, seminal management thinker and sound practitioner, "There is only one valid definition of business purpose: to create a customer. . . . It is the customer who determines what the business is. . . . Because it is its purpose to create a customer, any business enterprise has two—and only these two—basic functions: marketing and innovation" (1954, p. 37). According to Drucker (1974), "Any organization in which marketing is either absent or incidental is not a business and should never be managed as if it were one" (p. 62). Although marketing is now widely accepted as a critical organizational function, from a historical perspective, when compared to other sectors, health care has lagged in the adoption of a customer orientation. Marketing as an organizational function did not generally exist in health care before the 1980s (Berkowitz, 2011; Kotler et al., 2008; Thomas, 2005). In 1975, the appointment of a vice president of marketing at Evanston Hospital in Evanston, Illinois (now NorthShore University Health System), was one notable exception. With the growing significance of consumer-driven health care, the boom of the Internet on all frontiers, and increased demand for personalized services, understanding strategic marketing has become increasingly important.

WHAT IS MARKETING?

Many people mistakenly equate marketing with advertising, promotion, or selling. The American Marketing Association (2007, para. 2) defines **marketing** as "the activity, set of institutions, and processes for creating, communicating, delivering, and exchanging offerings that have value for customers, clients, partners, and society at large." What can we learn from this definition? First, it places marketing in the central role of satisfying customer needs. Second, all marketing activities center on building a sustainable value-driven system for customers, stakeholders, and society. These customers can include individual healthcare consumers, physicians, intermediaries, or other organizations. Third, healthcare organizations and managers with a relentless focus on creating long-term customer relationships will generally achieve superior performance over those who only focus on short-term results.

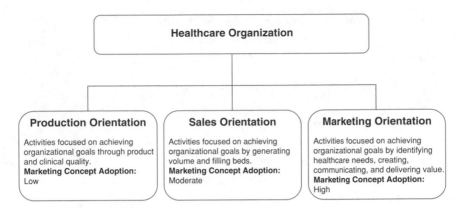

FIGURE 6-1 Production, Sales, and Marketing Orientation

Source: Adapted with permission from Eric N. Berkowitz, *Essentials of health care marketing* (Sudbury, MA: Jones & Bartlett Learning, 2011) 3rd ed., p. 12.

Key Components of the Marketing Concept

The discussion above introduces a managerial philosophy that suggests that *all* organizations, regardless of industry, must be in the business of satisfying customer needs. According to the **marketing concept**, an organization must create, communicate, and deliver customer value to selected target markets more effectively than its competition to achieve its goals and objectives (Kotler & Keller, 2009). **Customer value** is the difference between the benefits a consumer perceives from the purchase of a product, service, or idea and the cost to acquire those benefits. Through a coordinated set of well-defined activities, the marketing manager must do the right things at the right time to orchestrate individual strategies into a wholly integrated system. In general, an organization can be characterized as production oriented, sales oriented, or marketing oriented. Figure 6-1 depicts the sharp contrast between the three types of organizational orientations.

Social Marketing and Cause-Related Marketing

Two rapidly growing and distinct fields of marketing can be traced to the contribution of Philip Kotler and numerous colleagues who broadened the traditional marketing concept from the commercial for-profit to the not-for-profit realm (Cheng, Kotler, & Lee, 2011; Kotler & Andreasen, 1996; Kotler & Lee, 2008; Kotler & Levy, 1969; Kotler, Roberto, & Lee, 2002; Kotler & Zaltman, 1971). Kotler and Zaltman coined the term **social marketing** as "the design, implementation, and control of programs calculated to influence the acceptability of social ideas and involving consideration of product planning, pricing, communication, distribution, and marketing research" (Kotler & Zaltman, 1971, p. 5). In health care, **social marketing** is:

1. the application of commercial marketing principles and techniques;
2. used to influence behavioral change;
3. focused on a specific target audience;
4. used in order to promote public health;
5. intended to benefit society as a whole (Andreasen, 1995; Evans, 2006; Kotler et al., 2002).

FIGURE 6-2 Ribbon Used for Social and Cause-Related Marketing

Consider the marketing efforts inspired by Susan G. Komen for the Cure. Figure 6-2 depicts the ribbon that has come to symbolize breast cancer awareness. In 1982, Nancy Brinker, with the support of a handful of dedicated friends and a mere $200, founded the Susan G. Komen Breast Cancer Foundation in memory of her sister. According to the Komen website, the Susan G. Komen Race for the Cure series is today "the world's largest and most successful education and fund-raising event ever created" (Susan G. Komen for the Cure, n.d., para. 2). Since its inception, the non-profit has harnessed the power of social marketing principles and techniques to garner a vast array of strategic partners and sponsors that represent a global network for breast cancer awareness. Other non-profit organizations have followed and created their own ribbons in a variety of colors and patterns.

In contrast to social marketing, **cause-related marketing** links a for-profit company and its offerings to a societal issue, such as breast cancer, with the goal of building brand equity and increasing profits. In working with Komen, global networks of corporation partnerships have leveraged cause-related marketing techniques with significant benefits to both partners in the strategic alliance

A BRIEF HISTORY OF MARKETING IN HEALTH CARE

Because health care is a relative newcomer to marketing, it is useful to consider a historical perspective. As mentioned above, prior to the past few decades, marketing lacked widespread acceptance in the healthcare industry. During the 1970s and 1980s in particular, it was difficult for managers to agree on the role and value of marketing to healthcare organizations. As a result, most hospitals, insurers, managed care organizations, nursing homes, physician and dental practices, and other healthcare providers had limited use for marketing (Robinson & Cooper, 1980–1981). It is not surprising that books devoted to healthcare marketing did not appear until the late 1970s and the first formal conference on the topic did not take place until 1977 (Keith, 1985; MacStravic, 1990; Thomas, 2005).

As late as 1990, the future of marketing in health care remained unclear. In reviewing the slow progression, MacStravic (1990) presented the following reasons:

- Some managers supported marketing but chose not to disclose its success.
- Others were optimistic about marketing's potential but were experimenting.
- In a number of healthcare organizations, managers were frustrated but uncertain as to why marketing was not working.
- Other healthcare administrators and managers viewed marketing as a hoax.
- For the most part, organizations were only getting started in marketing.

Despite the differences in approach, early practitioners and scholars were asking precisely the same question we are asking today: "Why is marketing different in health care?" With roughly four decades of research into the nature and scope of marketing as it applies to health care, a number of issues are among the most mentioned. Among these issues are the following. First, in the past (and in some cases today), healthcare professionals scorned marketing activities based on the belief that, while suitable in non-healthcare entities, they were inappropriate and unethical for healthcare organizations (Thomas, 2005). With respect to this issue, there was a time when even the American Medical Association declared such activities as unethical. Second, healthcare professionals raise considerable doubt that health care is a "market" comparable to other industries. A chorus of practitioners and scholars say health care is uniquely different from other industries. Thomas perhaps best describes this view: "Healthcare is different from other industries in terms of characteristics inherent in the industry and the attributes of its buyers and sellers" (2005, p. 47). Even the most casual observer would agree that health consumers typically have not been responsible for paying all the associated costs of medical treatment. Additionally, imperfect knowledge about costs and services constrains consumer decision making. A third major shortcoming is a weak consumer-driven healthcare system, where third-party payers (e.g., employers and health insurance entities) are in charge and neither consumers nor their providers have direct decision-making power (Herzlinger, 2002, 2004). While a totally consumer-driven healthcare system seems unreasonable, empowering consumers to have a greater voice and more accountability is certainly an attainable goal.

A fourth issue is that the marketing function has been further constrained by the absence of value-based competition. As Porter and Teisberg (2006) point out, there is dysfunctional competition in health care where participants drive not to create value for patients but to capture more revenue, shift costs, and restrict services. They argue that:

> Consumers will only be able to play a bigger role in their care, and make better choices if providers and health plans re-align competition around patient results and disseminate the relevant information and advice. Reform does not require consumers to become medical experts or to manage their own care; it requires providers and health plans to compete on value, which will allow and enable consumers to make better choices and be more responsible. (Porter & Teisberg, 2006, p. 8)

Taken together, these arguments explain some of the reasons why marketing as a management tool has been neglected in the past. Today, healthcare managers are making the strategic choice to enable internal collaboration and enterprise-wide knowledge sharing in order to build a customer-driven healthcare organization. As a result, understanding and applying the essential elements of marketing falls squarely into the healthcare manager's domain of responsibility.

THE STRATEGIC MARKETING PROCESS

The emergence of a market orientation where sustainable distinctive advantage is based on the ability of an organization to create, communicate, and deliver customer lifetime value more effectively than its competitors is creating profound changes in the practice of healthcare marketing. The unforgiving global competitive environment is forcing organizations to derive value not just from the production of goods and services, but also from connecting with customers and patients. NorthShore University Health System recently commissioned a market research study to understand consumer motivation. By listening to patients, they learned that consumers were interested in talking about their medical conditions—not hospital offerings. They also learned that patients identify with physicians and nurses—not hospitals. With such market insights, the hospital staff was better prepared to integrate more relevant and compelling messages throughout the NorthShore University delivery system (Bendycki, 2010).

In response to many of the same market forces, challenges, and opportunities discussed in Chapter 5, the role of marketing continues to evolve as a critical strategic management function. Uncontrollable forces, i.e., the dramatic pace of technology, discontinuous change in U.S. health insurance reimbursement trends, and the prospect of more empowered consumers, have elevated marketing into the strategic realm (Berkowitz, 2011).

Although **external uncontrollable (marketplace)** and **internal controllable (organizational)** complexities present marketing issues, agile healthcare organizations can achieve extraordinary results by keeping the customer front and center as the focal point in all marketing activities. Figure 6-3 depicts the essential components of strategic marketing.

As shown in Figure 6-3, organizations can formulate an effective marketing strategy within the context of the organization's strategic plan and in concert with other functional areas (e.g., finance, human resources, operations, etc.). Once established, the mission, vision, and value statements dictate the broad direction for the organization, including strategic marketing planning. Marketing, in this sense, relies on the strategic plan to deliver a sound and reasonable fit between the external environment and internal organizational capabilities. However, from a managerial perspective, it is important to keep in mind that formulating an effective marketing strategy is not an easy task. Hence, organizations often

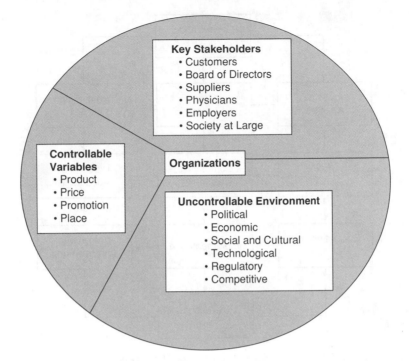

FIGURE 6-3 Components of Strategic Marketing

Source: Adapted with permission from Eric N. Berkowitz, *Essentials of health care marketing* (Sudbury, MA: Jones & Bartlett Learning, 2011) 2nd ed., 20.

assemble **cross-functional teams** (see Chapter 13 for more on teamwork) to provide input and insights throughout the strategic marketing process, as shown in Figure 6-4.

The development of a marketing strategy can be viewed at three main levels:

1. Establishment of a **core strategy**: An effective marketing strategy starts with a detailed and creative assessment of both the company's capabilities—its strengths and weaknesses relative to the competition—and the opportunities and threats posed by the environment.

2. Creation of the company's **competitive positioning**: At the next level, target markets are selected, which determines who the competitors are. At the same time, the company's differential advantage, or competitive edge in serving the customer targets, is defined. Together the identification of targets and the definition of differential advantage constitute the creation of the competitive positioning of the organization and its offerings.

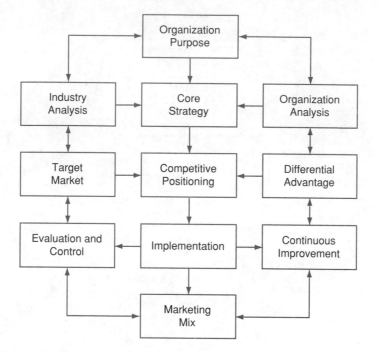

FIGURE 6-4 Strategic Marketing Strategy Process Framework

3. **Implementation** of the strategy: At the implementation level, a marketing-oriented organization must be capable of putting the strategy into practice. Implementation is also concerned with establishing the optimal marketing mix, which will be discussed in detail later in the chapter. Control concerns both the efficiency with which the strategy is put into operation and the ultimate effectiveness of that strategy.

UNDERSTANDING MARKETING MANAGEMENT

Healthcare marketers must continually scan the external environment and conduct a situation assessment to determine the **strengths, weaknesses, opportunities, and threats (SWOT)** for a given offering, set of offerings, or an entire portfolio of products and services. As such, healthcare marketing management is the art and science of selecting target markets and creating, communicating, and delivering value to selected customers in a manner that is both sustainable and differentiated from the competition (Kotler et al., 2008; Kotler & Keller, 2009).

Segmentation, Targeting, and Positioning (STP)

A market is a diverse group of organizations or individuals who have disparate needs for products and services. **Market segmentation** is the process of dividing the total market into groups or segments that have relatively similar needs for products and services. Segmentation enables organizations to design a marketing mix that will more precisely match the needs of individuals in a selected segment (Kotler et al., 2008). Using this method, segmentation is most useful when buyers in target segments have the budget, authority, need, and timeline (BANT) criteria with a propensity to purchase products and services. In other words, attractive healthcare market segments must also be measureable and actionable (Kotler et al., 2008). Again, it is important to note that since it is nearly impossible for a firm to serve an entire market, marketing managers often divide a diverse heterogeneous market into homogenous segments. Hence, a market segment consists of a more narrowly defined group of individuals or organizations with relatively similar wants and needs. Through segmentation, a healthcare organization seeks to match its offerings and services to the needs of the select segments.

Target Segment Selection

How do organizations choose some segments to serve and not others? The combination of target market needs and characteristics, the offering portfolio, and the organization's objectives and resources must be taken into consideration. Berkowitz (2011) distinguishes between the two categories of strategies as follows:

- *Concentration strategy.* This approach targets a single market in order to specialize with the objective of gaining a large share of the market. An orthodontic practice choosing to focus solely on children and adolescents as a niche market is an example. An advantage of this strategy is that specialization enables the healthcare provider to focus all marketing activities on creating, delivering, and sustaining long-term value to a distinct set of customers. The disadvantage, of course, is that specialization may preclude the organization from entering other attractive markets, such as treating adults in the orthodontic practice.
- *Multisegment strategy.* This approach targets several segments with differentiation among the selected group of customers. For example, a general dental practice might choose to serve both children and adults, but might also offer orthodontic services. Choosing this strategy extends the reach to a broader share of the total market. However, more organizational resources are required to satisfy the wants and needs of multiple customer segments.

To select target segments wisely, healthcare marketers need to determine whether the market is identifiable, divisible, accessible, and has enough potential to justify the allocation of organizational resources. After the organization identifies an appropriate marketing strategy, the next step in selecting a target market is determining which segmentation variables to use. The challenge of precisely meeting the needs of selected segments is addressed by dividing them into broad groups based on key distinguishing variables. As can be seen in Table 6-1, there are five broad groups of variables commonly used to segment health consumer markets.

TABLE 6-1 Segmentation Broad Categories, Variables, and Indicative Examples

Category	Variables	Example(s)
Demographic	Age; Gender; Ethnicity and race; Country of origin; Education; Occupation; Income; Generation; Life cycle stage	Changing U.S. demographics offer new opportunities to target retiring and aspiring retiree segments. A long-term care facility might develop an integrated communications plan to reach seniors 55 and older.
Geographic	State; City; County; Urban; Rural	Claritas, Inc., developed geoclustering using the Potential Rating Index by Zip Code Markets (PRIZM) to classify residential neighborhoods into 15 distinct clusters with a discrete marketing mix (Kotler, Shalowitz, & Stevens, 2008).
Psychographic	Values; Lifestyle; Personality; Motivation; Self-efficacy; Attitudes	Using a psychographic consumer segmentation framework, Wolff and her research colleagues (2010) identified four groups of distinct health information–seeking orientations that were significantly associated with certain prevention-related attitudes and behaviors. Using the screening instrument, respondents were segmented into four segments—*independent actives, doctor-dependent actives, independent passives*, and *doctor-dependent passives*.
Situational	Life events	Health insurance firms use situational segmentation to reach the employed and unemployed segments. Segment examples include: (1) employer-based health insurance coverage, (2) Consolidated Omnibus Budget Reconciliation Act (COBRA) coverage for 18 months after job termination, and (3) individual health plans beyond COBRA.
Behavioral	Usage rates; Tech-savvy users	In the midst of a recession and in a state with the highest unemployment rate in the nation in 2009, the Henry Ford Health System in Detroit led local competitors in inpatient growth, with a 7.4% increase in admissions over the previous year. Of the 8,201 new admissions, the seven-hospital system segmented the customer base to reach Internet users through social media and other online tools (Glenn, 2010).

Table 6-1 depicts the many layers of segmentation at the healthcare manager's disposal. Market segmentation based on demographics variables is a case in point. Perhaps the most widely used, demographic segmentation is a relatively easy way to estimate customer demand, i.e., wants and needs. Marketing in long-term care is a good example of the use of demographic segmentation. Consumers ranging from age 55 to 95+ represent a diverse range of people who are at various stages with respect to retirement, but at the same time, all have needs related to quality of life. In the United States, there are approximately 12 million Americans who belong to the pre-Depression generation (individuals born before 1930); the Depression generation (born between 1930 and 1945) is composed of another estimated 28 million; and the baby boomer generation (born between 1946 and 1964 and approaching the retirement phase of life) accounts for 80 million (Hawkins & Mothersbaugh, 2010). Various types of long-term care facilities (e.g., independent living, assisted living, skilled nursing) offer different levels of care. These different services suggest a need for long-term care facilities to market themselves in different ways to these demographic segments and to overcome the negative connotations associated with the words "nursing home" or "old folks home" (Laurence & Kash, 2010).

Positioning

The **positioning** aspect of the strategic marketing process brings healthcare marketing closer to tactical implementation. Once a healthcare system determines which portion of the larger market to serve, it then positions itself in the face of competition. Hence, healthcare organizations and providers must deliberately position the brand image and offerings in the mind of the target market. Kotler et al. (2008) argue that "good brand positioning helps guide marketing strategy by clarifying the brand's essence, what goals it helps the consumer achieve. . . . The result of positioning is the successful creation of a customer-focused value proposition" (p. 235).

HEALTHCARE BUYER BEHAVIOR

In creating and executing marketing strategy, managers face the central question of how healthcare buyers make decisions. There are fundamental differences between **organizational** and **consumer** markets. Healthcare managers need to gain a deep understanding of consumer and business behavior in order to meet customer needs. The following sections of this chapter will provide an overview of these important behaviors.

Organizational Buying Behavior

The business market has been defined as all organizations that acquire goods and services (Kotler et al., 2008). For the purposes of this discussion, both for-profit and non-profit organizations are considered business markets. **Business-to-business** (B2B) marketing concentrates on organizational buyers. Consider the following examples:

- Employers purchase health insurance coverage for employees.
- Local, state, and national governments hire managerial consultants.
- Hospital buying centers contract enterprise-wide electronic records solution providers.
- Medical devices, pharmaceuticals, and medical surgical supplies comprise a large share of virtually every hospital's total expenditures.
- Group purchasing organizations facilitate the complex task of sourcing and contracting products and services for hospitals and healthcare systems.

These illustrations are indicative of the degree of complexity associated with organizational purchase decisions as compared with consumer buyers. With respect to healthcare organizations, there are many people involved in the selling and buying process.

Additionally, both buyers and sellers typically follow formal policies and procedures. "**Derived demand**" is the term given to indicate that the demand for goods, services, and ideas in organizations is derived from consumer demand. Healthcare managers are expected to work with various decision-making units to influence either buying or selling decisions on behalf of the organization.

Consumer Buying Behavior

Consumer behavior refers to the totality of consumers' decisions with respect to the acquisition, consumption, and disposition of goods, services, time, and ideas by humans over time (Hoyer & MacInnis, 2008). The study of consumer behavior seeks to understand how people select, secure, use, and dispose of products, services, experiences, or ideas to satisfy their needs (Hawkins & Mothersbaugh, 2010). To understand consumer behavior, healthcare managers must draw heavily from the field of psychology. A number of psychological theories have been used to explain the consumer decision-making process. By understanding how people make decisions and the associated internal and external influences on the consumer decision-making process, a healthcare manager can anticipate consumer needs and develop solutions for those needs.

Internal influences include consumers' motivation, attitudes, perceptions, learning, memory and retrieval, personality, values, emotions, and behavioral intentions. External influences include consumers' family and friends, reference groups, situational factors, culture and subculture, and marketing stimuli.

In addition to understanding the many influences, it is helpful to be aware of the consumer decision-making process as depicted in Table 6-2.

It is fair to say that healthcare providers will continue to have a prominent role in the decision-making process in the foreseeable future. At the same time, the growing availability

TABLE 6-2 Consumer Decision-Making Process

Stage	Definition
I. Problem Recognition	The health consumer recognizes a difference between an actual and desired state. The individual or group is motivated to reach the desired state. For example, a person may feel that he or she is overweight and wish to reach a specific weight goal.
II. Internal Search	The consumer searches internal memory to find a solution to the problem. The person may remember a previous experience that led to solving the problem.
III. External Search	If the problem cannot be solved through an internal search, the health consumer is likely to seek external information that may lead to a solution. The health consumer might consult with family and friends, consult with a physician, or search the Internet or any number of external sources.
IV. Alternative Evaluation	In the fourth stage of the decision-making process, the consumer evaluates the various alternatives to arrive at a solution.
V. Purchase	The fifth stage involves the purchase by selecting the health product, service, or idea. For example, an individual might decide that gastric bypass surgery is the most viable solution.
VI. Post-Purchase Evaluation	In the final stage, the consumer evaluates his or her choice. Generally speaking, in a high-involvement purchase decision with several equally attractive alternatives, the consumer may experience cognitive dissonance, a state of anxiety where there is uncertainty about the selection.

of healthcare information due to the Internet, mobile computing, other unprecedented technological advancements, consumer empowerment, personalized healthcare trends, and more sophisticated and socially responsible marketing practices is giving consumers a greater role in their healthcare decisions.

MARKETING MIX

Putting the marketing strategy into practice requires attending to the controllable variables for the organization presented earlier in Figure 6-3. The **marketing mix** consists of these **four controllable P's**: (1) **Product**—goods, services, or ideas; (2) **Price**—value placed on the product; (3) **Promotion**—marketing activities used to communicate to the target market, including public relations, advertising, personal selling, and integrated marketing campaigns; and (4) **Place**—the offering delivery route (e.g., a pediatric optometrist office). The promotional component of the marketing mix (e.g., advertising, sales promotion, events, etc.) is too often considered to be marketing (Clarke, 2010). Instead, the effective marketing mix is closely aligned with the marketing strategy.

MARKETING PLAN

The **marketing plan** is a written document that serves to guide marketing initiatives across the organization. It is typically a part of the broader strategic plan with a long-term horizon. However, the marketing plan also contains specific tactical marketing activities that are more short-term in nature. Although the time frame varies from one organization to the next, organizations usually develop tactical implementation plans on an annual or biannual basis.

ETHICS AND SOCIAL RESPONSIBILITY

Any chapter on marketing would be incomplete without a discussion of **ethics and social responsibility**. At this mature stage, the marketing discipline must take into consideration the impact that marketing activities have on individual, group, organizational, and societal outcomes. There is also a dark side of marketing. There are firms that market unhealthy products such as cigarettes or encourage behaviors such as alcohol and video game addiction. In addition, there are ethical issues associated with advertising to children and vulnerable populations. Social responsibility and ethical behaviors need to be learned and applied to marketing (Hoyer & MacInnis, 2008). Every day, consumers are affected directly and indirectly by marketing influences. These influences can be subtle and insidious, as in the case of the food industry, food addiction, and the epidemic of obesity in the United States (Kessler, 2009). Healthcare leaders and their respective organizations should model ethically responsible marketing practices. Physicians also must practice ethically and avoid conflict of interest whenever possible in the delivery of health care, not seeking to induce demand for unnecessary procedures. Whether for-profit or non-profit, successful marketing practices should be developed to promote consumer well-being. Extending the reach through community-based intervention campaigns, influencing public policy, and emphasizing prevention are just some examples. There are huge implications. Future healthcare leaders must become increasingly aware of marketing ethics. They have both the responsibility and the opportunity to leverage the power of marketing to improve society as a whole.

CONCLUSION

There has never been a more exciting time for understanding the role of marketing in health care. Whereas this chapter places emphasis on the strategic view, healthcare marketing has many facets. Each healthcare organization, in its own way, leverages marketing to a greater or lesser extent. As remarkable technological advancements reach more and more customers, prudent healthcare managers must ensure that marketing is not a random activity. Even the most attractive Internet social networking site means little without an orchestrated marketing plan.

Marketing is a management orientation centered on customer satisfaction and an organizational function that is integrally related to the entire organization's mission, objectives, and resources. Consistent with this view, the role of marketing in the healthcare organization is to create, communicate, and deliver value to customers through mutually beneficial relationships. At the same time, marketing is a discipline in itself. Healthcare managers should seek assistance from marketing specialists, including internal marketing managers, strategic planners, advertising agencies, public relations firms, strategic alliances, and other consultants.

DISCUSSION QUESTIONS

1. Define marketing and describe why it is important for healthcare managers to understand the key components of the marketing concept.

2. Use an example to compare and contrast social marketing and cause-related marketing. Why is cause-related marketing often successful?

3. A few decades ago, the idea of marketing in many healthcare organizations was almost unthinkable. Discuss why healthcare organizations of the past were slow to integrate marketing principles and practices as compared to other industries.

4. Summarize how healthcare managers benefit from the study of marketing.

5. You have just inherited $1 million. After paying all your outstanding student loans, you decide to start a healthcare enterprise. What business are you in? Is it for-profit or non-profit? What segments would you choose to serve? Briefly describe the steps you would take to divide the broad market into your selected segments. Will you use a concentrated or differentiated targeting strategy? Refer to Table 6-1 in this chapter; identify the key segmentation variables that you would use, and explain why.

6. Locate an ad that seeks to influence the acquisition of a healthcare offering or service. Identify the specific consumer decision-making unit that might be affected by this ad. How do you think this ad will affect the consumer's behavior?

7. Differentiate between organizational and consumer buying behavior.

8. Today, healthcare marketing is a pervasive reality. What is the role of marketing ethics and social responsibility in health care today?

Cases in Chapter 17 that are related to this chapter include:

- All Children's Pediatrics: Changing with the Times—see p. 396

Additional cases, role-play scenarios, video links, websites, and other information sources are also available in the online Instructor's Materials.

REFERENCES

American Marketing Association (AMA). (2007). *About AMA.* Retrieved from http://www.marketingpower.com/AboutAMA/Pages/DefinitionofMarketing.aspx

Andreasen, A. (1995). *Marketing social change: Changing behavior to promote health, social developement and the environme*nt. San Francisco, CA: Jossey-Bass.

Bendycki, N. A. (2010). What do consumers want? *Journal of Health Care Marketing, 30*(1), 3.

Berkowitz, E. (2011). *Essentials of health care marketing* (3rd ed.). Sudbury, MA: Jones & Bartlett.

Cheng, H., Kotler, P., & Lee, R. (2011). *Social marketing for public health: Global trends and success stories.* Sudbury, MA: Jones & Barlett.

Clarke, R. (2010). Marketing health care services. In L. Wolper, *Health care administration: Planning, implementing, and managing organized delivery systems* (4th ed.). Sudbury, MA: Jones & Barlett.

Drucker, P. (1954). *The practice of management.* New York, NY: Harper and Row.

Drucker, P. (1974). *Management.* New York, NY: Harper and Row.

Evans, W. D. (2006). How social marketing works in health care. *British Medical Journal, 332*(7551), 1207–1210.

Glenn, R. (2010). Growth in a parched economy: The Henry Ford system's success story. *Journal of Marketing, 30*(2), 10–13.

Hawkins, D., & Mothersbaugh, D. (2010). *Consumer behavior: Building marketing strategy* (11th ed.). Boston, MA: McGraw-Hill/Irwin.

Herzlinger, R. (2002). Let's put consumers in charge of health care. *Harvard Business Review, 80*(7), 44–55.

Herzlinger, R. (2004). *Consumer-driven health care: Implications for providers, payers, and policy makers.* San Francisco, CA: Jossey-Bass.

Hoyer, D., & MacInnis, D. (2008). *Consumer behavior* (5th ed.). Mason, OH: South-Western Cengage-Learning.

Keith, J. (1985). Marketing health care: What the recent literature is telling us. In P. D. Cooper, *Health care marketing: Issues and trends* (2nd ed., pp. 13–26). Rockville, MD: Aspen Systems Corporation.

Kessler, D. A. (2009). *The end of overeating: Taking control of the insatiable American appetite.* Emmaus, PA: Rodale Press.

Kotler, P., & Andreasen, A. (1996). *Strategic marketing for nonprofit marketing* (5th ed.). Englewood Cliffs, NJ: Prentice Hall.

Kotler, P., & Keller, K. (2009). *Marketing management.* Upper Saddle River, NJ: Pearson Prentice Hall.

Kotler, P., & Lee, N. (2008). *Social marketing: Influencing behaviors for good.* Thousand Oaks, CA: Sage.

Kotler, P., & Levy, J. J. (1969). Broadening the concept of marketing. *Journal of Marketing, 33*(1), 10–15.

Kotler, P., Roberto, N., & Lee, N. (2002). *Social marketing: Improving the quality of life.* Thousand Oaks, CA: Sage.

Kotler, P., Shalowitz, J., & Stevens, R. (2008). *Strategic marketing for health care organizations: Building a customer-driven health system.* San Francisco, CA: Jossey-Bass.

Kotler, P., & Zaltman, G. (1971). Social marketing: An approach to planned social change. *Journal of Marketing, 35*(3), 3–12.

Laurence, J. N., & Kash, B. A. (2010). Marketing in the long-term care continuum. *Health Marketing Quarterly, 27*(2), 145–154.

MacStravic, R. S. (1990). The end of health care marketing? *Health Marketing Quarterly, 7*(1–2), 3–12.

Porter, M., & Teisberg, E. (2006). *Redefining health care: Creating value-based competition on results.* Cambridge, MA: Harvard Business School Press.

Pride, W., & Ferrell, O. (2009). *Foundations of marketing.* Boston, MA: Houghton Mifflin.

Robinson, L. M., & Cooper, D. P. (1980–1981). Roadblocks to hospital marketing. *Journal of Health Care Marketing, 1*(1), 18–24.

Susan G. Komen for the Cure. (n.d.). *About us.* Retrieved from http://ww5.komen.org/AboutUs/MediaCenter.html

Thomas, R. K. (2005). *Marketing health services.* Chicago, IL: Health Administration Press.

Wolff, L. S., Massett, H. A., Maibach, E. W., Weber, D., Hassmiller, S., & Mockenhaupt, R. E. (2010). Validating a health consumer segmentation model: Behavioral and attitudinal differences in disease prevention–related practices. *Journal of Health Communication, 15*(2), 167–188.

CHAPTER 7

Quality Improvement Basics

Eric S. Williams, Grant T. Savage, and Dennis G. Stambaugh

LEARNING OBJECTIVES

By the end of this chapter, the student should be able to:

- Define healthcare quality;
- Discuss the importance of quality;
- Define and apply key quality concepts;
- Describe the Baldrige criteria;
- Assess the leading models of quality improvement; and
- Apply the tools used in quality improvement.

INTRODUCTION

Quality, as an important policy consideration, gained significant public focus in the United States with two publications by the Institute of Medicine (IOM): *To Err Is Human* (Kohn, Corrigan, & Donaldson, 2000) and *Crossing the Quality Chasm* (Institute of Medicine, 2001). *To Err Is Human* first brought public attention to the issue of medical errors, concluding that between 44,000 and 98,000 people die every year from these errors. It also diagnosed the quality problem as not one of poorly performing people, but of people struggling to perform within a system that is riddled with opportunities for mistakes to happen. The second IOM report, *Crossing the Quality Chasm*, outlined a number of goals for improving the quality and performance of the U.S. healthcare system, as well as some of the methods for achieving those goals.

This chapter builds on these two significant reports. The first section presents several of the more common definitions of quality, discusses the importance of healthcare quality, and introduces key figures in quality improvement. The second section provides a strategic framework for improving quality and performance based on the Baldrige Award criteria. The third section expounds on the common elements of quality improvement, while the fourth and fifth sections examine several approaches for implementing quality improvement as well as discussing the tools and techniques of quality improvement.

DEFINING QUALITY IN HEALTH CARE

Healthcare quality may be defined in various ways, with differing implications for healthcare providers, patients, third-party payers, policy makers, and other stakeholders. The IOM provides the most widely accepted definition of healthcare quality as the "degree to which health services for individuals or populations increase the likelihood of desired health outcomes and are consistent with the current professional knowledge" (IOM, 1990). This definition highlights several aspects of quality. First, high-quality health services should achieve desired health outcomes for individuals, matching their preferences for variety. Second, they should achieve desired health outcomes for populations, matching the societal preferences of policy makers and third-party payers for efficiency. And third, they should adhere to professional standards and scientific evidence, consistent with the clinical focus and preferences of healthcare providers for effectiveness.

Another way to view quality is as the result of a system with interdependent parts that must work together to achieve outcomes such as those noted above. Avedis Donabedian defined quality in terms of **structures, processes, and outcomes** (Donabedian, 1966). The **structural elements** of quality involve the material and human resources of an organization and the facility itself. The quality of personnel is documented in their various certifications (registered nurse, board-certified physician, etc.), while the quality of facilities lies in accreditation (in hospitals through The Joint Commission). **Process** involves the actual delivery of care as well as its management. **Outcomes** are the resulting health status of the patients. As a physician, Donabedian championed the development of "**best practices**," i.e., "the ideal to which organizations should aspire" to improve care (Cooper, 2004, p. 827), linking structures, processes, and outcomes with a feedback loop, that is, information given back to providers to achieve better care. Moreover, he defined quality as having at least four components (Donabedian, 1986):

1. the technical management of health and illness;
2. the management of the interpersonal relationship between the providers of care and their clients;

3. the amenities of care; and
4. the ethical principles that govern the conduct of affairs in general and the healthcare enterprise in particular.

The four parts of this definition highlight the need to incorporate multiple stakeholder perspectives to understand healthcare quality. On one hand, the **technical management** of health focuses on the clinical performance of healthcare providers; on the other hand, the **management of interpersonal relationships** underscores the coproduction of care by both providers and patients. In other words, at the patient–provider encounter level, health service quality is driven both by clinical and nonclinical processes (Marley, Collier, & Goldstein, 2004). The "**amenities of care**" speak to the patient's interest in pursuing individual well-being (or variety); the "**ethical principles**" speak to the provider's interest in furthering societal and organizational well-being (or effectiveness).

A related, but more focused, view of quality represents two fundamental questions about any clinical service, procedure, or activity occurring in a healthcare setting: **(1) "are the right things done?"** and **(2) "are things done right?"** The first question assesses the effectiveness of clinical care; the second considers the efficiency of care services. Importantly, the performance of healthcare organizations depends on their effectiveness and their efficiency. Moreover, both effectiveness and efficiency are discussed in the IOM's *Crossing the Quality Chasm* as two of six specific aims for quality improvement. **Effectiveness** is defined as "providing services based on scientific knowledge to all who could benefit and refraining from providing services to those not likely to benefit (avoiding underuse and overuse)"; **efficiency** is defined as "avoiding waste, in particular waste of equipment, supplies, ideas, and energy" (IOM, 2001).

WHY IS QUALITY IMPORTANT?

One of the key issues in healthcare quality is the appropriate use of scarce resources to improve the health of both individuals and the entire population. Problems in this domain can take three forms: **underuse, overuse, and misuse**. Chassin (1997) defines these terms as follows:

> **Underuse** is the failure to provide a service whose benefit is greater than its risk. **Overuse** occurs when a health service is provided when its risk outweighs its benefits. **Misuse** occurs when the right service is provided badly and an avoidable complication reduces the benefit the patient receives.

Underuse is a problem since clinical research has produced a large number of proven, effective treatments that are not widely used. For example, beta blockers are effective in preventing heart attacks among patients who previously have had a heart attack. Soumerai and his colleagues (1997) found that eligible elderly patients were prescribed beta blockers upon hospital discharge after their first heart attack only 21% of the time. More recent studies suggest that the underuse of beta blockers not only in the United States but also in other parts of the world may occur because of hospital- and clinician-based prescribing patterns (Fonarow, 2005; Nicholls et al., 2001).

Overuse is also a quality problem, as certain treatments are provided despite evidence that the treatment is ineffective or even dangerous. Gonzales, Steiner, and Sande (1997) document the overuse of antibiotics among their sample of adults. They found that antibiotics were prescribed 51% of the time for common colds, 52% for upper respiratory infections, and 75% for bronchitis. The prescriptions are written even though these maladies are caused by viruses, not bacteria. Furthermore, the indiscriminant use of antibiotics has fed the rise of multi-drug-resistant strains of bacteria (Steinberg, 2000).

Misuse caught the public's attention with the publication of the first IOM report on patient safety (Kohn et al., 2000), which examined the high rate of medical errors in hospitals, noting, as pointed out earlier, that thousands of patients die every year from preventable adverse events and another million are injured. Moreover, in 1999, the IOM estimated that the costs to the U.S. economy totaled between $37.6 and $50 billion each year. Importantly, these figures only represent inpatient, hospital-based services. Recent studies estimate that 3.5% to 6% of outpatients will experience moderate to serious adverse drug events. Solberg and his colleagues used four years of claims data to identify potential drug-drug interactions that alter the effectiveness or toxicity of one or more drugs (Solberg et al., 2004). They found that about 3.5% of those prescribed drugs are at risk in any given year for moderate to severe drug interactions. Using a different methodology of chart auditing and patient surveys, Gandhi and his colleagues reported that 6% of outpatients experienced adverse drug events that were either serious and preventable or ameliorable (Gandhi et al., 2003).

The *Dartmouth Atlas of Health Care* (see www.dartmouthatlas.org/) illustrates the prevalence of healthcare service underuse, overuse, and misuse in the United States. The atlas, created by John Wennberg and associates, shows wide variation in medical practice. The variation has been shown to not result from severity of illness or patient preferences. The pattern is "often idiosyncratic and unscientific, and local medical opinion and local supply of resources are more important than science in determining how medical care is delivered" (Wennberg, 2002). For example, Boston and New Haven—demographically similar geographically close—might be expected to be fairly similar in their utilization of surgical services. However, "residents of New Haven were more than twice as likely to receive coronary bypass surgery and 50% more likely to undergo hysterectomy" than Bostonians. Bostonians "were two times more likely to undergo carotid artery surgery and 50% more likely to have their hip joints replaced than the residents of New Haven" (Wennberg, 2002).

KEY LEADERS IN QUALITY IMPROVEMENT

During the 1970s, oil shortages induced by the Organization of Petroleum Exporting Countries compelled many people in the United States to purchase fuel-efficient and inexpensive cars. Although U.S. automobile manufacturers tried to produce such cars, only the Japanese were manufacturing fuel-efficient yet inexpensive automobiles that were reliable and durable. In short, the quality of these small Japanese vehicles greatly surpassed those manufactured in the United States. Newspapers, magazines, and television news asked the question, "Can America compete with Japan?" This rapid shift in the marketplace created a new awareness among U.S. industrial leaders that quality mattered.

To address the quality deficit, automobile and other manufacturers in the United States sought the help of quality improvement experts. The contributions ensured that **Total Quality Management (TQM)**—referred to as **Continuous Quality Improvement (CQI)** in health care—became the new paradigm for quality improvement within the United States during the 1980s and 1990s. These quality gurus and advocates included Walter A. Shewhart, W. Edwards Deming, and Joseph M. Juran. They shared a common interest in improving the quality of production in manufacturing and other industries, and their extraordinary lives were intertwined by both industry experience and interest.

During the mid-1920s, Walter A. Shewhart, a physicist at Bell Laboratories, was asked to study the variations in Western Electric's production processes and formulate a means to ensure that products met specifications. Rather than inspecting each product for defects, Shewhart's practical perspective led him to try to control the source of quality variation in the production process. This led him to differentiate between **common-cause** and **special-cause variations**. He knew that common-cause variations in the production process—due to natural variations in raw materials, minor electrical voltage fluctuations, etc.—often were impractical to control. However, special-cause variations—due to operator behaviors, incorrectly calibrated machinery, the substituting of different types of raw materials, etc.—could be controlled (Kolesar, 1993). His book, *Economic Control of Quality of Manufactured Product* (Shewhart, 1931), articulated these principles of statistical process control (SPC) for reducing quality variation in production processes. With editorial assistance from his protégé, W. Edwards Deming, Shewhart also wrote a monograph on quality control, *Statistical Method from the Viewpoint of Quality Control*, which introduced the **Plan-Do-Check-Act (PDCA)** cycle model for improving production processes (Shewhart, 1939).

Known also as the **Shewhart cycle** in the United States, the PDCA cycle was popularized by W. Edwards Deming, and it is called the **Deming cycle** in Japan. A statistician, Deming further developed the principles underlying TQM/CQI while working with the

Japanese to reconstruct their industries after World War II. His approach with the Japanese was to help them fundamentally change work processes. Deming developed a management philosophy that encouraged worker participation in process change, focused on data-based decision making, and embraced a standardized approach to quality improvement. This management philosophy was eventually codified into 14 points (Deming, 2000).

Joseph M. Juran was a contemporary and colleague of Deming's. Born in Braila, Romania, in 1904, Juran immigrated to the United States with his family in 1912 and began working at the age of nine. He earned a bachelor's degree in engineering, but also excelled in mathematics and statistics. Upon graduating, he was hired as an engineer at Western Electric's Hawthorne Works in 1925. He was one of the first engineers trained by Shewhart to apply the principles of SPC. While at Western Electric, Juran championed the Pareto principle from economics, focusing attention and resources on those important quality problems that are attributable to a small number of factors (e.g., the 80/20 rule). During World War II, Juran worked as assistant to the administrator of the Foreign Economic Administration under the Office for Emergency Management. In this role, he oversaw the logistics for providing materials and supplies to allied governments and troops on both fronts. Building on this experience, another of Juran's important contributions was the "Juran Trilogy of quality planning, quality control, and quality improvement." All of these notions were first codified in the 1951 publication of the *Quality Control Handbook* (Juran, Gryna, & Bingham, 1974); his work now is carried on by the Juran Institute (see www.juran.com).

BALDRIGE AWARD CRITERIA: A STRATEGIC FRAME-WORK FOR QUALITY IMPROVEMENT

Effective quality improvement programs operate both at the top (strategic) level and at the operational (tactical) level of the organization. That is, quality improvement programs outline both an overall strategy (philosophy, framework) and a set of tactical processes and tools for quality improvement. Thus, prior to discussing the tactics of specific approaches to quality improvement, we present the **Baldrige Award Criteria**. These criteria provide a broad strategic framework organizations can use to improve quality. These criteria are named after Malcolm Baldrige, who was Secretary of Commerce under President Reagan and who died in office as a result of a rodeo accident on July 25, 1987. In his honor, the Malcolm Baldrige National Quality Award was created in 1988 for companies that display excellent performance across seven dimensions (the Award Criteria). These dimensions of quality have been continually refined and expanded from their original manufacturing base to include healthcare organizations (see Figure 7-1). The Baldrige Award models excellence using a structure-process-outcomes framework. At the left-hand side of the

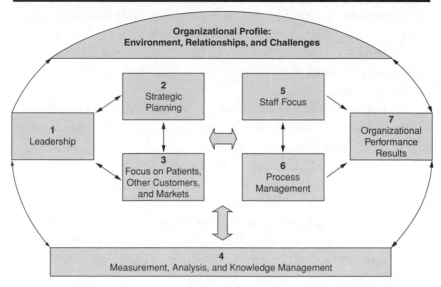

FIGURE 7-1 Baldrige Health Care Criteria for Performance Excellence Framework

Source: 2009–2010 Baldrige National Quality Program Criteria for Performance Excellence. The Baldrige National Quality Program at the National Institute of Standards and Technology in Gaithersburg, MD. Retrieved from http://www.baldrige.nist.gov/PDF_files/2009_2010_Business_Nonprofit_Criteria.pdf

figure is a set of three structural variables: **leadership, strategic planning, and focus on patient, other customers, and markets**. This reflects the notion that integration of customer needs (broadly defined) within the organization's leadership and strategic planning process is necessary for creating the conditions for quality. The two process variables are **staff focus and process management**, illustrating that quality improvement is recognized as an organization-wide responsibility. In other words, engaging staff in process management is another necessary condition for quality. Both structural and process variables interact to produce the organizational performance outcomes or results. At the bottom of the figure is the diffuse influence of measurement, analysis, and knowledge management, important elements that influence the structure, process, and outcome variables.

The goal of the Baldrige criteria is to enhance U.S. competitiveness in the international marketplace. The criteria give healthcare organizations a systematic framework to performance improvement, which results in:

- improved healthcare quality;
- enhanced organizational effectiveness; and
- gains in organizational and individual learning.

The strength of the Baldrige criteria is that it encourages a systemic approach to each of the six categories and specifically links them to measureable business outcomes. These criteria provide the overall strategy and framework for success but are not prescriptive in which approach (e.g., CQI, Six Sigma) should be used to drive improvements in organizational performance. Instead, they leave the organization to determine which approach best fits the organization.

Some see the Baldrige merely as an award, as an end in itself. Others see the Baldrige criteria as a tool to gauge the effectiveness of their organization's management system and do not apply for the Baldrige itself or any of the state-level awards. The Sisters of Saint Mary's Health Care's (SSMHC) journey to become the first healthcare organization to be awarded the Baldrige National Quality Award in 2002 is instructive (Dunn & Santamour, 2003; Ryan, 2004). In 1990, SSMHC began using Continuous Quality Improvement (CQI) as its quality improvement approach and began to use the Baldrige criteria as an assessment tool in 1995. As part of the effort to "get better, faster," they applied for both state and national quality awards, winning the Missouri Quality Award in 1999 and the Baldrige in 2002. One of its key lessons was to apply each year, not so much to get the award but as an organization-wide method of more fully understanding the criteria and how they apply to SSMHC. A further benefit of this approach is that it reinforces the value of quality improvement to SSMHC's organizational culture.

COMMON ELEMENTS OF QUALITY IMPROVEMENT

Before we consider **Continuous Quality Improvement** and **Six Sigma** as methods to improve quality, we need to discuss several key concepts common to all quality improvement methods. These common key concepts are: **measurement, process variation, and statistical process control**.

Measurement

The most basic concept in quality improvement is that of **measurement** and the **metrics** associated with it. Measurement is the translation of observable events into quantitative terms, while **metrics** are the means actually used to record phenomena. All quality improvement efforts require numerical data because "you can't manage what you can't measure." In this way, quality improvement is driven by data-based evidence rather than subjective judgments or opinions.

Good measurement begins with the rigorous **definition of the concept to be measured**. It then requires the use of a measurement methodology that yields reliable (e.g., consistent) and valid (e.g., accurate) measures of the concept. Rigorous definition means that the concept to be measured (e.g., wait times) needs to be defined in very specific terms. This definition should be written and should include the unit of measure. For example, wait times could be defined as the time interval between the arrival of a patient at the office and the time he or she is first seen by the doctor. The unit of measure is time, but the start and end points are important for assessing the reliability and validity of the measure.

Once a good definition of the concept is developed, one challenge is to measure it reliably. If every recorded wait time starts with the arrival of the patient and ends with the patient's first encounter with the doctor, then the measure should be consistent, or reliable. **Measurement reliability** means that if a measure is taken at several points over time or by various people, the measure will generally be consistent (that is, not vary too much). For example, if a person takes his or her temperature each morning, it should be close to 98.6 degrees Fahrenheit each time, assuming that he or she is not ill. If it substantially deviates from 98.6, then that person is ill, the thermometer is broken and not giving consistent readings, or the way in which the thermometer is used varies from day to day (e.g., length of time). Another example of reliability is that of reliability among people. If two nurses in a practice are measuring wait times but use different definitions of waiting, then their measurement of waiting time will not be consistent (i.e., reliable) because the two nurses are measuring the same concept, but in different ways.

Another challenge is to ensure that measurement of the concept is valid. Its validity depends on the accuracy of the measure. If two nurses use the same stopwatch to record waiting times, as long as the clock itself is accurate and the nurses adhere to the same definition of waiting, the wait times should be accurate. In other words, **validity** is the extent to which the measure used actually measures the concept. As with reliability, having a rigorous definition and method of data collection will yield a valid measure.

Process Variation and Statistical Process Control (SPC)

Process variation is the range of values that a quality metric can take as a result of different causes within the process. As Shewhart noted, these causes can take two forms: **special- and common-cause variation** (Shewhart, 1931). **Special-cause variation** is due to unusual, infrequent, or unique events that cause the quality metric to deviate from its average by a statistically significant degree. **Common-cause variation** is due to the usual or natural causes of variation within a process. Following Shewhart, quality improvement now involves (1) detecting and eliminating special-cause variation in a process; and (2) detecting and reducing, whenever feasible, common-cause variation within a process.

Statistical Process Control (SPC) is a method by which process variation is measured, tracked, and controlled in an effort to improve the quality of the process. SPC is a branch of statistics that involves time series analysis with graphic data display. The advantage of this method is that it often yields insight into the data in a way that is intuitive for most decision makers. In essence, it relies on the notion that "a picture is worth a thousand words" for its import. Quality data from a particular process is graphed across time. At some point when there is enough data, the mean and standard deviation are derived and a control chart constructed. The construction begins with graphing the data across time. It continues with the calculation of upper and lower control limits. Think of these limits as similar to the tolerances for machined parts. Complex machinery, like aircraft, requires parts that are manufactured to very tight tolerances so that they will fit together well. The larger the tolerance, the greater the likelihood that a part will not fit the way it is supposed to fit and will fall apart. These limits show the range of variation where the process is thought to be "in control." Typically these limits are set at plus and minus three standard deviations. With these control limits in place, the data can be interpreted and times when the process was "out of control" investigated and remedied.

TWO APPROACHES TO QUALITY IMPROVEMENT

Two quality improvement approaches that have been widely used in health care are Continuous Quality Improvement and Six Sigma. Each is discussed further below.

Continuous Quality Improvement

The concept of **Continuous Quality Improvement (CQI)** can be defined as an organizational process in which employee teams identify and address problems in their work processes. When applied across the organization, CQI creates a continuous flow of process improvements that meet or exceed customer—or patient—expectations. Inherent within this definition are five dimensions of CQI: (1) process focus, (2) customer focus, (3) data-based decision making, (4) employee empowerment, and (5) organization-wide impact.

CQI focuses on the process part of Donabedian's quality conception as key to developing high-quality health care. Specifically, CQI promotes the view that understanding and addressing the factors that create variation in an administrative or clinical process (e.g., long wait times, high rehospitalization rates) will produce superior patient care quality and organizational performance. Furthermore, quality improvement should not be a one-time activity; rather, it should be a normal activity, resulting in a continual flow of improvements.

Underpinning this approach are the concepts and tools of **statistical process control (SPC)** that Shewhart developed. For example, a manager of an ambulatory clinic tracked an increase in complaints about patient wait time from quarterly patient satisfaction surveys. For the next month, the wait time for each patient was collected, and the daily average was graphed. At the same time, data were collected about why waiting time increased, and the clinic manager found the special-cause variation was driven by (1) the number of medically complex, time-consuming patients each day; (2) the training needs of a new LPN and receptionist; and (3) the overscheduling of new patients. Armed with these findings, the manager was able to work with both clinical and administrative personnel to address these concerns and reduce both the variability and the average wait time.

The second element in CQI is the focus on the customer. That is, every effort in the organization must be taken in order to "delight the customer." CQI defines who a customer is in broad terms. Normally, patients are thought of as the main customers in health care. CQI's view is that any person, group, or organization that is impacted by a process at any point is a customer. For example, a doctor ordering an MRI can be considered a customer because she receives the service of the radiology department. Thus, CQI takes the position that each process has a variety of both **internal and external customers**. The customer focus is best exemplified in the widespread use of patient satisfaction surveys by hospitals and physician groups.

The third element in CQI is an emphasis on **using data to make all quality improvement decisions**. The foundation of SPC, as discussed earlier, rests on the collection, analysis, and use of data to improve processes and monitor the success of process interventions. The use of carefully collected data reduces both uncertainty and the dependence on uninformed impressions or biases for improving an organizational process. It also provides good evidence to convince skeptics that a process problem exists. Returning to our earlier example, the collected data on waiting times enabled not only the clinic manager to understand the special-cause factors creating waiting times but also helped physicians, nurses, and front desk and other staff understand the sources of the problem.

The fourth element of CQI is **employee empowerment**. This empowerment is manifested by the widespread use of quality improvement teams. The typical CQI team will consist of hourly employees whose day-to-day work gives them a unique perspective and detailed knowledge of patient care processes. Another important individual for a CQI team is the **facilitator**, who typically provides training on CQI tools and philosophy. Members of the CQI team are not only empowered to improve their work environment but can also become advocates for change, overcoming resistance among other employees. In our prior example, the clinic manager worked with both clinical employees (e.g., RNs, LPNs, and the nurse supervisor) and administrative employees (e.g., receptionists, admission and billing clerks, and their supervisor) to decrease the wait times and improve patients' satisfaction with the clinic.

The final element in CQI is its **strategic use across the organization**, accomplished through the coordinated and continuous improvement of various operational processes. Quality must be recognized as a strategic priority requiring executive leadership. Supporting this priority is substantial training in quality methods and tools supported by an organizational culture that values quality.

In order to make specific quality improvements, the Shewhart/Deming cycle of PDCA is generally used in manufacturing and other industries. However, during the early

1980s, the Hospital Corporation of America (HCA) modified the PDCA cycle to create the **FOCUS–PDCA framework**, which has become the most commonly used quality improvement framework in the healthcare industry. The addition of FOCUS clarifies the steps that need to be done prior to the implementation of any process change. The changes in the process will then be guided by the PDCA cycle.

FOCUS (Find, Organize, Clarify, Understand, and Select)

- **Find** means identifying a process problem, preferably a "high-pain" one, to address.
- **Organize** means to organize a team of people who work on the process. These people would then be trained on process improvement skills and tools.
- **Clarify** results in the team moving to clarify the process problem through some type of process mapping (flowcharting).
- **Understanding** the process problem comes next. It involves measurement and data collection of key metrics to document the dimensions of the process problem and to provide a benchmark for goal setting.
- **Select** means to identify a set of process improvements and then select from them for implementation.

PDCA (Plan, Do, Check, and Act)

- **Plan** means to take the process improvement from the S phase of FOCUS and create a plan for its implementation.
- **Do**, not surprisingly, means to actually implement the process improvement.
- **Check** means to check whether the process is involved using the measures identified and measured in the U phase of FOCUS.
- **Act** means to determine whether the process improvement was successful.

If the process improvement was successful, the cycle terminates. If the process improvement was not successful, then the cycle continues back to the planning stage to identify and plan the implementation of another process improvement.

Six Sigma

Six Sigma is an extension of Joseph Juran's approach to quality improvement and was developed by Motorola and popularized by Jack Welch at General Electric. It has been defined as a "data-driven quality methodology that seeks to eliminate variation from a process" (Scalise, 2001). Six Sigma, like CQI, is a resource-intensive tool requiring substantial up-front training in quality improvement tools and concepts, time and personnel resources to carry out quality improvement projects, and long-term management commitment. For these reasons, Six Sigma is best applied to important, costly issues in key processes.

Six Sigma employs a structured process called **DMAIC (Define, Measure, Analyze, Improve, and Control)**.

- **Define** includes delimiting the scope of work, determining due dates, and mapping the future state of the process, including improvements.
- **Measure** encompasses both the creation of measures or metrics and their application to determine how well a process is performing.
- **Analyze** further breaks down the understanding of the process and often includes flowcharting the process.
- **Improve** specifies the steps that will be taken to meet the goals outlined during the define step.
- **Control** is about ensuring that the improvements are permanent rather than temporary.

While DMAIC guides the actual improvement project, Six Sigma also features major training and human resource components. Because of these components, many large hospitals and health systems have begun adopting Six Sigma as a way to change the organization and establish a culture of quality. Such change begins with a CEO who supports the method; without top management support, efforts like this generally flounder. A **champion** is a senior executive (generally VP level or above) who has full-time responsibility for quality improvement efforts. Further into the organization are three levels of "belts." At the top are **master black belts**, who are full-time employees who provide technical leadership and training to those who are running QI projects. **Black belts** are those who direct multiple projects; **green belts** are those who lead specific projects; **yellow belts** have undergone a several day training program and have some experience working on projects; and **white belts** are novices who have very basic knowledge and have done a brief introductory course in Six Sigma but don't have project experience (Six Sigma Online, n.d.). (See also http://www.isixsigma.com, http://www.6sigma.us, or www.sixsigmaonline.org for possible offerings.)

QUALITY IMPROVEMENT TOOLS

Both CQI and Six Sigma use a variety of tools to help improve quality. These can be divided into three categories: data collection, process mapping, and process analysis.

Data Collection

The **check sheet** is a simple data collection form in which occurrence of some event or behavior is tallied. At the end of the data collection period, they are added up. The best check sheets are those that are **simple** and have **well-defined categories** of what constitutes a particular event or behavior. For example, a doctor's office staff wanted to find out the reasons why patients showed up late. The staff members brainstormed about the reasons for late arrivals, and after carefully defining each reason, they developed a check sheet. The check sheet was pilot tested, and several new reasons were added while other reasons were refined. The check sheet was then employed during a month-long data collection period. They found that transportation problems and babysitting problems jointly accounted for 63% of the late shows.

Another example is the use of **chart abstractions or chart audits**. In this process, a check sheet is used to collect information from a patient's medical record. Often this is a manual process that involves an individual looking at the medical record and finding the requested information and recording it on a check sheet. The use of electronic medical records may take some or all of the labor out of this process, as pertinent medical information can be collected more easily or, better yet, a complete report can be produced at the click of a mouse.

Geographic mapping is a pictorial check sheet in which an event or problem is plotted on a map. This is often used in epidemiological studies to plot where victims of certain diseases live, work, play, etc. For example, the Sudden Acute Respiratory Syndrome (SARS) outbreak initially occurred in China and, via air travel, quickly spread to a number of cities. Analysis by government public health agencies (e.g., U.S. Centers for Disease Control and Prevention) and the World Health Organization pinpointed the suspected origin of the outbreak and helped to direct prevention and treatment efforts.

A more focused application of geographic mapping is the **workflow diagram** (see Figure 7-2). Simply put, this reflects the movements of people, materials, documents, or information in a process. Plotting these movements on the floor plan of a building or around a paper document can present a very vivid picture of the inefficiency of a process. With the advancement of information technology, increasingly sophisticated geographic mapping and tracking programs have become available, making this complex task easier to do.

Mapping Processes

Flowcharting is the main way that processes are mapped (see Figure 7-3 for an example). A flowchart is nothing more than a picture of the sequence of steps in a process. Different action steps within the process are denoted by various geometric shapes. A basic flowchart outlines the major steps in a process. A detailed flowchart is often more useful in quality improvement. Developing a flowchart requires substantial investigation of each aspect of the process to be flowcharted. Determining the level of detail to be used should be driven by its

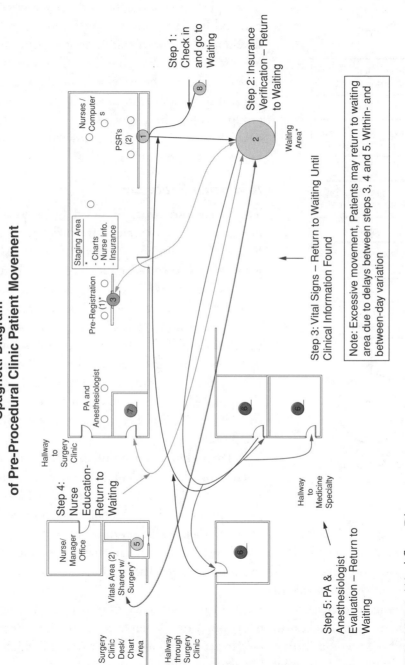

Spaghetti Diagram of Pre-Procedural Clinic Patient Movement

Step 1: Check in and go to Waiting

Step 2: Insurance Verification – Return to Waiting

Step 3: Vital Signs – Return to Waiting Until Clinical Information Found

Step 4: Nurse Education – Return to Waiting

Step 5: PA & Anesthesiologist Evaluation – Return to Waiting

Note: Excessive movement. Patients may return to waiting area due to delays between steps 3, 4 and 5. Within- and between-day variation

Nurses / Computers

PSR's (2)

Staging Area
* - Charts
  - Nurse info.
  - Insurance

Pre-Registration
(1)*

Waiting Area*

PA and Anesthesiologist

Nurse/Manager Office

Vitals Area (2) Shared w/ Surgery*

Surgery Clinic Desk/Chart Area

Hallway through Surgery Clinic

Hallway to Surgery Clinic

Hallway to Medicine Specialty

FIGURE 7-2 Workflow Diagram

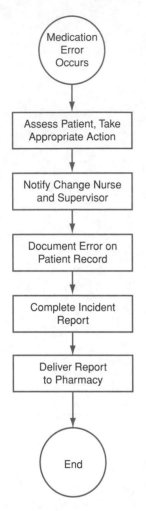

FIGURE 7-3 Medication Error Reporting Flowchart

use within the quality improvement process. A top-down flowchart is often used for providing an overview of large or complex processes. It shows the major steps in the process and lists, below each major step, the substeps. The development flowchart adds another dimension. Often it is useful for tracking the flow of information between people. That is, the development flowchart shows the steps of the process carried out by each person, unit, or group involved in a process. Since hand-offs are often where errors may occur, this flowchart provides a target for data collection efforts.

Analyzing Processes

The **cause-and-effect diagram** helps to identify and organize the possible cause for a problem in a structured format. It is commonly referred to as a **fishbone diagram** for its resemblance to a fish (see Figure 7-4). It is also called an **Ishikawa diagram**, in honor of Kaoru Ishikawa, who developed it. The diagram begins with the problem under investigation described in a box at the right side of the diagram. The fish's spine is represented by a long arrow within the box. The major possible causes of the problem are arrayed as large ribs along the spine. These are broad categories of causes to which smaller ribs are attached that identify specific causes of the problem.

A Pareto chart is a simple frequency chart. The frequency of each problem, reason, etc. is listed on the x-axis, and the number or percent of occurrences is listed on the y-axis. This analysis is most useful in identifying the major problems in a process and their frequency of occurrence. Another version of the frequency chart is the histogram, which shows the range and frequency of values for a measure. When complete, it shows the complete distribution of some variable. This is often useful in basic data analysis.

As mentioned earlier, quality improvement has its greatest impact if it becomes a part of the strategic mission of a healthcare organization. When that occurs, it is then possible to look beyond the boundaries of the organization and to consider ways in which the healthcare system at the local, regional, and national levels could be improved.

Materials/Supplies

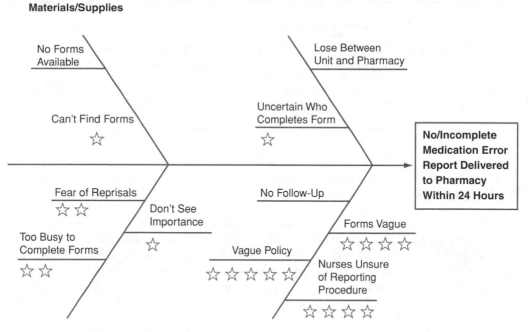

FIGURE 7-4 Fishbone Diagram

CONCLUSION

Quality, along with access and cost, are the three core policy issues for our healthcare system. Improving quality in a system that will be undergoing a vast expansion of access via health insurance reform and the continued cost pressure will be a challenge. The models and tools presented above show that quality can be dramatically improved, even in a challenging environment.

DISCUSSION QUESTIONS

1. Discuss the different stakeholders' views of healthcare quality.

2. Discuss how structure, process, and outcomes interact within a healthcare organization.

3. Compare and contrast CQI (TQM) and Six Sigma approaches to quality improvement.

4. Discuss the function of the Baldrige criteria and its interaction with CQI or Six Sigma.

5. Discuss the implications of underuse, overuse, and misuse for both quality and cost.

Cases in Chapter 17 that are related to this chapter include:

- Madison Community Hospital Addresses Infection Control Prevention—see p. 419
- Medication Errors Reporting at Community Memorial Hospital—see p. 459

Additional cases, role-play scenarios, video links, websites, and other information sources are also available in the online Instructor's Materials.

REFERENCES

Baldrige National Quality Program at the National Institute of Standards and Technology (2009–2010). Baldrige National Quality Program Criteria for Performance Excellence. Retrieved from http://www.baldrige.nist.gov/PDF_files/2009_2010_Business_Nonprofit_Criteria.pdf

Chassin, M. R. (1997). Assessing strategies for quality improvement. *Health Affairs, 16*(3), 151–161.

Cooper, M. R. (2004). Quality assurance and improvement. In L. F. Wolper (Ed.), *Health care administration: Planning, implementing, and managing organized delivery systems* (4th ed., p. 827). Sudbury, MA: Jones & Bartlett.

Deming, W. E. (2000). *Out of the Crisis.* Cambridge, MA: MIT Press.

Donabedian, A. (1966). Evaluating the quality of medical care. *Milbank Memorial Fund Quarterly, 44,* 194–196.

Donabedian, A. (1986). Quality assurance in our health care system. *Quality Assurance, 1*(1), 6–12.

Dunn, P., & Santamour, B. (2003). How health care won its first Baldrige. *Hospitals and Health Networks, 77*(9), 67–74.

Fonarow, G. C. (2005). Practical considerations of beta-blockade in the management of the post-myocardial infarction patient. *American Heart Journal, 149*(6), 984–993.

Gandhi, T. K., Weingart, S. N., Borus, J., Seger, A. C., Peterson, J., Burdick, E., . . . Bates, D. (2003). Adverse drug events in ambulatory care. *New England Journal of Medicine, 348*(16), 1556.

Gonzales, R., Steiner, J. F., & Sande, M. A. (1997). Antibiotic prescribing for adults with colds, upper respiratory tract infections and bronchitis by ambulatory care physicians. *Journal of the American Medical Association, 278,* 901–904.

Institute of Medicine. (1990). *Medicare: A strategy for quality assurance.* Washington, DC: National Academies Press.

Institute of Medicine. (2001). *Crossing the quality chasm: A new health system for the 21st Century.* Washington, DC: National Academies Press.

Juran, J. M., Gryna, F. M., & Bingham, J. (1974). *Quality control handbook.* New York, NY: McGraw-Hill.

Kohn, J. T., Corrigan, J. M., & Donaldson, M. S. (Eds.). (2000). *To err is human: Building a safer health care system.* Washington, DC: National Academies Press.

Kolesar, P. J. (1993). The relevance of research on statistical process control to the total quality movement. *Journal of Engineering and Technology Management, 10*(4), 317–338.

Marley, K. A., Collier, D. A., & Goldstein, S. M. (2004). The role of clinical and process quality in achieving patient satisfaction in hospitals. *Decision Sciences, 35*(3), 349–369.

Nicholls, S. J., McElduff, P., Dobson, A. J., Jamrozik, K. D., Hobbs, M. S. T., & Leitch, J. W. (2001). Underuse of beta-blockers following myocardial infarction: A tale of two cities. *Internal Medicine Journal, 31*(7), 391–396.

Ryan, M. J. (2004). Achieving and sustaining quality in healthcare. *Frontiers of Health Services Management, 20*(3), 3–11.

Scalise, D. (2001). Six Sigma: The quest for quality. *Hospitals and Health Networks, 75*(12), 41–45.

Shewhart, W. A. (1931). *Economic control of quality of manufactured product.* New York, NY: Van Nostrand.

Shewhart, W. A. (1939). *Statistical method from the viewpoint of quality control.* Washington, DC: The Graduate School of the Department of Agriculture.

Six Sigma Online. (n.d.). How does Six Sigma work? Retrieved from http://www.sixsigmaonline.org/index.html

Solberg, L. I., Hurley, J. S., Roberts, M. H., Nelson, W. W., Frost, F. J., Crain, A. L., . . . Young, L. R. (2004). Measuring patient safety in ambulatory care: Potential for identifying medical group drug-drug interaction rates using claims data. *American Journal of Managed Care, 10*(11 Pt 1), 753–759.

Soumerai, S. B., McLaughlin, T. J., Spiegelman, D., Hertzmark, E., Thibault, G., & Goldman, L. (1997). Adverse outcomes of underuse of beta-blockers in elderly survivors of acute myocardial infarction. *Journal of the American Medical Association, 277*(2), 115–121.

Steinberg, I. (2000). Clinical choices of antibiotics: Judging judicious use. *The American Journal of Managed Care, 6*(23 Supplement), s1178–s1188.

Wennberg, J. E. (2002). Unwarranted variation in healthcare delivery: Implications for academic medical centres. *British Medical Journal, 325*, 961–964.

CHAPTER 8

Information Technology
Tressa Springmann

LEARNING OBJECTIVES

By the end of this chapter, the student will be able to:

- Describe information systems common to all industries and those unique to health care;
- Identify key systems used by healthcare managers;
- Characterize the electronic medical record (EMR);
- Explain the challenges to clinical system adoption;
- Explore the future of healthcare information technology (HIT) and the vision of an integrated U.S. healthcare system;
- Assess the impact of HIT on the healthcare manager; and
- Describe the impact of HIPAA and other regulations, laws, and policies regarding confidentiality of patient information.

INTRODUCTION

Have you ever considered why it is so easy to get your money almost anywhere in the world from an automated teller machine (ATM) but impossible to have easy access to your health and medical history, even during a medical emergency? Information technology has traditionally been relegated to the administrative functions of health care—in the back office with payroll and accounting. Today, as pressures mount for safer and more cost-effective care, and as software applications become easier to use, the introduction of information technology into the clinical setting has accelerated. While introducing a new complexity, this also creates great opportunity for safer care, more standardized practice, greater accuracy of data and information, and achieving the elusive vision of electronic health records for U.S. citizens. The purpose of this chapter is to explain the current state of information technology in health care and to discuss the impact the acceleration of its implementation will have on managing an already complex environment for the health-care manager.

INFORMATION SYSTEMS USED BY MANAGERS

Similar to other industries, healthcare businesses, whether for-profit or not-for-profit, are supported by traditional software applications used to run the business. The key purpose of these systems is to manage the organization's expenses and revenues. For most health-care entities, you'll also find more sophisticated systems to manage two of their most costly resources—staff and equipment. These common systems, some of which healthcare organizations widely implement, include:

- Standard office applications such as word processing, spreadsheet management, and e-mail and other administrative tools to collaborate;
- Budget systems to manage their expenses and income;
- Cost accounting systems to model the profit (or loss) of key services/products;
- Enterprise resource planning (ERP) systems, which include human resource, payroll, accounts payable, materials management, and general ledger functions;
- Time and attendance, staffing and scheduling, and productivity systems to manage a diverse exempt and nonexempt, and oftentimes 24/7, 365-days-a-year workforce;
- Marketing systems including customer relationship management (CRM) and typically the organization's website;
- For those healthcare entities that are non-profit, fund-raising systems that play a key role in identifying and managing the contributions of donors; and
- Billing and accounts receivable systems used to bill clients and customers (e.g., patients and insurance companies) for the goods or services of the entity.

Prior to the 1990s, information technology found in most healthcare organizations—hospitals, physician practices, nursing homes, etc.—supported mostly the administrative transactions unique to health care. More specifically, these were systems that either assisted in the billing and accounts receivable processes, such as patient scheduling and registration systems, or systems that assist healthcare entities in meeting regulatory requirements, such as The Joint Commission (JCAHO), Medicare (CMS), American Association of Blood Banks (AABB), College of Pathologists (CAP), etc. For example, a clinical information system enables healthcare organizations to provide the ability for the hospital to document how they reconcile the medications that a patient brings into the hospital with those that are prescribed while visiting, as required by The Joint Commission. As technology has matured and its benefits around efficiency and patient safety have been identified, information technology has begun to be seen in more clinical areas.

The delivery of health care includes many repetitive workflows, such as filling prescriptions, resulting laboratory tests, and completing radiology images, to name but a few. These workflows lend themselves to becoming more effective and efficient through **automation**. As a result, clinical systems that supported these areas and the patient care process came to the forefront (see Table 8-1). Nonetheless, many of these systems didn't effectively communicate with each other within a single organization, let alone as patients moved from one part of the industry to another. In addition, through the 1990s, systems remained cumbersome enough that most direct care personnel (e.g., nurses, physicians, home health workers) were not asked to use them to support direct care processes. And if they had been asked, they probably would not have done so because of the amount of additional time it would have introduced into their workflow.

As efficiencies through automation were gained by these ancillary information systems, a parallel maturation of medical devices occurred. Many of these device types were oriented to enhancing workflow through increased throughput and reduced variation. Often they were physically connected to the ancillary system. These included robots in the pharmacy, which would pick medications for delivery to patients, and analyzers in the

TABLE 8-1 Examples of Typical Clinical Systems in Hospitals

Clinical System Name	Clinical System Function	Primary User(s)
Laboratory System	Tracks lab order and results	Laboratory department
Radiology System	Tracks radiology orders and results	Radiology department
Pharmacy System	Tracks medication orders including when dispensed	Pharmacy department
Clinical Data Repository (CDR)	Storage of all clinical data	Clinicians
Computerized Provider Order Entry (CPOE)	Electronic ordering of all orders for a patient by a provider such as a physician, pharmacist, or advanced practitioner	Providers
Nursing/Clinical Documentation	Online documentation of the care of patients by nursing, physical therapy, respiratory therapy, etc.	Nurses, therapists
Clinical Decision Support System (CDSS)	Alerts that indicate potentially harmful situations for patients	Physicians, pharmacists, nurses
Picture Archiving and Communications System (PACS)	System that stores actual digital imaging of radiology, cardiology, and other studies	Physicians

laboratory, which afforded high-speed and consistent processing of specimens. As more information about patients became available through the use of these systems, the promise of a complete and unified place to find patient information began to become reality. While traditional business systems have become standard and pervasive for effective daily management, the recent increase in the use of clinical systems presented and continues to present a unique challenge to those managing the impacted areas. In summary, healthcare managers must be comfortable and confident with information technology to manage their administrative responsibilities. Healthcare managers should anticipate the need to be flexible as these new tools become more pervasive in the areas they manage.

THE ELECTRONIC MEDICAL RECORD (EMR)

As early as 1991, the Institute of Medicine (IOM) issued a report concluding that computer-based patient records are "an essential technology" for health care (Institute of Medicine, 2001). Even so, adoption of these technologies continued to be low. Additional industry pressure came with another IOM report, *To Err Is Human* (Kohn, Corrigan, & Donaldson, 2000). The focus of this report was to highlight the need to build a safer healthcare system. The report identified that in the United States, clinical quality issues cause upwards of 99,000 preventable deaths annually. Recommendations from the report suggested the establishment of a federal Center for Patient Safety. One of the initial areas of attention was to "increase understanding of the use of information technology to improve patient safety (e.g., automated drug order entry systems, reminder systems that prompt nurses and other care providers when a patient's medication or other treatments are due)" (Kohn et al., 2000, p. 80). As clinicians have begun to realize the value of information technology, adoption of **electronic medical records (EMRs)** for patients has accelerated.

> An **EMR** is an application environment composed of the clinical data repository, clinical decision support, controlled medical vocabulary, order entry, computerized provider order entry, pharmacy, and clinical documentation applications. This environment supports the patient's electronic medical record across inpatient and outpatient environments, and is used by healthcare practitioners to document, monitor, and manage healthcare delivery within a care delivery organization (CDO). The data in the EMR is the legal record of what happened to the patient during their encounter at the CDO and is owned by the CDO. (Garets & Davis, 2006, p. 2)

The Healthcare Information and Management Systems Society (HIMSS) is a professional organization made up of members committed to leveraging information technology to better serve the healthcare industry. These are people who primarily have information

EMR Adoption Model[SM]	
Stage	Cumulative Capabilities
Stage 7	Complete EMR; CCD transactions to share data; Data warehousing; Data continuity with ED, ambulatory, OP
Stage 6	Physician documentation (structured templates), full CDSS (variance & compliance), full R-PACS
Stage 5	Closed loop medication administration
Stage 4	CPOE, Clinical Decision Support (clinical protocols)
Stage 3	Nursing/clinical documentation (flow sheets), CDSS (error checking), PACS available outside Radiology
Stage 2	CDR, Controlled Medical Vocabulary, CDS, may have Document Imaging; HIE capable
Stage 1	Ancillaries – Lab, Rad, Pharmacy – All Installed
Stage 0	All Three Ancillaries Not Installed

FIGURE 8-1 EMRAM MODEL

Source: Courtesy of HIMSS Analytics, 2010a.

technology jobs in hospitals, physician practices, pharmaceutical companies, insurance companies, software vendors, and so on (HIMSS, n.d.). HIMSS does significant work supporting the educational and networking needs of **information technology (IT)** professionals who've chosen health care as their industry of focus. By 2000, HIMSS Analytics had designed a model to track EMR progress at hospitals and health systems in the United States called the **Electronic Medical Record Analytical Model (EMRAM)**. See Figure 8-1. The EMRAM scores hospitals in the HIMSS Analytics database on their progress in implementing progressively more complicated clinical systems from stage 0 to stage 7, ultimately resulting in the ability to exchange their clinical information with external partners (such as labs or physician offices) (HIMSS Analytics, 2010).

The foundational implementation of an EMR is a hospital's ability to first automate data in individual areas within the hospital, as represented by stages 0 and 1. Next is the ability to bring this data together for clinical decision making, stage 2. Stages 3–6 include the implementation of advanced clinical systems primarily used by direct care personnel such as nurses and physicians. In a hospital where all of its key clinical processes are now automated, stage 7 represents the ability of that organization to then share or exchange data with external entities. It is at the achievement of this stage where real impacts on safety and efficiencies can be realized. Consider the impact of having all hospital-based information from a recent surgery available to your physician at your next follow-up appointment and/ or the availability of your medication history and recent lab and X-ray results to a hospital's emergency room (ER) when an unintended visit occurs. The physician can immediately identify any allergies you may have, understand what medications you are already on, and potentially avoid ordering duplicate tests and services.

As shown in Table 8-2, while the EMRAM scores from 2009 compared to 2008 reflect an increase of hospitals that have moved from lower to higher stages in the model, fewer than 6% of all hospitals in the United States have progressed past stage 4. And while we see movement to stage 7, this represents only 0.3% of all hospitals; a meager 29 of 5,167 hospitals. High cost and user "unfriendliness," combined with slow progress in developing standards for defining complex clinical information, have contributed to such slow movement to stage 7. This is further complicated by the highly sensitive confidential nature of patients' clinical data. Americans are fiercely protective of patient rights, including control over access to medical information. This lack of trust that electronic clinical information will remain secure has also had an impact on slow clinical system adoption; the primary stakeholder—the patient—isn't demanding it. This lack of trust is not entirely unfounded. Consider the risk of easily accessible health information on a preexisting medical condition and its impact on one's ability to get healthcare coverage at a reasonable rate. Or what about a sensitive lab result such as a positive HIV or pregnancy test? These aren't pieces of information most people would welcome having on the Internet, available to all.

Furthermore, the adoption rates are not just low in hospitals but are even lower in the setting where Americans receive most of their health care: physician offices. Think about

TABLE 8-2 Comparison of 2008 to 2009 EMRAM scores for American Hospitals, January 2010

EMRAM Stage	Q2 2008	Q2 2009
Stage 7	0.0%	0.3%
Stage 6	0.9%	1.0%
Stage 5	1.0%	4.5%
Stage 4	1.8%	3.6%
Stage 3	32.0%	38.4%
Stage 2	33.9%	31.6%
Stage 1	12.6%	7.2%
Stage 0	17.7%	13.4%
Total hospitals	5,048	5,167

Source: Courtesy of HIMSS Analytics, 2010.

your own experience: unless you've dealt with serious or chronic health issues, the times in which you sought care in the healthcare industry are largely identified through visits to your physician's office. In short, the setting where we receive most of our health care is the setting with the least amount of technology adoption.

Currently, while 89% of hospitals have some semblance of an EMR, only 37% of physician offices do (SK&A, 2010). For both care settings, the cost of purchasing and implementing EMR systems is the single greatest barrier (Hospitals and Health Networks, 2010). The larger the physician practice, the higher degree of administrative complexity and the higher the rate of EMR adoption—71% of practices with more than 26 physicians have adopted EMR (Miller & Sim, 2004). While seemingly positive, more than 40% of physician practices in the United States have between 1 and 5 physicians (Liebhaber & Grossman, 2007). In these smaller practices, the adoption rate is much lower. In short, physicians have had neither a compelling business reason nor the requisite resources to buy these systems. In addition, they have not had the depth of staffing to adequately select, implement, and support an EMR. To the extent that the patient record in the physician practice has remained on paper, physicians' notes, prescriptions, and lab and X-ray results have also remained in a format prohibitive to sharing. There are certainly exceptions to this. Kaiser Permanente has demonstrated that it is possible to have physicians practicing in an entirely automated environment with both efficiency and patient safety gains (McGee, 2010). Mohamoud, Byrne, and Samarth (2009) reported that long-term care settings face great challenges, including "regulatory and legal concerns, insufficient funding, technology fears, staff turnover, lack of interoperable standards and discontinuity of care" (pp. 21–22). Nonetheless, organizations like Kaiser currently are truly exceptions given the size of the challenges to clinical system adoption.

THE CHALLENGES TO CLINICAL SYSTEM ADOPTION

In the IOM report *Crossing the Quality Chasm*, numerous barriers to clinical adoption were detailed (IOM, 2001). Patient privacy and a patient's desire to ensure that others could not see their health information was one. Sharing of information is all the more challenging in health care because a "standard vocabulary" doesn't exist as it does in other industries such as banking, where information about your bank account can electronically move all over the world. This lack of one system being able to speak to another (e.g., physician's system to insurer's system) not only slows down productivity but also can contribute to delay of healthcare delivery (Zands, 2008). As noted previously, the cost to purchase, implement, and support these systems is a core barrier in an industry where recent and extreme focus on cost exists. Finally but not least, the majority of the healthcare industry–specific software applications were not developed in a manner in which the user interfaces were intuitive or easy to use, making the user, at least initially, frustrated and slower in implementing it. Based upon recent hospital EMR adoption numbers, these barriers continue to remain relevant (IOM, 2001). In 1996, Congress passed the **Health Insurance Portability and Accountability Act (HIPAA)** with the intent of developing standards for healthcare data and its exchange and regulations on privacy protections (Centers for Medicare and Medicaid, 1996). The concept of **Protected Health Information**, or PHI, and its implications on the healthcare workforce have been significant

> **Protected Health Information:** The Privacy Rule protects all *"individually identifiable health information"* held or transmitted by a covered entity or its business associate, in any form or media, whether electronic, paper, or oral. The Privacy Rule calls this information "protected health information (PHI)."
>
> "Individually identifiable health information" is information, including demographic data, that relates to:
>
> - the individual's past, present or future physical or mental health or condition,
> - the provision of health care to the individual, or
> - the past, present, or future payment for the provision of health care to the individual,
>
> and that identifies the individual or for which there is a reasonable basis to believe it can be used to identify the individual. Individually identifiable health information includes many common identifiers (e.g., name, address, birth date, Social Security Number).
>
> The Privacy Rule excludes from protected health information employment records that a covered entity maintains in its capacity as an employer and education and certain other records subject to, or defined in, the Family Educational Rights and Privacy Act, 20 U.S.C. §1232g. (U.S. Department of Health and Human Services, 2003, pp. 3–4)

It is critical that today's healthcare manager be educated on and understand the more significant concepts of HIPAA, such as the Notice of Privacy Practice (NOPP), and ensure that employees only have access to patients' PHI on a need-to-know basis. Even aside from struggles with standards and privacy, these systems are largely still seen as too costly and very difficult to use.

As the United States anticipated entering a new decade in 2010, there was mounting concern about the percentage of the gross domestic product (GDP) going to the cost of health care (Bartlett, 2009). Projections were made that suggested that within 10 years, Americans would spend one of every five dollars on health care. The Obama administration recognized the potential to reduce healthcare expenses through standards and automation and made the decision to jumpstart health information technology (HIT) investments. Understanding that an electronic medical record will provide organization to the complex and vast amount of clinical information on patients, thus leading to better clinical decisions, a higher quality of care, and a reduction in overutilization, aggressive measures were put forward in the American Recovery and Reinvestment Act (ARRA) in 2009 around EMR adoption (CMS, 2009). Under the Health Information Technology for Economic and Clinical Health Act (HITECH) portion of the ARRA, hospitals and physicians in the United States will receive funding incentives to adopt and implement clinical healthcare information technology. By 2015, organizations that have failed to do so will be unable to participate in the Medicare program and will be subject to fines and penalties. Whether by carrot or stick, the barriers appear to be lessening due to governmental involvement. Assuming the industry responds as anticipated, the adoption of EMR in physician practices and hospitals will increase. And once this previously elusive clinical information is stored in a system in a standard vocabulary, a foundation is set. This foundation provides for the acceleration of uses, increasing its value exponentially.

THE FUTURE OF HEALTHCARE INFORMATION TECHNOLOGY (HIT): THE VISION OF AN INTEGRATED U.S. HEALTHCARE SYSTEM

The era of carrying your personal EMR on a card in your purse or wallet with every conceivable piece of medical information about you is upon us. The ability to have a new physician evaluate your medical history without ever physically seeing you, and the ability to diagnose and treat you without you having to visit a doctor's office or clinic, is imminent. With our information being mobile, we don't need to be in the physician's office or in the hospital to be "seen."

This mobility, driven by a wireless world, will create the ability for virtual care. In 2010, there were 6.8 billion people worldwide and more than 4 billion active cell phones in use—more than TVs, PCs, and cars combined (D. Hesse, personal communication, 2010). Some of the possibilities of this wired and mobile world include medications that have embedded microchips that, after being ingested, would send information to either the patient or the physician (Mathews, 2010). Also feasible is the ability for a person wearing a "smart vest" to have the vest send physiological values (blood pressure, sugar levels, cardiac monitoring, etc.) to a remote location where nurses are monitoring them without the patient ever having to leave home.

As advances occur in information systems, a parallel and equally accelerated process has been and will continue to occur in medical devices and technology. Advanced genetics will become a predictive part of our health record, indicating potential treatments to avoid, or at least proactively manage, the expression of later-onset inherited illnesses. A large number of clinical decisions can be made by a computer programmed to respond to an X-ray or lab result rather than a physician—involving the specialist only when a set of conditions is unknown to the knowledge base. Admittedly, some of these possibilities may seem far fetched, perhaps as silly as the idea that a telephone would not have to be plugged into the wall in our home or place of business might have been in 1985. The availability of health information, combined with its ability to be mobile and shared, has the potential to transform the workplace of the future. The healthcare manager must be aware of and understand the impact of HIT to ensure that workers are productive, sensitive data is protected, and patients remain safe.

THE IMPACT OF INFORMATION TECHNOLOGY ON THE HEALTHCARE MANAGER

More than ever before, the healthcare work environment requires comfort with and knowledge of information systems. This means that managers need to have the competencies to effectively evaluate the experience of their staff in the use of required systems as well as their own ability to quickly adapt to new tools to manage their own workload. The nurse or medical coder who will not or cannot adapt to new automated tools will be unable to perform his or her job and has the potential to be terminated. This increasing dependency on computers creates new workplace challenges when those technologies are not available or are not working optimally. Downtime and upgrades that add extra steps for the workforce will create new situations to be effectively managed. And while clinical care cannot stop merely because a system is down, the gap in information during that downtime must be filled so a break in the documented care of the patient is addressed. The healthcare manager of the future must be able to navigate technology used by his or her team and understand the barriers to be addressed to increase productivity and enhance job satisfaction. Take, for example, a manager's commitment to ensure that healthcare employees are only accessing patient information on a need-to-know basis. Historically, this meant ensuring that charts were locked away when not used and not even accessible to those not physically in receipt of them. Today, with patient records online and able to be accessed by many simultaneously, the ability to uphold this obligation requires monitoring audit files to ensure that electronic "straying" doesn't happen, and if it does occur, it is addressed immediately. There is a human side of computing and IT: for every system created to ensure the security of health data and information, there is someone who can find a way around it and break into the system. New laws and policies regarding insurance and the confidentiality of patient information, such as the Health Insurance Portability and Accountability Act (HIPAA) (U.S. DHHS, 2003), create new challenges for the use, maintenance, and sharing of privileged health information. For an industry that is steeped in the creation and use of paper documentation and medical records, it is a difficult leap into the virtual world of EMR and enterprise systems. The textbox provides an example of a breach of privacy and the consequences.

TEXTBOX 8-1. BREACH OF PATIENT PRIVACY

In October 2008, a Little Rock, Arkansas, morning television news anchor, Anne Pressly, was taken from her home to St. Vincent Health System. Pressly had been severely beaten and ultimately died. She was a public and well known local figure, given her profession. During a routine patient privacy audit, the hospital concluded that six employees had inappropriately accessed her medical records. These individuals did not hold a job or perform a role in which they had any need to know the clinical information that they had accessed about Ms. Pressly. All six employees were fired.

As a HIPAA privacy rule violation, complaints are generally directed to the Office of Civil Rights (OCR) in the Department of Health and Human Services (DHHS). In this case, however, since the hospital dealt with the incident swiftly, the OCR did not take any further action.

Easy access to medical records information created a situation where the curiosity of these six individuals clouded their judgment, resulting in a very real punishment: job loss. Luckily for them, OCR did not press charges that might have resulted in further legal action (Healthcare Auditing Weekly, December 16, 2008).

CONCLUSION

Healthcare information technology (HIT) is having an increasingly large impact on the healthcare industry and therefore on the healthcare manager. Healthcare costs in the United States have risen, while quality has not. This situation within the global economy is unsatisfactory to both the public and private sectors. In what has traditionally been seen as a high-touch industry, the promise of increased clinical quality and cost-effectiveness through automation has become a significant and urgent goal. As the adoption of clinical systems increases, so does the need for more sophisticated knowledge about them. Effectively operating in this new environment will require that the successful manager be comfortable with using and taking advantage of the benefits of the use of HIT and carefully manage its risks. This chapter has provided the basics around the key systems used by healthcare managers and the significance of and challenges to adoption of the electronic medical record (EMR). The future of HIT creates a vision of seamless movement of clinical information to wherever and whenever it is needed for patient care. While achieving this vision appears almost impossible when one considers the current adoption levels, recent quality and cost concerns suggest that it is essential and inevitable. This inevitability will require new skills of and offer new opportunities for healthcare managers.

DISCUSSION QUESTIONS

1. Explain how the delivery of healthcare services can benefit from automation, and provide two examples.

2. What two pressures on the healthcare industry, the first in the 1990s and the second in the 2000s, conclude that electronic medical records are essential?

3. Jefferson Hospital has recently implemented computerized provider order entry (CPOE). What EMRAM stage are they in, and what projects might Jefferson undertake next to progress its EMR implementation?

4. Identify and describe the four primary barriers to healthcare information technology (HIT) adoption.

5. As a healthcare manager, it is critical that your employees value and preserve the privacy of patient information. What measures might you put into place to encourage and monitor this?

Cases in Chapter 17 that are related to this chapter include:

- Building a Better MIS-Trap—see p. 377
- The "Easy" Software Upgrade at Delmar Ortho—see p. 451

Additional cases, role-play scenarios, video links, websites, and other information sources are also available in the online Instructor's Materials.

REFERENCES

Bartlett, B. (2009, July 3). Health care: Costs and reform. *Forbes* magazine. Retrieved from http://www.forbes.com/2009/07/02/health-care-costs-opinions-columnists-reform.html

Centers for Medicare and Medicaid Services (CMS). (1996). *Health Insurance Portability and Accountability Act of 1996.* Retrieved from http://www.cms.gov/HIPAAGenInfo/01_Overview.asp

Centers for Medicare and Medicaid Services (CMS). (2009). *American Recovery and Reinvestment Act of 2009, HITECH.* Retrieved from http://www.cms.gov/Recovery/Downloads/CMS-2009-0117-0002.pdf

Employees fired after snooping in news anchor's medical records. (2008, December 16). *Healthcare Auditing Weekly.* Retrieved from https://www.hcpro.com/CCP-225052-1685/Employees-fired-after-snooping-in-news-anchors-medical-records.html

Garets, D., & Davis, M. (2006). *Electronic medical records vs. electronic health records: Yes, there is a difference.* A HIMSS Analytics white paper. Retrieved from http://www.himssanalytics.org/docs/WP_EMR_EHR.pdf

Health Care Auditing Weekly. (2008, December 16). Employees fired after snooping in news anchor's medical records. Retrieved from http://www.hcpro.com

HIMSS. (n.d.). About HIMSS. Retrieved from http://www.himss.org/ASP/aboutHIMSSHOme.asp

HIMSS Analytics. (2010). *The EMR Adoption Model.* Retrieved from http://www.himssanalytics.org/docs/HA_ARRA_100509.pdf

Hospitals & Health Networks (H&HN). (2010, January 9). IT challenges in physician practice management.

Institute of Medicine. (2001). *Crossing the quality chasm: A new health system for the 21st century.* Washington, DC: National Academies Press.

Kohn, J. T., Corrigan, J. M., & Donaldson, M. S. (Eds.). (2000). *To err is human: Building a safer health system.* Washington, DC: National Academies Press.

Liebhaber, A., & Grossman, J. M. (2007, August). *Physicians moving to mid-sized, single-specialty practices.* Center for Studying Health System Change, Tracking Report No. 18. Retrieved from http://www.hschange.com/CONTENT/941/#ib1

Mathews, A. (2010, March 2). Beep! It's your medicine nagging you. *Wall Street Journal,* D1.

McGee, M. K. (2010, March 10). *Kaiser Permanente finishes EMR rollout. Information Week.* Retrieved from http://www.informationweek.com

Miller, R., & Sim, I. (2004). Physicians' use of electronic medical records: Barriers and solutions. *Health Affairs, 23*(2), 166–126. doi: 10,1377/hlthaff,23.2.226

Mohamoud, S., Byrne, C., & Samarth, A. (2009, October). *Implementation of health information technology in long-term care settings: Finding from the AHRQ health IT portfolio.* Prepared by the AHRQ National Resource Center for Health IT under Contract No. 290-04-0016. AHRQ Publication No. 08-0087-EF. Rockville MD: Agency for Healthcare Research and Quality. Retrieved from http://healthit.ahrq.gov/portal/server.pt/document/907434/08-0087-ef_pdf?qid=32690600&rank=1

SK&A. (2010). *Physician office usage of electronic medical records software.* Irvine, CA: Author.

U.S. Department of Health and Human Services. (2003). *Summary of the HIPAA privacy rule.* Office for Civil Rights Privacy Brief. Retrieved from http://www.hhs.gov/ocr/privacy/hipaa/understanding/summary/privacysummary.pdf

Zands, D. (2008, July). *Challenges in healthcare communications: How technology can increase efficiency, safety, and satisfaction.* Cisco Internet Business Solutions Group (IBSG) White Paper. Retrieved from http://www.cisco.com/web/about/ac79/docs/wp/Communication_Healthcare_WP_0724FINAL.pdf

CHAPTER 9

Financing Health Care and Health Insurance

Nancy H. Shanks

LEARNING OBJECTIVES

By the end of this chapter, the student will be able to:

- Describe healthcare spending, how it has grown, and how it is expected to continue to grow;
- Identify the concepts of healthcare financing and payment for health care;
- Provide an overview of how health insurance works;
- Outline a brief history of how health insurance has evolved;
- Define the terms and characteristics of health insurance;
- Compare and contrast the different types of private health insurance;
- Delineate the types of social insurance;
- Evaluate data on health insurance coverage and lack thereof;
- Characterize the uninsured;
- Assess healthcare reform and changes to insurance resulting from it; and
- Explain the implications for management.

INTRODUCTION

As healthcare managers, there are a number of concerns relating to the overall costs of health care, how it is financed, how health insurance works, where the gaps in insurance are, and how to better manage these areas.

National Health Spending

Healthcare spending in the United States has grown over the last 40 years at what has been characterized as an alarming rate. While the increases have not, as yet, returned to the double-digit levels that existed in the 1980s and early 1990s, the Centers for Medicare and Medicaid Services (CMS) are predicting that the expansion in national healthcare spending will continue. "In 2008, U.S. health care spending growth slowed to 4.4 percent—the slowest rate of growth over the past forty-eight years" (Hartman, Martin, Nuccio, Catlin, & the National Health Expenditures Accounts Team, 2010, p. 147). Even with this slowing, healthcare expenditures in the United States were $2.3 trillion in 2008. Expenditures for 2012 were projected to reach $2.9 trillion and to account for 17.2% of gross domestic product (GDP), or $9,035 per capita (CMS, 2010a).

Expenditures for health care were directed to a variety of services, as shown in Table 9-1. Five areas accounted for more than four-fifths of those expenditures in 2008. Hospital care accounted for 30.7%; physician and clinical services represented another 21.2%; other professional, dental, and personal care services costs were 10.1%; prescription drug costs made up 10.0%; and nursing home and home health care comprised 8.7%.

In addition, CMS has also projected that healthcare spending will reach $4.5 trillion and will account for 19.3% of GDP by 2019 (CMS, 2010a). This will equate to an estimated $17,238 per capita. In sharp contrast, national health expenditures were $247.3 billion

TABLE 9-1 2008 National Health Spending by Type of Expenditure

Expenditure Type	Amount (in billions)
Hospital care	$ 718.4
Physician and clinical services	496.2
Other professional, dental, and personal care services	235.0
Prescription drugs	234.1
Nursing home and home health care	203.1
Program administrative*	159.6
Structures and equipment	112.9
Public health activities	69.4
Other medical products	65.6
Research	43.6
TOTAL	$2,337.9

Source: CMS, 2010a.
*Includes net cost of private health insurance.

in 1980 and accounted for only 8.9% of GDP (Levit et al., 1997). Chernew, Hirth, and Cutler (2009) argue that the continued growth in healthcare spending crowds out other areas and limits the resources that are available for other non-health-related types of goods and services and that efforts are needed to slow the rate of healthcare spending.

Paying for Health Care

Payments to cover these healthcare expenditures are derived from a variety of sources. These include individuals who pay out of pocket, private health insurance of a variety of types, other private funds, and public insurance programs. These categories are described below.

- **Out-of-pocket payments** include payments by individuals who buy individual insurance policies, pay for services themselves, and/or pay for part of those services through copayments and/or deductibles.
- **Private health insurance** includes payments made by individuals and/or their employers for health insurance premiums, which in turn cover the costs of payments made by various health plans, including indemnity plans, preferred provider organization plans (PPOs), point-of-service plans (POSs), health maintenance organizations (HMOs), and catastrophic plans, such as high-deductible health plans (HDHPs).
- Other private funds include, among other things, health spending accounts.
- Public sources include funding from federal, state, and local government programs, including, among others, Medicare, Medicaid, the Children's Health Insurance Program (CHIP), and the Military Health System.

The breakdown of expenditures by these sources of funding for 2008 is shown in Figure 9-1.

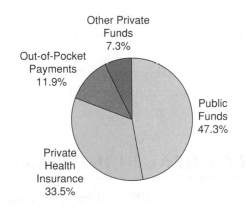

FIGURE 9-1 National Health Expenditures by Source of Funds, 2008

Data from: CMS, 2010a.

INTRODUCTION TO HEALTH INSURANCE

As with other types of insurance, the intent of health insurance is to provide protection should a covered individual experience a health event, adverse or otherwise, that requires treatment. When individuals purchase coverage, they join with others and pool their resources to protect against losses. In so doing, they pool the potential risk for losses that might be experienced. Two key concepts in insurance are that:

- **risk** is transferred from the individual to the group,
- with **sharing of the costs** of any covered losses incurred by the group members.

Fifty years ago, health insurance coverage was typically purchased on an individual basis, much like car insurance. Individuals bought policies to protect themselves and their families against catastrophic illness. This was at a time when health care was not as expensive as it is today and individuals paid for routine types of care out of pocket, thereby using health insurance to cover catastrophic expenditures and to protect against income loss. The latter, while technically a form of health insurance, is what we now think of as disability income insurance coverage.

During the second half of the 20th century, the demand for and use of health insurance changed in significant ways. Health insurance products have also changed in response to that demand. Of particular importance were the following:

- Most health insurance coverage included a comprehensive set of healthcare benefits, most frequently including hospital stays and physician care, as well as other types of services and benefits;
- Both the public and private sectors began to have expanded and increasingly important roles in the provision of health insurance coverage;
- Group health insurance policies began to be offered as an employee benefit, with the purchasing of coverage being handled by companies and fewer people taking out individual insurance policies;
- Mechanisms for reimbursing healthcare providers have expanded from solely paying on the basis of costs to reimbursing on a prepaid basis; and
- The cost of health care began to rise.

BRIEF HISTORY OF HEALTH INSURANCE

During the Great Depression of the 1930s, there were discussions about creating a national health insurance policy that would provide a system of universal health insurance coverage in the United States. While the proposal had some proponents, the American

Medical Association (AMA) and others opposed the move. With the subsequent U.S. involvement in World War II, the funding required for such a system was not available. While there continued to be interest in national health insurance after the war, the concept of a universal health insurance mechanism eventually became synonymous with "socialized medicine" and all the negative associations with Communism during the cold war of the 1950s. The end result was a health insurance system rooted in the private sector (Starr, 1982).

Although the expansionist social policies of President Lyndon B. Johnson's Great Society in the 1960s are credited with development of the largest social health insurance programs this country has ever known, now known as Medicare and Medicaid, the seeds of these programs were actually sown by Congress during the Eisenhower administration in the 1950s. At a time when private health insurance coverage was increasingly being provided for workers by their employers, the elderly had virtually no such coverage and yet were the group in society with the largest health costs and often the most limited financial resources. The ultimate passage of the Kerr-Mills Act by Congress in 1960 provided for federal matching grants to the states for a new category of "medically indigent" individuals, but still did not cover elders other than those who had become poor. However, this piece of legislation played a pivotal role as the precursor to Medicaid.

It was actually President John F. Kennedy, backed by senior interest groups and supported by labor unions and nurses, who proposed the first Medicare bill to Congress in 1962 in keeping with his strong belief in the need for federal health care for the elderly. Although this measure was defeated by legislative opponents in the Senate, it did serve to raise public awareness and support and set the stage for President Johnson to utilize his considerable political popularity, legislative liaisons, and persuasiveness in small groups (such as the leadership of the AMA) to lead the charge for passage of the Medicare and Medicaid legislation in 1965.

Over time, these public programs have been expanded to bring more eligible individuals into coverage, have added types of benefits, and have changed in a variety of other ways. One such major expansion took place with the creation of CHIP in 1997. CHIP provides health insurance coverage to many children in low-income families. The CHIP Reauthorization Act (CHIPRA) was signed in February 2009 by President Obama.

The most recent, and some would argue the most historic, change in health insurance occurred in March 2010 with the enactment of the Patient Protection and Affordable Care Act. The primary intent of this healthcare reform was to create an "individual mandate" that by 2014 requires "most legal residents of the United States to obtain health insurance." The law also mandates significant changes in health insurance practices for both the public and private sectors (Iglehart, 2010a). The legislation is described in greater depth later in the chapter.

Finally, the federal government also has an extensive program for providing health care to active-duty military personnel, veterans, and their dependents. The military medical system is one of the most advanced in the world and has come to serve as a model in many ways.

Private healthcare coverage has evolved significantly in the last 50 to 60 years, as well. Employers began to provide health insurance as an employee benefit, electing to offer the benefit in lieu of providing wage increases to employees. This was primarily the result of collective bargaining agreements, where unions negotiated increased benefits for workers and their families. Over the last 50 years, private insurance has evolved from indemnity policies to prepaid plans and managed care plans. Today, a variety of different types of coverage are used in the industry.

CHARACTERISTICS OF HEALTH INSURANCE

This section discusses some important aspects of health insurance, including how health care is financed, how costs are controlled, and the types of benefits offered.

Forms of Payment

Two forms of payment provide the basis for all types of health insurance coverage. These are:

- **Fee-for-service**—This approach was developed by Blue Cross-Blue Shield plans and is based on the idea of an insured individual purchasing coverage of a set of benefits, utilizing individual medical services, and paying the healthcare provider for the services rendered. The provider is paid either by the insurer of out of pocket by the insured, who, in turn, is reimbursed by the insurer. Typically, the insured must meet deductibles and make copayments for their care.
- **Prepayment**—In this approach, an insured individual pays a fixed, prespecified amount in exchange for services. Routine types of care are typically covered in full, with small copayments for selected services (e.g., prescriptions).

Cost Sharing

Most insurance policies require insured individuals to bear some of the cost of care out of pocket. Cost sharing may take different forms but may include some or all of the following:

- **Copayments**—are costs that are borne by the insured individual at the time of service. For example, a prescription medication or a physician office visit may require a $15 or $20 copay. Copayments are used in both fee-for-service and prepaid plans.

- **Deductibles**—are required levels of payments that the insured individual/family must meet before the insurer begins making its payments for care in a fee-for-service plan. Deductibles are regularly met at the beginning of each year and vary by policy type. They can range from relatively small amounts for traditional types of insurance to quite substantial amounts under high-deductible, catastrophic coverage plans.
- **Coinsurance**—Under a fee-for-service policy, insured individuals pay a portion of the cost of their care, while the insurer is responsible for the remaining costs. For example, the insured's coinsurance is often 20%, while the insurer pays 80%.

Policy Limitations

Often the insurance policy has various types of limitations—some that limit payments by the policy holder and some that limit how much total coverage the insurer will provide.

- **Maximum out-of-pocket expenditure**—This is an amount where the insured individual's cost sharing is capped. After reaching this point, the insurer will pick up 100% of the tab.
- **Lifetime limit**—This is the maximum amount that the policy will pay out over the lifetime of the insured individual. This type of limit usually only comes into play when there are catastrophic types of illnesses requiring very costly care. For example, in various types of transplants or spinal cord injuries, the treatment costs can escalate to hundreds of thousands of dollars. The limit can be $1 million or higher.

Types of Benefits

Different types of benefit packages can be purchased that offer varying types of coverage for individuals and families. These include:

- **Comprehensive policies**—These policies provide benefits that typically include physician and other types of outpatient visits, inpatient hospitals stays, outpatient surgery, medical testing and ancillary services, medical equipment, therapies, and other types of services. Prescription drugs are sometimes covered, as are rehabilitation services, hospice, and mental health care. Despite the name "comprehensive," most policies do not cover everything and thus have exclusions; in particular, most types of experimental treatments are excluded.
- **Basic, major medical, or hospital-surgical policies**—Referred to by several different names, the benefits provided by these policies are limited to types of illness that require hospitalization. Benefits include inpatient hospital stays, surgery, associated tests and treatments, related physician services, and other expenses incurred during an illness. There usually are limits on hospital stays and caps on expenditures.

- **Catastrophic coverage policies**—Benefits under these policies are intended to cover extraordinary types of illness; policies typically carry very sizable deductibles ($15,000 or higher) and lifetime limits on coverage.
- **Disease-specific policies**—In these policies, the benefits cover only the specific disease(s) covered (e.g., a cancer care policy).
- **MediGap policies**—These policies provide supplemental coverage of certain benefits that are excluded from other types of policies (e.g., prescription drugs).

Other Concerns Regarding Health Insurance

There are a number of issues that are important when managers and/or individuals are making decisions about healthcare coverage. These include the following:

- **Provider choice**—The concern here is whether the insured individuals have choices when they select care providers or whether there are limitations on which providers can be chosen.
- **Access to vs. restrictions on care**—This pertains to whether access to care is limited or controlled for the insured individual. Under some insurance policies, there is unlimited access, while under others, access is restricted by a gatekeeper.
- **Moral hazard**—This concept refers to the idea that existence of insurance coverage provides an incentive for insured individuals to secure and use the coverage. For example, a woman who knows she is going to become pregnant may be more likely to opt into coverage than a woman who is not expecting to have a need for this type of care.
- **Pre-existing conditions**—These are medical conditions that make a person a risk to an insurer, as the pre-existing condition may result in high expenditures. In the past, those who have had these types of conditions (e.g., cancer) have found it difficult or impossible to obtain coverage.
- **Buy-downs**—This is a situation that occurs with individual policies. "When insurers inform members of large premium hikes, they commonly suggest that the increase can be mitigated (or sometimes eliminated) by switching to a lower-cost policy (which means a policy with higher deductibles and/or greater limits on benefits) (Altman, 2010).
- **Coordination of benefits (COB)**—This is important when someone has two insurance plans: for example, a husband and wife both have coverage at work *and* have a family insurance plan. Each company seeks to ensure that it pays only that which it is obligated to pay.

The remaining sections of this chapter explore the different types of insurance coverage in greater depth. The chapter includes a discussion of the numbers and demographics of specific segments of the population who do and do not have health insurance coverage. Finally, the chapter concludes with a discussion of the implications of health insurance for healthcare managers.

PRIVATE HEALTH INSURANCE COVERAGE

Each type of private health insurance is described briefly below. Additionally, consideration is given to the pluses and minuses of the type of insurance with respect to access to care, choice of providers, and cost.

Conventional Indemnity Insurance

Most indemnity insurance products are based on the fee-for-service model. When the insured individuals utilize healthcare services, they pay for those services and seek reimbursement from the insurer. Care is rendered by independent healthcare providers, without gatekeeping or other restrictions. Management of care only comes into play in elective admissions, which require preauthorization. Table 9-3, provided later in this section, compares indemnity and other types of health plan coverages.

Managed Care Plans

Unlike indemnity plans, these health plans seek to manage cost, quality, and access to health services through control mechanisms on both patients and providers. These delivery systems attempt to integrate both the financing and provision of health care into one organization. The primary types include HMOs, PPOs, and POS plans and are described further below.

Health Maintenance Organizations (HMOs)

Individuals become members of the organization by paying a fixed prepayment amount. Once they become members, they are enrolled in the HMO. Enrollees are eligible to get care from the providers and facilities that are aligned with the HMO. Services are used at no charge, although minor copays are often required for prescription medications. Administration is centralized, with providers typically being reimbursed under a capitated rate. This means that providers are paid a set amount no matter how much care they need to provide. As described by Kongstvedt (2007), various types of contracting arrangements exist with providers, which may take the form of:

- **Closed-Panel HMO**—physicians practice only with the HMO, frequently in an HMO-owned health center;
- **Open-Panel HMO**—physicians practice within and outside the HMO;

- **Group Model HMO**—the HMO contracts with a multispecialty group practice to care for its enrollees;
- **Staff Model HMO**—groups of physicians are either salaried employees of the HMO or salaried employees of a professional group practice contracting exclusively with the HMO;
- **Independent Practice Association, or IPA Model**—the HMO contracts with an association of physicians practicing independently in their own offices; and
- **Network Model HMO**—the HMO contracts with several groups of physicians or with individual physicians or multispecialty medical clinics (physicians and hospitals) to provide a full range of medical services.

Preferred Provider Organizations (PPOs)

These plans reflect a combination of indemnity insurance and managed care options. In PPOs, insured individuals purchase coverage on a fee-for-service basis, with deductibles, copays, and coinsurances to be met. Care is managed in the sense that insured individuals pay less if care is obtained from a network of preferred provider with which the insurer contracts for discounted rates. Preferred providers include physicians, hospitals, diagnostic facilities, and other service providers. If care is not provided by a preferred provider, the insured individual pays a higher undiscounted rate and must meet higher deductibles and coinsurances for these services.

Point-of-Service (POS) Plans

These plans provide some flexibility to the HMO model described above and are sometimes referred to as open-ended plans. Under a POS plan, an enrollee can use services that are out of plan, in exchange for deductibles and coinsurance payments. The plan tries to address some of the shortcomings of the pure HMO approach.

High-Deductible Health Plan with Savings Option (HDHP/SO)

A form of consumer-driven health plan, these types of plans offer the enrollee catastrophic coverage for a relatively low premium that is coupled with a high deductible. The savings option is typically a Health Savings Account (HSA) or other some other type of vehicle. HSAs serve as a way to bank pretax dollars with an employer up to a certain amount to be used for medical expenses. If the consumer does not spend the HSA account down, she loses the money at the end of the year. Among the many provisions of the Medicare Prescription Drug, Improvement, and Modernization Act (MMA) of 2003, HSAs were mandated to "pair high-deductible plans that meet certain requirements with fully portable, employee-owned, tax-advantaged accounts" (Wilensky, 2006, p. 175). The underlying ideas behind HSAs are that consumers will become more educated users of health care, be more likely to utilize preventive and chronic care services, become more cognizant of the costs of care, be less likely to make poor decisions about using care that is not necessary or not appropriate, and be more prudent when using an account that is seen as containing "their own funds."

In the mid-1990s, many people thought managed care was the solution to the rising healthcare cost problem. While initially there was tremendous growth in managed care, particularly in HMOs, in recent years that trend has slowed. Additionally, consumer perceptions indicate negative views of managed care plans, concerns about the restrictions imposed in the plans, and the quality of care provided (Kaiser Family Foundation, 2006).

Evidence also suggests that PPOs have become the dominant form of coverage (Hurley, Strunk, & White, 2004). This represents a radical change in choice of plan since 1988, as shown in Table 9-2. At that time, the majority (73%) of covered workers were enrolled in conventional health insurance plans, 16% were in HMOs, 11% were in PPOs, and POS plans weren't even an option. By 2009, 60% of workers enrolled in health plans opted for a PPO, while only 20% and 10% were in HMOs and POSs, respectively. The penetration of HDHP/SOs into the health insurance market has increased from zero to 8% in the last 20 years. Only 1% of workers are still covered by conventional health plans (Kaiser Family Foundation and the Health Research and Educational Trust, 2009a).

The primary types of private health insurance coverage are compared across a number of important dimensions in Table 9-3. These include issues of access to care in general and to specialists, choice of providers, cost sharing, restrictions on utilization, administrative costs, paperwork, and several other dimensions. It is clear from reviewing this information that there are tradeoffs between plans. For example, those that provide unlimited access tend to have difficulties controlling costs, but afford higher quality. Those that are able to manage and control costs do so by limiting access and utilization.

TABLE 9-2 Health Plan Enrollment by Type of Plan, 1988–2009

Type of Plan	1988	1993	1998	2003	2008	2009
Conventional	73%	46%	14%	5%	2%	1%
HMO	16%	21%	27%	24%	20%	20%
PPO	11%	26%	35%	54%	58%	60%
POS	0%	7%	24%	17%	12%	10%
HDHP/SO	0%	0%	0%	0%	8%	8%

Source: Kaiser Family Foundation and the Health Research and Educational Trust, 2009a.

TABLE 9-3 Comparison of Insurance Plan Characteristics

	Indemnity Plans	Health Maintenance Organizations (HMOs)	Preferred Provider Organizations (PPOs)	Point-of-Service Plans (POSs)	High-Deductible Health Plans (HDHPs)
Access to Care	Unlimited	Limited and controlled; may require waiting up for care	Unlimited	Unlimited	Unlimited
Geographic Limitations	None	Limited to geographic regions served by HMO, except in emergencies	Unlimited	Unlimited	Unlimited
Choice of Provider	Unlimited choice of providers	Limited to in-network providers	Unlimited, but pay less when preferred (in-network) providers used	Can go out of network, but pay more	Unlimited
Access to Specialists	Unlimited; can self-refer	Limited; need referral from gatekeeper	Unlimited; can self-refer	Unlimited; may self-refer out of plan at a higher cost	Unlimited
Utilization Restrictions	None	Limitations may be imposed on certain services	Mostly unlimited; plan may place annual dollar or visit limits	Mostly unlimited; plan may place annual dollar or visit limits	Unlimited
Deductibles/ Copayments	Both typically must be met	No deductibles/small copays	Deductibles and copays required	Deductibles and copays required	High deductibles required
Coinsurance	Required	None	Required	Required for services received out of plan	None
Quality Issues	Likely to be high	May be lower, if patients have to wait for care	Likely to be high	Likely to be high, if patient gets second opinions	Likely to be high
Paperwork	Insured must complete to get reimbursed	Minimal; billing only needed on a small number of procedures	Excessive	Moderate for out-of-plan services	Minimal, unless catastrophic incident occurs
Administrative Costs	Moderately high	Low; controlled by not having to bill for most services	High; uncontrolled	Moderate to high	Low
Management of Costs	Costs difficult to manage; plans are cost inducing	Costs are known and can be managed	Costs are difficult to manage; costs are based on utilization	Costs are partially known for in-plan care; out-of-plan care is less known	Patients manage expenditures, unless catastrophic incident occurs

THE EVOLUTION OF SOCIAL INSURANCE

As with private insurance, many changes have taken place in how individuals can access care via social insurance or federal entitlement programs. The changes in both areas are discussed below, along with other key pieces of legislation that also relate to the private sector.

Major Legislation

The social health insurance programs of Medicare and Medicaid have continued to evolve over the past 45 years. The following discussion will address some of the major pieces of legislation shaping this evolution.

Social Security Act of 1965

The 1965 Amendments to the Social Security Act of 1935 established the two largest government-sponsored health insurance programs in the history of the United States. Medicare, Title XVIII of the Act, entitled persons 65 and over to coverage of hospital care under Part A and physicians' and other outpatient health services under Part B. Further eligibility for Medicare benefits has since been extended to younger people with permanent disabilities, individuals with end-stage renal disease (ESRD), and persons under hospice care. Medicaid, Title XIX, set up a joint federal-state program entitling financially qualified indigent and low-income persons to basic medical care. This program, too, has undergone numerous iterations at both the state and federal levels as these governments have attempted to strike a balance between equity in coverage for certain services (mandated at the federal level) and states' rights in controlling the use of public funds.

Employee Retirement and Income Security Act

"The Employee Retirement Income Security Act of 1974 (ERISA) protects the interests of participants and beneficiaries in private-sector employee benefit plans.... An employee benefit plan may be either a pension plan (which provides retirement benefits) or a welfare benefit plan (which provides other kinds of employee benefits such as health and disability benefits" (Purcell & Staman, 2009, p. 1). This federal law allows private companies to provide health benefits to employees through their own self-funded health insurance plan. The plan must meet the legal requirements of ERISA but can be customized to include only the benefits the company defines. While the law has been periodically amended to require these benefit plans to comply with other federal laws, such as the requirements of temporary coverage under the Consolidated Omnibus Budget Reconciliation Act (COBRA), the preexisting conditions provisions of the Health Insurance Portability and Accountability Act (HIPAA), the coverage requirements of the Mental Health Parity Act, and a couple of other specific coverage areas (Purcell & Staman, 2009; Pozgar, 2007), there are no requirements for these plans in terms of specific covered benefits. Additionally, since federal law preempts state law, companies that opt for this type of health plan have in almost all instances been exempted from the requirements of state health insurance mandates and laws.

TEFRA 1982 and OBRA 1989

In response to rapidly rising healthcare costs, Congress passed the Tax Equity and Fiscal Responsibility Act (TEFRA) in 1982, with particular emphasis on Medicare cost controls. Among its key provisions were the following:

- a mandate for a prospective payment system (PPS) for hospital reimbursement, with payment rates established up front for conditions known as Diagnosis-Related Groups (DRGs);
- the option of providing managed care plans to Medicare beneficiaries; and
- the requirement that Medicare become the secondary payer when a beneficiary had other insurance.

Similar payment arrangements have been mandated for other types of providers, such as compensation for physician office services to Medicare beneficiaries using the Resource-Based Relative Value System (RBRVS), mandated as part of the Omnibus Budget Reconciliation Act (OBRA) of 1989 and implemented in 1992. Under RBRVS, payments are determined by the cost of resources needed to provide each service, including physician work, practice expenses, and professional liability insurance.

Balanced Budget Act of 1997

Despite reductions in reimbursements for hospital admissions and physician visits, Medicare expenditures continued to soar throughout the 1990s. Congress passed the Balanced Budget Act (BBA) of 1997 in an attempt to control costs for other healthcare services, mandating some 200 changes (primarily restrictive) to the Medicare program alone, as well as changes to the Medicaid program. Medicare prospective payment systems were phased in and implemented in other healthcare settings beginning in 1998 as follows:

- Skilled nursing facilities (SNFs), in 1998, with RUGs (Resource Utilization Groups);
- Home health agencies (HHAs), in 2000, with HHRGs (Home Health Resource Groups);
- Hospital outpatient department services, in 2002, with OPPS (Outpatient Prospective Payment System); and
- Payment reductions and prospective payment arrangements for hospice care, rehabilitation hospitals, ambulance services, and durable medical equipment.

Other key provisions of the BBA, providing for cost controls in some areas and expansion of coverage in others, were:

- the creation of Medicare Part C, originally known as Medicare+Choice and referred to as "Medicare managed care," which was designed to move Medicare recipients into alternative forms of coverage, including HMOs and PPOs;
- provisions relating to fraud and abuse;
- improvements in protecting program integrity;
- restrictions on public benefits for illegal immigrants;
- addition of Medicare prevention initiatives (such as mammography, prostate cancer, and colorectal screenings);
- addition of rural initiatives; and
- establishment of CHIP to provide access for low-income children under Medicaid.

Medicare Prescription Drug, Improvement, and Modernization Act of 2003

Known as the Prescription Drug Benefit, Medicare Part D, and/or MMA, this produced the largest additions and changes to Medicare and was projected to cost $395 billion in its first decade alone. Effective January 1, 2006, this controversial entitlement to prescription drugs instigated a flurry of activities by individual states to mitigate uncertainties in its implementation and to temporarily provide prescription coverage for millions of seniors still in the process of meeting eligibility requirements. Tax breaks, subsidies, and other incentives to pharmaceutical companies and private, managed care insurers, along with significant pressure on seniors to enroll in Medicare Advantage Plans or risk significant out-of-pocket costs, were among the most contentious provisions of the drug benefit portion of this legislation.

With so much attention focused on the drug benefit, it has become easy for other provisions of this legislation to become lost in the discussion. Some of the more important ones include:

- increased prevention benefits;
- an extra $25 billion boost to often severely underfunded rural hospitals;
- a requirement for higher fees to be collected from wealthier seniors; and
- the addition of a pretax health savings account for working people.

Patient Protection and Affordable Care Act of 2010

President Obama signed Public Law 111-148 on March 23, 2010. This law calls for sweeping changes in health insurance, including both individual and employer mandates, creation of health insurance exchanges to allow choice in purchasing coverage, subsidies for small businesses, changes to Medicare, expansion of Medicaid to provide coverage for more children and low-income adults, cost-containment efforts for both Medicare and Medicaid, provisions for improving quality of care and performance, expansion of prevention and wellness programs, and elimination of cost sharing for these types of services, to name some of the key provisions (Iglehart, 2010c; Kaiser Commission on Medicaid and the Uninsured, 2010c; Kaiser Family Foundation, 2010c). Under the Community Living Assistance Services and Supports (CLASS) Act provisions, individuals will be able to purchase long-term care insurance coverage (Iglehart, 2010b; Kaiser Family Foundation, 2010c; Span, 2010a, 2010b, 2010c). Lifetime limits on health insurance coverage will be eliminated by 2014 (Iglehart, 2010a). The new healthcare reform legislation creates the Pre-Existing Condition Insurance Plan (PCIP) to allow access to coverage for individuals in this group (Kaiser Family Foundation, 2010c). A website was created by the federal government in July 2010 to begin to provide details about the new law (see http://www.healthcare.gov). The Kaiser Family Foundation (2010d) has also published a timeline for implementation of the new law, and numerous analyses of legislation are being prepared. While it is very early in the process of implementing this new legislation, concerns have already been raised and legal challenges have been filed. These relate to whether the federal government has the authority to mandate health insurance coverage, taxing of health benefits, and the impacts of the legislation on businesses (particularly small businesses), the states, insurers, and healthcare providers (Abelson, 2010; Helms, 2009; Kaiser Commission on Medicaid and the Uninsured, 2010a; Luo, 2010; Miller, 2010; Sack, 2010; Schwartz, 2010).

MAJOR "PLAYERS" IN THE SOCIAL INSURANCE ARENA

Medicare

As discussed previously, this federal program provides access to health care for the elderly over 65 years of age, for permanently disabled younger adults, and for those suffering from end-stage renal disease (ESRD). End-of-life "palliative" care (or comfort care) is also provided for terminally ill enrollees in their last six months of life. The primary benefits of this program, as delineated by the CMS (2010b), can best be summarized through description of its four "parts":

- **Part A—Hospital Insurance (HI)**, allowing 90 days of inpatient hospital coverage per benefit period (with a 60-day lifetime inpatient hospital reserve), inpatient skilled nursing facility (SNF) coverage of up to 100 days per episode (with a 90-day lifetime SNF reserve), currently prequalified home healthcare services, and hospice care for the terminally ill.
- **Part B—Supplemental Medical Insurance (SMI)**, providing coverage for visits to physicians, outpatient treatments, and preventive services, including flu and hepatitis B vaccines, mammography, and Pap smears.

- **Part C—Medicare Advantage Plans (MAs)**, allowing beneficiaries to enroll in a variety of capitated health insurance plans, which are required to provide the same types of services covered under traditional Medicare plans and may offer the option of additional benefits such as prescription drugs.
- **Part D—The Prescription Drug Benefit**, with drug coverage being available through Prescription Drug Plans (PDPs), Medicare Advantage Drug Plans (MA PDs), or other Medicare-approved prescription plans.

Administered federally by the Centers for Medicare & Medicaid Services (CMS), Medicare has been financed through three primary means. The first has been through assessments to employers and employees, contributing 2.9% of payroll (1.45% each), and is dedicated entirely to paying Part A benefits. The second means of financing has involved increased cost sharing by beneficiaries, including premiums (financing 25% of all Part B benefits and 25.5% of Part D benefits), deductibles, coinsurance, and balance billing. The third and largest financing source has increasingly been derived from allocations from general revenues (federal taxes). Total Medicare revenues from all sources were estimated at $513 billion in 2010 (Kaiser Family Foundation, 2010a). Figure 9-2 summarizes the relative percentages from major Medicare revenue sources.

Public policy circles have become increasingly concerned about the growth in Medicare program enrollment and the concomitant rise in expenditures. According to CMS data, 19.1 million individuals were enrolled in Medicare at its inception in 1966; this number

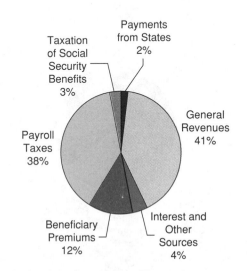

FIGURE 9-2 Estimated Medicare Revenues, 2010

Source: CMS, 2010a.

grew to 46 million in 2009 (CMS, 2009). Enrollment is projected to grow to 78 million by 2030 (CMS, 2009). Medicare's share of the U.S. economy is expected to increase from 2.7% (as a percentage of the GDP) in 2005 to 6.8% in 2030 (Boards of Trustees, Federal Hospital Insurance and Federal Supplementary Medical Insurance Trust Funds, 2009).

Another issue of concern surrounding Medicare expenditures is the distribution by percentages of dollars allocated to various sectors of the healthcare arena. Figure 9-3 summarizes this distribution.

These numbers are partially indicative of the aging of the population, with increased life expectancy. Healthcare services are being used by those 65 and older at a much higher rate than other age groups, and the huge baby boom generation (born between 1946 and 1964) began to turn 65 in 2011. Yet these factors do not tell the entire story. Why else have Medicare expenditures grown so dramatically? The following are among the most frequent and significant factors:

- a shift from treatment of acute illnesses to more chronic care as society ages and lives longer, with more substantial outlays of money to treat the latter;
- tremendous growth in hospital expenditures;
- initial lack of cost-conscious Medicare reimbursement, using retrospective fee-for-service (payments based on charges) methods;
- huge growth in pharmaceutical costs and in technological innovations in the medical field;

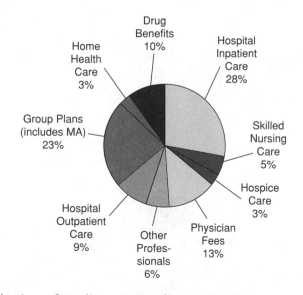

FIGURE 9-3 Distribution of Medicare Expenditures, 2009

Source: CBO, 2009.

- increased payments under Part C plans;
- the need for higher payments to rural health providers; and
- rising medical malpractice premiums related to increasing litigation.

During the early 1990s, federal policy makers were already alarmed by the dramatic rise in healthcare expenditures, particularly concerning Medicare. In fact, during the first Clinton administration in the early 1990s, there was a push toward legislation providing for a national healthcare system. Efforts to slow the rate of growth have been mandated. The 2010 healthcare reform legislation includes provisions for this, including changes to Medicare Advantage, reducing payments to hospitals and other providers, changing premiums for Parts B and D, promoting preventive care, and working to reduce fraud, to name a few (Kaiser Family Foundation, 2010c).

Medicaid

Medicaid, the second largest provider of socialized health insurance in the United States, provides healthcare coverage to the medically indigent (those below certain poverty-level determinations) and is jointly funded by state and federal governments. Mandatory services required by the federal government include the following basic health services: inpatient hospitalization, outpatient care, lab and X-ray services, nursing home facilities, and home health care (Kaiser Family Foundation, 2010b). Beyond this, each state has authority in administering Medicaid programs, including the amount and scope of services and differences in eligibility requirements.

There is huge variation in the types of benefits provided by various states. For example, some states provide a wide array of dental benefits to beneficiaries. Others provide mental health benefits and/or drug and alcohol treatment. Similarly, there are significant variations in coverage of the poor. Some "bare bones" Medicaid programs cover only individuals mandated by the federal government, while other states cover individuals with higher incomes. These differences, as well as differences in ages of individuals covered, result in wide gaps in Medicaid coverage from state to state, creating a phenomenon known as "welfare magnets," in which low-income individuals from less generous states travel across the borders to more generous ones.

Despite the considerable discretion given to the states in terms of eligibility requirements in relation to income, the following categories of medically indigent and low-income individuals must be included in state Medicaid programs:

- The medically indigent, historically linked to two federal assistance programs: Temporary Aid to Needy Families (TANF), which replaced Aid to Families with Dependent Children (AFDC) in 1996, and Supplemental Security Income (SSI);

- Low-income pregnant women, children, and infants, as mandated through the Omnibus Budget Reconciliation Act (OBRA) of 1986; and
- Children whose parents have income too high for Medicaid but too low for private insurance, through CHIP.

The primary problems caused by allowing such liberal state discretion have been the huge inequities in the numbers and percentages of residents being served and the types of benefits being received. Part of these discrepancies may be related to the differences in how Medicaid is financed. The federal government finances 50% to 77% of Medicaid costs in any given state, depending on the state's poverty status (i.e., the number of individuals living below the federal poverty level). This leaves state contributions ranging from 23% to 50%, with the poorer states contributing the lowest percentage. Many "richer" states, often feeling the pinch of reduced state coffers related to factors other than income, feel it is unfair that they must shoulder 50% of the health insurance burden of their poorest members and thus often contribute a smaller proportion of their General Fund to the provision of Medicaid services.

The recession of 2008 has had a significant impact on state Medicaid programs. According to the Kaiser Commission on Medicaid and the Uninsured (2010b), states experienced the largest single-year enrollment increase since the program's inception between June 2008 and June 2009; 3.3 million people were added to the Medicaid rolls, an increase of 5.4%.

The groups covered by Medicaid have remained relatively stable, with poor individuals, families, and children being eligible for benefits. What has changed radically, however, is the dollars consumed by different groups. For example, the aged, blind, and disabled numbered less than 28.0% of Medicaid beneficiaries but accounted for 62.0% of Medicaid spending in 2009 (CMS, 2009).

As with Medicare expenses, Medicaid expenditures have grown dramatically over the past couple of decades. "From CY 2000 through CY 2005, expenditures for Medicaid grew faster than did spending for the other major payers of health care. Medicaid increased at an average of 9.3 percent per year, while Medicare and private health insurance plans increased 8.6 percent and 8.0 percent per year on average, respectively" (Truffer, Klemm, Hoffman, & Wolfe, 2008, p. 21).

In 1966, at the inception of the Medicaid program, there were only 10 million recipients of Medicaid, with total spending at only $1.7 billion (in 1966 dollars). By FY 2009, total spending had risen to more than $371.9 billion, with more than 50 million recipients of Medicaid services (CMS, 2009). Other ways of looking at expenditures are in terms of types of services provided and populations served. Figure 9-4 summarizes the distribution of Medicaid expenditures by service.

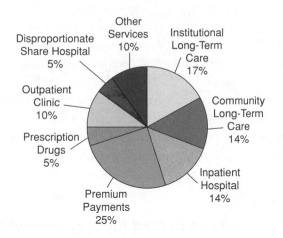

FIGURE 9-4 Distribution of Medicaid Medical Assistance Payments, FY 2009
Source: CMS, 2009.

As previously asked regarding Medicare expenditures, why have Medicaid expenditures grown so dramatically? The following are illustrative of the most significant reasons given for growth in spending and numbers of Medicaid recipients:

- Changes in Medicaid policies, particularly expansion of eligibility requirements.
- Expansion of types of services provided, including dental care, rehabilitation, preventive services, mental health care, and drug and alcohol treatment, in more generous states.
- Downturns in the economy and rising unemployment rates that have resulted in increasing numbers of the poor and uninsured since 2001. As mentioned above, the 2008 recession led to a sizable enrollment increase, which in turn resulted in a 6.6% growth in spending in FY 2009. It has been estimated that the growth continued, reaching double digits in FY 2010 (Kaiser Commission on Medicaid and the Uninsured, 2010a, 2010b).
- The unexpected significant increases in Medicaid expenditures as a result of higher payment rates to providers and more spending on those who "deserve" public support, including the aged blind, disabled, and children, according to some Republican governors.

As the federal government has been attempting to control escalating Medicare costs, the CMS and individual states alike have been active in implementing cost controls and reductions in Medicaid eligibility and benefits. At the federal level, one of the most important measures enacted has been the provision in the Balanced Budget Act of 1997 allowing states to enroll Medicaid recipients in managed care health plans. Additionally, the Deficit Reduction Act of 2005 attempted to reduce expenditures even more dramatically by calling for net Medicaid "reductions of $4.8 billion over the next five years and $26.1 billion over the next 10 years" (Kaiser Commission on Medicaid and the Uninsured, 2006, p. 1). The Medicaid Integrity Program resulted from this and created new efforts to reduce Medicaid fraud and abuse (CMS, 2009; Wachino, 2007).

Efforts to offset the 2009/2010 increases in spending have benefitted from a temporary increase in the federal Medicaid match that was authorized as part of the American Recovery and Reinvestment Act (ARRA) (Kaiser Family Foundation, 2010b). The growth in Medicaid enrollment spending has exacerbated state budgets deficits, led to cuts in other state programs, and resulted in other cost-containment efforts (Kaiser Commission on Medicaid and the Uninsured, 2010b; National Governors Association, 2010).

Insuring Veterans, Active and Retired Military Personnel, and Their Families

The Military Health System covers federal health benefits for veterans, military personnel, and their family members under the Department of Defense's (DOD) medical facilities and TRICARE plan, the medical facilities of the Department of Veterans Affairs (VA) and the VA's Civilian Health and Medical Program (CHAMPVA), and other specialized programs (TRICARE, 2007, 2008, 2010a, 2010b). While everyone who served in the military is a veteran, only those who served for an extended period (normally 20 years) are retired. Health benefits described in this section are federal benefits or entitlements—technically, not insurance.

TRICARE and DOD

TRICARE is not an abbreviation; it is the title of the military health program. It covers active duty military personnel, retired military personnel, and their family members. DOD's medical facilities are considered part of TRICARE. "VA's health care system now includes 153 medical centers, with at least one in each state, Puerto Rico and the District of Columbia. VA operates more than 1,400 sites of care, including 909 ambulatory care and community-based patient clinics, 135 nursing homes, 47 residential rehabilitation treatment programs, 232 Veterans Centers and 108 comprehensive home-care programs" (U.S. Department of Veterans Affairs, 2009a, p. 2). DOD has contracted with various companies to provide health care in the private sector both in the United States and overseas. Figure 9-5 shows the demographics of the population covered by TRICARE.

TRICARE offers three separate programs: an HMO, a PPO, and a fee-for-service option. All active duty members are automatically enrolled at no cost in the HMO option called PRIME. Other categories must enroll. Retirees and their families pay an annual enrollment fee; active duty families do not. All enrollees (except active duty) have copays for office visits, prescription medication, diagnostic tests, and hospitalization. Most preventive services are free. Individuals who do not elect to enroll in PRIME pay an annual deductible and have copays. Those who use the PPO (called TRICARE Extra) have a 20% copay, while those

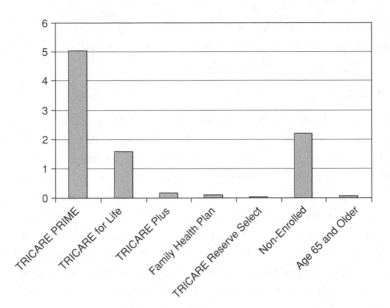

FIGURE 9-5 TRICARE Eligible Beneficiaries (in millions)

Source: TRICARE, 2008.

who use the fee-for-service option (called TRICARE Standard) are subject to a 25% copay. DOD offers all participants a mail-order pharmacy program. Dental services for active duty members are free; for others, there is an insurance plan where enrollees pay a monthly premium for covered services. There is no long-term care coverage under TRICARE.

The U.S. Army, Navy, and Air Force operate military medical facilities around the world and afloat. DOD (as opposed to the three military services organizations) manages the contracted arrangements, except in the limited case where contracts are issued by a medical facility—these are managed by the medical facility. Medical personnel from each of the three services provide staff to the DOD organizations that oversee the contracted arrangements. Utilization of VA healthcare facilities has continued to increase, with the provision of care to 5.5 million people in 2008. This represents a 29% increase from 2001 (U.S. Department of Veterans Affairs, 2009a).

Problems with TRICARE primarily focus on:

- the limited network of providers in rural areas;
- providing rehabilitative care to soldiers injured in 21st-century wars;
- providing care to National Guard and Reserve personnel who alternate from active duty to inactive duty; and
- ensuring that there are sufficient providers to meet the needs of the 9.2 million beneficiaries (Office of the Secretary of Defense, n.d.).

These problems are normally addressed within DOD and the services, but veterans' organizations and Congress take an active role in helping to ensure that beneficiaries receive access to quality services at a reasonable cost.

Veterans Affairs

Operated through the Veterans Health Administration (VHA), the VA manages the nation's largest healthcare delivery system with more than 160 medical centers and 1,000 community clinics. Every VA medical center is affiliated with a national medical school. Unlike the DOD, the VA does not differentiate between veterans who retired from the military and those who did not. Virtually all veterans are eligible for care in the VA, although those receiving less than honorable discharges or who left the service before serving 180 days may have limited or no benefits. The VHA operates its medical facilities in 22 regions called Veteran Integrated Service Networks (VISN). VISN directors are responsible for providing or arranging care for enrolled veterans, as well as some who are not enrolled. Individuals who enroll are placed in one of eight categories based on disability or service, as shown in Table 9-4. The VHA also purchases care from private providers when the VA does not have the needed service. Veterans who are in categories 1 through 4 are provided virtually all their medical needs by the VA. Those in categories 5 through 8 are provided care primarily for conditions that the veteran incurred while in the military—called service-connected conditions.

The VA leads the nation in providing quality care to veterans, as described in Table 9-5. Researchers, including the Congressional Budget Office (2007), tout the quality provided by the VA, with one pointing out that "at least in terms of process quality . . . the VHA has

---

TABLE 9-4 VA Enrollment Categories (abbreviated explanation)

Category 1: Service-connected (SC) veterans—50% or more disabled

Category 2: SC veterans—30–40% disabled

Category 3: SC 10–20%; former prisoners of war; Purple Heart recipients

Category 4: Vets receiving aid and attendance allowance or catastrophically disabled

Category 5: Low-income SC veterans with 0% disability and non-SC vets; vets receiving VA pension; vets eligible for Medicaid

Category 6: WWI vets; Mexican Border War vets; compensable SC vets with 0% disability; vets seeking care for herbicide exposure (Vietnam); vets exposed to ionizing radiation; vets with Gulf War illness; vets who articipated in Project SHAD

Category 7: Vets with income above a certain limit and below the HUD geographic index who agree to pay copays for services

Category 8: Same as Category 7 except above the HUD geographic index

---

Source: U.S. Department of Veterans Affairs, 2009b.

TABLE 9-5 VHA Performance Data

Clinical Performance Indicator	VA FY 05	HEDIS[2] Commercial 2004	HEDIS[2] Medicare 2004	BRFSS[5] 2004
Breast cancer screening	86%	73%	74%	54%
Cervical cancer screening	92%	81%	Not reported	65%
Colorectal cancer screening	76%	49%	53%	Not reported
LDL cholesterol < 100 after AMI, PTCA, CABG	Not reported[3]	51%	54%	29%
LDL cholesterol < 130 after AMI, PTCA, CABG	Not reported[3]	68%	70%	41%
Beta blocker on discharge after AMI	98%	96%	94%	85%
Diabetes: HgA1c done past year	96%	87%	89%	76%
Diabetes: Poor control HgA1c >9.0% (lower is better)	17%	31%	23%	49%
Diabetes: Cholesterol (LDL-C) screening	95%	91%	94%	80%
Diabetes: Cholesterol (LDL-C) controlled (<100)	60%	40%	48%	31%
Diabetes: Cholesterol (LDL-C) controlled (<130)	82%	65%	71%	51%
Diabetes: Eye exam	79%	51%	67%	45%
Diabetes: Renal exam	66%	52%	59%	47%
Hypertension: BP ≤ 140/90 most recent visit	77%	67%	65%	61%
Follow-up after hospitalization for mental illness (30 days)[6][7]	70%[4]	76%	61%	55%
Immunizations: influenza (note patients age groups)[6][7]	75% (65 and older or high risk)	39% (50–64)	75% (65 and older)	68% (65 and older)
Immunizations: pneumococcal (note patients age groups)[6]	89% (all ages at risk)	Not reported	Not reported	65% (65 and older)

1) Beginning with Quarter 4 of FY 2004, VA comparison data was obtained by abstracting medical record data using methodologies that matched HEDIS methodologies. The scores presented here are from those HEDIS mirrored extractions performed in the fourth quarter of FY 2004.
2) HEDIS data was obtained from the 2005 "State of Health Care Quality" report, available on the NCQA website: www.ncqa.org.
3) HEDIS mirrors for these measures were changed to include vascular diseases in addition to AMI. VHA initiated capture of expanded definition in FY 06. Scores will be posted when sufficent size threshold has been obtained.
4) HEDIS calculates score for MH follow-up in a calendar year (January–December); VHA calculates on fiscal year (October–September).
5) BRFSS reports are available on the CDC website: www.cdc.gov.
6) BRFSS (survey) scores are median scores. VA scores are averages obtained by medical record abstraction in 2003–2004 influenza seasons (September 2003–January 2004 and September 2004–January 2005).
7) The influenza vaccine shortage in the fall of 2004 resulted in disparities in distribution and a change in targeted populations that affected scores.
Source: U.S. Department of Veterans Affairs, Veterans Health Administration Office of Quality and Performance, 2005. See also raw data in Oliver (2007), Table 5.

improved substantially and now seems to be outperforming the rest of U.S. health care" (Oliver, 2007, pp. 11–12). The VA is also noted for being an early adopter of electronic medical records. When New Orleans was devastated by hurricanes in late 2005, not one veteran's medical record was lost.

Family members of selected veterans are provided care through the VA's special health benefits programs. If the veteran is not retired from the military and the military determines that the veteran is permanently and totally disabled or has died from a condition related to military service, family members are eligible for the CHAMPVA program. CHAMPVA is a fee-for-service program patterned after the TRICARE fee-for-service option with an annual deductible and a 25% copay. Unlike TRICARE, CHAMPVA is operated completely by the VA and not through contractors. If a veteran is a Vietnam veteran or served in Korea between 1967 and 1971 near the Demilitarized Zone (DMZ) and his or her child has spina bifida, the VA provides 100% coverage of medical care and supplies for these children under the Spina Bifida Healthcare Program (U.S. Department of Veterans Affairs, Health Administration Center, 2009). For women Vietnam veterans who have children with certain birth defects, the VA provides 100% coverage for the related condition under the Children of Women Vietnam Veterans Healthcare Program. Both the Spina Bifida Healthcare Program and the Children of Women Vietnam Veterans Healthcare Program were established because of veterans' exposure to Agent Orange, a defoliant used extensively in Vietnam and near the DMZ in Korea.

Figure 9-6 displays the VA population demographics.

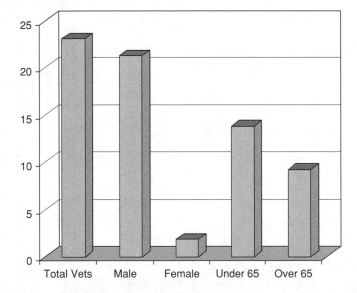

FIGURE 9-6 VA 2010 Demographics (in millions)

Source: National Center for Veterans Analysis and Statistics, 2010.

Problems with VA health programs are addressed through typical patient advocate activities. As with the DOD, veteran organizations and Congress play very active roles in the oversight of the VA's health system. The VA has problems providing services in rural areas, much like the DOD. Also, the large number of Guard and Reserve members serving in Operation Iraqi Freedom and Operation Enduring Freedom, who continually change status from active to inactive, sometimes have problems with continuity of care issues.

Financing for DOD and VA Health Programs

To obtain funds for their programs, the DOD and VA submit budgets to the Office of Management and Budget (OMB). The OMB validates the requests and includes them in the President's request to Congress, which appropriates funds for the operation of the health systems. The FY 2009 appropriation for the VA was $100 billion, while the FY 2010 has been estimated at $127 billion (National Center for Veterans Analysis and Statistics, 2010).

In sum, the Military Health System plays a large and critical role in providing care to veterans, active duty military personnel, and their families. It is, thus, a huge contributor to public sector health insurance.

STATISTICS ON HEALTH INSURANCE COVERAGE AND COSTS

As a part of the U.S. Census Bureau's Current Population Survey, health insurance coverage data are collected on an annual basis. The data from 2008 indicated that 84.6% of the population had some type of coverage (DeNavas-Walt, Proctor, & Smith, 2009). The data presented in Figure 9-7 show the breakdown of health insurance by type of coverage for those who were insured in 2008.

These data reflect only modest changes from the previous year. The individuals covered by some form of insurance increased by 1.6 million between 2007 and 2008. Coverage of individuals with employment-based private health insurance decreased slightly during that time period, while government health insurance programs absorbed the majority of this increase, with the largest increase coming in Medicaid (DeNavas-Walt et al., 2009). Several others have pointed out that changes in coverage are directly linked to the recession and job loss (Bernstein, 2009; Truffer et al., 2010).

At the outset of this chapter, there was a brief discussion of the increases in the expenditures for health care. While government programs are funded primarily from taxes, payments to the Social Security Trust Fund, and cost sharing by recipients, private health insurance must be financed by employers and employees. The costs of premiums for different

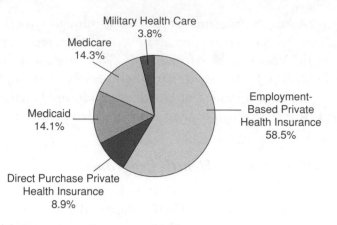

FIGURE 9-7 Health Insurance Coverage, 2008

Source: DeNavas-Walt, Proctor, and Smith, 2009.

types of health insurance, presented in Table 9-6, show the variation in the contributions toward premiums paid by employees and employers. Data are provided for individual policy holders, as well as for individuals opting for family coverage. These data also only reflect premiums and do not include deductibles, coinsurance, and/or copayments.

Premiums have increased 131% in the last 10 years. This was fairly evenly split between employer and worker contributions. The former increased 132% and the latter 128%

TABLE 9-6 Premiums Paid by Employees and Employers by Type of Plan, 2009

Type of Plan	Employee Contribution	Employer Contribution	Total Premium
Individual coverage			
All plans	$779	$4,045	$4,824
HMO	$817	$4,061	$4,878
PPO	$806	$4,116	$4,922
POS	$741	$4,093	$4,834
HDHP/SO	$540	$3,446	$3,986
Family coverage			
All plans	$3,515	$9,860	$13,375
HMO	$3,685	$9,785	$13,470
PPO	$3,470	$10,249	$13,719
POS	$4,146	$8,929	$13,075
HDHP/SO	$2,672	$8,411	$11,083

Source: Kaiser Family Foundation and the Health Research and Educational Trust, 2009b.

(Kaiser Family Foundation and the Health Research and Educational Trust, 2009b). Altman (2010) discussed the proposed 39% premium increase by Anthem Blue Cross Blue Shield in California, which is seen as a trend that may force companies and individuals to "buy-down" policies "to skimpier, less comprehensive coverage" and that "we may be reaching the point in the individual market where the policies many people have simply cannot be considered meaningful coverage" (para. 3).

THOSE NOT COVERED—THE UNINSURED

There were 46.3 million people without insurance coverage in the United States in 2008. This represented 15.4% of the population, a slight increase in the uninsured population over 2007. However, over the last 10 years, there has been a 19.5% increase, or the addition of 7.5 million, to the ranks of the uninsured (U.S. Census Bureau, 2009).

A breakdown of the data, as shown in Figure 9-8, indicates differences in those who are uninsured by racial group. For example, while Blacks made up 12.6% of the population in 2008, they accounted for 15.7% of the uninsured, and while Hispanics comprised only 15.8% of the population, 31.4% of the uninsured were from this ethnic group. These disparities are a function of many things, among them differences in employment, eligibility for public programs, and income.

Additionally, when these numbers are broken down by age, the distribution shows that those without insurance coverage spanned all age groups in 2008. Figure 9-9 indicates that,

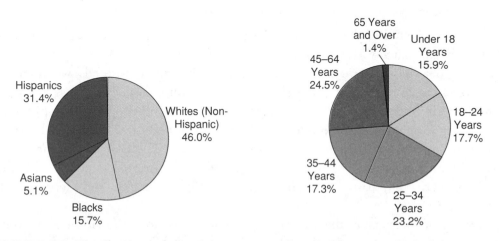

FIGURE 9-8 Distribution of the Uninsured by Race, 2008

Source: DeNavas-Walt, Proctor, and Smith, 2009.

FIGURE 9-9 Distribution of the Uninsured by Age, 2008

Source: DeNavas-Walt, Proctor, and Smith, 2009.

while only a small number of those 65 and over were uninsured (as would be expected due to Medicare coverage), all other age groups included several million uninsured individuals, with more than four-fifths being adults. The majority of the uninsured were individuals under 35 years of age, but the largest single group was the 11.4 million people ages 45 to 65.

Research about other characteristics of the uninsured also helps us to understand who this population includes (Abel, 1998; Rowland, Lyons, Salganicoff, & Long, 1994). The following are some of the key characteristics of these individuals.

- Approximately 25% were in families where income was below the poverty level.
- Most were individuals from families with incomes above the poverty level, but many had incomes below 300% of the poverty level.
- More than four-fifths were workers or dependents of workers who were employed in industries that do not typically provide health insurance coverage.
- The percentages of individuals without health insurance coverage vary across the states. More people in states in the South and the West tend be uninsured than those living in the Midwest and East.
- Those who are uninsured have been shown to use the healthcare delivery system in different ways. Without coverage and/or ability to pay, studies have shown that the uninsured:
  - do not typically have a primary care physician;
  - delay seeking care until they are sicker; and
  - utilize hospital emergency departments, the most expensive entry point to the healthcare system, to access the system and receive health care.

Additionally, the Kaiser Commission on Medicaid and the Uninsured (n.d.) has identified 10 myths associated with those who are uninsured (see Table 9-7).

Providing health care to the uninsured has fallen primarily to hospitals, where much of it becomes uncompensated care. There are some funds available to assist hospitals through the federal government's disproportionate-share program that provides some funding for providing large amounts of uncompensated care. There are also state and local programs that help to support these hospitals. The cost of care provided to the uninsured is borne by the taxpayers, as well as by insured patients, with the costs of that care being passed along in the form of higher taxation and higher health insurance costs.

Addressing the problem of the uninsured has now moved to the forefront of national health policy with the passage of the Affordable Care Act. With its individual mandate that requires all U.S. citizens to secure health insurance by 2014, the vast majority of the uninsured will have coverage (Kaiser Family Foundation, 2010c).

TABLE 9-7 Myths About the Uninsured

MYTH	FACT
1 The uninsured go without coverage because they believe they do not need it or don't want it.	The majority of uninsured, regardless of how young they are, say they forgo coverage because they cannot afford it, not because they don't need it.
2 Most of the uninsured do not have health insurance because they are not working and so don't have access to health benefits through an employer.	Most of the uninsured are either working full-time or have someone in their immediate family who does; the problem is that the majority of the uninsured are not offered benefits through their employers.
3 Most of the growth in the uninsured has been among those with higher incomes.	The majority of the growth in the uninsured since 2000 has been among people earning less than $38,000 a year for a family of four (commonly considered low-income).
4 Most of the uninsured are new immigrants who are U.S. citizens.	The large majority of the uninsured (79%) are American citizens.
5 The uninsured often receive health services for free or at reduced charges.	Free or even discounted health services are not common, and when the uninsured are unable to pay the full costs, the unpaid medical bills add to their providers' costs.
6 The uninsured can get the care they need when they really need it and are able to avoid serious health problems.	The uninsured are more likely to postpone and forgo care with serious consequences that increase their chances of preventable health problems, disability, and premature death.
7 Buying health insurance coverage on your own is always an option.	Individually purchased policies—vs. job-based group policies with similar benefits—are more expensive, and coverage can be limited or even denied to persons in less than good health.
8 We don't really know how large the uninsured problem is, and many are only uninsured for brief periods.	Depending on whether we count the number of people who are uninsured during a specific month, for an entire year, or just for short periods, the numbers will differ, and all measures are useful.
9 The health care the uninsured receive, but do not pay for, results in higher insurance premiums.	The large majority of uncompensated care is subsidized through a mix of federal and state government dollars, not cost-shifts to private payers.
10 Expanding health insurance coverage to all, or even a large share, of the uninsured will cost far more than the country currently spends on health care.	Because both the uninsured and government subsidies pay for a good share of their health care costs already, the amount of additional health spending to cover all of the uninsured is relatively small.

Source: Kaiser Commission on Medicaid and the Uninsured, n.d.

CONCLUSION

The changes that will occur over the next five years as healthcare reform is implemented will bring new and different challenges for healthcare managers. While much will change, much will remain the same. There will still be two primary ways that health insurance issues will affect healthcare managers. The first relates to managing the health insurance benefit for employees and their dependents. In this regard, managers need to understand the options available to them in selecting plans that meet the needs of their employees, as well as the needs of the company. For small businesses, new opportunities to provide coverage to workers will be in the offing. The affordability of providing health benefits to employees will continue to be an increasingly difficult proposition for all organizations, both large and small. Managers will be called upon to try to reduce the costs of coverage, to select cost-effective health plans, to encourage employees to manage their care better, and to take steps to have employees bear more of the cost of coverage.

The second way that health insurance will be important for managers is related to patients—their insurance coverage and how they receive reimbursement from their insurers. Managing the patient health insurance function well will be critical to the financial success and viability of the organization. Issues relating to coding, billing, and other aspects of financing are discussed further in Chapter 10.

DISCUSSION QUESTIONS

1. Compare and contrast fee-for-service and prepaid health plans.

2. What types of cost sharing in health insurance are most effective? Provide a rationale for your response.

3. What are the pros and cons of the different types of health insurance benefit packages that someone might purchase?

4. What is the best type of health insurance? Justify your answer.

5. Compare and contrast Medicare and Medicaid in terms of eligibility, benefit packages, access to care, and other key dimensions.

6. How does CHIP add to coverage provided under the Medicaid Program?

7. What issues and concerns have arisen relating to Medicare Part D? How can they be resolved?

8. Discuss the different types of healthcare coverage/health insurance that are provided to military personnel and their dependents.

9. What factors make it difficult to provide healthcare coverage for everyone in the United States? How will the Affordable Care Act bring more people into coverage?

The case in Chapter 17 that is related to this chapter is:

- A Small Healthcare Clinic Confronts Health Insurance Problems—see p. 441

Additional cases, role-play scenarios, video links, websites, and other information sources are also available in the online Instructor's Materials.

REFERENCES

Abel, P. (1998, April). *1997 Colorado health source book: Insurance, access & expenditures.* Denver: Colorado Coalition for Health Care Access and Coalition for the Medically Underserved.

Abelson, R. (2010, July 23). For insurers, fight is now over details. *New York Times.* Retrieved from http://www.nytimes.com/2010/07/24/business/24insure.html

Altman, D. (2010). *When premiums go up 39%.* Retrieved from http://www.kff.org/pullingittogether/031010_altman.cfm

Bernstein, J. (2009, August). *Impact of the economy on health care.* Retrieved from http://www.academyhealth.org/files/HCFO/findings0809.pdf

Boards of Trustees, Federal Hospital Insurance and Federal Supplementary Medical Insurance Trust Funds. (2009, May 12). *2009 annual report of the boards of trustees of the federal hospital insurance and federal supplementary medical insurance trust funds.* Washington, DC: Author. Retrieved from http://www.phrma.org/files/attachments/2009MedicareTrusteesReport.pdf

Centers for Medicare & Medicaid Services (CMS). (2009). *CMS financial report.* Baltimore, MD: Author. Retrieved from http://www.cms.gov/CFOReport/Downloads/2009_CMS_Financial_Report.pdf

Centers for Medicare & Medicaid Services (CMS). (2010a, January). *National health expenditure projections 2009–2019.* Retrieved from https://www.cms.gov/NationalHealthExpendData/downloads/proj2009.pdf

Centers for Medicare & Medicaid Services (CMS). (2010b). *Medicare & you.* Retrieved from http://www.medicare.gov/publications/pubs/pdf/10050.pdf

Chernew, M. E., Hirth R. A., & Cutler, D. M. (2009, September/October). Increased spending on health care: Long-term implications for the nation. *Health Affairs, 28*(5), 1253–1255.

Congressional Budget Office (CBO). (2007). *The health care system for veterans: An interim report.* Retrieved from http://www.cbo.gov/ftpdocs/88xx/doc8892/12-21-VA_Healthcare.pdf

Congressional Budget Office (CBO). (2009, March 24). *CBO's March 2009 baseline: MEDICARE.* Retrieved from http://www.cbo.gov/budget/factsheets/2009b/medicare.pdf

DeNavas-Walt, C., Proctor, B. D., & Smith, J. C. (2009, September). *Income, poverty, and health insurance coverage in the United States: 2008.* Current Population Reports. U.S. Census Bureau. Washington, DC: U.S. Government Printing Office, 60–236 (RV). Retrieved from http://www .census.gov/prod/2009pubs/p60-236.pdf

Hartman, M., Martin, A., Nuccio, O., Catlin, A., & the National Health Expenditures Accounts Team. (2010, January). Health Spending Growth at a Historic Low in 2008. *Health Affairs, 20*(1), 147–155.

Helms, R. B. (2009, November). *Medicaid: The forgotten issue in health reform.* Washington, DC: American Enterprise Institute for Public Policy Research. Retrieved from http://www.aei.org/ outlook/100087

Hurley, R. E., Strunk, B. C., & White, J. S. (2004, March/April). The puzzling popularity of the PPO. *Health Affairs, 23*(2), 56–68.

Iglehart, J. K. (2010a, May). The end of the beginning: Enactment of health reform. *Health Affairs, 29*(5), 758–759.

Iglehart, J. K. (2010b, January). Long-term care legislation at long last? *Health Affairs, 29*(1), 8–9.

Iglehart, J. K. (2010c, February). Medicaid expansion offers solutions, challenges. *Health Affairs, 29*(2), 230–232.

Kaiser Commission on Medicaid and the Uninsured. (2006, February). *Deficit Reduction Act of 2005: Implications for Medicaid.* Washington, DC: Author. Retrieved from http://www.kff.org/medicaid/ upload/7465.pdf

Kaiser Commission on Medicaid and the Uninsured. (2010a). *State Medicaid agencies prepare for health care reform while continuing to face challenges from the recession.* Washington, DC: Author. Retrieved from http://www.kff.org/medicaid/upload/8091.pdf

Kaiser Commission on Medicaid and the Uninsured. (2010b). *Medicaid's continuing crunch in a recession: A mid-year update for state FY 2010 and preview for FY 2011.* Washington, DC: Author. Retrieved from http://www.kff.org/medicaid/upload/8049.pdf

Kaiser Commission on Medicaid and the Uninsured. (2010c, July). *Expanding Medicaid to low-income childless adults under health reform: Key lessons from state experiences.* Washington, DC: Author. Retrieved from http://www.kff.org/medicaid/upload/8087.pdf

Kaiser Commission on Medicaid and the Uninsured. (n.d.). *Myths about the uninsured.* Washington, DC: Author.

Kaiser Family Foundation. (2006, January). *The public, managed care, and consumer protections.* Menlo Park, CA: Author. Retrieved from http://www.kff.org/spotlight/managedcare/upload/Spotlight_ Jan06_ManagedCare.pdf

Kaiser Family Foundation. (2010a). *Medicare: A primer 2010.* Menlo Park, CA: Author. Retrieved from http://www.kff.org/medicare/upload/7615-03.pdf

Kaiser Family Foundation. (2010b). *Medicaid: A primer 2010.* Menlo Park, CA: Author. Retrieved from http://www.kff.org/medicaid/upload/7334-04.pdf

Kaiser Family Foundation. (2010c, June 18). *Summary of new health reform law.* Menlo Park, CA: Author. Retrieved from http://www.kff.org/healthreform/upload/8061.pdf

Kaiser Family Foundation. (2010d, June 18). *Health reform implementation timeline.* Menlo Park, CA: Author. Retrieved from http://www.kff.org/healthreform/upload/8060.pdf

Kaiser Family Foundation and the Health Research and Educational Trust. (2009a). *Survey of employer health benefits 2009.* Menlo Park, CA: Author.

Kaiser Family Foundation and the Health Research and Educational Trust. (2009b). *Employer health benefits 2009 summary of findings.* Menlo Park, CA: Author.

Kongstvedt, P. R. (2007). *Essentials of managed health care.* Sudbury, MA: Jones & Bartlett.

Levit, K. R., Lazenby, H. C., Braden, B. R., Cowan, C. A., Sensenig, A. L., McDonnell, P. A., et al. (1997, Fall). National health expenditures, 1996. *Health Care Financing Review, 19,* 161–200.

Luo, M. (2010, March 26). Some states find burdens in health law. *New York Times.* Retrieved from http://www.nytimes.com/2010/03/27/health/policy/27impact.html?scp=1&sq=states+find+burdens+in+health+law&st=nyt

Miller, T. P. (2010, June). Health reform: Only a cease-fire in a political hundred years' war. *Health Affairs, 29*(6), 1101–1105.

National Center for Veterans Analysis and Statistics. (2010, April 28). *VA benefits & health care utilization.* Retrieved from http://www1.va.gov/VETDATA/Pocket-Card/4X6_spring10_sharepoint.pdf

National Governors Association and National Association of State Budget Officers. (2010, June). *The fiscal survey of states.* Washington, DC: National Association of State Budget Officers. Retrieved from http://www.nga.org/Files/pdf/FSS1006.PDF

Office of the Secretary of Defense. (n.d.). Health affairs senior leaders briefing.

Oliver, A. (2007). The Veterans Health Administration: An American success story. *The Milbank Quarterly, 85*(1), 5–35.

Pozgar, G. (2007). *Legal aspects of health care administration.* Sudbury, MA: Jones & Bartlett.

Purcell, P., & Staman, J. (2009, May 19). *Summary of the Employee Retirement Income Security Act (ERISA).* Washington, DC: Congressional Research Service. Retrieved from http://aging.senate.gov/crs/pension7.pdf

Rowland, D., Lyons, B., Salganicoff, A., & Long, P. (1994, Spring). A profile of the uninsured in America. *Health Affairs, 13*(2), 283–289.

Sack, K. (2010, July 27). Texas battles health law even as it follows it. *New York Times.* Retrieved from http://www.nytimes.com/2010/07/28/health/policy/28texas.html?scp=9&sq=kevin%20sack&st=cse

Schwartz, J. (2010, August 2). Virginia suit against health care law moves forward. *New York Times.* Retrieved from http://www.nytimes.com/2010/08/03/us/03virginia.html?scp=1&sq=virginia%20suit&st=cse

Span, P. (2010a, April 29). Details on the Class Act. *New York Times.* Retrieved from http://newoldage.blogs.nytimes.com/2010/04/29/details-on-the-class-act/

Span, P. (2010b, May 3). Details on the Class Act, pt. 2. *New York Times.* Retrieved from http://newoldage.blogs.nytimes.com/2010/05/03/details-on-the-class-act-pt-2/

Span, P. (2010c, May 3). Parsing the new law on long-term care. *New York Times.* Retrieved from http://www.nytimes.com/2010/05/04/health/policy/04land.html?_r=1&ref=the_new_landscape

Starr, P. (1982). *The social transformation of American medicine.* New York, NY: Basic Books.

TRICARE. (2007). *Anytime, anywhere, keeping warfighters ready, for life: 2007 TRICARE stakeholders report.* Falls Church, VA: TRICARE Management Activity. Retrieved from http://www.tricare.mil/stakeholders/downloads/stakeholders_2007.pdf

TRICARE. (2008). *Caring for America's heroes: 2008 MHS stakeholders' report.* Falls Church, VA: TRICARE Management Activity. Retrieved from http://www.tricare.mil/stakeholders/2007/downloads/stakeholders_2008.pdf

TRICARE. (2010a). *Sharing knowledge: Achieving breakthrough performance: 2010 MHS stakeholders' report.* Falls Church, VA: TRICARE Management Activity. Retrieved from http://www.tricare .mil/stakeholders/downloads/2010stakeholders-final.pdf

TRICARE. (2010b). *TRICARE for life.* Retrieved from http://www.military.com/benefits/tricare/ tricare-for-life/tricare-for-life-and-dual-eligibility

Truffer, C. J., Keehan, S., Smith, S., Cylus, J., Sisko, A., Poisal, J. A., et al. (2010, March). Health spend- ing projections through 2010: The recession's impact continues. *Health Affairs, 29*(3), 522–529.

Truffer, C. J., Klemm, J. D., Hoffman, E. D., & Wolfe, C. J. (2008, October). *2008 actuarial report on the financial outlook for Medicaid.* Washington, DC: CMS. Retrieved from http://www.centerforself- determination.com/docs/MedicaidReport2008.pdf

U.S. Census Bureau. (2009). *Health Insurance Historical Tables.* Retrieved from http://www.census.gov/ hhes/www/hlthins/data/historical/original.html

U.S. Department of Veterans Affairs. (2009a, January). *Facts about the Department of Veterans Affairs.* Retrieved from http://www1.va.gov/opa/publications/factsheets/fs_department_of_veterans_ affairs.pdf

U.S. Department of Veterans Affairs. (2009b, September 15). *All enrollment priority groups.* Retrieved from http://www4.va.gov/healtheligibility/eligibility/PriorityGroupsAll.asp

U.S. Department of Veterans Affairs, Health Administration Center. (2009, June). *Fact sheet 01-06: The spina bifida health care program.* Retrieved from http://www4.va.gov/hac/factsheets/spina/ FactSheet01-06.pdf

U.S. Department of Veterans Affairs, Veterans Health Administration Office of Quality and Perfor- mance. (2005). *VA's performance compared to non-VA.* Retrieved from the VA Intranet website.

Wachino, V. (2007, June). *The new Medicaid integrity program: Issues and challenges in ensuring program integrity in Medicaid—Executive summary.* Menlo Park, CA: Kaiser Family Foundation. Retrieved from http://www.kff.org/medicaid/upload/7650ES.pdf

Wilensky, G. R. (2006, January/February). Consumer-driven health plans: Early evidence and potential impact on hospitals. *Health Affairs, 25*(1), 174–185.

Managing Costs and Revenues

Kevin D. Zeiler

LEARNING OBJECTIVES

By the end of this chapter, the student will be able to:

- Describe the importance, purpose, and major objectives of financial management in healthcare organizations;
- Understand tax status implications of for-profit versus not-for-profit healthcare entities;
- Assess the primary methods of reimbursement to providers;
- Apply methods for classifying and controlling costs;
- Evaluate determinants and initial processes considered by healthcare managers in setting charges/prices for products and services;
- Define the purposes, primary sources, and major problems associated with managing working capital;
- Identify some of the important issues and major processes involved in managing accounts receivable in healthcare organizations;
- Describe the importance, basic tenets, and commonly accepted methods for managing materials and inventory; and
- Analyze the major characteristics and types of budgets utilized by healthcare managers.

INTRODUCTION

The purpose of this chapter is to give a general overview of the various components of financial management within healthcare organizations, providing examples and applications. Students in healthcare management and administration frequently become apprehensive about dealing with the financial management aspects of the field. However, it cannot be emphasized enough that an understanding of finance is critical to any student who desires to better understand the business function. The entry-level management position will, at the very least, require an understanding and grasp of the basic concepts of accounting and finance principles, budgets, and forecasting goals and techniques. Each section of this chapter will provide an overview that will help with future studies and lay the groundwork for continued research and application.

WHAT IS FINANCIAL MANAGEMENT AND WHY IS IT IMPORTANT?

Healthcare financial management is the process of providing oversight for the healthcare organization's day-to-day financial operations as well as planning the organization's long-range financial direction. Put simply, it involves working to increase the revenues and decrease the costs of the organization. This involves making organizational forecasts, while taking into consideration numerous external environmental variables such as the economy, insurance company policy changes, legislative rules and regulations, and so on. These can have profound impacts on the financial forecast. Ultimately, it is the goal of the finance department to put the organization in the best position possible.

Finally, in the dawn of healthcare reform, all students, health providers, and financial personnel must understand that financial management will be an ever-changing field that will continually be affected by outside influences. According to a recent poll concerning healthcare reform, "Nearly three-quarters of healthcare executives say healthcare reform will have a negative financial impact on their facilities, according to an AMN Healthcare poll" (Ledue, 2010, p. 1). This statement does not mean that reform is going to ruin the industry; instead, it means that the savvy financial manager will need to stay on top of industry changes in order to maintain the financial health of the organization.

Most healthcare organizations attempt to meet their economic goals by charging their finance departments with both accounting and finance tasks. These functions help to establish the groundwork for reaching the aforementioned goals.

Accounting consists of two types:

1. **Managerial accounting**, in which financial data are provided concurrently or prospectively to internal users (managers, executives, and the organization's governing board); and

2. **Financial accounting**, in which data are provided retrospectively to external users (stockholders, lenders, insurers, government, suppliers).

Finance generally includes:
1. Borrowing and investing funds; and
2. Analyzing accounting information to evaluate past decisions and make sound decisions that will affect the future of the organization.

While Nowicki (2004, p. 4) emphasizes financial management's primary purpose as being "to provide both accounting and finance information that assists healthcare managers in accomplishing the organization's purposes." Berger (2002, p. 7) takes this description of purpose one step further by noting that "a primary role of financial management [is] helping to analyze the financial implications of the data across the healthcare organization's setting." The latter implies the importance of involving managers at *all* levels of the organization in financial analysis and decision making. For example, the manager in the radiology unit of a hospital should be directly involved in looking at both the **revenues** generated by procedures (X-rays, ultrasound procedures, CT scans, etc.) performed in the department and the **expenses** incurred in running the department, in addition to being involved in hiring personnel, managing appropriate staffing ratios, making decisions involving the replacement or purchase of equipment, and so on.

TAX STATUS OF HEALTHCARE ORGANIZATIONS

In order to fully comprehend the financial needs and constraints of any given healthcare organization, it is important to first determine the tax status of that organization. Although healthcare organizations are primarily categorized as either for-profit or not-for-profit, Berger (2002) discusses three major types: one for-profit and two not-for-profit. For the student's clearer understanding, they have been arranged somewhat differently below, and additional comments have been included:

- **For-profit, investor-owned healthcare organizations:** These organizations are owned by investors or others who have an interest in making a profit from the services that are provided. These are normally viewed as the for-profit organizations that are required to pay taxes as a cost of doing business. Traditionally, this has included most physician practices and skilled nursing facilities.
- **Not-for-profit healthcare organizations:** Historically, these organizations have taken care of the poor, needy, and indigent residents of communities and thus have been granted **tax-exempt status**. They include the following two groups:
  1. **Business-oriented (private) organizations**, which are characterized as private enterprises with no ownership interests, that are self-sustaining from fees

charged for goods and services, are exempt from income taxes and may receive tax-deductible contributions from those who support their mission, and must provide a certain amount of charity care or community service. Based on their relationships with religiously affiliated organizations, it is not surprising that this group has included an overwhelming majority of hospitals.

2. **Government-owned organizations and public corporations**, which are influenced by political interests but are exempt from taxation and have the ability to issue directly (rather than through a state or municipal authority) debt that pays interest exempt from federal taxation. Included in this group are government-owned hospitals (especially research and training institutions or those serving the medically indigent) and public health clinics.

In addition, there are significant differences in financial management goals based on tax status, which can be summarized as follows:

- **Financial goals in for-profit organizations:** According to Berman, Weeks, and Kukla (1986, p. 4), "management must administer the assets of the enterprise in order to obtain the greatest wealth for the owner." That is, the goal is to maximize earnings and profits while minimizing risk to the organization.

- **Financial goals in not-for-profit organizations:** According to Berger (2002, p. 6), while these entities must still "produce the best possible bottom line . . . they simply need to do so in the context of providing optimal patient care in the most efficient manner." However, both Berger and Nowicki (2004) emphasize that nonprofit healthcare providers still place somewhat greater emphasis on community services and other social goals.

Table 10-1 delineates the primary differences between for-profit and not-for-profit healthcare organizations.

FINANCIAL GOVERNANCE AND RESPONSIBILITY STRUCTURE

The organizational structures of these healthcare organizations may also be affected by their tax status, although the largest differences are probably seen in the structures of their governing bodies, or **boards of directors or trustees**. While similar types of professionals (or "volunteers," in the case of not-for-profit boards) are specifically charged with financial accountability and stewardship, in smaller organizations one individual may perform several of the separate functions. Knowing the organizational structure of the financial components of the organization will allow all managers to access the appropriate individual(s)

TABLE 10-1 Comparison of For-Profit and Not-for-Profit Organizations

For-Profit	Not-for-Profit
Serve private interests	Serve public or community interests
Pay federal and state income taxes on profits, state and local sales taxes, and property taxes	Are exempt from taxes; healthcare organizations receive 501(c)(3) designation if they meet federal IRS criteria
Must file an annual for-profit tax return	Must file the IRS 990 annual corporate tax return, including a community services benefits report
Are motivated by profit, with income benefitting individuals	Revenues cannot benefit individuals, beyond payment of reasonable salaries
Must pay business fees	Are exempt from paying most business fees and licenses
Must adhere to taxable bond yields	Can access tax-exempt bond markets to raise capital
May participate in political campaigns and influence legislation	May not participate in political campaigns or influence legislation
Able to issue stock to raise capital and offer stock options to recruit and retain staff	May not issue stock or offer stock options to staff
Have limited obligation to provide indigent care	Must provide designated amounts of community benefit, including indigent care

in order to make judicious financial decisions for their departments or divisions. In order of responsibility:

- **The Governing Body, or Board of Directors:** As described by the American Hospital Association (1990) and reiterated by Nowicki (2004, p. 30), in its "fiduciary" role (persons in a position of trust), the board is ultimately "responsible for the proper development, utilization, and maintenance of all resources in the healthcare organization." In for-profit organizations, board members may be paid, but board members serve strictly as "volunteers" in not-for-profit organizations.
- **The chief executive officer (CEO)** is hired and delegated authority by the board and serves as chief administrator of the operations of the entire organization. The CEO's fiscal performance is monitored through the board's Finance Committee.
- **The chief operating officer (COO)**, often the senior vice president, is responsible for the day-to-day operations of the organization.
- **The chief financial officer (CFO)**, who may also serve as a vice president, is responsible for the entire financial management function of the organization. The CFO is in charge of two primary financial branches, involving (1) the accounting function

and (2) management of financial assets. The CFO directly supervises two officers (and occasionally one other) directly in charge of these functions. In some organizations, the COO and the CFO may be the same person.

- **The controller (also called the comptroller)** is the chief accounting officer responsible for the accounting and reporting functions, including financial record keeping. He or she oversees such departments and activities as patient accounts, accounts payable, accounts receivable, cost analysis, budgets, tax status, the generation of financial reports, and sometimes internal auditing.

- **The treasurer** is charged with the stewardship of the organization's financial assets, including cash management, commercial bank relations, investment portfolios, management of pensions or endowment funds, capital expenditures, management of working capital, and long-term debt obligations.

- **The internal auditor** is often a separate staff position from the CFO in large healthcare organizations and is responsible for ensuring that the accounting, bookkeeping, and reporting processes are performed in accordance with **generally accepted accounting principles (GAAP)**, the nationally accepted rules that determine how financial information is recorded and reported. GAAP includes, among other things, the overarching ideas of conservatism, consistency, and matching of revenues and costs. The internal auditor protects the organization's assets from fraud, error, and loss.

- **The chief information officer (CIO)**, present in many large healthcare organizations, is the corporate officer responsible for all information and data processing systems, including medical records, data processing, medical information systems, and admitting. The CIO reports either to the CFO or directly to the CEO.

- **The independent auditor**, generally a large accounting firm, is retained by the healthcare organization to ensure that all financial reports sent to external entities are accurate as to format, content, and scope in presenting the organization's true financial position.

- **All managers** in a healthcare organization are financial managers to the extent that they consider asset selection, charges, financing, reimbursement, and/or department budgets. This shared responsibility at all levels of the organization serves to maximize efficiency and accountability.

MANAGING REIMBURSEMENTS FROM THIRD-PARTY PAYERS

One of the major objectives of financial management involves facilitating and managing **third-party reimbursements**, which is vital to generating revenues for the daily operations, growth, and competitiveness of the healthcare organization. This section will discuss both the methods of payment to providers by managed care organizations (MCOs) and other private insurers and reimbursements to providers from public entities such as Medicare and Medicaid.

What Are the Primary Methods of Payment Used by Private Health Plans for Reimbursing Providers?

Private healthcare plans use a variety of methods for reimbursing the providers servicing the plan's enrollees. Some are utilized more frequently than others for payments to different provider groups. They are classified according to the amount of financial risk assumed by healthcare organizations and whether reimbursements are determined after or before healthcare services are delivered.

Retrospective Reimbursement

Under **retrospective reimbursement**, the amount of reimbursement is determined after the delivery of services, providing little financial risk to providers in most cases. It can involve the following methods:

- **Charges**, most commonly called **fee-for-service:** Healthcare providers are paid close to or at 100% of their submitted prices or rates for care provided. Because there is virtually no financial risk to providers, these are no longer common. Where full charges persist is with private-pay patients and uninsured individuals, who do not have insurance companies to negotiate discounted rates on their behalf.
- **Charges minus a discount** or **percentage of charges:** Healthcare organizations offer discounted charges to third parties in return for large numbers of patients. This is the second most common form of reimbursement to hospitals.
- **Cost plus a percentage for growth:** Healthcare institutions receive the cost for care provided, plus a small percentage to develop new services and products.
- **Cost:** The organization is reimbursed for the projected cost, expressed as a percentage of charges. While this method provides the smallest amount of reimbursement to providers, there is little risk unless full costs (**direct costs of providing care plus indirect costs or overhead for running the organization**) are not recognized.
- **Reimbursement modified on the basis of performance:** The provider is reimbursed based on quality measures, patient satisfaction measures, and so on. Obviously, this method poses more risk for providers.

Prospective Reimbursement

This method of reimbursement to providers is established before the services are provided to patients. These are the primary methods utilized by managed care organizations (MCOs):

- **Per diem**, in which a defined dollar amount per day for care is provided. This is the most common method of reimbursement to hospitals. It presents risks and incentives.

It tends to be bad for acute-only patients, for whom greater costs are incurred earlier in care without the opportunity to make up differences later, when less intense services may be needed.

- **Per diagnosis**, in which a defined dollar amount is paid per diagnosis. It provides risks and incentives. Most common are those similar to the rates utilized by CMS (Centers for Medicare & Medicaid) for Medicare reimbursements, including **DRGs (Diagnosis-Related Groups)** for hospitals, **RUGs (Resource Utilization Groups)** for nursing homes, and **HHRGs (Home Health Resource Groups)** for home health care. Additional rates have more recently been determined for outpatient and inpatient rehabilitation hospital services. In virtually all cases, fewer patient treatments or visits, and/or shorter hospital stays, are now being provided for any given diagnosis.

- **Bundles for hospital and physician services**, in which a fixed amount is paid by the MCO for treatment of a patient and is to be shared by all providers.

- **Fee schedule by CPT (Current Procedural Terminology) code, or procedure code**, which is the most common method for reimbursement of specialty physicians. In general, the more complex and time-consuming the procedure, the higher the rate of reimbursement.

- **Capitation**, which is an agreement under which a healthcare provider is paid a fixed amount per enrollee per month by a health plan in exchange for a contractually specified set of medical services in the future. Negotiated capitated payments are based on perceptions of expenses for a population. Thus, capitation shifts the risk of coverage from the insurer to the provider of care, providing the most financial risk but also the most opportunity. It is the most common reimbursement method for primary care physicians in MCOs, providing penalties and withholdings for too much care and bonuses as an incentive for ordering lower levels of care.

The third-party reimbursement system in the healthcare arena has become so complex that many healthcare providers (including hospitals and large physician practices) have been forced to hire employees specializing in different contract types within their insurance/finance departments to negotiate the labyrinth of rules and regulations. Accuracy is critical in today's healthcare industry, where improper coding or billing or untimely filing can lead to missed opportunity—or charges of fraud. Thus, reimbursement is a form of risk for the organization. Simply put, think about the risk as the way in which reimbursement affects profits and how it is uncertain (Gapenski, 2009). Remember, finance is forecasting, so you can see how a complex reimbursement system can and will affect an organization financially if billing is not done correctly.

What Are the Primary Methods of Payment Used for Reimbursing Providers by Medicare and Medicaid?

As discussed in Chapter 9, the largest government-sponsored healthcare programs in the United States are **Medicare and Medicaid**. Different methods are used to provide reimbursement to various providers of care by these programs, as discussed further below. The current regulations regarding reimbursement to providers in these programs are, however, reflective of various cost-containment efforts. It is also worth mentioning that health reform will also affect Medicare and Medicaid by creating the **Center for Medicare and Medicaid Innovation (CMI)**, which is in place to test innovative payment and service delivery models (Shafrin, 2010). As you enter the field or continue to study healthcare finance, keep in mind that reimbursement will continue to change and adapt to the numerous factors listed earlier in this chapter. Cost containment issues will continue to arise and will continue to force financial managers to adapt and change to this volatile environment.

Reimbursement to Hospitals and Contractual Allowances

Due to rapidly rising healthcare expenditures based on an initial retrospective, charge-based reimbursement system to providers, Congress passed the Tax Equity and Fiscal Responsibility Act (TEFRA) in 1982, with particular emphasis on Medicare cost controls. Included among its provisions was a mandate to hospitals for a prospective payment system (PPS) with reimbursement rates established up front for certain conditions, the option of providing managed care plans to Medicare beneficiaries, and the requirement that Medicare become the secondary payer when a beneficiary has other insurance.

Like most third-party payers for hospital services, the Centers for Medicare & Medicaid Services (CMS) substantially reduces reimbursement to hospitals (from original hospital charges to beneficiaries) based on a system of contractual allowances. As defined by McLean (2003, p. 53), a **contractual allowance** is the "difference between the charge for a bed-day in the adult medicine unit and the amount that the hospital has agreed to accept from the patient's insurance carrier."

In the case of Medicare-eligible patients, CMS reimburses a fixed amount per admission and per diagnosis, based on the patient's **Diagnosis-Related Group**, or **DRG**. For example, a patient being admitted for heart bypass surgery would receive a higher reimbursement rate than a patient admitted for observation after a fall in which he or she suffered a fractured humerus (arm bone). Berger (2002, p. 127) asserts that the International Classification of Diseases, ninth edition (ICD-9 codes) was "the most important element" in creating the DRG for reimbursement of an inpatient stay. Furthermore, the Omnibus Budget Reconciliation Act of 1990 later folded capital costs into DRG rates as well, with hospitals risking significant reimbursement losses if their buildings and equipment are not properly utilized (Nowicki, 2004).

On the other hand, the Medicaid reimbursement rate to hospitals for any given service varies from state to state, but in all cases includes a substantial contractual allowance. Individual states implement cost controls for Medicaid payments, using either DRGs (like Medicare) or case mix to set reimbursement rates. **Case mix**, also referred to as **patient mix**, is usually related to the mix of patients served by an organization based on the severity of illnesses. An example of differences in this type of reimbursement would be a nursing unit primarily serving patients on ventilators that would be reimbursed at a substantially higher rate than a nursing unit serving patients with orthopedic problems, due to the greater expenses incurred by the former. In all cases, providers must accept reimbursement as payment in full and follow designated efficiency and quality standards.

Reimbursement to Physicians

A **Resource-Based Relative Value System (RBRVS)** was implemented in 1992 for reimbursement for physician office services rendered to Medicare beneficiaries. This system pays a prospective flat fee for physician visits and is based on **HCPCS (Healthcare Common Procedure Coding System)** codes used by outpatient healthcare providers and medical suppliers to code their professional services and supplies. Current Procedural Terminology (CPT) (American Medical Association, 2010) is the generally accepted coding methodology utilized. An example of this system is the higher reimbursement rate afforded to a physician for an extended initial patient visit to fully assess a patient's medical condition, versus the lower reimbursement provided for a brief follow-up visit to assess how well a prescribed medication was working.

Similarly, state Medicaid programs have implemented cost controls for reimbursement to physicians, initially through fee schedules, but with many states more recently requiring beneficiaries to enroll in capitated managed care plans. As defined by Gapenski (2003, p. 576), **capitation** is "a flat periodic payment per enrollee to a healthcare provider; it is the sole reimbursement for providing defined services to a defined population. . . . Generally, capitation payments are expressed as some dollar amount per member per month (PMPM)."

Medicare Reimbursements to Other Providers

Despite reductions in reimbursements for hospital admissions and physician visits, Medicare expenditures continued to soar throughout the 1990s. Congress passed the Balanced Budget Act of 1997 in an attempt to control costs for other healthcare services. Prospective payment systems were implemented in other settings beginning in 1998, as follows:

- **Skilled nursing facilities (SNFs)**, in 1998, with RUGs (Resource Utilization Groups);

- **Home health agencies (HHAs)**, in 2000, with HHRGs (Home Health Resource Groups); and
- **Outpatient hospitals and clinics**, in 2002, with OPPS (Outpatient Prospective Payment System).

How Are Providers Reimbursed by Private Pay Patients and Individuals with No Health Insurance?

As discussed above, those individuals who are not covered by any type of health plan, whether private or public, are often billed for full charges (generally well above costs) by the healthcare organization delivering the care. This is largely due to the inability of the individual to negotiate a discounted rate for his or her care that is usually afforded patients covered by group health plans. This phenomenon has had the consequence of substantially increasing the number of personal bankruptcies related to medical bills. As revealed in a frequently cited article in the journal *Health Affairs*, approximately half of the 1.458 million personal bankruptcies filed in 2001 were related to medical bills caused by injury and illness (Himmelstein, Warren, Thorne, & Woolhandler, 2005). As a direct result, there have been increases in the amount of uncompensated, or unreimbursed, care.

Not-covered, or uncompensated, care is a measure of total hospital care provided without payment from the patient or an insurer. This accounted for 5.6% of hospital total expenses in 2004, down from 6.2% in 1999 (American Hospital Association, 2005). The two major types include:

- **Bad debt**, in which the healthcare organization bills for services but receives no payment. These operating expenses are based on charges, not costs, and are written off by the organization. This term is usually used with for-profit organizations.
- **Charity care**, in which the not-for-profit organization provides care to a patient who it knows will be unable to pay. Level of charity care (based on either costs or charges) must be documented in footnotes to the financial statements; otherwise, the organization's tax status can be questioned.

Although uncompensated care may be written off as bad debt or charity care by the healthcare organization, and although it is even required to a certain extent with a not-for-profit organization to maintain its 501(c)(3) status, it is important for managers to recognize that providing too much of this type of care could serve to financially cripple the organization, both in terms of difficulty in maintaining current operations and inability to maximize investment opportunities. Some for-profit organizations question the tax status of not-for-profit organizations and their ability to write off debt as "charity care." They also decry the use of the term "bad debt," because it implies that the manager who extended the credit used poor judgment. This is a controversial topic and one that bears watching.

CONTROLLING COSTS AND COST ACCOUNTING

Historically, healthcare organizations, especially hospitals, have been provided strong financial incentives to maximize reimbursements rather than to control costs. However, as can be seen in the preceding discussion, there has been a major movement during much of the past two decades to decrease the levels of reimbursement to providers in almost all sectors of the industry. It has thus become increasingly important for healthcare organizations to understand how to estimate and manage their costs. This changing environment has also resulted in separation of "cost accounting systems from financial accounting systems" and movement "from traditional allocation-based cost systems to activity-based cost systems" (Zelman, McCue, Millikan, & Glick, 2003, p. 15).

While Nowicki (2004, p. 145) describes its purpose as providing managers with cost information for such reasons as "setting charges and profitability analysis," it is important to note that cost accounting ultimately leads to decision making. This might include enhancing departments that are making money, eliminating services that are losing money, and carefully managing loss leaders (i.e., procedures provided cheaply or below cost to attract customers to the organization). Cost accounting also provides methods for classifying and allocating costs, as well as more precisely determining product costs, all of which will be described briefly in this section.

Classifying Costs

Although there are a number of ways in which costs may be classified, the purpose of Table 10-2 is to illustrate a sampling of the most frequently utilized methods. The importance of such systems is merely to provide a point of departure for controlling costs.

While many authors provide a concise summary of the major methods of classifying costs, such as those shown in Table 10-2 (Nowicki, 2004; Zelman et al., 2003), they do not show how these classifications are often combined by managerial accountants to demonstrate the complexity of cost analysis within healthcare organizations. For example, concerning salaries and wages in hospitals, the salaries of radiology department managers are both direct and fixed, the wages of on-call nurses are direct but variable, and the salaries of the CEO and CFO are fixed but indirect.

Allocating Costs

Cost allocation involves the determination of the total cost of producing a specified healthcare service through assigning costs into revenue-producing departments and then further allocating the costs down to the unit-of-service or procedure level based either on departmental revenue or volume. The purpose of this methodology is:

- To ensure that patients are paying [theoretically] "for only the costs of the services and products they received" (Nowicki, 2004, p. 147) and

- "To separate costs at the unit-of-service level to allow managers to:
  - Measure the effects of change in intensity and case mix;
  - Identify those costs that can be converted from fixed to variable; and
  - Identify inefficient functions and demonstrate the nature of the problem, such as price, volume, or practice" (Berger, 2002, p. 216).

Although a number of methods have been identified for cost-allocation purposes, in each case the process ends when all of the organization's costs (including those generated in non-revenue-producing departments, such as housekeeping and medical records) are allocated to the cost centers of revenue-producing departments (radiology, pediatrics, and so forth). These methods have been widely used for pricing and reimbursement purposes in the past but are beginning to be replaced by more accurate methods of determining product costs.

TABLE 10-2 Frequently Utilized Methods of Classifying Costs

METHOD	CLASSIFICATION	EXAMPLE
By behavior	Fixed costs—stay the same in relation to changes in volume of services	Electricity for lighting
	Variable costs—change directly in relation to changes in volume	Number of sutures used to close incisions
	Semivariable costs—partially fixed and partially variable	Labor costs are the same for patients 1–8; then with The Joint Commission standards, need another RN to take care of the ninth person
By traceability	Direct costs—can be traced to a particular patient, product, or service	Gauze pads used in dressing a wound
	Indirect costs, aka overhead—cannot be traced to a particular patient or service	Amount of water used during a typical hospital stay
	Full costs—both direct costs and indirect costs	Treatments provided plus utilities used
By decision-making capability	Controllable costs—under the manager's influence	Wages of certified nursing assistants (CNAs) per shift
	Uncontrollable costs—cannot be controlled by the manager	Upper administrative hours allocated to department
	Sunk costs—already incurred and cannot be influenced further	Cost of insurance paid in advance
	Opportunity costs—proceeds lost by rejecting alternatives	No purchase of X-ray machine if money spent on new ultrasound machine

Determining Product Costs

A number of methods for determining **product costs** (e.g., home health visits or patient days) have been posed, each of which crosses department lines of responsibility. However, one method, **activity-based costing (the ABC method)**, has enjoyed increasing popularity in healthcare organizations because of its greater accuracy. This change in methodology is also due to the fact that cost allocations are no longer made on the basis of **cost center characteristics** (e.g., number of office visits or percentage of square feet) but rather on the basis of **cost drivers**, or "the activities that go on in preparation for and during a unit of service" (McLean, 1997, p. 142). As explained by Zelman et al. (2003, p. 426), "ABC is based on the paradigm that activities consume resources and products consume activities. Therefore, if activities or processes are controlled, then costs will be controlled."

Break-Even Analysis

The ultimate goal of managing costs is minimally to break even and not run a deficit. **Break-even analysis** is the method of determining at what level of volume the production of a good or service will equal the revenues created. It is used by healthcare managers for the purpose of determining profit or loss. The **break-even point** is the volume of production in units and sale of goods or services where total costs equal total revenue. As noted by Nowicki (2004, p. 159), "After the break-even point has been reached and fixed costs have been covered, each subsequent unit produced contributes to profit." McLean (2003), however, emphasizes that the break-even quantity (e.g., total number of visits) does not necessarily need to be reached for a healthcare organization to decide to keep a specified service. He states, "If [a] unit covers its direct costs (fixed and variable) and makes any contribution to overhead, it is worth keeping, even in the long run," since the organization would incur overhead expenses even without the unit (McLean, 2003, p. 142). In the long run, "if the unit cannot meet its own (direct) total costs, it should be eliminated unless some outside entity or another revenue center is to subsidize it" (McLean, 2003, p. 142).

SETTING CHARGES

Only after costs have been determined can healthcare organizations go about the business of **setting rates or charges** for their services and products. While the earlier section on "Managing Reimbursements from Third-Party Payers" describes a number of methods used by third-party payers and healthcare organizations to negotiate payments for services, a more complete picture of what is involved when setting charges should be taken into consideration by any provider.

A first step in this discussion might be to differentiate the meanings of charges versus actual prices set by the organization. *Pam Pohly's Net Guide*, in its "Glossary of

Terms in Managed Health Care," defines "charges" in terms of "**published prices**" (Pohly, 2005).

Prices in health care, on the other hand, involve opportunity costs, what consumers or third-party payers give up in order to acquire medical goods or services, including:

- Money actually spent and
- The perceived value of:
  - These goods or services;
  - Time sacrificed in acquiring these services; and
  - Other opportunities forgone (purchases, activities).

In other words, charges posted by the organization do not necessarily translate into actual prices paid for services.

Other Determinants of Setting Charges and Prices

Although not claiming to be all-inclusive, the following factors are provided to make sure that the healthcare manager gives due consideration to each when involved in setting prices for services or products.

- State and federal laws and regulations;
- The Joint Commission and other accrediting body regulations;
- Antitrust and other fair-pricing laws; and
- Profit-oriented pricing, including profit maximization, satisfactory profits, or break-even strategies.

Setting charges or rates remains a highly complex activity within any healthcare organization due to the need to consider a huge number of variables, both internal and external to the organization. While individual healthcare managers may be involved in providing substantial input into this process, larger organizations employ experts dedicated to this task in order to sustain revenue maximization and competitiveness in the healthcare market.

MANAGING WORKING CAPITAL

"**Working capital** refers both to **current assets**," that is, inventory, cash on hand, accounts receivable, and other such items that can be converted to cash in less than one year, "and to **current liabilities**," meaning "those liabilities that will be paid within the current accounting period" (McLean, 2003, p. 288). Virtually all experts, however, define net working capital as "current assets minus current liabilities," a concept that seems to remind us that healthcare organizations are never without accumulation of debt.

What Are the Purposes of Working Capital Management?

There are two sets of purposes in managing working capital. The end result of the first set of purposes is to increase revenues and reduce expenses in order to:

- **Serve as the "catalyst"** to make capital assets (buildings and equipment) productive by wisely managing such current assets as labor and inventory.
- **Control the volume of resources** committed to current assets. McLean (2003, p. 288) states that "financing working capital by the least costly means available can allow one's organization to deliver the same amount of care at lower cost, or can allow an organization with a limited budget to deliver a greater amount of care."
- **Conserve cash** by cutting the organization's financing costs in order to take advantage of short-term investments.
- **Manage cash flow,** that is, the amount of inflows and outflows, and the cash conversion cycle, which is the process (measured in days) through which initial cash is converted into the inventory, labor, and supplies needed in healthcare operations that in turn generate accounts receivable and that finally are collected in the form of cash revenues.
- **Manage the liquidity** of an organization, that is, "how quickly assets can be converted into cash" (Zelman et al., 2003, p. 488).
- The second set of purposes involves enhancing "**goodwill**" toward the organization by:
  - Paying vendors and employees on time and
  - Demonstrating to lenders that the organization is "creditworthy" by showing it has sufficient resources to repay loans or at least pay interest on short-term funds.

Why Is Working Capital Management in Healthcare Environments Problematic?

Managing working capital tends to be more problematic with healthcare organizations because, with the exception of patient copays, which are miniscule in the big picture of the organization's finances, healthcare organizations generate very little immediate cash. This is largely due to the huge preponderance of third-party payers and the substantial delays in payment. Also, even if paid by private parties, the large costs incurred for most medical services result in payment after the billing cycle, by credit card, or in negotiated installments.

Another area of concern for many healthcare financial managers is how best to make decisions in managing working capital when faced with such a wide array of options. Even new and inexperienced managers might take heart by heeding the advice of Sachdeva and Gitman (1981, p. 45), who offer a simple decision rule when faced with alternative choices between possible means of managing current assets and liabilities: "Undertake changes in working capital management practices that *add value* to the organization."

MANAGING ACCOUNTS RECEIVABLE

Accounts receivable (AR) have been defined as a "current asset, created in the course of doing business, consisting of revenues recognized, but not yet collected as cash" (McLean, 2003, p. 352). Zelman et al. (2003, p. 175) estimate that AR comprise "approximately 75 percent of a healthcare provider's current assets." Also called "**patient accounts**" in many healthcare organizations, accounts receivable provide no interest for the provider unless they have been converted into interest-bearing loans to allow patients to pay out their debts for services over time. Therefore, management of AR becomes exceedingly important in order to collect revenues generated to ensure cash flow for management of the operations of the organization. It is essential to note that the ultimate collection of AR becomes less likely as the amount of time since services were rendered increases. More and more providers are becoming aggressive about collecting these revenues, sometimes resorting to telephone scripts more typical of collection agencies to obtain payments.

Major Steps in Accounts Receivable Management

Managing accounts receivable involves collaboration and cooperation among almost all departments of a healthcare organization, although some departments are more directly involved than others. Table 10-3 provides examples of involvement in a typical hospital setting.

TABLE 10-3 Hospital Departmental Involvement in Managing Accounts Receivable

Department	AR Involvement
Contracts	Relationships and contract negotiation with third-party payers
Admissions/registration	Precertification, preadmission, insurance verification
Patient care unit (nursing, lab, radiology, rehab, etc.)	Documentation capture, charge capture for services rendered
Medical records	Coding, utilization review, QA (quality assurance audits)
Billing	Bill preparation, billing audits
Compliance	Fraud and abuse internal audits
Collections	Collection policy and procedures, financial counseling, third-party, and self-pay follow-up
Legal	Contracts, litigation policy, federal regulations, patient rights

Some additional thoughts and clarification are warranted concerning the "overriding importance" of managing accounts receivable in all departments:

- **Documentation capture** emphasizes the importance of the quality of the written record of patient care by all healthcare professionals.
- Ultimately**, interdependence among departments** affects the reduction in the AR collection period. For example, accurate documentation supports the coding, and the timeliness of the coding greatly affects the ability of the billing department to send out a timely bill. Cooperation among managers is essential.
- **AR outcomes** are often measured by first determining a baseline of the progress to be measured and then monitoring the outcomes periodically by looking at the organization's balance sheet and income statements. This process is often referred to as "benchmarking," in which the current year's results can be measured against prior results to see whether things are getting better or worse.

MANAGING MATERIALS AND INVENTORY

Formerly referred to as "**inventory management**" and more recently designated as "**supply chain management**," materials management refers to the process of managing the clinical and nonclinical goods and inventory purchased and used by the personnel of a healthcare organization in order to perform their duties.

Why Is Materials Management Important?

There are at least three important reasons why materials management is so important to the healthcare organization. The first involves delivery of appropriate patient care, for which the organization must have the right kind and right amount of supplies, delivered in the right time frame. Stock-outs (not having enough of a product) are considered totally unacceptable in healthcare organizations, as they may result in unnecessary deaths or poor outcomes. A second reason involves cost control. Inventory, a nonproductive asset, loses value over time, increasing the costs to the healthcare facility. If items spend too much time in inventory, they may become contaminated, lost, stolen (referred to as "shrinkage"), or expired. Furthermore, cash tied up in excessive inventory cannot be used for assets that produce income. The third reason involves improvement of the organization's profitability. Skillful materials management can improve the organization's bottom line through such techniques as reducing utilization of overused supplies, obtaining best pricing for supplies and equipment through negotiation, and standardizing the organization's supplies to provide purchasing discounts (Berger, 2002).

What Are the Basic Tenets of Materials Management?

It is also important to adopt the most appropriate method for stocking inventory. This includes keeping a safety stock level of inventory, below which the healthcare facility will not allow units on hand to fall. It further involves understanding and adopting one of the commonly accepted methods for valuing inventory:

- **FIFO, or "first-in, first-out,"** in which the first item put in inventory is the first taken out; it produces an inventory of newer items and thus values the cost of inventory at the price paid for the newest items;
- **LIFO, or "last-in, first-out,"** in which the last item put in inventory is the first taken out; it produces an inventory of older items and thus values the cost of inventory at the price paid for the oldest items;
- **Weighted average,** in which the average cost of inventory items is multiplied by the number of units in inventory; and
- **Specific identification,** in which the actual cost of each item is included. This tends to be used with high-cost (and relatively few) items.

Finally, adopting the most appropriate method for stocking inventory includes application of either the **JIT or ABC inventory methods** in terms of when to order or deliver products to the healthcare facility:

- **Just-in-time (JIT):** With this technique, products are literally delivered to the organization "just in time" for use. This method is preferred by Berger (2002, p. 306) in order to decrease the "chance for obsolescence and shrinkage (theft)" and to reduce holding costs associated with warehousing items in the healthcare facility.
- **ABC inventory method:** With activity-based costing (ABC), each supply item is categorized as belonging to one of three groups. Group A includes very expensive items that must be monitored closely, such as certain expensive drugs. Group B consists of intermediate-cost items, where order and inventory quantities change "as interest rates and unit prices vary." Group C, the largest group, consists of items that represent little cost but are important to the day-to-day operations of the healthcare organization (e.g., bandages, tissues, pain relievers). Zelman et al. (2003) and Nowicki (2004) describe the ABC method in detail, providing examples of how it is applied.

While it may be the ultimate responsibility of the materials manager to ensure that all goods needed by both the clinical and nonclinical users in a healthcare facility are available when required and in the most cost-efficient manner, every manager in the organization must be held accountable for timely ordering and judicious use of materials. Physicians and other users of high-cost equipment and supplies should also be educated about the procedures involved in the ordering and stocking process. Table 10-4 provides examples of the most commonly used inventory management techniques.

TABLE 10-4 Inventory Management Techniques

FIFO Example

Date	Purchased			Sold			Balance		
August 3							200	@ $10 =	$2,000
August 9				100	@ $10 =	$1,000	100	@	10 = 1,000
August 11	300	@ $11 =	$3,300				100	@	10 = 1,000
							300	@	11 = 3,300
August 12				100	@	10 = 1,000	200	@	11 = 2,200
				100	@	11 = 1,100			
August 20	50	@	14 = 700				200	@	11 = 2,200
							50	@	14 = 700
August 26				200	@	11 = 2,200	50	@	14 = 700
August 29	200	@	12 = 2,400				50	@	14 = 700
							200	@	12 = 2,400
Total August 30	550		$ 6,400	500		$ 5,300	250		$ 3,100
2,000 + 6,400 − 5,300 − 3,100 = 0									

LIFO Example

Date	Purchased			Sold			Balance		
August 3							200	@ $10 =	$2,000
August 9				100	@ $10 =	$1,000	100	@	10 = 1,000
August 11	300	@ $11 =	$3,300				100	@	10 = 1,000
							300	@	11 = 3,300
August 12				200	@	11 = 2,200	100	@	10 = 1,000
							100	@	11 = 1,100
August 20	50	@	14 = 700				100	@	10 = 1,000
							100	@	11 = 1,100
							50	@	14 = 700
August 26				50	@	14 = 700			
				100	@	11 = 1,100			
				50	@	10 = 500	50	@	10 = 500
August 29	200	@	12 = 2,400				50	@	10 = 500
							200	@	12 = 2,400
Total August 30	550		$ 6,400	500		$ 5,500	250		$ 2,900
2,000 + 6,400 − 5,500 − 2,900 = 0									

(*continued*)

TABLE 10-4 Inventory Management Techniques (Continued)

Weighted-Average Example

Date	Purchased	Sold	Balance
August 3			200 @ $ 10 = $2,000
August 9		100 @ $ 10 = $1,000	100 @ 10 = 1,000
August 11	300 @ $11 = $3,300		400 @ 10.75 = 4,300
August 12		200 @ 10.75 = 2,150	200 @ 10.75 = 2,150
August 20	50 @ 14 = 700		250 @ 11.40 = 2,850
August 26		200 @ 11.40 = 2,280	50 @ 11.40 = 570
August 29	200 @ 12 = 2,400		250 @ 11.88 = 2.970
Total August 30	550 $ 6,400	500 $ 5,430	250 $ 2,970

2,000 + 6,400 − 5,430 − 2,970 = 0

MANAGING BUDGETS

One of the most critical functions for managers in healthcare organizations is management of the departmental or division budget. While the facility's Finance Department is generally involved in working with the manager in developing both operational and capital budgets for the department, it is the responsibility of each manager to ensure that expenditures (for items such as labor, equipment, and supplies) and revenues (if the department supplies services or products for patients/consumers) are monitored carefully on an ongoing basis.

Sorting Out the Definitions and Distinguishing Characteristics of Budgeting

Budgeting means different things to different people, even in healthcare organizations, and it does not help that not all authors or organizations utilize the same terms in discussing their budgeting processes. The purpose of the current section is to try to sort out some common budgeting terms that are used in the financial management departments of healthcare entities.

Budgeting is, quite simply, the process of converting the goals and objectives of the organization's operating plan into financial terms: expenses, revenues, and cash flow projections. The budget, then, is a financial plan for turning these objectives into programs for earning revenues and expending funds. Listed below are characteristics of budgeting important to healthcare managers.

- The budget should be a dynamic working document, to be utilized on an ongoing basis by every manager in the organization.

- Managers must have access to a budget manual and last year's data regarding volumes, revenues, expenses, and cash flows on a monthly basis to provide guidance for their departments' budgeting process.
- Budgets provide a tool for ex post facto evaluation of managers concerning their performance in efficiently running their departments and for assessing how well the organization as a whole has met its financial performance goals.
- The budget period is the time frame for which a budget is prepared, often one fiscal year (McLean, 2003).
- The budget calendar is a planning tool used to design and maintain all of the organization's projects falling under the budget, with separate calendars being prepared for the operating and capital budgets (Berger, 2002). Included in this calendar are the budget activities, time frame expectations, the parties responsible, and follow-up meeting times.

What Are the Specific Types of Budgets?

The **operating budget** generally refers to the annual budget that follows the strategic financial and operating plan. Berger (2002, pp. 145–148) describes 24 steps in preparing the operating budget, including 5 distinct "segments": strategic planning, administrative, communications, operational planning, and budgeting segments. He further asserts that these steps "involve managers in every facet of operations. In addition, a critical set of stakeholders who must be accessed, solicited, and appeased are the physicians linked to the organization, either in an employment capacity or in an affiliate relationship."

"**Cash budget**" is a term sometimes used interchangeably with "operating budget," but it is specifically distinguished from the latter by some authors and organizations. Prepared by the finance department staff, this budget is described by Berger (2002, p. 235) as "the necessary step that allows the organization to determine how to optimize the value of the cash being generated by its operations." McLean (1997, p. 355) more specifically defines a cash budget as "a forecast of cash inflows, cash outflows, and net lending or borrowing needs for the months ahead." This 52-week budget attempts to forecast the receipts (most often from third-party payers) and disbursements (expenses) of the organization. These budgets are comprised of the following:

- An **expense budget**, which is a prediction of the total expenses that the organization will incur, typically includes such items as labor, supplies, and acuity levels (case mix) and is included on the left-hand side (the debit side) of accounting entries. Remember, an expense is an outflow or an asset that has been used up, and a cost is the resources necessary to provide the service or product you are producing.

- A **revenue budget**, shown on the right-hand (credit) side of accounting entries, includes data on forecasted utilization of specific services within the organization and third-party payer mix.

Three other terms generally associated with cash budgets are:

- **Cash outflows**, which include such expenses as mortgage payments or rents, salaries and wages, benefits, utilities, supplies, and interest paid out;
- **Cash inflows**, which include cash payments up front, 30-day and 60-day collections, government appropriations, donations, and any interest earned each month; and
- **Ending cash**, which comprises both the cash balance at the end of the month and the following month's beginning cash level. The following formula is used to determine this amount: Ending cash = Beginning cash + Cash inflows − Cash outflows.

There are two other types of budgets with which healthcare managers should become familiar. The term **statistics budget** is given to the initial statistics delineated in the operating plan that forecasts service utilization (by service type, acuity level or case mix, and payer mix), resource use, and policy data (employment data, occupancy rates, staffing ratios, etc.). The **capital budget** refers to the plan for expenditures for new facilities and equipment (often referred to as fixed assets). The following discussion will focus on the latter.

The Importance of Capital Budgeting

Capital budgeting may be defined as the process of selecting long-term assets, whose useful life is greater than one year, according to financial decision rules. The capital budget determines funding amounts, what capital equipment will be acquired, what buildings will be built or renovated, depreciation expenses, and the estimated useful life to be assigned to each asset. Berger (2002, p. 157) states that its main purpose "is to identify the specific capital items to be acquired. The problem in almost all healthcare organizations is which capital projects should be funded" in light of scarce resources. McLean (2003, p. 189) further asserts that "[t]he basic question that any capital budgeting system must ask is, 'Does this asset or project, in a time value sense, at least pay for itself? If not (if it requires a subsidy), is there a subsidy forthcoming?' If the answer is yes, then the project is worth doing."

The following are types of items typically included in such budgets:

- Land acquisition, including land to be used for expansion of service offerings;
- Physical plant or facility construction, expansion, acquisition, renovation, or leasing, possibly including medical office space for physician practices;
- Routine capital equipment, including items used in clinical areas (radiology, lab, surgery, rehab, and nursing departments);

- Information technology infrastructure or upgrades for financial systems, medical records, and clinical use; and
- Recruitment and acquisition of staff physicians (more recently included), either through purchasing existing physician practices or establishing new practices by employing physicians.

While the capital budgeting process often involves substantial outlays of time by managers at different levels of the organization, it is important to consider some essential steps that are frequently followed. Determination of the capital budget often begins with a wish list of various items requested by staff, physicians, or any other individuals who must obtain or use equipment within the department. It is important to note that engaging physician leaders in this process cannot be overemphasized, because they ultimately make the majority of diagnostic and clinical decisions regarding patient care in healthcare organizations.

Department managers must then complete and submit designated capital budget requests to the Finance Department. Once all requests have been submitted, the finance staff reviews them for consistency and completeness. Reviewers of the technical aspects of the capital requests make sure each contains all of the data required. This group often includes accounting staff, information systems management, materials management, and facilities management. Designated evaluators assess the merits of the requests, how each compares to all other project requests on a criteria basis, and whether each adheres to strategic plan criteria. Administrative approval and approval by the governing body completes the process.

While there are a number of methods utilized to make capital budgeting decisions, most healthcare organizations establish criteria-based decision rules. These range from a simple accept/reject decision, which merely addresses "whether or not to acquire an asset or initiate a project," to capital rationing, in which a fixed dollar amount is placed on annual capital spending by governing bodies and those with the highest profitability index are selected (McLean, 2003, pp. 193–195). However, as a "safety valve" in the decision process, some organizations have found that it is necessary to include a mechanism that allows some needed capital acquisitions "to be purchased no matter what," that is, despite not being able to meet formal evaluation criteria. Berger (2002) calls this non-criteria-based capital budgeting.

CONCLUSION

Managing costs and revenues in the healthcare arena is a complex and often technical process that involves understanding of the interrelatedness of the processes involved, the interplay of many departments and managers within the organization, and the importance of influences external to the organization. This chapter has addressed the importance and objectives of financial management and the impacts of tax status and organizational structure and has taken a cursory look at how effective management of a variety of organizational support functions contribute to maximizing revenues and controlling costs. More specifically, the chapter has provided the healthcare administration student with a nonfinancial career path a basic understanding of managing costs, reimbursements from third-party payers and other sources, budgeting, capital acquisition, working capital, accounts receivable, setting charges and prices, and managing materials and inventory. Managers at all levels of the organization are often involved in addressing these functions.

What this chapter did not address more specifically were investment decisions, short-term versus long-term financing, managing endowments, financial ratios, or financial statement preparation and analysis. This is largely due to the fact that these functions are most often handled by professionals within the Finance Department of the healthcare organization, who in turn provide managers with pertinent related information on an as-needed basis. However, for healthcare managers more directly involved in financial management as a major part of their jobs, it is imperative that they avail themselves of this and other detailed financial management information to help ensure the financial viability of their organizations.

All managers employed within the healthcare arena must continue to monitor the changes taking place in health care and, more precisely, with healthcare reform. The key to understanding healthcare finance is to take the concepts one step at a time until you are able to build them into one cohesive unit of understanding. Furthermore, getting involved and applying what you have learned in the classroom and through the textbook is an excellent way to hone your financial skills. Never pass up the opportunity to put your financial skills to work in a real-world setting, as this is how you will learn to apply the principles discussed in this chapter.

DISCUSSION QUESTIONS

1. Define healthcare finance and provide several examples of how it affects managers at all levels within the organization.

2. Compare and contrast the different inventory management techniques and discuss how each technique might play a role within different healthcare organizations.

3. How are health services paid for? Provide a definition for the term "third-party payer," discuss the different payers currently operating in the market, and assess the importance of each.

4. Define and give examples (other than from the table in the text) of fixed, variable, and semivariable costs.

5. Explain why budgets are important to all organizations. Expand this discussion by illustrating how different types of budgets are used.

6. How is working capital important to the healthcare organization of today? Why is it different in health care as opposed to other industries?

7. Discuss the various ways in which healthcare reform has affected and may affect the financial delivery of health care today and into the future.

Cases in Chapter 17 that are related to this chapter include:

- Managing Costs and Revenues at Happy Town Neurology—see p. 471
- Problems with the Pre-Admission Call Center—see p. 390
- Negotiation in Action—see p. 403

Additional cases, role-play scenarios, video links, websites, and other information sources are also available in the online Instructor's Materials.

REFERENCES

American Hospital Association (AHA). (1990). *Role and functions of the hospital governing board.* Chicago, IL: Author.

American Hospital Association (AHA). (2005, November). *Uncompensated hospital care cost fact sheet.* Retrieved from http://www.aha.org/ahapolicyforum/resources/content/0511UncompensatedCare FactSheet.pdf

American Medical Association (AMA). (2010). Current procedural terminology (CPT). Retrieved from http://www.ama-assn.org/ama/pub/physician-resources/solutions-managing-your-practice/coding-billing-insurance/cpt.shtml

Berger, S. (2002). *Fundamentals of health care financial management: A practical guide to fiscal issues and activities* (2nd ed.). San Francisco, CA: Jossey-Bass.

Berman, H. J., Weeks, L. E., & Kukla, S. F. (1986). *The financial management of hospitals* (6th ed.). Chicago, IL: Health Administration Press.

Gapenski, L. C. (2003). *Understanding healthcare financial management* (4th ed.). Chicago, IL: Health Administration Press.

Gapenski, L. C. (2009). *Fundamentals of health care finance.* Chicago: Health Administration Press.

Himmelstein, D. U., Warren, E., Thorne, D., & Woolhandler, S. (2005, February). Market watch: Illness and injury as contributors to bankruptcy. *Health Affairs, 10*(W5), 63–73, Web exclusive.

Ledue, C. (2010, April 23). Healthcare executives believe reform will negatively affect facilities. *Healthcare Finance News.* Retrieved from http://www.healthcarefinancenews.com/news/healthcare-executives-believe-reform-will-negatively-affect-facilities

McLean, R. A. (1997). *Financial management in health care organizations.* Clifton Park, NY: Thomson Delmar Learning.

McLean, R. A. (2003). *Financial management in health care organizations* (2nd ed.). Clifton Park, NY: Thomson Delmar Learning.

Nowicki, M. (2004). *The financial management of hospitals and healthcare organizations* (3rd ed.). Chicago, IL: Health Administration Press.

Pohly, P. (2005). Glossary of terms in managed health care. *Pam Pohly's net guide, 1997–2005.* Retrieved from http://www.pohly.com/terms.html

Sachdeva, K. S., & Gitman, L. J. (1981). Accounts receivable decisions in a capital budgeting framework, *Financial Management, 10*(4), 45–49.

Shafrin, J. (2010, June 30). Center for Medicare and Medicaid innovation. *Healthcare Economist.* Retrieved from http://healthcare-economist.com/2010/06/30/center-for-medicare-and-medicaid-innovation/

Zelman, W. N., McCue, M. J., Millikan, A. R., & Glick, N. D. (2003). *Financial management of health care organizations: An introduction to fundamental tools, concepts and applications* (2nd ed.). Malden, MA: Blackwell.

Managing Healthcare Professionals

Sharon B. Buchbinder and Dale Buchbinder

LEARNING OBJECTIVES

By the end of this chapter, the student will be able to:

- Distinguish between the education, training, and credentialing of physicians, nurses, nurses' aides, midlevel practitioners, and allied health professionals;
- Identify five factors affecting the supply of and demand for healthcare professionals;
- Analyze reasons for healthcare professional turnover and costs of turnover;
- Propose strategies for increasing retention and preventing turnover of healthcare professionals;
- Define and provide examples of conflict of interest; and
- Discuss issues associated with the management of the work life of physicians, nurses, nurses' aides, midlevel practitioners, and allied health professionals.

INTRODUCTION

Healthcare organizations employ a wide array of clinical, administrative, and support professionals to deliver services to their patients. The Bureau of Labor Statistics (BLS), which lists more than 30 different categories of healthcare professionals at its website, notes that "as the largest industry in 2008, healthcare provided 14.3 million jobs for wage and salary workers" and that "most workers have jobs that require less than four years of college education, but health diagnosing and treating practitioners are highly educated" (Bureau of Labor Statistics, 2010a).

The largest category of healthcare workers is registered nurses, with 2.6 million jobs, 60% of which are in hospitals (BLS, 2010b). According to the BLS, there were 661,000 physicians and surgeons who held jobs in 2008, and "approximately 12 percent were self-employed. About 53 percent of wage-and-salary physicians and surgeons worked in offices of physicians, and 19 percent were employed by hospitals. Others practiced in Federal, State, and local governments, educational services, and outpatient care centers." (BLS, 2010c). In 2008, physician assistants held 74,800 jobs, "over 50% of which were in physician practices, about a quarter were in hospitals, and the rest in outpatient care centers" (BLS, 2010d). Allied health professionals constitute a broad array of 22 health science professions, including anesthesiologist assistants, medical assistants, respiratory therapists, and surgical technologists (Commission on Accreditation of Allied Health Education Programs, 2010).

These statistics mean that, as a healthcare manager, in many instances you will be working with a mix of people with either more or less education than you have. It also means that you will not have the clinical competencies that these healthcare providers have—an intimidating scenario, to say the least. Instead of clinical expertise, you will bring a background that enables you to enhance the environment in which these highly specialized personnel deliver healthcare services. You will be the person responsible for making sure that nurses, doctors, and other healthcare professionals have the resources to provide safe and effective patient care. Your role will be to provide and monitor the infrastructure and processes to make the healthcare organization responsive to the needs of the patients and the employees. The more you understand clinical healthcare professionals, the better prepared you will be to do your job as a healthcare manager. The purpose of this chapter is to provide you with an overview of who your future colleagues are, how they were trained, and ways to manage the quality of their work environment.

PHYSICIANS

Physicians begin their preparation for medical school as undergraduates in premedical programs. Premedical students can obtain a degree in any subject; however, the Association of American Medical Colleges (AAMC) indicates that the expectation is that they will graduate with a strong foundation in mathematics, biology, chemistry and physics (Association of American Medical Colleges, 2010). Entry into medical school is competitive; applicants must have high grade point averages and high scores on the Medical College Admission Test (MCAT).

There are some shorter, combined Bachelor of Science/Medical Doctor (BS/MD) programs; however, the majority of medical school graduates will have 8 years of post–high school education before they go through the National Residency Matching Program (NRMP) (2010), a matching process whereby medical students interview and rank their choices for graduate medical education (GME), also known as residencies, and the residency training programs do the same. Once matched with a residency training program, physicians are prepared in specialty areas of medicine. Depending on the specialty, the length of the residency training program can be as short as 3 years (for family practice) or as long as 10 years (for cardio-thoracic surgery or neurosurgery). According to the Accreditation Council for Graduate Medical Education (ACGME), "When physicians graduate from a residency program, they are eligible to take their board certification examinations and begin practicing independently. Residency training programs are sponsored by teaching hospitals, academic medical centers, healthcare systems and other institutions" (Accreditation Council for Graduate Medical Education, 2010a). Depending on the type of healthcare organization where you are employed, you may be working with residents-in-training and medical students, as well as physicians who have been in independent practice for decades.

In addition to having a long time before they can practice independently, residents work extensive hours as part of their training programs. At one time, it was not uncommon for residents to be on call continuously for 48 hours, because ceilings on hours of work for residents varied by residency training program. However, that all changed due to the death of Libby Zion, an 18-year-old college student, who was seen at the Cornell Medical Center in 1984 and allegedly died due to resident overwork (American Medical Association, 2010). Although the hospital and resident were exonerated in court, the battle over resident work hours had begun. New York was the first state to institute limits on resident work hours in 1987. Over the past two decades, various specialty societies, medical associations, and legislators fought over the definition of "reasonable" work hours for physicians in training. The battle has continued, and new rules have been updated from those published in 2003. Per these new rules, hospitals and residency training program directors will be required to limit resident work hours to no more than 80 hours per week, inclusive of in-house call activities and all moonlighting (i.e., side jobs or extra work in addition to the 80 hours per week). No first-year residents (PGY-1) are permitted to moonlight (ACGME, 2010b). Furthermore,

> Duty periods of PGY-1 residents must not exceed 16 hours in duration. Duty periods of PGY-2 residents and above may be scheduled to a maximum of 24 hours of continuous duty in the hospital. Programs must encourage residents to use alertness management strategies in the context of patient care responsibilities. Strategic napping, especially after 16 hours of continuous duty and between the hours of 10:00 p.m. and 8:00 a.m., is strongly suggested (ACGME, 2010b, p. 17).

Additionally, the same document describes the need for continuity of patient care and appropriate patient "handoff" procedures; that is, when the resident goes home, the next person taking care of the patient must be briefed to ensure that the patient care team has all relevant information (ACGME, 2010b). These new rules are supposed to become effective July 1, 2011; however, the ACGME is under pressure to delay implementation until 2012 (Iglehart, 2010). Regardless of the exact date of implementation, this controversy will not disappear. These work-hour rules and new patient handoff protocols underscore the fact that residents are in the hospital for education, not to provide service to the hospital, a major departure from the way graduate medical education was conducted a few decades ago. They also emphasize the need for a culture of safety and patient-centric care.

The implications of limits on resident work hours are multifold. While residency training program directors are responsible for monitoring resident work hours, they must be in compliance with the healthcare institution's policies as well. You may be responsible for ensuring compliance by collecting work-hour data for your managers. Healthcare managers are obligated to ensure adequate coverage of the hospital with physicians. Resident work-hour restrictions may mean that you need to employ more physicians or midlevel practitioners—physician assistants and nurse practitioners. And your organization may need to hire ancillary staff and allied health professionals, such as intravenous therapists and surgical assistants, to do tasks previously covered by resident physicians.

Most physicians are eligible to obtain a license to practice medicine after one year of post-graduate training. **Licensure**, granted by the state, is required for physicians, nurses, and others to practice and demonstrates competency to perform a scope of practice (National Council of State Boards of Nursing, 2010a). Limited licensure is granted for PGY-1s in hospital practice under supervision. State Boards of Physician Quality Assurance (BPQA) establish the requirements for medical licenses. These requirements are lengthy and strenuous. For example, the state of Maryland requires the following (Annotated Code of Maryland, 2010):

- Good moral character;
- Minimum age of 18 years;
- A fee;
- Documentation of education and training; and
- Passing scores on one of the following examinations:
    - All parts of the National Board of Medical Examiners' examinations, and/or a score of 75 or better on a FLEX exam, or a passing score on the National Board of Osteopathic Examiners, or a combination of scores and exams; or
    - State Board examination;
    - All steps of the U.S. Medical Licensing Examination (USMLE).

Candidates must demonstrate oral and written English-language competency and supply the following:

- A chronological list of activities beginning with the date of completion of medical school, accounting for all periods of time;
- Any disciplinary actions taken by licensing boards, denying application or renewal;
- Any investigations, charges, arrests, pleas of guilty or *nolo contendere*, convictions, or receipts of probation before judgment;
- Information pertaining to any physical, mental, or emotional condition that impairs the physician's ability to practice medicine;
- Copies of any malpractice suits or settlements, or records of any arrests, disciplinary actions, judgments, final orders, or cases of driving while intoxicated or under the influence of a chemical substance or medication; and
- Results of all medical licensure, certification, and recertification examinations and the dates when taken.

Thirty-four states now have the "authority to run criminal background checks (CBCs) as a condition for licensure" for physicians (Federation of State Medical Boards, 2010). The reasons are numerous and include but are not limited to increasing societal concerns about alcohol and drug abusers, sexual predators, and child and elder abusers. If a CBC contains information about convictions, the licensure board will examine the application on a case-by-case basis. The reviewers will be looking for level and frequency of the criminal behavior, basing their decision on that, along with other materials submitted by the applicant, such as proof of alcohol and drug rehabilitation.

In addition to obtaining a license, physicians may voluntarily submit documentation of their education, training, and practice to an American Board of Medical Specialists (ABMS) member board for review (American Board of Medical Specialists, 2010a). Upon approval of the medical specialty board (i.e., successful completion of an approved residency training program), the physician is then allowed to sit for examination. Successful completion of the examination(s) allows the physician to be granted certification, and she is designated as **board certified** in that specialty (e.g., a board-certified pediatrician or a board-certified general internist). Certificates are time-limited; physicians must demonstrate continued competency and retake the exam every 6 to 10 years, depending on the specialty. The purpose of American Board of Medical Specialties Maintenance of Certification (ABMS MOC) is to ensure that physicians remain up-to-date in their specialties (ABMS, 2010b). Board certification is a form of **credentialing** a physician's competency in a specific area. For staff privileges and hiring purposes, most hospitals, HMOs, and other healthcare organizations require a physician to be board certified or **board eligible** (i.e., preparing to sit for the exams) because board certification is used as a proxy for determining the quality of health professionals' services. This assumption of quality is based on research that more education and training leads to a higher quality of service (Donabedian, 2005; Tamblyn et al., 1998).

Most states require that physicians complete a certain number of **continuing medical education (CME)** credits to maintain state licensure and to demonstrate continued competency. Additionally, hospitals may require CME credits for their physicians to remain credentialed to see patients (National Institutes of Health, 2010a). Seven organizations, the ABMS, the American Hospital Association (AHA), the American Medical Association (AMA), the Association of American Medical Colleges (AAMC), the Association for Hospital Medical Education (AHME), the Council of Medical Specialty Societies (CMSS), and the Federation of State Medical Boards, Inc. (FSMB), are members of the **Accreditation Council for Continuing Medical Education (ACCME)** (Accreditation Council for Continuing Medical Education, 2010b). The ACCME establishes criteria for determining which educational providers are quality CME providers and gives its seal of approval only to those organizations meeting their standards (ACCME, 2010a). The ACCME also works to ensure "uniformity in accreditation" of educational offerings to maintain the quality of continuing physician education (ACCME, 2010b).

Physician credentialing is the process of verifying information that a physician supplies on an application for staff privileges at a hospital, HMO, or other healthcare organization. Most healthcare organizations have established protocols, and as a healthcare manager, you will be required to follow that protocol. Physicians are tracked by the AMA from the day they graduate from medical school until the day they die. Information about every physician in the United States is in the AMA Physician Masterfile, which has been in existence for more than 100 years. Originally created on paper index cards to establish biographic records on physicians, it is now a computer database "used by the medical community for credentials verification, research, manpower planning, and other public good efforts" (Eiler, 2006). Physician credentialing is a time-consuming, labor-intensive, costly process that must be repeated every two years. When physicians apply for privileges at a hospital, they must specify what they want by specialty and, within the surgical specialties, by procedure. For example, a general surgeon who wants to do laparoscopic cholecystectomies (i.e., removal of the gall bladder through a very small incision, using an instrument like a tiny telescope) would apply for both general surgery privileges and for that specific procedure. Using extensive documentation, the surgeon must demonstrate competency for those privileges.

Normally, physician credentialing criteria are established by the department where the physician would be affiliated. **Core privileges** cover a multitude of activities that a physician is allowed to do in a healthcare services organization. Using family practice (FP) as an example, the Department of Family Practice in a hospital would establish the criteria for privileges. Core privileges for an FP could include: "admission, evaluation, diagnosis, treatment and management of infants and children, adolescents and adults for most illnesses, disorders and injuries" (American Academy of Family Practice, 2010). **Specific privileges** would be those activities outside the core privileges and would require documentation of required additional training and expertise in a procedure. In this example, if the FP also wanted to be allowed to deliver babies at a hospital, that FP might be required to provide documentation that he or she had completed "at least 2 months obstetrical rotation during family practice residency with 40 patients delivered" (AAFP, 2010). If there are two departments with physicians who do the same thing (e.g., Obstetrics and Gynecology and Family Practice), each department is responsible for its own criteria. The Medical Staff Office would enforce, but not establish, the criteria. A hospital must conduct diligent research on physicians before granting privileges, or it can be held liable in a court of law for allowing an incompetent physician on its staff, should there be a bad outcome. The same is true for HMOs, ambulatory care centers, and other healthcare delivery organizations.

It is preferable to obtain primary, meaning firsthand, verification and documentation by contacting each place of education, training, and employment individually by phone and obtain original documents, such as transcripts with raised seals. Verification can include, but is not limited to, the following elements (Government Accounting Office, 2010):

- Name, address(es), and telephone numbers;
- Birthdate and place of birth;
- Medical school;
- Residency training program and other graduate education, including fellowships;
- State licensure details, including date of issue and expiration;
- Specialty and subspecialty, including board certification and eligibility;
- Continuing medical education;
- Educational and employment references;
- Drug Enforcement Agency (DEA) registration status; and
- Licensure, Medicare/Medicaid, and other state or federal sanctions.

The importance of primary verification of these elements has been underscored by an audit of the credentials of physicians employed by six Veterans' Affairs Medical Centers (VAMCs) (GAO, 2010). The auditors "looked for evidence of omissions by physician applicants related to medical licenses, malpractice, and at five of six VAMCs visited, gaps in background greater than 30 days" (GAO, 2010, p. 42). They found that of 180 physician files they reviewed, 29 lacked proper verification of state licensure and 21 physicians failed to disclose malpractice information (GAO, 2010).

As a healthcare manager, you may find yourself working in the physician relations and credentialing department of a hospital, HMO, or other healthcare delivery organization, and you may be responsible for determining whether the credentials offered by a physician are legitimate. Physician credentialing requires excellent interpersonal skills, organizational skills, persistence, an eye for details, and the ability to identify inconsistencies in data.

Since physicians are tracked from the moment they graduate from medical school, the first thing to verify is that there are no gaps in their resumes. Physicians rarely take time off "to find themselves." If there is a significant gap between educational or employment placements (e.g., nothing on the resume for four years between a residency training program and an evening-shift job working at a clinic with a poor reputation), you need to question what has transpired in this individual's life. Physicians are human, and they can have events in their lives such as mental illness, addiction, or imprisonment. Since you will be responsible for safe, effective patient care, you must be mindful about who is providing that care. The first clue will be in the credentials, especially in the chronology of life events.

Occasionally, you will come across an individual who claims to be a physician but is not. In this Internet and computer age, physician imposters can obtain fraudulent credentials from medical schools in other countries, or even in the United States. Physician imposters are rare, but potentially dangerous, individuals. There is no substitute for personal interaction with the institution where someone claims to have been educated or employed. This is where an eye for details and inconsistencies and interpersonal skills come into play. You will be required to handle telephone inquiries with the utmost tact to ensure that you obtain verification. If no one at an institution knows the individual, or if the medical school has "burned down, leaving no records," alarm bells should be ringing in your head, and you should notify your manager immediately that there may be a problem with the application.

A comprehensive review of a physician's credentials involves making electronic queries to the **National Practitioner Data Bank (NPDB)**. At one time, physicians who were disciplined or lost their license in one state could simply move to another state and get a license there. Other than person-to-person contacts, there were few ways to track "bad docs" who moved across state borders. The NPDB was created to have a system, whereby state licensing boards, hospitals, professional societies, and other healthcare entities could identify, discipline, and report those who engage in unprofessional behavior. "The intent of the NPDB is to restrict the ability of incompetent physicians, dentists, and other healthcare practitioners to move from state to state without disclosure or discovery of previous medical malpractice payment and adverse action history. Adverse actions can involve licensure, clinical privileges, professional society membership, and exclusions from Medicare and Medicaid" (National Practitioner Data Bank, 2010). One of the main criticisms of the NPDB is that a physician can be reported for having been sued, but the outcome of the lawsuit, even when dismissed, is not reported, and the lawsuit remains on the physician's record. In an era of increasingly litigious consumers of health care, this is not a minor complaint. Physicians may dispute the report, but it can take much time and effort, much like trying to get a correction on a credit report. Per the NPDB, "The information contained in the NPDB should be considered together with other relevant data in evaluating a practitioner's credentials; it is intended to augment, not replace, traditional forms of credentials review" (NPDB, 2010).

When credentialing physicians, it is critical to have other physicians review the application to ensure that experts who understand the nuances of the data contained in an application render the final judgment as to whether to approve or disapprove privileges. Using the example of a surgeon applying for general surgical privileges at a hospital, after the physician credentialing department receives a physician's application for privileges and does due diligence in verifying each and every claim on the application, the materials are submitted to a surgical credentialing committee. Unless the hospital is very small, each department will have its own credentialing committee. In this case, if the department of surgery's credentialing committee approves the application, it then recommends that the documents be forwarded to a medical executive committee, which is a subcommittee of the hospital board of directors. The medical executive subcommittee then makes a recommendation to the board, which then approves or disapproves the application. Under certain circumstances, temporary credentials can be granted. Usually, however, the time from submission of the application to final approval can take three to six months. If there are problems with the application or missing documents, the process can take even longer.

Physician credentialing is one of the most important jobs in any healthcare delivery setting. By approving a physician's privileges, the healthcare organization indicates that it believes that this physician will provide safe, effective patient care. It is not a responsibility to be taken lightly. The lives of patients and the financial survival of the healthcare organization depend on how well this process has been done.

International Medical Graduates

International Medical Graduates (IMGs), formerly referred to as Foreign Medical Graduates (FMGs), can be U.S. citizens who attend school abroad or foreign-born nationals who come to the United States seeking educational and professional opportunities and filling voids in healthcare services delivery for the U.S. population. "In 2008, International Medical Graduates (IMGs) represented 25.7% of the total physician population" in the U.S. physician workforce, or approximately 245,005 physicians (Smart, 2010). In 2004, the top three countries for sending foreign-born physicians to the United States were India, the Philippines, and Cuba, trailed by Pakistan, Iran, Korea, Egypt, China, Germany, and Syria (McMahon, 2004).

Researchers have repeatedly demonstrated that IMGs are more likely to go where U.S. medical graduates (USMGs) prefer *not* to go (i.e., inner-city and rural areas) and to serve populations increasingly at risk of medical abandonment (Hagopian, Thompson, Kaltenbach, & Hart, 2003; Hallock, Seeling, & Norcini, 2003; Mick & Lee, 1999a, 1999b; Mick, Lee, & Wodchis, 2000; Polsky, Kletke, Wozniak, & Escarce, 2002). In 2008, nearly 60% of the IMGs in the United States were in primary care (internal medicine, pediatrics, family medicine) or specialized in psychiatry, anastehesiology, obstetrics/gynecology, general surgery, or cardiovascular disease (Smart, 2010). More than three-quarters of the IMGs in practice were in direct patient care. At one time, the quality of care provided by non-USMGs was a major concern. Over the past decades, however, a formidable system of checks and balances has been implemented, and foreign-trained and foreign-born medical graduates (FBMGs) are now required to pass rigorous English-language and written and clinical skills assessment examinations prior to being allowed to apply for GME, that is, residency training positions (Whelan, Gary, Kostis, Boutlet, & Hallock, 2000). This arrangement has improved the quality of the IMG applicant pool that continues to fill graduate medical education positions still left unfilled by USMGs (Cooper & Aiken, 2001; McMahon, 2004). Additionally, a study examining quality of care provided by IMGs in Pennsylvania found the quality of care provided to be as good as or better than that given by those who graduated from U.S. medical schools (Norcini et al., 2010).

Research indicates that the U.S. primary care physician (PCP) workforce of the future will include more IMGs, most of whom will be citizens or permanent residents of the United States and graduates of Caribbean medical schools (Brotherton, Rockey, & Etzel, 2005). In addition, contrary to previous predictions of a glut in the medical labor pool, many experts now predict a shortage of physicians resulting, in part, from the aging of the baby boomer population, physician retirements, changing ethnic and racial demographics, increased utilization of services, a hostile malpractice environment, and an increasing number of medical school graduates (both female and male) who desire reasonable work hours (Bureau of Health Professions, 2003; Cooper, 2002, 2003). While some experts argue over the exact numbers of physicians in the workforce and whether to use the American Medical Association Masterfile or the U.S. Census Bureau Current Population Survey for workforce projections, they agree that the physician workforce will continue to be smaller and younger and will work fewer hours per week regardless of gender (Steiger, Auerbach, & Buerhaus, 2009, 2010).

Newspapers have been reporting on difficulties some PCPs are encountering in seeing patients and shortages in internal medicine (Bell, 2005). In response to these pressures, some authors and organizations—including the AAMC—called for increases in the number of U.S. medical schools and the expansion of U.S. medical school classes to increase the number of graduates (Blumenthal, 2003; AAMC, 2006a). In response to anticipated shortages of physicians, since 2007, "more than a dozen allopathic schools have started the Liaison Committee on Medical Education accreditation process. Another 10 are under discussion, and five osteopathic medical colleges have opened" (O'Reilly, 2010).

Some authors have questioned the ethics of a country that continues to rely heavily on IMGs (AAMC, 2006a, 2006b; Biviano & Makarehchi, 2002). Mullan (2005) points out that, in a global economy, the United States and other developed countries had a disproportionate share of physicians compared to lower-income nations. Others have reported on the expense involved in IMGs coming to America, only to be exploited and placed in poor or unfair working conditions—a situation not unlike indentured servitude (Hagopian et al., 2003). Clearly, these abuses and ethical concerns must be addressed. And at a time when our nation is escalating the production of physicians, it might seem to some that we don't need to import more. In fact, the preeminent organization representing U.S. medical schools stated that "AAMC will continue to support opportunities for IMGs to train and practice in the U.S., and is committed to increase its involvement in international medical education while finding ways to reduce the drain of valuable human resources from less developed nations" (AAMC, 2006b, p. 2).

Regardless of politics, as the United States comes to terms with the knowledge that its physician supply is not keeping up with demand, healthcare managers will struggle with recruitment, retention, and optimal utilization of physicians, whether USMG or IMG. Some of the issues you will be most likely to encounter with IMGs will surround the physician credentialing process and the J-Visa, which provides legal entry to the United States for training purposes. Physicians who graduate from foreign medical schools will have to provide, in some instances, additional documentation and verification that the information they have provided is true and correct. The Educational Commission for Foreign Medical Graduates (ECFMG) offers online credential verification services that can ease some of the burden but not all of the responsibility or liability in the granting of privileges (Educational Commission for Foreign Medical Graduates, 2010).

In summary, physicians are critical to the provision of safe, effective patient care. Ensuring the quality of the physicians practicing in an organization is one of the roles of the healthcare manager. To fulfill this responsibility, you will need to know all the steps in the education, training, and credentialing of physicians. It will take attention to detail, organizational skills, and excellent interpersonal skills to do it well.

Employed Physicians and Turnover

At one time, the majority of physicians in the United States were self-employed, solo practitioners, or in partnership with one or two other physicians. Recent data suggest that the old images of the independent physician practitioner need to be updated to reflect the growing numbers of physicians who are now employed by organizations such as hospitals and large single- or multispecialty group practices (Isaacs, Jellinek, & Ray, 2009). One recruiter reported that in some communities, as many as 90% of the physicians may be employees (Butcher, 2008). In 2008, about one-third of all physicians, male and female, between the ages of 45 and 54 were full-time hospital employees (Smart, 2010). The reasons for the trend toward increasing numbers of employed physicians are numerous, not the least of which are the newer generations of medical school graduates who expect a balanced work–family life, uncertainties and volatility in reimbursement and payment mechanisms, medical malpractice concerns, and the hassle factor of fighting with insurance companies for dwindling amounts of money (Spatz, 2006).

Consolidation of physicians' practices and enrollment growth in managed care organizations has accelerated these trends. Buchbinder, Wilson, Melick, and Powe (2001), using data from a nationally representative sample, studied a cohort of 533 post-resident, non-federal, employed PCPs who were younger than 45 years of age, had been in practice between two and nine years, and had participated in national surveys in 1987 and 1991. They combined data from this sample with a national study of physician compensation and productivity and physician recruiters to estimate recruitment and replacement costs associated with **turnover** (i.e., the proportion of job exits or quits from a facility in a year). The authors found that by the 1991 survey, slightly more than half ($n = 279$, or 55%) of all PCPs in this cohort had left the practice in which they had been employed in 1987; 20% ($n = 100$) had left two employers in that same five-year period. Estimates of recruitment and replacement costs for individual PCPs for the three specialties were $236,383 for family practice (FP), $245,128 for internal medicine (IM), and $264,645 for pediatrics (Peds). Turnover costs for all PCPs in the cohort by specialty were $24.5 million for FP, $22.3 million for IM, and $22.2 million for Peds. They concluded that turnover was an important phenomenon among the PCPs in this cohort and that PCP turnover has major fiscal implications for PCP employers. Loss of PCPs causes healthcare organizations to lose resources that could otherwise be devoted to patient care.

A physician retention study conducted by Cejka Search and American Medical Group Association (AMGA) (Cejka Search & American Medical Group Association, 2007) reported that many medical groups are having more trouble recruiting and hiring physicians and have increased the use of PAs in their practices. Physician turnover remained at about the same level from the previous year; however, women and older male physicians were more likely to opt for part-time employment. One of the more effective retention strategies found in this national survey was the use of mentoring. Half of the medical groups surveyed "assigned mentors to new employee physicians" (Cejka Search & AMGA, 2007, p. 8). In addition, "setting clear expectations" for new hires was also cited as another useful retention strategy (Cejka Search & AMGA,

2007, p. 8). These are clearly management issues related to physician recruitment, retention, and turnover.

Employee turnover has been clearly linked to job dissatisfaction and job burnout. **Job satisfaction** is the "pleasurable or positive emotional state resulting from the appraisal of one's job or job experiences" (Locke, 1983). **Job burnout** is "a prolonged response to chronic emotional and interpersonal stressors on the job" (Maslach, 2003). In the past, most solutions to job burnout involved removing the affected individual from the job. However, it is the *organization* that is the primary cause of job burnout (due to heavy workload, poor relations with coworkers, etc.) and job dissatisfaction. Therefore, it is the healthcare manager's role to address these issues. Healthcare managers employed in these kinds of settings must be alert to signs of physician job dissatisfaction and burnout, the harbingers of turnover. "Achieving a patient-centered and professionally satisfying culture and closing the quality chasm in cost-effective ways depend on accountable organizational arrangements, strong primary care, and effective team performance" (Mechanic, 2010, p. 556). As a healthcare manager in a medical group practice, you will be expected to work with the physicians to help create a positive practice environment and to provide recommendations for interventions to improve retention.

Employed Physicians and Conflict of Interest

There has long been a requirement for researchers to disclose funding sources for biomedical research because of concerns that the outcomes of the research could be biased in favor of the company that has, in essence, paid for the research. The NIH and the majority of biomedical journals require investigators to disclose any financial relationships that might exist between the researcher and the funding entity (Drazen et al., 2010; NIH, 2010b). Related to these concerns have been growing fears about the influence of gifts and other financial incentives on physicians' prescribing practices and purchasing behaviors. Some states, such as Massachusetts, Minnesota, and Vermont, enacted laws earlier than others to prohibit pharmaceutical or medical device companies from giving more than $100 in gifts to a physician (Ross et al., 2007). These laws have led to a greater urgency for organizations to create their own conflict of interest policies for physicians employed by healthcare organizations.

Conflict of interest is a term used to describe when an individual can be influenced by money or other considerations to act in a way that is contrary to the good of the organization for whom he or she works or the patient for whom he or she should be advocating in their best interests. The American Medical Association created Conflict of Interest Guidelines for Organized Medical Staffs, which served to act as a model for hospitals and healthcare organizations (AMA, 2005). These documents, which are required for all employees who make purchasing decisions—including physicians and administrators—include a series of questions to which the individual must respond no or, if yes, must explain. These questions include but are not limited to the topics of:

- Financial interests (including stocks and company ownership interests) of the physician or spouse or other immediate family members;
- Compensation, gifts, or other payments from a biomedical, pharmaceutical, or medical device company in exchange for changing orders of products, goods, or services;
- Speaking and consulting services in exchange for compensation, gifts, or other payments from a biomedical, pharmaceutical, or medical device company;
- Attendance at meetings, conferences, or other events in exchange for compensation, gifts, or other payments from a biomedical, pharmaceutical, or medical device company; or
- Other potential conflicts (Medstar Health, 2010).

There must be full disclosure if a conflict exists, and the individual must remove himself or herself from the decision-making role. The individual must then certify that his or her responses to all of the above questions are complete and accurate to the best of their knowledge and that if anything changes, they must update their disclosure document. Conflict of interest documents must be updated annually (Medstar Health, 2010).

Your job as a healthcare manager will be to ensure that first and foremost you complete the same type of document that you will expect to have physicians complete. Even the appearance of any potential conflict of interest or possible impropriety should be avoided. Your reputation and the reputation of the healthcare organization where you are employed depend on ethical behaviors of all employees.

REGISTERED NURSES

At one time, all nurses were trained in hospital-based programs and received diplomas upon graduation. Before 1917, nursing was essentially an apprenticeship, without a set curriculum, which then morphed into hospital-based diploma schools that produced their own nursing workforce. The hospital-based diploma nursing school is part of a passing era; in 2010, there were only 68 left in the United States (Sweeney, 2010). In 2008, only 20.4% of the RNs in practice were graduates of diploma schools of nursing (Health Resources and Services Administration, 2010). Currently, the majority of nursing education is provided in degree-based settings. In 2008, 45.4% of the U.S. RN population was educated in community colleges, earning an associate's degree in two to three years. Slightly more than one-third (33.7%) were educated in university and college baccalaureate programs for professional nursing practice, earning a bachelor's of science in nursing (BSN) in four years. Many graduates of associate degree programs go back to school while they work full-time to earn a BSN to improve their opportunities for career advancement (HRSA, 2010).

Nurses with BSNs can continue their education and enter a wide array of graduate educational programs including but not limited to postbaccalaureate certificates, master's of science in nursing (MSN) degrees for community health nursing and nurse education; advanced practice degrees (nurse practitioner, clinical nurse specialist, nurse midwife, nurse anesthetist); and doctoral degrees, such as the nursing doctorate (ND), doctorate in nursing science (DNs), or a doctor of philosophy (PhD).

The undergraduate nursing school curriculum (BSN) is rigorous and demands a good understanding of the biological sciences. At Towson University, for example, students are eligible to apply for admission to the major only after completing a minimum of 42 undergraduate credits, including at least four laboratory sciences and an English composition course. Admission is based on the cumulative grade point average, only one grade below a C is allowed in prerequisite or general education courses, and no more than two non-nursing courses may be repeated (Towson University, 2010).

The current shortage of nursing faculty means fewer slots for nursing students—there are fewer faculty to teach (American Association of Colleges of Nursing, 2005). Many nursing programs are so competitive that there are three applicants for every acceptance. Due to a crisis-level national nursing shortage and demands for workers, state legislators are pressuring universities and colleges to increase the number of graduates from nursing programs. However, unlike other undergraduate degrees, nursing students must learn clinical skills and be carefully supervised in healthcare organizations by master's or doctorally prepared nursing faculty. The nursing faculty clinical supervisor is only allowed to have a specific number of student nurses. Exceeding that number could endanger the lives of patients and the faculty member's nursing license.

As nursing students progress through their program of study, meeting state requirements for licensure and passing the National Council Licensure Examination (NCLEX) is uppermost in everyone's mind. A student must pass the NCLEX to become a licensed registered nurse (RN) in the United States, and nursing programs' pass rates on the NCLEX are used as a proxy for the quality of their educational curriculum. With the current nursing shortage, many graduating nurses have a job offer in hand before they graduate—contingent upon obtaining state licensure and passing the NCLEX (NCSBN, 2010b, 2010c).

As of 2008, 32 states required criminal background checks (CBCs) for nurse applicants for licensure (NCSBN, 2008). Again, the reasons are multifold and include but are not limited to increasing societal concerns about alcohol and drug abusers, sexual predators, and child and elder abusers. If a criminal background check contains information about convictions, the licensure board will examine the application on a case-by-case basis. As noted previously, the reviewers will be looking for level and frequency of the criminal behavior, basing their decision on that, along with other materials submitted by the applicant, such as proof of alcohol and drug rehabilitation.

After graduation, RNs, unlike physicians, do not have postgraduate programs that last from 3 to 10 years. In the past, new RNs have been hired to work in hospitals or other healthcare organizations, given a brief orientation, then placed on a nursing unit and left to sink or swim. This Darwinian approach to nurse staffing has led, in part, to massive turnover. Although the vast majority of nurses are female (only 6.6% are male), women now have career choices other than nursing, teaching, or homemaking; and older nurses continue to retire faster than new ones come into the field (HRSA, 2010; Steiger, Auerbach, & Buerhaus, 2000). Nursing turnover costs have been estimated to be 1.3 times the salary of a departing nurse, or an average of $65,000 per lost nurse (Department for Professional Employees AFL-CIO, 2010; Jones & Gates, 2007). Multiply that by the number of nurses who quit their jobs and the costs can be in the millions of dollars for healthcare organizations. Healthcare managers cannot afford to ignore the loss of nurses from the workforce.

Any strategy that improves the retention of nursing staff saves the organization the costs of using agency or traveler nurses, replacing lost nurses and training new ones, as well as the loss of productivity from burdening the remaining staff. A survey conducted among 67 new nurses from 13 hospital departments indicated that new graduates were concerned about communicating with physicians and were afraid of "causing accidental harm to patients." Additionally, this group identified a desire for "comprehensive orientation, continuing education and mentoring" (Boswell, Lowry, & Wilhoit, 2004, p. 76). Nurse residency programs (NRPs) have been identified by The Joint Commission (2002) and the Robert Wood Johnson Foundation (Kimball & O'Neill, 2002) as a strategy for improving RN retention. One study of an NRP for intensive care unit (ICU) nurses demonstrated increased job satisfaction, improved retention, and decreased turnover (Williams, Sims, Burkhead, & Ward, 2002). Another study describing the planning, implementation, and evaluation of a model NRP for ICU and medical-surgical nurses found that new RNs who participated in the NRPs "demonstrated improved retention, critical thinking, socialization, ability to manage stress, and problem-solving skills" (Herdrich & Lindsay, 2006, p. 55). Calls for NRPs increased, and in 2008, the Commission on Collegiate Nursing Education (CCNE) promulgated standards for the accreditation of postbaccalaureate nurse residency programs to be implemented in 2009 (Commission on Collegiate Nursing Education, 2008; Dracup & Morris, 2007). NRPs desiring CCNE accreditation must go through a number of procedures, including a self-study and a site visit (CCNE, 2009). A difficult transition into practice isn't the only reason that nurses leave healthcare organizations. Nurses quit jobs where they feel overworked, underpaid, and disrespected by their coworkers and managers. Using national focus groups, on behalf of the Robert Wood Johnson Foundation, Kimball and O'Neil (2002) found that RNs are concerned about being unable to physically continue to do the work, increases in their daily workloads, and the lack of ancillary staff to support them. These groups also indicated that they were confused about healthcare financial issues, felt powerless to change things in their work environments, and thought their nurse managers were overextended and unable to help them. The respondents gave a list of suggestions to improve the retention of nurses, including:

- Decreasing workloads;
- Providing support staff;
- Empowering nurse managers;
- Increasing salaries;
- Encouraging physicians to treat nurses as colleagues;
- Improving the orientation process; and
- Providing paid continuing education (Kimball & O'Neil, 2002, p. 46).

Overwork of nurses and high patient-to-nurse ratios lead to patient mortality, nurse burnout, and job dissatisfaction (Aiken, Clarke, Sloane, Sochalski, & Silber, 2002). Aiken et al.'s (2002, p. 1991) benchmark article reported "that the difference from 4 to 6 and from 4 to 8 patients per nurse would be accompanied by 14% and 31% increases in mortality, respectively." The Joint Commission (2002, p. 6) report called a high patient-to-nurse ratio "a prescription for danger" and indicated that "staffing levels have been a factor in 24% of 1,608 sentinel events (unanticipated events that result in death, injury, or permanent loss or function)." In addition, Aiken and her colleagues reported that more nurse education and training led to higher quality of service and lower patient mortality (Aiken, Clarke, Cheung, Sloane, & Silber, 2003). In light of these data, it makes financial sense to employ more RNs per patient and to hire RNs with a baccalaureate level or higher. Given the nursing shortage, the healthcare manager's next best choice would be to hire RNs with an associate degree, provide tuition assistance, and create incentives for them to return to school for their BSN.

Conflict and Communication: Creating a Culture of Safety

Encouraging physicians to treat nurses as colleagues has always been a challenge. Recommendations for collaborative practice between physicians and nurses have been in place for decades, going back to nursing shortages in the 1980s and the National Commission on Nursing's 1983 *Summary Report and Recommendations*, calling for nurse-physician joint practice (National Commission on Nursing, 1983). One of the problems in this dyad has been the gap between physician and nursing education. In previous years, when diploma schools dominated nursing education, physicians had at least 20 more years of formal education than the RNs they worked with. In that era, when a physician walked into a room, a nurse would stand as a sign of respect—and give him her chair. Nurses now have formal educational programs in degree-granting settings, and the educational gap between the two healthcare professional groups is diminishing. Women have also "come of age" since the women's rights movement in the 1970s, and nurses are no longer the doctor's handmaidens. They, too, are healthcare professionals.

Teamwork is essential to a culture of safety. Physician resistance to acknowledging nurses as professionals and colleagues leads to poor teamwork and interpersonal conflict and can result in poor patient outcomes. One study found that physicians and nurses differed widely in their opinions about teamwork in an ICU setting. Almost three-quarters of the physicians reported high levels of teamwork with nurses, but less than half of the nurses felt the same way (Sexton, Thomas, & Helmreich, 2000). As noted in a subsequent chapter on teamwork, despite demonstrated need and effectiveness of interdisciplinary teamwork, formal educational training in this important skill for physicians and nurses is rare (Baker, Salas, King, Battles, & Barach, 2005; Buchbinder et al., 2005). A poll conducted in 2004 by the American College of Physician Executives (ACPE) revealed that about one-quarter of the physician executive respondents were seeing problem physician behaviors almost weekly (Weber, 2004). Approximately 36% of the respondents reported conflicts between physicians and staff members (including nurses), and 25% reported that physicians refused to embrace teamwork.

Intimidating and **disruptive behaviors** include "overt actions such as verbal outbursts and physical threats as well as passive activities such as refusing to perform assigned tasks or quietly exhibiting uncooperative attitudes during routine activities" (The Joint Commission, 2008). Disruptive behaviors, whether from physicians or nurses, are unacceptable and counterproductive to a patient-centric culture of safety. Disruptive behavior is considered a "**sentinel event**, i.e., an unexpected occurrence involving death or serious physical or psychological injury, or the risk thereof" (The Joint Commission, 2010). People who behave like schoolyard bullies in healthcare organizations must be dealt with through counseling sessions, disciplinary actions, or terminations. Trust and good communication are central to excellence in healthcare delivery.

Communication between physicians, nurses, and other healthcare professionals is critical to a culture of safety. The Joint Commission established new standards to address communication and published a book for clinicians and healthcare managers with strategies to improve communication between staff members, patients, and teams (The Joint Commission, 2009). In this book, as well as in peer-reviewed articles, physicians and nurses are tasked to focus on patient-centered care and patient safety (Levinson, Lesser, & Epstein, 2010; Nadzman, 2009). However, nurses and physicians rarely receive education on effective communication in their professional programs. While it is hoped that medical and nursing school curricula will respond to the need for this important skill, those courses are not in place at this time. For this reason, it may become *your* duty as a healthcare manager to ensure that resources such as educational seminars and teamwork training are in place to support a culture of safety at your healthcare organization.

Organizational climate is critical to promoting job satisfaction and retention of nursing staff. Laschinger and Finegan (2005) found that nurses who perceived that they had access to opportunity, experienced honest relationships and open communication with peers and managers, and trusted their managers were more likely to be retained and to have higher job satisfaction. The American Association of Colleges of Nursing (AACN, 2002) published a white paper titled *Hallmarks of the Professional Nursing Practice Environment.* The attributes of hospitals with work environments that support professional nursing practice were reviewed and the questions a new graduate should ask were listed. They are: Does your potential employer:

- Manifest a philosophy of clinical care, emphasizing quality, safety, interdisciplinary collaboration, continuity of care, and professional accountability?
- Recognize the contributions of nurses' knowledge and expertise to clinical care quality and patient outcomes?
- Promote executive-level nursing leadership?
- Empower nurses' participation in clinical decision making and organization of clinical care systems?
- Maintain clinical advancement programs based on education, certification, and advanced preparation?
- Demonstrate professional development support for nurses?
- Create collaborative relationships among members of the healthcare provider team?
- Utilize technological advances in clinical care and information systems?

The AACN also recommends that applicants inquire about RN staff education, vacancy, tenure, and turnover rates; patient and employee satisfaction scores; and the percentage of registry/traveler nurses used. The questions posed by the AACN challenge healthcare organizations to rise to higher standards and to reach for American Nurses Credentialing Center Magnet Recognition Program status (ANCC, 2010a). Unless these questions are answered in the affirmative, nursing turnover will continue to be one of the largest human and financial costs that the healthcare manager will be forced to control.

Like physicians who sit for board certification examinations, RNs can take ANCC or other nursing specialty organizations' (e.g., the Wound, Ostomy, and Continence Nurses' Society; the American Association of Critical Care Nurses, etc.) examinations to demonstrate additional competence in a specialty, after they have practiced for a specific number of hours (usually 1,000 hours, or about a year) in a specialty area. Nursing Professional Development requires 2,000 hours of practice (American Association of Critical Care

Nurses, 2010b). Thus nurses can be certified in a large number and variety of specialty areas, including but not limited to:

- Ambulatory care;
- Cardiac rehabilitation;
- Cardiac vascular;
- Case management;
- Critical care;
- Gerontological;
- High-risk perinatal;
- Hospice and palliative
- Maternal child;
- Medical-surgical;
- Nursing administration;
- Nursing professional development;
- Operating room;
- Pain management;
- Pediatric;
- Perinatal;
- Psychiatric and mental health;
- School;
- Vascular; and
- Wound care.

Nurses who are credentialed in specialty areas must demonstrate continuing competency by fulfilling requirements for certification renewal via one or several of the following mechanisms: continuing education hours, academic courses, presentations and lectures, publications and research, or preceptorships.

In many states, nurses are required to obtain nursing continuing education units (CEUs) to renew and maintain their nursing licenses. The ANCC Commission on Accreditation, the credentialing unit of the American Nurses Association (ANA), reviews and approves providers of nursing CEUs (ANCC, 2010b). There are literally hundreds of providers of nursing CEUs and multiple ways to obtain nursing CEUs, including but not limited to online courses; magazine or journal articles; workshops and conferences; audiotapes, CDs, DVDs; and the previously noted academic courses, presentations and lectures, publications and research, or preceptorships. Nurses can even attend other healthcare providers' workshops that have been approved for awarding nursing CEUs. There is no dearth of opportunities for nurses to obtain continuing education. It is the responsibility of the RN to maintain his or her license. Your role as healthcare manager will be to ensure that resources (i.e., money and time) are available for nurses to participate in these educational opportunities.

Foreign Educated Nurses

The nursing shortage, caused by a confluence of the aging of the U.S. nursing work-force, declining enrollments in nursing schools, higher average age of new graduates from nursing school, and organizational retention and turnover difficulties, would have been difficult enough for healthcare managers on its own. However, we have what some people call "the perfect storm" in health care because the nursing shortage is now combined with demographic forces and market forces, such as aging baby boomers, increasing racial and ethnic diversity, increased demand for healthcare services, increasing longevity of U.S. citizens, new treatments for chronic diseases that used to kill people (like asthma, diabetes, hypertension), and educated and demanding healthcare consumers (HRSA, 2003).

Since U.S. healthcare organizations are experiencing a crisis in the nursing workforce and cannot survive without nurses to deliver care, it is not surprising that foreign-educated nurses are coming to the United States to fill gaps in nursing services. In 2004, about 3.5% (100,791) of the RNs practicing in the United States received their basic nursing education outside the country (HRSA, 2004). A little over 50% of these nurses come from the Philippines, 20% from Canada, 8% from the United Kingdom, and the remaining from a variety of countries. About half of the foreign-educated nurses have a baccalaureate degree or higher.

Most U.S. state nursing boards require foreign-educated nurses to successfully complete the Commission on Graduates of Foreign Nursing Schools (CGFNS) certification program (Commission on Graduates of Foreign Nursing Schools, 2010). This program consists of three parts: a credentials review, a qualifying exam of nursing knowledge, and an English-language proficiency examination. The CGFNS program is designed to predict an applicant's likelihood of passing the NCLEX-RN examination and becoming licensed as a registered nurse in the United States. The CGFNS Certification Program removes a major burden from an employer. However, as a healthcare manager, your job may require you to ensure that foreign-educated nurses have fulfilled all the requirements of the State Board of Nursing and that they are legally allowed to work in the United States.

Due to the stringent requirements the United States has for RN licensure, concerns about the United States depleting other nations of their nursing workforce are not based on hard data (Aiken, Buchan, Sochalski, Nichols, & Powell, 2004). However, these types of misperceptions can influence coworker relationships and may contribute to conflicts between U.S.-educated and foreign-educated nurses and between physicians and foreign-educated nurses. Different cultures bring varying expectations to the work setting. These expectations may well be at odds with those of their coworkers. Excellent interpersonal skills, conflict management, cultural proficiency, and sensitivity to diversity issues are critical for you to be able to be an effective healthcare manager for these employees.

LICENSED PRACTICAL NURSES/LICENSED VOCATIONAL NURSES

In 2008, there were about 753,600 **Licensed Practical Nurses (LPNs) or Licensed Vocational Nurses (LVNs)** working under the supervision of physicians and nurses in the United States. According to the Bureau of Labor Statistics (2010d), about one-quarter were employed in hospitals, about one-quarter in nursing care facilities, and another 12% worked in physicians' offices. Others worked for home health services, employment services, community care facilities for the elderly, public and private educational services, outpatient centers, and federal, state, and local government services. After graduation from high school, LPNs are trained in one-year, state-approved programs. Most are trained in technical or vocational schools, although some high schools offer it as part of their curriculum. In order to be employed as an LPN, students must graduate from a state-approved program, then pass the LPN licensing exam, the NCLEX-PN (BLS, 2010d). LPNs are trained to do basic nursing functions such as checking vital signs, observing patients, and assisting patients with **activities of daily living (ADLs)**, such as bathing, dressing, and feeding. With additional training, where state laws allow, they can also administer medications. LPNs are the backbone of the long-term care (LTC) sector of the healthcare industry, providing around-the-clock care and supervision of **certified nurse's assistants (CNAs)** in nursing homes and convalescent centers. Many LPNs go on to earn their RN, and in some states, LPNs can take challenge examinations to earn their RN licensure. LPNs are an important part of the healthcare team and should be included in the healthcare manager's tuition assistance plan to encourage key personnel to return to school for additional education.

NURSING AND PSYCHIATRIC AIDES

In 2008, there were about 1.5 million nursing and psychiatric aides employed in nursing and residential care facilities, hospitals, and psychiatric and substance abuse facilities (BLS, 2010e). Nursing aides, nursing assistants, certified nursing assistants (CNAs), orderlies, and other unlicensed patient attendants work under the supervision of physicians and nurses. They answer call bells, assist patients with toileting, change beds, serve meals, and assist patients with ADLs. Regardless of employment setting, aides are frontline personnel. Since nursing aides held the most jobs, at 1.5 million, and were employed most often by nursing care facilities, that will be the focus of the remainder of this section.

Nurse's aides have made the news in negative ways in recent years. In the past, CNAs were not required to have criminal background checks (CBCs), and elder abusers, sexual predators, and thieves saw the elderly population as easy prey. Now the majority of states and employers require CBCs. However, a clean CBC doesn't guarantee that the person hasn't abused or won't abuse a patient. Therefore, it is incumbent upon the healthcare organization to have policies about neglect and abuse prevention in place, and the healthcare manager must enforce them. Some nursing homes have installed "granny-cams," video surveillance systems, to keep an eye on caregiver behavior and to document misbehavior. When working with vulnerable populations, the healthcare manager must be in a state of constant vigilance for neglect and abuse.

CNAs are often trained on the job in 75 hours of mandatory training and are required to pass a competency examination. CNAs provide direct care to patients over long periods of time and are often the most overlooked group of workers in terms of pay, benefits, and opportunities for advancement. Seavey (2004) conducted a literature review and found that estimates of turnover from LTC facilities ranged from 40% to 166%, with indirect and direct costs per lost worker ranging from $951 to $6,368. She estimated a minimum direct cost of $2,500 per lost worker.

It's a vicious cycle: poor quality of work life begets turnover, which begets poor quality of work life, which begets more turnover. And it's not just the CNAs and other aides who are affected. Once the CNAs are gone, the LPNs will go, then the RNs will be stressed, become emotionally burned out, and leave (Kennedy, 2005). Then who will provide the care? The job of the healthcare manager is to improve retention to slow down or stop turnover by addressing the quality of work life. The place to start is with a comparable market wage analysis. Are the workers being paid the same as or better than workers with comparable jobs at other comparable facilities? Nursing home administrators have confided that CNAs will leave one facility to go to another one for a pay raise of 25 cents per hour. Is the pay fair? Does the facility pay tuition assistance for CNAs? What kind of benefits package is being offered?

After looking at these basic items, the healthcare manager then needs to assess the work environment, including employee job burnout and satisfaction, preferably using an outside organization so workers can respond freely without fear of retribution. While not an exhaustive list, some of the items to be included in a work life analysis include worker perceptions of

- Job autonomy, variety, and significance;
- Fairness of pay and benefits;
- Opportunities for promotion and advancement;
- Relationships with supervisors;
- Relationships with coworkers;
- Level of job burnout; and
- Overall job satisfaction.

All healthcare workers, not just nurses, want to be treated as colleagues and with respect. If you conduct a survey of the organizational climate—as seen by the workers—you must be prepared to respond and to intervene. If you do nothing, you will lose employees' trust, and the revolving door of turnover will continue.

HOME HEALTH AIDES

In 2008, there were 1.7 million home health and personal care aides employed in the United States (BLS, 2010f). Hospitals are discharging patients quicker and sicker, which means that more and more health care that used to be provided strictly in hospital settings is now given at home (Landers, 2010). In addition, due to the demographic tsunami of aging baby boomers who wish to age in place (i.e., at home) and due to the increasing longevity of individuals with chronic diseases and disability, this area of employment is expected to grow dramatically over the next decade. Many of the same issues associated with nursing and psychiatric aides will come along with this dramatic employment surge in home health aides. Since these individuals go to people's homes to provide their services, all of the concerns noted above related to the need for criminal background checks (CBCs), prevention of abuse of vulnerable populations, and turnover apply here as well. In addition, "home health aides who work for agencies that receive reimbursement from Medicare or Medicaid must receive a minimum level of training. They must complete both a training program consisting of a minimum of 75 hours and a competency evaluation or state certification program" (BLS, 2010f). Many hospitals and healthcare organizations have branched out into home healthcare services. While you may think that you will be employed by a hospital and work only on inpatient services, the reality is that you may very well become a manager for these outpatient, in-home services. It will be your responsibility to ensure that the people who are hired for these jobs are trustworthy and competent.

MIDLEVEL PRACTITIONERS

Midlevel practitioners include advanced practice nurses (APNs), such as nurse practitioners (NPs), clinical nurse specialists (CNS), nurse anesthetists, and nurse midwives, as well as physician assistants (PAs). "In 2008, an estimated 250,527 RNs reported that they were prepared as an advanced practice nurse in one or more advanced specialties or fields, an increase of 4.2 percent from 2004, when there were 240,460 prepared for advanced practice" (HRSA, 2010, p. 19). According to the Bureau of Labor Statistics, "Physician assistants held about 74,800 jobs in 2008. The number of jobs is greater than the number of practicing PAs because some hold two or more jobs" (BLS, 2010g). These data are consistent with those from the American Academy of Physician Assistants (AAPA), who reported that about 15% of actively practicing PAs worked more than one clinical job concurrently in 2008 (American Academy of Physician Assistants, 2009). These health-care professionals are called **midlevel practitioners** because they work midway between the level of an RN and that of an MD. Midlevel practitioners serve in a variety of set-tings, including hospital emergency rooms or departments, community health clinics, physician offices, and health maintenance organizations. They may also cover hospital floors for physicians. Midlevel practitioners are usually less expensive than physicians, often replacing MDs at a 2:1 ratio. Although APNs were resisted by many state medical societies early in the 1970s, over time physicians realized that APNs could increase their productivity and ease their workload. Midlevel practitioners are much sought after by healthcare organizations because they can provide many of the same services as physicians at a lower cost.

Advanced Practice Nurses

There are many organizations and accrediting bodies that certify advanced practice nurses (APNs). The following discussion is not intended to be an exhaustive listing of the spe-cialty certifications that are available. Rather, it is meant to be illustrative of the variety of roles that APNs can assume. In addition to the educational preparation noted below, all APNs must demonstrate continuing competency by obtaining CEUs. APN certification must be renewed every five years, either by documenting evidence of practice or by retak-ing the examination. Below are some examples of APNs.

Nurse practitioners (NPs) are prepared in either an NP MSN, a post-master's certifi-cate, or a doctoral program. To become certified in adult, gerontologic, and family nurse practice by the American Academy of Nurse Practitioners (AANP), candidates must pro-vide documentation that they are "graduates of approved master's or post-master's level adult, gerontologic, and family nurse practitioner programs" (American Academy of Nurse Practitioners, 2010). They must also take a competency-based exam. "The examination is recognized by all states as well as by Medicare, Medicaid, the Veterans Administration, and private insurance companies" (AANP, 2010). This means they can bill for services rendered, as can the organization that employs them. NPs can also become certified in areas of care that include but are not limited to acute, adult psychiatric/mental health, advanced diabetes management, family psychiatric/mental health, medical-surgical, school, and pediatric. They must pass a certification exam and maintain their competency through continuing nursing education and recertification exams (ANCC, 2010c). Only eleven states permit nurse practitioners to practice independently, that is, without physi-cian supervision. However, in light of the looming physician shortage, these laws may change (Christian, Dower, & O'Neil, 2007).

Clinical nurse specialists (CNSs) have in-depth education in the clinical specialty area at a master's or doctoral degree level. To be certified as a CNS, the RN must have all of the same educational qualifications as an NP, but in their area of focus, plus a minimum number of hours of supervised clinical practice as specified by each specialty area. Areas of certification include but are not limited to advanced diabetes, adult health, adult psychiatric/mental health, child/adolescent psychiatric/mental health, gerontological, home health, pediatric, and public/community health. They, too, must pass a certification exam and maintain their competency through continuing nursing education and recertification exams (ANCC, 2010c).

Certified registered nurse anesthetists (CRNAs) are APNs who specialize in providing anesthesia. According to the American Association of Nurse Anesthetists (AANA), nurses have been providing anesthesia care since the U.S. Civil War (American Association of Nurse Anesthetists, 2010). They work in cooperation with anesthesiologists, surgeons, dentists, and other healthcare professionals. The AANA lists the requirements to become a CRNA as follows:

- A bachelor of science in nursing (BSN) or other appropriate baccalaureate degree.
- A current license as a registered nurse.
- At least one year of experience as a registered nurse in an acute care setting.
- Graduation with a minimum of a master's degree from an accredited nurse anesthesia educational program. As of April 2010, there were 108 nurse anesthesia programs in the United States utilizing more than 1,700 approved clinical sites. These programs range from 24 to 36 months, depending upon university requirements. All programs include clinical training in university-based or large community hospitals.
- Pass the national certification examination following graduation (AANA, 2010).

A review of six years of data from the Centers for Medicare & Medicaid Services (CMS) found no adverse outcomes in states where nurse anesthetists were allowed to practice solo, that is, without the supervision of a physician (Dulisse & Cromwell, 2010). Nurse anesthetists and anesthesiologists have similar postgraduate training; these data provide evidence that the positive health outcomes for patients of solo nurse anesthetists are similar to those of physicians.

Certified nurse midwives (CNMs) are licensed as independent practitioners in all 50 states (American College of Nurse-Midwives, 2010a). More than 80% of all nurse midwives have master's degrees; another 7% have doctoral degrees. Nurse midwives were introduced to the United States in 1925 with the Frontier Nursing Service (FNS), founded by Mary Breckenridge (Frontier Nursing Service, 2010). As of 2010, all CNM applicants are required to have graduate degrees and to graduate from a nurse-midwifery education program accredited by the American College of Nurse-Midwives and pass a national certification examination (ACNM, 2010b).

Physician Assistants

According to the Bureau of Labor Statistics (BLS, 2010g), in 2008 there were 74,800 physician assistants (PAs) in the United States. PAs were created in the 1960s in response to a primary care physician shortage in the United States. Vietnam veteran medical corpsmen were selected for a "fast-track" training program and trained to assist physicians wherever they practiced (AAPA, 2010a). Once a male-dominated profession, now almost two-thirds (65%) are female. Since that time, the education and training of PAs has changed dramatically. In 2010, there were more than 140 accredited PA educational programs affiliated with two- and four-year colleges, universities, and schools of medicine (AAPA, 2010b). Only graduates of accredited PA programs are eligible to take the Physician Assistant National Certifying Examination (PANCE). PAs must demonstrate competency and be recertified every six years, and must earn 100 CME hours every two years (National Commission on Certification of Physician Assistants, 2010a). PAs are licensed to practice in every state in the United States, the District of Columbia, and Guam, and physicians can delegate prescribing authority to them (NCCPA, 2010b). PAs practice in every conceivable setting, although the major employers of PAs are "hospitals (38%), group physician practice (35%), solo physician practice (9%), rural community health (8%) and other settings (10%)" (AAPA, 2009, p. 2). PAs are versatile and valuable members of the healthcare team and are highly sought after by physician practices, hospitals, and other employers.

ALLIED HEALTH PROFESSIONALS

The term "**allied health professionals**" refers to more than 2,100 programs in more than 20 health science occupations (CAAHEP, 2010). Allied health professionals assist physicians and nurses in providing comprehensive care to patients in a variety of settings. Many of the occupations, such as anesthesiologist assistant and surgical assistant, have grown from the unmet demand for help in the highly specialized operating room environment. Other occupations, such as perfusionist and electroneurodiagnostic technician, have grown out of the technological boom and the need for people to operate highly specific equipment. Radiologic technologists and technicians (often shortened to "rad techs") assist radiographers in imaging technologies, which are changing with dizzying speed. The rate of accreditation of licensed rad techs is not keeping up with the speed of change in technology, and shortages are predicted for this high-demand field (BLS, 2010h).

Laboratories that analyze clinical specimens with increasingly sophisticated technologies need to be staffed with qualified personnel. The National Accrediting Agency for Clinical Laboratory Sciences (NAACLS) is responsible for maintaining the quality of programs in the clinical laboratory sciences. "Accredited programs include Clinical Laboratory Scientist/ Medical Technologist, Clinical Laboratory Technician/Medical Laboratory Technician, Cytogenetic Technologist, Diagnostic Molecular Scientist, Histologic Technician, Histotechnologist, and Pathologists' Assistant" (National Accrediting Agency for Clinical Laboratory Sciences, 2010). The Bureau of Labor Statistics indicates that job growth will be brisk in the coming years for clinical laboratory technologists and technicians and that the majority of this growth will occur in hospitals; however, other settings will need these workers as well (BLS, 2010i).

The following is a list of the occupations described at the CAAHEP website, www.caahep.org/, and is not meant to be exhaustive of all allied health professions. Each has its own body of knowledge, program requirements, and competency expectations.

- Anesthesia technician/technologist;
- Anesthesiologist assistant;
- Athletic trainer;
- Cardiovascular technologist;
- Cytotechnologist;
- Diagnostic medical sonographer;
- Electroneurodiagnostic technologist;
- Emergency medical technician/paramedic;
- Exercise physiologist;
- Exercise scientist;
- Kinesiotherapist;
- Lactation consultant;
- Medical assistant;
- Medical illustrator;
- Orthotist/prosthetist;
- Perfusionist;
- Personal fitness trainer;
- Polysomnographic technologist;
- Recreational therapist;
- Specialist in blood blanking technology;
- Surgical assistant; and
- Surgical technologist.

Respiratory Therapists (RTs)

This section will address one allied health occupation in greater detail: respiratory therapists (RTs). In 2008, RTs held about 106,000 jobs, with more than 80% in hospital departments of respiratory care, anesthesiology, or pulmonary medicine (BLS, 2010j). RTs evaluate, treat, and care for patients with respiratory disorders, such as asthma, emphysema, pneumonia, and heart disease. An associate's degree is required for entry into the field to become a certified respiratory therapist (CRT). Additional education is required for advanced practice and eligibility for the registered respiratory therapist (RRT) designation. RTs are certified by the National Board for Respiratory Care (NBRC), and registration is available only to graduates of accredited programs in respiratory care of the Commission on Accreditation for Respiratory Care (CoARC) (National Board for Respiratory Care, 2010). All states except Hawaii and Alaska, as well as the District of Columbia and Puerto Rico, require RTs to obtain a license (American Association for Respiratory Care, 2010). In addition, most employers require cardiopulmonary resuscitation (CPR) certification because RTs are usually members of hospital rapid response teams.

Shortages exist in almost all the allied health occupations, but respiratory therapy continues to be particularly affected, along with radiology technologists and certified nursing assistants. A 2002 survey of these three groups found a disturbing picture of work life for these healthcare professionals (AFT Healthcare, 2002). All three groups were dissatisfied with current work life and claimed inadequate staffing was the "number one problem they face." They felt that healthcare professional shortages compromised patient care and that turnover was affecting retention and recruitment. Recommendations from the three groups included increased salaries, improved staffing ratios, better health benefits, more input into decisions, flexible schedules, increased support staff, and continuing education.

CONCLUSION

This chapter has described the education, training, and credentialing of physicians, nurses, nurses' aides, midlevel practitioners, and allied health professionals and has given an overview of the supply of and demand for healthcare professionals. In addition, some of the reasons for healthcare professional turnover and costs of turnover have been discussed, along with some strategies for increasing retention and preventing turnover. Conflict of interest as it relates to employed physicians has been addressed, and issues related to the management of the work life of physicians, nurses, nurses' aides, midlevel practitioners, and allied health professionals have been interwoven through all of these topics. These are issues that can and should be addressed by you, the healthcare manager, with respect for each and every healthcare professional. The challenges await you; there will be no shortage of problems for you to solve.

DISCUSSION QUESTIONS

1. Delineate the steps in attaining state licensure for physicians.

2. Describe the steps in attaining state licensure for nurses.

3. What is the difference between licensure and credentialing?

4. Distinguish between core privileges and specific privileges in physician credentialing.

5. Why is physician credentialing one of the most important jobs in a hospital?

6. What is the National Practitioner Data Bank, and why was it created?

7. What is an international medical graduate, and what populations have they traditionally been most likely to serve?

8. Why might we begin to see more foreign-educated nurses in the United States?

9. Define the following terms: "job burnout," "job satisfaction," "retention," and "turnover." Why are they of importance in managing healthcare professionals?

10. What is conflict of interest, and why is it an important issue among employed physicians?

11. What is the relationship between nursing education, nursing burnout, job dissatisfaction, and patient mortality?

12. What are the attributes of hospitals that support professional nursing practice?

13. Distinguish between the following: advanced practice registered nurse, certified registered nurse, and physician assistant.

14. Distinguish between licensed practical nurses, certified nurses' assistants, and home health aides. What are some of the healthcare manager's challenges with these groups?

15. Who are allied health professionals? What are some healthcare management issues in working with them?

Cases in Chapter 17 that are related to this chapter include:

- Managing Healthcare Professionals: Mini-Case Studies—see p. 388
- Such a Nice Young Man—see p. 392
- The Brawler—see p. 382
- The New Toy at City Medical Center—see p. 449
- I Love you...Forever—p. 386

Additional cases, role-play scenarios, video links, websites, and other information sources are also available in the online Instructor's Materials.

REFERENCES

Accreditation Council for Continuing Medical Education (ACCME). (2010a). *Board of directors.* Retrieved from http://www.accme.org/index.cfm/fa/about.directors.cfm

Accreditation Council for Continuing Medical Education (ACCME). (2010b). *Recognition requirements.* Retrieved from http://www.accme.org/index.cfm/fa/RecognitionRequirements.home/RecognitionRequirements.cfm

Accreditation Council for Graduate Medical Education (ACGME). (2010a). *ACGME fact sheet.* Retrieved from http://www.acgme.org/acWebsite/newsRoom/ACGMEfactsheet.pdf

Accreditation Council for Graduate Medical Education (ACGME). (2010b). *Common program requirements effective: July 1, 2011.* Retrieved from http://acgme-2010standards.org/pdf/Common_Program_Requirements_07012011.pdf

AFT Healthcare. (2002). *Empty hallways: The hidden shortage of healthcare workers.* Retrieved from http://www.aft.org/pdfs/healthcare/staffing/Empty-Hallways.pdf

Aiken, L. H., Buchan, J., Sochalski, J., Nichols, B., & Powell, M. (2004, May/June). Trends in international nurse migration. *Health Affairs, 23*(3), 69–77.

Aiken, L. H., Clarke, S. P., Cheung, R. B., Sloane, D. M., & Silber, J. H. (2003). Educational levels of hospital nurses and surgical patient mortality. *Journal of the American Medical Association, 290* (12), 1617–1623.

Aiken, L. H., Clarke, S. P., Sloane, D. M., Sochalski, J., & Silber, J. H. (2002). Hospital nurse staffing and patient mortality, nurse burnout, and job dissatisfaction. *Journal of the American Medical Association, 288* (16), 1987–1993.

American Academy of Family Practice (AAFP). (2010). *Hospital priviliging.* Retrieved from http://www.aafp.org/online/en/home/practicemgt/privileges.html

American Academy of Nurse Practitioners (AANP). (2010). *What is a nurse practitioner?* Retrieved from http://www.aanp.org/NR/rdonlyres/A1D9B4BD-AC5E-45BF-9EB0-DEFCA1123204/4271/FAQsWhatisanNP83110.pdf

American Academy of Physician Assistants (AAPA). (2009). *National physician assistant census report.* Retrieved from http://www.aapa.org/images/stories/Data_2009/National_Final_with_Graphics.pdf

American Academy of Physician Assistants (AAPA). (2010a). *Our history.* Retrieved from http://www.aapa.org/about-pas/our-history

American Academy of Physician Assistants (AAPA). (2010b). *Becoming a physician assistant.* Retrieved from http://www.aapa.org/about-pas/becoming-a-physician-assistant

American Association for Respiratory Care (AARC). (2010). *State licensure.* Retrieved from http://www.aarc.org/advocacy/state/licensure_matrix.html#matrix

American Association of Colleges of Nursing (AACN). (2002, January). *Hallmarks of the professional nursing practice environment.* AACN white paper. Retrieved from http://www.aacn.nche.edu/Publications/positions/hallmarks.htm

American Association of Colleges of Nursing (AACN). (2005, June). *Faculty shortages in baccalaureate and graduate nursing programs: Scope of the problem and strategies for expanding the supply.* AACN white paper. Retrieved from http://www.aacn.nche.edu/Publications/WhitePapers/FacultyShortages.htm

American Association of Nurse Anesthetists (AANA). (2010). *Certified registered nurse anesthetists (CRNAs) at a glance.* Retrieved from http://www.aana.com/ataglance.aspx

American Board of Medical Specialists (ABMS). (2010a). *What board certification means.* Retrieved from http://www.abms.org/About_Board_Certification/means.aspx

American Board of Medical Specialists (ABMS). (2010b). *About ABMS maintenance of certification.* Retrieved from http://www.abms.org/Maintenance_of_Certification/

American College of Nurse-Midwives (ACNM). (2010a). *Essential facts about midwives.* Retrieved from http://www.midwife.org/Essential-Facts-about-Midwives

American College of Nurse-Midwives (ACNM). (2010b). *Mandatory degree requirements for entry into midwifery practice.* Retrieved from http://www.midwife.org/siteFiles/position/Mandatory_Degree_Req_for_Entry_Midwifery_Practice_7_09.pdf

American Medical Association (AMA). (2005). *Conflict of interest guidelines for organized medical staffs.* Retrieved from http://www.ama-assn.org/ama1/pub/upload/mm/395/coiguidelines111805.pdf

American Medical Association (AMA). (2010). *Resident work conditions.* Retrieved from http://www.ama-assn.org/ama/pub/about-ama/our-people/member-groups-sections/medical-student-section/advocacy-policy/resident-work-conditions.page?

American Nurses Credentialing Center (ANCC). (2010a). *ANCC magnet recognition program.* Retrieved from http://www.nursecredentialing.org/Magnet.aspx

American Nursing Credentialing Center (ANCC). (2010b). *ANCC nurse certification.* Retrieved from http://www.nursecredentialing.org/certification.aspx#

Annotated Code of Maryland (COMAR). (2010). *Licensure: Qualifications for initial licensure.* Retrieved from http://www.dsd.state.md.us/comar/comarhtml/10/10.32.01.03.htm

Association of American Medical Colleges (AAMC). (2006a, June). *AAMC statement on physician workforce.*

Association of American Medical Colleges (AAMC). (2006b, February). *Questions and answers about AAMC's new physician workforce position.*

Association of American Medical Colleges (AAMC). (2010). *Making the decision to study medicine.* Retrieved from https://www.aamc.org/students/considering/exploring_medical/

Baker, D. P., Salas, E., King, H., Battles, J., & Barach, P. (2005, April). The role of teamwork in the professional education of physicians: Current status and assessment recommendations. *Journal on Quality and Patient Safety, 31*(4), 185–202.

Bell, J. (2005, October 16). Symptoms of a doctor shortage: Growing population, physicians' desire to cut work weeks add up to a deficit. *Baltimore Sun,* 1, 6A.

Biviano, M., & Makarehchi, F. (2002, April 25). *Globalization and the physician workforce in the United States.* Sixth International Medical Workforce Conference, Ottawa, Ontario, Canada, April 25, 2002.

Blumenthal, D. (2003). Toil and trouble? Growing the physician supply. *Health Affairs, 22* (4), 85–87.

Boswell, S., Lowry, L. W., & Wilhoit, K. (2004). New nurses' perceptions of nursing practice and quality patient care. *Journal of Nursing Care Quality, 19*(1), 76–81.

Brotherton, S. E., Rockey, P. H., & Etzel, S. (2005). US graduate medical education, 2004–2005: Trends in primary care specialties. *Journal of the American Medical Association, 294,* 1075–1082.

Buchbinder, S. B., Alt, P. M., Eskow, K., Forbes, W., Hester, E., Struck, M., & Taylor, D. (2005). Creating learning prisms with an interdisciplinary case study workshop. *Innovative Higher Education, 29*(4), 257–274.

Buchbinder, S. B., Wilson, M. H., Melick, C. F., & Powe, N. R. (2001). Primary care physician job satisfaction and turnover. *American Journal of Managed Care, 7*(7), 701–713.

Bureau of Health Professions (BHPr). (2003, Spring). *Changing demographics: Implications for physicians, nurses and other health workers.* U.S. Department of Health and Human Services, Health Resources and Services Administration, Bureau of Health Professions, National Center for Health Workforce Analysis. Retrieved from http://bhpr.hrsa.gov/healthworkforce/reports/changingdemo/default.htm_

Bureau of Labor Statistics (BLS). (2010a). *Career guide to industries, 2010–2011 edition, healthcare.* Retrieved from http://www.bls.gov/oco/cg/cgs035.htm

Bureau of Labor Statistics (BLS). (2010b). Registered nurses. *U.S. Department of Labor, career guide to industries, 2010–2011 edition.* Retrieved http://www.bls.gov/oco/ocos083.htm

Bureau of Labor Statistics (BLS). (2010c). Physicians and surgeons. *Occupational Outlook Handbook, 2010–11 edition.* Retrieved from http://www.bls.gov/oco/ocos074.htm

Bureau of Labor Statistics (BLS). (2010d). Licensed practical and licensed vocational nurses. *Occupational outlook handbook, 2010–11 edition.* Retrieved from http://www.bls.gov/oco/ocos102.htm

Bureau of Labor Statistics (BLS). (2010e). Nursing and psychiatric aides. *Occupational outlook handbook, 2010–11 edition.* Retrieved from http://www.bls.gov/oco/ocos165.htm

Bureau of Labor Statistics (BLS). (2010f). Home health aides and personal and home care aides. *Occupational outlook handbook, 2010–11 edition.* Retrieved from http://www.bls.gov/oco/ocos326.htm

Bureau of Labor Statistics (BLS). (2010g). Physician assistants. *Occupational outlook handbook, 2010–11 edition.* Retrieved from http://www.bls.gov/oco/ocos081.htm

Bureau of Labor Statistics (BLS). (2010h). Radiologic technologists and technicians. *Occupational outlook handbook, 2010–11 edition.* Retrieved from http://www.bls.gov/oco/ocos105.htm

Bureau of Labor Statistics (BLS). (2010i). Clinical laboratory technologists and technicians. *Occupational outlook handbook, 2010–11 edition.* Retrieved from http://www.bls.gov/oco/ocos096.htm

Bureau of Labor Statistics (BLS). (2010j). Respiratory therapists. *Occupational outlook handbook, 2010–11 edition.* Retrieved from http://www.bls.gov/oco/ocos321.htm

Butcher, L. (2008, July). *Many changes in store as physicians become employees.* Retrieved from http://www.managedcaremag.com/archives/0807/0807.physicians.html

Cejka Search & American Medical Group Association (AMGA). (2007). *2007 physician retention survey: Supplemental edition.*

Christian, S., Dower, C., & O'Neil, E. (2007). *Overview of nurse practitioner scopes of practice in the United States: Discussion.* San Francisco: Center for the Health Professions, University of California, San Francisco. Retrieved from http://www.acnpweb.org/files/public/UCSF_Discussion_2007.pdf

Commission on Accreditation of Allied Health Education Programs (CAAHEP). (2010). *About CAAHEP.* Retrieved from http://caahep.org/Content.aspx?ID=63

Commission on Collegiate Nursing Education (CCNE). (2008, April). *Standards for accreditation of post-baccalaureate nurse residency programs.* Retrieved from http://www.aacn.nche.edu/accreditation/pdf/resstandards08.pdf

Commission on Collegiate Nursing Education (CCNE). (2009, April 23). *Procedures for accreditation of post-baccalaureate nurse residency programs.* Retrieved from http://www.aacn.nche.edu/accreditation/pdf/ProceduresResidency.pdf

Commission on Graduates of Foreign Nursing Schools (CGFNS). (2010). *The certification program.* Retrieved from http://www.cgfns.org/sections/programs/cp/

Cooper, R. A. (2002). There's a shortage of specialists. Is anyone listening? *Academic Medicine, 77,* 761–766.

Cooper, R. A. (2003). Medical schools and their applicants: An analysis. *Health Affairs, 22*(4), 71–84.

Cooper, R. A., & Aiken, L. H. (2001). Human inputs: The health care workforce and medical markets. *Journal of Health Politics, Policy and Law, 26,* 925–938.

Department for Professional Employees AFL-CIO (DPEAFLCIO). (2010). *Fact Sheet: The costs and benefits of safe staffing ratios.* Retrieved from http://dpeaflcio.org/pdf/DPE-fs_2010_staffratio.pdf

Donabedian, A. (2005). Evaluating the quality of medical care. *The Milbank Quarterly, 83*(4), 691–729.

Dracup, K., & Morris, P. E. (2007, July). Nurse residency programs: Preparing for the next shift. *American Journal of Critical Care, 16* (4): 328–330.

Drazen, J. M., de Leeuw, P. W., Laine, C., Mulrow, C., DeAngelis, C., Frizelle, F. A., et al. (2010). Toward more uniform conflict disclosures — the updated ICMJE conflict of interest reporting form. *New England Journal of Medicine, 363,* 188–189.

Dulisse, B., & Cromwell, J. (2010, August). No harm found when nurse anesthetists work without supervision by physicians. *Health Affairs, 29*(8), 1469–1475.

Educational Commission for Foreign Medical Graduates (ECFMG). (2010). *International credentials services.* Retrieved from http://www.ecfmg.org/eics/index.html

Eiler, M. A. (2006). Helping doctors help patients for 100 years: Happy birthday AMA physician masterfile. *AMA Physician Credentialing Solutions, 9*(2).

Federation of State Medical Boards (FSMB). (2010). *Criminal background checks: Overview by state.* Retrieved from http://www.fsmb.org/pdf/grpol_criminal_background_checks.pdf

Frontier Nursing Service (FNS). (2010). *Frontier nursing service.* Retrieved from http://www.midwives.org/whoweare/fnshistory.shtm

Government Accounting Office (GAO). (2010, January). *VA health care: Improved oversight and compliance needed for physician credentialing and privileging processes.* Report number GAO-10-26. Washington, DC: Author. Retrieved from http://www.gao.gov/new.items/d1026.pdf

Hagopian, A., Thompson, M. J., Kaltenbach, E., & Hart, L. G. (2003). Health departments' use of international medical graduates in physician shortage areas. *Health Affairs, 22*(5), 241–249.

Hallock, J. A., Seeling, S. S., & Norcini J. J. (2003). The international medical graduate pipeline. *Health Affairs, 22*(4), 64–96.

Health Resources and Services Administration (HRSA). (2003, Spring). *Changing demographics: Implications for physicians, nurses and other health workers.* U.S. Department of Health and Human Services, Health Resources and Services Administration, Bureau of Health Professions, National Center for Health Workforce Analysis.

Health Resources and Services Administration (HRSA). (2004). *The registered nurse population: Findings from the March 2004 national sample survey of registered nurses.*

Health Resources and Services Administration (HRSA). (2010, March). *The registered nurse population: Initial findings from the 2008 national sample survey of registered nurses.*

Herdrich, B., & Lindsay, A. (2006). Nurse residency programs: Redesigning the transition into practice. *Journal for Nurses in Staff Development, 22*(2), 55–62.

Iglehart, J. K. (2010). The ACGME's final duty-hour standards—Special PGY-1 limits and strategic napping. *New England Journal of Medicine.* Retrieved from http://www.nejm.org/doi/pdf/10.1056/NEJMp1010613

Isaacs, S. L., Jellinek, P. S., & Ray, W. L. (2009). The independent physician—going, going… *New England Journal of Medicine. 360*, 655–657.

The Joint Commission. (2002). *Health care at the crossroads: Strategies for addressing the evolving nursing crisis.* Retrieved from http://www.jointcommission.org/assets/1/18/health_care_at_the_crossroads.pdf

The Joint Commission. (2008, July 9). *Behaviors that undermine a culture of safety.* Sentinel Event Alert, Issue 40. Retrieved from http://www.jointcommission.org/sentinel_event_alert_issue_40_behaviors _that_undermine_a_culture_of_safety/

The Joint Commission. (2009). *The Joint Commission guide to improving staff communication* (2nd ed.). Oak Brook, IL: Joint Commission Resources.

The Joint Commission. (2010). *Sentinel events.* Retrieved from http://www.jointcommission.org/ sentinel_event.aspx

Jones, C., & Gates, M. (September 30, 2007). The costs and benefits of nurse turnover: A business case for nurse retention. *OJIN: The Online Journal of Issues in Nursing. 12*(3), Manuscript 4. Retrieved from http://www.nursingworld.org/MainMenuCategories/ANAMarketplace/ANAPeriodicals/ OJIN/TableofContents/Volume122007/No3Sept07/NurseRetention.aspx

Kennedy, B. R. (2005, December). Stress and burnout of nursing staff working with geriatric clients in long-term care. *Journal of Nursing Scholarship, 37*(4), 381–382.

Kimball, B., & O'Neil, E. (2002, April). *Health care's human crisis: The American nursing shortage.* Retrieved from http://www.rwjf.org/files/publications/other/NursingReport.pdf

Landers, S. H. (2010). Why health care is going home. *New England Journal of Medicine, 363*(18), 1690–1691.

Laschinger, H. K. S., & Finegan, J. (2005). Using empowerment to build trust and respect in the workplace: A strategy for addressing the nursing shortage. *Nursing Economic$, 23*(1), 6–13.

Levinson, W., Lesser, C. S., & Epstein, R. M. (2010). Developing physician communication skills for patient-centered care. *Health Affairs, 29*(7), 1310–1316.

Locke, E. A. (1983). The nature and causes of job satisfaction. In M. Dunnette (Ed.), *Handbook of industrial and organizational psychology* (pp. 297–1349). New York, NY: John Wiley & Sons.

Maslach, C. (2003, October). Job burnout: New directions in research and intervention. *Current Directions in Psychological Science, 12*(5), 189–190.

McMahon, G. T. (2004). Coming to America: International medical graduates in the United States. *New England Journal of Medicine, 350*, 2435–2437.

Mechanic, D. (2010). Replicating high-quality medical care organizations. *Journal of the American Medical Association, 303*(6), 555–556.

Medstar Health. (2010). *Conflict of interest corporate policy.* Retrieved from http://www.medstarhealth .org/documents/conflict_of_interest_policy.pdf

Mick, S. S., & Lee, S. D. (1999a). International and US medical graduates in US cities. *Journal of Urban Health: Bulletin of the New York Academy of Medicine, 76*(4), 481–496.

Mick, S. S., & Lee, S. D. (1999b). Are there need-based geographical differences between International Medical Graduates and US Medical Graduates in rural US counties? *The Journal of Rural Health*, Winter, *15*(1), 26–43.

Mick, S. S., Lee, S. D., & Wodchis, W. P. (2000). Variations in geographical distribution of foreign and domestically trained physicians in the United States: "Safety nets" or "surplus exacerbation." *Social Science & Medicine, 50*, 185–202.

Mullan, F. (2005). The metrics of the physician brain drain. *New England Journal of Medicine, 353,* 1810–1818.

Nadzman, D. M. (2009). Nurses' role in communication and patient safety. *Journal of Nursing Care Quality, 24*(3), 184–188.

National Accrediting Agency for Clinical Laboratory Sciences (NAACLS). (2010). *Programs.* Retrieved from http://www.naacls.org/program-center/

National Board for Respiratory Care (NBRC). (2010). *Examinations.* Retrieved from http://www.nbrc .org/examinations/rrt/tabid/60/default.aspx

National Commission on Certification of Physician Assistants (NCCPA). (2010a). *Continuing medical education.* Retrieved from http://www.nccpa.net/ContinuingMedicalEducation.aspx

National Commission on Certification of Physician Assistants (NCCPA). (2010b). *PA facts.* Retrieved from http://www.nccpa.net/PDFs/PAfacts.pdf

National Commission on Nursing (NCN). (1983). *Summary report and recommendations.* Chicago, IL: Hospital Research and Educational Trust.

National Council of State Boards of Nursing (NCSBN). (2008, December). *State information regarding criminal background checks.* Retrieved from https://www.ncsbn.org/CBC_SxS.pdf

National Council of State Boards of Nursing (NCSBN). (2010a). *About NCSBN.* Retrieved from https://www.ncsbn.org/about.htm

National Council of State Boards of Nursing (NCSBN). (2010b). *Nursing practice, licensure and certification.* Retrieved from https://www.ncsbn.org/1427.htm

National Council of State Boards of Nursing (NCSBN). (2010c). *Quarterly examination statistics: Volume, pass rates & first-time internationally educated candidates' countries.* Retrieved from https:// www.ncsbn.org/NCLEX_Stats_2010.pdf

National Institutes of Health (NIH). (2010a). *Frequently asked questions.* Retrieved from http://www .nih.gov/news/calendar/calendarfaq.htm#cmecredit

National Institutes of Health (NIH). (2010b). *Financial conflict of interest.* Retrieved from http://grants .nih.gov/grants/policy/coi/

National Practitioner Data Bank (NPDB). (2010). *National practitioner data bank: About us.* Retrieved from http://www.npdb-hipdb.com/topNavigation/aboutUs.jsp

National Residency Matching Program (NRMP). (2010). *How the NRMP process works.* Retrieved from http://www.nrmp.org/about_nrmp/how.html

Norcini, J. J., Boulet, J. R., Dauphinee, W. D., Opalek, A., Krantz, I. D., & Anderson, S. T. (2010). Evaluating the quality of care provided by graduates of international medical schools. *Health Affairs, 28*(8), 1461–1468.

O'Reilly, K. B. (2010, March 29). New medical schools open, but physician shortage concerns persist. *American Medical News.* Retrieved from http://www.ama-assn.org/amednews/2010/03/29/ prl20329.htm

Polsky, D., Kletke, P. R., Wozniak, G. D., & Escarce, J. (2002). Initial practice locations of international medical graduates. *HSR: Health Services Research, 37,* 907–928.

Ross, J. S., Lackner, J. E., Lurie, P., Gross, C. P., Wolfe, S., & Krumholz, H. M. (2007). Pharmaceutical company payments to physicians: early experiences with disclosure laws in Vermont and Minnesota. *Journal of the American Medical Association, 297*(11), 1216–1223.

Seavey, D. (2004, October). *The cost of frontline turnover in long-term care.* Retrieved from http://www .directcareclearinghouse.org/download/TOCostReport.pdf

Sexton, J. B., Thomas, E. J., & Helmreich, R. L. (2000). Error, stress, and teamwork in medicine and aviation: Cross sectional surveys. *British Medical Journal, 320*, 745–749.

Smart, D. R. (2010). *Physician characteristics and distribution in the US*. Chicago, IL: AMA Press.

Spatz, D. (2006, March 16). Where have all the doctors gone? Doctors, administrators have varied view of turnover causes. *The Dallas Chronicle*.

Steiger, D. O., Auerbach, D. I., & Buerhaus, P. I. (2000). Expanding career opportunities for women and the declining interest in nursing as a career. *Nursing Economic$, 18*(5), 230–236.

Steiger, D. O., Auerbach, D. I., & Buerhaus, P. I. (2009). Comparison of physician workforce estimates and supply projections. *Journal of the American Medical Association, 302*(15), 1674–1680.

Steiger, D. O., Auerbach, D. I., & Buerhaus, P. I. (2010). Trends in the work hours of physicians in the United States. *Journal of the American Medical Association, 303*(8), 747–753.

Sweeney, E. (2010, September 30). Teaching nurses for over 100 years: Brockton Hospital school is the last of its kind in Mass. *Boston Globe*. Retrieved from http://www.boston.com/news/local/articles/2010/09/30/brockton_hospital_school_of_nursing_is_the_last_of_its_kind/

Tamblyn, R., Abrahamowicz, M., Brailovsky, C., Grand'Maison, P., Lescop, J., Norcini, J., et al. (1998). Association between licensing examination scores and resource use and quality of care in primary care practice. *Journal of the American Medical Association, 280*(11), 989–996.

Towson University. (2010). *Department of nursing: Nursing basic program*. Retrieved from http://www.towson.edu/nursing/undergraduate/basic/index.asp

Weber, D. O. (2004, September-October). Poll results: Doctors' disruptive behavior disturbs physician leaders. *The Physician Executive, 30*(5), 6–14.

Whelan, G. P., Gary, N. E., Kostis, J., Boutlet, J. R., & Hallock, J. A. (2000). The changing pool of international medical graduates seeking certification training in US graduate medical education programs. *Journal of the American Medical Association, 288*, 1079–1084.

Williams, T., Sims, J., Burkhead, C., & Ward, P. M. (2002). The creation, implementation, and evaluation of a nurse residency program through a shared leadership model in the intensive care setting. *Dimensions of Critical Care Nursing, 21*(4), 154–161.

CHAPTER 12

The Strategic Management of Human Resources

Jon M. Thompson

LEARNING OBJECTIVES

By the end of this chapter, the student will be able to:

- Explain why human resources management includes strategic and administrative actions;
- Assess current environmental forces influencing human resources management;
- Analyze the key role of employees as drivers of organizational performance;
- Describe major federal legislation affecting human resources management;
- Define human resources functions that address employee workforce planning/ recruitment, and employee retention;
- Identify the key responsibilities of human resources management staff and line management staff in recruitment and retention;
- Classify methods of compensating employees;
- Demonstrate knowledge of methods of evaluating employees; and
- Discuss examples of human resource management issues in healthcare settings.

INTRODUCTION

The management of human resources is one of the most important and challenging responsibilities within health services organizations. Health services organizations need to be high-performing organizations, and human resources are considered the most important factor in creating such organizations (Pfeffer, 1998). A high-performing health services organization provides high-quality services and excellent customer service, is efficient, has high productivity, and is financially sound.

Human resources management involves both administrative and strategic elements. From a strategic perspective, health services organizations compete for labor. They desire an adequate labor supply and the proper mix of quality and committed healthcare professionals to provide needed services. The strategic perspective acknowledges that organizational performance is contingent on individual human performance. Health services organizations need to view their human resources as a strategic asset that helps create competitive advantage (Becker, Huselid, & Ulrich, 2001). Additionally, organizations must have the capability to understand their current and future manpower needs and develop and implement a clear-cut strategy to meet those needs to achieve the organizational business strategy. Administratively, there are a number of specific functions and action steps that need to be carried out in support of managing the human resources of the health services organization to ensure high levels of performance.

Fundamentally, **human resources management** addresses the need to ensure that qualified and motivated personnel are available to staff the business units operated by the health services organization (Hernandez, Fottler, & Joiner, 1998). Human resources management encompasses a variety of functions and tasks related to recruiting, retaining, and developing staff in the health services organization. These staff include **administrative staff** who carry out nonclinical administrative functions such as patient accounting, quality management, and community relations; **clinical staff** who provide diagnostic, treatment, and rehabilitation services to patients; and **support staff** who assist in the delivery of clinical, administrative, and other facility services. The human resources activities that support administrative and clinical staff are carried out by dedicated human resources personnel who work in human resources or personnel departments, and are also carried out by line managers who have primary responsibility for directing staff and teams and who are charged with hiring, supervising, evaluating, developing, and, when necessary, terminating staff.

Management of human resources is complex, and human resources actions address a variety of issues and situations. Consider the following examples of human resources management in various health services organizations:

- A large physician practice is in need of hiring someone to head up its information management area. The practice has grown from 7 to 23 physicians in the past five years, and the practice administrator has realized that the clinical and financial records needs of the practice have outpaced current administrative expertise. The administrator wants to define the job by analyzing job duties and then recruiting personnel to fill the position.
- A large system-affiliated hospital desires to train patient care technicians to assist in direct clinical care of patients. The hospital has experienced a shortage of RNs in the

past three years and has found that a multidisciplinary team approach using patient care technicians will help the organization meet patient and manpower needs. The vice president of Patient Care desires to know the best way to train these teams.

- An assisted living facility is developing a new position for a marketing specialist, who will be tasked with marketing the facility in an effort to increase its census. The facility administrator desires to conduct a job analysis to determine the specific responsibilities of the marketing specialist's job.

- An ambulatory care clinic plans to add new diagnostic imaging equipment in order to compete for more patients in its service area. The purchase of this equipment raises several questions for the organization, including: What are the specific human resources needed to staff the new technology, and are they available? How will the addition of new technology and services affect the operating budget and the achievement of the business strategy of the clinic?

Each of these scenarios provides a good illustration of the diverse nature of human resources activities from both strategic and administrative perspectives and suggests how these activities contribute to the effective performance of the organization.

This chapter provides an overview of the specific activities that take place strategically and administratively to manage the human resources of the health services organization. First, environmental forces affecting the management of human resources in health services organizations will be reviewed. Second, the importance of employees as drivers of organizational performance will be addressed. Key functions within human resources management will then be identified and discussed. Finally, conclusions regarding management of human resources in health services organizations will be presented.

ENVIRONMENTAL FORCES AFFECTING HUMAN RESOURCES MANAGEMENT

There are several key environmental forces that affect the availability and performance of human resources within health services organizations (HSOs) (see Table 12-1). The **environment** for HSOs is the external space beyond the organization that includes other organizations and influences that affect the organization.

First, *declining reimbursements* from government payers and other third parties have reduced the revenues coming to HSOs. In efforts to contain their expenses, the Medicare and Medicaid programs, private insurance, and managed care organizations have reduced their payments on behalf of covered beneficiaries. Declining reimbursements for health services organizations have left HSOs with fewer resources to recruit, compensate, and develop their workforces. Because other organizations in local and regional markets are

TABLE 12-1 Environmental Forces and Impacts on Human Resources Management

Force	Impact
Declining reimbursement	Less resources to recruit, compensate, and develop workforce
Declining supply of workers	Shortage of skilled workers; changes in recruiting and staffing specialized services; lower satisfaction of workers
Increasing population need	Increased volumes of patients and workload for HSOs
Increasing competition among HSOs	Competition for healthcare workers and pressure for higher wages
External pressure on HSOs	HR must ensure high performance in HSO for accountability and performance

also competing for the same labor, this has made recruitment and retention of staff more difficult for many HSOs.

Second, the *low supply of healthcare workers*—particularly highly specialized clinical personnel—has made recruitment of needed healthcare personnel very challenging (Fottler, Ford, & Heaton, 2002). Many areas of the country have experienced shortages of nursing, diagnostic, and treatment personnel, a phenomenon that has left many HSOs understaffed, requiring remaining staff to work longer hours per week (Shanahan, 1993). This has also contributed to lower levels of staff satisfaction and higher rates of turnover in certain staff positions, which has in turn increased human resources costs to the HSOs (Izzo & Withers, 2002; Shanahan, 1993). In addition, recruiting staff members who are highly specialized and who are in short supply tends to raise human resources costs as HSOs have to pay these staff members higher wages and provide other incentives to appeal to these potential workers (Shanahan, 1993).

Third, *competition among health services organizations* has increased dramatically in the past 20 years due to an increase in supply of traditional HSOs, such as hospitals and nursing homes, as well as the influence of newly emerging HSOs, such as retirement communities, assisted living facilities, and ambulatory care programs. HSOs have engaged in service competition and, to a lesser degree, price competition in trying to outperform their rivals. Competition in services and competition for labor has contributed to increased demands on human resources management.

Fourth, *the population's needs for health and medical care have increased* in the past two decades and will continue to grow during the next 25 years as the population ages and baby boomers approach retirement and qualify for Medicare. Older adults require more health services, and therefore, HSOs will require more healthcare workers to care for the increasing volumes of patients served at their facilities. This is further complicated by the fact that much of the current healthcare workforce is nearing retirement age themselves (Burt, 2005). Thus, in the future, health services organizations will be faced with declining workforces due to retirements, on the one hand, and expanded demands from the population on the other hand. Projections of the future number of healthcare workers show significant opportunities for employment (see Table 12-2). However, this puts HSOs in a difficult situation: additional workers are needed to care for the increased patient workload, while the supply of workers in many categories continues to be low. This creates additional challenges for recruiting as well as retaining HSO staff.

Finally, *increasing regulation and scrutiny of health services organizations* by external organizations have increased pressures for high-quality and high-performing organizations. While licensing and accrediting organizations monitor HSO conformance to standards, they also make these performance indicators available to the public, legislators, and other stakeholders. In addition, reimbursement organizations and government payers like Medicare and Medicaid are increasing requirements on HSOs for accountability and performance by mandating reports on quality, morbidity, and mortality, as well as efficiency and costs. For HSOs, this means that human resources management must help the HSO

TABLE 12-2 Projected Growth in Healthcare Occupations Employment, 2008–2018

Occupation	Total Employment, 2008	Projected Total Employment, 2018	Difference (percentage)	Median Annual Earnings in 2008
Physician Assistants	74,800	103,900	29,100 (39%)	$81,230
Physical Therapists	185,500	241,700	56,200 (30%)	$72,790
Emergency Medical Technicians and Paramedics	210,700	229,700	19,000 (9%)	$29,328
Nursing Aides, Orderlies, and Attendants	1,469,800	1,745,800	276,000 (19%)	$23,837
Physicians and Surgeons	661,400	805,500	144,100 (22%)	$186,044 (primary care) $339,738 (medical specialties)
Medical and Clinical Laboratory Technicians	155,600	180,700	25,100 (16%)	$53,500
Registered Nurses	2,618,700	3,200,200	581,500 (22%)	$62,450
Medical and Health Services Managers	283,500	328,800	45,300 (16%)	$80,240

Source: Bureau of Labor Statistics, 2010.

become a high-performing, high-quality organization that can demonstrate quality processes and outcomes to these external stakeholders. Human resources can help accomplish this by hiring staff that are high quality, retaining those that are high quality, and reinforcing the culture of a high-performing organization.

In addition to the noted external factors, internal factors also affect human resources management. Increasingly, senior management of HSOs view human resources in terms of its contribution to the success of the HSO and look to human resources indicators in their assessment of overall organizational performance (Becker et al., 2001; Galford, 1998; Griffith, 2000; Pieper, 2005). As they do with other departments and services, HSO senior management wants to see a return on their investment in human resources functions and a contribution to the bottom line (Becker et al., 2001). Although a support function to the core focus of delivery of patient care services, human resources activities are evaluated in terms of the contribution to recruitment, training, and development for staff, as well as employee satisfaction and retention. Therefore, human resources strategies and programs to address recruitment and retention needs are being developed and assessed, not in terms of whether they look good or because other organizations are doing them, but rather because they contribute to the organization's mission and goals for the creation of a high-performing, high-quality organization.

UNDERSTANDING EMPLOYEES AS DRIVERS OF ORGANIZATIONAL PERFORMANCE

The core services provided by HSOs—patient care services—are highly dependent on the capabilities and expertise of the organization's employees. It has been said that successful business strategy is directly connected to having committed, high-performance employees (Ginter, Swayne, & Duncan, 2002). HSOs are only as good as their employees. Why is this so for health services organizations?

There are three primary reasons why this is the case. First, HSOs are service organizations, unlike traditional businesses or manufacturing firms that make and distribute a specific product. Being a service organization means providing a service that is needed and/or desired by a consumer who decides to take advantage of what the HSO has to offer. Providing services involves doing things to help others, and HSOs require employees who have a desire to help others, a "service orientation" (Fottler et al., 2002). Second, HSOs are highly specialized service organizations that provide a range of specific services that include inpatient, outpatient, surgical, rehabilitation, diagnostic, therapeutic, and wellness services. To provide these specialized services, healthcare workers need to carry out many highly specialized tasks, and they need to have the proper knowledge, training, and experience to do those tasks well. Finally, because of the variety of services provided in HSOs and the fact that specialized staff provide only specific "pieces" of the overall service experience, healthcare workers from different departments and units must work together to provide a comprehensive service that meets all the needs of each patient (Liberman & Rotarius, 2000). Therefore staff must work together as teams to ensure that all required services are provided and that the total needs of the patient or healthcare client are met. Therefore, teamwork is necessary in order for the HSO to provide the high-quality, coordinated, and comprehensive services that are required for it to be a high-performing organization.

In essence, all HSO employees need to work together to ensure the best service possible, centered on the patient's needs. Managers, therefore, must be able to hire good people with the proper knowledge, skills, and attitudes and provide them the resources and support necessary to do their jobs effectively and efficiently.

KEY FUNCTIONS OF HUMAN RESOURCES MANAGEMENT

In this section, the major functions within human resources management will be reviewed. The primary areas of human resources management activity include job analysis; workforce planning; establishing position descriptions; recruitment, selection, and hiring of employees; orienting new employees; managing employee relations and engagement; providing training and development; managing compensation and benefits; assessing performance; offering leadership development programs; providing employee assistance services; and offering employee suggestion programs. Typically, these key functions can be collapsed into two major domains called **workforce planning/recruitment** and **employee retention** (see Table 12-3). In the discussion below, the reader should note that activities

TABLE 12-3 Human Resources Functions

Function	Related Tasks
Workforce Planning/Recruitment	Job analysis Manpower planning Job descriptions Recruitment, selection, negotiation, and hiring Orientation
Employee Retention	Employee relations and engagement Training and development Compensation and benefits Employee assistance programs Assessing performance Labor relations Leadership development Employee suggestion programs

in these two domains are typically carried out by human resources staff professionals who are under the supervision of a vice president, director, or manager of human resources. In some HSOs, this office may be called "personnel," but most health services organizations—particularly large HSOs—now have a department or office of human resources that reflects both a strategic and administrative focus.

The human resources department or office develops and maintains all employee policies and procedures that reflect hiring, evaluating, promoting, disciplining, and terminating employees. In addition, policies and procedures related to assessing employee satisfaction, giving employee awards, compensating employees, and providing benefits are also developed and managed by the human resources staff. Furthermore, all employee records are maintained in the human resources office and in the human resources information system.

It should be noted that many federal and state laws affect human resources management in HSOs. There is a lengthy history of federal legislation that has been enacted to protect the rights of individual employees and to ensure nondiscrimination in the hiring, disciplining, promoting, compensating, and terminating of employees on the basis of age, sex, religion, color, national origin, or disability. Many states have also enacted specific laws that protect employees. Other employment issues such as sexual harassment, whistleblowing (identifying wrongdoing), and workplace harassment are also addressed under federal and state law and offer employees protection. The legal environment for HSOs related to human resources management is constantly changing, and employers must carry out their activities with full knowledge of applicable laws and emerging rulings from court cases. Table 12-4 provides a summary of key federal legislation affecting human resources management in HSOs.

WORKFORCE PLANNING/RECRUITMENT

Human resources functions carried out within the workforce planning/recruitment domain are directed to analyzing jobs needed within the HSO; identifying current and future staffing needs; establishing position descriptions; recruiting, selecting, negotiating, and hiring employees; and orienting new employees.

Job Analysis

One of the fundamental tasks of human resources is to conduct an analysis of all jobs or positions that are a part of the HSO. Every position in the HSO—whether administrative, support, or clinical—needs to be justified in terms of its specific responsibilities and day-to-day activities. **Job analysis** involves identifying those unique responsibilities, duties,

---

TABLE 12-4 Key Federal Legislation Affecting Human Resources Management

1935	**National Labor Relations Act** (as amended in 1974). Provides for bargaining units and collective bargaining in hospitals and health services organizations.
1938	**Fair Labor Standards Act** (as amended many times). Employees who are nonexempt from minimum wage and overtime provisions must be paid minimum wage and time and a half for hours beyond 40 hours per week. Special provisions for health services organizations.
1963	**Equal Pay Act.** Prohibits discrepancies in pay between men and women who perform the same job.
1964	**Civil Rights Act** (as amended many times). Prohibits discrimination in screening, hiring, and promotion of individuals based on gender, color, religion, or national origin (Title VII).
1967	**Age Discrimination in Employment Act.** Prohibits employment discrimination against employees age 40 and older.
1970	**Occupational Safety and Health Act.** Requires employers to maintain a safe workplace and adhere to standards specific to healthcare employers.
1973	**Rehabilitation Act.** Protects the rights of handicapped people (physically or mentally impaired) and protects them from discrimination.
1974	**Employee Retirement Income Security Act (ERISA).** Grants protection to employees for retirement benefits to which they are entitled.
1978	**Pregnancy Discrimination Act.** Requires employers to consider pregnancy a "medical condition" and prohibits exclusion of pregnancy in benefits and leave policies.
1986	**Consolidated Omnibus Budget Reconciliation Act (COBRA).** Gives employees and their families the right to continue health insurance coverage for a limited time due to various circumstances such as termination, layoff, death, reduction in hours worked per week, and divorce.
1986	**Immigration Reform and Control Act.** Establishes penalties for employers who knowingly hire illegal aliens.
1987	**Worker Adjustment and Retraining Notification Act.** Requires employers who will make a mass layoff or plant closing to give 60 days' advance notice to affected employees.
1989	**Whistleblower Protection Act.** Protects employees who report employer misconduct or wrongdoing with respect to compliance with federal and state law.
1990	**Americans with Disabilities Act (ADA).** Gives people with physical and mental disabilities access to public services and requires employers to provide reasonable accommodation for applicants and employees.
1993	**Family and Medical Leave Act (FMLA).** Permits employees in organizations to take up to 12 weeks of unpaid leave each year for family or medical reasons.
2003	**Health Insurance Portability and Accountability Act (HIPAA).** Affords employee protection from outside access to personal health information and limits employers' ability to use employee health information under health insurance plans.
2010	**Patient Protection and Affordable Care Act.** Enacts various health insurance reforms, including requiring employers to offer coverage, prohibiting denial of coverage/claims based on preexisting conditions, and extending insurance coverage for dependent children to age 26.

Sources: Busse, 2005; Kaiser Family Foundation, 2010; Lehr, McLean, & Smith, 1998; U.S. Department of Labor, 2006.

and activities specific to every position in the HSO. This is necessary to clarify individual responsibilities but is also critical to avoid duplication of tasks and responsibilities across positions. The outcome of job analysis is to clearly state the responsibilities, duties, and tasks of every position within the HSO.

Human resources experts have suggested that HSOs should focus on those positions that contribute most directly to the completion of the organization's business objectives (Huselid, Beatty, & Becker, 2005). This is important because filling these critical positions with the best personnel—"A" players—will then increase the organization's ability to perform.

Workforce Planning

For every position established for the HSO, there needs to be an estimate of the number of staff members needed to carry out those responsibilities at the present time, as well as projections of the number of staff members needed at some future target date. For example, how many RNs does our hospital currently need for all the various services that we currently offer, and how many will we need in five years? This is a very complex decision process, and it must be based on consideration of many factors. For example, consider a hospital. Will the hospital be downsizing or eliminating any services in the next five years? Will the facility be adding any new services that are not presently offered? How will the addition of new technology, or the addition of nursing assistants, affect the need for RNs in the future, across all services of the hospital?

Identifying current numbers of staff is based on volume statistics that reflect the current performance of the HSO. The need for clinical staff is based typically on patient care statistics, such as the number of patients admitted, number of outpatient visits, or the number of patients receiving a specific service. In some cases, need will be determined by licensure standards that govern the minimum number of staff for certain services. For non–patient care areas, including such support functions as medical records, information technology, and financial services, the number of staff needed is contingent on the current volume of records and patient accounts that must be processed. Each support person in these areas can handle a minimum number of accounts or records per day, which becomes the basis for estimating current need. This is a called a **ratio method of determining needs**. The managers in various units calculate these estimates and forward them to human resources for the development of aggregate estimates of staffing needs for the total facility.

Projections of staffing needs for a future target date are based on a similar method. **Projections of future service volumes** are made and associated staffing requirements are projected as well to serve that anticipated volume. Again, line managers usually develop these projections. Future volumes are typically determined through a consensus-based strategic planning process where there is agreement on future service volumes. In this process, consideration is also made for retiring staff, transfers, and service changes (such as eliminations or expansions of beds and services) to arrive at the needed number of staff to recruit or to acquire on a temporary basis from outside staffing firms. Once the projected staffing needs are identified for the total facility, strategies and timeframes are established for recruiting. Projections of staffing needs are revisited every year as annual performance is assessed to see if projections remain accurate.

Accuracy of projections has important implications for preparing budgets and evaluating financial performance of the HSO. For example, future staffing levels may be unrealistic if forecast revenues don't match projected expenses. Therefore, planned positions may remain unfilled and flexible staffing arrangements used as necessary. In addition, if demand shifts occur, some services may not realize projected patient volumes, and cutbacks in staffing arrangements may be necessary. In conclusion, projections of future staffing requirements are just that—projections that may or may not hold up given the uncertain and dynamic nature of the health services environment. Many factors affect these projections, and a thorough and periodic assessment is needed to ensure that projections are realistic and revised as appropriate.

Establishing Job Descriptions

Position descriptions or job descriptions are required for every position within the HSO. **Job descriptions** are necessary to define the required knowledge, skills, responsibilities, training, experience, certification or licensure, and line of reporting for a specific job within the HSO. Such descriptions are important to both the organization and employee. The **position description** elaborates on the findings from the job analysis and provides a means by which the organization clarifies each position in terms of expectations, locus within the organizational structure, and how it contributes to the organization's overall performance. For the employee, the position description clarifies expectations and duties and allows prospective employees a means to evaluate the "fit" between a position and their own individual knowledge, skills, and experience.

Position descriptions are developed through joint efforts of line managers and human resources staff. Line managers specify job requirements; human resources staff keep job descriptions in a consistent format and ensure accuracy of the positions as they are included in the HSO's Human Resources Information System. An example of a position description for a hospital is shown in Figure 12-1.

Recruitment, Selection, Negotiation, and Hiring of New Employees

A key principle of human resources recruitment is making sure that HSO positions are filled with competent and highly skilled personnel. Once recruitment needs are made known by line managers, it is the responsibility of human resources to follow the

BON SECOURS HEALTH CORPORATION
St. Francis Medical Center
POSITION DESCRIPTION

TITLE:	Environmental Services Aide	**JOB CODE: 950**
DEPARTMENT:	Environmental Services	
REPORTS TO:		**FLSA: Non-exempt**

I. GENERAL PURPOSE OF POSITION:

The primary responsibility of this position is to perform cleaning tasks to maintain designated areas in a clean, safe, orderly and attractive manner. The employee is expected to follow detailed instructions and/or written task schedules to accomplish assigned duties. This position serves all populations of visitors, employees, physicians and patients.

II. EMPLOYMENT QUALIFICATIONS:

1. Ability to communicate and interpret assignments issued through a computerized paging system.
2. Dependability and flexibility demonstrated through previous work or school history.
3. Previous housekeeping work experience preferred.

III. ESSENTIAL JOB FUNCTIONS:

1. Communicates all hospital-related issues to Supervisor.
2. Performs the duties necessary to maintain the sanitary conditions of the hospital, including routine cleaning and maintenance of all floor types.
3. Prepares patient rooms for new admissions through the proper utilization of the Bedtracking® system. (Login|Logout)
4. Cleans and sanitizes isolation rooms and other contaminated areas following written techniques appropriate for that type of isolation (i.e., tuberculosis, HIV, hepatitis).
5. Performs general cleaning tasks using the 7 Steps process.
6. Follows hospital policy regarding storage and security of housekeeping chemicals.
7. Accurately uses Bedtracking® system to meet departmental response and cleaning time standards.
8. Responsible for the use and care of equipment and other hospital property. Maintains equipment by proper cleaning and storage; reports dangerous or broken equipment to team leader. Makes sure EVS cart is clean, box locks, and wringer free of lint.
9. Understands basic safety procedures. (RACE, PASS, MSDS, etc.)

IV. OTHER JOB EXPECTATIONS:

1. Actively participates in the hospital's Continuing Educational Improvement programs (i.e., Essential Skills, Safety Fairs, etc.)
2. Assists in the orientation of new employees in departmental methods and procedures.
3. Responds to unusual occurrences such as flood, spillage, etc.

V. WORKING CONDITIONS:

Works in all areas of the hospital and off-site properties. May be exposed to hazardous chemicals, but potential for harm is limited, if safety precautions are followed.

The individual performing this job may reasonably come into contact with human blood and other potentially infectious materials. The individual in this position is required to exercise universal precautions, use personal protective equipment and devices, when necessary, and learn the policies concerning infection control.

VI. BON SECOURS MISSION, VALUES, CUSTOMER ORIENTATION AND

CONTINUOUS QUALITY IMPROVEMENT FOCUS:

It is the responsibility of all employees to learn and utilize continuous quality improvement principles in their daily work.

All employees are responsible for extending the mission and values of the Sisters of Bon Secours by understanding each customer, treating each patient, staff member, and community member in a dignified manner with respect, kindness, and understanding, and subscribing to the organization's commitment to quality and service.

VII. APPROVALS   DATE

Department Manager

Administration ———————————————————

Human Resources

The above statements are intended to describe the nature and level of work being done by individuals assigned to this classification and are not to be construed as an exhaustive list of all job duties. This document does not create an employment contract, and employment with Bon Secours Richmond Health System is "at will".

FIGURE 12-1 Position Description

Source: Reprinted with permission from Bon Secours St. Francis Medical Center, Midlothian, Virginia.

appropriate procedures to fill those positions. In some cases, existing employees will have an interest in a new position for which they are qualified, and internal candidates will be considered. Human resources recruitment personnel use a standard process for external recruiting. These steps include advertising, screening applicants, determining those to be interviewed, conducting interviews, selecting the candidate, negotiating, and hiring. Activities for both human resources staff and line managers related to recruitment are identified in Table 12-5.

Advertising

Different modes of **advertising** are used to target candidates and generate interest. These sources include local newspapers and electronic media including radio and television, organizational websites, and Internet job search engines, for example, www.monster.com and www.CareerBuilder.com. The human resources department uses standards for communication that address the position, required degrees, training and/or certification, experience, functional line of reporting, and general expectations of the position. Applicants submit information in response to the advertising and submit their credentials electronically to be reviewed and evaluated by human resources staff.

Candidates are recruited also through **private recruitment** or **"headhunter"** firms, and these may include firms that engage in general staff recruiting or firms that specialize

---

TABLE 12-5 Responsibilities of HR Staff and Line Managers in Recruitment

HR Staff Person

Prepares position description
Prices jobs
Prepares advertisements/recruitment materials
Keeps track of applicants/maintains HR Information System
Checks applicant references
Maintains personnel files
Narrows candidate pool

Line Manager

Clarifies job function/provides input into position description
Interviews candidates
Ranks candidates
Selects candidate
Negotiates with candidate
Hires candidate

in health services organization staff by recruiting nurses, technicians, financial analysts, or office personnel. Arrangements with recruiters usually involve paying a percentage of the first-year salary to the recruiter if the candidate referred by the recruitment firm is selected for the position. This method of recruiting will result in costs that exceed the normal expected costs of filling position vacancies. However, this technique may be a necessary option when recruiting for highly specialized positions where the candidate pool is limited.

Another frequently used option in recruiting is to work with **educational programs** that prepare specialized health personnel, such as nurses, physical therapists, and diagnostic technicians (Shanahan, 1993). Sending announcements of positions to these educational programs, attending recruitment open houses, and developing important referral relationships with faculty and staff of these programs is helpful in building interest and identifying candidates. Other sources include placing ads in targeted professional journals that are read by healthcare professionals, disseminating recruitment materials to healthcare workers identified through association membership listings, and attending regional or annual meetings of professionals where human resources representatives can meet with interested candidates. A final option to identify interested candidates is for human resources staff to attend **healthcare recruitment or job fairs** held locally or regionally, or for the HSO to hold its own.

Some observers have suggested that HSOs use a pre-employment assessment by the candidate of the fit between their credentials and the job (Liberman & Rotarius, 2000). This is recommended to ensure that only appropriate, well-qualified applicants apply.

Interviewing, Selection, Negotiation, and Hiring

Most applications for positions in HSOs are handled online through the organization's employment website, and tracking is also handled online. Human resources staff complete the preliminary review and analysis of candidates based on their applications, check candidate references, and identify past employers' satisfaction with the candidates. As a result, human resources staff narrow down the pool to those candidates that provide the best fit for the position based on training, experience, and other factors such as motivation and attitude. These applicants are then discussed with the line manager to select those to be interviewed. The candidates are invited to come to the organization and interview and spend some time with management, staff, and others. From the HSO's perspective, this is important for two reasons. It enables the HSO to assess firsthand the candidates and verify their knowledge and skills; also, it enables the assessment of the candidates' fit and compatibility with the organization and staff with whom they would be working. From the candidate's perspective, an interview is important to get a close look at the organization and staff, and to assess their fit and interest in the position and the organization.

Depending on the position, human resources staff may participate in candidate interviews, and line managers will definitely participate in interviews with candidates. **Structured interviews** with clearly defined questions are thought to be best for assessing candidates (Foster & Godkin, 1998). Increasingly, peer interviews and behavioral-based interview questioning are used to assess candidates (Studer, 2003). **Behavioral-based questioning** focuses on the candidate's response to questions that yield insight into actions taken in particular situations (e.g., Tell me a time when a project could not be completed and how you resolved the problem).

Subsequent to the interviews, the staff who have interviewed candidates meet to review the candidates, determine how the candidates match with position requirements, and rank order candidates. Once the staff agree on the applicant they would like to hire, an offer is extended.

An **offer of employment** is made in writing, and the offer letter must specify the position for which the offer is made, start date, associated salary/compensation and benefits, and any other key information regarding the offer. Although an offer has been extended, the recruitment process is not complete. Depending on the position, there may be a period of negotiation over salary, benefits, start time, flexible scheduling, and other issues. Once agreement is reached, the position is assumed filled, and the candidate responds with a formal letter of acceptance agreeing to the position and conditions of acceptance. Background checks, physical examinations, and proof of immunizations are frequently required. Completion of hiring paperwork is necessary at the time that the person starts the job. It should be noted that if agreement is not reached with the first-choice candidate, then the offer would be extended to the next best candidate, and then the next, until agreement with a suitable candidate is reached.

Orientation

One of the key requirements of a new staff member is to attend an **orientation program** coordinated by human resources. This program is important for several reasons. An orientation program informs the new employee of policies, procedures, and requirements, and it offers an opportunity for the new employee to ask questions and clarify understanding about the organization. The Employee Staff Manual is provided to each new employee. During orientation, various policies and procedures are highlighted, including expectations for the work day, proper attire and behavior, employee assessment, disciplinary actions and grievances, probationary period, and opportunities for training and development. The organization's values, mission, vision, and goals are reviewed, as are strategic and long-range plans. Specific employee benefits are identified and reviewed, and employees are informed about options concerning benefits and associated costs. Safety and security policies and practices are reviewed, and in large HSOs such as hospitals and nursing homes, special codes are revealed so that employees know when and how to respond to emergency situations such as fires, patient medical emergencies, patient problems, intruders, and chemical and environmental emergencies. With the passage of the Health Insurance Portability and Accountability Act (HIPAA) in 1996, training in the requirements of this law regarding confidentiality of health information has been incorporated into many HSO's employee orientation sessions. Training in compliance with Medicare rules and regulations, along with the dissemination of Whistleblower Protection Act of 1989 information, is also becoming a part of new employee orientation in many HSOs.

Orientation is usually held once a month to coincide with the start date for new employees. Part-time, full-time, and short-term temporary employees are typically required to attend orientation. New employees have an opportunity to meet the senior management team, who typically provide an overview of their respective management domains during orientation. This helps new staff gain an understanding of their respective roles in the HSO. Subsequent to the formal orientation session, most HSOs now require new employees to complete a required number of online and in-person courses related to the organization and other pertinent topics, such as sexual harassment, communications, customer service, and teamwork. Employees are tested on their knowledge after completing the training and must show competency as a part of their employment.

EMPLOYEE RETENTION

Employee retention functions include all of those key activities that address care, support, and development of employees to facilitate their long-term commitment to the organization. The key functions under **employee retention** include employee relations and engagement, training and development, managing compensation and benefits, providing employee assistance programs, assessing performance, managing labor relations, providing leadership development programs, and offering employee suggestion programs.

Employee Relations and Engagement

The purpose of employee relations and engagement efforts coordinated by the human resources staff is to identify and address the needs of employees so that they will be satisfied and remain with the organization. It has been shown through empirical study that satisfied workers provide better service and care (Angermeier, Dunford, Boss, & Boss, 2009). As a result, HSOs have increased their efforts recently to address staff concerns, improve the work environment, and redesign jobs and administrative structures to provide for personal learning and professional growth (Becker et al., 2001; Osterman, 1995). Initiatives to increase participative management, through greater employee decision making about aspects of their work and sharing of organizational metrics about performance with employees, have been shown to increase employee satisfaction and lessen the likelihood of leaving the organization (Angermeier et al., 2009). Also, there have been major efforts at implementing recognition and reward programs, such as employee of the month, staff appreciation events, and greatest improvement by department or unit in balanced scorecard measures.

The human resources department works with managers to determine appropriate employee relations activities, and typically, cross-functional committees are established to spearhead these efforts. Employee engagement and satisfaction surveys are commonly used to assess satisfaction and to help human resources staff and individual managers identify operational areas in need of improvement. Sometimes HSOs contract with consulting firms to survey employees in an anonymous fashion, usually once a year; to collect employee perceptions and suggestions; and to assess progress on addressing prior issues. Improvements in communications and teamwork, in addition to common areas of concern such as compensation and benefits, are issues that are frequently identified through engagement surveys.

Another common tactic for HSOs to gauge employee perceptions and satisfaction is through manager walk-arounds, town hall meetings, employee neighborhood meetings, daily huddles, and employee focus groups. These efforts can be used in addition to engagement surveys, and those organizations that practice high-involvement employee relations will use these additional techniques with regularity. These methods allow for greater clarity of employee issues and concerns through dialogue with a manager. Follow-up responses to employees by managers are critical to closing the loop on concerns and suggestions. Moreover, observation of work units and meeting with employees through rounding creates a connection between management and employees that signals managerial interest in employees and a greater sense on the part of management as to employee daily job tasks and challenges (Studer, 2003). Observations are recorded on logs or diaries and are used to identify needed improvements. Sometimes, employees may feel constrained in their input and discussion with managers—particularly their own manager—as they may view their input as complaining. However, in most HSOs where there is a positive relationship between management and staff, and where input and exchange is a key part of the organizational culture, employees will feel open to expressing their concerns. In addition, some senior administrators now use blogs and intranet postings to inform staff about decisions and solicit input on key issues.

Training and Development

Training and development of the workforce are extremely important human resources functions for several reasons. First, the organization's need for specific knowledge and skills is always changing because of the rapid changes being experienced by HSOs. For example, HSOs frequently add new medical technologies that require different technical skills of employees. Another example of additional skills needed is in the information technology area, where new computer information systems, electronic medical records, databases, and integrated patient and financial data systems are being acquired to generate, store, and retrieve patient-level and organizational information. Second, training is necessary to provide for continuing education of some staff. For clinical staff that require continuing education as part of their licensure and/or certification, HSOs may coordinate the provision of hands-on training that is provided either on-site or at remote locations. Some clinical training and training for nonclinical staff can be provided online through the organization's intranet or a third party's website. While it is clear that not all the training and development needs of staff can be met due to resource limitations, the human resources staff determines priorities for annual training and education efforts and implements and manages those programs. Human resources staff typically accomplish this through organization-wide needs assessments or through identification of specific training needs that are made known to human resources staff by managers. Typically, the cost of training and development programs is provided for in the human resources budget; in some cases, other departments or services within the HSOs may cover the cost of training that is coordinated by human resources. In most cases, the costs of training can be reduced if the training is provided online.

The goal of any training or development effort is to provide value for the organization by returning benefits, such as increased productivity, greater effectiveness, higher quality, greater coordination of care, and enhanced patient or customer service. Therefore, training and development programs are evaluated by human resources for cost-effectiveness to ensure that training is effective in terms of return on investment and that methods of training are appropriate (Phillips, 1996). Training programs cover a range of topics, including technical training on equipment and software programs, customer service training, and training to improve interpersonal communications and leadership skills, among others. Training and development of teams within HSOs are also increasingly common, as HSO staff work frequently in teams to coordinate the delivery of care. The effectiveness of team leaders has been shown to influence team learning, development, and performance (Edmonson, Bohmer, & Pisano, 2004).

Managing Compensation and Benefits

The following sections describe the management of employee compensation and benefits in healthcare organizations and how it can contribute to a high-performing organization.

Compensation

The human resources department has the specific responsibility of managing the pay or **compensation and benefits** associated with all positions held within the HSO. This is no easy task, as specific pay ranges and benefits must be established for each position, which in the hospital industry includes more than 300 distinct jobs or major job classifications

(Metzger, 2004). The management of compensation begins with a clear definition of the HSO's compensation philosophy, which reflects the organization's mission, values, and strategy regarding human resources, as well as consideration of internal (e.g., equity) and external (e.g., competitive) factors (Gering & Conner, 2002; Joiner, Jones, & Dye, 1998).

Determining compensation refers to the establishing of a specific financial value for a job. Compensation for each position is set based on the consideration of a number of factors, including the specialized knowledge and skills associated with the position, the experience required for the position, the relative availability of skilled individuals to fill the position, and average wages that are specific to the local labor market. This is called "**job pricing**" (Joiner et al., 1998). Some positions are hourly rated (i.e., nonexempt and eligible for overtime pay), where a compensation rate per hour of work is established (e.g., for maintenance staff and floor nurses). Some positions are salaried (i.e., exempt and not paid overtime), where an annual salary is paid the employee (e.g., nurse managers and other managerial staff). In short, compensation is set to account for the special skills and experiences required of employees and to enable the organization to be competitive in the market in securing and retaining needed employees. Pay ranges will vary by type of position, but within a position class there must be equity. However, HSOs typically account for differences in training, experience and special considerations of the job (working weekends or evenings) by allowing for pay/shift differentials. Also, some jobs are subject to significant external market pricing, because the skill set is unique and the market is national or international.

The typical large HSO, such as a hospital or hospital system, has a separate, designated staff to handle the administration of compensation on the one hand and benefits on the other. Human resources staff responsible for compensation keep records of wages and salaries, compensation adjustments, and the basis for compensation adjustments in individual employee personnel files and in the Human Resources Information System. Every few years, human resources administers a compensation or salary survey for positions within the HSO in order to **benchmark** current compensation to local and regional markets. This comparative market analysis of wages is then used to adjust salary ranges for positions as appropriate to remain competitive.

Job pricing is used to establish equitable pay scales by position within HSOs, but reward systems beyond base pay are frequently considered of greater importance to employees (Joiner et al., 1998). In addition to base compensation tied to expectations for a specific job, many HSOs have embraced **incentive compensation**. While compensation plans focus on individual performance and allocating rewards such as raises to high performers based on individual performance, incentive plans are designed to improve organizational performance (Gibson, 1995). In an incentive or **pay-for-performance plan**, the purpose of the plan is to stimulate employees to higher levels of achievement and performance that benefit the organization. Meaningful measures such as profits (return on investments), productivity, attendance, safety, quality, and customer satisfaction are a few examples of financial and nonfinancial organization-wide performance indicators that can be used in developing incentive plans. The incentive plan would work in the following way. The organization would set target goals for performance in a specific time period. At the end of that time period, the organization would collect and review relevant information to measure the status of performance. If the measurement of performance on specific indicators met the target goals, the organization would then reward employees for the "organization-wide" performance. These programs are also known as **gainsharing** or **goal-sharing** programs, and payouts (revenues derived from savings, increased productivity or volumes, increased customer retention, and quality) would be shared with employees as a bonus for their contributions to high performance within the HSO (Gomez-Mejia, Welbourne, & Wiseman, 2000).

Incentive compensation plans have long been thought to be associated with higher levels of organizational performance (Bonner & Sprinkle, 2002). The theory behind this approach is that use of incentives such as compensation bonuses positively affects motivation, which leads to higher performance (Gibson, 2002). Many health services organizations have begun to follow the lead of businesses and industries that pioneered these programs, but published literature addressing the impact of incentive compensation on organizational performance in health care is limited (Griffith & White, 2002). There is evidence to show that more HSOs are using incentive programs for executives that are tied to organizational performance (Healthcare Financial Management Association, 2001). However, other research in the business literature has shown that the relationship between incentive pay and performance may not hold up.

Beer and Katz (2003) found in their survey of senior executives from among many firms that bonuses have little to no positive effect on performance and that their real function may be to attract and retain executives. They looked at firms that had implemented executive bonus compensation systems and assessed relationships to performance but found that the only key explanatory factor was that the incentive system promoted teamwork. Similarly, Luthans and Stajkovic (1999) found in their analysis of research on pay-for-performance that social recognition and administrative feedback to employees on performance were just as influential as pay-for-performance in achieving higher levels of performance in a manufacturing setting. Moreover, Beer and Cannon (2004) found that many senior managers view incentive compensation programs with concern and question whether the benefits outweigh the costs. However, none of the studies cited above were specific to health services organizations.

Benefits

The human resources staff is responsible for managing benefits provided to employees working in an HSO. A **benefit** is defined as any type of compensation provided in a form other than salary or direct wages, that is paid for totally or in part by an employer (Jenks & Zevnik, 1993). As benefits extended to workers in general have increased over the past two decades, the number and type of benefits made available to HSO employees have increased as well (Griffith & White, 2002; Runy, 2003). However, the HSO is faced with a dilemma. On the one hand, HSOs are under pressure to manage costs, and employee benefits have been a high-cost item for HSOs, which directly affects the HSO's cost management strategy, financial status, and competitive position. On the other hand, benefits as a portion of total compensation have increased in importance, as more and more employees indicate that benefits are important in their choice of an employer (Runy, 2003).

Benefits may differ by level within the organization, as management may receive one set of benefits to offset the higher level of skill needed to complete the job, versus lower-level employees who may receive fewer benefits due to a lower level of skills required for the job. The availability of benefits, as well as the percentage of employee cost sharing, varies widely by HSO. Typical benefits offered by HSOs include the following:

Sick leave. A certain number of days per year are allocated for the employee being unable to be on the job due to illness or injury.

Vacation. A certain number of vacation days are allocated to employees for them to use as free time. In many HSOs, this is combined under a paid-time-off (PTO) plan with sick leave days and holidays.

Holidays. Designated national holidays are given to employees with pay as part of their benefits.

Health insurance. Medical coverage for the employee and optional coverage for dependents are typically made available. Depending on the type of health insurance plan offered to employees (and there may be one or more plans offered by the HSO), the total plan cost for the employee may be shared by the employer and employee. HSOs, like other organizations, have turned to managed care plans as a way to reduce health benefits expense for the HSO. Typical plan features include greater cost-sharing and out-of-pocket expenses for employees, along with the trend of increased access to out-of-network and specialty care. In addition, much of the coverage by health insurers today focuses on the management of certain chronic clinical conditions, such as cardiovascular problems and diabetes. These disease management programs are offered in an attempt to help the employee or dependent manage their conditions to promote better quality of life and reduce cost.

Life insurance. Coverage is provided that will help offset the loss of earnings for a limited time and to cover burial and other expenses related to the death of an employee. The employee is typically provided a base amount of life insurance with an option to increase coverage for an additional cost.

Flexible health benefits. Flexible or "cafeteria" benefits are increasing in popularity as they are offered to employees as options. Flexible benefits most often include health insurance, dental insurance, eye coverage, and other health benefits (such as disability insurance and long-term care insurance) and provide the employee with a choice of benefits for specific costs. Flexible benefits offer advantages to the employee in that the employee can tailor benefits to meet individual needs at varying costs (Joiner et al., 1998). For the HSO, overall benefit costs can be reduced under flexible benefit plans due to the fact that the employer is no longer paying for a specific base package of benefits for all employees (Joiner et al., 1998).

Retirement benefits. Many HSOs have retirement plans in place where employees are granted a certain percentage of their compensation over and above their compensation that is put into a retirement fund. This fund can be a pension fund that is set up specific to the HSO or, more likely, a 401(k) or 403(b) plan where employees can manage their retirement dollars in mutual fund investments (Jenks & Zevnik, 1993). Many HSOs also have included the option in the retirement plan of offering to "match" employees' contributions to the plan with employer-paid funds up to a maximum amount. Retirement funds can only be accessed at the age of retirement, or fund withdrawals are subject to penalties.

Flexible spending accounts. These are also called reimbursement accounts and are offered by the HSO to help the employee and their dependents by allowing pre-tax dollars to be placed in a healthcare or dependent care account. These accounts are then used to reimburse for out-of-pocket costs incurred by the employee and dependents that are not covered under other benefits or for the care of a child or dependent, disabled parent (Jenks & Zevnik, 1993).

Other benefits. Several other categories of benefits are also made available to HSO employees, although the degree to which they are offered and the scope of coverage will vary considerably. These benefits may include personal health benefits (complementary and alternative health care, yoga and Pilates classes, wellness/fitness center memberships, health education programs, and personal health risk appraisals); transportation (use of a van pool); educational reimbursement (tuition for employee or dependent's college); employee incentives (profit sharing, stock options, sign-on bonuses, relocation/moving assistance); flexible work scheduling, part-time work, job-sharing, and telecommuting; child care assistance and on-site child care; concierge services for information and referral on a variety of personal services; and savings programs (matched savings plans), among many others (Jenks & Zevnik, 1993). Flexible scheduling, part-time work, telecommuting, and job sharing are examples of what many employee-focused organizations offer employees in terms of work–life balance benefits. These benefits are viewed as a means to strengthen the commitment to the organization, reduce turnover, increase satisfaction, and provide flexibility in order to meet personal needs of employees (Osterman, 1995). Part-time work and telecommuting through a "virtual office" have increased in HSOs for some staff, and offer several benefits for the individual and the HSO, which include lower absenteeism, increased morale, greater schedule flexibility, creation of a wider talent pool, perception of fewer distractions, and perceived higher productivity (Corwin, Lawrence, & Frost, 2001; Hill, Miller, Weiner, & Colihan, 1998; Kurland & Bailey, 1999). However, challenges resulting from this workplace practice include social and professional isolation, where employees believe that interactions with others and promotional opportunities are limited (Cooper & Kurland, 2002). Managerial resistance to part-time workers and telecommuters, as well as unsupportive cultures, have also been identified as key barriers mitigating use of flexible work arrangements (Corwin et al., 2001; Kossek, Barber, & Winters, 1999). Perceived inequity among employees in terms of job structure and oversight may be another dilemma for management that results from adoption of this policy. Certainly, not all direct-care HSO employees could even consider telecommuting, due to their skills needed where the patient or client is located. For some HSO employees—such as information technology, business development and marketing, and finance—such flexible scheduling options may work well. In general, offering of these benefits is linked to several advantages, including lower turnover, higher satisfaction, and greater financial performance (Huselid, 1995; Konrad & Mangel, 2000; Perry-Smith & Blum, 2000),

Occupational safety and health. The human resources department contributes to the organization's efforts to maintain a safe and healthy work environment. Responsibilities are carried out in several ways to address this concern. First, workers' compensation coverage is required for organizations under state law, in order to protect workers who may get sick due to the job or become injured or incapacitated due to working conditions. This coverage is separate from any health insurance provided. Second, the HSO monitors federal and state regulations for occupational safety, monitors risk in the organization, and works to eliminate safety risks. Sometimes these human resources staff activities are conducted in conjunction with the risk management activities within the HSO.

Employee Assistance Programs

Employee assistance programs (EAPs) are HSO-sponsored programs that are made available to employees, and in many cases their dependents, to assist with personal or family problems that also affect the employee's job performance (Howard & Szczerbacki, 1998). Such problems include stress and mental health problems; parenting issues; family dysfunction and divorce; alcohol and substance abuse problems; financial problems; legal issues; physical and emotional abuse; poor work relationships; and adjustment issues stemming from a death in the family, loss of a job, or severe illness. In addition, the patient care services provided in an HSO are often challenging and stressful, and providing care to individuals who are sick, injured, and in some cases dying or near death is very trying and stress inducing for employees (Blair, 1985). This may lead to feelings of helplessness, guilt, or grief that negatively affect attendance and threaten the employee's focus, effectiveness, and productivity. Workplace stress may also be exacerbated by personal and family stress outside the HSO. As a result, HSOs have recognized the value of EAPs to help employees in their times of need by making available counseling, stress reduction programs, health education programs, and other interventions based on need to lessen the impact of these problems. A problem-free, happy employee is an employee who is more likely to be focused and productive on the job. This results in positive performance for the individual employee as well as the HSO. The cost of services to the employee will vary depending on how the EAP is structured; some of the needed EAP services may be covered under other current employee benefits. EAP services can be offered on-site at the HSO or offered at remote locations under contract with other providers, which facilitates greater confidentiality for users. Employees are also afforded protection from harassment and job loss due to use of the EAP.

In summary, the benefit package has become more important to employees in recent years as employees balance tradeoffs between compensation and an appropriate array of benefits that are important to the employee and his/her dependents. For example, many employees with young families may be more interested in a broad range of benefits, such as those discussed above, rather than the highest salary possible. Such benefits help employees meet their own unique needs and become a significant factor in employee recruitment and retention. In the end, benefits may be one of the most critical factors in making the HSO competitive in attracting and retaining staff.

Assessing Employee Performance

The human resources department is charged with developing and maintaining a system for measuring employee performance for all employees of the HSO. The central theme of this chapter is that organizational performance is paramount and that individual employee performance in an HSO is highly contributory to organization-wide performance. Therefore, assessing individual employee performance is critical to understanding and achieving high levels of organizational performance.

Under human resources department leadership, a performance appraisal system is established for the HSO. **Performance appraisal** means assessing the job performance of an individual employee. In order for the HSO to know how individuals are performing and to develop a plan and program for employees to improve performance, an annual performance assessment is required. The assessment form includes several criteria that are determined to be important for the HSO in evaluating performance. These criteria may include measures of both quality and quantity of the work as specified in the position description and include technical skill assessment as well as other criteria that address the employee's motivation, attitude, and interpersonal skills in carrying out their respective work. Human resources, in conjunction with senior management of the HSO, will determine what specific criteria are included in the performance appraisal. Performance appraisals also include an assessment of the degree to which an individual's annual goals and objectives have been achieved as spelled out in the yearly management plan. See Figure 12-2 for an example of a performance appraisal used by Bon Secours St. Francis Hospital.

Kirkpatrick (2006) argues that a performance appraisal system must be part of the organization's efforts for continuously improving performance. Performance assessment is conducted by line managers for their subordinates on an annual basis, at the time of the employee's anniversary date or, more commonly, at a standard time to coincide with the budget development process for the upcoming year. Using the agreed-upon form, the manager will complete an assessment of each subordinate's performance for the assessment period. The manager then will sit down with the employee and review the appraisal and discuss areas of favorable performance, as well as areas of improvement opportunity. This will also give the subordinate an opportunity to express any concerns and/or seek clarification as to the basis for the evaluation ratings. Many managers also ask subordinates to complete a self-evaluation for the performance period under review, using the same criteria, for discussion at the meeting. It should be noted that good managers communicate with their subordinates about employee performance regularly throughout the year, with an interest in monitoring, correcting, and improving performance on an ongoing basis.

At the designated annual performance appraisal meeting between a manager and a subordinate, a meaningful exchange can be carried out in order to frankly discuss performance, identify opportunities for improving performance, and develop a specific plan for achieving higher levels of performance. A two-way discussion of these matters is the most fruitful for both parties, as the employee will understand the manager's concern and interest in the employee and the sincere desire for improving performance. In addition, the employee can express likes and dislikes about the job, which the manager needs to know (Butler & Waldroop, 2005). However, it is essential that clarity be provided in communicating performance, as perceived by the supervisor, so that there is no confusion as to the intent of the evaluation (Timmreck, 1998). A key outcome of the performance evaluation is the setting of performance improvement goals, actions to achieve the improvements, and priorities for action (Kirkpatrick, 2006). In addition to an annual performance appraisal, the HSO may require some or all employees to be reviewed for satisfactory performance at

Management Summary Form	**Development Level:**	_____ Annual Review
	1 = Performs below standard	_____ Other
Confidential	2 = Inconsistently meets the standard	
	3 = Consistently meets the standard	(For the initial review, please
	4 = Frequently exceeds the standard	use the "Introductory
	5 = Consistently exceeds the standard	Performance Review" Form)

Instructions: The Performance Improvement Plan is a tool designed to assist in managing, developing and reviewing an employee's effectiveness and efficiency. It also provides a common understanding of job expectations for present and future performance review periods. *Please note all supporting comments on the Development Plan.*

I. Values (includes integration of Quest for Excellence Behaviors) *(see page 6-7 of the Process Guide)*

Developmental Level

		1	2	3	4	5
A.	Respect - commitment to treat people well (e.g., responsive - returns calls/emails).	1	2	3	4	5
	Justice - supporting and protecting the rights of all people.					
	Integrity - honest in dealings (e.g., honors commitments, keeps promises).					
	Compassion - experiencing empathy with another's life situation.					
B.	Stewardship - responsible use of Bon Secours resources (e.g., consistently on time).	1	2	3	4	5
	Innovation - creating or managing new ideas, methods, processes and/or technologies.					
	Quality - continuous improvement of service; involved in Gallup/Quest planning.					
	Growth - developing and improving services and promoting self-renewal; completion of previous year's Development Plan. (e.g., thinks "Big Picture").					

Average Developmental Level for Section I (A + B/2):

II. Leadership Competencies (see page 10-14 of the Process Guide)

Developmental Level

	1	2	3	4	5
Change Management & Organization Development - planning & designing change strategies as needed; integrating individual dev. & organizational dev. into strategies.	1	2	3	4	5
Communication & Interpersonal Skills - listening & responding in constructive manner; promoting understanding while building productive working relationships.	1	2	3	4	5
Critical Thinking - examining underlying causes & determining best course of action.	1	2	3	4	5
Human Resource Development - facilitating others to achieve professional dev. goals.	1	2	3	4	5
Planning & Strategic Direction Setting - determining shape of present & future job environment; efficiently maintaining & improving practices; setting direction for dept./org.; **developing Gallup Impact, PRC, Quest for Excellence Plans.**	1	2	3	4	5
Promotion of Mission & Values - setting an example by integrating org. standards into day-to-day functions; guiding others to a common Mission & Vision.	1	2	3	4	5
Self-Knowledge & Insight - using personal understanding to promote positive self-change.	1	2	3	4	5
Team Building - promoting teamwork to accomplish dept./org. objectives.	1	2	3	4	5
Proficiency in Field - subject matter expert in field; resource to others.	1	2	3	4	5

Average Developmental Level for Section II (Sum of 9 Leadership Competency Dev. Levels/9):

III. Essential Job Functions
(This section is determined by the Job Description and will vary with the Position being evaluated)

Average Developmental Level for Section III:

Overall Average: *(Average Level for Section I x .5) + (Average Level for Section II x .25) + (Average Level for Section III x .25)*

FIGURE 12-2 Performance Evaluation

Source: Reprinted with permission from Bon Secours St. Francis Medical Center, Midlothian, Virginia.

Development Plan

Name: _____

Facility & Dept.: _____

The Purpose of the Development Plan is to aid in the process of developing specific skills and behaviors. The Plan is reviewed and finalized during the performance review meeting. At a minimum, progress toward reaching agreed-upon goals should be discussed once during the year. **This form must be completed by each employee and returned prior to the performance review.**

1 **Previous Objectives, Goals, and Accomplishments.** Review learning and development objectives, goals, and accomplishments achieved since last performance review; include knowledge and skill strengths used to accomplish objectives and goals.

_____

_____

_____

_____

_____

_____

2 **New Objectives and Goals.** Identify new learning and development objectives and goals for the coming year, which include addressing opportunities for growth. Include issues, which may need to be addressed and opportunities needed to successfully implement, including implementation of Quest/Team Player improvements.

_____

_____

_____

_____

_____

_____

3 **Employee and/or Manager's Comments.** Additional comments may be made on a separate sheet of paper and attached to this form.

_____

_____

_____

_____

_____

_____

_____

_____

_____

FIGURE 12-2 (*Continued*)

the end of their first 90 days of employment (often referred to as the probationary period) and at other times as specifically requested by a manager or if conditions warrant.

Performance appraisals are helpful to management and employees in the following ways (Longest, Rakich, & Darr, 2000):

- The manager can compare absolute as well as relative performance of staff;
- Together, the manager and employee can determine a plan for improving performance if such improvement is needed;
- Together, the manager and employee can determine what additional training and development activities are needed to boost employee performance;
- The manager can use the findings to clarify employee desires to move up to higher-level positions and/or expand responsibilities;
- The manager can document performance in those cases where termination or reassignment is necessary;
- The manager can determine adjustments to compensation based on performance; and
- The manager can determine promotional or other advancement opportunities for the employee.

In addition to the traditional method of assessing performance described above, many HSOs are now employing **360-degree performance appraisal systems**. While this method also includes a manager–subordinate evaluation, it provides for multisource feedback on employee performance from a number of other stakeholders—including peers, the employee's subordinates, and internal and external customers, if applicable. Feedback is aggregated and communicated to the employee through a neutral third party such as a human resources staff member. The advantages to using the 360-degree evaluation are reduction of fear of repercussion from evaluative comments and a greater range of feedback from a larger number of observers of the employee/manager (Garman, Tyler, & Darnall, 2004). However, there are some disadvantages as well. These include the higher cost of administration of a 360-degree evaluation, compared to a traditional evaluation, and the lack of an instrument suitable for health services managers (Garman et al., 2004). In addition, peer feedback included in 360-degreee evaluation may also be biased or inaccurately given, due to difficulties in determining an individual's contribution to the unit or service or fear of providing negative feedback to a colleague (Peiperl, 2005).

One of the most challenging outcomes of the performance appraisal process is the need to terminate an employee. Although the goal of human resources management is to retain high-performing staff, not all employees will be retained. There are many reasons why an employee can be discharged, but in every case, the primary reason must relate to performance deficiency. Terminating an employee is not easy and is uncomfortable at times for managers who have the authority to discharge an employee. However, failure to act decisively will jeopardize the HSO's performance and will certainly reflect negatively on the manager's ability as a leader (Hoffman, 2005). In situations where an employee is not likely to be retained, it is essential that the manager not wait until the appraisal to assess the employee's performance. In fact, ongoing monitoring of performance, efforts to correct performance problems, and documentation of the steps taken in any corrective processes are all typically required prior to discharge. This process should be done by the line manager in close consultation with the human resources manager. The HSO policies and procedures must be adhered to carefully to prevent subsequent allegations of wrongful discharge and potentially avert a lawsuit against the HSO and/or the line manager.

Managing Labor Relations

Labor relations is a general term that addresses the relationships between staff (labor) and management within HSOs. Labor relations is associated with **collective bargaining** where a union, if certified (i.e., voted in by the workers), represents the interests of employees who become members of that union. Nationally, about 20% of HSOs have at least one union represented in their organizations (Longest et al., 2000). In the period 1980–1994, there were 4,224 certification elections held in health services organizations: 31% of these were in hospitals, 40% in nursing homes, and 29% were in other healthcare facilities (Scott & Lowery, 1994). Union elections in health services organizations vary by type of healthcare setting, but overall about 60% of elections result in a union being approved (Deshpande, 2002). Unions have a higher-than-average win rate in hospitals, and hospitals have been the focus of increased union organizing efforts in recent years (Deshpande, 2003). In 2009, union membership in healthcare was about 14% of the healthcare workforce (Malvey, 2010). However, this represents an increase of 270,000 unionized healthcare workers since 2000, with much of the growth occurring in registered nurse and other non-physician occupations (Malvey, 2010).

Why do unions get involved in HSOs? As seen in manufacturing, the fundamental reason for unionization in health care is that employees are dissatisfied with some aspects of the work and/or the work environment and feel that management is insensitive to their needs. Unions often step in where management has failed to do its job and become the "voice" of the employees. If staff are strongly dissatisfied with various aspects of the HSO, view senior management as poor communicators, and/or perceive that management is insensitive to staff issues, they may believe that a union is the only way to have their voices heard and needs met. If elected to represent employees in an HSO, a union is then authorized to engage in collective bargaining with management of the HSO regarding wages, working conditions, promotion policies, and many other aspects of work (Longest et al., 2000).

The National Labor Relations Act of 1935, as amended, enables union organizing and collective bargaining in health services organizations. The Act also created the National

Labor Relations Board (NLRB), which recognizes several bargaining units for healthcare employees, including nurses, physicians, other professional employees, and nonprofessional employees, among others. The NLRB has the authority to oversee and certify the results of union elections. There are many rules and regulations that must be followed in unionization activity, and there are certain restrictions placed on management as well as staff that govern what can and cannot happen regarding union discussions, organizing, and elections.

The presence of a union creates significant challenges for management of an HSO. From management's perspective, unions create an unnecessary third party in decisions that affect the employment relationship and work of the HSO's staff, which raises potential for conflict. Union requirements may restrict the administrator's ability to use the number and type of staff in desired ways, and compensation negotiated by the union may reduce management's ability to directly control staffing expenses. Labor unions can also limit an HSO's discretionary authority to make changes in the workplace and in workplace practices (Holley, Jennings, & Wolters, 2001). Also, some research has shown that productivity may be negatively affected after unionization (Holley et al., 2001).

Beyond general impact on administration, unionization has been shown to significantly affect the human resources function in HSOs. Deshpande (2002) found in a study of hospital unionization activity that the presence of unions resulted in higher numbers of employees who were screened, a higher number of employee training programs, a greater number of job classifications, greater use of employee performance appraisal methods, and lower productivity, as reported by CEOs of hospitals.

Various strategies have been discussed with respect to the administrative stance vis-à-vis unions (Deshpande, 2003). To reduce the possibility of union discussions and union organizing, administrators are encouraged to keep communication open and fluid, provide competitive salaries and benefits, establish grievance policies and procedures, and ensure staff participation and involvement in decision making as much as possible. In all respects, administrators and human resources staff should continuously assess staff satisfaction and needs, as well as opportunities for staff and management to work together for the betterment of the organization and larger community. There are many challenging issues that affect HSOs, including lowered reimbursements from managed care and government payers, cost reduction practices, and lower staffing ratios. These can lead to employee dissatisfaction, and management needs to be cognizant of the negative impact of some of their decisions on staff motivation, satisfaction, and commitment.

If one or more unions are certified to represent employees in an HSO, then much of the time and effort of the human resources staff will be spent in addressing unionization issues. These include negotiating (bargaining) aspects of the union contract, ensuring that specific aspects of the contract are met, communicating with union representatives, and being the focal party in carrying out all union discussion and negotiation under the auspices of federal labor law (Longest et al., 2000).

Leadership Development

It is widely accepted that health services managers must practice effective leadership in order for their staffs, and thus the organizations, to perform at the highest possible level. Leadership and leadership practices are increasingly addressed in the current healthcare literature, and leadership is seen as one of the key competencies of health services managers. Because of the complexity and rapid change within the environment of HSOs and within HSOs themselves, managers need to engage in learning consistently to upgrade their knowledge and skills so that they can be effective leaders (Sukin, 2009).

Many HSOs have followed the lead of business and industry and are now embracing the concept of leadership development for their managers. Recent data show that 21% of freestanding hospitals and about one-half of hospital systems have a leadership development program for senior executives (McAlearney, 2010; Squazzo, 2009). Leadership development includes both formal and informal efforts. The formal efforts include completion of courses with satisfactory scores on assessment, usually on an annual basis, which are required to advance to higher levels of management within the HSO or to keep knowledge and skills current. Some HSOs separate leadership development for existing managers, executive managers, and aspiring managers. Courses and self-study may be completed online through organizational staff Web portals or through seminars with trainers who are either HSO staff or contracted consultants. Required training may include topics that are priorities of the HSO, such as customer service or process improvement, or it may reflect special topics of executing leadership, such as organizational change, effective communications, and building effective teams. Many times, leadership development training is tied to a personal development plan for a manager, or conversely, for an aspiring manager. Informal methods are where the HSO has its executive and mid-level managers work unofficially with selected staff through mentoring, advising, and coaching. This also may include job enlargement based on successful job performance, where the staff member may be assigned additional work tasks or tasks that reflect cross-discipline work where that staff member can gain different perspectives and gain visibility throughout the organization.

As noted in Chapter 2, leadership development efforts in HSOs are also employed to provide for succession planning for senior/executive and mid-level managers. Because many senior executives are nearing retirement, and given the high demand for healthcare managers across all sectors of the industry due to keen competition for leadership talent, organizations have decided to groom from within. Providing for succession to positions by filling from within offers several advantages. These include seamless continuation of organizational leadership, proven fit with the organizational culture, commitment to the organization, and prior demonstration of effective working relationships across disciplines.

Leadership development initiatives also serve as a recruitment tool for bringing highly qualified candidates to the organization in both clinical and nonclinical roles. For example, clinical staff who have an interest in management may find that the organization that provides extensive leadership development and career track options is better than those that do not. Accordingly, leadership development can serve as a differentiator for HSOs. This has been a strategy of businesses for many years, where individuals with bachelor's and master's degrees can begin their careers with an organization that will provide opportunities for leadership development and advancement.

Employee Suggestion Programs

Employee suggestion programs (ESPs) are increasingly being considered by HSOs in an effort to encourage creativity on the part of employees and to identify needed improvements in processes and outcomes. Employee suggestion programs have been in existence for quite some time (Carrier, 1998), but the primary locus has been in manufacturing and other business enterprises as opposed to HSOs.

An ESP works simplistically by soliciting employee suggestions for change and acknowledging and rewarding those suggestions that offer the most potential to meet organizational goals and implementing those suggestions. These programs usually are formally structured, widely communicated throughout the organization, and managed by human resources staff. Current ESPs have gone far beyond the old suggestion box model and include elements of electronic submission and Web-based applications, as well as formal recognition and reward (Fairbank, Spangler, & Williams, 2003).

ESPs are part of an overall effort by HSOs to stimulate innovation and creativity by generating ideas that will help the HSO. The underlying rationale for the program is that employees of HSOs, as key providers of its services and activities, are in the best position to know what can be improved and may have good ideas as to how such improvements can be made. ESPs are built on the premise that innovation in organizations can be understood from a problem-solving approach (Fairbank et al., 2003). Goals of ESPs can include organizational improvements, such as reducing costs, improving methods and procedures, improving productivity, improving equipment, and cutting waste, as well as increasing job satisfaction and organizational commitment on the part of employees (Carrier, 1998). This second goal of ESPs is very important and should not be overlooked by the human resources staff. Part of the overall satisfaction in working in an HSO is the belief that management understands and appreciates its employees and is interested in their input. ESPs are not, however, without their limitations. Drawbacks to the program include difficulties in designing a program, effectively administering it, and sustaining the program over several years (Kim, 2005).

CONCLUSION

The management of human resources is an important function within HSOs because the performance of HSOs is tied directly to the motivation, commitment, knowledge, and skills of clinical, administrative, and support staff. Human resources actions of HSOs are undertaken for both strategic and administrative purposes. A variety of activities are included within the human resources area, and these activities typically fall within the domains of workforce planning/recruitment and employee retention. While human resources serves as a support function for line managers within HSOs, line managers and staff managers carry out human resources management roles as well, because they are involved in hiring, supervising, evaluating, promoting, and terminating staff. Therefore, human resources staff and other managers work closely to ensure that HSOs perform well. The contribution of the human resources management function is increasingly being evaluated by senior management, similar to other organizational functions, to determine the net contribution of human resources staff to organizational success. It is likely that management of human resources will increase in importance in the future, as HSOs face heightened external and internal pressures to recruit and retain committed and high-performing staff.

DISCUSSION QUESTIONS

1. Describe why human resources management is comprised of strategic and administrative actions.

2. For each human resources scenario described in the introduction to the chapter, identify the steps you would take to address the specific human resources issue being faced. From your perspective, which is the most challenging issue, and why?

3. Two key domains of human resources management are workforce planning/recruitment and employee retention. Describe several human resources functions that fall under each and describe their importance to human resources management.

4. Identify and describe some environmental forces that affect human resources functions in health services organizations.

5. Define and contrast "employee assistance programs" and "employee suggestion programs."

6. Why do HSOs offer incentive compensation programs? How do these programs differ from base compensation programs?

7. Describe the importance of employee relations and engagement efforts by HSOs, and give some examples of these activities.

Cases in Chapter 17 that are related to this chapter include:

- The Case of the Complacent Employee—see p. 379
- I Love You...Forever—see p. 386
- A Nightmare Job Interview—see p. 438
- Recruitment Challenge for the Middle Manager—see p. 454
- Sexual Harassment at the Diabetes Clinic—see p. 412
- Staffing at River Oaks Community Hospital: Measure Twice, Cut Once—see p. 424
- Such a Nice Young Man—see p. 392
- The Brawler—see p. 382
- The Merger of Two Competing Hospitals—see p. 406

Additional cases, role-play scenarios, video links, websites, and other information sources are also available in the online Instructor's Materials.

REFERENCES

Angermeier, I., Dunford, B. B., Boss, A. D., & Boss, R. W. (2009). The impact of participative management perceptions on customer service, medical errors, burnout, and turnover intentions. *Journal of Healthcare Management, 54*(2), 127–142.

Becker, B. E., Huselid, M. A., & Ulrich, D. (2001). *The HR scorecard.* Boston, MA: Harvard Business School Press.

Beer, M., & Cannon, M. D. (2004, Spring). Promise and peril in implementing pay-for-performance. *Human Resources Management, 43*(1), 3–48.

Beer, M., & Katz, N. (2003). Do incentives work? The perceptions of a worldwide sample of senior executives. *Human Resource Planning, 26*(3), 30–44.

Blair, B. (1985). *Hospital employee assistance programs.* Chicago, IL: American Hospital Publishing, Inc.

Bonner, S. E., & Sprinkle, G. B. (2002). The effects of monetary incentives on effort and task performance: Theories, evidence and a framework for research. *Accounting, Organizations and Society, 27*, 303–345.

Bureau of Labor Statistics. (2010). *Employment and wage estimates and projections between 2008 and 2018.* Retrieved from http://www.bls.gov/emp/ep_projections_methods.htm

Burt, T. (2005, November/December). Leadership development as corporate strategy: Using talent reviews to improve senior management. *Healthcare Executive, 20*(6), 14–18.

Busse, R. C. (2005). *Your rights at work.* Naperville, IL: Sphinx Publishing.

Butler, T., & Waldroop, J. (2005). Job sculpting: The art of retaining your best people. In *Harvard Business Review on appraising employee performance* (pp. 111–136). Boston, MA: Harvard Business School Press.

Carrier, C. (1998, June). Employee creativity and suggestion programs: An empirical study. *Creativity and Innovation Management, 7*(2), 162–172.

Cooper, C. D., & Kurland, N. B. (2002). Telecommuting, professional isolation, and employee development in public and private organizations. *Journal of Organizational Behavior, 23*, 511–532.

Corwin, V., Lawrence, T. R. B., & Frost, P. J. (2001, July/August). Five successful strategies of successful part-time work. *Harvard Business Review*, 121–127.

Deshpande, S. P. (2002). The impact of union elections on human resources management practices in hospitals. *Health Care Manager, 20*(4), 27–35.

Deshpande, S. P. (2003). Labor relations strategies and tactics in hospital elections. *Health Care Manager, 22*(1), 52–55.

Edmondson, A., Bohmer, R., & Pisano, G. (2004). Speeding up team learning. In *Harvard Business Review on teams that succeed* (pp. 77–97). Boston, MA: Harvard Business School Press.

Fairbank, J. F., Spangler, W. E., & Williams, S. D. (2003, September/October). Motivating creativity through a computer-mediated employee suggestion management system. *Behavior and Information Technology, 22*(5), 305–314.

Foster, C., & Godkin, L. (1998, Winter). Employment selection in health care: The case for structured interviewing. *Health Care Management Review, 23*(1), 46–51.

Fottler, M. D., Ford, R. C., & Heaton, C. (2002). *Achieving service excellence: Strategies for healthcare.* Chicago, IL: Health Administration Press.

Galford, R. (1998, March/April). Why doesn't this HR department get any respect? *Harvard Business Review, 76*(2), 24–32.

Garman, A. N., Tyler, J. L., & Darnall, J. S. (2004, September/October). Development and validation of a 360-degree-feedback instrument for healthcare administrators. *Journal of Healthcare Management, 49*(5), 307–322.

Gering, J., & Conner, J. (2002, November). A strategic approach to employee retention. *Healthcare Financial Management, 56*(11), 40–44.

Gibson, V. M. (1995, February). The new employee reward system. *Management Review, 84*(2), 13–18.

Ginter, P. M., Swayne, L. E., & Duncan, W. J. (2002). *Strategic management of health care organizations* (4th ed.). Malden, MA: Blackwell.

Gomez-Mejia, L. R., Welbourne, T. M., & Wiseman, R. M. (2000). The role of risk sharing and risk taking under gainsharing. *Academy of Management Review, 25*(3), 492–507.

Griffith, J. R. (2000, January/February). Championship management for healthcare organizations. *Journal of Healthcare Management, 45*(1), 17–31.

Griffith, J. R., & White, K. R. (2002). *The well-managed healthcare organization* (5th ed.). Chicago, IL: Health Administration Press/AUPHA Press.

Healthcare Financial Management Association (HFMA). (2001, August). More healthcare organizations using quality measures to reward executives. *Healthcare Financial Management Association, 55*(8), 22–25.

Hernandez, S. R., Fottler, M. D., & Joiner, C. L. (1998). Integrating management and human resources. In M. D. Fottler, S. R. Hernandez, & C. L. Joiner (Eds.), *Essentials of human resources management in health services organizations*. Albany, NY: Delmar Publishers.

Hill, E. J., Miller, B. C., Weiner, S. P., & Colihan, J. (1998). Influences of the virtual office on aspects of work and work/life balance. *Personnel Psychology, 51*, 667–683.

Hoffman, P. B. (2005, November/December). Confronting management incompetence. *Healthcare Executive, 20*(6), 28–30.

Holley, W. H. Jr., Jennings, K. M., & Wolters, R. S. (2001). *The labor relations process* (7th ed.). Orlando, FL: Harcourt College Publishers.

Howard, J. C., & Szczerbacki, D. (1998). Employee assistance programs in the hospital industry. *Health Care Management Review, 13*(2), 73–79.

Huselid, M. A. (1995). The impact of human resource management practices on turnover, productivity, and corporate financial performance. *Academy of Management Journal, 38*(3), 635–672.

Huselid, M. A., Beatty, R. W., & Becker, B. E. (2005, December). "A players" or "a positions"? The logic of workforce management. *Harvard Business Review,* 110–117.

Izzo, J. B., & Withers, P. (2002). Winning employee-retention strategies for today's healthcare organizations. *Healthcare Financial Management, 56*(6), 52–57.

Jenks, J. M., & Zevnik, B. L. P. (1993). *Employee benefits.* New York, NY: Collier Books/Macmillan Publishing Company.

Joiner, C. L., Jones, K. N., & Dye, C. F. (1998). Compensation management. In M. D. Fottler, S. R. Hernandez, & C. L. Joiner (Eds.), *Essentials of human resources management in health services organizations.* Albany, NY: Delmar Publishers.

Kaiser Family Foundation. (2010). *Summary of new health reform law.* Retrieved from www.kff.org/healthreform/upload/8061.pdf

Kim, D.-O. (2005, July). The benefits and costs of employee suggestions under gainsharing. *Industrial and Labor Relations Review, 58*(4), 631–652.

Kirkpatrick, D. L. (2006). *Improving employee performance through appraisal and coaching* (2nd ed.). New York, NY: American Management Association/AMACOM.

Konrad, A. M., & Mangel, R. (2000). The impact of work-life programs on firm productivity. *Strategic Management Journal, 21,* 1225–1237.

Kossek, E. E., Barber, A. E., & Winters, D. (1999, Spring). Using flexible schedules in the managerial world: The power of peers. *Human Resource Management, 38*(1), 33–46.

Kurland, N. B., & Bailey, D. E. (1999, Autumn). Telework: The advantages and challenges of working here, there, anywhere and anytime. *Organizational Dynamics, 28*(2), 53–67.

Lehr, R. I., McLean, R. A., & Smith, G. L. (1998). The legal and economic environment. In M. D. Fottler, S. R. Hernandez, & C. L. Joiner (Eds.), *Essentials of human resources management in health services organizations.* Albany, NY: Delmar Publishers.

Liberman, A., & Rotarius, T. (2000, June). Pre-employment decision-trees: Jobs applicant self-election. *The Health Care Manager, 18*(4), 48–54.

Longest, B. B., Rakich, J. S., & Darr, K. (2000). *Managing health services organizations and systems.* Baltimore, MD: Health Professions Press.

Luthans, F., & Stajkovic, A. D. (1999, May). Reinforce for performance: The need to go beyond pay and even rewards. *The Academy of Management Executive, 13*(2), 49–57.

Malvey, D. (2010). Unionization in healthcare—background and trends. *Journal of Healthcare Management, 55*(3), 154–157.

McAlearney, A. S. (2010). Executive leadership development in U.S. health systems. *Journal of Healthcare Management, 55*(3), 206–224.

Metzger, N. (2004). Human resources management in organized delivery systems. In L. F. Wolper (Ed.), *Health care administration* (4th ed.). Sudbury, MA: Jones & Bartlett.

Osterman, P. (1995). Work/family programs and the employment relationship. *Administrative Science Quarterly, 40,* 681–700.

Peiperl, M. A. (2005). Getting 360-degree feedback right. In *Appraising employee performance* (pp. 69–109). Boston, MA: Harvard Business School Press.

Perry-Smith, J. E., & Blum, T. C. (2000). Work-family human resource bundles and perceived organizational performance. *Academy of Management Journal, 43*(6), 1007–1117.

Pfeffer, J. (1998). The human equation. Boston, MA: Harvard Business School Press.

Phillips, J. (1996, April). How much is the training worth? *Training and Development, 50*(4), 20–24.

Pieper, S. K. (2005, May/June). Reading the right signals: How to strategically manage with scorecards. *Healthcare Executive, 20*(3), 9–14.

Runy, L. A. (2003, August). Retirement benefits as a recruitment tool. *Hospitals and Health Networks, 77*(8), 43–49.

Scott, C., & Lowery, C. M. (1994, Winter). Union election activity in the health care industry. *Health Care Management Review, 19*(1), 18–27.

Shanahan, M. (1993). A comparative analysis of recruitment and retention of health care professionals. *Health Care Management Review, 18*(3), 41–51.

Squazzo, J. D. (2009, November/December). Cultivating tomorrow's leaders: Comprehensive development strategies ensure continued success. *Healthcare Executive, 24*(6), 8–20.

Studer, Q. (2003). *Hardwiring excellence.* Gulf Breeze, FL: Fire Starter Publishing.

Sukin, D. (2009, Winter). Leadership in challenging times: It starts with passion. *Frontiers of Health Services Management, 26*(2), 3–8.

Timmreck, T. C. (1998, Summer). Developing successful performance appraisals through choosing appropriate words to effectively describe work. *Health Care Management Review, 23*(3), 48–57.

CHAPTER 13

Teamwork

Sharon B. Buchbinder
Jon M. Thompson

LEARNING OBJECTIVES

By the end of this chapter, the student will be able to:

- Distinguish between a team, a task force, and a committee;
- Compare and contrast disciplinary, interdisciplinary, and cross-functional teams;
- Describe the challenges associated with teamwork in healthcare organizations;
- Summarize current trends in the use of teams in healthcare;
- Compare and contrast the benefits and costs of teamwork;
- List key features of wicked problems;
- Identify ways to fit into a team and to select team members;
- Apply current thinking on emotions to teamwork scenarios;
- Discuss the importance of communication on teams;
- Describe strategies for managing conflict on a team; and
- Provide examples of teams in healthcare settings.

INTRODUCTION

Unless you've lived alone your entire life, by the time you obtain your first job in the healthcare arena, you will have been on a team. Family teams organize chores, vacations, and household projects. In school, students are assigned tasks—almost from the sandbox—that require small group work and cooperation. Extra-curricular activities—Girl Scouts, Boy Scouts, Junior Achievement, Habitat for Humanity—all require young people to work in cooperative groups. And let us not forget the soccer moms and dads, who chauffer their offspring from preschool through high school to participate in sports teams. So why does the thought of teamwork assignments make entire classes of healthcare management students cringe? Despite years of teamwork experiences, few students in any discipline are actually educated and trained in the "how-to" of working in teams. Yet in healthcare management, from the day you enter the door of your first job, your role will include being part of a team. Teamwork requires leadership, strategic thinking, diverse groups of people with different perspectives and disciplines, excellent organizational and interpersonal skills, and a good sense of humor. The purpose of this chapter is to help you understand the formation and operation of teams, the benefits and costs of teams, and tools to navigate the sometimes tricky waters of teamwork.

WHAT IS A TEAM?

Most simply, a **team** is a group of people, working together to achieve a common goal (Grumbach & Bodenheimer, 2004). Teams typically include individuals with complementary skills who are committed to a common approach for which they hold themselves mutually accountable (Katzenbach & Smith, 2004). The formation and operation of teams are central to the effective functioning of healthcare organizations. In healthcare organizations, teams can be composed of one or more disciplines, for example, the nursing team, the physician leader team, the management team, or the quality improvement team. In Chapter 1, you learned about the internal structure of healthcare organizations. For example, a senior Vice President has several directors who report to him, which constitutes a management team. Likewise, the administrator or CEO and all Vice Presidents that report to her comprise an executive team.

One of the distinguishing characteristics of healthcare organizations is that the professional staff needs to work closely and collaboratively to meet patient needs. In other words, the tasks of individual employees affect, and are dependent upon, the work of others. This is known as task interdependency. Because the healthcare needs of patients cut across an organization's different disciplines or functions, it is important that interdisciplinary clinical teams be set up to ensure the delivery of safe, effective, and timely care. In addition, teams can be organized to address a short-term, quality assurance problem, such as "Why did Mrs. Jones fall out of bed?" or long-term problems, such as preventing harm to all patients in all aspects of care (Ball, 2005). (See Textbox 13-1.) Moreover, **cross-functional teams (CFTs)** are common in healthcare organizations to address specific organizational needs, such as service excellence, environmental sustainability and green initiatives, and clinical services marketing (Thompson, 2010). These CFTs include representatives from clinical and nonclinical areas of the organization. It is widely believed that the use of clinical and cross-functional teams will become more critical in the future as healthcare organizations become more complex and the demands for effective patient management increase (Jain, Thompson, Chaudry, McKenzie, & Schwartz 2008). (See Textbox 13-2.)

TEXTBOX 13-1. QUALITY IMPROVEMENT TEAMS IN A HOSPITAL

The West Florida Regional Medical Center established a Continuous Quality Improvement (CQI) process for its hospital in Pensacola, Florida. The purpose of the CQI process was to improve the way that services were provided to patients. The approach the hospital took was to place employees into teams of individuals that analyzed the clinical (e.g., patient care) and nonclinical processes (e.g., support services) that were in need of improvement. For example, teams were formed that examined the labor/delivery/recovery/postpartum (LDRP) services and the distribution and use of medications within the hospital. The teams critically reviewed these processes and came up with suggestions for improving quality. For LDRP, changes were identified to develop package pricing for having a baby, as well as ensuring that LDRP met the needs of consumers. The team examining the use of medications found that listing medications for physicians in order of increasing costs per average daily dose rather than alphabetically resulted in an annual savings of about $200,000. This illustrates the impact of team decision making through a CQI process on improving cost and quality of operations in a hospital.

Source: McLaughlin, 2004.

TEXTBOX 13-2. USING CROSS-FUNCTIONAL CLINICAL TEAMS TO IMPROVE PATIENT ACTIVITIES OF DAILY LIVING

Cross-functional teams (CFTs) have been advocated as a means to ensure effective care that results in positive patient outcomes. Prior research has found that CFTs are associated with more creative solutions, better quality decisions, increased organizational effectiveness, and lower turnover rates among treatment staff. However, a noted gap in the literature is the limited number of studies that address the relationship of team process measures of team performance. Researchers carried out a longitudinal, multilevel analysis in Veterans Affairs hospitals to assess the relationship of team participation and team functioning to patients' ability to perform activities of daily living. "Team participation" was defined as the extent to which staff members engage jointly with others in making patient care decisions. "Team functioning" was defined as how well team members work together in discharging the team's responsibilities. They collected staff and patient data from 40 teams within patient care units treating seriously mentally ill patients in 16 facilities across the United States. Findings indicate that the level of participation by the team as a whole may be more important than the team's smooth functioning. The findings of this study show the value of managerial interventions to encourage and facilitate member investment in team processes.

Source: Alexander et al., 2005.

Task forces require teamwork, but don't have the life of a **committee**. A blue-ribbon task force may be commissioned for several years by a professional association or institute to examine issues in healthcare services delivery, such as medical errors and patient safety (Institute of Medicine, 2001). These groups focus on a specific agenda, have a limited term of tenure, and disband when a report or book is issued. At the intra-organizational level, a quality assurance committee comprised of individuals from many departments may have people appointed to 3-year terms. At the end of that time, a person whose term has expired steps down, but the committee and the work of the committee lives on. Committees such as these usually have a person for whom this area is their full-time job, but representatives of multiple disciplines and areas of the organization are required to examine problems and to implement organizational policy decisions.

THE CHALLENGE OF TEAMWORK IN HEALTHCARE ORGANIZATIONS

Originally, hospitals grew out of religious orders, and nuns and monks provided health care to the poor. If you were wealthy, uneducated nurses tended to you at home, and physicians made house calls. Prior to the late 1700s and early 1800s, medical training was an apprenticeship, and there were no university-trained nurses. The U.S. Civil War and the Crimean War fueled the development of the nursing profession. The first nurse training school in the United States was created in 1798 at New York Hospital, by a physician. Florence Nightingale, a nurse, founded the first training school for nurses at St. Thomas Hospital in England in 1860 after the Crimean War and published her landmark book, *Notes on Nursing*, in 1890 (Donahue, 1985). Over time and as the field of nursing evolved, nursing education moved out of strictly hospital training programs into university-based settings (Donahue, 1985).

The American Medical Association (AMA) was formed in 1842, and its first meeting was to discuss the appalling lack of quality in U.S. medical schools and their products—physicians. The AMA Council on Medical Education was formed in 1847. Abraham Flexner, working at the Carnegie Foundation, traveled around the United States and Canada to examine the structure, processes, and outcomes of the more than 300 medical schools that existed at that time. His 1910 report, *Medical Education in the United States and Canada*, often referred to as "The Flexner Report," called for dramatic reorganization in the medical education system. Those schools that were at the "A" level (such as the Johns Hopkins School of Medicine) were the standards by which all other schools were evaluated. The report recommended that "B"-level schools either get the resources to become "A"-level schools or go out of business. Flexner urged all "C"-level schools, which were considered substandard (some had no books!), to cease production of physicians (Flexner, 1910).

Compared to medicine and nursing, healthcare management is a young discipline. The University of Chicago founded the first program in health administration in 1934 under the leadership of Michael M. Davis, who had a PhD in sociology. Davis recognized that there was no formal training for hospital managers and that an interdisciplinary program of education was needed. Envisioning the role of the healthcare manager as both a business and social role, he utilized the expertise of medical, social service administration, and business faculty to create an interdisciplinary model that has been replicated repeatedly across the United States and throughout the world (University of Chicago, n.d.). Schools with a degree in healthcare management or administration were originally all master's degrees, geared to preparing hospital administrators. Now, in addition to master's degrees, there are baccalaureate and doctoral programs in healthcare management. More jobs in healthcare management are being created outside of hospital settings than within (Bureau of Labor Statistics, 2010). Increasing specialization of health care, burgeoning allied healthcare disciplines, a diversity of healthcare organizations, greater variety in jobs, higher expectations for healthcare outcomes, and demanding consumers mean that healthcare organizations must be able to respond appropriately, effectively, and efficiently. Interdisciplinary teams and teamwork provide the mechanism for improved responses to these demands.

Despite demonstrated need and effectiveness of interdisciplinary teams, formal educational training in this skill for physicians and nurses is rare (Baker, Salas, King, Battles, & Barach, 2005; Buchbinder et al., 2005). A poll conducted in 2004 by the American College of Physician Executives (ACPE) revealed that about one-quarter of the physician executive respondents were seeing problem physician behaviors almost weekly (Weber, 2004). Thirty-six percent of the respondents reported conflicts between physicians and staff members (including nurses), and 25% reported that physicians refused to embrace teamwork. The Institute of Medicine has recommended that healthcare organizations develop effective teams (Institute of Medicine, 2001). Physicians and nurses work from a clinical framework of advocating at the individual level for patients and families. Healthcare managers, on the other hand, are trained to look at population level and organization-wide issues. Sometimes, clinicians and managers have head-on collisions due to these contrasting worldviews (Edwards, Marshall, McLellan, & Abbasi, 2003). Developing teams and facilitating team activities are recognized competencies for healthcare managers (Stefl, 2008). However, there is little formal preparation in teamwork in undergraduate and graduate healthcare management education programs (Leggat, 2007), and therefore, much of the manager's understanding of team dynamics and operations is learned on the job. Developing and managing teams is a skill that you will want to build as you progress in your healthcare management career.

Healthcare executives recommend that to engage medical staff, managers need to promote alignment between hospitals and physicians. This alignment can be accomplished through the use of shared goals, especially those relating to patient safety (Sherman, 2006). Understanding physicians is key to getting them on board with teamwork and reducing medical errors. Physicians are pulled in multiple directions by multiple demands, and their time is at a premium. Valuing a physician's time means organizations must have competent team members in place to whom physicians can delegate tasks that they might otherwise have to do themselves. Promoting interdependence on trustworthy teammates is critical in achieving safe, effective patient care. As a healthcare manager, you will be responsible for working with and encouraging all healthcare professionals to become good team members. It will not always be an easy task, but in the long run, it will be rewarding.

THE BENEFITS OF EFFECTIVE HEALTHCARE TEAMS

One of the best ways to convince a clinician that interdisciplinary teamwork is important is to show them the relationship to patient care. According to Mickan (2005), some of the **benefits of effective teams** include improved coordination of care, efficient use of healthcare services, increased job satisfaction among team members, and higher patient satisfaction. Ruddy and Rhee (2005) echoed these findings in their literature review of primary care for the underserved. Roblin, Vogt, and Fireman (2003) demonstrated that primary healthcare teams in ambulatory care settings could improve quality of care and corporate productivity when employees were empowered to be innovative and rewarded for performance. Additional benefits of teams include sharing different areas of knowledge and expertise, learning from different perspectives, and realizing innovative ideas that come from other team members (Thompson, 2010; Quinlan & Robertson, 2010). For example, Alexander et al. (2005) found in their study of teams providing treatment to mental health patients that patients experienced greater improvements in activities of daily living when teams had higher levels of sharing and staff participation. (See Textbox 13-2.) Specialized hospital services also can benefit from "service line" team approaches that show increased trust among staff, shared goals, and greater patient satisfaction (Liedtka, Whitten, & Sorrells-Jones, 1998). (See Textbox 13-3.)

Clinical research has underscored the importance of excellence in teamwork in the operating room (OR). A multisite retrospective study of 74 Veterans Health Administration (VHA) facilities found that "participation in the VHA Medical Team Training program was associated with a lower surgical mortality rate" (Neily et al., 2010, p. 1693). By *lower*, the authors mean an 18% reduction in annual mortality rates. The findings from this study are significant not only in a research sense, but also in a true clinical sense: that figure represents lives saved through improved teamwork. Dissemination of this information throughout all surgical training programs in the United States will require enormous effort because surgeons often believe "they alone are responsible for patient outcomes" (Pronovost &

TEXTBOX 13-3. COLLABORATION OF STAFF IN A SERVICE LINE APPROACH

The existing literature suggests that collaboration should make possible simultaneous improvement in both quality and cost-effectiveness of care. Collaboration supports ongoing learning for providing good care and can assist with effective redesign of care processes. An academic medical center, with a bed capacity of 500 beds, reorganized from a traditional departmental structure to a service line approach, which included 12 service centers. The service line structure used "focused teams." Focused teams, in contrast to functional or coordinated teams, are distinguished by the fact that non-nursing professionals report to unit or service managers rather than to a central department.

The medical center staff designed a questionnaire to assess perceptions of effectiveness of the service line model in promoting collaboration and improving care outcomes. Overall, respondents—including administrators, physicians, and nurses—indicated that the successful service line collaboration was associated with a sense of greater ownership, a high level of trust, realistic expectations, and shared goals. However, there were differences in perceptions of effectiveness of the service line approach as viewed by administrators, physicians, and nurses. This showed that staff may be at different places regarding their view of the value of service line models. For example, nurses expressed feelings of being left out of decision-making processes and believed that unrealistic expectations were placed on them. Physicians also viewed input into the decision-making process as important and expressed the need to have a clear sense of strategic direction. Outcome data, in terms of patient satisfaction, cost per case, and length of stay, remained consistent for the period of time studied. The authors note that the lack of positive change in these indicators may be due to the newness of the implementation of the service line model and the possibility that chosen measures may not be sensitive enough to capture positive outcomes associated with service line collaboration. The authors concluded that the diversity of staff perspectives and experiences with service line management models makes for significant challenges for leaders of healthcare institutions and that successful collaboration can result only when these professional differences are understood and addressed.

Source: Liedtka et al., 1998.

Freischlag, 2010, p. 1721). It will take a major culture shift to move many physicians and surgeons from this solo savior mentality to the "there is no I in teamwork" approach.

Clinicians are not always the reluctant team builders. Sometimes higher-level management is uncertain that teamwork is worth the effort and short-term costs. For this audience, the answer lies in the bottom line: improved communication, increased productivity, increased job satisfaction, and decreased nursing turnover (Amos, Hu, & Herrick, 2005; Institute for Healthcare Improvement, 2004). In an era when nurses are retiring faster than new ones are coming into the field, healthcare managers cannot afford to ignore the loss of nurses from the workforce (Health Resources and Services Administration 2003, 2004, 2010). As noted in Chapter 11, nursing turnover costs have been estimated to be 1.3 times the salary of a departing nurse or an average of $65,000 per lost nurse (Department for Professional Employees AFL-CIO, 2010; Jones & Gates, 2007). Multiply that by the number of nurses who quit their jobs and the costs can be in the millions of dollars for healthcare organizations.

Any strategy that improves the retention of nursing staff saves the organization the costs of using agency or traveler nurses, replacing lost nurses and training new ones, and the loss of productivity from burdening the remaining. In a large system, like the Veterans Health Administration, High Involvement Work Systems that include teamwork can mean lower service costs in the millions of dollars (Harmon et al., 2003). Show higher-level management improvements in patient satisfaction scores, as well as the money to be saved in the long run with effective teamwork, and their approvals will follow.

THE COSTS OF TEAMWORK

Despite all the benefits of teamwork noted above, there can be a downside with its associated costs. The **costs of teamwork** include the costs of having meetings, along with a place to meet and food and coffee; the costs of trying to arrange a time that's convenient for most of the participants; time spent in meeting and the accompanying opportunity costs, that is, how that time might have been better spent; the hard-to-measure interpersonal costs associated with having to work with other people (such as a perceived loss of autonomy and the need for compromise, which is very hard for some persons); the development of mutually respectful behaviors and trust; the costs of risk taking associated with letting go of one's turf; and the potential embarrassment of looking bad in a group.

In 1995, Lucente, Rea, Vorce, and Yancey reported on the impact of creating a patient-focused care delivery model. (See Textbox 13-4.) Due to the merger of two acute care facilities, the hospital decided to create a patient-focused care model and a new team organization for case management to streamline care and reduce costs. A multidisciplinary steering group developed the model, and nurse managers, physicians, and patient care technicians implemented it. The authors found that patient education and quality of care improved; overtime decreased, with a savings of $112,000; and patient satisfaction was unchanged. However, when they attempted to survey 500 employees to obtain staff satisfaction levels in 1992 and 1993, only 4 surveys were returned. The poor initial response to the staff satisfaction questionnaire could have been due to methodology—or the fact that people dislike change. Resistance to organizational change is always a potential cost in teamwork, and one that shouldn't be readily discounted.

TEXTBOX 13-4. USE OF TEAMS IN A "PATIENT-FOCUSED CARE MODEL" IN A COMMUNITY HOSPITAL

In 1994, Augusta Medical Center in Fishersville, Virginia, opened its new facility and instituted a redesign of its patient care delivery system. The redesign project embodied the "future care model," which is a patient-focused care delivery system that focuses on the value for the patient through a continuous quality improvement process. The "patient-focused care model" is based on the following assumptions:

1. Services at the point of delivery would reduce wait times and improve patient services.
2. Patients will be grouped according to resources needed.
3. High-volume and low-risk services will be decentralized.
4. For all patient services, professional staff will be assisted by cross-trained, multidisciplinary, nonlicensed extenders, which will result in improved cost-effectiveness and efficiency.
5. Physician—nurse communication and collaboration are essential for appropriate care, resource utilization, and preventing patient problems.

Implementation of the model began in 1992 in the existing facility on a pilot basis with the formation of patient care teams including a case manager (an RN), an RN team leader, an LPN, a patient care technician, and a patient care assistant. The latter two team members were unlicensed assistive personnel used by the hospital to address the shortage of RNs and to reduce the non-nursing time being experienced by RNs. The patient care teams were assigned to care for a defined group of patients in particular clinical units within the hospital. In addition, certain non-nursing clinical and support services—such as selected respiratory therapy activities, phlebotomy, patient transport, specimen collection, patient registration, and environmental services—were decentralized to the care unit levels.

Evaluation of the pilot project was conducted in 1992–1993 to assess quality, patient satisfaction, and cost-related outcomes in a 22-bed medical unit. Findings from interviews with 400 medical-surgical patients indicated a 6% increase in the number of patients demonstrating patient education knowledge upon discharge, and a record review of 100 medical-surgical patients indicated a 50% increase in the number of medical records of discharged patients with patient educational interventions documented. In addition, the hospital experienced an average hourly wage reduction of 26 cents per hour as a result of using unlicensed, multiskilled extenders. Length of stay decreased by 12% for all patients in the pilot project unit, and for those patients who were actively case managed, length of stay decreased by 17% during the study period. Patient satisfaction levels did not change considerably during the pilot project. However, physicians reported that the patient-focused care model improved the quality of care the patient receives, and that the new roles of nurses in the team approach have enhanced the quality of care the patient receives.

Source: Lucente et al., 1995.

Tuckman (1965) conducted a comprehensive literature review of small group behavior in therapy group, t-group, natural, and laboratory group studies. After examining the literature, he devised a classification scheme for small group dynamics. In this classic article, Tuckman provided the following five stages that teams go through: **forming**, **storming**, **norming**, **performing**, **and adjourning**. When teams are **forming**, they are getting oriented to the team goals and each other, finding out what the tasks are and who they will be working with. Then the **storming** begins. With storming, there is intragroup conflict; there can be attempts at dominance, passive-aggressive behavior along with information withholding, and other forms of resistance to team tasks and goals. Peace breaks out when the storming stage passes, and team members actually begin **performing** the work at hand, have open dialogue with one another, and share information to accomplish the team's goals. Winding down and **adjourning** brings its own emotional turbulence. Team members who may have disliked each other at the start have worked together over a long period of time and have developed respect for one another. They've grown to like each other as individuals and the team as a whole and become sad that they are disbanding (Tuckman, 1965).

When teams don't work well together, there are significant costs to the organization in terms of human resources and opportunity costs. These costs mean that teamwork may not always be as efficient as other forms of problem solving and decision making. According to Drinka and Clark (2000), "To become efficient... the team members must learn to define the scope of the problem... and select the least disciplines needed to address the problem well." The more is not always the merrier. Efficient team function can only occur when each carefully selected team member knows the goal(s) of the team. It takes less time (usually) for one person to decide on a potential strategy than a group of people. However, without having team advocates in each of the areas affected by the decision, implementing a unilateral decision can become a healthcare manager's worst nightmare.

One of the emerging trends in healthcare organizations is the use of virtual teams. With the availability of the Internet and other innovative communication technologies, virtual teams are gaining popularity for some activities in healthcare organizations (Tompkins & Orwat, 2010). Most patient care cannot be addressed effectively through virtual or remote teams, however. Some positive results from virtual teams are related to the use of telemedicine, which promotes healthcare interventions over geographic distances (Tompkins & Orwat, 2010). As noted in Chapter 12, for some staff in nonclinical areas of healthcare organizations, who have flexible work schedules and can telecommute, such communication technologies allow for less face-to-face team activities and more remote team activities. This can work both for and against team unity, and the manager must guard against problems in employee relationships and team effectiveness that may result from the use of remote and virtual teams.

REAL-WORLD PROBLEMS AND TEAMWORK

Real-world healthcare problems are vexing—complex, complicated, and messy (Buchbinder, 2009a). Rittel and Webber (1973, p. 160) wrote on planning, and first dubbed these "wicked problems." Drinka and Clark (2000, p. 37) wrote about "tame versus wicked problems." **Tame problems** can be defined and, while not easy, they can be solved. **Wicked problems** are difficult to define and not easily resolved—and sometimes can never be truly solved due to multiple layers of issues, such as we see in health care. Rittel and Webber (1973) described ten key features of wicked problems.

1. "There is no definitive formulation of a wicked problem.
2. Wicked problems have no stopping rule.
3. Solutions to wicked problems are not true-or-false, but good-or-bad.
4. There is no immediate and no ultimate test of a solution to a wicked problem.
5. Every solution to a wicked problem is a 'one-shot operation;' because there is no opportunity to learn by trial-and-error, every attempt counts significantly.
6. Wicked problems do not have an enumerable (or an exhaustively describable) set of potential solutions, nor is there a well-described set of permissible operations that may be incorporated into the plan.
7. Every wicked problem is essentially unique.
8. Every wicked problem can be considered to be a symptom of another problem.
9. The existence of a discrepancy representing a wicked problem can be explained in numerous ways. The choice of explanation determines the nature of the problem's resolution.
10. The planner has no right to be wrong" (Rittel & Weber, 1973, pp. 161–166).

Most healthcare problems fall along the continuum of tame to wicked, with many levels of messiness along the way. Conklin (2008) speaks of fragmentation as a result of vexing, wicked problems interacting with social complexity. By having only one discipline examining an issue, problems can actually be *exacerbated*, rather than ameliorated. When different factions stare at their pieces of the puzzle and don't attempt to see the perspectives of others, problems are addressed in a piecemeal, not holistic, manner.

Here are some examples of wicked problems:

- An 80-year-old woman has had hip replacement surgery and used up her post-op Medicare paid days at the skilled nursing facility (SNF). Her walking has improved but is not back to pre-injury status. In her home, her bedroom is on the second floor and she has a flight of stairs to climb to get to her front door. Her only daughter lives in another state and has two teenagers (one of whom is struggling with depression), and her husband just lost his job.

- A Hispanic man has sustained burns over much of his upper torso, including his arms. He is uninsured and needs extensive therapy to prevent contracture (immobilization) of his arms. Neither he nor his family members are fluent in English. They don't understand what he needs or how to access healthcare resources to help him return to his activities of daily living (ADLs).
- A young woman who is addicted to heroin gives birth. The baby is born with low Apgar scores (a numerical score on a scale from 1 to 10, given at 1 and 5 minutes after birth; a lower score indicates a sicker newborn) and is in withdrawal. Eventually, the baby is ready for discharge. The social services department is not keen on handing the baby over to the mother, who is still using heroin. However, the mother's mother (the baby's grandmother) says *she* can take care of the baby—except grandmother arrives to pick up the infant drunk (she failed to mention that she was an alcoholic) and her husband (the grandfather) is also high when he arrives because he is addicted to prescription painkillers.

As you can see from the above examples, wicked problems cannot be solved by one person or one discipline. You need to have every involved area's input to analyze a wicked problem, because it won't be solved by one person—or one discipline. Because of these complexities, members of a team must be selected with care.

WHO'S ON THE TEAM?

When you first start out in healthcare management, it is unlikely that you will be able to choose your teammates. It will be *your* job to learn the culture of the organization and to determine how best to fit into a team. Some of the questions that you can ask when you are assigned to a team are:

- What are the goals of the team?
- How will they be measured?
- What are the short-term and long-term deadlines?
- When and where does the team meet?
- To whom do I report? (Sometimes staff members are loaned to teams, so this is an important issue to resolve.)
- What is my role on the team?
- What are my responsibilities in that role?

Good managers don't mind if a new staff member makes a list of questions and asks for clarification and direction. Coaching, mentoring, and guiding are all part of the manager's role, and healthcare management is a continuous learning experience. Managers *do* mind, however, if you don't ask questions, and go off and do the wrong thing. Additionally, good managers want thoughtful observations from a new perspective: yours.

Over time, as you assume more responsibilities and learn the organization, you may be asked to recommend team members or to convene a team to address a specific organizational issue. Getting the right people on a team is one of the most critical tasks a healthcare manager can have. When this opportunity comes, ask for counsel and advice from your manager and your coworkers. The last thing you want to do is exclude the chairman of surgery on a team that's addressing operating room productivity. As noted previously, real-world healthcare management problems are complex, complicated, and messy. As a healthcare manager, you will need to assess the strengths and weaknesses of each potential team member before inviting him or her onto your team. You will need to ask the following questions.

Does this person:

- Belong to an area that's affected by the problem at hand?
- Have the knowledge, skills, and disposition to do the tasks at hand?
- Have a clearly defined role on the team?
- Have the authority to make decisions and implement recommendations?
- Follow through on assignments and tasks and meet deadlines?
- Think beyond the confines of a department or discipline?
- Work collaboratively and respectfully with other disciplines?
- Have the ability to defuse tensions and de-escalate conflict?
- Have a sense of humor?
- Have a good reputation within the organization as a team player?
- Value perceptions and ideas of others?
- See organizational goals as superseding individual goals?

One tool that is sometimes used for understanding differences in team members' personalities is the **Myers-Briggs Type Indicator (MBTI)**, a personality inventory based on Jung's theory of psychological types (Rideout & Richardson, 1989). The MBTI assesses four domains and four subsets within those domains on a four-by-four grid (Wideman, 2003). On the vertical axis of this grid is the **Introvert-Extrovert scale**; on the horizontal axis is the Sensing-Intuitive scale. Within each of the four quadrants of this grid are two more axes—the **Perceiving-Judging axis** and the **Thinking-Feeling axis**. After taking this paper-and-pencil, self-administered inventory, the individual finds her "Myers-Briggs Type" on a large square. The types are designated by letters, so when a search firm is looking for a strong executive, they would want an "ESTJ," someone who is "responsible, dependable, highly organized, likes to see things done correctly, tends to judge in terms of standard operating procedures, realistic, matter-of-fact, and loyal to institutions" (Wideman, 2003, p. 11).

When building a team, you may not want everyone to be a leader. As noted in Chapter 2, you also need good followers, that is, people who are willing to bring their strengths to the group process, who may be more on the sensing, introverted, intuitive end of the axis on the MBTI, rather than the extroverted end. Wideman (2003) suggests that, while project management and teamwork are becoming mandatory in most employment settings, not everyone in the workforce population is suited, by their personality type, to function well on a team. He suggests judicious use of the MBTI to see where people fit in the leadership versus followership mode and to be cautious about who is placed on a team.

Many healthcare recruiters utilize the MBTI to help them select candidates for healthcare placements. In addition, many healthcare management professional organizations offer seminars and workshops for individuals to learn about their personality styles. The key thing to know about this popular tool is that it is one of many ways to understand healthcare team members, but it is not the only way. Oftentimes, experience and the oral history of the healthcare organization where you work is the best predictor of selecting good team members.

EMOTIONS AND TEAMWORK

Psychological researchers have known for decades that infants learn emotions through observation and mimicry of caregivers' facial expressions (Buchbinder, 2009c). In addition, Laird and Bresler (1992) demonstrated in laboratory research that when subjects' faces were arranged into frowns, the subjects reported feeling angry—even in the absence of any cues that would induce such emotions. Muscle memory appeared to create the mood associated with the facial expressions. Recently, neuroscientists have discovered that a cluster of premotor and parietal cells called "mirror neurons" or the "mirror neuron system" (MNS) is responsible for enabling humans to learn motor skills, language, communication, and social behaviors (Iacoboni & Depretto, 2006; Rizzolatti & Craighero, 2004; Society for Neuroscience, 2008).

According to Hatfield, Cacioppo, and Rapson (1993), people who are emotionally in tune with others can read emotions within *nanoseconds* of observing facial expressions. The ability to read other people's emotions has been measured through the **Emotion Contagion (EC) scale**. Doherty, Orimoto, Singelis, Hatfield, and Hebb (1995) found that women and physicians scored higher on the EC scale and that there were significant correlations between self-report of "catching emotion" and "judges' ratings of participants actual emotional reactions" (Doherty et al., 1995, p. 369).

When Totterdell, Kellett, Teuchmann, and Briner (1998) looked at the relationship between mood and work groups of community nurses, they discovered "significant associations between people's moods and the moods of their teammates at work over time" (Totterdell et al., 1998, p. 1513). The term used by these researchers and others for why this happened was "emotional contagion." In other words, the teammates caught each others' moods.

To summarize:

- We are hardwired to learn emotions through mimicry and mirroring.
- Emotions are communicated in a flash—literally within microseconds.
- Women and people in the helping professions are more sensitive to reading emotions.
- Emotions are contagious and can spread within moments.

Kanter (2004) found that optimistic leaders focus on specific tasks ahead, rather than dwelling on past failures and negativity. Although we are experiencing challenging times in health care, leaders *can* moderate the impact of this volatile environment. With all the women and helping professionals in healthcare settings, the majority of employees are highly sensitive to other people's moods. Enthusiasm, confidence, and optimism are critical to leading others. Emotionally aware team members can change an organization's emotional environment and improve the quality of employees' and patients' lives by helping others to become "infected" with positive emotions (Buchbinder, 2009b).

As noted in Chapter 2, emotional intelligence (EI), the concept made famous by Daniel Goleman in the late 1990s, encompasses self-awareness, self-regulation, self-motivation, social awareness, and social skills, and within each of these areas, specific skill sets (Consortium on Research for Emotional Intelligence in Organizations, 2009; Goleman, 1998). In 2006, Goleman moved to the terminology *social intelligence* (SI) to separate out the last two components of EI, social awareness and social skills, and began using the term "social facility" instead of "social skills" (Goleman, 2006). These two are defined as:

"Social Awareness
- Primal empathy: Feeling with others; sensing nonverbal emotional signals.
- Attunement: Listening with full receptivity; attuning to a person.
- Empathic accuracy: Understanding another person's thoughts, feelings, and intentions.

Social Facility
- Synchrony: Interacting smoothly at the nonverbal level.
- Self-presentation: Presenting ourselves effectively.
- Influence: Shaping the outcome of social interactions.
- Concern: Caring about others' needs and acting accordingly." (Goleman, 2006, p. 84)

Currently there is a controversy in the industrial-organizational psychology literature regarding the definitions, models, and measurement of EI, SI, and now, emotional social competencies (ESC). Cherniss (2010, p. 184) defined ESC as "those emotional abilities, social skills, personality traits, motivations, interests, goals, values, attachment styles, and life narratives that can contribute to (or detract from) effective performance across a variety of positions." The bottom line is that being aware of one's emotional and social skills and being able to effectively use them is an important ability for leaders and followers. In health care, these competencies and the ability to assess when and how to utilize these competencies are essential to good leadership and effective teamwork. Protocols such as the EI360, a 360-degree assessment of an individual's EI, help to identify an individual's emotional and social strengths and weaknesses (Buchbinder, 2009c). With coaching and specific behavioral goals that are applied in the workplace, healthcare managers can learn how to move to the next level of their EI, SI, and ESC abilities—and how to best apply them in the workplace.

TEAM COMMUNICATION

Frequent, positive communications improve team interactions and increase trust. Organizations that empower their employees promote employee job satisfaction. Laschinger and Finegan (2005) found that nurses who felt they had access to opportunity, honest relationships, open communication with peers and managers, and trusted their managers were more likely to be attached to their organizations and have higher job satisfaction. Similarly, it has been shown that healthcare employees who view their work unit climate as participative as opposed to authoritarian provide higher levels of customer service, commit fewer clinical errors, and express less likelihood of leaving the organization (Angermeier, Dunford, Boss, & Boss, 2009).

Dreachslin, Hunt, and Sprainer (1999) conducted research to assess how diversity affected patient-centered team communication and to improve communication and patient care. Focus groups were convened to elicit key issues and to develop recommendations. The authors concluded that healthcare managers should facilitate open and honest dialogue between management and care production teams and within the teams themselves. The process should involve care production team members in process improvement. To improve relationships between team members and nurse managers, more training is needed, both in the clinical and relationship management arenas. Diversity training has to be part of team and leadership training. The **patient-centered care model** must emphasize caring for patients, as well as 360-degree feedback, where nurses and technicians evaluate each other, should be implemented for assessment, communicated to team members, and used as a management tool for continuous quality improvement.

In a classic article on management teams, Eisenhardt, Kahwajy, and Bourgeois (1997) observed teams in 12 technology companies. Much like health care today, these companies operated in a high-stakes, fast-paced environment, where today's technology is tomorrow's dinosaur. Teams had to be lightning fast in their responses and almost precognitive to stay ahead of the competition. The authors found that teams with minimal interpersonal conflict had the same six strategies. "Team members: worked with more, rather than less information, and debated facts; developed multiple alternatives to enrich the level of debate; shared commonly agreed upon goals; injected humor into the decision process; maintained a balanced power structure; and resolved issues without forcing consensus" (Eisenhardt et al., 1997, p. 78). By keeping the focus on the facts and not on personalities, and communicating in an open, honest, and safe forum, the teams were able to have fun and be productive.

The airline industry has become a model of how to build teams in hospitals and other healthcare organizations (Nance, 2008). Pilots are trained to be team players because a plane full of people may die if they don't pay attention to their teammates' observations. **Crew resource management** has been developed to address attitudes, change behavior, and improve performance. Sexton, Thomas, and Helmreich (2000) have applied crew resource management research to hospitals, where stakes are also high and lives depend on the smooth functioning of the healthcare team. Senior surgeons were least likely to be in favor of teamwork and flat hierarchies. Medical staff responded that teamwork was imperative, but that they were not encouraged to report safety concerns. Doctors and nurses differed widely in their opinions regarding teamwork. Almost three-quarters of surveyed intensive care physicians reported high levels of teamwork with nurses, but less than half of the nurses felt the same way. These results point to the need for a more realistic appraisal of safety concerns, improved communication between team members, and enhanced team training for healthcare professionals, in all disciplines and specialties.

METHODS OF MANAGING TEAMS OF HEALTHCARE PROFESSIONALS

Koeck (1998) observed that, while healthcare delivery demands extensive teamwork, the reality is that healthcare teams often fail due to resistance to organizational change and lack of effective leadership. Effective leadership, addressed in the second chapter of this book, is needed at every level of the healthcare organization, but especially in teamwork. Because, by definition, interdisciplinary health teams are made up of people from different fields, it's the healthcare manager's job to take the lead and to establish team guidelines and foster good communication. It's the responsibility of the team leader to establish communication networks. At the first meeting, the leader should obtain names, all phone numbers, e-mail addresses, and any other ways the team members can be contacted. One of the things a team leader can do to facilitate good communication early in the life of the team is to establish guidelines for expected behaviors, processes, and outcomes in a written document. A manager can facilitate effective team functioning within her unit by providing support for struggling teams and by allowing teams to share their successes in improving teamwork and team results (Scott, 2009).

As can be seen in **Figure 13-1, Guidelines for Teamwork**, the document does not have to be complicated. This tool can be used to evaluate the performance of individual members of the team, thus avoiding the **social loafer** or **free-rider syndrome**, where a member of the team does nothing but gets credit for the work done by others. Managing social loafers and other problem teammates can be the biggest part of managing a team. As an effective team leader, your job is to get the best out of each team member. Attaining top performance requires understanding who your teammates are, what they need, and

---

The purpose of Team XYZ is to _____ <**goals**> _____ .

Our deadline for solving this problem is _____ <**date**> _____ .

The team will meet _____ <**number of times or frequency of meetings**> _____ .

Representatives from each affected area have been asked to serve on Team XYZ.

Those representatives are: _____ <**List names of team members**> _____

Team members will:
- Attend all team sessions, unless there is an emergency;
- Prepare for each session;
- Listen to each other with respect:
- Work collaboratively to identify and meet session goals;
- Be an active participant in group discussions;
- Keep an open mind, be willing to modify opinions or conclusions to keep the project moving forward;
- Present ideas concisely;
- Be considerate and tactful when participating in group discussions;
- Submit/delegate work on time and fulfill responsibilities as agreed; and
- Work actively to achieve group consensus on issues and problems.

By _____ <**deadline**> _____, Team XYZ will have the following outcomes:*
- Reports of proceedings, data analyses, recommendations, and an evaluation plan for implementation of the recommendations.

Note: The Leader of Team XYZ is responsible for presentation of this report, with all team members present, if possible, to the administration for review and approval.

Interim deadlines may be needed, so consider those as you discuss these guidelines.

FIGURE 13-1 Guidelines for Teamwork

the ability to build consensus, being aware that you may not have 100% agreement on every decision.

After introductions and establishing the purpose of the team in a written document, Maginn (1995) recommends that the team leader go around the table and ask each person his or her ideas about the problem. The leader should acknowledge each idea, recording it as the team member speaks. Be sure to wait for people to respond to the question—and to each other. Don't interrupt, and don't let others interrupt a person when he/she has the floor. Ask critics for ideas and suggestions, getting those negative comments out on the table so they can be addressed. Remain calm, open-minded, and nondefensive. At the end of each meeting, thank everyone for their thoughtful comments, summarizing what you thought you heard and asking for clarification.

Before the meeting ends, it's time to ask people to do some homework. Who is willing to do what task? Will there be research needed? What process should be used for reporting to each other? Send a summary of the meeting to everyone on the team, and include a list of steps that need to be taken before the next meeting. Communication that includes everyone is key. Establish an e-mail list and be sure all correspondence regarding the project goes through it. The more information team members have, the more buy-in and cooperation will occur.

To build trust, meet commitments and do what you say you are going to do. Bring reliable information to the team. Accurate data and demonstrated skill at your work informs the team members that you are competent—and trustworthy (Maginn, 1995). Even when team members trust each other, conflict happens. At some point in time, there will be disagreement about which choices and decisions the team should make. Maginn (1995) recommends five potential strategies for conflict resolution in teams: **bargaining, problem solving, voting, research, and third-party mediation**.

Bargaining is when someone says, "If you go along with me this time, I'll back you up next time." If the choices are equally good, then bargaining can be a good tool; if the choices aren't equal, then it may not be a good tool. **Voting** is democratic, but also bears the weight of potentially taking a team to the incorrect choice. **Problem solving** may be the better way to go. This means taking time to answer the "what if" scenarios of each alternative. "If we do this, then that might happen?" How will you assess if it's the right option? You may not know until you try it. Doing more **research** is safe, but you may have time pressures that preclude the team from doing an in-depth study. When all else fails, **third-party mediation** is probably a win-win, especially if the third party is the boss. Oftentimes, the team presentation to the boss will include choices that have been laid out, like a menu, for an upper-level manager to select. The alternatives are listed, the pros and cons of each alternative are provided, and the assessment plan for each alternative is in place. You win, your team wins, and your organization wins.

CONCLUSION

This chapter has described what a team is and some of the challenges associated with teamwork in healthcare organizations. Some current trends in using teams and the benefits of teamwork, as well as costs, have been described. Tame and wicked problems were defined and related to the need for interdisciplinary teams to solve them. Fitting into teams and selecting team members were discussed, along with the Myers-Briggs Type Indicator personality inventory. The importance of emotional contagion, emotional and social intelligence, and emotional and social competencies was discussed in relation to effective teamwork. In addition, communication on teams and some methods of managing teams of healthcare professionals have been reviewed. And, finally, some examples of teams in healthcare settings have been presented. You have the background and tools; now you can begin to build your team.

DISCUSSION QUESTIONS

1. What are the differences between a team, a task force, and a committee? What are some of the potential differences in dynamics between people in these different groups?

2. Compare and contrast disciplinary, interdisciplinary, and cross-functional teams.

3. What are some of the unique challenges associated with teamwork in health care? Describe three benefits and three costs of teamwork in healthcare organizations.

4. After working in a hospital for 6 months, you have been selected to head up the team to conduct hand-washing audits on all the nursing units. Whom do you want on your team and why?

5. A member of the hand-washing audit team comes to you and complains that another team member is not pulling her weight. This individual is not your employee, but she is on your team. What should you do?

6. Define and give an example of a wicked problem in a healthcare setting.

7. List and describe five potential strategies for conflict resolution in teams. Which method is likely to be most successful if your manager likes to be involved in every decision?

8. What are the five stages of team development? Describe each stage and how that might appear in a healthcare setting.

9. What is the Myers-Briggs Type Indicator personality inventory, and why is it a useful tool for healthcare executives?

10. Over the past month, every member of the Intravenous (IV) Therapy Team has complained to you about the IV Team supervisor. Her direct reports, all RNs, agree that she is technically superb. However, their comments include statements that she is "hyper-critical," "demeaning," and that they "feel bad" about coming to work. It would be extremely difficult to find a replacement for this supervisor; however, if you don't do *something*, it looks as if the entire IV Team will resign. What should you do?

Cases in Chapter 17 that are related to this chapter include:

- Seaside Convalescent Care Center—see p. 422
- The New Toy at City Medical Center—see p. 449
- Problems with the Pre-Admission Call Center—see p. 390
- Heritage Valley Medical Center: Are Your Managers Culturally Competent?—see p. 430
- Emotional Intelligence in Labor and Delivery—see p. 434

Additional cases, role-play scenarios, video links, websites, and other information sources are also available in the online Instructor's Materials.

REFERENCES

Alexander, J. A., Lichtenstein, R., Jinnett, K., Wells, R., Zazzali, J., & Liu, D. (2005). Cross-functional team processes and patient functional improvement. *Health Services Research, 40*(5), 1335–1355.

Amos, M. A., Hu, J., & Herrick, C. A. (2005, January/February). The impact of team building on communication and job satisfaction of nursing staff. *Journal for Nurses in Staff Development, 21*(1),10–16.

Angermeier, I., Dunford, B. B., Boss, A. D., & Boss, R. W. (2009). The impact of participative management perceptions on customer service, medical errors, burnout, and turnover intentions. *Journal of Healthcare Management, 54*(2), 127–141.

Baker, D. P., Salas, E., King, H., Battles, J., & Barach, P. (2005, April). The role of teamwork in the professional education of physicians: Current status and assessment recommendations. *Journal on Quality and Patient Safety, 31*(4), 185–202.

Ball, M. J. (2005, October 25). Culture of safety. *Advance for Nurses, 7*(23), 31–32.

Buchbinder, S. B. (2009a, September 17). Can we tame the wicked problems in health care? Retrieved from http://portfolio.jblcarning.com/health/2009/9/9/can-we-tame-wicked-problems-in-health-care.html

Buchbinder, S. B. (2009b, November 23). Infectious leadership. Retrieved from http://portfolio .jblearning.com/health/2009/11/23/infectious-leadership.html

Buchbinder, S. B. (2009c, July 29). Emotional intelligence and leadership. Retrieved from http:// portfolio.jblearning.com/health/2009/7/29/emotional-intelligence-and-leadership.html

Buchbinder, S. B., Alt, P. M., Eskow, K., Forbes, W., Hester, E., Struck, M., & Taylor, D. (2005). Creating learning prisms with an interdisciplinary case study workshop. *Innovative Higher Education, 29*(4), 257–274.

Bureau of Labor Statistics (BLS). (2010). Medical and health services managers. *Occupational outlook handbook, 2010–11 edition.* Retrieved from http://www.bls.gov/oco/ocos014.htm

Cherniss, C. (2010). Emotional intelligence: New insights and further clarifications. *Industrial and Organizational Psychology, 3*, 183–191.

Conklin, J. (2008). Wicked problems and social complexity. Retrieved from http://www.cognexus.org/ wpf/wickedproblems.pdf

Consortium on Research for Emotional Intelligence in Organizations. (2009). *The emotional competence framework.* Retrieved from http://www.eiconsortium.org/reports/emotional_competence_ framework.html

Department for Professional Employees AFL-CIO (DPEAFLCIO). (2010). *Fact sheet: The costs and benefits of safe staffing ratios.* Retrieved from http://dpeaflcio.org/pdf/DPE-fs_2010_ staffratio.pdf

Doherty, R. W., Orimoto, L., Singelis, T. M., Hatfield, E., & Hebb, J. (1995). Emotional contagion: Gender and occupational differences. *Psychology of Women Quarterly, 19*, 355–371.

Donahue, M. P. (1985). *Nursing: The finest art: An illustrated history.* St. Louis, MO: CV Mosby.

Dreachslin, J. L., Hunt, P. L., & Sprainer, E. (1999). Communication patterns and group composition: Implications for patient-centered care team effectiveness. *Journal of Healthcare Management, 44*(4), 252–268.

Drinka, T. J. K., & Clark, P. G. (2000). *Health care teamwork: Interdisciplinary practice and teaching.* Westport, CT: Auburn House.

Edwards, N., Marshall, M., McLellan, A., & Abbasi, K. (2003, March 22). Doctors and managers: A problem without a solution? *British Medical Journal, 326*(7390), 609–610.

Eisenhardt, K. M., Kahwajy, J. L., & Bourgeois, L. F. (1997). How management teams can have a good fight. *Harvard Business Review, 75*(5), 77–85.

Flexner, A. (1910). *Medical education in the United States and Canada.* New York, NY: Carnegie Foundation for the Advancement of Teaching.

Goleman, D. (1998, December). What makes a leader? *Harvard Business Review*, 93–102.

Goleman, D. (2006). *Social intelligence.* New York, NY: Bantam Books.

Grumbach, K., & Bodenheimer, T. (2004). Can primary health care teams improve primary care practice? *Journal of the American Medical Association, 291*(10), 1246–1251.

Harmon, J., Scotti, D. J., Behson, S., Petzel, R., Neuman, J. H., & Keashly, L. (2003, November/ December). Effects of high-involvement work systems on employee satisfaction and service costs in veterans healthcare. *Journal of Healthcare Management, 48*(6), 393–406.

Hatfield, E., Cacioppo, J. L., & Rapson, R. L. (1993). Emotional contagion. *Current Directions in Psychological Sciences, 2*, 96–99.

Health Resources and Services Administration (HRSA). (2003, Spring). *Changing demographics: Implications for physicians, nurses and other health workers.* U.S. Department of Health and Human

Services, Health Resources and Services Administration, Bureau of Health Professions, National Center for Health Workforce Analysis.

Health Resources and Services Administration (HRSA). (2004). *The registered nurse population: Findings from the March 2004 national sample survey of registered nurses.*

Health Resources and Services Administration (HRSA). (2010, March). *The registered nurse population: Initial findings from the 2008 national sample survey of registered nurses.*

Iacoboni, M., & Dapretto, M. (2006). The mirror neuron system and the consequences of its dysfunction. *Nature Reviews: Neuroscience, 7*, 942–951.

Institute for Healthcare Improvement. (2004). *Transforming care at the bedside.* Retrieved from http:// www.ihi.org/IHI/Results/WhitePapers/TransformingCareattheBedsideWhitePaper.htm

Institute of Medicine. (2001). *Crossing the quality chasm: A new health system for the 21st century.* Washington, DC: National Academies Press.

Jain, A. K., Thompson, J. M., Chaudry, J., McKenzie, S., & Schwartz, R. W. (2008). High-performance teams for current and future physician leaders: An introduction. *Journal of Surgical Education, 65*(2), 145–150.

Jones, C., & Gates, M. (September 30, 2007). The costs and benefits of nurse turnover: A business case for nurse retention. *OJIN: The Online Journal of Issues in Nursing, 12*(3). Retrieved from DOI: 10.3912/OJIN.Vol12No03Man04

Kanter, R. M. (2004). *Confidence: How winning streaks and losing streaks begin and end.* New York, NY: Crown Books.

Katzenbach, J. R., & Smith, D. K. (2004). The discipline of teams. In Teams that succeed. Boston, MA: Harvard Business School Press.

Koeck, C. (1998, November 7). Time for organizational development in healthcare organisations: Improving quality for patients means changing the organisation. *British Medical Journal, 317*(7168), 1267–1268. Retrieved from http://www.pubmedcentral.nih.gov/articlerender .fcgi?artid=1114203

Laird, J. D., & Bresler, C. (1992). The process of emotional feeling: A self-perception theory. In M. Clark (Ed.), *Review of Personality and Social Psychology* (Vol. 13). Newbury Park, CA: Sage. As cited by Hatfield, E., Cacioppo, J. L., & Rapson, R. L. (1993). Emotional contagion. *Current Directions in Psychological Sciences, 2*, 96–99.

Laschinger, H. K. S., & Finegan, J. (2005). Using empowerment to build trust and respect in the workplace: A strategy for addressing the nursing shortage. *Nursing Economic$, 23*(1), 6–13.

Leggat, S. G. (2007). Teaching and learning teamwork: Competency requirements for healthcare managers. *The Journal of Health Administration Education, 24*(2), 135–149.

Liedtka, J. M., Whitten, E., & Sorrells-Jones, J. (1998). Enhancing care delivery through cross-disciplinary collaboration: A case study. *Journal of Healthcare Management, 43*(2), 185–206.

Lucente, B., Rea, M. R., Vorce, S. H., & Yancey, T. (1995). Redesigning care delivery in the community hospital. *Nursing Economics, 13*(4), 242–247.

Maginn, M. (1995). *Effective teamwork.* West Des Moines, IA: American Media Publishing.

McLaughlin, C. P. (2004). West Florida Regional Medical Center. In J. S. Rakich, B. B. Longest, & K. Darr. *Case in health services management* (4th ed.). Baltimore, MD: Health Professions Press, Inc.

Mickan, S. M. (2005). Evaluating the effectiveness of health care teams. *Australian Health Review, 29*(2), 211–217.

Nance, J. (2008). *Why hospitals should fly.* Bozeman, MT: Second River Healthcare Press.

Neily, J., Mills, P. D., Young-Xu, Y., Careney, B. T., West, P., Berger, D. H., et al. (2010). Association between implementation of a medical team training program and surgical mortality. *Journal of the American Medical Association, 304*(15), 1693–1700.

Pronovost, P. J., & Freischlag, J. A. (2010). Improving teamwork to reduce surgical mortality. *Journal of the American Medical Association, 304*(15), 1721–1722.

Quinlan, E., & Robertson, S. (2010). Mutual understanding in multi-disciplinary primary health care teams. *Journal of Interprofessional Care, 24*(5), 565–578.

Rideout, C. A., & Richardson, S. A. (1989, May). A teambuilding model: Appreciating differences using the Myers-Briggs Type Indicator with developmental theory. *Journal of Counseling and Development, 67*(9), 529–533.

Rittel, H., & Webber, M. (1973). Dilemmas in a general theory of planning. *Policy Sciences, 4,* 155–169. In N. Cross (Ed.). (1984). *Developments in design methodology* (pp. 135–144). Chichester, UK: Wiley & Sons.

Rizzolatti, G., & Craighero, L. (2004). The mirror-neuron system. *Annual Review of Neuroscience, 27,* 169–192.

Roblin, D. W., Vogt, T. M., & Fireman, B. (2003, January–March). Primary health care teams: Opportunities and challenges in evaluation of service delivery innovations. *J Ambulatory Care Management, 26*(1), 22–35.

Ruddy, G., & Rhee, K. (2005). Transdisciplinary teams in primary care for the underserved: A literature review. *Journal of Health Care for the Poor and Underserved, 16,* 248–256.

Scott, G. (2009). Teamwork. *Healthcare Executive, 24*(2), 46–47.

Sexton, J. B., Thomas, E. J., & Helmreich, R. L. (2000). Error, stress, and teamwork in medicine and aviation: Cross sectional surveys. *British Medical Journal, 320,* 745–749.

Sherman, J. (2006, March/April). Patient safety: Engaging medical staff. *Healthcare Executive, 21*(2), 20–23.

Society for Neuroscience. (2008, November). Mirror neurons. *Brain Briefings.* Retrieved from http:// www .sfn.org/index.cfm?pagename=brainBriefings_MirrorNeurons

Stefl, M. (2008). Common competencies for all healthcare managers: The healthcare leadership alliance model. *Journal of Healthcare Management, 53*(6), 360–374.

Thompson, J. M. (2010). Collaboration in health care marketing and business development. In B. Freshman, L. Rubino, & Y. Reid Chassiakos (Eds.), *Collaboration across the disciplines in health care.* Sudbury, MA: Jones and Bartlett.

Tompkins, C., & Orwat, J. (2010). A randomized trial of telemonitoring heart failure patients, *Journal of Healthcare Management, 55*(5), 312–323.

Totterdell, P., Kellett, S., Teuchmann, K., & Briner, R. B. (1998). Evidence of mood linkage in work groups. *Journal of Personality and Social Psychology, 74,* 1504–1515.

Tuckman, B. W. (1965). Developmental sequence in small groups. *Psychological Bulletin, 63,* 384–399. Reprinted in *Group Facilitation: A Research and Applications Journal* - Number 3, Spring 2001. Retrieved from http://dennislearningcenter.osu.edu/references/GROUP%20DEV%20ARTICLE.doc

University of Chicago, School of Social Service Administration, Chicago, IL, The Graduate Program in Health Administration and Policy. (n.d.). *About GPHAP*. Retrieved from http://gphap .uchicago.edu/aboutgphap.shtml

Weber, D. O. (2004, September–October). Poll results: Doctors' disruptive behavior disturbs physician leaders. *The Physician Executive, 30*(5), 6–14.

Wideman, M. (2003). *Project teamwork, personality profiles and the population at large: Do we have enough of the right kind of people?* Retrieved from www.maxwideman.com/papers/profiles/profiles.pdf

Addressing Health Disparities: Cultural Proficiency

Nancy Sayre and Ruth Chavez

LEARNING OBJECTIVES

By the end of this chapter, the student will be able to:

- Define the concepts of health disparities, cultural competency, and cultural proficiency;
- Develop a cogent argument for addressing health disparities;
- Identify trends in demographics in the United States and the expected impact on the patient population and the healthcare workforce;
- Describe initiatives to foster cultural proficiency within healthcare organizations;
- Explain the benefits of implementing cultural proficiency programs; and
- Discuss new paradigms relating to health disparities in research and practice.

INTRODUCTION

Unprecedented scientific and medical discoveries, continuous innovation, and new evidence-based interventions have improved the health of American residents. Simultaneously, participants in the public and private sectors of the healthcare economy have made enormous investments, and Americans' healthcare utilization and spending have increased. Not all individuals, groups of individuals, or organizations have benefited, however, from these scientific breakthroughs or these financial investments in diagnosis and treatment. For decades there has been, and even now there continues to be, a disproportionate burden of illness and injury among **underserved populations**. According to the U.S. Department of Health and

Human Services' Health Resources and Services Administration (HRSA), the definition of an underserved population is a group with economic barriers or cultural and/or linguistic barriers to primary medical care services (Health Resources and Services Administration, 1995). Researchers compared segments of the population in the United States and found very different measures of wellness, healthcare utilization, and outcomes of illnesses and injuries. Called **health disparities**, this concept is complicated, and the causes are multifactorial.

The word "disparity" means a great difference. The term "health disparity" is widely used in public health, although the term has different meanings. In one report, 11 different definitions were identified from various sources, including the National Institutes of Health (NIH), *Healthy People 2010*, and the Health Resources and Services Administration (Carter-Pokras & Baquet, 2002). The NIH definition reads "a population is a health disparity population if . . . there is a significant disparity in the overall rate of disease incidence, prevalence, morbidity, mortality, or survival rates in the population as compared to the health status of the general population" (National Institutes of Health, n.d.). The Agency for Healthcare Research and Quality (AHRQ) considers these priority populations in terms of research, policy, support, and funding. These include the following priority populations: inner-city, rural, low-income, minority, women, children, elderly, and those with special health care needs, including those who have disabilities, need chronic care, or need end-of-life health care (Agency for Healthcare Research and Quality, 2003).

Outside the United States, in countries such as the United Kingdom and Australia, the terms "**health inequality**" or "health **inequity**" are more commonly used. An **inequality** refers to conditions being unequal, whereas an **inequity** signifies a subjective value judgment of unjustness. The ethical judgment of the fairness of a health disparity and whether one is avoidable leads to the sometimes subjective nature of the term. Most would agree that a **health disparity** signifies a difference in access, utilization, or quality of care, health status, health environment, or health outcome between groups.

Some of the most striking disparities include shorter life expectancy and higher rates of cancer, infant mortality, and birth defects, as well as a higher incidence of diseases such as asthma, diabetes, stroke, cardiovascular disease, sexually transmitted diseases, and mental illness, among multiethnic populations. The National Institutes of Health has published numerous reports on health disparities; the following are but a few examples (NIH, n.d.; NIH, 2006).

- **Diabetes**—The Pima Indians of the Gila River Indian Community near Phoenix, Arizona, have the highest rates of diabetes in the world. The NIH has researched contributing factors such as genetics, in utero exposures, and lack of exercise (NIH, n.d.). Also, Hispanics, African Americans, and some Asian Americans, Native Hawaiians, and Pacific Islanders, including Japanese Americans and Samoans, are at particularly high risk for developing type 2 diabetes (NIH, n.d.).

- **Infant mortality**—Even when controlling for socioeconomic factors, the rate of infant mortality has been twice as high among African Americans as compared to whites during the last decade. Infants of Native American and Alaskan descent also have a death rate almost double that of whites (NIH, n.d.).

- **Heart disease and stroke**—Cardiovascular disease rates consistently have been higher in the African American population than in whites. Stroke death rates, when adjusted for age, are almost 80% higher for African Americans than those of whites (NIH, n.d.).

- **Cancer**—Cancer deaths vary by gender, race, and ethnicity. Whites have higher survival rates than many racial and ethnic groups for most cancers. Colorectal cancer rates are higher among Alaska Natives than the national average, and Asian Americans suffer disproportionately from stomach and liver cancers (NIH, n.d.).

- **Mental health**—American Indians and Alaska Natives suffer disproportionately from mental health disorders, and this population experiences a higher suicide rate (Suicide Prevention Resource Center, n.d.).

- **Eye disease**—Latinos living in the United States have higher rates of eye disease and visual impairments compared to other ethnic groups. This includes diabetic retinopathy, cataracts, and glaucoma (NIH, 2006).

- **HIV and AIDS**—In 2002, the AIDS diagnosis rate among African Americans was nearly 11 times the rate among whites; African American women had a 23 times greater diagnosis rate than white women. In addition, the AIDS incidence among Hispanics in 2000 was more than three times the rate for whites (NIH, n.d.).

As illustrated by the preceding examples, health disparities can be measured by comparing the health of one group to a reference group, although who should be included in the comparison group is often debatable. Another complicating factor in health disparities is the fact that knowledge of *why* they exist is limited. The causes of disparities are multifactorial, but the largest contributors are related to determinants outside the healthcare delivery system. Factors that impact health disparities include biology and genetics, behaviors, living or working conditions, income and socioeconomic status, education, age, race, ethnicity, culture, sexual orientation, and access to insurance. Access to health insurance is often identified as the most serious contributing factor. Of the 45.7 million non-elderly Americans without health insurance in 2008, more than half of the citizens affected were racial and ethnic minorities (Thomas & James, 2009). Other root causes that have been explored are the patient's health beliefs, the patient's recognition of symptoms, and the patient's adherence to preventive and therapeutic measures (Betancourt, Green, Carrillo, & Ananeh-Firempong, 2003). Separating the sociocultural issues from the health and medical issues is difficult with health disparities. The complicated interrelationships among these variables and their individual causal contributions have not been determined.

Cultural competence is one strategy to begin to address health disparities and to drive toward equity in health and health care. It is just one competency among many needed by healthcare managers to be proficient in the workplace. Healthcare managers must evaluate whether the delivery of care is aligned with the program or institutional priorities related to the health outcomes of the populations they serve. Similar to health disparities, the term "cultural competence" has many definitions, interpretations, and limitations. In 1989, the seminal work of Cross established a foundation for the discipline and provided a definition of cultural competence. Since then, the definition has been adapted and modified; however, the core concepts remain applicable today. Cross defined **cultural competence** as a set of congruent behaviors, attitudes, and policies that come together in a system or agency or among professionals and enable the system, agency, or professions to work effectively in cross-cultural situations (Cross, Bazron, Dennis, & Isaacs, 1989). According to the National Center for Cultural Competence, cultural competence requires that organizations have a defined set of values and principles and demonstrate behaviors, attitudes, policies, and structures that enable them to work effectively cross-culturally (National Center for Cultural Competence, n.d.). The Office of Minority Health has defined cultural competence as the capacity to function effectively as an individual and an organization within the context of cultural beliefs, behaviors, and needs presented by consumers and their communities (Office of Minority Health, 2005). According to The Joint Commission, a **culturally competent organization** is one that is vigilant for ethnic disparities in screening, prescriptions, procedures, and health outcomes and has policies and procedures in place to address any disparities found (McDaniel, 2000). Generally, cultural competency refers to the "ability and willingness to respond respectfully and effectively to people of all cultures, classes, races, ages, ethnic backgrounds and religions in a manner that recognizes and values the worth and dignity of all" (McDaniel, 2000). Cultural competence includes both interpersonal and organizational interventions for overcoming differences.

Concerns with the term cultural competence are prevalent among practitioners, public health experts, and sociologists. One concern is whether anyone or any organization can truly be culturally competent because culture changes over time and the attitudes and skills needed change as well. Another limitation of the term is the implication that prior to training or at some point in time, people may have been culturally incompetent, obviously a negatively charged sentiment. Cultural competence is really a growth process or a journey, not a destination. It is a continuum starting with cultural destructiveness and blindness leading to competence and then proficiency (Rose, 2011). Also, it is difficult to demonstrate that individuals have achieved cultural competence because it is extremely difficult to measure. While many have published surveys or scales to measure this important ability, a 20-year study of cultural competency measures published between 1980 and 2003 found that *none* of the instruments had been validated (Gozu et al., 2007). Other terms that are sometimes used include "culturally effective care," "cultural conditioning," "cultural sensitivity," or "cultural excellence training." The term preferred by these authors is "**cultural proficiency**," because just like other skills, cultural proficiency needs continual updating. The terms cultural competence and cultural proficiency will be used interchangeably here. No matter what terminology is used and whether it can be ultimately attained, the underlying principles of cultural competence for healthcare managers remain salient and timely. Healthcare organizations and healthcare professionals must journey toward delivering culturally effective care and work toward reduction in disparities.

CHANGING U.S. DEMOGRAPHICS AND PATIENT POPULATIONS

In 1900, the United States had a population of 76 million and the percentage of whites was 90% or more in all but two states (Hobbs & Stoop, 2002). According to projections from the U.S. Census Bureau, by midcentury, the nation will be more racially and ethnically diverse, as well as much older. Now approximately one-third of the population, minorities are expected to become the majority in 2042 and represent 54% of the population by 2050, as shown in Figure 14-1. The Hispanic American, Asian

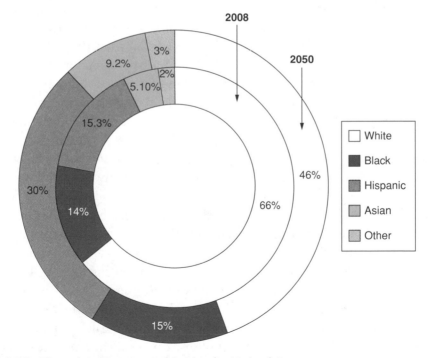

FIGURE 14-1 Changing Demographics in the United States

Source: U.S. Census Bureau, 2008

American, and African American populations are all expected to climb (U.S. Census Bureau, 2008).

As the United States becomes more diverse, healthcare systems will increasingly see patients of every race, ethnicity, age, culture, language, sexual orientation, and language proficiency. Patients may present symptoms differently from textbooks, may not speak or read English as their primary language, or may have varying beliefs about health and illness. Healthcare organizations and healthcare managers must be ready to understand and address these issues.

ADDRESSING HEALTH DISPARITIES BY FOSTERING CULTURAL COMPETENCE IN HEALTHCARE ORGANIZATIONS

Until the 1980s and 1990s, the field of health disparities and cultural competency was ill-defined. In 1986, the Office of Minority Health was established by the United States Department of Health and Human Services. Its focus was on public health programs affecting American Indians and Alaska Natives, Asian Americans, Blacks/African Americans, Hispanics/Latinos, Native Hawaiians, and other Pacific Islanders. In 1992, the results of a study conducted by the American College of Healthcare Executives (ACHE) on diversity in healthcare management spurred the creation of the Institute for Diversity in Health Management, an affiliate of the American Hospital Association. In 1998, the First National Conference on Quality Health Care for Culturally Diverse Populations was held in New York City. These served as watershed events because they placed the issues of health and healthcare delivery for underserved populations front and center on the national agenda.

The year 2000 brought forth much activity in the area of health disparities and cultural competency. In January 2000, *Healthy People 2010* was released. Building upon previous public health initiatives from the Surgeon General and the U.S. Department of Health and Human Services and in collaboration with many federal and state agencies, other public and private organizations, and nonprofit agencies, *Healthy People 2010* delineated a set of health objectives for the nation to achieve. The second goal of Healthy People was to eliminate health disparities among different segments of the population in the United States, and it listed 467 objectives (Office of Disease Prevention and Health Promotion, 2005). Also, in 2000, the U.S. Congress passed Public Law 106-525, also known as the "Minority Health and Health Disparities Research and Education Act." This established the National Center on Minority Health and Health Disparities to lead, coordinate, support, and assess the NIH efforts to eliminate health disparities. The outcomes were a strategic plan and a definition of disparity as mentioned previously (NIH, n.d.). In addition, the Office of Minority Health issued National Standards on Culturally and Linguistically Appropriate Services (CLAS) in 2000, as shown in Table 14-1. Some

TABLE 14-1 National Standards on Culturally and Linguistically Appropriate Services (CLAS)

Standard 1	Healthcare organizations should ensure that patients/consumers receive from all staff members effective, understandable, and respectful care that is provided in a manner compatible with their cultural health beliefs and practices and preferred language.
Standard 2	Healthcare organizations should implement strategies to recruit, retain, and promote at all levels of the organization a diverse staff and leadership that are representative of the demographic characteristics of the service area.
Standard 3	Healthcare organizations should ensure that staff at all levels and across all disciplines receive ongoing education and training in culturally and linguistically appropriate service delivery.
Standard 4	Healthcare organizations must offer and provide language assistance services, including bilingual staff and interpreter services, at no cost to each patient/consumer with limited English proficiency at all points of contact, in a timely manner during all hours of operation.
Standard 5	Healthcare organizations must provide to patients/consumers in their preferred language both verbal offers and written notices informing them of their right to receive language assistance services.
Standard 6	Healthcare organizations must ensure the competence of language assistance provided to limited English proficient patients/consumers by interpreters and bilingual staff. Family and friends should not be used to provide interpretation services (except on request by the patient/consumer).
Standard 7	Healthcare organizations must make available easily understood patient-related materials and post signage in the languages of the commonly encountered groups and/or groups represented in the service area.
Standard 8	Healthcare organizations should develop, implement, and promote a written strategic plan that outlines clear goals, policies, operational plans, and management accountability/oversight mechanisms to provide culturally and linguistically appropriate services.
Standard 9	Healthcare organizations should conduct initial and ongoing organizational self-assessments of CLAS-related activities and are encouraged to integrate cultural and linguistic competence-related measures into their internal audits, performance improvement programs, patient satisfaction assessments, and outcomes-based evaluations.
Standard 10	Healthcare organizations should ensure that data on the individual patient's/consumer's race, ethnicity, and spoken and written language are collected in health records, integrated into the organization's management information systems, and periodically updated.
Standard 11	Healthcare organizations should maintain a current demographic, cultural, and epidemiological profile of the community as well as a needs assessment to accurately plan for and implement services that respond to the cultural and linguistic characteristics of the service area.
Standard 12	Healthcare organizations should develop participatory, collaborative partnerships with communities and utilize a variety of formal and informal mechanisms to facilitate community and patient/consumer involvement in designing and implementing CLAS-related activities.
Standard 13	Healthcare organizations should ensure that conflict and grievance resolution processes are culturally and linguistically sensitive and capable of identifying, preventing, and resolving cross-cultural conflicts or complaints by patients/consumers.
Standard 14	Healthcare organizations are encouraged to regularly make available to the public information about their progress and successful innovations in implementing the CLAS standards and to provide public notice in their communities about the availability of this information.

Source: Office of Minority Health, 2001.

of these (Standards 4, 5, 6, and 7) are mandates that must be complied with in order to receive federal funds, whereas the others are guidelines or recommendations. These impact patient care, language services, and organizational practices.

Since the establishment of these standards, the field of health disparities and cultural competency has evolved significantly. Grants have been provided to support innovation and research, standards and policies have been adopted at state and national levels, and accrediting bodies and professional associations have established common practices. All medical schools in the United States are now required by the Association of American Medical Colleges to integrate cultural competence into their curricula. Similarly, residency programs are also adhering to cultural competence standards of the American Council on Graduate Medical Education, and associations like the American Nurses Association and the American Public Health Association support the agenda as well (Betancourt, et al., 2003).

In 2007, the American Hospital Association (AHA) convened a special advisory group to study how to improve care and eliminate disparities for minority populations. Two specific AHA initiatives included:

1. Developing a trustee training program to help hospitals expand the diversity of their governing boards, and
2. Developing a Disparities Toolkit, a Web-based toolkit to collect uniform race, ethnicity, and language data (Armada & Hubbard, 2010).

The National Committee for Quality Assurance (NCQA), which accredits and certifies healthcare organizations, specifically health insurance plans, released its Multicultural Health Care Standards in 2010 (National Committee for Quality Assurance [NCQA], 2010). These standards pertain to data collection of race/ethnicity and language; language services; cultural responsiveness and accountability; and quality improvement, including using data to improve culturally and linguistically appropriate services. In a similar manner, The Joint Commission is proposing accreditation requirements for hospitals to promote effective communication, cultural competence, and patient-centered care; implementation of the proposed requirements is anticipated in 2011. Issues addressed include staff training on cultural sensitivity, use of demographic data, and accommodation of patients' cultural and personal beliefs and religious and spiritual practices. Healthcare managers should monitor both The Joint Commission's and NCQA's requirements to develop or modify organization-specific initiatives to ensure compliance. In recognition of the importance of disparities in public health, the National Center on Minority Health and Health Disparities recently became the National Institute on Minority Health and Disparities (NIH, 2010).

In addition to complying with standards, mandates, and recommendations, driving toward cultural competence in a healthcare organization is simply a good business practice.

It is becoming a new standard of care in delivering quality service. The website called the Provider's Guide to Quality and Culture, a joint project of the Management Sciences for Health and the U.S. Department of Health and Human Services' Health Resources and Services Administration and Bureau of Primary Health Care, assists healthcare organizations in providing high-quality, culturally competent services to multiethnic populations (Manager's Electronic Resource Center, n.d.). Initiatives addressing cultural competence have the potential to make care more effective, as well as improve staff productivity, customer satisfaction, and market share for hospitals or medical practices.

BEST PRACTICES

Healthcare managers must recognize the issues of health disparities and build a framework to link interventions to eliminating disparities. Cultural proficiency requires that organizations and interdisciplinary staff value diversity and manage the dynamics of difference. Healthcare organizations should pursue initiatives to acquire the awareness, knowledge, and skills in continual pursuit of greater cultural competence. Essential components of a culturally proficient healthcare organization include:

1. A diverse healthcare workforce,
2. Management practices including supportive leadership and culture and appropriate human resource policies,
3. Assessment,
4. Education and training for all staff,
5. Effective multilingual services and support materials,
6. System capacities such as evaluation and research data collection for tracking health outcomes, and
7. The ability to adapt to the context of and respond to and engage the community served.

The Healthcare Workforce

In 1992, the American College of Healthcare Executives (ACHE) joined with the National Association of Health Services Executives (NAHSE), an association of African-American healthcare executives, to investigate the career advancement of their members. The study found that minorities held less than 1% of top management positions, although they represented more than 20% of hospital employees. It also documented that African-American healthcare executives made less money, held lower positions, and had less job satisfaction than their white counterparts. A 1997 follow-up study, expanded to include Latinos and Asians, found that, although the gap had narrowed in some areas, not much had changed (Institute for Diversity in Health Management, 2008). Newer data on ACHE and NAHSE members is certainly needed; however, the more recent study by Weil (2009) confirms these findings. Given U.S. demographic trends, achieving greater diversity in the healthcare workforce continues to be an issue and challenge for healthcare leaders. The reported benefits are a more culturally competent workforce; greater access for the underserved; fostering of research in neglected areas; enriching the pool of talent to meet future needs of society; and cost savings by decreasing turnover, absenteeism, and the number of lawsuits (Cohen, Gabriel, & Terrell, 2002; Cordova, Beaudin, & Iwanabe, 2010). The Institute for Diversity in Health Management is a good resource for strategies, programs, and leadership initiatives in the area of workforce diversity. The ultimate goal is to have the healthcare workforce in the United States reflect the makeup of the communities served.

Management

Cultural competence needs to be incorporated into many aspects of the healthcare organization, particularly to be embraced by the leadership, human resource management, administration, and service delivery. It requires cross-disciplinary healthcare professionals who are sensitive and respectful of others to collaborate and advance the cause of cultural proficiency within an organization. Cultural proficiency means being able to understand the organizational forces that either support or negate achieving cultural sensitivity. Management must ensure that there is not differential access to resources, opportunities, and influence. In order for managers to be change agents, they must understand the implications of power and privilege within the institution.

First and foremost, the leaders of an organization need to be role models in cultural sensitivity and establish a supportive culture for diversity and cultural competence initiatives. Healthcare executives should incorporate underlying principles into the mission and vision of the organization and place initiatives in the organization's strategic plan to underscore their importance. Examining the return-on-investment of cultural proficiency training can be a worthwhile exercise. Researchers have examined the positive business benefits of diversity management in health care (Dreachslin, 2007). Although some benefits can be intangible and others can be long term and difficult to quantify, specific measures, such as better customer satisfaction, enhanced employee productivity, greater market share, or fewer malpractice claims, can be evidence supporting the business rationale. Managers need to be wary of falling into the trap of cultural proficiency training becoming the "fad" project of the month. This important competency development must be a long-term commitment of the management team in order to make progress on the issue.

Human resource policies play a key role in addressing diversity in the workforce. Healthcare managers must ensure that salary, benefit, recruitment, and promotion practices are fair to all regardless of age, sex, race, or ethnic background. A recent study demonstrated that racially and ethnically diverse employees represented a growing percentage of the healthcare workforce, although they held only a small percentage of top healthcare management positions (Weil, 2009). To address this problem, the study recommended that healthcare executives offer residencies and fellowships, embrace mentoring, encourage transparency in organizational decisions, develop programs that diversify managerial ranks, and promote professional societies' policy statements on equal employment.

Structural barriers to care sometimes arise when patients are facing a complex, bureaucratic organization. Even relatively simple changes like expanding hours of operation to match work schedules can bring greater access to care. The clinical patient-provider encounter must be appropriately cross-cultural. Studies have shown that the communication between providers and patients is directly related to patient satisfaction, adherence to treatment regimens, and ultimately outcomes (Betancourt et al., 2003). Organizations should design and implement patient services that offer equal access and are nondiscriminatory, tailored to match the needs of the community they serve, and determined by client-preferred choices. Managers must monitor the impact of these programs; developing reports to examine inequalities in care may be a good management practice. The National Center for Cultural Competence translates policy into specific practices and provides helpful advice for programs and personnel in healthcare delivery.

Assessment

To address disparities and work toward cultural sensitivity in a healthcare organization, assessment must occur on several personal and organizational levels. The first step is for healthcare leaders to examine their own personal biases in order to become role models. Informal self-assessment of one's own attitudes and behaviors should include questions such as: What is my worldview and what are my biases? Am I aware of my prejudices toward other cultural groups? Do I seek out encounters with individuals who are different from me? How do I react when someone does not speak English? An online assessment tool has been designed by the National Center for Cultural Competence for healthcare practitioners (National Center for Cultural Competence, n.d.). Although not designed for healthcare managers, the tool can be used as part of the learning experience for all individuals working in the healthcare system. Another assessment tool for organizations based on the CLAS standards is available from the Center on Cross-Cultural Health, and a third was developed by researchers at Creighton University Medical Center (National Center for Cultural Competence, n.d.; O'Brien et al., 2006). An easy-to-use assessment tool for executives, staff, and providers has been prepared by a health educator in her textbook (Rose, 2011). Other assessment tools are available and are often used in conjunction with consultants in this field; one example is the Intercultural Development Inventory (IDI), which is often used to assess individuals before and after an intercultural training intervention (Hammer, Bennett, & Wiseman, 2003). These instruments and their results should be interpreted with care, as they provide a snapshot of an individual at that particular moment in time on a test and may not reflect the individual's real-world application of the needed information. After examining these issues on a personal level, next, the organization must reflect on and assess whether it appropriately reflects and serves its community.

On an organizational level, assessment in terms of tracking patient data on race, ethnicity, and language is currently being performed by 78% of hospitals in the United States. Although some cite limitations due to self-reporting or observational reporting, the data is a starting point. Sadly, less than 20% of surveyed hospitals report tying patient race and ethnicity information to patient outcomes and quality improvements (Armada & Hubbard, 2010). If healthcare organizations want to be top-notch, then they need to keep racial, ethnic, and language assessment data at the forefront of management attention. After all, how can an organization deliver best practices in clinical care if they don't know who their patients are?

The American College of Healthcare Executives (ACHE) has partnered with three other national organizations to develop a **Diversity and Cultural Proficiency Assessment Tool for Leaders** (American Hospital Association, 2004). This tool helps organizations address the issue of cultural competence and presents case studies of successful diversity and cultural proficiency programs from America's hospitals. Action steps are presented as well. Other assessment tools are available for healthcare organizations (Andrulis, Delbanco, Avakan, & Shaw-Taylor, n.d.).

An assessment can provide a tool to understand what an organization does well in delivering care to diverse populations, where there are gaps, and how it can determine an agenda for improving services. Most importantly, assessment can lead to a dialogue on diversity and cultural proficiency within the organization. The very act of conducting an assessment indicates to the workforce that the organization values diversity and wishes to increase its cultural competence.

Education and Training

Although experts agree that behavioral change is key in cultural proficiency, most training in the workplace surrounds building awareness and changing attitudes (Curtis, Dreachslin, & Sinioris, 2007). Interactive and stimulating courses can be employed to train all healthcare personnel about health disparities and cultural competence. Learning about cultural competence is not easy. Culture happens within a context; memorizing simple facts about disparities can lead to stereotyping. Healthcare professionals who have typically been trained in the absolute of scientific methodology sometimes have a difficult time learning how to tolerate gray areas, particularly in human interactions. Cultural proficiency implies being open and accepting ambiguity. Training can include watching videos or having speakers present on health disparities or cultural competence. Former patients who have encountered situations of intolerance or professionals who have participated in health care for underserved groups make for interesting presentations. In addition to the didactics, opportunities should be provided for practicing cross-cultural communications through role playing and for developing conflict resolution skills. Some institutions embrace mentoring as a way to encourage cultural sensitivity. Consultants are often used to introduce new training programs. The training should be documented and evaluated for effectiveness using outcome measurement tools.

Multilingual Services

According to the American Hospital Association, 80% of members encounter an individual with limited English proficiency frequently, 43% reported daily encounters, and 20% weekly encounters (Armada & Hubbard, 2010). To understand an organization's starting place in terms of competency in this area, the American Medical Association (AMA) is developing a self-assessment tool for patient-centered communications. The goal is to help hospitals and physicians assess their organizations to determine how well they communicate with diverse patient populations. It focuses on those groups at risk of poor health outcomes because of vulnerability to ineffective communication during patient encounters (American Medical Association, 2010).

Healthcare professionals need to be able to effectively communicate and convey information in an easily understood manner to a diverse audience, including people of limited or no English proficiency, those who are illiterate or disabled, and those who are deaf or hard of hearing. **Linguistic competency** requires staff to be able to interact and respond to the community they serve. Two publications that may be helpful to healthcare managers are the AMA's *Office Guide to Communicating with Limited English Proficient Patients* (AMA, n.d.) and *Bridging the Language Divide: A Pocket Guide to Working Effectively with Interpreters in Health Care Settings* (Grey, Yehieli, & Rodriguez-Kurtovic, 2006). Healthcare organizations must have the policies, practices, and resources to support this capacity. Services need to be delivered in the preferred language of the population served. Those qualified to be medical interpreters should be bilingual with superior language proficiency, have studied medical vocabulary, have training in interpreting techniques, and be culturally sensitive. Written materials need to be modified to meet the needs, reading abilities, and preferences of the community. When necessary, they should be translated from English into other languages. Interpretation and translation services need to comply with federal, state, and local mandates as well as the requirements of accrediting agencies. In addition to meeting compliance standards, language services may improve the outcome of the patient/provider encounter, decrease medical errors, equalize healthcare utilization, and increase patient and provider satisfaction. Consumers of healthcare services should be engaged in evaluating language and communication services of the healthcare organization to ensure quality and satisfaction. An organization should monitor its performance regularly using structure, process, and outcome measures, and make appropriate adjustments as needed.

Evaluation

Interventions in addressing health disparities and fostering cultural proficiency should be evaluated for their impact. Toolkits and guides are available for collecting racial and ethnic data in a culturally competent manner (Center for Cross-Cultural Health, 2010; Martin, 2007). Questions to be addressed include: Did the intervention achieve its goal? Did it affect the process of care? Was utilization improved? Did it affect patient behavior or satisfaction? Was practitioner, manager, or patient satisfaction improved? How were the patient health outcomes impacted? Was the cost-effectiveness of delivery altered? The evaluation of interventions can provide managers with insights about how to address health disparities and improve cultural proficiency within their organizations.

Research

Research findings are used to justify evidence-based practice in health care. In the area of culturally competent interventions, the research has not kept pace in terms of documenting disparities and the outcomes of implementing new measures. Greater collection and reporting on patient data related to race, ethnicity, and culture is needed, particularly identifying sources of disparities. The Office of Minority Health and the Agency for Healthcare Research and Quality support investigations on how cultural competence affects healthcare delivery and health outcomes. Other organizations, such as the National Center for Healthcare Leadership, are investigating the impact of improved culturally competent healthcare leadership on patient safety and other measures of organizational performance. This additional research is required to document the impact of culturally competent healthcare interventions and their outcomes. In 2006, the federal government established the Federal Collaboration on Health Disparities Research, with the purpose of supporting and disseminating research aimed at reducing or eliminating disparities (Rashid et al., 2009). Organizations on national and local levels must continue to pursue research to support an evidence-based approach for cultural competency interventions in health care and eliminating inequities in health.

Community Outreach and Engagement

A healthcare organization must demonstrate inclusivity with the community it supports. Community engagement is defined as "an exchange of information, ideas, and resources between individuals, community members and mainstream organizations or institutions" (Center for Cross-Cultural Health, 2010). According to the Center for Cross-Cultural Health, there are five steps to **community engagement**, including education, input, advisory, interface, and partnership. The key point is participation (Rodgers, 2008). To pursue community engagement, healthcare managers may put into action a public health education campaign, the use of a focus group or an advisory panel, a community health fair, or employment of community health workers.

ADDRESSING HEALTH DISPARITIES BY ENHANCING PUBLIC POLICY

Most public health experts would agree that a health disparity indicates that a discussion among policy makers is needed to address whether the inequality can be reduced or eliminated. The American Public Health Association (APHA) is working with members of the U.S. Senate and House of Representatives to explore legislation addressing the underlying causes of disparities in health status and healthcare access and to develop policy recommendations to reduce and ultimately eliminate health disparities (American Public Health Association, 2010). Addressing the components of socioeconomic status (income, education, and occupation) with public policy could help to begin the process of addressing health disparities. Freudenberg and Olden (2010) have proposed several specific initiatives to enhance public policy, including:

- *Improve access to primary care*—Lack of access to primary care has been reported to contribute to disparities in health. Authors have advocated for a change in the U.S. healthcare system toward greater investment in primary care, including screening and counseling, particularly to address the burden of chronic disease in underserved populations.
- *Enforce consumer and environmental protection laws*—A public health advocate has suggested that consumer and environmental policies leave vulnerable populations more exposed to risks. For example, manufacturers of unhealthy products like tobacco or high-fat fried foods have directed their marketing efforts at vulnerable populations contributing to chronic disease and exacerbating health disparities.

Healthcare providers and government agencies have an obligation to be responsive to the communities they serve. Health for all is a complex and complicated undertaking, and it can only be achieved by creating a culturally proficient workforce within these organizations. The interrelationships are illustrated in Figure 14-2. Healthcare managers can help the nation move toward the long-term goal of health equity for all Americans.

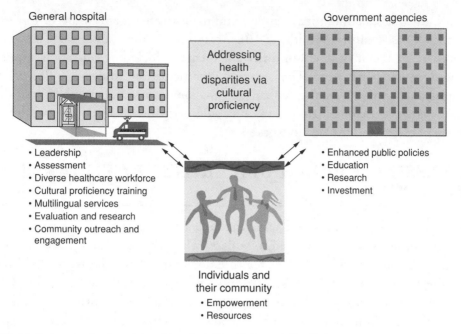

FIGURE 14-2 Interrelationships Needed for Cultural Proficiency

CONCLUSION

Major gaps exist in understanding the causal relationships in complicated health disparities, and more research is needed to support the cost and quality improvements from cultural competency initiatives. Healthcare managers who are committed to the issues of diversity, equity, and equality need to be aware of and implement best practices in cultural competency. Healthcare managers must take leadership roles within their institutions to facilitate developing cultural competence within their staffs. Although cultural proficiency alone may not solve the problems of health disparities, managers who understand the diversity of their communities will be better able to serve diverse patient populations and ensure that their organizations both reflect and support the communities they serve.

DISCUSSION QUESTIONS

1. Explain why cultural competence alone cannot address health disparities.

2. What are the benefits of implementing programs to address cultural competence within a healthcare organization?

3. What are some of the limitations of the term "cultural competence"? Which term do you prefer and why?

4. Describe a time when you witnessed or experienced cultural incompetence in the delivery of health care. Knowing what you now know, what do you think could have been done to avoid that incident?

5. Describe how you would put in place initiatives for cultural proficiency at a medical clinic.

6. How do you convince the reluctant healthcare professional to participate in cultural proficiency training?

7. What public policies might help to address health inequities?

Cases in Chapter 17 that are related to this chapter include:

- Are We Culturally Aware or Not?—see p. 436
- Heritage Valley Medical Center: Are Your Managers Culturally Competent?—see p.430
- Humor Strategies in Healthcare Management Education—see p. 455

Additional cases, role-play scenarios, video links, websites, and other information sources are also available in the online Instructor's Materials.

REFERENCES

Agency for Healthcare Research and Quality (AHRQ). (2003). *AHRQ policy on the inclusion of priority populations in research.* Retrieved from http://grants.nih.gov/grants/guide/notice-files/not-hs-03-010.html

American Hospital Association (AHA). (2004). *Strategies for leadership: Does your hospital reflect the community it serves? A diversity and cultural proficiency assessment tool for leaders.* Retrieved from http://www.aha.org/aha/content/2004/pdf/diversitytool.pdf

American Medical Association (AMA). (2010). C-CAT *patient centered communication: Organizational assessment resources.* Retrieved from http://www.ama-assn.org/ama/pub/physician-resources/medical-ethics/the-ethical-force-program/patient-centered-communication/organizational-assessment-resources.shtml

American Medical Association (AMA). (n.d.). *Office guide to communicating with limited English proficient patients* (2nd ed.). Retrieved from http://www.ama-assn.org/ama1/pub/upload/mm/433/lep_booklet.pdf

American Public Health Association (APHA). (2010). *Advocacy and policy: Eliminating health disparities.* Retrieved from http://www.apha.org/advocacy/priorities/issues/disparities/

Andrulis, D., Delbanco, T., Avakan, L., & Shaw-Taylor, Y. (n.d.). *Conducting a cultural competence self-assessment.* Retrieved from http://www.consumerstar.org/pubs/Culturalcompselfassess.pdf

Armada, A. A., & Hubbard, M. F. (2010). Diversity in health care: Time to get real! *Frontiers of Health Services Management 26*(3), 3–17.

Betancourt, J. R., Green, A. R., Carrillo, J. E., & Ananeh-Firempong, O. (2003). Defining cultural competence: A practical framework for addressing racial/ethnic disparities in health and healthcare. *Public Health Reports, 118*(4), 293–302.

Carter-Pokras, O., & Baquet, C. (2002). What is a health disparity? *Public Health Reports, 117*(5), 426–434.

Center for Cross-Cultural Health. (2010). *Community engagement.* Minneapolis, MN: Center for Cross-Cultural Health.

Cohen, J. J., Gabriel, B. A., & Terrell, C. (2002). The case for diversity in the healthcare workforce. *Health Affairs, 21*(5), 90–102.

Cordova, R. D., Beaudin, C. L., & Iwanabe, K. E. (2010). Addressing diversity and moving toward equity in hospital care. *Frontiers of Health Services Management, 26*(3), 19–34.

Cross, T. L., Bazron, B. J., Dennis, K. W., & Isaacs, M. R. (1989). *Towards a culturally competent system of care* (Vol. 1). Washington, DC: CASSP Technical Assistance Center, Georgetown University Child Development Center.

Curtis, E. F., Dreachslin, J. L., & Sinioris, M. (2007). Diversity and cultural competence training in health care organizations: Hallmarks of success. *Health Care Manager, 26*(3), 255–262.

Dreachslin, J. L. (2007). Diversity management and cultural competence: Research, practice, and the business case. *Journal of Healthcare Management, 52*(2), 79–86.

Freudenberg, N., & Olden, K. (2010). Finding synergy: Reducing disparities in health by modifying multiple determinants. *American Journal of Public Health, 100*(Supp 1), S25–S29.

Gozu, A., Beach, M. C., Price, E. G., Gary, T. L., Robinson, K., Palacio, A., et al. (2007). Self-administered instruments to measure cultural competence of health professionals: A systematic review. *Teaching and Learning in Medicine,19*(2), 180–190.

Grey, M. A., Yehieli, M., & Rodriguez-Kurtovic, N. (2006). *Bridging the language divide: A pocket guide to working effectively with interpreters in health care settings.* Cedar Rapids: University of Northern Iowa.

Hammer, M. R., Bennett, M. J., & Wiseman, R. (2003). The Intercultural Development Inventory: A measure of intercultural sensitivity. *International Journal of Intercultural Relations, 27*(4), 421–443.

Health Resources and Services Administration (HRSA). (1995). *Shortage designation: Medically underserved areas and populations.* Retrieved from http://bhpr.hrsa.gov/shortage/muaps/index.html

Hobbs, F., & Stoop, N. (2002). *Demographic trends in the 20th century.* U.S. Census Bureau, Census 2000. Special Reports, Series CENSR-4. Washington, DC: U.S. Government Printing Office.

Institute for Diversity in Health Management. (2008). *About the institute.* Retrieved from http://www.diversityconnection.org/diversityconnection_app/about-us/About-the-Institute.jsp

Manager's Electronic Resource Center. (n.d.). *The provider's guide to quality and culture.* Retrieved from http://erc.msh.org/mainpage.cfm?file=1.0.htm&module=provider&language=English

Martin, C. (2007). *Reducing racial and ethnic disparities: A quality improvement initiative in Medicaid managed care toolkit.* Hamilton, NJ: Center for Health Care Strategies, Inc. Retrieved from http://www.rwjf.org/files/research/racialethnichealthdisparities.pdf

McDaniel, G. (2000). Cultural competency: A new standard of care. *Advance for Medical Laboratory Professionals.* Retrieved from http://laboratorian.advanceweb.com/Article/Cultural-Competency-A-New-Standard-of-Care.aspx

National Center for Cultural Competence. (n.d.). *Cultural competence: Definition and conceptual framework.* Retrieved from http://nccc.georgetown.edu/foundations/frameworks.html

National Committee for Quality Assurance (NCQA). (2010). *About NCQA.* Retrieved from http://www.ncqa.org/tabid/675/Default.aspx

National Institutes of Health (NIH). (2006). *Fact sheet: Health disparities.* Bethesda, MD: National Institutes of Health.

National Institutes of Health (NIH). (2010). *National Institutes of Health statement of organization, functions, and delegations of authority.* Retrieved from http://www.federalregister.gov/articles/2010/09/13/2010-22666/national-institutes-of-health-statement-of-organization-functions-and-delegations-of-authority

National Institutes of Health (NIH). (n.d.). *NIH health disparities strategic plan, fiscal years 2004–2008.* Retrieved from http://www.nimhd.nih.gov/about_ncmhd/Strategic%20Plan%20FY%202004-2008%20vol%201.pdf

O'Brien, R. L., Kosoko-Lasaki, O., Cook, C. T., Kissell, J., Peak, F., & Williams, E. H. (2006). Self-assessment of cultural attitudes and competence of clinical investigators to enhance recruitment and participation of minority populations in research. *Journal of the National Medical Association, 98*(5), 674–682.

Office of Disease Prevention and Health Promotion. (2005). *Healthy People 2010: The cornerstone for prevention.* Retrieved from: http://www.healthypeople.gov/Publications/Cornerstone.pdf

Office of Minority Health. (2001). *National standards for culturally and linguistically appropriate services in health care.* Retrieved from http://minorityhealth.hhs.gov/assets/pdf/checked/executive.pdf

Office of Minority Health. (2005). *What is cultural competency?* Retrieved from http://minorityhealth.hhs.gov/templates/browse.aspx?lvl=2&lvlID=11

Rashid, J. R., Spengler, R. F., Wagner, R. M., Skillen, E. L., Mays, R. A., Heurtin-Roberts, S., et al. (2009). Eliminating health disparities through transdisciplinary research, cross-agency collaboration, and public participation. *American Journal of Public Health, 99*(11), 1956–1961.

Rodgers, D. (2008). Five approaches to community engagement. Minneapolis, MN: Center for Cross-Cultural Health.

Rose, P. R. (2011). *Cultural competency: For health administration and public health.* Sudbury, MA: Jones and Bartlett.

Suicide Prevention Resource Center. (n.d.). *Suicide among American Indians/Alaska Natives.* Retrieved from http://www.sprc.org/library/ai.an.facts.pdf

Thomas, M., & James, C. (2009). The role of health coverage for communities of color. *Kaiser Family Foundation Issue Brief.* Retrieved from http://www.kff.org/healthreform/upload/8017.pdf

U.S. Census Bureau. (2008). An older and more diverse nation by midcentury. *U.S. Census Bureau News* August 14, 2008. Retrieved from http://www.census.gov/newsroom/releases/archives/population/cb08-123.html

Weil, P. (2009). A racial/ethnic comparison of career attainments in healthcare management: By taking action, healthcare executives can help narrow the gaps. *Healthcare Executive, 24*(6), 22–31.

Additional Websites to Explore

Agency for Healthcare Research and Quality	www.ahrq.gov
Healthy People 2010	www.healthypeople.gov
Institute for Diversity in Health Management	www.diversityconnection.org/
The Joint Commission	www.jointcommission.org
Manager's Electronic Resource Center	http://erc.msh.org/
National Center for Cultural Competence	http://nccc.georgetown.edu/
National Center for Healthcare Leadership	www.nchl.org
National Committee for Quality Assurance	www.ncqa.org
Office of Minority Health	www.omhrc.gov

And search on these key terms:

Health disparity, cultural competence, cultural proficiency, cross-cultural sensitivity, workforce diversity, CLAS standards

CHAPTER 15

Ethics and Law

Kevin D. Zeiler

LEARNING OBJECTIVES

By the end of this chapter, the student will be able to:

- Describe the distinctions and overlaps between ethics and law;
- Define the concepts of respect for persons, beneficence, nonmaleficence, and justice;
- Define common law, statutes, rules, regulations, and executive orders;
- Distinguish between civil and criminal law;
- List the elements of a contract and describe the relationship to torts;
- Identify the types of torts;
- Define malpractice;
- Provide an overview of patient and provider rights and responsibilities; and
- Identify some of the legal issues in managed care, biomedical care, and beginning- and end-of-life care.

INTRODUCTION

Ethics and the law are often mentioned in the same breath, but for all of the instances in which they are similar, there are many ways in which they are different. In this chapter, we will discuss the meaning of each as well as how they work together and apart to form and shape the legal system in the United States. The topics surrounding law and ethics are extremely important to the aspiring healthcare manager as they touch and affect the daily activities of every organization. Our discussion will begin with a definition of both ethics and law so that a foundation can be laid in order to proceed more easily through the chapter.

The two categories, law and ethics, overlap, with ethical principles underlying the development of laws, but they approach the world of health care from somewhat differing perspectives. In America, laws are publicly enforced standards and rules that are created by courts, legislatures, executive orders, and administrative agencies. Each of those bodies has a unique process, creating laws in varying ways. There are also differences between the authority of federal and state lawmaking entities. Ethical viewpoints, on the other hand, stem primarily from family, community, and religious traditions. It is worth noting that this is how we get many of our laws; the rights and wrongs that we hold dear to our hearts often become the laws of our country. Therefore, it must be noted that those who write and enforce our laws bring their ethical beliefs to the table when making decisions affecting the law. Even though the premise behind legal decision making is to be an unbiased adjudicator, it is extremely difficult to leave your personal, ethical beliefs behind. As we have seen in such cases as that of Terri Schiavo, clashes between and among individuals' deeply held ethical principles and legal interpretations can cause major disruptions in the healthcare system (Dresser, 2004). Before continuing, take a look at Table 15-1 to see the ways in which law and ethics differ.

TEXTBOX 15-1. TERRI SCHIAVO CASE

Terri Schiavo suffered a heart attack in 1990 that led to a massive brain injury from a lack of oxygen. A court battle ensued and lasted nearly 16 years, dealing with issues surrounding the right to life and who had the legal right to make such decisions on behalf of Terri. Furthermore, the case addressed issues surrounding life-sustaining treatment, as well as the withdrawal of such treatment. Ultimately, Terri Schiavo died in 2005 after her feeding tube was removed.

Source: Conigliaro, 2005.

TABLE 15-1 Legal and Ethical Comparison

LEGAL	ETHICAL
Action is required by law.	No legal requirements to act, but professional organizations may require it.
Legal consequences may occur if no action is taken.	Censure by the governing body may occur if unethical behavior occurs.
Many professionals have a duty to report based on law, that is, physicians, nurses, social workers, and so on.	Ethics oftentimes helps to define the duty of care owed to a patient by a professional caregiver.
Results from numerous areas of law such as rules of professional responsibility, legislative action, court rulings, and so on.	Standards are defined by governing bodies that license professionals.
Individuals may face criminal sanctions if they deviate from the law.	Violation of standards may result in loss of license or professional privileges.

There are numerous examples like the Schiavo case, but most recently, healthcare reform followed this same pattern. Many believe that every individual is entitled to health care, while others feel that it must be earned, and in the middle, numerous constitutional and other legal precedents tug at the issue as well. In this sense, law and ethics are inseparable, but this is exactly what makes the law in the United States work. However, on many occasions law and ethics are at polar opposites and often lead to much controversy. Without a doubt, many of you have heard the statement that it is legal, so it must be ethical. This is where the line between the two disciplines becomes distorted, and in healthcare organizations, questions between law and ethics force managers to make difficult decisions.

This chapter will begin by defining **ethics** and **law** as they apply to health care, and then will discuss patient, provider, and organizational rights and responsibilities. Ethical management will be examined in the broad sense so that the reader can see how it affects the overall health delivery system. Also, in the wake of healthcare reform, the chapter will focus on how changes in ethical and legal thought have brought us to this current point in health care. Finally, ethical management will be examined, with a particular focus on managed care settings, and we will discuss some biomedical areas of ethical and legal concern and provide an overview of a few key beginning- and end-of-life issues affecting the administration of healthcare services. Table 15-2 illustrates the overlap of perspectives on what is legal and ethical in healthcare settings. There is very little absolute agreement about what actions belong in each cell, but in health care, these types of choices must be made on a daily basis.

LEGAL CONCEPTS

In order to provide a solid background for understanding the law, **legal concepts** will be discussed first, then we will move to a discussion of **ethical considerations**. Many of us may feel that we have a good handle on the law in the United States, but to fully understand the way in which law is carried out, we must learn how law is developed, what entity

TABLE 15-2 Overlap of Legal and Ethical Activities

	Is it legal?		
Is it ethical?	Yes	Uncertain	No

enforces it, and when it applies. First and foremost, we must understand what the law does. Pozgar provides a usable definition that is easy to understand. "**Laws** govern the relationships between private individuals and organizations and between both of these parties and government" (Pozgar, 2007).

Thus, the law is used to help determine our actions and the actions of others when it comes to dealing with individuals, organizations, and other such entities. Look at the law as a body of official rules of conduct, subject to interpretation and change over time. In most cases, federal laws take precedence over state laws; this is called **preemption**. In other words, federal law trumps state or local law if the federal government has passed legislation in the field of law being disputed. Also, states can always be more stringent than the federal government, meaning that they may enforce laws that are "tougher" than what the federal government has mandated. In addition to the **U.S. Constitution** (National Archives, n.d.), each state also has a **constitution**, setting the basic principles for its legal system. It is these constitutions that form the basis for legal decisions in our country.

The constitutions provide a basic understanding of what our laws are, but how can a constitution possibly cover every single issue that arises in society? The answer is that we use **interpretive justice** or **judicial authority** to set precedents in order to have a sound understanding of what the law says. As the judiciary interprets previous precedents for each particular case, they create what is known as **common law**. The common law was developed through court decisions and is used to ensure that fairness and consistency exist when similar issues are faced by the court (Pozgar, 2007). Remember, **judge-made**, or common, law sets what is known as a **precedent**, and it is this precedent that is followed by courts in similar cases. Before we leave the common law, think about how a judge's decision not only follows the law when setting precedent, but how his or her own ethical viewpoints may help to create the law. It is easy to see how the line between law and ethics can be extremely thin.

TEXTBOX 15-2. KEY TERMS

Common law: A form of law that depends on judicial decisions as opposed to legislative acts. It is often referred to as judge-made law.

Interpretive justice: An academic approach to defining the justice system so that legal standards can be better understood—for example, defining what the U.S. Constitution means and how it applies to specific cases.

Precedent: The term "precedent" refers to legal cases (at common law) that were decided by judges. When issues arise that are similar to those in a previous case, those same principles will be used to decide the current case.

Another way in which laws are created is by the **legislature**. Legislatures create law by passing **statutes**, which will be able to overrule common law findings for a given jurisdiction unless the judiciary finds the statutes to be unconstitutional. Think about ways in which politicians attempt to stop, for example, Supreme Court decisions that they are not happy with. Oftentimes, statutes are used to gain an advantage over precedent by creating such statutes and forcing society to abide by the new law. However, **constitutional challenges** exist, and the statutes must be able to pass this review. Also, laws are created by **administrative agencies**, which establish the necessary rules and regulations to carry out statutes. Administrative agencies exist to govern numerous industries in society, and healthcare is no exception. Administrative agencies dictate many of the ways in which healthcare organizations do business. Finally, **executive orders** are also used on occasion to establish a **binding policy**, rather than waiting for the legislature or courts to act.

TEXTBOX 15-3. KEY TERMS

Legislature: The legislature is the government body that makes rules and laws that society abides by. Normally, legislators are elected officials such as congressional representatives and senators.

Statutes: A statute, in this context, refers to an act by a legislative body such as a law. The statute is the form in which the law is expressed.

Executive orders: An executive order is a requirement that the President makes of individuals or organizations under the jurisdiction of the executive branch of government. It is respected much like a law.

Binding policy: A policy is a requirement that an organization, group, or government agency adopts to make its organization run more smoothly. Therefore, a binding policy means that the policy is final and must be followed when it applies.

As if the above variants on the law weren't confusing enough, we must also keep in mind the distinction between civil and criminal laws. **Criminal law** is concerned with wrongs against society as a whole, even if only a particular individual is harmed. There appears to be a growing willingness to use criminal law charges in the healthcare field, including in cases of malpractice, Medicare fraud, abortion, and the unlicensed practice of medicine. **Civil law**, on the other hand, is concerned with wrongs against a particular person or organization. It encompasses contractual violations involving voluntary agreements between two or more parties. **Torts** also fall under civil law, as a category of "wrongful acts" committed against another person without a preexisting contract, for which courts seek to determine and apply remedies. The following sections will address tort and contract law in more detail, as they are important in the delivery of health services.

TORT LAW

Tort law is viewed by some as an area of the law that is in need of reform, but this type of law is common and touches many everyday events. Tort law plays an important role in the delivery of health services. For example, the new healthcare reform that was passed in March 2010 is as much about tort reform as it is about medical systems reform. The new health bill has dedicated some $50 million for organizations, physicians, and state and local governments to look at alternative ways in which to adjudicate medical/legal claims (Sorrel, 2010). These alternatives include items such as health courts, medical review panels, and apology programs, which are all geared at cutting legal costs, making people healthy, and keeping medical issues out of the court system (Sorrel, 2010).

Tort law encompasses several key areas within the healthcare industry, including:

1. **Negligence**, which involves the unintentional commission or omission of an act that a reasonably prudent person would or would not do under the same circumstances;
2. **Intentional torts**, such as assault and battery, false imprisonment, defamation of character, and invasion of privacy; and
3. The **infliction of mental distress**.

Managers must understand tort law and its implications to the organization. It is an active area of the law that affects many aspects of health care.

In order for **negligence** to be proven, there must be four key factors involved: (1) the negligent party must have a **duty** toward the harmed party. In health care, this includes the practitioner exercising the level of skill expected in routine practice while treating a person with whom he/she has a patient–provider relationship; (2) there must have been a **breach of duty**, by failing to meet the appropriate **standard of care**; (3) the plaintiff must prove that he or she suffered **injury or damages** from the interaction; and (4) **causation** must be proven. In other words, the breach of duty has to have been directly connected to the harm that occurred. Negligence charges are usually brought against the practitioner involved, but they can also be brought against an organization under the doctrine of **respondeat superior** (meaning that organizations can be liable for harm caused by their employees or agents). There are various types of negligent acts:

- **Misfeasance**, or performing the correct action incorrectly and causing injury;
- **Malfeasance**, or performing an unlawful act (such as abortion in states where it is illegal); and
- **Nonfeasance**, or failing to act where there is a duty that a reasonably prudent person would have fulfilled (perhaps failing to test for an obvious cause of a person's symptoms).

Intentional tort cases depend on proving that the harm was committed deliberately. In assault and battery cases, for example, there must be a deliberate threat on one person by another for **assault** to apply, and actual physical contact for the situation to be considered **battery**. One example in the healthcare field would be surgery mistakenly performed on an unconscious patient without his/her consent. **False imprisonment** is another form of intentional tort. This could include inappropriately restraining a patient or keeping someone in a more restrictive level of care than necessary. **Defamation of character** can be slander or libel—oral or written false representations of a person's character that will hold that person up to shame or ridicule. Another important aspect of intentional torts in healthcare settings is **invasion of privacy**, which violates the right to privacy implicit in the Constitution. **Confidentiality of patient records** (more on this later in this chapter) constitutes a major concern under this heading, as does the need to evaluate when a "need to know" overrides privacy, as in the legal requirement to report child or elder abuse, sexually transmitted diseases, or other public health concerns.

MALPRACTICE

A major emphasis of tort law in health care involves **medical malpractice**. Malpractice is the negligence or carelessness of a professional person; it can be either a civil (tort) concern or a criminal one, depending on whether it involved "reckless disregard" for the safety of another (criminal) or simple carelessness (civil). The legal dictionary definition states that: "malpractice is a professional's improper or immoral conduct in the performance of duties, done either intentionally or through carelessness or ignorance. Furthermore, the term is commonly applied to a physician, surgeon, dentist, lawyer, or public officer to denote the negligence or unskillful performance of duties resulting from such person's professional relationship with patients or clients" (Gifis, 1996). For a healthcare administrator, this is a central concern in hiring, training, and monitoring the performance of employees and those with admitting privileges, both in order to protect the patients from harm and out of concern for the reputation and financial stability of the organization itself.

Again, as has been discussed earlier in this chapter, tort reform, healthcare reform, and other legislative and legal actions are all focused on eliminating many of the medical malpractice claims in the United States today. However, many people believe that medical malpractice claims in and of themselves help to deter malpractice by forcing the organization or individual to focus on poor outcomes and be more cognizant of best practices and patient outcomes (Shi & Singh, 2008). It may be true that the threat of being sued is a deterrent to many, but this is not always the case. The downside of malpractice is that a fear of litigation has actually led to many organizations hiding the truth and ignoring patient harms, as they don't want to face fines, sanctions, or in some cases prison time (Shi & Singh, 2008). In addition, fear of malpractice can also drive up costs of care when practitioners order unnecessary tests so they won't miss something—or out of fear of malpractice suits (Bishop, Federman, & Keyhani, 2010).

Medical malpractice will continue to be a problem in the United States as long as individuals perceive that they have been harmed. According to the Kaiser Family Foundation, "in some areas of the country medical malpractice is considered a crisis" (Kaiser Family Foundation, 2005). This area of law carries with it both legal and ethical implications and is very difficult to control. The fact that many look at this issue as a crisis should make you aware that as a manager it is critical to understand the law surrounding this topic and work within your organization to ensure that training and education are being provided to mitigate the risk.

CONTRACT LAW

No legal discussion would be complete without discussing the law of contracts. Much like most areas of the law, contracts can be very specialized and difficult to understand, but most of us have been a party to one kind of contract or another. The easiest example is that of a patron who walks into a restaurant and orders a meal. He or she has what is considered an **implied contract**, which means that by ordering a meal and consuming it, they have agreed to pay for their purchase. This example also helps to illustrate that a contract does not have to be in writing, and this is very important when it comes to issues in health care. Let's begin by looking at the necessary elements of a contract.

In order for a contract to exist, there must be **four key elements**:

1. The agreement must be between two or more parties;
2. The parties must both be competent to consent to such an agreement;
3. The agreement must be for something of value; and
4. The agreement must be lawful.

If any of these elements are missing, the parties are not bound by their agreement. The above elements are used to inform each party that they are bound by either a written or verbal agreement. In complex organizations, such as the healthcare industry, contracts are usually written documents and are signed by both parties. The purpose of this practice is to force the parties to ensure that they are getting what they bargained for and to help eliminate undue litigation, cost, and time to both parties (Pozgar, 2007).

Contract law is another area that requires the attention of healthcare managers, and Table 15-3 delineates several of the differences between contract and tort law and ways in which the two interrelate.

TABLE 15-3 Contract and Tort Law

CONTRACT	TORT
Duties are determined by the parties who are privy to the contract	Duties are determined by law
Parties are known as those that have been contracted with	Parties are generally unknown
Consented to	Individuals do not consent
No legal action for the contract itself	Legal action is available
The damages awarded are not for the contract itself, only for the particular breach that occurred	Damages are awarded and are the only remedy
Damages are normally determined by the writing contained in the contract; in other words, the intent of the contracting parties will determine the legal remedy	Damages are normally decided by a judge or jury that makes a decision based on the evidence

---

TEXTBOX 15-4. KEY TERM

Competent: Competence speaks to an individual's ability to make decisions or perform tasks. For example, an individual must be competent to agree to a medical procedure, meaning that they are of sound mind, of legal age, and so on. Competent also means that a professional has the skills to perform a task, that is, a surgeon is educated, trained, and licensed to practice surgery.

ETHICAL CONCEPTS

"Ethics" is a term that has been used in many different (sometimes contradictory) ways. We talk of **ethical behavior**, meaning the ability to tell the difference between right and wrong. But where does one's "sense of right and wrong" come from? At an individual level, ethical perspectives generally come from family upbringing and/or religion. We are also members of communities (ethnic, residential, national) and of professions that have codes, traditions, and practices setting out standards of ethical behavior. At the organizational level, we speak of similar standards, which may vary depending on the type of organization under examination (public/private; for-profit/nonprofit; religiously based/nonsectarian). In all these settings, we must also distinguish between "normative" ethics, which set a standard of what ought to be done, and "descriptive" ethics, illustrating what is actually done.

On the theoretical level, ethics discussions in health care hark back to moral philosophies such as, among others, utilitarianism, deontology, natural law, and the hybrid philosophy of John Rawls (which uses portions of several of these philosophical approaches to address a particular issue or problem, i.e., ethics). As crises in human subject research came to the public's attention in the 20th century, a whole new field of "bioethics" emerged, examining not just the physician–patient relationship, but also areas such as the allocation of scarce resources, genetics, transplantation, and end-of-life care.

In documents, including the World Medical Association's 1964 Declaration of Helsinki, and the 1978 report of the National Commission for the Protection of Human Subjects of Biomedical and Behavioral Research, a simplified listing of key ethical principles for health-care research was created and widely circulated. Callahan and Jennings (2002) (and many others) make a persuasive argument for the application of those same ethical principles to a much wider array of healthcare settings. These central principles are: **respect for persons, beneficence, nonmaleficence, and justice**.

Respect for Persons

Several key aspects of medical ethics fall under this heading, including **autonomy**, **truth-telling**, **confidentiality**, and **fidelity**. Individuals have the right to make informed decisions about and consent to their care when they are **competent** to do so, and to have **respectful guardianship** when they cannot be self-determining. The principle of truth-telling implies that those involved in health care are to be honest with patients/clients as much as possible. Confidentiality, which requires keeping information about others involved in the healthcare interaction private, is a critical part of any healthcare manager's job and is being closely scrutinized in the electronic world. Fidelity, the fourth element of the respect-for-persons concept, requires keeping one's word. This includes practitioners' and administrators' responsibility to provide care as promised, whether a formal contract exists or not.

Beneficence and Nonmaleficence

Beneficence and **nonmaleficence** are common ethical principles and will be discussed briefly as they are key to understanding medicine and ethics. Beneficence requires doing the best one can for the recipient of one's services. Stemming from the Hippocratic tradition, it requires a positive duty to care. In other words, it is a balancing of treatment versus the risks and cost involved. For a health administrator, this would mean approaching cost-benefit analysis carefully, and always with the requirement of putting the patient's welfare first. Under this standard, practitioners are to use the full array of their skills for all patients, regardless of demographic or cultural factors that might separate them and (as much as possible) regardless of the ability to pay.

The parallel concept, **nonmaleficence**, is the "do no harm" or at least "don't make it worse" principle. Healthcare workers and administrators are admonished to not increase patients' difficulties by their actions (or inactions). Of course, this principle can't always be followed to the letter, as some risks and harms may be inevitable in the attempt to make the situation better. Such tradeoffs are acceptable only with patient understanding and consent. Where possible, practitioners and organizations are to minimize risk and need to always protect against active, intentional harm to patients.

Justice

As a healthcare principle, justice is a bit harder to pin down than the preceding three. **Justice,** however, is tied to ethical philosophy and implies fairness. Authors and policy makers have defined "fairness" according to an array of definitions, ranging from exactly equal treatment for all to having individuals receive the treatment they "deserve." For example, if someone pays for an item, they would receive the item as opposed to the person not paying for it. Thus, not all are equal. In health care, justice and ethics, as a theory, are often very complicated.

It may seem that ethics and the law are further apart than ever after reading the previous sections, but one only needs to look through a newspaper or view the nightly news in order to see that the values system in this country is on the decline. Pozgar hit the nail on the head when he described instances that include "questionable political decisions, numbers-cooking executives with exorbitant salaries, health care executives working for both profit and non-profit organizations," among others (Pozgar, 2010). What can we do to remedy this? Will more laws help us get on track ethically, or will better ethics lead to more enforcement of our existing laws? It is a dilemma that every healthcare executive must face, and it is critical to the success of any organization. Law and ethics are very much intertwined, and the savvy manager must find a way to walk the thin line between the two in order to bring order and discipline to the organization.

PATIENT AND PROVIDER RIGHTS AND RESPONSIBILITIES

Both the healthcare provider and the patient have rights and responsibilities in a host of different areas relating to the provision of care, compliance, respect, and numerous other areas. Of course, as noted above, one key provider responsibility is to avoid harming patients and to use one's skills to (ideally) better their situation. This has both legal and ethical underpinnings and is directly connected to concerns about malpractice. The legal notion of "duty" is critical, as it flows both from the provider's training and professional oath and from the existence of a relationship (contractual or implied) with the patient. In the case of people seeking emergency care, for instance, the federal Emergency Medical Treatment and Active Labor Act (EMTALA) of 1985 requires that hospitals participating in Medicare must provide screening examinations and treatment in their emergency departments unless they can prove that a patient requested a transfer (having been fully informed about EMTALA) and/or that the hospital cannot provide the necessary care for the patient's condition.

Another critical responsibility of the healthcare organization itself is its fiduciary duty to the patient. **Fiduciary duty** means that people or organizations have an obligation to those who have placed their trust in them. The healthcare organization, its board of trustees, and its staff are in a position of relative power with the patients. This entails fiduciary duties to protect the organization's assets, abide by its articles of incorporation, and refrain from personal gain at the organization's or patient's expense.

Marketing presents numerous concerns as well and can be a particularly sticky ethical area for any organization or practitioner. Some issues to consider in this regard are:

- How far is it acceptable to go in convincing potential patients that they "need" your services?
- When does providing public information cross over into creating demand in order to increase your own income?
- Is it ethical to attract or keep patients in your institution or professional practice when they might be served better elsewhere?

In addition to their responsibilities to patients, healthcare organizations have the responsibility to ensure that all employees and attending staff are treated fairly and with dignity. Providers are to be protected from sexual or other harassment and have been generally allowed to excuse themselves from patient care with which they disagree, although this is an area under litigation and pressure for legislative change (Stein, 2006).

Individual medical providers are obliged to abide by the requirements of their licenses, living up to the standards of their professions. This includes protecting patient information, providing the best quality of care, serving as advocates for their patients within the healthcare organization, keeping their own training up-to-date, and reporting any unethical behavior by their coworkers. For their part, patients have the responsibility to understand and consent to care, to ask questions of their care providers, to provide accurate information to them (including insurance information, medications, etc.), and to attempt to follow the directions and take prescriptions given for their care.

In America, legal and ethical standards support the notion of **patient self-determination** as a central aspect of health care. Closely linked to this concept is the requirement for confidentiality of patient information. The federal Health Insurance Portability and Accountability Act (HIPAA) of 1996 is one effort to protect patient information in the modern hospital. According to the U.S. Department of Health and Human Services (2003), a portion of HIPAA was designed to protect patient privacy and confidentiality in secure environments, particularly through electronic transactions. The regulations protect medical records and other individually identifiable health information, whether on paper or in electronic or oral communications. Key provisions of these new standards include rules and regulations regarding access to medical records, notice of privacy practices, limits on the use of personal and medical information, prohibitions on marketing, stronger state laws, confidential communications, and provisions for patient complaints in case they feel their rights have been violated.

TEXTBOX 15-5. KEY TERM

Patient self-determination: Patient self-determination is a law that requires healthcare organizations to inform patients of their rights as they pertain to their ability to determine their own health care. For instance, a patient would be informed about their right to consent, their ability to accept and refuse care, and advanced directives.

Long before HIPAA, however, there was an acknowledged legal right of patients to make **informed decisions** about their own care. **Consent** cannot be considered valid if the person giving it did not fully understand the situation, including the potential benefits and risks involved. Adult patients (or their surrogates) also have an absolute right to decline care, even if medical practitioners disagree.

LEGAL/ETHICAL CONCERNS IN MANAGED CARE

By definition, "managed" care imposes limits on patient and provider choices. When it was originally developed, the goal was to avoid "unnecessary" care and to encourage the use of preventive care as much as possible. However, the more recent concerns are that care is being "rationed," that doctors' hands are tied, and/or that managed care disproportionately harms those dependent on public funding for their care (hence unable to pay higher premiums to ensure a wider range of choices). As most employers have moved to requiring some version of managed care for their employees, the last concern (of unfair treatment of recipients of medical assistance) has waned somewhat. But the issues of rationing and physicians' divided loyalties remain.

In order to be able to treat patients in a managed care plan, the physician must be found acceptable to the plan because of his/her treatment record and charges. Once in the plan, a physician is expected to use only approved medications (also called a **formulary**), treatments, and referrals in order to save money and to stay within the plan's budgetary restrictions—and good graces. Such cases as *Wickline v. California* (1986) established that physicians are obliged to act as advocates for their patients and resist inappropriate care determinations made by managed care organizations. Other cases have reiterated the point that both the physician and the managed care organization are legally liable for harm caused to the patient by inadequate care due to cost containment. Managed care organizations are also obliged to hire and retain competent physicians and to ensure that they remain qualified to practice (Perry, 2002).

Healthcare organizations are in the somewhat unique situation of choosing which managed care plans to belong to as providers, as well as choosing which to offer to employees in their own health benefits packages. This can bring home rather bluntly the cost-benefit decisions involved. However, the new healthcare reform law may be changing the landscape for these organizations, as it is felt that they may be in a better position to offer more competitive benefits to recipients. Because managed care organizations have successfully fought off a national health plan, the opportunity to service more individuals under the umbrella of the new healthcare reform may bring new prosperity and expansion to the industry (Kaiser Health News, 2010).

BIOMEDICAL CONCERNS

While healthcare managers do not have to personally make life-and-death medical decisions, the organization's policies can strongly influence what happens under its supervision. One area of ongoing concern is the question of resource allocation implicit in most healthcare decisions and explicit in managed care settings. As long as equal access to particular levels of care and/or treatments is not available, this will continue to occur. It is possible that healthcare reform will answer some of these questions, but nonetheless, these will still be the types of questions that managers will need to address.

Another overarching issue is that of consent. As mentioned above, informed consent is a keystone of medical practice, requiring the practitioner to provide the patient with sufficient information to participate in decisions about his/her care. With laws such as the Americans with Disabilities Act, this responsibility has been expanded to require providing information that is understandable to the patient or, if the patient is not able to decide, to a surrogate decision maker. Particularly in highly emotional situations, such as beginning- and end-of-life care decisions, this process needs to occur. Most hospitals have **patient advocate offices** for the specific purpose of having staff dedicated to walking through difficult decisions with patients and their families.

BEGINNING- AND END-OF-LIFE CARE

As medical science has advanced, the variety and complexity of decisions to be made has also expanded. Two places where this is particularly apparent are in beginning- and end-of-life care. When *Roe v. Wade* was decided in 1966, morning-after pills and various forms of nonsurgical abortions weren't available. In vitro fertilization didn't exist, and medical science wasn't able to keep infants alive when they were born many months early. Provision and funding of contraception, provision and funding of abortion, and balancing parental, societal, and practitioner rights and responsibilities are all issues to be discussed in the context of an organization's mission, vision, and values.

Likewise, end-of-life care has become more complicated than in previous eras. Healthcare organizations now must pay close attention to obtaining advance directives and identifying surrogate decision makers, providing ethical care in the absence of clear directives, making crucial decisions about life-sustaining treatment, and balancing familial, societal, and practitioner rights and responsibilities.

Similarly, the previous end-of-life cases would have been much more complicated with today's increased array of end-of-life technologies. Also, we now face divergence between state and federal law about physician-assisted suicide. Of course, not every healthcare organization has the desire or the facilities to provide complicated care. In addition, the particular organization's mission and values will shape what it is willing to provide. Aside from the requirements of the Emergency Medical Treatment and Active Labor Act for those hospitals with emergency facilities and/or obstetrics departments, facilities are free to decide and publicize the types of care that their (often religious) standards will or will not allow them to provide.

CONCLUSION

Health care is one of the most regulated industries in the nation. Laws have been put in place to protect patients based on ethical concerns and precedents. Every time an organization provides healthcare services, the potential for legal violations of patients' rights should loom large in the healthcare manager's consciousness. This chapter has provided you with the vocabulary and some context for addressing legal issues in healthcare organizations. Since these laws can change and the cases vary, it is incumbent upon the healthcare manager to stay abreast of developments in healthcare ethics and law. Furthermore, the new healthcare reform act of 2010 will provide numerous changes that will affect all healthcare providers and organizations. It is critical that managers are able to understand the complex issues presented in these new laws and apply them in a both just and ethical manner.

DISCUSSION QUESTIONS

1. Provide several examples of legal behavior and ethical behavior. In what instances are the two similar, and in what instances are they different?

2. How do the legal concepts discussed in this chapter, that is, criminal, tort, civil, and so on, work to dictate the ways in which organizations must operate?

3. As you think about the new healthcare reform bill, what type of lawmaking action instituted it? In other words, was it developed from the common law, executive order, or legislative process? Was this the best way to institute the new reform? Explain your answer.

4. Think of several examples of both ethical and legal circumstances where you can apply the concepts of beneficence and nonmaleficence. How do these concepts work within your examples to provide protection to both the organization and the patient?

5. There are numerous end-of-life issues that we have all heard about in the news, but how are these laws established? Is it okay for a patient and provider to make these decisions on their own, outside of the law? Aren't these privileged physician/patient decisions?

6. What do you see for the future of healthcare reform as the law applies? Will healthcare reform spawn new laws, or will new laws be enacted to guide reform?

7. Return to the tort section in your text and answer the following question based on the information provided by the chapter. Is reporting child abuse a legal obligation or an ethical one? Does it matter what your position is within the organization, that is, nurse, manager, clerk, and so on? What if you find out about child abuse from a patient encounter, but the law does not allow you to report from the official record? Do you have an ethical obligation to do so?

8. Look back at Table 15-2 and try to determine where tort and contract law come together and in what areas there may be conflict between law and ethics. Explain your thinking and final decisions.

9. In thinking about biomedical issues, address the following questions: How do we decide which patient will receive an organ transplant? Can we be positive that a particular combination of genetics, age, demographics, and lifestyle factors will enable one person to have a longer and more productive life than another? Should we be influenced by the available level of family support, or by the family's need to

be involved in a relative's care? How can a healthcare organization best reflect the ethical preferences of its community while abiding by the law? Should the ability to have care reimbursed affect the decision to provide it?

Cases in Chapter 17 that are related this chapter include:

- Dr. Nugget's Medical Practice—see p. 465
- End Days—see p. 384
- Sundowner or Victim?—see p. 394
- Sexual Harassment at the Diabetes Clinic—see p. 412

Additional cases, role-play scenarios, video links, websites, and other information sources are also available in the online Instructor's Materials.

REFERENCES

Bishop, T. F., Federman, A. D., & Keyhani, S. (2010). Physicians' views on defensive medicine: A national survey. *Arch Intern Med, 170*(12), 1081–1083.

Callahan, D., & Jennings, B. (2002). Ethics and public health: Forging a strong relationship. *American Journal of Public Health, 92*(2), 169–176.

Conigliaro, M. (2005). Abstract appeal: *The Terri Schiavo Information Page.* Retrieved from http://abstractappeal.com/schiavo/infopage.html

Dresser, R. (2004). Schiavo: A hard case makes questionable law. *Hastings Center Report, 34*(2), 8–9.

Gifis, S. H. (1996). *Barron's law dictionary.* Hauppauge, NY: Barron's Educational Series.

Kaiser Family Foundation. (2005). *Medical malpractice law in the United States.* The Henry J. Kaiser Family Foundation Online. Retrieved from http://www.kff.org/insurance/upload/Medical-Malpractice-Law-in-the-United-States-Report.pdf

Kaiser Health News. (2010). *Health law having affects on managed-care firms, medical suppliers.* Retrieved from http://www.kaiserhealthnews.org/Daily-Reports/2010/May/28/Health-Overhaul-and-Business.aspx

National Archives. (n.d.). United States Constitution. Retrieved from http://www.archives.gov/exhibits/charters/constitution.html

Perry, F. (2002). *The tracks we leave: Ethics in healthcare management.* Chicago, IL: Health Administration Press.

Pozgar, G. D. (2007). *Legal aspects of health care administration* (10th ed.). Sudbury, MA: Jones and Bartlett.

Pozgar, G. D. (2010). *Legal and ethical issues for health professionals* (2nd ed.). Sudbury, MA: Jones and Bartlett.

Shi, L., & Singh, D. A. (2008). *Delivering health care in America* (4th ed.). Sudbury, MA: Jones and Bartlett.

Sorrel, A. L. (June 7, 2010). Health reform has liability insurers looking at tort alternatives. *American Medical News Online.* Retrieved from http://www.ama-assn.org/amednews/2010/06/07/prl20607.htm

Stein, R. (2006, January 30). Health workers' choice debated: Proposals back right not to treat. *Washington Post,* A01.

U.S. Department of Health and Human Services (DHHS). (2003). Fact sheet: Protecting the privacy of patient's health information. Retrieved from http://www.hhs.gov/news/facts/privacy.html

Wickline v. California. 192 Cal. App. 3d 1630, 1636, 239 Cal Rptr 810 (2d Dist. 1986).

CHAPTER 16

Fraud and Abuse

Kevin D. Zeiler

LEARNING OBJECTIVES

By the end of this chapter, the student will be able to:

- Explain the difference between fraud and abuse;
- List examples of fraud and abuse and compare the extent of occurrences;
- Discuss the types of civil and criminal penalties incurred for violating rules and regulations;
- Describe the history of the False Claims Act and its application to health care;
- Discuss the managerial and organizational implications of the Emergency Medical Treatment and Active Labor Act (EMTALA);
- Explain the major objectives of the U.S. antitrust laws related to the healthcare industry;
- Describe the major provisions of the Stark I and Stark II laws and safe harbor regulations;
- List the major components of compliance, risk management, and internal control programs;
- Discuss qui tam and the whistle-blower role; and
- Explain the desirable role of a healthcare manager in fraud and abuse cases.

INTRODUCTION

Fraud and abuse have always been a concern to the federal government with regard to Medicare, Medicaid, and other federally funded healthcare programs. Many remedies have been implemented through the years. In 1995, Operation Restore Trust (ORT) was put in motion by the U.S. Congress to give the Department of Health and Human Services (DHHS) the investigative and enforcement authority necessary to deal with fraud and abuse violations. With ORT in motion, the delivery of healthcare in the United States has dramatically and definitively changed for the provider, the beneficiary, and the payer of federally funded healthcare benefits. Whether these measures were taken for political, fiscal, or quality-of-care reasons, the landscape has changed. The Department of Health and Human Services (DHHS) Office of Inspector General (OIG) reported to government officials in 2010 that "the sums lost each year to fraud and abuse reached into the tens of billions of dollars, though there's little agreement on a specific estimate" (Blesch, 2010). These numbers are staggering and still seem to be rising. As you try to understand the fact that tens of billions of dollars are lost to fraud, is it the number that is troublesome or the fact that nobody can agree on an estimate? What is being and can be done to reduce the fraud and prevent it? Clearly, this is a major issue facing healthcare managers.

This chapter will focus on the beginnings of the fraud and abuse prevention programs that started with the decentralized home health agencies (HHA) and have broadened to include various types of compliance programs. The chapter will also look at the investigative processes used to uncover fraud and abuse, the enforcement role of governmental programs, and the responsibilities of employees of healthcare organizations.

For the federal government, ORT was successful, but it still wasn't enough. New programs such as the Tax Relief and Healthcare Act of 2006, which instituted Recovery Audit Contractors (RAC) and the Health Care Fraud Prevention and Enforcement Action Team (HEAT) in 2009, have continued to turn up the heat and keep the pressure on fraud and abuse in the healthcare industry. Furthermore, the new healthcare reform bill, passed in March 2010, provides an additional $350 million in new funding to fight fraud and abuse over the next 10 years (Lexology, 2010).

WHAT IS FRAUD AND ABUSE?

Fraud is an intentional act of deception, while **abuse** consists of improper acts that are unintentional but inconsistent with standard practices. Oftentimes, abuse is so labeled because the investigator cannot determine if fraud occurred, or in other words, if the party acted willfully. The more common forms of fraud and abuse are providers billing for services that were not provided or did not meet medical necessity criteria (false claims), submitting duplicate bills, upcoding services to receive higher reimbursement, and receiving kickbacks for referrals.

HISTORY

The history of compliance as it relates to healthcare fraud and abuse dates back to the Civil War. The False Claims Act (FCA) was enacted in 1863 by the federal government as the primary civil remedy for fraudulent or improper healthcare claims. In 1986, the first major amendments were added to the FCA. These changes removed the clause requiring that there be specific intent to defraud the federal government and that the government need only show that the claim submitted is false and submitted knowingly. Violations of this act include fines of $5,500 to $11,000 per claim, plus up to three times the amount of the damages caused to the federal program (31 USC, 1986a). The Act's qui tam provision permits private individuals to file false claims actions on behalf of the federal government and receive 15% to 30% of any recovery (31 USC, 1986b). A qui tam (Latin for "who as well") is used to indicate that the plaintiff is bringing the action on behalf of the government as well as himself. This individual is also known as a "whistle-blower" or a "relator." The qui tam provision has been key to getting individuals to come forward, as it offers monetary incentives and shelter from backlash and/or prosecution.

While the number of civil healthcare fraud cases rose dramatically in the 1990s, the rate of increase in the number of cases has stabilized since then, but the dollars recovered in suits and investigations has increased. In the fiscal year ended September 30, 2003, $1.7 billion was recovered through violations of the False Claims Act as it relates to healthcare fraud. This represents 81% of the total $2.1 billion recovered for the year as reported by the Department of Justice (DOJ) for fraud-related claims (Department of Justice, 2003). Numbers for the recently instituted RAC program are not currently available, but full implementation should likely occur in 2010 (Centers for Medicare & Medicaid Services, 2009).

Operation Restore Trust

Operation Restore Trust (ORT) started in 1995 to counter charges about healthcare fraud and abuse. Initially, the program involved the five states with the heaviest volume of Medicare beneficiaries. The first services investigated were those provided outside of normal treatment facilities (e.g., hospices, home health agencies, etc.). These investigations led to recovery of $190 million from fraudulent healthcare activities. In 1997, the program was expanded to include 12 more states.

Operation Restore Trust now includes all 50 states, and more healthcare delivery systems are covered. The program not only investigates and applies penalties for fraud, but also provides advisories to prevent violations. It uses statistical data to select claims for audits and investigations. DHHS has organized state and federal agencies to monitor activities under ORT.

The Tax Relief and Health Care Act of 2006

In 2009, the Centers for Medicare & Medicaid Services (CMS) introduced Recovery Audit Contractors (RACs) in response to the continuing fraud and abuse problem faced by both programs. The beauty of the RAC program is that examiners work on a contingency basis, meaning that they only get paid when they find a mistake (Omdahl &

Warmack, 2009). The RAC program is the biggest effort since ORT in the mid-1990s. The goal is to use computer systems to find data that will lead to discrepancies so that information can be obtained that will lead to a monetary recovery. Since contractors are not being paid unless the program is recovering money, the incentive to uncover fraud and abuse is very large. Time will tell if this program is able to generate as much return as ORT, as it was not used in all 50 states until sometime during 2010 (CMS, 2009).

Health Care Fraud Prevention and Enforcement Action Team

The newest member to the fraud and abuse team is the President's Health Care Fraud Prevention and Enforcement Action Team, or HEAT, as it is known. This program, much like the others, is geared toward stopping fraud and abuse of Medicare and Medicaid claims. However, this Act is different in the sense that the President is also using it as an enforcement tool against the agencies directed to stop such fraud and abuse (Blesch, 2010). In the past, CMS acted to investigate fraud and abuse, but this law gives muscle to agencies and assists CMS with enforcement against those individuals or organizations that are violating the law and attempting to defraud the system. Since so many agencies are working to reduce this problem, it is only reasonable that some type of accountability must take place. Time will tell if a more concerted government effort will prove to be the difference in this ongoing battle.

THE SOCIAL SECURITY ACT AND THE CRIMINAL-DISCLOSURE PROVISION

The Criminal-Disclosure Provision of the Social Security Act makes it a felony for a healthcare provider or beneficiary to possess "knowledge of the occurrence of any event affecting his initial or continued right to any such benefit or payment, or the initial or continued right to any such benefit or payment of any other individual in whose behalf he has applied for or is receiving such benefit or payment conceals or fails to disclose such event with an intent fraudulently to secure such benefit or payment either in a greater amount or quantity than is due or when no such benefit or payment is authorized" (42 USC, 1987a). Violation of this provision is a felony and may include punishment of up to 5 years in prison and/or fines of up to $25,000 (42 USC, 1987a).

This provision of the Social Security Act (SSA) also imposes a requirement to disclose overpayments to the government regardless of intent at the time the claim was submitted (42 USC, 1987a). By obligating this disclosure, the government may start collection efforts. If the provider acts in good faith to reimburse the program, it may limit its liability under the False Claims Act (FCA). It does not, however, loosen any criminal liability under this provision.

There are at least two cases that follow the Criminal-Disclosure Provision of the Act. These include several defendants who were charged with conspiracy to knowingly misstate certain interest expenses on providers' cost reports filed with the government. Documents show that the conspiracy involves the defendants knowingly failing to notify the government of the fiscal intermediary's audit error concerning interest expense. The defendants were convicted on the conspiracy count, but no separate finding was made on the failure-to-disclose allegation (42 USC, 1987b).

Another case involves three individuals in California who were charged with conspiracy to defraud the U.S. government in connection with a scheme to submit fraudulent medical necessity certification for certain medical equipment. It is critical that all healthcare managers, whether it be the highest ranking executive, the line, or the unit manager, understand that the federal government intends to prosecute these types of cases to the fullest extent of the law. *All* members of an organization are now going to be held liable for the actions or inactions of those within the organization and will be held to standards established by criminal statutes. In other words, it is getting more and more difficult for CEOs or high-ranking executives to hide behind the corporate shield.

THE EMERGENCY MEDICAL TREATMENT AND ACTIVE LABOR ACT

The Emergency Medical Treatment and Active Labor Act (EMTALA) was enacted in 1986 to prevent patient dumping. It is also known as the Anti-Dumping Act. It was used to prevent emergency rooms from refusing treatment or transferring a patient to another facility because of the patient's inability to pay for treatment. The Act mandates that an appropriate medical screening exam (MSE) be given to any patient who presents to any department that is established as a provider of emergent or urgent care. If an MSE is performed and shows that an emergency condition exists, the patient must be either treated and discharged or admitted as an inpatient and transferred from the dedicated emergency department. The EMTALA obligations cease at this point. However, EMTALA also restricts the emergency room staff from discussing financial or insurance information until after the MSE has been performed and the emergent condition has been stabilized. As long as the treatment is not delayed, hospitals may continue the registration process.

The CMS has the authority to enforce EMTALA and can impose financial penalties on providers who do not comply. In addition, the OIG has separate authority to impose sanctions for EMTALA violations. Violators may incur monetary penalties of up to $50,000 per violation and have their Medicare program participation terminated. The final EMTALA rule became effective on November 10, 2003.

Hospital Compliance with EMTALA

To avoid EMTALA violations, providers should:

- Require all clinical, administrative, and contact staff to review and understand the EMTALA requirements and to document this training;
- Ensure that all patients who have an emergent admission and either "refuse" or withdraw treatment are offered a medical screening exam and treatment before they leave the hospital and that refusal to accept treatment is documented (informed consent);
- Ensure that the ER staff understands all statutory rules regarding transfer of patients to another facility; and
- Enforce the requirement that prevents staff from asking for financial and accounting information before the medical screening exam has been completed and the patient is stabilized.

Review the chart (shown in Table 16-1) so you have a good understanding of the acts that have been covered thus far in the chapter.

TABLE 16-1 Criminal Disclosure Provisions

ACT	FUNCTION
Criminal-Disclosure Provisions of the Social Security Act	a) Provider must disclose overpayments so that the government can initiate collection efforts. b) Imposes penalties for failure to disclose such payment information. c) Disclosure may provide a defense if the government attempts to collect. d) Provider liability includes: 　i) Felony offense 　ii) Up to $25,000 fine 　iii) Up to five years in jail 　　(Cleverley & Cameron, 2007, p. 76).
False Claims Act	a) Federal government's primary civil remedy for fraudulent claims. b) Providers who make improper claims are fined $5,500–$11,000 per claim. c) The Act is also applied to improper billing, claims for services not rendered, unnecessary services, misrepresenting credentials, and substandard quality of care (Cleverley & Cameron, 2007, p. 75).
Emergency Medical Transfer and Active Labor Act (EMTALA)	a) Requires all Medicare and Medicaid hospitals with an emergency department to provide appropriate medical screening to all seeking care. b) Often referred to as the anti-dumping law because it prohibits hospitals from transferring an emergency patient to another hospital because of an inability to pay (Cleverley & Cameron, 2007, p. 77).

ANTITRUST ISSUES

Antitrust laws were implemented to protect the citizenry from the negative effects of monopolies. Three Acts form the basis of antitrust law.

- The Sherman Antitrust Act—Section 1 prohibits all conspiracies or agreements that restrain trade.
- The Clayton Act—Section 7 of the Act prohibits mergers and acquisitions that may substantially lessen competition "in any line of commerce . . . in any section of the country." This was enacted in 1914.
- The Federal Trade Commission Act—Section 5 of the Act prohibits various types of unfair competition, such as collusion, price fixing, and the like.

The Department of Justice (DOJ) and the Federal Trade Commission (FTC) revised the Statements of Antitrust Enforcement Policy in Health Care in 1996. The revision was intended to ensure that policies did not interfere with activities that reduce healthcare costs.

In order to prevent violations of the Antitrust Act, Congress passed **the** Hart-Scott-Rodino Antitrust Improvements Act of 1976. This required hospitals and all other parties who enter into certain mergers, acquisitions, joint ventures, or tender offers to notify the DOJ and FTC before finalizing all agreements. This is a requirement for hospitals with assets greater than $100 million acquiring a hospital with more than $10 million in assets. The DOJ and FTC then decide if the transaction should be approved.

Table 16-2 provides an overview of the main antitrust acts and their functions.

TABLE 16-2 Antitrust Acts

ACT	FUNCTION
Sherman Antitrust Act	a) Applies to agreements that unreasonably restrain trade. These include, but are not limited to: price fixing, boycotting other organizations, dividing market territories, and using coercive tactics with the intent to harm or injure another party.
	b) Applies to virtually all businesses in the country, including health care (Cleverley & Cameron, 2007, p. 78).
Clayton Act	a) Prohibits mergers and acquisitions that may lessen competition.
	b) Unlike the Sherman Act, the Clayton Act only imposes civil penalties (Cleverley & Cameron, 2007, p. 82).
Federal Trade Commission Act	a) Prohibits unfair methods of competition. This may include techniques such as larger businesses using their size to gain lower prices from suppliers and suppliers giving discounts to larger companies without providing the same for smaller ones (Cleverley & Cameron, 2007, p. 78).

PHYSICIAN SELF-REFERRAL/ANTI-KICKBACK/ SAFE HARBOR LAWS

Two laws have been enacted to prevent conflicts of interest in Medicare patient referrals. The Physician Self-Referral Laws are also known as Stark I and Stark II. The Stark II Law "prohibits physicians from referring patients to providers with which the physician has a financial relationship" (Furrow et al., 2004). This law is an extension of the **Stark I** Law, which only applies to physicians referring to laboratories in which they have a financial interest. Examples of violations of the Stark Laws include paying a physician for a referral and a hospital offering rental space to a physician below fair market value. Physicians who receive benefits not given to other doctors or staff may be considered in violations of the rule, too.

The second law is the Anti-Kickback Act (42 USC, 1987a), which is designed to prevent the offer or payment of bribes or other remuneration as an inducement to refer Medicare patients for treatment or services (Manning, 1996). These rules, especially the Anti-Kickback statute, were so stringent that many providers were being wrongly accused of conduct that was not inherently illegal, leading Congress to ask CMS to develop and enforce **safe harbor** provisions, under which physicians can receive remuneration in specific instances. Each of these is discussed further in this section.

Under Stark II, if a physician or immediate family member has a specified financial relationship with an entity, the physician may not refer Medicare or Medicaid patients to that entity to receive health services (Furrow et al., 2004, p. 1034). Thus, the provision may be implicated when a referring physician has an ownership or investment interest, or when a physician or immediate family member receives compensation or other remuneration from the entity providing healthcare services. Additionally, the recipient of the referral may not present a claim for any designated health services provided due to this referral.

Before continuing in with this section, take a moment to expand your knowledge as it applies to Stark I and II, as shown in Table 16-3.

TABLE 16-3 Stark Laws

STARK I	STARK II
Enacted to deal with physician self-referrals.	Expanded Stark I laws.
Often referred to as the Ethics in Patient Referrals Act.	Any amounts billed illegally must be refunded.
Makes it illegal for a physician to make a Medicare-financed referral to an organization in which he or she or a family member has a financial interest.	Applies to Medicaid services as well as Medicare.
Also prohibits billings by a laboratory for services provided pursuant to illegal referrals.	Knowingly billing or failing to make a refund is subject to a civil fine of $15,000 per item billed.

Source: Furrow et al., 2004, p. 1033.

The Anti-Kickback Act, formerly known as the "Medicare and Medicaid Anti-Kickback Act," is the law of choice for federal enforcement authorities. This Act imposes criminal liability for the knowing and willful payment, solicitation, or receipt of remuneration (remuneration is any kickback, bribe, or rebate, direct or indirect, overt or covert, in cash or in kind, and any ownership interest or compensation interest) in return for referring an individual to a person for, or in return for purchasing, leasing, ordering, arranging for, or recommending the purchase, lease, or ordering of items or services reimbursable by the federal healthcare program. This Act affects a vast array of healthcare industry business relationships.

The Anti-Kickback Act has broadened the original Act's reach to encompass all federal healthcare programs, excluding the Federal Employees Health Benefits Program, which is the health plan for federal employees. This was done in 1996 with the passage of the Health Insurance Portability and Accountability Act (HIPAA). In addition, the Balanced Budget Act of 1997 imposes civil monetary penalties of $50,000 for each violation of the Anti-Kickback Act and damages of up to three times the total amount of remuneration offered, paid, solicited, or received in violation of the Act (HR 2015, 1997).

Federal enforcement authorities continuously review application of the Act. They are currently reviewing doctors and drug samples, incentives for therapeutic switches, and provision of free goods or value-added services to nursing homes. OIG staffers have stressed that the most important aspect of the Anti-Kickback Act violation is the intent to induce referrals and that no safe harbor exists for conduct that may also benefit patients because enforcement authorities do not believe that such services are provided with only patients' interests in mind. In contrast to the Anti-Kickback Act, Stark I and II describe prohibited conduct explicitly. Unlike the Anti-Kickback Act, Stark I and II are strict liability statutes, meaning that individuals or organizations are liable "for damages that their actions or products cause regardless of fault on their part;" they do not require proof of intent, nor do they have regulatory safe harbors that give rise to gray areas (Pozgar, 2007).

Safe harbor regulations were put in place in 1987 by DHHS after a congressional mandate. Initially, 11 safe harbor provisions were implemented in 1991. These gave guidelines that, when complied with in full, would ensure compliance with this very vague statute. The goal of the safe harbors laws is to "immunize certain payment and business practices that are implicated by the anti-kickback statute from criminal and civil prosecution under the statute" (Office of Inspector General, 1999). "In 1993, the OIG proposed to include within the list of safe harbor provisions, payments made to surgeon-investors in Ambulatory Surgery Centers (ASCs), provided that the facility was wholly owned by the referring surgeons and that these surgeons performed the surgery themselves on patients they had referred to the ASC, so this safe harbor could be justified because the ASC facility was an extension of the referring surgeon's practice and of little risk for fraud and abuse" (Kinkade, 2000).

On November 19, 1999, the OIG published a final rule, which established 8 new safe harbors and clarified 6 of the original 11 that went into effect in 1991 (Kinkade, 2000).

The following key points, as delineated by Kinkade (2000), help to outline the standards established by the safe harbor rules:

1. Both surgeon-owned and single-specialty ASC safe harbors, which differ only by types of physicians who may hold ownership interest in the ASC, impose an additional requirement that examines each investor's income from the ASC. Under this rule, one-third of each physician-investor's medical practice income for the previous year must be derived from the physician's performance of surgical procedures at an ASC or hospital surgical setting. According to the OIG, this will ensure that a physician's investment in an ASC actually represents an extension of the physician's office.

2. The multispecialty ASC safe harbor is identical to surgeon-owned and single-specialty ASC safe harbors, but requires that at least one-third of the physician's surgical procedures are performed at the ASC in which they are investing. Like the practice income test applicable to surgeon-owned and single-specialty ASCs, this requirement is intended to prohibit passive investment among physicians in different specialties. This situation, according to the OIG, creates the greatest risk of prohibited payments or other remuneration for referrals.

3. The hospital/physician ASC is somewhat different from the above-described safe harbors. This safe harbor requires the same five criteria, but does not require the examination of practice income arising from the facility. Instead, the safe harbor imposes three stringent requirements on the hospital investor that may well keep all hospital/physician ASCs outside the scope of the safe harbor.

4. Perhaps the most important feature of the new ASC safe harbor is the OIG's decision to do away with a requirement of 100% physician ownership. Under the final safe harbor, individuals who are neither an existing nor potential source of referrals are permitted to invest in the facility.

5. Also significant in the new safe harbors is the OIG's decision not to expand the scope of the safe harbor to include facilities that are not traditionally considered "surgical" facilities, such as lithotripsy centers, end-stage renal disease facilities, comprehensive outpatient rehabilitation facilities, radiation oncology facilities, cardiac catheterization centers, and optical dispensing facilities, despite support for inclusion (Kinkade, 2000, para. 6–10).

The government has successfully prosecuted cases under the FCA by contending that either the Stark laws or Anti-Kickback Statute violation constitutes making a false statement. These cases have primarily been ones in which a provider submits claims to the government certifying that, either implicitly or explicitly, all services or items were provided according to applicable laws (Kinkade, 2000).

MANAGEMENT RESPONSIBILITY FOR COMPLIANCE AND INTERNAL CONTROLS

According to the Committee of Sponsoring Organizations (COSO) of the Treadway Commission, "internal control is a process effected by an entity's board of directors, management, and other personnel designed to provide reasonable assurance regarding the achievement of objectives in the following categories: effectiveness and efficiency of operations, reliability of financial reporting, and compliance with applicable laws and regulations" (Committee of Sponsoring Organizations (COSO) of the Treadway Commission, 2010).

Under the new structure of corporate compliance, it is important to note that the internal control of compliance programs is now the responsibility of the board, management, and other internal personnel. The responsibility clearly rests in the hands of management. The CEO is no longer able to merely place the blame on the executive staff. The COSO (2010) lists five interrelated components of internal control:

- Control environment sets the tone of an organization, influencing the control consciousness of its people. It is the foundation for all other components of internal control, providing discipline and structure.
- Risk assessment is the entity's identification and analysis of relevant risks to achievement of its objectives, forming a basis for determining how the risks should be managed.
- Control activities are the policies and procedures to help ensure that management directives are carried out.
- Information and communication—pertinent information must be identified, captured, and communicated in a form and time frame that enable people to carry out their responsibilities.
- Monitoring [is] a process that assesses the quality of the system's performance over time (COSO, 2010, p. 2).

CORPORATE COMPLIANCE PROGRAMS

The OIG strongly recommends the adoption of a corporate compliance plan as it helps limit the risk of compliance errors and limits the liability of management and directors. An effective program can also limit liability under the Federal Sentencing Guidelines, which are rules that demand consistency in sentencing as it applies to felonies only, not misdemeanors. Most importantly, an effective corporate compliance plan gives employees the guidelines necessary to follow the laws and allows management to know that the laws are being followed. In addition, more and more organizations are appointing a designated corporate compliance officer as opposed to the past when it was often tasked to numerous individuals. In 2006, the OIG released an integrated approach to corporate compliance that helps organizations to understand the roles and responsibilities of all involved in the discipline (OIG, 2006).

The OIG has published a list of eight **essential elements of an effective compliance program**. They are part of the Federal Sentencing Guidelines and are shown in Table 16-4.

For the compliance plan to be effective, all employees must be aware of the plan. The OIG will survey employees when auditing an institution to measure compliance knowledge and awareness. To develop an effective plan, the first step is to conduct a risk assessment facing the organization.

TABLE 16-4 Effective Compliance Program Essentials

ELEMENT	REQUIREMENT
1) Written policies, procedures, and standards of conduct.	These must speak to the organization's commitment to comply with all applicable federal and state standards.
2) Designation of a compliance officer.	Sponsor must have: a) compliance officer in place b) compliance committee in place c) established protocol for overview d) compliance officer if responsible for fraud and abuse program
3) Training and education.	Must have a training and education program in place.
4) Effective lines of communication throughout the organization.	Sponsor must have: a) organized lines of communication to effectively provide information as it pertains to compliance issues b) mechanisms are in place for capturing concerns and risks
5) Enforcement procedures.	Must enforce standards through disciplinary guidelines.
6) Procedures for effective internal monitoring and auditing.	These requirements are as follows: a) must have a monitoring and auditing program b) must monitor and audit contractors c) must allow CMS to audit financial records d) must allow the federal government to perform an onsite audit e) contractors must allow CMS access to their records
7) Procedures for corrective action.	The organization must ensure: a) prompt response to violations b) appropriate corrective action is taken
8) Fraud and abuse plan must be in place.	Must have a plan in place to detect and prevent fraud and abuse.

The greatest threat to healthcare compliance is erroneous or fraudulent billing. A snapshot of the corporation's billing practices should be created for a risk analysis under the supervision of the organization attorneys, and once the risk areas are identified, a written compliance plan should be developed. This plan should be distributed to all personnel, with all employees being trained to follow it. Once the plan is in force and operational, it will only be effective if it has management support, as well as effective communication, continuous monitoring, and accountability. Also, a key to making a compliance program work is to provide the appropriate organizational response to a violation (OIG, 2004). Without proper reporting, the program is merely an expensive tool to the organization.

CONCLUSION

Fraud and abuse are constantly changing in response to the environment. For instance, as new statutes or laws are passed, clever violators find new ways to get around them. It is for this reason that all healthcare managers must be cognizant of even the most subtle changes within their organization. The key to handling fraud and abuse issues is to keep the staff informed, prepared, and ready and willing to work together in order to protect not only the organization but the industry as well.

This chapter has merely provided an overview of the many complicated laws and issues surrounding fraud and abuse. Recent laws, statutes, and healthcare reform all are proposing new ways to address this difficult issue, but there are no easy answers. As Furrow et al. (2004) state, "the particular statutes, regulations, cases and interpretive rulings and guidelines that fraud has spawned, are also bewilderingly complicated and have generated confusion and cynicism in the health care industry." Therefore, a diligent compliance program is the best way to combat this growing problem.

DISCUSSION QUESTIONS

1. Discuss the differences between fraud and abuse. During your discussion, provide examples of each and how healthcare managers might deal with them.

2. How has the history of healthcare compliance changed since its inception? Hint: Look at the ways in which penalties have increased in various ways. What do you think will be the key to getting control of the issue of fraud and abuse in the future?

3. Choose one of the recent laws that have been enacted that are included in the chapter and discuss why it is or isn't an effective stop-gap to healthcare fraud and abuse.

4. EMTALA is a far-reaching act; explain several of its benefits and describe how it is effective at preventing fraud and abuse as opposed to detecting it.

5. Describe your responsibilities as a healthcare manager as it applies to fraud and abuse. What if you were a unit manager? A department manager? A member of the executive division?

6. As you try to understand the fact that tens of billions of dollars are lost to fraud, is it the number that is troublesome or the fact that nobody can agree on an estimate? What is being done and can be done to reduce fraud and prevent it?

7. You are the new compliance manager for a healthcare organization. Describe the steps you will take to ensure that your compliance plan is legal and effective.

8. A physician and his colleague decide to set up a laboratory owned by a dummy corporation in their wives' names and begin to refer patients to this laboratory. What (if any) laws have they violated?

9. A psychiatrist bills for 10 hours of psychotherapy and medication checks for a deceased woman. Has he committed fraud or abuse? Can the deceased woman's estate press charges if the bills were sent to Medicare, and not to the family?

10. An attorney sees a plastic surgeon and is so happy with her face-lift that she begins to refer all her friends and family. At her 6-month follow-up, she says, "So, Doc, I've sent you all these patients, where's my 30% cut of your fees?" What should the plastic surgeon do?

Cases in Chapter 17 that are related this chapter include:

- Oops Is Not an Option—see p. 375
- Fraud and Abuse: Help Me, the Feds Are Coming!—see p. 468

Additional cases, role-play scenarios, video links, websites, and other information sources are also available in the online Instructor's Materials.

REFERENCES

Balanced Budget Act of 1997 (HR 2015) (Public Law 105-33). Title IV, Subtitle D, Chapter 1, Section 4304 (b) (2).

Blesch, G. (2010). Targeting fraud. *Modern Health Care*. Retrieved from http://www.modernhealthcare.com/article/20100621/MAGAZINE/100619919

Centers for Medicare & Medicaid Services (CMS). (2009). *Recovery audit contractor overview.* Retrieved from http://www.cms.gov/RAC/

Cleverley, W. O., & Cameron, A. E. (2007). *Essentials of health care finance* (6th ed.). Sudbury, MA: Jones & Bartlett.

Committee of Sponsoring Organizations (COSO) of the Treadway Commission. (2010). *Internal control-integrated framework.* Retrieved from http://www.coso.org/IC-IntegratedFramework-summary.htm

Department of Justice (DOJ). (2003, November). *Memorandum 613:11-10-03.* Retrieved from http://www.justice.gov/opa/pr/2003/November/03_civ_613.htm

Furrow, B. R., Greaney, T. L., Johnson, S. H., Jost, T. S., & Schwartz, R. L. (2004). *Health law: Cases, materials and problems* (5th ed.). St. Paul, MN: Thomson-West.

Kinkade, W. A. (2000). *Anti-kickback act safe harbor provisions finalized.* Retrieved from http://library.findlaw.com/2000/Dec/8/126843.html

Lexology. (2010). *The fraud-and-abuse provisions of the health care reform act.* Retrieved from http://www.lexology.com/library/detail.aspx?g=1a1ece1c-87bf-41c4-b4c7-65adc56b3d67

Manning, W. L. (1996). *Summary of the Medicare and Medicaid Patient Protection Act of 1987 (42 U.S.C. 1320a-7b).* Retrieved from http://www.netreach.net/~wmanning/fasumm.htm

Office of Inspector General (OIG). (1999). *Federal anti-kickback law and regulatory safe harbor.* Retrieved from http://oig.hhs.gov/fraud/docs/safeharborregulations/safefs.htm

Office of Inspector General (OIG). (2004). *An integrated approach to corporate compliance.* Retrieved from http://www.oig.hhs.gov/fraud/docs/complianceguidance/Tab%204E%20Appendx-Final.pdf

Office of Inspector General (OIG). (2006). *Prescription drug plan sponsors' compliance plan.* Retrieved from http://oig.hhs.gov/oei/reports/oei-03-06-00100.pdf

Omdahl, D. J., & Warmack, P. (2009). *Surviving a RAC attack: Strategies to reduce financial risk.* Retrieved from http://www.beaconhealth.org/pdfs/mz80607_summer_ac_brochure_web_3.pdf

Pozgar, G. D. (2007). *Legal aspects of health care administration* (10th ed.). Sudbury, MA: Jones & Bartlett.

Title 31 United States Code (31 USC). 31 U.S.C. §§ 3729 (7) et seq. (1986a).

Title 31 United States Code (31 USC). 31 U.S.C. §3730 (d1) (1986b).

Title 42 United States Code (42 USC). 42 U.S.C. 1320a-7b, 1903m; Title 42 Consolidated Federal Registry (CFR) § 1001.952 (1987a).

Title 42 United States Code (42 USC). 42 U.S.C. CFR 489.24 and 42 CFR 413.65. (1987b).

CHAPTER 17

Healthcare Management Case Studies and Guidelines*

Sharon B. Buchbinder, Donna M. Cox, and Susan Judd Casciani

INTRODUCTION

A case study is the presentation of an organizational scenario. The case will usually present a description of the organization and its market, as well as the major players in the organization and their interactions regarding a specific situation. The objective in analyzing a case study is to develop and test a proposed "solution" to address the described situation. As praised in the *Case Study Handbook from the Harvard Business School*, "The case method is not only the most relevant and practical way to learn managerial skills, it's exciting and fun" (Hammond, 2002, p. 1). Hammond states further:

> Simply stated, the case method calls for discussion of real-life situations that business executives have faced. Casewriters, as good reporters, have written up these situations to present you with the information available to the executives involved. As you review their cases, you will put yourself in the shoes of the managers, analyze the situation, decide what you would do, and . . . [be] prepared to present and support your conclusions. (Hammond, 2002, p. 1)

*Each case study is followed by a list of related chapters. These chapters are listed in order of relevance, the first listed is most closely related to the case study.

Case studies are thus widely used as learning methods in the education of healthcare managers and administrators. Cases require the student to think, reason, develop critical thinking and analytic skills, identify underlying causes of problems, use creative abilities, make decisions, and, in the case of group work, deal with personality conflicts and change. Generally, healthcare management utilizes two types of case studies: **diagnostic** and **descriptive**. In a **diagnostic case study**, a major issue or problem will need to be identified and addressed. A **descriptive case study** usually presents a theme or describes a situation or series of events. There is not necessarily a major problem presented, and thus the objective is more of discussing the theme in terms of management challenges. Regardless of the type, case studies can be daunting at first, and a good strategy for how to tackle the case study is needed.

CASE STUDY ANALYSIS

Based on more than two decades of experience using the case study method in the classroom and in faculty workshops, we recommend that students work in teams and use the following guidelines for case studies.

- Read (or watch) the case carefully several times. The first time you read it, read it quickly, trying to pick up the high-level issues and players. In successive readings, become absorbed in the situation in such a way that you see yourself intimately involved with the personalities, problems, and conflicts.

  TIP: Highlight sentences that may be important in identifying the main issue or theme of the case, and strike out those sentences that are "nice to know" but not critical to the issues in the case. This will help you to filter out the "noise" in the case.

- As the case starts to become more familiar to you, begin to ask yourself the following types of questions and jot down your thoughts:

  1. What is *really* going on this case? Generally speaking, what types of managerial issues are there (e.g., human resources, leadership, legal, confidentiality, quality control, conflict management, etc.)?
  2. Can you describe *in one sentence* the major issue/problem? Make a list of all of the problems you can identify. Analyze this list to see if you can determine how these problems relate to each other. Are some problems the *cause* of other problems? If so, highlight the causal problems to see if a pattern develops. For example, a problem that is usually rather easy to identify is a loss of

revenue, but you must dig deeper—*why* is there a loss of revenue? What is causing it?

- This will lead you to begin to understand the secondary, or underlying, issues. It is important to note here that you may end up with more than one "major" problem; your challenge is to identify the one that has the greatest potential to alter the situation for the better if addressed successfully.

  TIP: Sketch out the relationships between your major and secondary problems in a flowchart-like manner. Apply reasoning to how and why the problems developed; always answer the question, "WHY?" While we only know what the case tells us, we need to think about underlying motivators while we read. Play "devil's advocate" to test these causal relationships to help ensure you are on the right track.

- Conduct some initial research on your identified major problem/issue. The research will likely help frame the major problem and reinforce its relationships to your potential secondary problems. For example, if the problem you have identified deals with employee supervision, research what types of things need to be considered when supervising employees (e.g., performance reviews, hiring/firing processes, related potential legal issues, discrimination and/or diversity issues, mentoring, confidentiality, etc.). Be sure to consider any potential diversity issues and the impact they may have. Only by gaining an understanding of the relevant management issues surrounding the major problem can you begin to develop potential solutions.

  TIP: Utilize academic and trade journals as the major focus of your research. Websites can only get you so far, and academic/trade journals will provide you with more in-depth and directly relevant **information**.

- *Important note:* If you are working in teams on the case study, we highly recommend you complete all of the above steps *individually*, and then come together as a group to compare notes. This will help to ensure you have done the best job of analyzing the case.

- Now that you have identified the major problem, decide from which management level you want to "solve" the problem. Is the problem best addressed from a departmental perspective (e.g., supervisor, director, manager); a senior executive perspective (e.g., vice presidents); an organizational perspective (e.g., CEO, board of directors); or perhaps from an outside perspective (e.g., consultant)? Note that in order to best make this decision, you *must* understand the roles and responsibilities of each of these levels as they relate to the problem and identify the strengths and weaknesses of each approach.

■ Identify at least two, but no more than three, potential alternative "solutions" to address the major problem *from the management level you have selected.* This is where you are being asked to "think outside of the box." Were there possibilities not suggested by the text? How would each of these solutions improve the situation, and to what degree? Identify the strengths and weaknesses of each approach. The best choice may not be affordable; as managers we have to "satisfice," that is, make the best choice available at that time. Is one more cost-effective than the other(s)? Would one of them take too long to implement before experiencing the needed results? Do you have the expertise and resources to implement the solution? In developing your alternative solutions, keep in mind the strengths and weaknesses of the organization *as they relate to the major problem.* Having a great community reputation, for example, will likely have little bearing on whether you should fire the head of surgery. However, significant financial reserves may be relevant in trying to increase access for patients in outlying areas. Remember, there is no one right or wrong solution, only better or worse solutions. The difference will be in how you analyze and present them.

■ Select the best alternative solution to implement. In the step above, you analyzed each potential alternative in terms of the strengths and weaknesses of each. Through this process it should have become evident which alternative has the best chance of successfully addressing the major problem. Your final challenge is to identify *how* and *when* you will know whether your proposed alternative solution worked. To do this, you must identify ways to evaluate your solution. For example, if the desired outcome of your solution is increased revenue, when will this occur, and to what degree? Increased revenue will be one of your evaluation metrics, but you will need to outline specifically what you expect to happen. A sufficient response in this example could be "increase revenue by 5% by end of third quarter." Note that regardless of which metrics you choose, you need to be able to *measure* them. At this point in the case it may be necessary to "assume" some things. For example, if a desired outcome is increased patient satisfaction, you can assume the organization already measures this and simply state your expected quantitative improvement and time frame (e.g., "improve patient satisfaction by 10 percentage points within six months"). However, be sure to *state any assumptions* you are making (e.g., "We assume the organization already tracks patient satisfaction and it is currently at 30%").

CASE STUDY WRITE-UP

Prepare a written report of the case using the following format.

Background Statement

What is going on in this case *as it relates to the identified major problem*? What are (only) the key points the reader needs to know in order to understand how you will "solve" the case? Summarize the scenario in your own words—do not simply regurgitate the case. Briefly describe the organization, setting, situation, who is involved, who decides what, and so on.

Major Problems and Secondary Issues

Specifically identify the major and secondary problems. What are the real issues? What are the differences? Can secondary issues become major problems? Present analysis of the causes and effects. Fully explain your reasoning.

Your Role

In a sentence or short paragraph, declare from which role you will address the major problem, whether you are a senior manager, departmental manager, or an outside consultant called in to advise. Regardless of your choice, you *must* justify in writing *why* you chose that role. What are the advantages and disadvantages of your selected role? Be specific.

Organizational Strengths and Weaknesses

Identify the strengths and weaknesses that exist *in relation to the major problem*. Again, your focus here should be in describing what the organization is capable of doing (and not capable of doing) with respect to addressing the major problem. Thus, the identified strengths and weaknesses should include those at the managerial level of the problem. For example, if you have chosen to address the problem from the departmental perspective and the department is understaffed, that is a weakness worthy of mentioning. Be sure to remember to include any strengths/weaknesses that may be related to diversity issues.

Alternatives and Recommended Solutions

Describe the two to three alternative solutions you came up with. What feasible strategies would you recommend? What are the pros and cons? State what should be done—why, how, and by whom. Be specific.

Evaluation

How will you know when you've gotten there? There must be measurable goals put in place with the recommendations. Money is easiest to measure; what else can be measured? What evaluation plan would you put in place to assess whether you are reaching your goals?

> *TIP:* Write this section as if you were trying to "sell" your proposed solution to the organization. Convince the reader that your proposed solution is the best available and that it will work as planned. Make sure the goals you identify are worth the effort required to achieve them!

TEAM STRUCTURE AND PROCESS FOR COMPLETION

We recommend that teams select a team leader and a team recorder, although *all* should take notes. The team should decide how to divide the tasks to be accomplished. In our classes, we expect to see written responses to the aforementioned questions, and the written, typed case studies to be a minimum of five pages long. Teams should indicate who had responsibility for different tasks/sections on the written materials that are handed in.

Team findings should be presented in no more than 10 minutes to the rest of the class. Individual grades are given for each of the student's designated sections and a group grade for the case study as a whole from peers on the presentation, plus teammates are required to grade each other's efforts and teamwork within the group. The average of the three grades becomes each individual's case study grade. Copies of forms utilized for each evaluation (individual sections, group presentation, and teamwork) are provided in this chapter (Figure 17-1, Figure 17-2, and Figure 17-3).

Guidelines for Effective Participation

1. Attend all team sessions. Eighty percent of life is showing up. It's important here too.
2. Prepare before coming to team sessions, and take careful notes. Think about the project and be prepared for each session.
3. Help establish the purpose of the session and the direction to be followed by the group.
4. Have an open mind and be willing to modify your conclusions. Welcome the stimulation of having your ideas challenged.
5. Strike a balance between your speaking time and that of others.
6. Be respectful, considerate, and tactful of the feelings of others—especially when you disagree.
7. Present the substance of your thinking concisely and to the point.
8. Help the team reach some conclusions within the allotted time.
9. Really pull your weight on the team. Assist in accomplishing the work of the team by putting the needs of the group ahead of your own needs.
10. *Have fun!*

	A Level	B Level	C Level	D Level
Introduction (10 pts)	The section introduction • Was well organized • Smoothly pulled the reader into the topic • Presented the main focus of the case study section • Included adequate content • Was written for the correct audience	The section introduction had one limitation: • Disorganized • Not smooth • Did not present the main focus of the case study section • Too detailed or too sketchy • Rocky first sentences	The section introduction had two of these limitations: • Disorganized • Not smooth • Did not present the main focus of the case study section • Too detailed or too sketchy • Rocky first sentences	The section introduction had three or more limitations listed at left or required major changes
Content (20 pts)	The content of the case study section • Was clear • Had a unified focus • Focused on important information • Adequately explained concepts • Was correct	The content of the case study section had one of these limitations: • Hard to understand • Included irrelevant or too much detailed information • Failed to explain concepts • Had a disjointed focus • Incorrect information	The content of the case study section had two of these limitations: • Hard to understand • Included irrelevant or too much detailed information • Failed to explain concepts • Had a disjointed focus • Incorrect information	The content of the case study section was not clearly written and difficult to understand OR had three or more limitations listed at left
Paragraph organization (20 pts)	Paragraphs in the case study section • Had clear topic sentences • Were about a single topic • Were organized at the paragraph level • Had transitions from one paragraph to another	Paragraphs in the case study section had one of the following limitations: • Poor topic sentences • Run-on paragraphs or paragraphs were too brief • Lacked organization within the paragraph • Lacked transitions from one paragraph to another	Paragraphs in the case study section had two of these limitations: • Poor topic sentences • Run-on paragraphs or paragraphs were too brief • Lacked organization within the paragraph • Lacked transitions from one paragraph to another	Paragraphs in the case study section had three or more of the limitations at left
Case study section organization (20 pts)	The case study section's organization • Was easy to follow • Was presented in a logical manner • Integrated information • Summarized information when needed • Used headers	The case study section had one of the following limitations: • Organization was not logical • Information was not consistently integrated together • Information was not summarized when needed • Headers were missing	The case study section had two of the following limitations: • Organization was not logical • Information was not consistently integrated together • Information was not summarized when needed • Headers were missing	The case study section was disorganized and illogical OR had three or more of the limitations listed at left.
Writing style (10 pts)	The style of writing is professional • Easy to understand • Uses appropriate vocabulary • Shows mature syntax style	Writing is affected by one of the following limitations: • Jargon • Wordiness • Redundant phrasing • Awkward syntax structures • Choppy sentences • Run-on sentences • Incorrect use of vocabulary	Writing is affected by two of the following limitations: • Vocabulary jargon • Wordiness • Redundant phrasing • Awkward syntax structures • Choppy sentences • Run-on sentences • Incorrect use of vocabulary	Writing is affected by three or more limitations occurring three or more times
Writing mechanics (10 pts)	The case study section is free of spelling, grammar, and punctuation errors.	The case study section has fewer than 5 errors in spelling, grammar, or punctuation.	The case study section has 6–10 errors in spelling, grammar, or punctuation.	The case study section has more than 10 errors in spelling, grammar, or punctuation.
APA (10 pts)	All APA rules are followed for citations, numbers, quotes, references, headers, etc.	The case study section has fewer than 5 APA rule errors.	The case study section has 6–10 APA rule errors.	The case study section has more than 10 APA rule errors.

FIGURE 17-1 Detailed Rubric for Grading Written Case Studies

Source: With permission of Sharon Glennen.

PEER EVALUATION CRITERIA FOR CASE STUDY PRESENTATIONS SCORING SHEET	
Presentation Title and Author's Name	**Your Name**
Use a scale of 1 to 10, where 1 is poor and 10 is excellent. **(You must explain any scores below 3 and above 8.)**	
How well did the presenter:	**Points**
Indicate the purpose of the presentation and its relevance to the course?	0
Ensure the presentation was relevant to the current state of health care?	0
Demonstrate knowledge about the *case study*?	0
Contribute to peer knowledge?	0
Use proper grammar, punctuation, and vocabulary?	0
Adhere to length constraints (*10 slides maximum*, excluding references)?	0
Use current references and cite properly in presentation?	0
Provide appropriate main points?	0
Use legible fonts with appropriate colors/background and clip art?	0
Accomplish the stated objectives?	0
TOTAL	**0**
Comments	

FIGURE 17-2 Peer Evaluation Criteria for Group Presentations

CONFIDENTIAL TEAMMATE EVALUATION CRITERIA			
Use a scale of 1 to 10, where 1 is poor and 10 is excellent. **(Do NOT evaluate yourself.)**			
How well did your teammates:	**Name**	**Name**	**Name**
Attend all team sessions?	0	0	0
Prepare for each session?	0	0	0
Work collaboratively to identify and meet session goals?	0	0	0
Actively participate in group discussions?	0	0	0
Keep an open mind or modify opinions or conclusions to keep the project moving?	0	0	0
Present ideas concisely?	0	0	0
Submit assigned work on time?	0	0	0
Interact with teammates in a respectful, considerate, and tactful manner?	0	0	0
Fulfill responsibilities as agreed?	0	0	0
Work actively to achieve group consensus on issues/problems?	0	0	0
TOTAL	0	0	0
Would you be willing to work with this teammate again on another team? (YES or NO)			
(You must evaluate ALL teammates and explain any scores below 3 and above 8.)			

FIGURE 17-3 Confidential Teammate Evaluation Form

REFERENCES

Hammond, J. S. (2002, April 16). Learning by the case method. *Harvard Business Review*, Industry and Background Note 9-376-241. Retrieved from http://hbr.org/product/learning-by-the-case-method/an/376241-PDF-ENG?N=0&Ntt=Case+method&referral=00269&cm_sp=endeca-_-spotlight-_-link

Oops Is Not an Option—Case for Chapter 16

Maron J. Boohaker

Bill Salamander is a consultant working in the medical records department of a medical center. As would any vendor doing business with this hospital, Bill's company has signed a Business Associate Agreement. This agreement confirms that the vendor will abide by the hospital's compliance and Health Insurance Portability and Accountability Act (HIPAA) policies.

Bill has friends all through town, and they know how much access he has to patient information. One such friend is a personal injury attorney, Anna Anywaican. This attorney is full of ideas. One of her schemes includes a network of associates at hospitals around the state. She hadn't yet made inroads into this one facility, but now she had Bill.

It was a simple plan—Bill would provide Anna access to trauma patients, and for every case he recruited, she would award him 10% of any monies she recovered.

In his first assignment, Bill was paid $25,000 after Anna's client accepted a settlement. However, Bill still had one problem. His access to the medical records was limited to post-discharge. Sometimes, a trauma patient's record would not arrive to the medical records department for months. Bill had to find help.

Bill decided to go to the Emergency Room and scout the third-shift employees. Eventually, he comes to you, Micah Makaliving. On your break, he asks you to provide him access to the patients who register in the ER as trauma patients. He offers you two choices: either pass out Anna Anywaican's cards or hand him a list of patient names and addresses. Bill will pay you 50% of what he makes. Micah, what will you do?

DISCUSSION QUESTIONS

1. What law is Bill violating?

2. Why was this law enacted?

3. What are the penalties for violating these laws?

4. If you agree to help out and Bill and Anna get caught, what do you think is the probability that they will roll over and give you up to the authorities?

5. Do you think you should be updating your resume and looking for a new job? Or should you find out where the whistle-blower number is?

6. Do you think Bill and Anna should be thinking about how they'll make new friends in jail?

Building a Better
MIS-Trap—Case for Chapter 8

Sharon B. Buchbinder

You are the CEO of a large health services organization (HSO) in Florida. Your HSO has inpatient and outpatient facilities, home healthcare services, and every other service your patient population needs. You also have a world-renowned AIDS treatment center that has been considered by many to be a model for the rest of the United States. Your HSO has always enjoyed an excellent reputation, and your quality of care is known to be excellent. You have been very happy in your work, knowing that your HSO provides good care to people who truly need it in a caring and cost-effective manner.

Your HSO has recently been featured in every media vehicle known to every man, woman, and child in the United States and beyond. The reason: someone downloaded the names of 4,000 HIV+ patients who had been seen in your world-renowned HIV clinic and sent the list to newspapers, magazines, and the Internet.

You and your board of trustees are completely blown away. The board is furious and wants to fire you. You have been able to convince them that they need to keep you on to fix the HSO's management information system (MIS). Their last words to you were "You had *better* come back with plans for building a better MIS, or you're fired!"

You hire a computer security consultant, and she comes into your organization under disguise as a nurse manager to help you determine where the security leak might be. She returns to you in three days with the following report.

"While I was undercover in your organization for a mere three days, I observed the following breaches in computer security. These are the highlights (or lowlights):

- Nurses log in with their passwords, walk away, and leave the system open and up and running;
- Dr. Jones leaves his password taped to the PC on a piece of paper;
- Fax machines and printers are often in areas of high traffic and in rooms without locks;

- With my one password, I had remote access to every database in the hospital, including Human Resources, from my home;
- There are no programs reminding people to change their passwords on a regular basis;
- When I pretended to forget my password, other nurses gave me theirs; and
- When I requested sensitive patient files on flash drive, even after this incident, people rarely questioned me.

In short, you have a major problem with your MIS—and your staff!"
What should you do?

DISCUSSION QUESTIONS

1. What law is being violated by the employees at this health services organization?

2. Why was this law enacted?

3. What are the penalties for violating this law?

4. If an employee shares confidential medical information about a celebrity and is caught, what should the penalty be?

5. Do you think you should be updating your resume and looking for a new job?

The Case of the Complacent Employee—Case for Chapter 12

Sharon B. Buchbinder

It was the end of an exhausting Wednesday for Bob Miller. He had spent all day with a 10-year-old girl who kept saying she was going home and taking all the pills she could find to kill herself. He had kept talking with her, trying to determine what had triggered this response, as he'd simultaneously searched for her mother by phone. When the mother had arrived at his office, panic-stricken and crying, she had also been in need of support. It was four o'clock by the time the mother and daughter left. Now he had to document everything.

Bob looked up from the pile of papers on his desk as his office door opened. His boss stood there in her signature lime green suit, looking grim.

"Harriet! What brings you out today?"

She closed the door and looked around the cramped office.

"Do you have a chair, Bob? It would be good if I could sit down and chat with you."

"Um, sure, hold on a minute."

Bob stood up and grabbed a pile of papers off the threadbare visitor's chair. "There you go."

This couldn't be good. Not only were Harriet's visits rare, but when she did appear at Louisa May Alcott Elementary School, they were always grab-and-grins, and then out she went. This was the first time she'd ever sat down in his broom closet of an office.

"So, Bob, how are you doing?" Her eyes bored into his head.

"Well, you know, we're really busy here. Lots of kids with problems, families in crises, almost nonexistent support systems, no money, no resources, the usual."

Harriet nodded, still staring at Bob.

Sweat trickled down his back. The office air-conditioner had broken two weeks before. He'd meant to write up a work order but had been too busy. Today, for certain, after Harriet left, he was doing it.

"Bob, I feel really badly about this, and it's not as if we haven't given it a lot of thought. Administration has decided to cut your position."

"What?"

"There doesn't seem to be enough work here for a full-time child psychologist, Bob. This school will be covered part-time by a psychologist from Melville Middle School."

This can't be happening to me, Bob thought. I've fallen asleep at my desk and I'm having a nightmare. He pinched his leg under the desk. *Nope. That hurt.*

"I've been overworked here from day one," Bob said. "I never leave here before six o'clock. The principal told me the teachers and the kids love me! How did administration make this decision?"

"Remember those e-mails we sent out, asking you to complete those workload reports? You never answered them."

"Who has time to fill out workload reports when a suicidal child is sitting in your office, crying her heart out?"

"How about the monthly forms we asked you to complete, describing the population you serve and the kinds of problems you're seeing?"

"I have a hard enough time trying to keep up with the Medicaid paperwork so we can get some kind of reimbursement for the work I do here!"

"And, the newsletter, Bob? We never got any submissions from you."

"That piece of trash?"

Harriet flinched. "Some people think it's a very important form of communication for our school mental health professionals."

Bob had forgotten Harriet was the editor of "that piece of trash."

"Have you spoken to the principal? She loves me," he said. "The teachers love me. The kids love me! What are they going to do without me?"

"Principal Daniels did tell me she thought you were working hard, Bob. But, she also said she had no idea how many kids you were seeing, or how often. She said you pretty much kept to yourself."

"Kept to myself? Yeah, you could say that! I'm up to my eyeballs in work, I spend every day with kids in crisis, the most emotionally draining work in the world, and I have an air-conditioner that died two weeks ago! When I eat lunch, it's at my desk, because I'm trying to keep up with the paperwork between crying, screaming kids, or being pulled into classrooms to help with a crisis, or to evaluate kids that teachers are worried about. Keep to myself? I can't even find myself!"

"I'm sorry, Bob. It's nothing personal."

Harriet stood to leave and Bob jumped to his feet.

"Why didn't you say something sooner? I've been doing my job! What could I have done differently?"

DISCUSSION QUESTIONS

1. Whose responsibility should it be to complete those reports? Explain your answer.

2. Is Bob right? Was he really doing his job? Provide a rationale for your answer.

3. Describe what Bob should have done differently.

4. Did Harriet handle this termination properly? Explain your answer.

5. What part did Harriet play in this scenario? Is she a good manager? Provide a rationale for your responses.

The Brawler—Case for Chapters 11 and 12

Sharon B. Buchbinder and Dale Buchbinder

Dr. O'Connor was known for his hot temper and drinking. Although he claimed never to come to work under the influence, nurses, physicians, and other coworkers had their doubts, and several expressed their alarm to their supervisors. The emergency room needed coverage, and it was hard to find physicians who would work the graveyard shift, so little was done to address these concerns. One night, Dr. O'Connor walked across a clearly marked wet floor that the custodian had just mopped. When the angry janitor protested loudly and pointed to the bright yellow sign and the offending footprints, Dr. O'Connor took a swing at the other man and a fistfight ensued.

DISCUSSION QUESTIONS

1. What should the hospital do to deal with the good doctor? Who should handle this?

2. What role, if any, did the janitor play in this incident? What could he have done differently?

3. Where should Dr. O'Connor be referred—anger management, Alcoholics Anonymous, psychiatric evaluation? Provide a rationale for your response.

4. How can this incident be turned into a "teachable moment" for the staff, physicians, and others?

5. How could this have been prevented?

ADDITIONAL RESOURCES

DesRoches, C. M., Rao, S. R., Fromson, J. A., Birnbaum, R. J., Iezzoni, L., Vogeli, C., et al. (2010). Physicians' perceptions, preparedness for reporting, and experiences related to impaired and incompetent colleagues. *Journal of the American Medical Association, 304*(2), 187–193.

Gillespie, G. L. (2008). Consequences of violence exposures by emergency nurses. *Journal of Aggression, Maltreatment & Trauma, 16*(4), 409–418.

Hesketh, K. L., Duncan, S. M., Estabrooks, C. A., Reimer, M. A., Giovannetti, P., Hyndman, K., et al. (2003). Workplace violence in Alberta and British Columbia hospitals. *Health Policy, 63,* 311–321.

Kowalenko, T., Walters, B. L., Khare, R. K., & Compton, S. (2005). Workplace violence: A survey of emergency physicians in the state of Michigan. *Annals of Emergency Medicine, 46*(2), 142–147.

End Days—Case for Chapter 15

Sharon B. Buchbinder and Dale Buchbinder

In 2005, Hurricane Katrina struck New Orleans and left a path of destruction and devastation. Caught in the midst of this were hundreds of healthcare professionals who were forced to make difficult and, in one highly publicized case, horrific choices of life and death for patients under their care. Dr. Anna Maria Pou, a cancer specialist, stayed with her critically ill patients at Memorial Hospital despite the lack of electricity, diminishing supplies of water, and rising temperatures. Feeling she had no choice but to relieve their suffering, she administered pain medications to four elderly patients. The for-profit hospital lost 34 patients in the days following Katrina, four of whom were Dr. Pou's. In the aftermath of the disaster, inquiries began, and in July 2006, Dr. Pou was accused, but never charged, of murder (Okie, 2009). Dr. Pou was considered a hero, not a mass murderer, by many citizens of New Orleans. At a time when others abandoned patients, she stayed with them in the tropical heat and the darkness. The grand jury failed to indict her, but the debate continues, with healthcare professionals being uncertain about how to handle such situations (Nossiter, 2007). Many wonder if they, too, will be considered criminals if they make the choice to give their patients comfort *in extremis*.

DISCUSSION QUESTIONS

1. What should healthcare professionals do in times of disaster?

2. How does this case relate to the concepts of respect for persons, beneficence, nonmaleficence, and justice?

3. What are the pros and cons for them in terms of their responsibilities in caring for their patients in such situations?

4. Why did Dr. Pou feel she fulfilled her provider rights and responsibilities?

ADDITIONAL RESOURCES

Nossiter, A. (2007, July 25). Grand jury won't indict doctor in hurricane deaths. *New York Times.* Retrieved from http://www.nytimes.com/2007/07/25/us/25doctor.html

Okie, S. (2009). Dr. Pou and the hurricane: Implications for patient care during disasters. *New England Journal of Medicine, 358*(1), 1–5.

I Love You...Forever—Case for Chapters 12 and 11

Sharon B. Buchbinder and Dale Buchbinder

Nurse Practitioner Nancy Masters broke up with her control freak boyfriend, Joe Jerque, after a three-year relationship that was going nowhere but down. Despite her repeated pleas for counseling, he refused help, and his short temper and terrifying tantrums were only getting worse. Fearful of retaliation, she moved out while he was at work, didn't leave a forwarding address, and changed her phone number and e-mail address. One evening as she walked to her car in the poorly lit parking lot next to the clinic where she worked, Joe showed up and confronted her, begging to be taken back. She told him it was over and to please leave her alone. The following night, Joe appeared again, and again she told him to go away. On the third evening, she asked the security guard to walk her to her car. When she arrived at her vehicle, she found a note under her windshield wiper alongside an envelope: "I will never let you go. You are mine forever, even in death." Inside the envelope was a .38 caliber bullet. Terrified, she immediately called the police to report the incidents, and the security guard took the matter to his supervisor. The clinic administrator told Nancy and the security guard that it was a personal matter she had to pursue with the police and the legal system, and that the clinic was not responsible for her safety once she left the premises. Nancy is terrified; she is familiar with the stalking literature. There is a direct association between the number of stalking incidents and the likelihood of violence—including homicide. She petitions the court and obtains a restraining order against Joe, but worries that he will violate it. She is considering getting a permit to carry a concealed weapon for self-protection.

DISCUSSION QUESTIONS

1. What is the clinic's responsibility in these types of situations?

2. What could the clinic do to help remedy the situation?

3. What do you recommend that Nancy do above and beyond what has already been done?

4. Do you think Nancy is wise in considering carrying a gun to the clinic?

ADDITIONAL RESOURCES

Baum, K., Catalano, S., & Rose, K. (2009). *Stalking victimization in the United States.* U.S. Department of Justice, Office of Justice Programs, Bureau of Justice Statistics, Special Report. Retrieved from http://www.ovw.usdoj.gov/docs/stalking-victimization.pdf

Centers for Disease Control and Prevention, National Institute for Occupational Safety and Health (NIOSH). (n.d.). *Women's safety and health issues at work.* Retrieved from http://www.cdc.gov/niosh/docs/2001-123/pdfs/2001-123.pdf

Concannon, D. (2005). The association between stalking and violence in interpersonal relationships. *Dissertation Abstracts International: Section B: The Sciences and Engineering, 67*(2-B), 2006, 1203.

Hoskins, A. B. (2005). Occupational injuries, illnesses, and fatalities among women. *Monthly Labor Review, 128*(10), 31–37. Retrieved from http://www.bls.gov/opub/mlr/2005/10/art4full.pdf

Mullen, P. E., Mackenzie, R., Ogloff, J. R. P., Pathé, M., McEwan, T., & Purcell, R. (2006). Assessing and managing the risks in the stalking situation. *Journal of the American Academy of Psychiatry Law, 34*(4), 439–450.

Mullen, P. E., Pathé, M., & Purcell, R. (2001). Stalking: New constructions of human behavior. *Australian and New Zealand of Psychiatry, 35*(1), 9–16.

U.S. Department of Justice, Office of Violence Against Women (OVW). (n.d.). *Violence Against Women Act (VAWA) offenses.* Retrieved from http://www.ovw.usdoj.gov/docs/federal_violence.pdf

Wattendorf, G. E. (2000, March). Stalking-investigation strategies. *FBI Law Enforcement Bulletin, 69*(3), 10–14. Retrieved from http://www.fbi.gov/stats-services/publications/law-enforcement-bulletin/2000-pdfs/mar00leb.pdf

Managing Healthcare Professionals— Mini-Case Studies for Chapter 11

Sharon B. Buchbinder and Dale Buchbinder

1. You are a new administrator at Jonestown Medical Center. You receive a telephone call from the nurse manager of the emergency room. Dr. Smith, an emergency room physician who is an employee of your hospital, has just reported for duty. The nurse manager suspects that Dr. Smith is intoxicated. What do you do?

2. You are the CEO of Sleepy Hollow Retirement Community and Nursing Center. A resident's family has come to you to complain that their loved one, who is on pain medication, is in intolerable pain. Her medications appear not to be working anymore. One of the family members states, "My 90-year-old mother saw the nurse put the pain medicine in her pocket." What do you do?

3. You are the practice manager of Docs R Us, Ltd., a large multispecialty medical practice employing more than 100 physicians. You are conducting a random review of billing for doctors in the practice and you discover that one of the internists in your group who treats mostly Medicare recipients has been checking off the wrong code for her procedures on the billing form. The procedures on the patient record do not match the billing form codes. You pull up her files for the past 3 months and find a pattern of upcoding. When you meet with her to review this miscoding, she becomes very defensive and angry. What do you do?

4. You are the assistant director of the hospital medical staff office at the Rural Outreach Community Hospital in a tiny town in Arkansas. It is your job to verify physician credentials for staff privileges. Your hospital receives an application from a physician for staff privileges. On his application, it states that he graduated from medical school in El Salvador. When you call to verify this, you are told that the medical school burned down two years ago and all the records were destroyed. What do you do?

5. You are a new administrator at a hospital, well known for pulmonary medicine. The physicians in the ICU, the ER, and the department of pulmonary medicine have

demanded to meet with you about the shortage of respiratory therapists. You stall them for 48 hours so you can gather data. What types of information will you need to collect to have an intelligent conversation with this powerful group of physicians?

6. Dr. White ordered an unusual dose of a medication. May Patterson, RN, sees the order and believes it to be the wrong dose. She calls Dr. White, who insists that she give the medication—as written. Nurse Patterson calls you, the administrator on call for the weekend, to resolve this crisis. What do you do?

Problems with the Pre-Admission Call Center—Case for Chapters 13 and 10

Sharon B. Buchbinder and Dale Buchbinder

South Street Hospital (SSH) is one of 12 hospitals in the Great West Hospital System, a not-for-profit healthcare system. SSH serves a largely blue-collar and elderly population. This patient-centric hospital prides itself on high patient satisfaction scores and good financial management.

Dr. Canton is a busy colorectal surgeon who has brought hundreds of cases to SSH in the past year. The day before one of his patients, Mr. Gutsy, was scheduled for an extensive bowel resection, Dr. Canton's office received an irate phone call from the patient stating that he was not having the surgery "because a woman from SSH called and demanded he bring money to the admitting center." Shocked, Dr. Canton personally called the patient to find out what happened.

Mr. Gutsy stated that a woman "insisted that I bring cash or credit cards with me to pay my copayment. I have Medicare and other insurance. There are *no* copays. The more I tried to explain that to the woman, the nastier she became."

Dr. Canton apologized and asked if Mr. Gutsy was able to recall the woman's name.

"No, she didn't give me a name, but she sure gave me attitude." Despite Dr. Canton's best efforts, the patient said he wasn't going *anywhere* that made these types of demands.

Dr. Canton complained to the chairman of surgery, Dr. Kutup, who in turn called the head of SSH pre-admissions, Mrs. Mintz. She was appalled and said, "No one makes those calls from *this* hospital. Great West has a corporate call center for all 12 hospitals in the system. They're *supposed* to be following a script." Mrs. Mintz told Dr. Kutup she'd look into it and get back to him ASAP.

A short time later, Dr. Kutup was scrubbing for his next case and related the story to an anesthesiologist, Dr. Gasser.

Dr. Gasser laughed and said, "Tell your patient they did the same thing to me—but they told me to bring $2,000 in cash to admissions. I almost asked them if they wanted it in unmarked bills."

"Did you bring the money?"

"No, I did *not*. I knew I had coverage, so I just agreed with the woman and ignored her."

"Well, you work here, you're one of their physicians, and they told you that—which makes me think they're doing this to everyone." Dr. Canton shook his head. "Will you tell Mrs. Mintz about this with me?"

"Sure, just don't ask me for my credit card or gold bullion."

The next day, Drs. Kutup, Canton, and Gasser sat down with Mrs. Mintz.

"When I talked to Mr. Count de Money at headquarters, he said the call center used a script and they were 'just following it.'" Mrs. Mintz shook her head. "I tried to tell him that it wasn't true, that they were *harassing* people and patients were complaining—but more will just vote with their feet and go elsewhere. He asked me if I thought the system should lose money on these deadbeats? I tried to reason with him, but he hung up on me! Great West talks a good game about how we're a '*team with 12 hospitals.*' He didn't treat me like a member of the team. He was nasty—and he's in charge of the call center!"

Dr. Canton said, "I have privileges at another hospital. If they don't stop this, I'll be taking my cases there."

Dr. Kutup pointed at his colleague. "This guy is one of our busiest surgeons. SSH is going to lose a *lot* of business if something isn't done about this."

DISCUSSION QUESTIONS

1. Who should Dr. Kutup and Mrs. Mintz approach next with this problem? Provide a rationale for your choice(s).

2. Is Mr. Count de Money responding in an emotionally intelligent way to Mrs. Mintz and her concerns? What aspects of emotional contagion do you think apply to this case?

3. What type of team should SSH form to address this problem? Who should be selected to be on this team? Provide a rationale for your choices.

4. Identify and delineate the top three issues that the team should address in its deliberations.

5. Since SSH is part of the larger hospital system, who should be the person designated to take the matter to corporate headquarters?

6. How should the team evaluate whether a change in corporate policy is needed? Who should take the lead on this evaluation?

Such a Nice Young Man—Case for Chapters 11 and 12

Sharon B. Buchbinder and Dale Buchbinder

Mrs. Davenport is a vivacious septuagenarian living in Whispering Willows Continuing Care Retirement Community. An attractive lady, she spends her days with a large group of friends, playing cards and going on day trips to museums and shows. She enjoys kidding around with the staff, especially Joe, who works in the dining room. A handsome young man, she tells him that he reminds her of her dearly departed husband and calls him "eye-candy." One day, when she doesn't appear for her bridge game, her best friend, Mrs. Atkins, goes to her apartment and knocks on her door—which swings open. Mrs. Davenport is in bed, sobbing. When Mrs. Atkins asks her what's wrong, all Mrs. Davenport can say is, "I thought he was such a nice young man." Mrs. Atkins summons help, and the Nursing Home Administrator (NHA) arrives with an RN from the Nursing Center. Mrs. Davenport will not get out of bed and refuses to get out from under the covers. The NHA is very concerned and suspicious. To Mrs. Davenport's horror, the NHA calls the police. Mrs. Davenport refuses to speak to the RN or the female police officer and sits in her bed, weeping. The NHA tries to convince the shaking resident to go to the ER. Mrs. Davenport shakes her head and says, "No, no, no! It's too shameful. I brought it on myself. Just go away. Please. Just leave me alone." Leaving the RN at the bedside to secure the scene, the NHA and the police officer step out into the hall to discuss the next steps. The police officer asks to speak with Joe. The NHA sends the Administrator in Training (AIT) to find Joe and bring him to the NHA's office—but the AIT returns and reports he is not in the dining room, and a coworker reported seeing Joe jump into his car and take off like a "bat out of hell." Upon review of Joe's criminal background check at hire, all that appear are minor misdemeanors. Can Whispering Willows be sure they are not responsible for hiring a sexual predator? Or is Joe just a victim of circumstances?

DISCUSSION QUESTIONS

1. What are the facts in this situation? What is known and not known so far?

2. What steps should be taken to investigate this further?

3. Do you think the NHA did the correct thing by bringing in the police?

4. Do we know if elder sexual abuse has taken place?

5. Circumstantial evidence seems to point to Joe as the perpetrator of this offense. What does the police officer have to do to ensure collection of physical evidence to support her case?

6. What should the facility do to train the staff and try to prevent these types of incidents from happening again?

7. What liability does Whispering Willows have in this case? Be sure to check out the resources below before answering this question.

ADDITIONAL RESOURCES

ABC2 News. (2010, August 23). Police investigating the rape of an assisted living facility resident. Retrieved from http://www.abc2news.com/dpp/news/national/police-investigating-the-rape-of-an-assisted-living-facility-resident

Burgess, A. W. (2006, December). *Elderly victims of sexual abuse and their offenders.* Retrieved from http://www.ncjrs.gov/pdffiles1/nij/grants/216550.pdf

National Sexual Violence Resource Center. Retrieved from http://www.nsvrc.org/

Ovalle, D. (2008, January 16). Assisted-living facility investigated after rape alleged. Retrieved from http://ombudsman.myflorida.com/press/011608.pdf

Rosenfeld, J. (2010). Nursing home abuse blog: Sexual abuse and assault. http://www.nursinghomesabuseblog.com/sexual-abuse-assault/

Russell, R. (2010, November 18). I-Team: Janitor charged with rape had personal relationship with employer. Retrieved from http://www.khou.com/news/investigative/khou-109056619.html

Schlachtenhaufen, M. (2009, March 3). Report backs allegations against nursing home: Alleged rapist dies days after being charged. Retrieved from http://www.edmondsun.com/local/x1472022038/Report-backs-allegations-against-nursing-home

Sundowner or Victim?—Case for Chapter 15

Sharon B. Buchbinder and Dale Buchbinder

Mr. Nathan, an elderly male patient hospitalized for prostatic surgery, woke up in the middle of the night, dressed himself, and attempted to leave the nursing unit. An RN approached him to ask him where he was going and tried to detain him. He shoved the woman into a wall and she struck her head, sustaining a concussion. The unit clerk called for help. The patient ran toward the exit and was stopped by two male orderlies and a security guard. As they took him by the arms, he screamed, "I'm being held prisoner! I have the right to leave!" A physician wrote restraining orders to be checked in an hour, and the patient was given an intramuscular sedative. Mr. Nathan sustained some bruises and abrasions in the struggle. The nurse was taken to the ER and was out of work for two weeks. The patient is now suing the hospital for false imprisonment and aggravated assault.

DISCUSSION QUESTIONS

1. What are the known facts in this situation? What else may be going on?

2. What are the responsibilities of the hospital with regard to caring for Mr. Nathan?

3. What should the hospital do about the nurse's injuries?

4. Was the physician justified in giving the patient a sedative and ordering physical restraints? Provide a rationale for your position.

5. Do you think his suit will hold up in court? Why or why not?

ADDITIONAL RESOURCES

False imprisonment: Nursing Law. (2002, May). Home patient can sue. (2007, April 1). *Free Library*. Retrieved from http://www.highbeam.com/doc/1G1-161077192.html

Haldol given, patient taken to nursing home: No battery, false imprisonment. (2002, May). *Legal Eagle Eye Newsletter for the Nursing Profession.* Retrieved from http://www.nursinglaw.com/haldol.pdf

Lanza, M. L., Zeiss, R., & Rierdan, J. (2006). Violence against psychiatric nurses: Sensitive research as a science and intervention. *Contemporary Nurse, 21*(1), 71–84.

Lippman, M. (2007). *Contemporary criminal law: Cases, concepts and controversies.* Thousand Oaks, CA: Sage.

Sanders, R. (2003, December). Double offense problems in kidnapping and false imprisonment cases. *The Florida Bar Journal, 77*(11), 10–17.

Tammello, A. D. (2001, April). TX: Nurse supervisor blocks exit with chair: Terminated nurse sues for false imprisonment. *Nursing Law's Regan Report, 41*(11), 3.

Tammello, A. D. (2008, March). Nurse sued employer & dr. for assault/false imprisonment by dr. Case on point: Baker v. Cook Children's Physician Net. *Nursing Law's Regan Report, 48*(10), 4.

All Children's Pediatrics: Changing with the Times—Case for Chapter 6

Ruth Chavez

Part I

Dr. Quon, president of All Children's Pediatrics (ACP), started the business meeting at the annual retreat for his single-specialty group. As usual, there was a full slate of topics to discuss, ranging from continuing medical education (CME) and best practices to negotiating contracts with health insurance companies. ACP had forged collaborative partnerships with several obstetricians/gynecologists throughout the region.

"The main topic for discussion this morning is marketing. In order to maintain and grow the practice, it is necessary to think about ways to incorporate a marketing mindset. What does the group think about this?"

Dr. Carter, a senior member of the practice, responded harshly to Dr. Quon's inquiry, "Advertising is not ethical. It is beneath us!" As a traditional physician, he believed that doctors who were as exceptionally good as the ones at ACP should not have to advertise. He argued that marketing did not work. After all, for many years, the American Medical Association (AMA) had told the medical community not to advertise. From his perspective, the best approach was to keep patients happy by giving them great care and staying on time. One happy parent would give word-of-mouth recommendations to friends and neighbors.

Dr. Stein, another senior member, was open to the idea that soft marketing and advertising might be beneficial. She suggested, "Perhaps we can gauge how well a parent likes our pediatric patient care and then determine the parent's receptiveness to giving a testimonial on our website."

Abruptly, Dr. Carter protested, "No, we shouldn't even do that."

DISCUSSION QUESTIONS

1. Why is Dr. Carter having such a hard time with the idea of marketing?

2. What should Dr. Quon say to reassure Dr. Carter that ACP will continue to have the same values?

3. Is Dr. Stein's idea of patient testimonials a good one? What about HIPAA and privacy laws?

Part II

Dr. Harp, although being in the group for only two short years, was excited at the opportunity to build the practice. He was especially interested in increasing the number of newborn patients at ACP and blurted out, "For those of us who are not as seasoned as you three, I feel that going out to the neighborhood hospitals and speaking at the lactation nurses' prenatal lectures would be a great way to introduce myself and the practice to parents-to-be."

All the physicians were aware that in recent years ACP had been facing increasing and fierce competition. Neighborhood chain drug stores offered "Doc in the Box" clinics staffed with ancillary caregivers rather than MDs. At the other end of the spectrum were staff model health maintenance organizations, which were fully integrated provider groups that offered economies of scale with seamless pediatric health care.

Dr. Quon's worry was that ACP lacked a comprehensive strategic marketing plan to promote the practice's particular niche. He reminded his partners, "We are an 'all physician' pediatric practice without ancillary caregivers. When you come to us, your child will always see an MD—a trusted source—and no one else." At ACP, if a parent wanted his or her child to be seen on the same day, the team made it happen. Unlike other providers, ACP had a full physician staff on Saturdays to see patients until noon. Saturday hours were not limited to sick visits, but also included routine well check-ups. In this way, the practice accommodated households with two working parents.

In fact, the practice over the last decade had the distinction of being recognized for outstanding patient care and satisfaction. Other ideas were proposed, including promoting the accolades through media coverage and advertising in newspapers, local hospital newsletters, and the ACP website. One of the doctors also suggested that the group participate in events to raise money for organizations such as brain cancer and diabetes awareness groups. Parents and their children would be able to meet the ACP physicians at these events.

The ideas were far reaching and continued for a few hours. As the discussion progressed, Dr. Quon suggested that the best way to grow the practice was for the physician group at

ACP to continue what they did best. "I know our job is to keep kids healthy, but we need to change with the times. We must find ways to keep the practice healthy."

After hearing his colleagues make the case and being reassured that the ACP values would continue to be good care and good service, Dr. Carter also suggested that the practice seek the help of a marketing consultant.

Dr. Quon agreed that this sounded like a good idea and asked the others what they thought. They all responded positively to this idea. Dr. Stein suggested working with a healthcare marketing professor and her students from a local college to help ACP develop its marketing strategy and plan for implementation. Dr. Harp enthusiastically volunteered to be the primary contact between ACP and the marketing consultant. In concluding the meeting, Dr. Quon added that later that day a group of obstetricians/gynecologists (Drs. Berkeley, Hamilton, and Azana) would be in to discuss prenatal care and early childhood development along with a number of other related topics. Dr. Quon remarked, "Let's see how we might incorporate this partnership and these other great ideas into our new marketing strategy."

DISCUSSION QUESTIONS

1. What are some key messages that ACP should build into its marketing campaign?

2. What opportunities for improvement in the practice do you see in this case?

3. Why is organizational change a challenge in healthcare settings?

High Employee Turnover at Hillcrest Memorial Hospital—Case for Chapter 3

Amy Dore

You are on a newly formed "Service Excellence Committee" at Hillcrest Memorial Hospital. Your area of expertise includes leadership issues such as mentoring, team building, motivation, and empowerment. Over the past year, employee turnover has dramatically increased throughout the organization with no obvious reason. The hospital CEO has asked the committee to survey and research reasons for the turnover. Upon careful review of the surveys, you notice that normal reasons for turnover, such as low pay and poor benefits, are not the problem. However, one trend stands out—dissatisfaction with job autonomy. You surmise the reason this is a problem is because Hillcrest operates with a traditional hierarchy, including traditional manager roles that appear more dictatorial than participative. Employees have limited freedom when it comes to their work and are neither motivated nor empowered by managers. You mention this to the committee and a vote is quickly taken to explore this theory. Empowerment is a controversial topic to members of the committee, as their initial fear is that once an employee is empowered they will run amok and the organization will suffer. Upper management ignores the concept of employee motivation due to the misconception that motivating employees means it will cost the organization money. The committee assigns you the task of writing a draft response to present to the CEO and the committee.

DISCUSSION QUESTIONS

1. In light of the committee's agreement on the causes of the high employee turnover, why should upper management give attention to the concepts of employee motivation and empowerment?

2. What are the costs and benefits of high turnover and of reducing it?

3. How might Hillcrest develop and implement an employee program that encompasses employee motivation and empowerment?

4. How could the committee ensure success of such a program?

5. Should the committee consider other strategies and opportunities to help Hillcrest overcome the issue of high employee turnover?

6. Should you be updating your resume in case the CEO doesn't like your recommendations? Explain your response.

Set Up for Failure?—Case for Chapter 3

Amy Dore

Allison began her healthcare career with an established general dentistry practice consisting of one dentist, Dr. Gable. Shortly after she started her job, Dr. Gable decided to add a second dentist, even though his past ventures with adding a partner had not been successful. Dr. Gable hired an expensive consulting firm to handle all the specifics, such as developing the contract with this new dentist, helping with hiring additional staff, purchasing additional equipment, and helping the current staff adapt during the transition. Even though Allison was new to the dental field, Dr. Gable kept her up-to-date with the process, but only to a certain point. Furthermore, Allison's input was not wanted, so she politely stepped back and observed the process. Both dentists had big ideas of a successful partnership and expected instant success. They even looked for land to build and move the current practice because they expected the practice to double or triple in size since there would be two dentists to serve their expanding patient base.

Watching the beginning of the partnership develop was exciting for Allison, and she was anxious for the partnership to succeed. The thought of managing such a large, successful practice would certainly be good experience for her. However, Allison noted a couple of negative factors that made her question the wisdom of adding a second dentist. Those factors included:

1. The new partner had just graduated from dental school and did not have a patient base to bring to the practice.
2. The discussions between the two dentists and the consulting firm did not indicate how the new dentist would market himself.
3. The new dentist would be paid a set salary, increasing each year, without consideration of how much revenue he actually generated.

Furthermore, several issues quickly came to the surface:

1. Expenses quickly exceeded profits.
   a. The new dentist wanted all the best and newest equipment, which was very expensive.
   b. Increased staff for the new dentist meant a larger salary expense (not to mention the salary of the new dentist).
2. The new dentist was neither motivated to nor interested in marketing himself. He was drawing a salary, which would increase each year, so he was not motivated to seek new patients.
   a. This meant he was treating the existing patients and, therefore, taking away business from Dr. Gable.
   b. In turn, little additional revenue was being generated, and expenses were going through the roof.
3. The morale of the office quickly deteriorated.
   a. The tension between the dentists and staff was obvious. Due to the increased expenses, the year-end bonuses for staff were eliminated and employee hours were cut.
   b. Allison was also feeling demoralized.

Now, after keeping Allison out of this process, both dentists expect her to fix the situation. Allison feels like her job is on the line, along with the morale of the staff and the outcomes of the practice. Plus, Allison is positive neither dentist will be open to accepting responsibility for the situation. She is trying to decide what to do and how to address these problems.

DISCUSSION QUESTIONS

1. How might she draw upon and apply the theories of management and motivation to address these issues?

2. How might she approach the dentists?

3. What are the most urgent issues?

4. What actions might she suggest to improve the situation?

5. What strategies might be used to motivate the dentists and the employees in working to begin to address the issues?

6. Should Allison be updating her resume and looking for another job? Explain your response.

Negotiation in Action—Case for Chapter 10*

Daniel F. Fahey

The following negotiation case study is designed to provide the student with a simulation of an actual negotiation scenario involving a medical group (or IPA) and an HMO. This case study will allow students to participate in a negotiation using real-life issues so they may experience the actual negotiation process.

Process

Approximately 10 students are directly involved in the simulation. The IPA and HMO will each field a team of 5 to represent their respective interests, as follows:

Majestic Health Plan	**EveryDoc IPA**
(HMO)	(Medical Group IPA)
Regional VP for Provider Relations (Chief Negotiator)	Director of Managed Care Contracting (Chief Negotiator)
Medical Director	Chief Executive Officer
Director of Utilization Management	Medical Director
Director of Pharmacy	Chief Operations Officer
Scribe or note taker	Chief Financial Officer

Other students may serve as observers and provide feedback regarding the process and outcomes of the negotiation.

Negotiations are expected to consume a minimum of six class sessions (90 minutes each) including time for research and caucus. Students will be graded on participation and negotiating skills.

Associated Case Documents

Associated with this case are the following three supporting documents:

- **Position Paper (Figure 17-4):** A position paper has been provided to assist the medical group (IPA) with the negotiations. This position paper is not to be shared with the HMO.

EveryDoc IPA

Capitation Rate: The current professional capitation rate is $40 per member per month (pmpm). Specialty costs have been increasing at more than 15% per month, somewhat due to adverse selection as the result of a new large employer contract negotiated by Majestic HMO. The IPA has evidence that supports its position that a new capitation rate of $45 pmpm would allow the IPA to continue providing services.

OB Volume: The IPA has data that support the contention that its patient population has a substantially higher birth rate than other IPAs contracted with Majestic HMO. The IPA estimates that it should receive an additional $1 pmpm to offset the cost of providing obstetrical services to its members.

Stop-Loss Insurance: The current cost to the IPA for Stop-Loss Insurance, which is provided by the HMO, is $1.80 pmpm. The IPA has a bid from an outside insurance carrier in the amount of $0.60 pmpm. The IPA wants to be allowed to purchase the Stop-Loss at a lower amount and not have the HMO deduct the $1.80 pmpm from the IPA's capitation rate.

New Benefits/Procedures: The IPA wants language in the new agreement that prevents the HMO from offering new benefits or procedures that are not currently provided without consultation with the IPA and additional capitation for expensive procedures or services.

Retroactive Capitation Payment: The IPA wants the HMO to guarantee that capitation for new members added before the 15th of each month will be retroactive to the 1st of the month, instead of the current practice of increasing the capitation rate at the second month of enrollment.

Pharmacy Risk: The IPA is currently responsible for a portion of the pharmacy cost. The IPA wants the HMO to assume all risk for pharmacy cost with the new agreement.

Quality Improvement Incentive: The IPA currently receives an additional $1 pmpm if certain quality improvement measures are met, including better-than-average HEDIS and patient satisfaction scores. This effort consumes a great deal of resources, and the IPA wants $2 pmpm.

Specialty Claims Processing: The IPA currently is required to reimburse specialists for services rendered within 45 days of submittal of a clean claim. This time period is too short, and the IPA wants the period extended to 60 days.

FIGURE 17-4 Position Paper

- **Letter (Figure 17-5):** A letter from the Majestic Health Plan HMO to EveryDoc IPA describes proposed changes that must be addressed during upcoming contract negotiations.
- **Attachment (Figure 17-6):** The attachment to the letter above further details proposed changes to the agreement between the organizations.

* **Instructor:** please note that an instructor's guide for this case is available in the online resources.

MAJESTIC HEALTH PLAN OF THE INLAND EMPIRE, INC.

400 North Main Street
Any Town, USA 12345
December 10, 20XX

Chief Executive Officer
EveryDoc IPA
100 Hospitality Way
Suite 500
Any Town, USA 12345

Dear CEO:

This letter is to inform you that Majestic Health Plan wishes to enter into negotiations for the contract year effective July 1, 20XX. We apologize for the lateness of this letter, but we have recently reorganized and this is the first opportunity we have had to enter into negotiation for the renewal of our agreement with your IPA affecting approximately 10,000 of our members.

We have enclosed our proposed changes from the current agreement. As you are well aware, this past year has not been kind to the managed care industry. A number of our competitors have either ceased business in the Inland Empire or have merged with other health plans. The business community continues to expect high-quality care at relatively low premium levels. We have been informed recently by one of the major industry purchasing groups that they do not expect any increases in premiums for the coming year, which means that we are not in a position to enrich our agreement with you. Furthermore, the managed care industry continues to see escalating costs for medical services and must take specific measures to contain costs.

All this means that the coming year will be difficult for all concerned. We value our relationship with your IPA and hope we can reach agreement on a new contract before the termination date of the existing contract.

Sincerely,

John Jones
Vice President, Provider Relations

FIGURE 17-5 Negotiation Letter

The following are changes to the Agreement between Majestic Health Plan of the Inland Empire, Inc. (MHP) and EveryDoc Independent Physician Organization, Inc. (IPA), effective July 1, 20XX.

1. The current capitation rate of $40 pmpm will remain in place for the duration of the agreement to take effect July 1, 20XX and will continue thereafter unless modified by mutual written agreement.
2. The Division of Financial Responsibilities (DOFR) will be modified with the new agreement as set forth in the attached, which will become part of the new agreement. Among other issues in the DOFR, the revised DOFR will reflect that the cost of any prescription drugs not currently on the Formulary will be assigned to the IPA.
3. The new capitation rate will be paid based on an adjusted age–sex formula that will be prepared and presented before implementation of the new agreement.
4. We are requesting that the IPA expand its network of primary care physicians and specialists to the Palm Springs area. The details of this request will be discussed during the negotiations.
5. We will be making a change in the timing of capitation payments for newly enrolled members. Effective July 1, capitation for any new enrollee joining Majestic Health Plan will be paid beginning the second month of enrollment, except in the case of Medicare Seniors, which will be paid to the IPA within one month of receipt of funds from CMS.
6. Effective July 1, all specialist claims must be paid within 30 days of submittal. Any claim paid beyond 30 days will result in an automatic 10% penalty to the IPA and will be deducted from the next month's capitation payment.
7. Effective July 1, all referrals for liver transplant and bone marrow transplant will be to the Mayo Clinic as our Center of Excellence.
8. These negotiations depend on the successful completion of a new agreement with your PHO partner, St. Elsewhere Hospital.
9. We are asking that your IPA obtain and maintain Directors and Officers liability insurance for your Board in the amount of $5 million effective July 1, 20XX.
10. Majestic Health Plan reserves the right to present additional negotiation issues by February 28, 20XX.

FIGURE 17-6 Attachment

The Merger of Two Competing Hospitals—Case for Chapters 5, 2, and 12

Mary Anne Franklin, Dale Mapes, Audrey McDow, and Karin Mithamo

This case highlights the process of merging two fully accredited hospitals, both of which have a full complement of state-of-the-art diagnostic technology, including MRI and CAT scanners, 24-hour physician-staffed emergency care centers, and specialized women's centers. Both of these facilities are located in a community of 60,000 in the southeastern part of Idaho.

The success of the merger hinges on the timely resolution of several issues that the executive staff implemented, mutually enhancing solutions in the areas of: (1) leadership, (2) culture adaptation, (3) human resource management, (4) staffing, and (5) benefit issues.

Overview

Hospital A: Porter Regional Medical Center (PRMC)

Located on the east side of town, Porter Regional Medical Center (PRMC) was a for-profit hospital, consisting of 110 hospital beds, 8 of which were reserved for transitional care. PRMC was a privately owned facility. Mountain Health Care (MHC), a large healthcare organization in the Rocky Mountain region, owned the facility. Built in 1990, the facility was designed to efficiently handle patient flow from the emergency room to the pharmacy and to be a point of referral for more complicated patient conditions. PRMC services consisted of general and same-day surgery and full-service rehabilitation and radiology departments. Other services included a kidney dialysis center, on-site retail pharmacy, a regional Red Cross blood bank, 24-hour laboratory, home health, Infusion/Home IV, and a women's center, including obstetrics and numerous other amenities.

Other assets owned by PRMC were the adjacent medical office buildings, a day care center, the land on which an assisted living center was located adjacent to the hospital, and the sports medicine complex adjacent to the state university's arena. These assets represented 188,000 square feet of facility space housed on 63 acres. The hospital employed 450 personnel.

Last year, the hospital's operating budget was $34 million. However, in the same year, the hospital experienced a $1 million loss, and a projected $500,000 loss was anticipated for the following year. After three years of red ink, PRMC decided to liquidate.

Hospital B: Banner Regional Medical Center (BRMC) and Turner Geriatric Center

Built in 1951, Banner Regional Medical Center (BRMC), a county-owned hospital, was located on the west side of town. The hospital structure included 154 inpatient beds and a geriatric healthcare center that consisted of 100–106 beds, 13 transitional care beds, and 7 rehabilitation beds. A medical office building with a parking structure was located adjacent to the hospital. The campus consisted of 561,366 square feet of building space, housed on 6 acres. The hospital's operating budget for last year was $79 million. BRMC had a reserve fund of $20 million earmarked for major renovations to the existing facility's emergency room and intensive care unit. BRMC's services included the Herman Cancer Center, Family Centered Care (Ob/Gyn), a newborn intensive care unit, a women's center, Life Flight (mobile intensive care), a regional pediatric unit, a geriatric center, and a sports/industrial medicine clinic. The hospital had a staff of 914 employees.

While the majority of the services were housed at BRMC, the home health administrative offices and the physical therapy departments were housed at different locations in the same town. For strategic planning purposes, management knew that the hospital's viability depended on the necessary action to expand and renovate the facility to meet the needs of its current market.

The stage was set for the consolidation of the two competing hospitals: PRMC, crippled with three years of losses, and BRMC, struggling with aging facilities. The process would take the next three years to complete the merger and create a new facility. BRMC's board of directors offered the facility to the county, so as not to let an outside organization compete for its resources and patients. The county would pay $25 million, to be paid in increments of $15 million at the time of purchase and $10 million over the next two to three years, interest free. The CEOs of PRMC and BRMC, Pat Herman, MHA, FACHE, and Scott Johns, MBA, had applied for the single hospital management slot. A consulting firm from Seattle was hired to review the resumes, experiences, and job performances of both men. In the end, the commissioners voted to hire Herman, who had more than 20 years as an administrator for a Catholic institution and had been the chief communication officer for a military academy.

Consolidation

In the fall, the chairs of each hospital's board met to discuss options for cutting healthcare costs, addressing the shortage of healthcare personnel, and improving the delivery of health care in the community. The following spring, a letter of intent to consolidate was sent from BRMC to MHC. Three months later, an agreement was solidified with the following requirements:

1. The consolidated hospital would have a new name; and
2. A transitional team, including the previous CEO of PRMC, would be assembled to deal with management changes and employee benefit packages.

Other requirements included a new mission statement, a policy that no workers would be laid off as a result of the merger, and a newly elected 15-member hospital board, comprised of 10 BMRC board members and 5 PMRC members. Public meetings were held by board members and hospital administrators to answer questions and explain the merger process. During the meetings, the public voiced concerns that consolidation would destroy competition in the area, leading to an increase in healthcare costs and a decrease in services and quality. In preliminary employee meetings, the staff expressed concerns over seniority, job placement, compensation, and benefit packages.

Leadership

Leadership style at BMRC could be characterized as participative, autonomous, and self-governing. As CEO of BRMC, Pat Herman's initial job was to rebuild the executive team that had been depleted by the retirement of the outgoing CEO, the serious illness of the director of nursing services, and the departure of the vice president of human resources.

PRMC operated as a subsidiary of MHC, whose corporate office made all policy and strategic management decisions. Lower-level managers were not highly involved in the decision-making processes at MHC. Management, therefore, was highly structured and centralized. Consequently, the management team at PRMC relied on the corporate office for the day-to-day operations of the hospital.

To embrace the new entity, the community decided to name the consolidated hospital Portsmith Regional Medical Center. At the time of the merger, there was a combined staff of more than 1,400 employees. The staff at both PRMC and BRMC in duplicate management positions had to compete for their jobs. Approximately 90 employees decided to retire. By the conclusion of streamlining positions, 1,200 employees were part of the new organization.

Herman conducted 30 to 40 meetings with the staff and met weekly with the managers to answer their questions and concerns. The employees were encouraged to express their feelings. Employees were given access to the EAP program, social workers, and one employee relations person to help cope with their fears and apprehensions.

Culture Adaptation

Cultures in organizations are manifested in language, physical settings, values, symbols, and formal procedures. As a single entity, BRMC had developed an autonomous, independent, self-directed culture. PRMC's culture was much less independent and relied heavily on the corporate office for its decision making, policy development, and operating procedures. These factors greatly influenced the culture of each organization and the final impact on the consolidation of the new entity.

PRMC and BRMC referred to each other in competitive language. There were many references to "them" versus "us" within the organizations. The language was indicative of the entrenched processes, cultures, loyalty, and systems that had to be addressed in the consolidation.

Both organizations had symbols that represented their cultures. Each organization had a logo that symbolized who they were and what they represented. PRMC had a vision and mission statement developed and defined by the corporate office, while BRMC, on the other hand, did not have a clearly defined mission and vision statement. Although BRMC's board and Pat Herman had determined their vision and mission statements for the future, these statements were not clearly defined and were not communicated to the staff.

Human Resource Management

A year after the merger, a new vice president of human resources, Dale Miller, was recruited from a Catholic healthcare system in Kentucky to handle the newly merged hospital. Miller had extensive experience in mergers and acquisitions. Soon, he realized that the merger included more than the consolidation of duplicated services. The merger also brought together two different hospital boards, two separate groups of physicians and staff, and two different benefit packages.

Staffing

There were several major staffing concerns for the consolidated hospital. Six months prior to consolidation, PRMC and BRMC had to develop a joint medical structure that included leadership, credentialing, bylaws, rules and regulations, and peer review. Both hospitals had three medical staff leadership positions: chief of staff, vice-chief, and secretary, for a total of six physicians. A process was developed to consolidate these six positions to four. Four of the existing physicians' names were recommended to the medical staff, and subsequently, the staff voted to retain all four to lead the new, consolidated medical staff. BRMC's Dr. Gene Roberts became the new chief of staff of Portsmith Regional Medical Center.

The next step required evaluating the different bylaws, rules, and regulations for each medical staff at PRMC and BRMC. Through a ballot, the two medical staffs decided to adopt bylaws, rules, and regulations that reflected their joint decision-making efforts. Credentialing the two medical staffs required interventions by a legal team. Since every physician must be credentialed every two years, both hospitals had to develop a timeline that would meet The Joint Commission's standards that would keep physicians' credentials current with the time of consolidation. For example, if a physician's time for credentialing would put him/her out of compliance, then the credentialing timeline had to move to the shortest time in order to maintain his/her current license. Since each hospital had different peer review/quality standards, the newly elected medical executive team and staff voted to modify and adopt PRMC's more stringent, well-documented standards. By the time of consolidation, 160 physicians at PRMC and 180 medical staff at BRMC had completed a smooth transition with only five physicians choosing to leave.

Another staffing issue was with the nursing department. An analysis of the combined workforce revealed that in nursing services, the ratio of RNs to LPNs was disproportionate (70% LPN to 30% RN). This ratio was opposite what was needed for the planned high-tech services to be offered by the merged organization, which included cardiovascular, open heart, heart cauterization labs, cancer centers, and four call centers of excellence. These centers of excellence required a higher level of specialty nursing than was needed previously. The nursing staff ratio needed to be changed to a 60:40 RN to LPN ratio as rapidly as possible.

In addition, the staff analysis revealed that the skill levels of other existing staff needed to be developed rapidly in order to perform in a more technically advanced environment that included picture archiving computerization systems, electronic medical records, and new patient systems technology.

Benefits

Each hospital offered its employees benefits that included sick leave, paid time off, health insurance, life insurance, and retirement plans. Paid time off and sick leave were accrued at different rates at each hospital. BRMC was self-insured, while PRMC offered its employees a fully insured healthcare plan. In addition, healthcare coverage, deductibles, premiums, and out-of-pocket costs varied between the hospitals. PRMC employees feared that they would lose benefits if they moved to the BRMC retirement system. In the end, 90 BRMC employees opted to leave the organization for fear of losing their benefits. Another group opted to stay in order to obtain a better benefit package.

Two months later, the newly formed board and executives, including Herman and Miller, met at a planning retreat in Jackson, Wyoming, to decide how to best resolve leadership, culture adaptation, human resource management, staffing, and benefits issues.

DISCUSSION QUESTIONS

1. What specific steps should the board take to create an executive team to manage the newly created organization?

2. Given the diversity of cultures embedded in the merged organization, what should the management team do to facilitate a working culture in the new organization?

3. How should management deal with the physical structures at the time of the consolidation?

4. How should the duplication of services and departments be handled?

5. What are the risk management issues and legal issues associated with the merger?

6. How can the board and administrators calm the fears of the staff before, during, and after the consolidation?

7. How do the physicians work with administration to share power and resources within the new consolidated hospital?

Sexual Harassment at the Diabetes Clinic—Case for Chapters 12 and 15*

Kenneth L. Johnson and Barry G. Gomberg

Part A

The diabetes clinic is one of four academic hospital–based clinics that Tim Jorgenson has been managing for the past three months. Tim earned an MBA and has worked in hospital administration for about five years. This is his first experience as a medical group manager. While the clinic staff members are impressed with Tim's management background, he has no clinical experience, so some of the nurses and a few of the physicians are questioning Tim's ability to understand their needs.

All four of the clinics Tim has been hired to manage are connected by a rear hallway and are home to physicians from the internal medicine department (see Figure 17-7). The diabetes clinic is located at the western end of the area; next comes the general internal medicine clinic, then the oncology clinic, and finally the infectious disease clinic. Physicians using the diabetes clinic are specialists in endocrinology; however, they do not keep the clinic busy every day of the week. When the endocrinologists are not using the rooms, they are used by gastroenterology, pulmonary, and cardiology specialists. The other connected clinics represent general internal medicine and rheumatology, infectious diseases, oncology, and the heart and lung transplant programs. Some of the physicians bring their own nurses to the clinics when they work there, but in the diabetes clinic alone, Tim manages four clerks, two medical assistants, two licensed practical nurses (LPNs), and four registered nurses (RNs), who serve whatever group of doctors happens to be using the clinic. Among the four clinics, the different specialties practice on different days. Monday is very busy with endocrinology GI patients, general internal medicine, infectious diseases, oncology, and some pulmonary. Tuesday is heavy cardiology, pulmonary, oncology, and internal medicine. Wednesday is heart transplant, pulmonary, and so on. Tim never seems to have enough rooms or enough staff to meet the demands. That includes the overwhelming

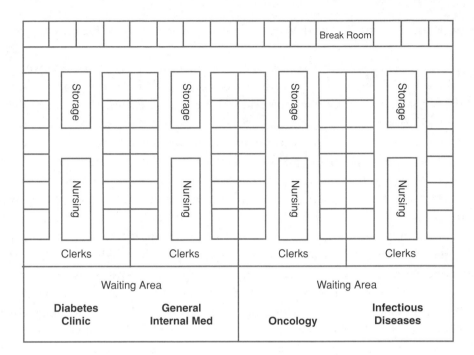

FIGURE 17-7 The Internal Medicine Clinics

number of phone calls and check-ins handled by the clerks at the front. He is always concerned about turnover and works hard to keep the staff he has.

While the other three clinics seem to be functioning well, the diabetes clinic never seems to run smoothly. In particular, Tim is concerned about the lack of camaraderie and teamwork among the staff. The nurses seem to be more concerned about each other's work habits than they are their own. One of the medical assistants, just out of high school, doesn't respond to the nurses' requests and has come to Tim arguing that she shouldn't report to the nurses. One of the LPNs has worked for the clinic for 12 years and doesn't like the newer RNs taking over. Some of the RNs think their first priority is the physicians, even if it means putting coworkers and clinic patients on the back burner. Other RNs think the patients in the clinic should come first.

Tim has decided to hold regular staff meetings with all four clinics combined in order to discuss some of the issues he has noticed. No minutes of previous staff meetings or training sessions exist in the clinic. He's not sure what has happened in the past.

While the clinical staff struggles a bit, Tim is pleased that he has a group of clerks who seem to be comfortable with their jobs, are well-trained, and seem to be able to handle the overwhelming challenges they are faced with each day in the clinic. It is one of the clerks, however, a young woman named Maggie Connelly, who has made it to the top of Tim's list of worries.

Maggie has been a clerk at the diabetes clinic for nearly three years. She works most specifically with the endocrinologists who have expressed their appreciation for her work. She's one of the few clerks working for Tim who can take the sometimes heated demands of the endocrinologists in stride. In fact, she shows no fear and has earned their respect. Tim's concern centers around a few comments made by one of Maggie's coworkers, who indicated that Maggie speaks and jokes openly with other clerks—all women—about sex, sometimes talking about her dates the night before. While no official complaints have come to Tim's attention, he has sensed from a couple of her coworkers that Maggie may be creating a situation that is uncomfortable for them. In the back of his mind, Tim knows that the entire endocrinology team will soon be moving to a new building. Maggie will be moving with them and will most likely be joined by another clerk, who will be a new hire. She will no longer be working directly with the other clerks who have shown some concern.

William Peterson is the only male clerk in the four-clinic area and now works in the oncology area. William is a 22-year-old man who has worked in the oncology clinic for about eight months. William has proven to be the type of individual who always solves problems. He is well liked by everyone he works with, and Tim wishes that more of his employees had William's initiative. William is also the type of individual who likes to visit and joke with his coworkers.

While focusing on the diabetes clinic, prioritizing the problems he could begin to work on, Tim heard a knock on his door and found Maggie standing there.

"William's bugging me," she said. Maggie came in and began telling Tim she was feeling very uncomfortable with William. "He's always stopping by my station and making jokes about sex," she said. "Sometimes he touches me on the arm or shoulder and it really makes me feel uncomfortable. He does the same thing any time we both end up together in the break room or some other area of the clinics when no one is around."

"Wow, I haven't seen that in William when I'm around," said Tim. "Have you asked him to stop?"

"Well, no, not really," Maggie said.

"Tell me more about it. How long has this gone on?"

"Maybe for two or three weeks," Maggie answered.

"Have other people been around you when this has happened?" Tim questioned.

"I don't think so."

"What would you like me to do?" Tim asked sincerely. He knew not to just ignore her, even though the irony of the situation struck him immediately.

"Well, I can't work here with him around," she answered.

What would you do in Tim's situation?

Part B

Tim has decided on a couple of alternative solutions to the problems presented by Maggie and William. First, Tim discussed with Maggie what she wanted him to do. She indicated that she just wanted William to leave her alone. She isn't asking that he be fired. As a result, Tim has spoken with William and indicated Maggie's concerns. William indicated that he was surprised to learn that Maggie was so bothered by what he considered friendly chats. In fact, he felt they had a good relationship. Tim suggested to William that he be courteous and respectful with Maggie, but avoid being alone with her. This not only protects Maggie, Tim thinks, but it will protect William from any allegations that aren't true since witnesses will be nearby.

Tim has also decided to pursue training for his entire staff. This training will include specifics about harassment, that is, what it is, what it's not, policies surrounding the issues, the rights of those involved, how to document and report it, and other important concerns. A second type of training will focus on communication skills. Tim suspects that part of the problem in his clinic is due to the fact that some people might not be able to communicate that they are offended, and some, perhaps as in the case of William, may not know that what they say and do may be offensive to others.

As he is preparing his training outline and deciding how to approach his staff on this issue, Maggie again comes to his office. Now, she alleges, William has gone too far. She reports, "He grabbed my butt." Again, she has no witnesses.

Does this change what Tim should do? If so, what does he do now?

* **Instructor:** please note that an instructor's guide for this case is available in the online resources.

Prelude to a Medical Error—Case for Chapters 4 and 7

Sheila K. McGinnis

Mrs. Bee was lying in her bed after her morning physical therapy with Mr. Traction and felt like she couldn't breathe. "Is something bothering you, Mrs. Bee?" asked Nurse Karing. "I know you had a disagreement with your husband regarding rehabilitation last night," she said. Nurse Karing knew that Mrs. Bee had had a bad fall and that therapy was going to be tough for her to deal with. She had discussed with Mrs. Bee's husband the support issues that were important during stressful hospitalizations, and it seemed like he was going to be a good support system for her. She felt that the disagreement wasn't the real problem.

The previous night, Mrs. Bee had terrible spasms in her left calf and told Nurse Karing right away. Nurse Karing proceeded to order a STAT venous Doppler X-ray to rule out thrombosis. She also paged Dr. Cural to notify him that Mrs. Bee was having symptoms of thrombosis. Dr. Cural, upset that he was being bothered after a long day of work, shouted into the phone, "I evaluated that patient this morning, and nothing was wrong with her. I don't need incompetent nurses calling me at night to tell me that my patient is having leg cramps. Don't bother me again! And by the way, cancel that test!" [Click.] Nurse Karing was upset. She felt humiliated and distracted. She canceled the venous Doppler test as ordered by Dr. Cural, thinking he was right. Mrs. Bee was probably just having leg cramps from being sedentary that day. And besides, she thought, Dr. Cural had always claimed to know his patients inside and out. Yet Nurse Karing went home that night feeling bothered by the lack of respect and communication displayed by her coworkers lately.

But today, Mrs. Bee was short of breath, pale, and had elevated blood pressure. Something was wrong. Nurse Karing ordered a STAT VQ scan to rule out a pulmonary embolus. This was serious. Mrs. Bee was starting to go unconscious. Nurse Karing immediately called for help. The nursing team and Dr. Krisis (from the ER) came immediately to the room to help stabilize Mrs. Bee. "Looks like we have another problem from one of the nursing floors," observed Dr. Krisis. "Someone must have not had time again to call the doctor yesterday to see if a venous Doppler was necessary. Now she's really critical!" Nurse Karing ignored Dr. Krisis's comment and quickly collected Mrs. Bee's chart to notify Dr. Cural of the situation. Dr. Cural was angry. "Why didn't anybody call me to tell me that my patient was having problems? I am the physician! Can't you nurses do anything right? Don't you know that you need to focus on what symptoms Mrs. Bee is having? Get Mrs. Specimen up here to draw some blood. I want STAT ABGs now! Get ICU on the phone!"

At the same time, Mr. Friendly, the social worker, happened to be walking by and said to Dr. Cural and Nurse Karing, "Mrs. Bee's paperwork is all ready. Her insurance will allow her to go to a rehabilitation facility for one week of physical therapy. The MediCar will be here in one hour to pick her up." Nurse Karing was furious. She thought to herself, "It's time for administration to hear this one."

DISCUSSION QUESTIONS

1. Identify and discuss examples of preconceptions, assumptions, and mental models evident in this scenario. What are the consequences of the ways these health providers are thinking about the situation?

2. Discuss some strategies each actor could use to deal with the preconceptions, assumptions, and mental models evident in this scenario. Role-play the scenario using those strategies.

3. What retraining would you recommend for the physicians and nurses in this scenario?

Source: Scenario courtesy of Jennifer Krapfl, RN, MHA.

The Finance Department at Roseville Community Hospital—Case for Chapters 4 and 10

Sheila K. McGinnis

Kelly Munson, the new finance manager of Roseville Community Hospital, is reviewing a recent staff meeting in which the staff discussed reorganizing the finance department. Louise Smith, who has been with the department for 8 years, agrees that outdated computer systems compromise the level of service provided to patients but is unenthusiastic about making major changes. Frank Williams, who applied for the finance manager position for which Kelly was hired, seems unwilling to cooperate with the rest of the department. John Evans, who recently completed his MHA degree, is eager to try new approaches that he learned about in grad school. Kelly sighs, thinking how difficult it can be to help department members understand how their work fits together and to decide how to change operations to better serve patients and the hospital.

Activity A: Role-play a discussion between Louise, Frank, John, and Kelly as they discuss whether to reorganize the finance department. Following the role-play, describe the **assumptions and thought patterns** that seemed to emerge in this scenario and discuss how they may be hindering the finance department's ability to effectively solve this problem.

Activity B: Role-play a discussion between Louise, Frank, John, and Kelly on whether to reorganize the finance department. Use the principles of **Action Inquiry** during the discussion to check each others' assumptions. Discuss how the conversation differs when you address underlying assumptions.

Madison Community Hospital Addresses Infection Control Prevention—Case for Chapter 7*

Michael Moran

The Quality Issue

Hospitals across the country have seen an increase in methicillin-resistant staphylococcus aureus (MRSA), a bacterial infection that is highly resistant to some antibiotics. Patients who contract this infection can develop serious complications, sometimes leading to death. Area hospitals with MRSA outbreaks have been featured in recent media programs, resulting in a loss of public confidence and declining admissions. As the director of an inpatient unit at Madison Community Hospital (MCH), you understand the potential for an increase of MRSA at your hospital. Your infectious disease physicians are concerned about the potential for an outbreak at your hospital. Infection prevention studies have reported that only 40% of healthcare workers sanitize their hands before treating patients. Handwashing and other hand-sanitizing methods have been proven to reduce the transmission of dangerous infections from one patient to another.

Preliminary Actions at MCH

The MCH products committee has evaluated several hand-sanitizing products and selected an alcohol-based product that effectively eliminates the majority of bacterial microorganisms that can be transmitted by contact. The hand hygiene policy at MCH requires staff members, physicians, and volunteers to apply the hand sanitizer before entering and after leaving a patient's room. The Infection Prevention staff estimates an average of 15–20 individuals enter a patient's room each day.

You have been appointed to serve on a task force charged with improving hand hygiene compliance. The Infection Prevention personnel have gathered preliminary data from various inpatient nursing units (see Table 17-1). Staff on these units were observed in order

TABLE 17-1 Madison Community Hospital Hand Hygiene Compliance Observation Data

	Number of Staff Observed	Number Sanitizing Hands	Percent Sanitizing Hands
2 North	15	8	53%
2 South	18	12	67%
2 East	16	6	38%
3 North	19	10	53%
3 South	13	7	54%
3 East	15	6	40%
4 North	18	9	50%
4 South	17	7	41%
4 East	14	6	43%
Total	145	71	49%

to assess whether they sanitized their hands prior to entering and upon leaving a patient's room. The Infection Prevention staff observing the inpatient unit personnel are routinely seen on these units as part of their surveillance activities. Staff members were not aware their hand hygiene practices were being observed. At first glance, the data indicates hand hygiene is not practiced, as required by the policy, in more than half the observations.

MCH has adopted the FOCUS-PDCA improvement model and utilizes various tools for collecting data and analyzing processes. The hand hygiene task force will be applying these methods to address the hand hygiene concern.

DISCUSSION QUESTIONS

1. How would your task force use the FOCUS model and the data collection, process mapping, and process analysis tools to plan for a process change?

2. What are some of the issues associated with caregivers sanitizing their hands? Why do you suppose only 40% of caregivers sanitize their hands? What other department personnel, besides nursing, may need to enter a patient's room during their stay? What are some of the issues associated with caregivers sanitizing their hands?

3. Who should be on this task force to represent what hospital functions and why? To whom should the taskforce report their results and why?

4. What are the possible causes for noncompliance? Are there other factors contributing to the issue? (Hint: develop a flowchart to lay out the sequence of events for staff

members entering and leaving patient rooms, develop a workflow diagram to identify barriers, and use these to construct a fishbone diagram.)

5. What data are needed to determine the factors involved in the noncompliance?

6. How would the problem look different if it turned out only a handful of personnel were noncompliant? How would this affect the improvement process?

7. Do you have enough data to complete the analysis? What data are needed to determine the factors involved in the noncompliance?

8. What process should be selected for improvement?

9. What aspects of the FOCUS model would be most useful to target the improvement efforts?

10. How can MCH motivate its staff to be more compliant? Do you think posters and recognition awards for units with the best results would help move the numbers in the right direction? Why or why not?

11. What do you think about the idea of installing a *poka-yoke*, that is, an engineering approach to prevent an error before it occurs, such as the one seen in this video, Poka Yoke: Lean Hand Washing Error Proofing at MetroWest Medical Center http://www.youtube.com/watch?v=0sK--VfyR7E and discussed on this video podcast, LeanBlog Video Podcast #2 - Kevin Frieswick, MetroWest Medical Center http://www.youtube.com/watch?v=njiUpmWDTsA.

* **Instructor:** please note that an instructor's guide for this case is available in the online resources.

Seaside Convalescent Care Center—Case for Chapters 13 and 3

H. Wayne Nelson

Mindy Alternot has been the administrator of Seaside Convalescent Care Center (SCCC) for seven months. This was her first job after earning her Nursing Home Administrator's license, and despite her initial enthusiasm, she began having second thoughts about her career choice. Things weren't going well at SCCC. Actually, things hadn't gone well there for several years. Mindy had hoped to turn things around, but the facility's last survey was terrible. The inspectors had found several deficiencies indicating a pattern of "potential for more than minimal harm" to the residents. There were other significant problems relating to resident care, resident rights, and quality of life. Consequently, SCCC was denied payment for new admissions and was being fined $3,000 a day for noncompliance.

Mindy blamed her nurse's aides (NAs). After all, they provided more than 90% of the hands-on patient care. She found it nearly impossible to find good ones, and even when she did, she couldn't keep them. Their turnover rate was well over 100% a year (not rare in troubled facilities). Even those who seemed to enjoy working with the elderly would inevitably leave during the summer when it was easy to find more lucrative tourist-trade work.

Mindy had tried to motivate her aides by improving their training and by making their job more meaningful. She tried to encourage their input in matters related to patient care—and wanted to work with the licensed nurses to make the aides part of the total primary care team (which didn't sit well with the nurses). She wanted the aides to assume more responsibility for solving everyday resident problems. Moreover, she tried to build good relationships with them. She wanted to lead by being visible, available, engaged, and in tune with what was going on in the interactive caregiving environment. After two months of "beating her brains out" trying to build relationships, Mindy finally conceded to her Director of Nursing Services, Ann, that the task was hopeless. This was a bitter pill for Mindy, who had been warned by Ann that "touchy-feely schoolbook approaches" just wouldn't work with this crowd.

Ann was a top-notch nurse and a veteran nursing manager. She found the nurse's aides to be a sullen lot, generally, and very hard to manage. Her experience showed them to be young, immature, poorly educated, untrustworthy, undependable, and condescending (to residents), with very poor work habits and almost no motivation. "Besides," she complained "most of them barely speak English, and even those that can, don't really like working here—they do it only because they can't get work elsewhere."

Mindy didn't buy this at first, but quickly became frustrated by the aides' lack of commitment. Soon, she resigned herself to the fact that she couldn't develop the aides' competence, especially when they left before they really got to know their jobs or the patients' individual needs. Moreover, because she had to maintain the minimum required staff-to-patient ratios, she couldn't be too choosy and was compelled to hire warm bodies just to avoid fines.

Stressed, exhausted, and feeling defeated, Mindy began to resent her ignorant and "uncaring" nursing assistants and began to avoid them. By her third month at SCCC, she had delegated their direct oversight to Ann. Mindy felt this was feasible because Ann had worked in nursing homes for years and had a clear vision and the strength of character to whip a poorly motivated workforce into shape. Ann was a strict disciplinarian who understood how to deal with workers who only wanted a paycheck.

"You set clear rules and guidelines, you punish infractions, and you ride them all the time," she explained. "It sounds tough, but unskilled and reluctant workers need clear direction, and they only respect strong, determined leadership. You know, there is such a thing as being too supportive—and this type of workforce sees that type of boss as a sucker."

Ann set about to "clean up the place." But due to high turnover and staff shortages, Ann required a good deal of overtime. Double-shifting was not uncommon. Ann knew this would take a toll on the aides' resilience, but she reasoned that it's "better to use 'em while you got 'em, as they'll quit for better bait during the tourist season anyway."

This delegation of responsibility to Ann allowed Mindy to focus on managing the budget—where Mindy had excellent skills. In fact, she was highly adept at all the technical aspects of managing a nursing home.

DISCUSSION QUESTIONS

1. Do you think this change in management responsibility bodes well for Seaside Convalescent?

2. Which theory of motivation does Mindy represent in this case? Explain your response.

3. Which theory of motivation does Ann represent in this case? Explain your response.

4. Reread the case carefully. What is the underlying reason for the aides not staying on the job?

5. Should Mindy have handed over the reins to Ann? Explain your rationale.

6. Brainstorm 10 alternatives Mindy could have come up with before giving up. Compare and contrast these alternatives and select the two best options. Explain your reasoning.

Staffing at River Oaks Community Hospital: Measure Twice, Cut Once—Case for Chapter 12*

Dawn M. Oetjen, Woody D. Richardson, and Donna J. Slovensky

The CEO began the meeting: "The census for all units and all programs has decreased dramatically from 75% inpatient occupancy to just 50%. The Community Residential Center occupancy, formerly at 90%, has fallen to 40%, and we've dropped from 40 outpatients/partial hospitalizations a week to 15. With these decreased census numbers, we must make staff reductions." Now Debbie Davis, director of operations, and the other directors knew the reason for the emergency executive committee meeting. The CEO not only expressed concern, but also mandated that each of the directors make staff reductions in their departments. "Have your recommendations ready for tomorrow's regularly scheduled meeting, and remember: no department shall remain untouched, period."

River Oaks Community Hospital (ROCH)

River Oaks Community Hospital (ROCH) was a 70-bed, private, for-profit healthcare facility established to treat alcohol/drug abuse and mental illness. Built on vacant farmland, the facility, which had been in existence for 10 years, sat well hidden in a growing urban area surrounded by shopping malls and neighborhoods. Competing facilities and their proximity to ROCH are shown in Table 17-2.

TABLE 17-2 Market Area Facilities

Type of Facility/Programs	Miles Away
New private, for-profit general hospital/inpatient and outpatient psychiatry units	2
Private, for-profit alcohol and drug rehabilitation center	2
State-owned hospital/inpatient and outpatient psychiatric units	7
State-owned alcohol and drug treatment facility	10
Established private, for-profit general hospital/inpatient and outpatient psychiatry units	10
Several private psychiatric practices offering outpatient programs	2–15
Private, for-profit community residential program	50

ROCH had adult, youth, and residential inpatient units and outpatient and partial hospitalization programs. The adult unit outpatient and partial programs treated individuals 18 years of age and older. The youth unit outpatient and partial programs treated children from 3 to 17 years of age.

Some exceptions were made with 17- and 18-year-olds, depending on their maturity level (e.g., an immature 18-year-old might be placed on the youth unit, and an independent, mature 17-year-old might be treated on the adult unit). The community residential center (CRC) was fairly unique in the clientele it treated. It treated very violent youths, ages 12 to 17, who needed long-term (four months or longer) psychiatric and/or addiction treatment in a structured environment. The partial hospitalization program provided treatment for both adults and youths.

Outpatients reported to their respective units between the hours of 7:00 and 8:00 a.m. and were free to leave after the last session, usually around 5:00 p.m. The outpatient program provided adults and youths several group and individual sessions to choose from every week.

Staffing

ROCH maintained around 100 employees on three shifts (24-hour coverage), 7 days a week and 365 days a year. The executive management team consisted of the chief executive officer and directors of operations, nursing/clinical staff, finance, marketing/advancement, and outpatient/CRC services.

With a new master's degree in health administration and 8 years of experience in healthcare management, Debbie had been in her position as the director of operations for only a few weeks. Her responsibilities included the following departments: medical records (two full-time employees), utilization review (one full-time and one part-time employee), quality management, risk management, housekeeping (two full-time employees), maintenance (two full-time employees), dietary services (five full-time employees), education/school (two full-time employees), and an administrative assistant (one full-time employee). Two of the departments, quality management and risk management, were not staffed, and Debbie was performing those duties.

ROCH, in addition to clinical treatment, also provided educational services with one full-time teacher for the youth unit and one for the CRC, and one full-time and one part-time dual-diagnosis educator for adults who acted as "counselors" for other adult patients. Two full-time activity therapists were also on staff to provide recreational and creative activities and programs throughout the day to all patients. The youth educators reported to Debbie while the dual-diagnosis educators reported to the director of nursing.

Despite the diverse clinical and special programs offered at ROCH, admissions were declining. This was partly due to the increasing competition from both inpatient and outpatient facilities (new and established) and private practice physicians (solo and group practices) in the area. A second cause was attributable to recent reimbursement changes due to an increased number of managed care–type insurers. These changes encouraged shorter lengths of inpatient stay with more intense treatments and more outpatient visits and partial hospitalizations. Whereas an inpatient may have been allowed 21 to 28 days of treatment in the past, current reimbursement allowed for 14 days.

The Reaction

After the CEO left the conference room, Debbie looked around for reactions from the other directors. They looked dumbfounded, but only for a few seconds. Heated and emotional statements filled the air for the next 10 minutes. A sampling from the other directors included the following:

> I am already functioning with a skeleton crew. I cannot—no, make that will not—allow my staff to be cut any more; it's just not safe! Sure, this might help meet today's budget, but what about a few months down the line? Fire today, rehire tomorrow, then fire 'em again—that's a great way to build a quality staff.

Debbie chimed in with "I'm already doing two of my employees' jobs in addition to my own. If we keep up these cutbacks, I'm going to be admitted here myself."

Debbie's Dilemma

Debbie left the conference room, went to her office, and closed the door. Was it too late to return her diploma and sign up for a residency instead? Her mind (and eyes) wandered out to the courtyard where she saw a few of her employees eating lunch. These same employees had, just two days ago, shared with her their concerns of downsizing and their feelings of being overwhelmed with their workloads. They had asked Debbie to consider hiring some temporary staff to help them get caught up, and she agreed to look into it. At the time, it did not seem unreasonable, even with low census numbers, due to a scheduled site visit from The Joint Commission less than a year away. She had planned on requesting temporary help for the quality management, medical record, and maintenance departments. Quality management and medical record requirements for The Joint Commission were some of the most important, detailed, and time-consuming parts of the entire survey. She knew extra attention and time should be given to each area for one to two years prior to the survey, and with less than a year until the visit, ROCH was already behind. Maintenance also needed extra staff to ensure that the facility was in compliance in terms of safety, cleanliness, and appearance.

With this new mandate, not only were these moot points, but Debbie now needed to consider how to "get blood from a stone." She had only a day to create a new staffing plan for her departments that reflected the required staff reductions. She pulled out the "cheat sheet" that she had created to help her identify each of her employees (Table 17-3) and the staffing sheet (Table 17-4) she was given at the meeting only an hour ago. It was going to be a long night.

TABLE 17-3 Staff Profiles for Debbie's Direct Reports at ROCH

Name	Department and Position	Full- or Part-Time	Years with ROCH	Years in Field	Sex and Age	Performance Appraisal Score (4 being best)
S. Buford, RRA	Medical Records Supervisor	Full	8	17	F 49	3.25
D. Fitzgerald	Medical Records Clerk	Full	3	13	F 52	3.5
S. Carpenter	Medical Records Transcriptionist	Part	2	5	F 27	3
M. Burke	Housekeeping Housekeeper	Full	10	35	F 58	4
T. Snyder	Housekeeping Housekeeper	Full	7	10	F 32	2.75
D. Bogues	Maintenance Interior Specialist	Full	10	20	M 41	4
T. Dimatteo	Maintenance Exterior Specialist	Full	1.5	22	M 40	3.25
A. Pensa	Dietary–Cafeteria Cook	Full	10	37	M 55	2.75
J. Jones	Dietary–Cafeteria Cook	Full	3	6	M 28	3.75
P. Tucker	Dietary–Cafeteria Server, Preparer	Full	10	20	F 37	4
C. Black	Dietary–Cafeteria	Full	1	3	F 24	3
T. Burns	Dietary–Cafeteria Server, Preparer	Full	2.5	8	M 32	3
M. Carter, RD	Dietary–Cafeteria Dietician	Full	1	7	F 29	3.75
Y. Fredericks, RN	Utilization Review Case Reviewer	Full	10	20	F 42	4
B. Stephens, LPN	Utilization Review Case Reviewer	Part	6	12	F 36	3.75
P. Johnson	School/Education Teacher (youth unit)	Full	10	12	F 34	4
B. Patterson	School/Education Teacher (CRC unit)	Full	3	22	F 45	3.75
P. Stanton	Administrative Assistant	Full	7	25	F 47	3

TABLE 17-4 ROCH Staffing Report

Department Positions	Shifts		
	7:00 a.m.–3:00 p.m.	3:00 p.m.–11:00 p.m.	11:00 p.m.–7:00 a.m.
Nursing			
R.N. (nurse)	6 (2/2/2)	6 (2/2/2)	3 (1/1/1)
R.N. supervisors	2	2	1
P.C.A. (patient care assistant)	3 (1/1/1)	3 (1/1/1)	3 (1/1/1)
A.T. (activity therapist)	2	-	-
S.W. (social work)	3 (1/1/1)	-	-
S.W. supervisor	1	-	-
Intake (admission screeners)	2	1	1 (on call)
Intake supervisor	1	-	-
D.D. (dual diagnosis educators)	1.5	-	-
Nursing director	1	(on call)	(on call)
Operations			
M.R. (medical records)	1.5	-	-
M.R. supervisor	1	-	-
Maintenance	2	(on call)	(on call)
Housekeeping	2	-	-
Dietary—Cafeteria	3	2	-
Dietician	1	-	-
Q.M. (quality management)	(vacant)		
R.M. (risk management)	(vacant)		
U.R. (utilization review)	1.5	-	-
Teachers—School	2	-	-
Administrative assistant	1	-	-
Operations director	1	(on call)	(on call)
Marketing			
Marketing associates	2	-	-
Administrative assistant	1	-	-
Marketing director	1	-	-
Finance			
Business office staff	7	1	-
Operator	1	1	-
Business office supervisor	1	-	-
Administrative assistant	1	1	-
Finance director	1	-	-
Outpatient/CRC			
Staff	2	1	1
CRC supervisor	1	(on call)	(on call)
Outpatient supervisor	1	-	-
Administrative assistant	1	-	-
Director	1	(on call)	(on call)
Administrative			
CEO	1	-	-
Administrative assistant	1	-	-

DISCUSSION QUESTIONS

1. Discuss the CEO's decision to lay off employees in light of the reduced census figures. Are layoffs the appropriate response?

2. What effects will layoffs have on the organization?

3. Design a role-play to discuss the layoffs from the perspectives of the CEO, operations director, and employees.

4. Develop a plan for implementing immediate employee layoffs. Give specific details concerning departments/positions affected, the use of seniority versus merit (performance appraisals), the amount of notice, and outplacement activities. What additional information, if any, would you need? Provide a rationale for each recommendation together with reasons other alternatives were not chosen.

* **Instructor:** please note that an instructor's guide for this case is available in the online resources.

Heritage Valley Medical Center: Are Your Managers Culturally Competent?—Case for Chapters 14 and 13

Velma Roberts

Heritage Valley Medical Center was very proud of its reputation for providing quality services for all citizens in the community. Over the last 20 years, the Medical Center had flourished, and both staff and health professionals in the organization were committed to its shared values and its respect for all patients and their families. Services were provided to a community whose residents were 80% Caucasian, 15% African American, and 5% Hispanic. However, in the last 5 years, the population had gradually changed to 50% Caucasian, 40% African American, and 10% Hispanic and Asian American. The Center's occupancy rates were down to 40%, given that many of its traditional, more affluent, private-pay patients had moved out into the suburbs to escape the urban sprawl that comes with development.

The Medical Center administrator first noticed a change when the patient mix became more diverse. After the State Health Indigent Care Fund was established, Medicaid reimbursement increased, making it comparable to those of managed care organizations. It was strategically imperative to capture this new market and these potential revenues, particularly since most of the indigent and Medicaid recipients were minorities. Heritage Valley started a major marketing campaign and developed alliances with physicians, community clinics, and public health agencies to increase its referrals of Medicaid and indigent patients to capitalize on this new source of revenue.

By year 3 of this strategic initiative, the increase in minority patients had jumped from approximately 10% to 40% (primarily African American and Hispanics). Many of the Hispanics were immigrants with work permits for the construction boom in the affluent areas of the county and surrounding suburbs. Even though there was an increase in minority patients, the ethnicity of the service providers remained at previous levels. Eighty-five percent of the clinical staff members, including physicians, nurses, laboratory technologists, pharmacists, and therapists, were Caucasian. There were two African American managers and one Hispanic manager. The executive management team was 100% Caucasian, with one female. The majority of the support and administrative staff (secretaries, human resource technicians, nurse's aides) were African American. In some of the support areas (e.g., dietary or environmental services), the staff was 100% African American. There was little turnover, and the clinical and support staff were like family, since the majority of them had worked at Heritage for more than 15 years, and shared similar values and principles about valuing every patient and treating each patient with respect.

At a management meeting with administrative directors, the vice president of community relations, Ms. Harper, shared the results of a recent patient satisfaction survey, which indicated that while 80% of the Caucasian patients were very satisfied with their care, only 30% of African Americans, 10% of Hispanics, and 20% of Asians were satisfied. She was very concerned about the reasons for dissatisfaction. At the top of the list for all three ethnic groups was the reason "I don't feel welcomed here." The second was "people talk down to me," and the third was "the nurses don't seem to understand me." When asked for feedback and how to improve these results, the nursing director immediately defended her staff. She made it clear that she had one of the most caring, attentive, and qualified nursing staffs in the county. She could not understand how these minority patients could be so ungrateful.

"These people will never be satisfied unless they can get something for nothing. Half of them can't even speak English and the others mess up the King's English so badly you don't know what they want. We can't help it if these people are uneducated, can't speak the language, and don't know how to communicate with professional people. My nurses and nurse aides are doing the best they can to work with these people, even when they are too limited to understand basic information." Following this feedback, several other managers also voiced their support for the nursing staff because their employees had complained about these same issues. They wanted to let the vice president know their opinions, of which the following comments were representative:

- Most of these patients won't even look us in the eye. We can hardly get any information out of them.
- It takes twice as long to deal with Hispanics and Asians because they can barely speak English. They should learn to speak English and get with the program. It's not the employees' fault that these people can't speak the language.
- There is absolutely no excuse for those Black patients. They were born here and still cannot speak English. We have done everything for them—given them a free ride for

education, jobs, and housing. If anything, they are driving away our few remaining paying patients with their loud conversations and by bringing family members and children with them who are always acting ghetto and foolish.

- These patients are not satisfied? Has anybody considered what we have to put up with? These people are just ungrateful complainers!

The two African American managers were asked what they thought about the patients' feedback. Both of them agreed with their colleagues, saying:

"Those Hispanics and Asians need to learn how to speak English. This is America—what do they expect? We can only do so much. As for those Asians, they should speak up and stop being so passive. You can't get them to talk; they bring every family member with them and they speak Chinese or Vietnamese while you're trying to help them. Sometimes I think they are talking about us right in front of our faces. Plus, they think they are better than other minorities; they are cliquish and they don't want to be a part of anything. How can we ever understand them when they won't talk to us?"

The male Hispanic manager was very upset about the African Americans' and Caucasians' feedback about Hispanics. He felt that Hispanic patients were being unnecessarily targeted because they were the most vulnerable. He knew that they were hard-working people just trying to make a living, doing work no one else would. To blame them for the way they felt about their treatment at the Medical Center was wrong. He went on to say the following:

"How dare the African American managers say anything? They are only here because of affirmative action and diversity initiatives. The only reason they are agreeing with the white managers is because they want to keep their jobs. The Blacks are ashamed of their culture and are afraid to be associated with the low-income Black patients, even though they probably came from the same ghetto neighborhood."

Ms. Harper was completely shocked and dismayed at the responses of these managers. As she left the meeting, she was at a loss as to how to explain these attitudes to the Medical Center's executive team. And more importantly, what could be done to change these managers' beliefs and attitudes about minority patients? Or was it too late?

DISCUSSION QUESTIONS

1. Reread this case. Using Figure 17-3, the Confidential Teammate Evaluation Form at the start of this chapter, compare the behavior of these managers with the expected behaviors of teammates. Score each manager (the nurse, the African American manager, and the Hispanic manager) as if he or she were your teammate. What scores did they earn?

2. Would you want to work with them on a team? Explain your response.

3. Thinking back to the chapter on teamwork, do you think Ms. Harper is a good team leader? Explain your response.

4. Do you think any of these managers demonstrated cultural proficiency?

5. What should Ms. Harper do about her managers' knowledge about other cultures? Compare and contrast two different approaches to fixing this organization's issues.

Emotional Intelligence in Labor and Delivery—Case for Chapters 2 and 13

Louis Rubino and Brenda Freshman

It is Sunday night in Labor and Delivery. An obviously pregnant full-term mother, Mrs. Ford, presents herself, saying her doctor, Dr. Jones, told her to come to the hospital to deliver her baby. The mother tells Ms. Smith, the nurse manager of L&D, that the doctor has informed her that the baby has anencephaly, and she understands that the baby will not be expected to live very long after delivery. Ms. Smith is very concerned, since the unit did not receive any prior word about Mrs. Ford coming to the hospital, nor did the unit receive the prenatal record, which is required to be submitted by the 36th week of pregnancy per hospital policy.

Ms. Smith proceeds to call Dr. Jones to ask for orders and to get more information regarding Mrs. Ford's condition. Dr. Jones gets very upset with the phone call, says that he just completed a delivery and was trying to get a couple hours of sleep before he came to the hospital to deliver Mrs. Ford's anencephalic baby. He yells that he will be there shortly now that she has woken him and tells her to start prepping for a C-section and hangs up. Ms. Smith realizes the survivability of the baby is not possible and that no measure will be able to save the life of the baby once delivered. Ms. Smith understands that in these cases, it is the nurses' job to use whatever measures necessary to make the baby and mother as comfortable as possible so the baby can have a dignified death.

Ms. Smith is agitated at Dr. Jones's response. First, he was obviously in the wrong in not notifying the hospital about Mrs. Ford coming in, let alone not sending in the prenatal record. When Dr. Jones enters the unit, he is obviously upset but gets even more upset when Ms. Smith questions why he intends to do a C-section. Ms. Smith could tell that Mrs. Ford was not expecting a C-section based on her comments to her. Dr. Jones dismisses Ms. Smith's comments about doing a vaginal delivery and begrudgingly he does do a vaginal birth, complaining during it about how he will now have to reschedule his whole day, since it will take much longer than a C-section.

The baby is delivered. It is clear that the baby is anencephalic and has very poor circulation. The nurses wrap the baby in blankets and hand the baby to Mrs. Ford for her to view.

Dr. Jones says there is no reason to call in a neonatologist and that this baby will obviously only live a few hours at most. Mrs. Ford requests to have her baby fed. Dr. Jones says it is okay to do that and requests the baby be put on a cardio-respiratory monitor with an IV tube for feeding. Ms. Smith is concerned about this, since she knows it will prolong the life of the child, and this would be considered futile care. She wonders how to handle this concern since she realizes Dr. Jones will probably yell at her if she is to question his orders again.

DISCUSSION QUESTIONS

1. What is your opinion of Dr. Jones's emotional intelligence (EI)? Based on a scale of 1–10, with 1 being lowest, how would you rate Dr. Jones? Why?

2. Repeat this process for Ms. Smith, the nurse manager.

3. Do you think there should be any consequences for Dr. Jones as a result of his behavior? What can be done?

4. Should Ms. Smith question Dr. Jones's orders for feeding the terminal baby? How would she do this?

5. What about the patient, Mrs. Ford? What is her stake in all this? Should she get involved in the obvious conflict occurring around her?

6. What should the hospital do to try to educate the staff about emotional intelligence? Explain your answer.

7. How could teamwork training help this Neonatal ICU team? Explain your answer.

Are We Culturally Aware or Not?—Case for Chapters 14 and 5

Nancy Sayre

A growing, profitable internal medicine practice of 10 physicians, 2 physician assistants, a physical therapist, and a massage therapist is located in a city of 150,000 people. The clinical personnel are mostly from the majority group in the area and consider themselves open-minded, altruistic, and culturally aware. The administrative support staff is representative of the makeup of the patient population—mostly minority groups in the local community. The patient population is growing and becoming more diverse from those newly arrived in the city. The practice is currently facing several challenges.

DISCUSSION QUESTIONS

1. The practice manager wants to have the local hospital expert on cultural competency come talk to the staff. The administrative support staff does not feel that they need training. How should the practice manager proceed?

2. The practice needs to hire a new administrative assistant to work with the front desk staff. The practice wishes to hire someone from the local minority community rather than an equally qualified individual from another state. How should the practice manager proceed? Justify the rationale for this recommendation.

3. With the recent growth, the practice is considering relocating its office to another, larger office facility. Several options are being discussed. Should they relocate to a more affluent area of the city that is less diverse? Or should they stay in the same neighborhood, even if it is less profitable? What are the pros and cons of staying in this neighborhood versus moving to another area? If the rent is higher in the more diverse area, is that enough to justify not moving there? Or is diversity responsiveness a "cost of doing business"? How should the practice manager proceed?

4. The practice wants to maintain its good standing in the community. What initiatives could it undertake to remain connected to its local patient population?

5. The practice manager decides to do a strategic plan to answer some of her questions. Who should she invite to participate in focus groups? What might be some ethical incentives that she can use to encourage participation?

A Nightmare Job Interview—Case for Chapter 12

Nancy H. Shanks

The Scenario

Susie Q. is the current administrative assistant in the transplant department of the University of Timbuktu (UT) Medical Center, a not-for-profit state school. Susie Q. has held her position for three years, since graduating from UT's Health Care Management (HCM) Program. She has done a terrific job, has just received a promotion, and will be leaving the department in a couple of weeks. Ms. Hardman, the transplant nurse manager, is the hiring authority for the position and thus has the responsibility for selecting Susie Q.'s replacement. This position will report to Ms. Hardman and Dr. Kidney, the chief of the department. In the interest of a smooth transition, Ms. Hardman has asked Susie Q. to assist with the recruitment and hiring of her replacement. Susie Q. and Ms. Hardman have met to discuss the process; the job description has been prepared and approved by HR and the department. The job has been posted online, advertised in the local paper, and sent to a couple of professors at the UT HCM Program. The response has been terrific, with a very strong pool of applicants being identified for the position. Susie Q. has completed preliminary telephone interviews with each candidate in an effort to narrow the pool and has scheduled in-person interviews with the three finalists. Now it's time for the interviews. Ms. Hardman will be conducting the interview, and Susie Q. will participate as needed.

The Interview

Both Susie Q. and Ms. Hardman have reviewed Mary's resume. She is a UT HCM graduate and is the strongest candidate based on her resume and phone interview. Susie Q. starts the process by introducing Ms. Hardman to Mary.

"Mary, it's great to meet you in person. I'd like you to meet my boss, Ms. Hardman. She's the manager of our department and will be conducting the interview."

438

"Welcome, Mary, nice to meet you. Let's get started with you giving us a brief overview of your background."

"Thank you, Ms. Hardman. I'm very pleased to have the opportunity to interview for this position. I am a new college graduate with a bachelor's degree in healthcare administration. After marrying young and having a couple of kids, I returned to school to complete my degree. I am very proud to have achieved this. I have experience working part-time in a similar position as an administrative assistant in the UT English department during college. This position allowed me to gain lots of experience that is generalizable to the transplant department."

"Can you elaborate on this for us?"

"Well, as an example, I have provided general office support to professionals, mainly faculty, been responsible for appointment and meeting scheduling, prepared reports, helped manage our budget, ordered supplies, provided customer service to students, and the like."

Susie Q. chimes in: "That's great, Mary, but do you have any experience in the health-care industry?"

"I do have some experience in the field. I had a fabulous internship experience at Planned Parenthood. I was involved in developing job descriptions, doing preliminary applicant screenings, making revisions to an employee handbook, and performing other HR duties as assigned. I also was able to assist in one of the clinics, doing patient scheduling, learning about registering patients, and using the electronic medical records system. It's not a lot of experience, but it's a start."

"What is the ideal job for you?"

"I am looking for a full-time position in health care, where I can get more experience, learn new areas and skills, be delegated new responsibilities, be given autonomy, have a collegial work environment, and begin to apply what I've learned in school. I'm a quick study, could learn a great deal from Susie Q. before she leaves, and think I would do a great job for the department."

Susie Q. and Mary both think to themselves that this is going great. All of a sudden and out of the blue, Ms. Hardman asks a question that changes the tone and direction of the interview: "Mary, do you smoke?"

Susie Q. sits stunned, not knowing what to do. Mary is completely taken aback and hesitates to respond. Finally, after a very lengthy pause, she nervously, but truthfully, replies: "Yes, I have smoked for a long time, but am currently trying to quit. I have started taking Chantix, a prescription medication used to help people quit smoking, and my quit day is this coming Sunday."

Ms. Hardman butts in: "Sorry, but that's a deal breaker for me. Thanks for coming in."

Desperate to save the interview, Mary adds the following explanation: "I get terrible sores when I am without nicotine. This is medically documented by my dentist and physician. But I am committed to quitting."

Ms. Hardman stands up and as she leaves the room says: "It's tacky when healthcare workers smoke. This is a smoke-free campus. I can't hire people who smoke. Sorry, but you're not in a protected class. That's it, this interview is over. Thanks again for taking the time."

DISCUSSION QUESTIONS

1. Was this a good way to handle this situation?

2. How could each party have handled this differently?

3. Was this a legitimate question to ask? Was Ms. Hardman legally correct? Ethically?

4. What are the key learnings from this case for you as a potential interviewee? As a potential interviewer or hiring manager?

5. If Mary was able to prove that Ms. Hardman was out of line asking that question and was begrudgingly offered the job, should she take it?

A Small Healthcare Clinic Confronts Health Insurance Problems—Case for Chapter 9

Nancy H. Shanks

After working for a small physician practice for several years, you've decided that it's time for a change. Having had some experience assisting a practice manager with management, you've sought out and been hired as the administrator of a small nonprofit clinic that provides primary care services to an ethnically diverse population in a mid-size metropolitan area.

The Clinic's History

The organization started as a broader community effort, with a group of volunteers coming together over concern that residents of a low-income area of the community didn't have access to basic health care. A group of retired physicians, nurses, a nurse practitioner, a healthcare administrator, and a couple of community volunteers put their heads together to strategize about how to address the problem. The result was a new organization that was incorporated as a non-profit, with the founders serving as the board of directors.

Each of the board members agreed to make an initial contribution of $10,000, providing $100,000 in seed money to the clinic. A local church had a small building that wasn't being used that was made available to house the clinic; used equipment, exam tables, office furniture, and a couple of computers were secured from other local healthcare facilities that had remodeled; and board members recruited friends and associates to volunteer their time to serve the patients and to make donations to assist in the venture.

The clinic's mission was to serve all comers as best they could and to not turn anyone away, even if they had little or no ability to pay for their care. This approach was successful in getting the organization off the ground.

The Patient Population

Many of the patients served come from the low-income community where the clinic is located. There are many younger individuals who are beginning to start families, are employed as seasonal workers or in types of jobs and industries that don't provide health insurance coverage, and are relatively healthy. There is a growing population of elderly individuals who have moved into the area because housing is less expensive in the community. Some of the patients are undocumented. Many are uninsured; some can pay out-of-pocket for care, but some can't.

The Current Scenario

The organization has been in existence for 10 years and has experienced some significant changes. The founders have stepped down from their leadership roles, making way for a new group of younger board members. While in the beginning many services were provided for free and costs were kept to a minimum, now expenditures on staffing, new equipment, and operations have escalated. The organization still has numerous volunteers, with many medical, nursing, and other students donating their time. However, the clinic had to hire several part-time workers a few years ago. Now, they have a part-time medical director, a couple of young physicians who work 1 day per week, two nurses, three medical assistants, and a couple of administrative staff to meet the steady growth in patient volume and the increased complexity of the organization. Ability to pay, even on a sliding-fee-scale basis, and the lack of insurance coverage have become increasingly problematic. While the original model of operating the business worked for a while and was admirable in terms of meeting community needs, it is not sustainable over the long run. Now, the organization has some new challenges.

DISCUSSION QUESTIONS

There are three areas of particular concern that the new board of directors would like you to address:

1. The clinic has never provided health insurance benefits to its employees. As the new administrator, you concur that this is a problem and would like to find a way to address it. While the board members don't have much background in or knowledge about how to do this, they are willing to consider your proposal. They have requested that you present them with a proposal that addresses the following:

   a. What are the pros and cons of providing coverage?
   b. What types of coverage are available? Which are options for the organization?
   c. How much would the options cost? How much would the organization be required to pay? Should the employees share in the cost? What would be the employees' share?
   d. What is the best option?

2. Another major issue is the lack of health insurance coverage of the patients. With the recent recession and job losses that have occurred, more of the clinic's patients seem to be uninsured clients. Again, the board would like a proposal that covers:

   a. What are the options that may potentially be available to patients?
   b. What are the pros and cons of these?
   c. Which seem to offer the best potential, given the current circumstances?
   d. How can the clinic assist its patients with learning about the options?

3. There is a possibility that the clinic might be able to apply for federal grants to keep afloat. Review the materials at this website about Federally Qualified Health Centers (FQHC) http://www.raconline.org/info_guides/clinics/fqhcfaq.php#whatis

   a. Identify the pros and cons of applying for status as an FQHC for the clinic.
   b. Make a recommendation about what is needed and what additional steps the board might take.

Choosing a Successor—Case for Chapters 1 and 2

W. Carole Shepherd and Louis Rubino

Objectives

1. Recognize and describe the complex criteria often used to select a candidate to be the next leader.
2. Evaluate and select the correct candidate for a leadership position.
3. Apply critical thinking skills in a complex and multifaceted decision-making model.

The Case

Paul is the 62-year-old administrator of the multispecialty Ambulatory Care Center. He has worked at the Center for many years. He is planning his retirement one year from now, and he wishes to begin the process of training a successor. He has three possible internal candidates for the position. Your job is to evaluate these managers and help Paul choose the best new leader for the organization.

Important Facts to Know

The Ambulatory Care Center is a medium-sized facility serving an average of 80 patients on a daily basis. There has been little growth over the last few years, and the direction of the Center needs to change in order for it to remain viable. Historically, the Center has served a predominance of senior citizens, reflective of the surrounding community; however, the neighborhood is changing. More and more young families are moving in, and there are now many young adults and school-age children in the surrounding community. Additionally, the ethnicity of the neighborhood is changing, with more and more families of Hispanic or African American origin.

The financial base that supports the Center is gradually changing from payments that come predominantly from Medicare and private pay to a financial base where payments are mainly coming from a combination of group insurance, Medicaid, and cash patients. Many of the adults work at the car manufacturing plant that was recently built in their city. These individuals and their families have high-quality group insurance. The Center would like very much to "tap into" this insured group and is interested in contracting with them for services for their employees.

Because of these changes in the surrounding community and the resulting impact on their financial base, the Center wants to change direction for the future. They wish to redesign their image and how the community views them. They no longer wish to be identified as just a clinic mostly for seniors, but as a Center for *all* who need medical care.

The Center wants it to be known that they can care for all ages. They are particularly interested in making sure that people are aware of the many services they can provide for children, including newborn screening for metabolic, sickle cell, and other genetic disorders; special programs for diabetic children; and specialty treatments for children with ADHD, autism, and Asperger's syndrome. The addition of a specialized pediatric group to their physician base has made these services possible, and they want to get the word out to the community as to their availability.

The Candidates
Candidate #1

The first person being considered for the new leadership job is Taneshia. She is an African American woman, age 36, who has worked for the Center for the last three years. She has her bachelor's degree in health administration and is a registered record administrator. Her college minor was in human resources management.

She is currently the director of health information management systems, has done well in her job, and has increased reimbursement for the Center. One of the ways in which Taneshia was able to increase the reimbursement figures was by implementing electronic medical records in her department. The transition from paper to electronic record-keeping has been difficult, but Taneshia is very good with technology, and she has led her department with a sure hand. The introduction of electronic medical records has also decreased record-keeping errors. Taneshia makes a point of keeping up-to-date with all the latest advances in her field of expertise. She is entrepreneurial and innovative.

Taneshia has a directive management style when she is training those under her. Unfortunately, she is also somewhat pompous and opinionated and feels no one knows as much about the work of her department, or about computers, as she does. However, the training of her staff, despite her style, has achieved the goal of having her people do better and more accurate coding work. Correct coding has resulted in fewer appeals and more payments for the Center. She accomplishes her goals—but tends to push her people a little too hard.

She has done outstanding work in regulatory compliance by volunteering to make sure that all reporting for the entire Center is completed. There was, at one point, some question as to whether her reporting methods were accurate or whether she was just reporting what the Department of Health wanted to hear. However, no improper conduct was ever proven, and the Center remains in good standing with the local regulators.

Additionally, she has created a strong liaison with the physicians by providing them with extensive peer comparison statistics. She has created a great deal of transparency with her new and improved record-keeping methods, and this has motivated the doctors to work better and smarter. They have increased their productivity, and this has also helped to increase revenue.

Taneshia is married and has no children. At this time, she has no plans for a family. She and her husband are busy with their respective careers. She is unsure if she wants to pursue a further degree, such as a master's. She works whatever hours are necessary to get the job done.

Candidate #2

The second person being considered for the new leadership job is Felipe. He is a Hispanic male, age 29, who has worked for the Center for the last five years. He started with them directly out of college and has worked his way up to where he is now—the director of community outreach. He has his bachelor's in health administration, and he just finished his master's in business administration.

His duties include marketing and contracting with managed care companies. He has done well in his job and is seen as a talented negotiator. He understands contracts and is good with people. He has signed a number of lucrative contracts for the Center.

Felipe has no employees directly reporting to him. However, now that he has his master's degree, he is interested in moving into operations in his next healthcare job. He feels that he would be good at leading, directing, and managing employees, and he would like to take on this added responsibility. He has already started to look around for new job possibilities.

Felipe has a participative management style, and he is professional in his demeanor. He is well liked both at the Center and out in the community. He has improved the reputation of the Center in the surrounding neighborhood simply with his engaging personality and his involvement in community outreach. His youth, good looks, and charming personality have made him popular with his female employees; however, there has never been any hint of scandal associated with his name. Felipe is considered to have high integrity, and he cares deeply what people think of him.

Due to his external community focus, Felipe is not required to be at the Center on a daily basis. He is expected, though, to be out in the field 40 hours per week developing new and nurturing old business relationships. There were rumors that he was attending his MBA classes when he was supposed to be working and did not have Paul's permission to do so.

Felipe is single and has no intention of getting married anytime soon. He works many hours of overtime and appears to be willing to go the extra mile and give the time necessary to get something done.

Candidate #3

The third person being considered for the new leadership job is Amanda. She is a Caucasian woman, age 45, who has worked for the Center for the last 10 years. She started as a front office receptionist in order to "get in" and has worked her way up to the job of business office manager. She has a bachelor's degree in health administration. Amanda has a professional style and dresses well. She is a confident woman with a positive outlook on life. She is highly motivated to do a good job and motivates those around her.

Amanda oversees a large and varied group of workers, ranging from receptionists to billing clerks. She has done well in her job and has increased reimbursement for the Center. She has done this by first teaching and training those in her department to do effective billing and collection, resulting in faster claims turnaround and fewer denials. Second, she has improved information collection at the front desks. The receptionists now make sure that all information on the intake forms is filled out completely, that copayments and deductibles are collected, and that correct authorizations are in place before a patient is seen. Amanda was instrumental in the purchase and installation of a new billing system that helps her people do an excellent job.

Amanda is well liked by her employees. She has good coaching skills and gives her people credit for their accomplishments. She rarely takes credit for herself. She has a great deal of confidence and is able to easily instill confidence in those around her. She has integrity and is well known throughout the Center as the "go to" person if you have a problem. When the current leader is out of town on business or goes on vacation, Amanda fills in for him. She has done this on numerous occasions.

Over the years, the employee base at the Center has gradually changed, and now there is great variety in the ethnicity and nationality of the employees. Amanda is not that comfortable working with people of backgrounds different from her own. She is aware of this insecurity and is working to correct it by meeting and greeting all those who work for her on a daily basis.

Because of her assertive leadership and the aggressive collection methods that she has her people use, both at the front desk and later via telephone collection, the patients tend to complain to their doctors. The doctors, in turn, complain to Amanda, asking her to "soft pedal" the requests for money. She has no sympathy and tells the doctors it is her job to collect money and she's going to do it in every way that she can.

Amanda is married and has two adolescent children and a busy life. As a result, she has never pursued her master's degree. She has never felt she had the time. Because of her children, she rarely works past 5 p.m. She puts in her 40 hours faithfully and then heads for home.

DISCUSSION QUESTIONS

1. Identify the strengths and weaknesses of each candidate for the leadership role.

2. Which of the factors you consider important would most favor Taneshia? Felipe? Amanda?

3. Do you think the ethnicity of the candidate is important or irrelevant? Why?

4. How would a change in the environment influence the person selected?

5. Which of the three candidates would you recommend to be the next leader? Why?

6. If Taneshia is chosen, what do you think would be her biggest problems as a leader and being able to work with the others? Felipe? Amanda?

7. Should Paul have considered an outside candidate to be his successor?

The New Toy at City Medical Center—Case for Chapters 11 and 13

Windsor Sherrill and Dale Buchbinder

Capsule endoscopy is used to examine parts of the gastrointestinal tract that cannot be seen with other types of endoscopy. The process uses a very small camera attached to a long flexible tube to view the intestinal tract. The technology is particularly useful when disease is suspected in the small intestine and can sometimes diagnose sources of bleeding or causes of abdominal pain such as Crohn's disease or peptic ulcers.

A group of gastroenterologists at the City Medical Center proposed the purchase of the capsule endoscopy equipment through the Capital Equipment Purchasing process. After the equipment was approved and the purchase initiated, providers began the process of applying for specific privileges to use it. Three gastroenterologists, Drs. Smith, Sams, and Amalfi, applied for credentials and were approved by the department of gastroenterology and, ultimately, the Medical Center Board of Directors to use capsule endoscopy.

After the three gastroenterologists began to use the new equipment, they discovered that a surgeon, Dr. Jones, intended to use the capsule endoscopy equipment for procedures, too. Having done this procedure at another competing hospital on numerous occasions, Dr. Jones had also been privileged through the department of surgery and, ultimately, the City Medical Center Board of Directors. When Dr. Jones put his first case on the schedule for the Gastroenterology Suite where the capsule endoscopy was to be performed, Nurse Tattler called the gastroenterology department and alerted them to this potential intrusion.

Drs. Sams, Smith, and Amalfi were outraged. They had advocated for the equipment, and this poacher was attempting to enter their domain. While each of them told Dr. Jones that they liked him "as a person," they were *not* willing to share their new toy with him or the surgery department. They felt strongly that they "owned" the equipment and the suite. He would just have to go elsewhere.

Dr. Jones pointed out to the trio that the *hospital* purchased the equipment with capital equipment dollars; the department of gastroenterology did not pay for it. In addition, the suite and the nurses who staffed the suite were employees of City Medical Center, not of the department of gastroenterology. And he had been privileged by his department and the City Medical Board of Directors.

Tempers flared, and the chairs of the two departments were informed of this escalating conflict. Since Dr. Jones had scheduled the procedure and the patient was expecting to have it the next morning, the chairs called an emergency meeting with all the involved parties.

DISCUSSION QUESTIONS

1. What questions do you think the chairs of each department should ask?

2. Dr. Jones has a busy practice and is the second highest revenue producer from general surgery. City Medical Center is dependent on revenue from the surgical service. How might this impact how the situation should be handled? What specific steps should be taken to avoid this situation in the future?

3. The goal of physician privileging is to ensure that providers practicing in an organization have appropriate credentials to provide safe and effective treatment. What are three challenges illustrated by this case?

4. Who are the stakeholders in the privileging process at City Medical Center?

5. Who is responsible for communicating about specific privileges?

6. Would these physician behaviors be considered "patient-centric"?

7. Are these physicians "team players"? Explain your response.

8. Reread this case. Using Figure 17-3, the Confidential Teammate Evaluation Form at the start of this chapter, compare the behavior of these physicians with the expected behaviors of teammates. Score each physician as if he or she were your teammate. What scores did they earn?

The "Easy" Software Upgrade at Delmar Ortho—Case for Chapters 8 and 13

Tressa Springmann and Sharon B. Buchbinder

Delmar Orthopedics is a 42-physician orthopedic group; its physicians command the local market in terms of the orthopedic specialty—operating in several of the nearby hospitals and seeing patients in their five sites around the city. Delmar works like a machine. The physicians, the structure around their practice, and the employees who support them are extremely efficient and predictable. Recently, their margins have declined due to reductions in reimbursement, but they have been doing a good job of squeezing every penny out of each clinical day. And, they finally smoothed things out after the somewhat rocky implementation of their electronic medical records (EMR) system the prior year. Everything seemed to be under control.

Patrick McCain joined Delmar Orthopedics a month ago as the practice manager. Prior to joining the practice, he'd been managing a bank for 2 years after working his way up through the teller ranks in his college years. A hard worker, Patrick felt relatively comfortable in his ability to manage people and a budget. He was excited about his new job with the challenge of managing a large team—more than 40 people—and having responsibility for all practice administrative functions excluding finance, legal, and information technology (IT).

Years ago, the practice instituted a bimonthly meeting of the leadership (management team members and a number of the key physicians) to discuss volumes and patient care issues and announce upcoming activities/events. Yesterday's meeting was Patrick's second since joining. During the meeting, it appeared that a number of the physicians were not paying attention. One played a game on his smart phone during the entire meeting, and another one kept leaving the meeting to take phone calls. Two of the team members had a running sidebar conversation about their weekend plans, and a third one actually fell asleep. Although the meeting was relatively noneventful—and, in fact, this seemed to be the team's usual meeting behavior—there *was* one item that concerned him.

Terry, the practice's IT director, announced to the group that it was time for the annual upgrade of the system. The schedule wasn't yet finalized, but he recommended completion within the next 90 days. This would be their first upgrade to the system and would require five hours of downtime for the vendor to complete. Plus, it had to occur on a weekday, when physicians would be seeing patients. Terry did say that this would be their first time the system had been down since it was installed the prior year; however, he did not provide any additional details or offer contact information for follow-up.

Patrick knew this upgrade would be an important chance to prove himself, but he was the "new kid" on the block. He worried that there might be alliances of which he was unaware and "sacred cows" that no one wanted to disturb. He lived through many systems upgrades in the banking world and was painfully aware that these supposedly "easy" upgrades never were. He wanted to alert the practice to the problems that could occur and how to avoid them. As he sat at his desk thinking about all the issues, Terry strolled by, grinned at him and said, "Don't worry, I've got it all under control." At those words, Patrick's heart sank.

As he learned more about the project, it was clear that all of the staff and physicians needed to be retrained. And there had been no accommodations made for testing the changes. He increasingly felt as though Terry had not appropriately informed the leadership team about the scope and risk of the upgrade. Terry appeared to be held in high regard by the practice.

DISCUSSION QUESTIONS

1. How can Patrick address these risks without embarrassing Terry?

2. Why do you think that a number of the team members don't pay attention to this important event? As a future manager, what do you think should have occurred in this meeting?

3. How would you handle the discussion that needs to take place with Terry? What measures might you take to plan for the worst?

4. What research should Patrick do on the prior's year's project that might assist him in assessing the risk in the upgrade?

5. How might Patrick ensure that he understands the impact of the project before putting too much time and effort into it himself?

6. What are some of the questions Patrick should pose to understand how this upgrade would affect his staff? The physicians? Delmar's patients?

7. Are the physicians "team players"? Explain your response.

8. Reread this case. Using Figure 17-3, the Confidential Teammate Evaluation Form at the start of this chapter, compare the behavior of these physicians and managers with the expected behaviors of teammates. Score each one as if he or she were your teammate. What scores did they earn?

Recruitment Challenge for the Middle Manager—Case for Chapter 12

Jon Mase Thompson

You are the director of strategic planning and marketing in a large, multihospital-based health system. The office includes 10 professional positions (including yours), and you currently have five professional staff members and one support staff member who report directly to you. Your office has responsibility for managing and updating the organization's annual strategic planning process, including managing external (e.g., competitor and market information) and internal databases (e.g., service volumes and projections, patient origin data, and payer data), as well as managing all public relations and marketing activities. You are engaged in the process of filling a newly approved position that reports to you, called senior planning analyst, which will have a leadership role in managing the planning process. Currently, there are two planning analysts who report to you. Of all the candidates you are considering, one has the appropriate education and significant experiences in planning in other healthcare settings and is the best fit for the job. However, her salary demand for the job is $9,000 more than the salary range for the position allows.

Use your knowledge of human resources management, the role of the line manager in recruitment and supervision of staff, and the role of the human resources department staff to effectively address this situation and to respond to the following questions.

DISCUSSION QUESTIONS

1. How do you convince your boss and the human resources department that this is the candidate you want to fill the job?

2. What steps would you undertake to get the salary approved?

3. What problems does this situation present for you, and how can you effectively address each problem?

4. What options do you have if the salary remains a "sticking point"?

Humor Strategies in Healthcare Management Education—Case for Chapter 14

Rosalind Trieber

Educators and managers have a critical role in creating a learning environment that initiates emotion, attracts attention, creates meaning, and subsequently builds lasting memories. When we learn in such a rich environment, it then becomes possible to apply what we've learned to a real-life situation. Research demonstrates that there is a significant correlation between humor and leadership effectiveness (Priest & Swain, 2002). Organizational culture supports the use of humor by leaders in appropriate ways. In addition, the humor employed by managers and leaders achieves three specific ends: (1) it reduces stress in the workplace, (2) it helps employees understand management concerns by enhancing communication patterns, and (3) it motivates followers (Davis & Kleiner, 1989). A majority of good leaders are shown to have quick wit, see the point of jokes, maintain group morale through extraverted humor vs. mean-spirited humor, have infectious laughs, and tell humorous satires in dialect (Priest & Swain, 2002).

The greatest challenge in the college classroom is to prevent death by lecture with material that is thought to be boring, difficult, and stress producing. According to Mehrabian's Communication Model, what determines a speaker's impact on an audience is based on the following: (a) what you say accounts for 7%; (b) how you say it accounts for 38%; and (c) how you look accounts for 55%. The rate of retention of material also varies, depending upon the instruction mode used, as follows: (a) lecture and reading—15% retention rate; (b) audio-visual—20%; (c) demonstration—30%; (d) discussion group—50%; (e) practice by doing—75%; and (f) teaching others—90% (NTL Institute for Applied Behavioral Science, n.d.). Humor and collaborative strategies have a significant role in teaching. The goal of collaborative learning is to develop autonomous, articulate, thinking people (Sawyer, 2004).

The use of humor in the classroom has the ability to grab students' attention, increase interest in the topic, make topic learning fun, and facilitate understanding of the topic (Berk, 2003).

How can educators use effective humor strategies to help students learn to develop the capacity to relate effectively to others, cooperate and achieve agreed-upon outcomes, and develop an understanding of themselves and of the groups (teams) to which they belong? Studies suggest that people learn in direct proportion to how much fun they are having (Pike, 1989). The following case study of a healthcare management team combines both fun and learning by using exaggeration in a dramatization, combined with exaggerated nonverbal behavior, spontaneous responses, and class participation.

Case: To Discharge or Not to Discharge (Koppet, 2001)
Overview

All participants, other than the interpreter, are instructed to speak in a nonsense language, as if they are from a foreign country or cannot speak the same language. Gibberish can be anything, such as blah, blah, unah, hoah, and so on. Everyone practices a minute of gibberish to get the idea.

Topic Identification

In this case, the patient did not want to be discharged from the hospital. The daughter was not sure about the options her mother had in terms of recovery. The surgeon and occupational health therapist felt the patient was ready to go home, with an occupational therapist making home visits.

The Task

The task is to provide explanations to both the patient and her daughter as to why the patient would have a successful recovery having the occupational therapist make home visits.

Players

Five volunteers and the remaining students in the class assume the roles below:

- A 65-year-old hospitalized female recovering from hip replacement surgery who does not speak English.
- A 30-year-old female daughter of the patient who had a hip replacement and does not speak English.
- An occupational health therapist assigned to the case who does not speak the same language as the patient or her daughter.
- The surgeon who speaks only English.
- An interpreter who speaks the foreign language of the patient and her daughter as well as English.
- The remaining students in the class.

Procedure

The case role-play should proceed as follows:

- The patient, in animated body language and with multiple inflections using gibberish, explains her concerns.
- The interpreter explains the patient's concerns in English to everyone.
- The daughter responds with her concerns with animated body language and gibberish.
- The interpreter explains the daughter's concerns, in English, to everyone.
- The occupational therapist explains how she can be helpful to both the patient and the daughter, in gibberish.
- The surgeon explains to everyone his prognosis and how accessible he would be if necessary, in gibberish.

Tips and Added Guidelines

While conducting the dramatization, keep in mind the following:

- The only person who speaks English is the interpreter.
- The class also has the opportunity to ask questions that can be interpreted into gibberish by the interpreter.
- This process can last from 5 to10 minutes.
- Whatever is said in gibberish or English is correct.
- The idea is to accept the information (that which is being said), acknowledge it, add more information, and lead to new discoveries.
- The interpretations should be based on the information taught in class.

DISCUSSION QUESTIONS

These questions are to be asked of the volunteers and the class:

1. What communication cues do we have, other than words?

2. Did the translation match the interpretations you made in your heads?

3. What did you learn about the group in general?

4. How did people contribute to the success?

5. How did you feel about what you communicated to the group?

6. How or what helped you learn?

7. What did you learn?

These questions are asked specifically of the volunteers who played the specific roles:

1. How did it feel to communicate without words?

2. How do you feel about what you created as a group?

OUTCOMES

Below is a list of desired outcomes of this case study:

- Everyone is involved.
- Team building occurs because everyone is helping each other to be successful.
- Everyone is actively listening to one another.
- There is a conscious review of the material needed taught by the instructor.
- Participants learn to think spontaneously and recover from mistakes.
- Everyone has fun and rarely forgets the substantive learning points.

REFERENCES

Berk, R. A. (2003). *Professors are from Mars and students are from Snickers.* Sterling, VA: Stylus Publishing.

Davis, A., & Kleiner, B. H. (1989). The value of humor in effective leadership. *Leadership and Organizational Development Journal, 10*(1), 1–3.

Koppet, K. (2001). *Training to imagine.* Sterling, VA: Stylus Publishing.

NTL Institute for Applied Behavioral Science (NTL). (n.d.). http://www.ntl.org/

Pike, B. (1989). *Creative training techniques: Tips, tactics, and how-to's for delivering effective training.* Minneapolis, MN: Lakewood.

Priest, R., & Swain, J. E. (2002). Humor and leadership effectiveness. HUMOR: *International Journal of Humor Research, 15*(2), 169–189.

Sawyer, R. K. (2004). Creative teaching: Collaborative discussion as disciplined improvisation. *Educational Researcher, 33*(2), 12–20.

Medication Errors Reporting at Community Memorial Hospital—Case for Chapter 7

Eric Williams and Grant Savage

Part I

Frances Ballentine, RN, MSN, VP for Nursing Services, has a problem. A recent Joint Commission inspection found several deficiencies at her hospital, including incomplete reporting of medication errors. The CEO gave her six months to fix this situation. Frances, who had been on the job for less than a year, already knew that the reporting of medication errors was problematic. She often found it difficult to complete her own monthly report on the number and causes of medication errors. She did not receive timely incident reports from every department, and many times these reports were incomplete. She also suspected that some incidents were going unreported.

In her investigation, Frances learned that although there was a clearly defined process (Figure 17-8) in the procedure manuals that each floor used, the process seemed to be inconsistently applied when a medication error occurred. She also knew that there were some other issues but could not pin them down without some additional investigation. From her observations, she estimated that 20–30% of medication error incident reports were not completed correctly, not completed on a timely basis, or not completed at all.

The next step of her investigation was to discuss the situation with the director of quality improvement (QI), Ally Ray. Together they agreed it would be worth creating a QI team to study the current work process of "reporting medication errors." The discussion ended with Ally asking Frances to put together the necessary information to present to the hospital's quality council for approval of the QI project. In the next quality council meeting, the Medication Errors Quality Improvement (MEQI) project was approved.

The initial meeting of the MEQI project team consisted of representatives from the pharmacy and the six hospital units (north, south, east, west, northeast, southeast) who were knowledgeable about the reporting of medication errors. The meeting was devoted to training on basic TQM/CQI principles and tools. The group decided to

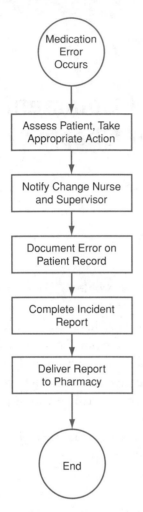

FIGURE 17-8 Medication Error Reporting Flowchart

use the FOCUS-PDCA framework as their guide for completing the MEQI project. The group had clearly completed the first two steps: F (Find a process to improve) and O (Organize a team that knows the process).

The second meeting focused on the C part of the framework—to clarify current knowledge of the process. Several MEQI members were surprised when Francis pulled out the current medication error reporting process (Figure 17-8). In preparation for the third meeting, each team member was asked to develop a cause-and-effect chart (fishbone or Ishikawa diagram; Figure 17-9) based on their discussions with other unit members. This began work on the U part of the framework—to understand the sources of variation. Additionally, the six hospital units were asked to create a daily checklist of medication errors for the month of July (Figure 17-10). Pharmacy would keep a corresponding checklist of medical error incident reports received (Figure 17-11). Comparing the two checklists would allow for the identification of the number of missing reports and reveal other patterns.

The third meeting turned out to be a fruitful one. To open the meeting, Frances presented a chart (Figure 17-11) showing the incident reports received from each unit for each day in July 2003. She also showed the corresponding checklist of medication errors from each unit (Figure 17-10).

DISCUSSION QUESTIONS

1. Compare and contrast the two charts. What proportion of errors identified on the unit checklist was also reported on the pharmacy checklist?

2. Which units had the poorest reporting records?

3. During what days did the number of reported errors decline?

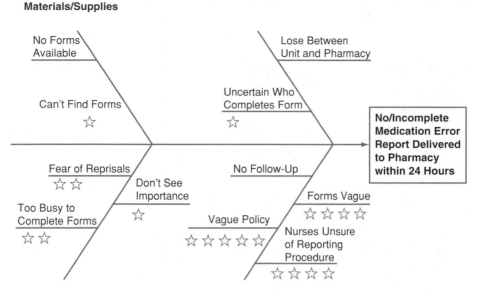

FIGURE 17-9 Fishbone Diagram

Part II

After a break, each team member reported on their cause-and-effect diagram, and the team, after several hours of discussion, created a composite cause-and-effect diagram (Figure 17-9). As a further refinement to the diagram, each of the 10 team members was asked to vote for the two most important causes of problems in the medication errors reporting process (these are indicated by the stars that appear after the problems identified in the cause-and-effect diagram; more stars reflect more votes that the problem is serious).

DISCUSSION QUESTIONS

1. Looking at the composite cause and effect diagram (Figure 17-9), what were the three principle causes?

2. After identifying the three principle causes, it is now your job to individually create a list of potential solutions.

3. Working with your group, your next task is to create a composite list of solutions and discuss them. What are the best solutions to this problem?

FIGURE 17-10 Combined Unit Checklists for July

Unit	T	W	T	F	S	S	M	M	W	T	F	S	S	M	T	W	T	F	S	S	M	T	W	T	F	S	S	M	T	W	T
	1	2	3	4	5	6	7	8	9	10	11	12	13	14	15	16	17	18	19	20	21	22	23	24	25	26	27	28	29	30	31
N	1	1	1	1	1	1	1			1		1	1	1	1			2	1	1				2		1	1	1		1	
S	1	1	1	1	1	1	1	2		1		1	1	1		1				1					2		2	1			
E		2	1	1	1	1	1	1			1	2	1	1		1	1	1	1	1		1	1	1		1			1		1
W	1		1		1	1	1	1		1	1		1	1			1	1	1			1	1		1		1			1	
NE	1	2	1		1	2	1	1		1	1	1	1	2			1	1	1						2		1	2			
SE				1	1		1		2					1	1	1		1	1			1									2

FIGURE 17-11 Report Received by Pharmacy for July

Unit	T	W	T	F	S	S	M	M	W	T	F	S	S	M	T	W	T	F	S	S	M	T	W	T	F	S	S	M	T	W	T
	1	2	3	4	5	6	7	8	9	10	11	12	13	14	15	16	17	18	19	20	21	22	23	24	25	26	27	28	29	30	31
N	1	1	1	1		1	1			1		1	1	1	1			2		1				2			1	1		1	
S		1		1	1	1	1	2			1	1	1	1		1									2					1	
E	2	2		1	1		1	1				1				1	1			1		1	1	1		1					
W							1	1		1		1	1	1			1	1	1				1		1				1		
NE	1	1	1			2					1	1	1	1			1	1	1						1			2			
SE				1	1				2						1	1					1	1									1

Part III

Once the solutions were determined, the team moved to the P part (Plan the solution) of the PDCA cycle. In the fifth team meeting, Frances tasked two subgroups to make specific plans about how to carry out the plan. The first subgroup recommended that the QI team implement the policy and form revision and a second group, made up of human resources staff, would design and implement a Web-based training program. Over the next three meetings, the QI team focused on revising the policy and forms. Once this was done, the human resources staff prepared the Web-based training program.

The D or "Do" part of the process began with a general announcement to the hospital staff and a series of meetings between the QI team and the nurse manager of each wing to discuss the implementation of the new policy, forms, and training program. Over the next month (September), each floor was familiarized with the policy and forms, and the policy was reinforced with the online training program. The committee set a goal of 95% of medication errors being reported on time. To see if this goal would be met, check sheets, like those prepared for July, were also prepared for September through December.

The C or "Check" part of the cycle began with an initial examination of the September data, which revealed a modest improvement, with 72% of medication error reports received (up from 66% in July), but showing the same problems with certain units and the weekend shift. The QI team was somewhat dismayed by the results and felt that the online training was not being taken seriously. The team then asked the CEO to meet with the wing nurse managers to reinforce the importance of medication error reporting. The October data revealed that 87% of medication error reports were received and that the three problem units improved considerably. The weekend reporting problem remained. The data showed improvement through November and December, with 93% and 96% of medication errors being properly reported, respectively. The three problem units still had lower reporting rates, but the gap had narrowed considerably. The weekend reporting remained somewhat lower than the weekday report.

DISCUSSION QUESTIONS

1. Brainstorm 10 ideas for what Frances can do to get the employees to understand the importance of reporting. Pick the two best ideas and indicate how they should be implemented.

2. Should employees who do not comply be punished? Should those who do comply be rewarded? What are the pros and cons of the stick-and-carrot approach?

Part IV

The A or "Act" part (Acting to hold gains) began in mid-January with a meeting between the CEO and the QI team. The CEO praised the team's hard work and success. One member of the QI team asked about the weekend problem. Both the CEO and QI team recognized this as an issue but decided to continue to monitor the reporting process via the two check sheets. They did ask the human resources department to continue to use the online training program in its orientation sessions. At the end of this meeting, the QI team disbanded. Frances continued to monitor the reporting process while Ally moved on to helping other QI teams within the hospital.

DISCUSSION QUESTIONS

1. Should this team be disbanded? Why or why not?

2. What should Frances do if she sees the units are backsliding?

3. Who is responsible for ensuring the new policies are enforced?

Dr. Nugget's Medical Practice—Case for Chapter 15

Kevin D. Zeiler

You work for Dr. Nugget, a successful medical practitioner who deals with OB/GYN healthcare issues and is looked upon as a pillar of both the local and medical community. Part of his good will with the community focuses on the fact that he is outspoken about abortion and proudly boasts that he would never perform an elective one solely because someone elected to not raise a child. The community backs this belief strongly, and it has given Dr. Nugget a position of great standing with the people of the community.

The normal type of business in the office deals with pregnancy exams, high-risk pregnancy, GYN exams, and child delivery. The practice has been in business for more than 15 years and has never been subject to any lawsuits or negative publicity. Certainly, patients from time to time have been unhappy with certain aspects of the practice, but Dr. Nugget has always been successful at handling them. Generally, the practice is what you would consider your dream job.

You are the practice manager and have been working for Dr. Nugget for just over a year and are still very excited about your position with the organization. As the practice manager, you have the opportunity to view all aspects of the practice from financial and legal to, clinical and patient follow-up. Dr. Nugget has always treated you well, and you feel that he is a very ethical person and an extremely competent physician. You have never heard anyone utter a negative word about him.

During your normal work routine, you begin looking through medical records to determine if patient bills are being paid on time or if there are any outstanding balances that have yet to be collected. As you maneuver through this process, you notice a lot of referrals to a private clinic that you know does abortions, both early and late term. It strikes you as odd, because Dr. Nugget advertises that he would never condone such a practice. Nonetheless, you push them to the side and continue with your work. A few weeks later, as you are reviewing some invoices, you happen to notice money coming to Dr. Nugget from the abortion clinic where the referrals have been taking place. A further review indicates that these are the same patients whose records you happened upon earlier in the month.

As the practice manager, you are motivated by your own organization making a profit within the bounds of the law, but you are concerned about the fact that what is being advertised may not be the reality of the practice. Your concern leads you to investigate further, and you come to find out that Dr. Nugget is a shareholder in the abortion clinic where the referrals are being sent. You have now stumbled upon a situation that you are completely confused about, but you aren't certain how you should approach it. Furthermore, you aren't sure if you should approach it at all.

Your interest leads you to continue looking through the medical records, and you find occasions where Dr. Nugget has actually performed the abortions at the clinic. Furthermore, you begin to realize that many of these abortions are late term (16th–20th week of gestation), and you believe that in your particular state, these are illegal. However, you are not certain about this assumption based on Supreme Court decisions, so you begin to wonder what you might do to further investigate this situation.

Because of the circumstances that you have uncovered, you find yourself falling behind in your work, and you are having trouble concentrating. When Dr. Nugget approaches you about your work performance, you tell him that you have been having issues at home and that you will rectify them. However, you are unable to deal with the stress, as you feel that you are being betrayed and that you are living a lie at work. Ultimately, you can no longer hold back your anxiety, and you begin taking medical records home at night so that you can research them very carefully. While the records are sitting on your dinner table, an acquaintance who is in your home for a visit notices a name that he recognizes on the record and, in your absence, reads the chart. You are not aware of this, nor are you aware of the fact that this particular patient was one of his ex-girlfriends. When you return to the dining room, your friend says he must leave and does so abruptly.

You don't realize that anything is out of place and continue about your business until the next day at work, when you begin taking phone calls about Dr. Nugget being an abortion doctor. Local community members begin calling on the doctor for answers, and patients call to cancel appointments. Also, the local news is knocking at the door, and Dr. Nugget is in a panic about what is taking place. He approaches you as the practice manager and seeks your advice as to what he should do to stop what he calls false allegations. You are left speechless and with a dilemma on your hands.

Finally, the patient record that you took home surfaces in the local newspaper in bits and pieces. The patient is outraged and wants to know how her medical information became public. As you field these calls, you begin to put the pieces of the puzzle together and realize what happened. Your situation has gone from bad to worse, and it looks like there is no way out.

DISCUSSION QUESTIONS

1. Putting aside your personal feeling about the abortion issue, what seems to be the major issue in this case?

2. In the beginning, you are told that Dr. Nugget is an outstanding and well-respected physician within his community, but in the end you find out that he may not be who he says he is. Who is at fault?

3. Did the practice manager handle the situation as well as she should have? What could she have done to mitigate the ultimate outcome? Think about the following:

    a. Did she have a right to look through medical records?
    b. Was she entitled to take medical records home?
    c. If she thought a crime was committed, what should she have done?

4. Looking back on the case, what are the ethical dilemmas presented?

5. What are the legal ones?

6. What could you do to determine if late-term abortion is legal in your state? What area of law governs these types of matters?

7. If late-term abortions are legal in this jurisdiction, has any crime been committed? Think about all of the circumstances surrounding the facts: if late-term abortions are legal, what crime or crimes have been committed?

8. Dr. Nugget has asked for your help, and as the practice manager, you are trained to handle such situations, but you are not certain where your allegiance is on this day. What duty do you have to Dr. Nugget? To the practice? The community? To the law?

9. Could this entire situation have been avoided? How? Go back through the case and pick out the key points on a timeline, so that you can see where there was opportunity for handling this situation in a more professional manner.

10. What do you do now that all of this has occurred? Where and to whom can you turn?

11. Do you think it's time to update your resume and start searching for a new job in a medical practice that doesn't deal with obstetrical patients? Or should you be thinking about how you'll be making new friends in jail? Explain your response.

Fraud and Abuse—Help Me, the Feds Are Coming!—Case for Chapter 16

Kevin D. Zeiler

I'm in need of your help. I have been working for a healthcare organization for several years and have always enjoyed it, but I am concerned with the way they are doing business. I am a financial assistant in the hospital's billing department, where I specialize in Medicare and Medicaid billing. I do not have an academic background in finance, but I feel that has been taught to me during my current tenure. Nonetheless, I am concerned about some issues, and I'm hopeful that your expertise and background in healthcare management will provide me with the answers I seek.

There has been a lot of buzz taking place in my office lately about government inspections of our financial records as they pertain to Medicare and Medicaid, and I have even heard that fraud investigators are milling around. I have never seen so much concern as in the past weeks, and they have even started calling in employees one at a time. My boss told me that I should just tell them that I have no idea how the bills are being processed and that I merely ensure that addresses are correct. However, this is not the case at all. As a matter of fact, I have oftentimes approved billing statements for Medicare and Medicaid, and I also fill out cost reports that are filed with the federal government. I was never fully trained on how to do these things, and honestly, I have no idea what happens to them when they leave my office. However, I have heard many employees state that our books are never correct and our billing is not accurate. This certainly doesn't seem like a problem for me, as I'm just doing my job and collecting a paycheck.

I would like to add that I was recently speaking with an attorney friend of mine, and he said that I could potentially be liable for any fraudulent billing practices that have taken place, especially if I was the one that approved them. He seems to think I should speak with the government officials and inform them that I have knowledge of fraudulent billing and that I have signed numerous government forms. Mind you, I have no knowledge of the content of these forms. I just fill them out and send them along, so I have no idea how that could be fraudulent. I think it might be best to stay out of it and do what my manager told me to do. I really think attorneys take things too seriously. Maybe I need a new friend, as the old one is really scaring me.

I have also been told that I could not be held liable, since I work for a large hospital. I believe that as long as I am doing what I am told, I will be okay, and the executives are the ones who will get in trouble with the federal investigators. I think this is correct because I really don't know what I am doing. There are times I change a billing code so the organization gets more money, but I think everyone does that. It is a standard practice in the industry, so that isn't any reason to be concerned. Furthermore, my supervisor told me that, when I see certain code designations, I should automatically change them to another code because it is a mistake. I have a list of these particular changes I follow every day. It just makes good business sense. Also, I have submitted the same claim multiple times, but since I don't know if the previous ones were paid, it only makes sense to continue to do so. I was telling my spouse that oftentimes a procedure is not covered, so I will bill it to another code in order to get it paid. I'm doing this for the patient, as that way they won't receive a bill, since they have enough to deal with. In the end it all helps, as our hospital gets paid as well. I think I am a great employee, and I'm truly doing the best I can to ensure that patients and the organization are reimbursed. In some ways, I am a one-man health reformer.

I am scared a little, though, as I keep hearing about fraud and abuse. These terms don't make sense to me, but my aunt's friend, Rosy, said as long as I didn't know what I was doing, I will still be okay. Rosy used to work for a doctor, so I think she is really on top of the issues facing health care today. Just because I get a little extra money on my paycheck every time I change a code doesn't mean I did something wrong, does it? I mean, I wouldn't get extra pay unless I was helping the company, and in a tough economy, you want to make sure you are taking care of your employer so he or she takes care of you.

Anyway, you are now well aware of my situation, and I would appreciate any feedback/advice that you can provide me. I know I will be okay when they call my name in a few minutes, but I think I would rest easier if you gave me your opinion before I go in to the interview. I am going to list some questions if you don't mind discussing them and providing me with your thoughts. Hurry though, I hear footsteps coming down the hall. . . .

DISCUSSION QUESTIONS

Our finance friend needs our help, so let's see if we can answer a few questions for him. Before we begin, it is necessary to remember that fraud and abuse, or what has come to be known as the two-headed monster, are really two distinct violations that can be enforced. Fraud is an "intentional" act of deception, while abuse is improper behavior not consistent with standard practices. As to abuse, it does not matter if the act was unintentional, it will be punished the same way. With that in mind, let's see if you can answer the following key discussion questions and then provide a remedy for our finance friend.

1. First, do you think that there are any indications that either fraud or abuse has occurred? If so, provide examples of each and discuss what makes them fraud and what makes them abuse.

2. Do you think that our friend has anything to fear? Is he an innocent bystander who is truly unaware of his actions? Does it matter?

3. What legal implication is his lawyer friend referring to when he tells him to come clean and explain what he has been involved with? What do you think about this approach, and do you think that he would be protected?

4. Speak to the coding issues that were mentioned in the case. What implications are there for this type of behavior?

5. What about Rosy's advice? Is it sound? Does it speak to the legality issues required to meet fraud and abuse charges?

6. If you were in the position that our finance friend is in, what would you do? What is the best advice you can provide?

7. Based on your knowledge of the topic and case reviews, what do you think the outcome of a case like this will be? If there are penalties, what will they be?

8. Do you think our friend should be updating his resume and looking for a new job? Or should he be thinking about how he'll be making new friends in jail?

Managing Costs and Revenues at Happy Town Neurology—Case for Chapter 10*

Kevin D. Zeiler

Part I

You have been working as an assistant to the financial manager at Happy Town Neurology for the past three and a half years, and there is finally an opportunity for you to advance to a lead position within the finance department. You are excited about this new position, but first, you must be able to accomplish a task that the current CFO is assigning to you. He is going to evaluate you on your ability to understand a cash budget and provide the neurology center with the necessary information to obtain the operating loans that they will need for the next calendar year. This process is more important than ever before because new federal legislation is putting a pinch on lending institutions by restricting their lending practices, and therefore, the new legislation will impact most. It is your goal to use sound financial management principles, utilize the department employees as time allows, fully calculate third-party reimbursement, and ultimately determine Happy Town's borrowing requirements.

DISCUSSION QUESTIONS

1. Describe the department or clinic personnel that you might utilize to help you with this process. Why would you choose these people?

2. What is a third-party payer, and why do you care about their forecasted reimbursement?

Part II

You feel prepared because of the experience you have within the finance department, but you also know that cash budgets are never certain, and that financial forecasting can help the organization to be prepared. First, you fully understand that you need to budget for the next 12-month period, so you decide to look at the historical data from the last several years. Also, you determine that you must also look at what cash is on hand today and what needs to be paid. Finally, you must consider each and every inflow and outflow that may affect your budget and, ultimately, your organization.

DISCUSSION QUESTIONS

1. Define a cash budget as you understand it.

2. What type of historical data will you consider? How far back should you look?

3. Explain what is meant by outflows and provide examples.

4. Explain what is meant by inflows and provide examples.

Part III

After looking at the available data, you realize that the neurology center is in an envious position because the patient revenues are extremely consistent throughout the year. This makes preparing your budget very easy, as you will be able to more readily break down the numbers and manage them on a monthly basis. As you continue your research, you find that more than 60% of your collections are from third-party payers. This is also something that is beneficial to you, as you will be able to compute the amount of income that the clinic will make on a per-procedure basis. Also, you have found that about 20% of your collections come from private pay and the final 20% comes from other sources such as government programs, local charities, and so on. It is in this arena that you find numerous inconsistencies, so you are uncertain how this may affect your final financial forecast. To fully understand and present this data, you will develop a revenue budget.

DISCUSSION QUESTIONS

1. Above, you comprised a list of outflows and inflows, and now you need to better understand how they are costing or benefitting the organization. For instance, let's say that you have established your budget and you feel it is in tune with the current needs of the organization. What outflows and inflows could change to implode your current budget? How might you prepare for these types of circumstances? Think both about third-party payers (inflows) and lending organizations, medical supply companies, real property, and so on. (outflows).

2. How would a minimum balance on a term loan affect your organization? What techniques might you employ to ensure that the minimum balances are always met?

Part IV

Through your coursework, you understand that finance by definition is forecasting, and as such, it is not going to provide 100% accuracy all the time. You must consider this when you are preparing a cash budget, especially a cash budget that is 12 months in duration. As you know, there are several factors that you and your organization cannot control, and this makes this type of forecasting all the more difficult. Also, you will have to ensure that you consider loans that may be paid off during the term of the cash budget. Both inflows and outflows must be carefully considered to allow for consistent and accurate accounting practices. Taxes, both local and federal, and other items such as insurance, licenses, and so on, must also be in the mix. It is key to fully account for all items that affect your organization.

We can now return to the opening paragraph and look at your goals for this project. As you look at the issues presented by your CFO, you will need to ensure that you have accomplished what you set out to do. Were you thorough? Did you consider all inflows and outflows? By understanding the limits of finance, you are in a great position to complete what is required to benefit the organization and its cash needs.

DISCUSSION QUESTIONS

1. How do local and federal legislation, policy, and the economy affect your cash budget decisions? How do you think healthcare organizations plan for these changes?

2. If you followed the steps outlined above, would you accomplish the goals of the organization? What might you add or delete to streamline the process as you understand it?

3. Once you are finished putting the above information together, is the process complete? Do you believe that budgeting is something that is used on a daily, weekly, monthly, or annual basis? Explain your answer.

* **Instructor:** please note that an instructor's guide for this case is available in the online resources.

A

AACN. *See* American Association of Colleges of Nursing

AAMC. *See* American Association of Medical Colleges

AAN. *See* American Academy of Nursing

ABC Inventory method, 203

ABMS. *See* American Board of Medical Specialists

Abuse
  antitrust issues, 359
  in billing for services, 354
  Criminal-Disclosure Provision of Social Security Act and, 356–357
  definition of, 354
  EMTALA and, 357–358, 358*t*
  forms of, 354
  Operation Restore Trust and, 353, 355

Access to care restrictions, for health insurance, 154

ACCME. *See* Accreditation Council for Continuing Medical Education

Accounting
  billing and accounts receivable systems, 134
  financial, 186
  managerial, 186

ACGME. *See* Accreditation Council for Graduate Medical Education

Accounts receivable management, 201–202, 201*t*

Accreditation, and information systems, 134

Accreditation Council for Continuing Medical Education (ACCME), 218

Accreditation Council for Graduate Medical Education (ACGME), 215

ACGME. *See* Accreditation Council for Graduate Medical Education

ACHCA. *See* American College of Health Care Administrators

ACHE. *See* American College of Healthcare Executives

ACPE. *See* American College of Physician Executives

Act, in FOCUS-PDCA framework, 124

Action Inquiry, 72

Activities of daily living (ADLs), 234

Activity-based costing, 198

ADA. *See* Americans with Disabilities Act

Adam's Equity Theory, 45

Adaptive Leadership, 22, 23*t*

Adjourning, of teams, 298

ADLs. *See* Activities of Daily Living

Administrative agencies, in creating rules and regulations, 339

Administrative staff, 252

Advanced practice nurses (APNs), 237–239

Advertising methods, for recruitment, 263–264

African Americans, 316, 317

Age/aging
  health/medial care needs and, 254–255
  uninsured population and, 176–177, 176*f*

Age Discrimination in Employment Act, 259*t*

AHA. *See* American Hospital Association

AHCLA. *See* Asian Health Care Leaders Association

Airlines industry team building model, 305

Alaska Natives, 317

Alderfer's ERG Theory, 44

Allied health professionals, 214, 239–241

AMA. *See* American Medical Association

Ambulatory Surgery Centers (ASCs), safe harbor regulations, 361–362

"Amenities of care", 115

American Academy of Nursing (AAN), 35*t*

American Association of Colleges of Nursing (AACN), 227, 231–232

American Association of Medical Colleges (AAMC), 214, 222

American Board of Medical Specialists (ABMS), 217

American College of Health Care Administrators (ACHCA), 34*t*

American College of Healthcare Executives (ACHE), 33, 33*t*, 35*t*, 323

American College of Physician Executives (ACPE), 35*t*

American Hospital Association (AHA), 320, 322

American Medical Association (AMA), 150–151, 225, 292

American Nurses Association (ANA), 232

American Nurses' Credentialing Center Magnet Recognition Program, 231

American Public Health Association (APHA), 329

American Recovery and Reinvestment Act (ARRA), 141, 168

Americans with Disabilities Act (ADA), 259*t*, 348

ANA. *See* American Nurses Association

Analyze, in DMAIC, 125

ANCC Commission on Accreditation, 232

Antibiotics, overuse of, 116

Anti-Dumping Act. *See* Emergency Medical Treatment and Active Labor Act

Anti-Kickback statutes, 360, 361

Antitrust issues, 359, 360

APHA. *See* American Public Health Association

APNs. *See* Advanced practice nurses

ARRA. *See* American Recovery and Reinvestment Act

ASCs. *See* Ambulatory Surgery Centers, safe harbor regulations

Asian Americans, 316, 317

Asian Health Care Leaders Association (AHCLA), 35*t*

Assault, 341

Association for University Programs in Health Administration (AUPHA), 35*t*

Attribution theory/error, 64–66

AUPHA. *See* Association for University Programs in Health Administration

Authentic leadership, 23–24

Autonomy, 344

B

Bad debt, 195

Balanced Budget Act of 1997 (BBA)
   enforcement tools, 361
   key provisions, 160–161
   Medicaid and, 160, 167
   Medicare and, 160–161, 194

Baldrige, Malcolm, 118

Baldrige National Quality Award, 34, 118–120, 119*f*

Bargaining, in teams, 307

Basic health insurance policies, 153

Battery, 341

BBA. *See* Balanced Budget Act of 1997

Beginning-of-life, ethics of, 349

Behavioral-based interview, 265

Beliefs
   ethical, 336
   healthcare, 317
   perceptual expectations, 61*t*, 62, 64, 65
   sharing with others, 71–72

Benchmarking, 202, 269

Beneficence, 344

Benefits, employee, 270–273

"Best practices" in quality, 114, 118–120

Beta blockers, underuse of, 115–116

Bias, 61–64, 61*t*, 65, 69–70, 70–71, 325–326

Billing for services, fraud and abuse in, 354, 365

Binding policy, 339

BLS. *See* Bureau of Labor Statistics

Board certified physicians, 217

Board eligible physicians, 217–218

Board of directors, 17, 29–31, 31*t*, 188–189

BPQA. *See* State Board of Physician Quality Assurance

Breach of duty, 340

Break-even analysis, 198

Budget
   capital, 207–208
   cash, 206
   definition of, 205–206
   expense, 206
   management of, 205–208
   operating, 206
   types of, 206–208

Budgeting
   definition of, 205
   importance of, 205–206
   systems, 134

Bundle payments, for hospital and physician services, 192

Bureau of Labor Statistics (BLS), 2, 213–214, 234, 236–237, 255*t*

Business-to-business marketing, 106

Buy-downs, 154

C

Cancer incidence, 317

Capital budgets, 207–208

Capitation, 155, 192, 194

Case mix and reimbursement, 194

Case studies by topic,
   call center management, 392–393
   communication, 458–461
   cultural competence, 433–436, 439–440, 458–461
   emotional intelligence, 437–438
   end-of-life, 386–387
   ethical issues, 386–387, 468–470
   financial issues, 392–393, 405–407, 420, 474–476
   fraud and abuse, 377–378, 471–473
   health information systems, 379–380, 454–456
   health insurance, 444–446
   health professionals, 384–385, 388–389, 390–391, 394–395, 452–453
   hospital merger, 408–411
   human resources management, 381–383, 384–385, 388–389, 394–395, 408–413, 414–417, 427–432, 441–443, 457
   leadership issues, 408–413, 447–451

legal issues, 396–397, 414–417, 468–470
managed care, 405–407
Management Information System, 379–380, 454–456
marketing, 398–400
motivation, 401–402, 403–404, 424–426
negotiation, 405–407
quality improvement, 418–419, 421–423, 462–467
sexual harassment, 414–417
strategic management, 408, 439–440
teamwork, 392–393, 424–426, 433–436, 437–438, 452–453, 454–456
Case study guidelines, 369–376
analysis, 370–372
effective participation, guidelines for, 374
grading rubric for, 375*f*
group presentations, peer evaluation criteria for, 376*f*
guidelines for, 369–376
peer evaluation criteria, 376*f*
purpose of, 369
teammate evaluation forms, 376*f*
team structure and process for completion, 374
types of, 370
write-up, 372–374
Cash budget, 206
Cash conversion cycle, 200
Cash inflows, 207
Cash outflows, 207
Catastrophic health insurance policies, 150, 154, 156–157
Causation, in negligence, 340
Cause and effect diagram, 128
Cause-related marketing, 98
CBCs. *See* Criminal background checks
Centers for Medicare & Medicaid Services (CMS)
administration of Medicare and Medicaid, 163
enforcement of EMTALA, 357
healthcare payments and, 82
Medicaid cost control measures, 167–168
national healthcare expenditures, 148–149, 148*t*
reimbursements for hospital services, 193–195
Centers for Medicare & Medicaid Innovation (CMI), 193
CEO. *See* Chief Executive Officer
Certified Nurse Midwives (CNMs), 138–239
Certified nurses' aides (CNAs), 234–236
Certified Registered Nurse Anesthetists (CRNAs), 238
CEUs. *See* Continuing education units
CFO. *See* Chief Financial Officer
CGFNS. *See* Commission on Graduates of Foreign Nursing Schools
CHAMPVA program, 168, 172

Charges
determinants of, 199
fee-for-service, 191
goals/objectives for, 198–199
minus a discount or percentage, 191
setting, 198–199
vs. prices, 198–199
Charity care, 195
Chart audits, 116, 126
Check sheets, 125–126
Chief accounting officer, 190
Chief Executive Officer (CEO), 189
Chief Financial Officer (CFO), 189–190
Chief Information Officer (CIO), 190
Chief Operating Officer (COO), 189
Children of Women Vietnam Veterans Healthcare Program, 172–173
Children's Health Insurance Program (CHIP), 151, 161, 166
CIO. *See* Chief Information Officer
Civil laws, 339
Civil Rights Act, 259*t*
Clarify, in FOCUS-PDCA framework, 124
CLAS. *See* National Standards on Culturally and Linguistically Appropriate Services
CLASS. *See* Community Living Assistance Services and Supports Act
Clayton Act, 359, 359*t*
Clinical Data Repository (CDR), 135*t*
Clinical Decision Support System (CDSS), 135*t*
Clinical Nurse Specialists (CNSs), 238
Clinical staff, 252
Clinical systems, 135, 135*t*
Closed-panel health maintenance organizations (HMOs), 155
CME. *See* Continuing medical education
CMI. *See* Centers for Medicare & Medicaid Innovation
CMS. *See* Centers for Medicare & Medicaid Services
CNAs. *See* Certified nurses' aides
CNMs. *See* Certified Nurse Midwives
Coaching style of leadership, 26, 26*t*
COBRA. *See* Consolidated Omnibus Reconciliation Act
Code of Ethics, 32–33, 33*t*
Coercive style of leadership, 26, 26*t*
Cognition, 58, 60–61
Cognitive biases, 63–64
Coinsurance, 153, 156, 158*t*
Collaboration. *See* Teamwork

Collection period, for accounts receivable, 201, 202
Collective bargaining, 152, 279
Commission on Graduates of Foreign Nursing Schools (CGFNS), 233
Committee of Sponsoring Organizations (COSO) of the Treadway Commission, 363
"Common cause" variations, 117, 121
Common law, 338
Communication
  barriers, 71–72
  case study, 458–461
  cross-cultural, 321t, 327–328
  definition of, 71
  in strategic planning, 88–89, 91–92
  team, patient-centered, 304–305
  in teams, 304–307
Community engagement, in addressing health disparities, 328–329, 330f
Community Living Assistance Services and Supports Act (CLASS), 162
Compensation, employee, 47, 49, 235, 268–270
Competence, 343, 344
Competencies of healthcare managers, 1–5, 8, 9–13
Competition
  human resources management and, 254
  setting charges and prices and, 198–199
Compliance
  with Criminal Disclosure Provisions of the Social Security Act, 358t
  with EMTALA, 358, 358t
  with False Claims Act, 358t
  history of, 354–355
  officer, 363, 364t
  program essential, 364, 364t
  program oversight, 363–365
Comprehensive health insurance policies, 150, 153
Comptroller, 203
Computer-based patient records, 136
Computerized Provider Order Entry (CPOE), 135
Confidentiality, 142, 341, 344
Conflict of interest, 225–226
Consent to care, 343, 347
Consolidated Omnibus Budget Reconciliation Act (COBRA), 159, 259t
Constitutions, 338
Consumer buying behavior, 106–107, 107t
Consumer-driven health care, 99–100
Consumer-driven health plans, 156–157
Contingency Theory of Leadership, 21, 23t
Continuing education units (CEUs), 232
Continuing medical education (CME), 218

Continuous Quality Improvement (CQI)
  Baldrige National Quality Award for, 118–120
  case studies, 418–419, 421–423, 462–467
  data-driven decision making, 118, 120–128
  definition of, 122
  dimensions of, 122–124
  employee empowerment and, 122–123, 125
  executive leadership in, 119, 119f, 123, 125
  focus of, 122
  FOCUS-PDCA framework, 123–124
  history of, 21–22, 117–118
  in patient-focused care model, 297
  PDCA cycle model, 117, 124
  statistical process control and, 120–122
  in strategic planning, 118–120, 123
Contract law, 342–343, 343t
Contracts, legal, elements of, 342
Contractual allowance, 156, 193
Control in DMAIC, 125
Control activities, for internal control, 363
Control environment, for internal control, 363
Controller, 190
COO. See Chief Operating Officer
Copayments, 152, 158t
Corporate compliance programs, 363–365
COSO. See Committee of Sponsoring Organizations (COSO) of the Treadway Commission
Cost accounting, 196–198
  systems, 134
Cost allocation, 196–198
Costs
  allocation of, 196–198
  classification of, 196, 197t
  control of, 193, 196–198, 202
  definition of, 191
  direct, 191, 196, 197t
  indirect, 191, 196, 197t
  of inventory, 202
  of malpractice, 342
  of nursing turnover, 228, 296
  of physician turnover, 224
  plus percentage for growth, 191
  product, determination of, 198
  projected, 191
  of teamwork, 296–298
Cost sharing, 150, 152–153
  by employees, 271
Costs/revenues, 187–209
CPOE. See Computerized Provider Order Entry
CQI. See Continuous Quality Improvement and Total Quality Management

Credentialing, of physicians, 217–218
Crew resource management, 305
Criminal background checks (CBCs), 217, 227, 234–236
Criminal-Disclosure Provision. *See* Social Security Act
    Criminal-Disclosure Provision
Criminal laws, 339
CRNAs. *See* Certified Registered Nurse Anesthetists
Cross-functional teams, 101, 290, 291
Crossing the Quality Chasm (Institute of Medicine), 113,
    115, 139
Cultural competency, 323–337
    assessment, 325–326
    assessment tools, 325–326
    benefits of, 323
    best practices in, 323
    case studies, 433–436, 439–440, 458–461
    community outreach and engagement, 328–329
    continuum of, 318–319
    definition, 318
    education and training in, 326–327
    evaluation of, 328
    initiatives, 323
    leadership and, 24, 324
    management, 324–325
    multilingual services, 327–328
    research on, 328
Cultural conditioning, 319
Cultural excellence training, 319
Cultural proficiency
    assessment, 325–326
    assessment tools, 325–326
    benefits of, 323
    best practices in, 323
    case studies, 433–436, 439–440, 458–461
    community outreach and engagement, 328–329
    continuum of, 318–319
    definition, 319
    education and training in, 326–327
    evaluation of, 328
    initiatives, 323
    interrelationships of, 329, 330*f*
    leadership and, 24, 324
    management, 324–325
    multilingual services, 327–328
    research on, 328
Cultural sensitivity, 319
Culturally competent organizations, 318
Culturally effective care, 318
Current assets, 199
Current liabilities, 199
Current Procedural Terminology, 192

Customer focus, of Continuous Quality Improvement, 123
Customers, in health care, 96

D
Dartmouth Atlas of Health Care, 116
Data, for Continuous Quality Improvement, 120–126, 128
Data collection tools, in quality improvement, 125–126
Declaration of Helsinki, 344
Deductibles, 153, 156, 158*t*
Defamation of character, 344
Deficit Reduction Acts, 167–168
Define, in DMAIC, 125
Deming, W. Edwards, 117–118
Deming cycle, 117–118
Department of Defense (DOD)
    financing, 173
    medical facilities of, 168
    TRICARE plan and, 168–170, 169*f*
Department of Health and Human Services (DHHS)
    Operation Restore Trust, 353, 355
Department of Justice (DOJ), 359
Derived demand, 106
DHHS. *See* Department of Health and Human Services
Diabetes incidence, 316
Diagnosis-related groups (DRGs), 160, 192, 193
Direct costs, 191, 196, 197*t*
Disability income insurance coverage, 150
Disease incidence, 316
Disease management programs, 271
Disease-specific health insurance policies, 154
Disparities. *See* Health disparities
Distributors, 222
Diversity. *See also* Cultural competence
    of healthcare workforce, 323–324
    leadership, 24, 324
    management of, 24, 324–325
    of population, 319–320, 319*f*
    of teams, 304
    toolkit, 322
    training, 322, 326–327
Diversity and Cultural Proficiency Assessment Tool
    for Leaders, 326
DMAIC, 125
DME. *See* Durable medical equipment
Doctoral degrees, in nursing, 227
DOD. *See* Department of Defense
DOJ. *See* Department of Justice
Donabedian, Avedis, 114, 122
DRGs. *See* Diagnosis-related groups
Drug-drug interactions, 116
Duty to care, in negligence, 340, 345–346

E

EAPs. *See* Employee Assistance Programs
ECFMG. *See* Educational Commission for Foreign
        Medical Graduates
Economic market conditions, in setting charges and prices,
        198–199
Education
    of nurses, 227–228
    of physicians, 214–215
Educational Commission for Foreign Medical Graduates
        (ECFMG), 223
Effectiveness in care delivery, 115
Efficiency of care delivery, 115
EI. *See* Emotional intelligence
Eisenhower administration, 151
Elder abuse prevention, 235, 236
Electronic Medical Record Analytical Model (EMRAM),
        137–139, 137*f*
Electronic medical records (EMRs)
    adoption of, 136–139, 137*f*
    challenges, 139–141
    conversion from paper records, 139, 142
    in hospitals, 138–139
    in long-term care facilities, 139
    in physician practices, 139
    Kaiser Permanente and, 139
    leadership and, 32
    privacy of, 139–140
    sharing, 139, 142
    Veterans Affairs and, 171
E-mail communication, 134
Emergency Medical Treatment and Active Labor Act
        (EMTALA), 82, 346, 349, 357–358, 358*t*
Emotional contagion, 302–303
Emotional intelligence (EI), 23, 23*t*, 303–304
    case study, 437–438
Empathy and emotional intelligence, 22, 23*t*
Employee Assistance Programs (EAPs), 273–274
Employee empowerment, in Continuous Quality
        Improvement and, 123
Employee Retirement and Income Security Act of 1974
        (ERISA), 159–160, 259*t*
Employees
    benefits for, 47, 270–2732
    compensation for, 268–270
    case studies, 381–383, 384–385, 388–389, 394–395,
        414–417, 427–432, 441–443, 457
    costs of turnover of, 224, 228, 235
    as drivers of organizational performance, 256–257
    exempt vs. non-exempt, 269
    hiring process, 265–266

hourly vs. salaried, 269
interviewing/selection process, 231, 264–265
job analysis, 258, 260
job descriptions, 261, 262*f*
manpower planning, 260–261
manual, 265
motivation, 39–52
negotiations, 265
orientation, 265–266
performance appraisals, 274–279, 276*f*, 277*f*
recruitment, 261–263, 262*t*, 263–265, 263*t*
retention of, 266–282
staffing needs, 260–261
termination of, 278–279
training/development of, 267–268, 326–327
Employee satisfaction, 254
    assessment of, 267
    CNAs, 235
    and motivation, 40–42, 48–51
    nurses, 231
    and unions, 279
Employee Staff Manual, 265
Employee suggestion programs (ESPs), 282
Employment offer, 265
EMRAM. *See* Electronic Medical Record Analytical
        Model
EMRs. *See* Electronic medical records
EMTALA. *See* Emergency Medical Treatment and Active
        Labor Act
Ending cash, 207
End-of-life, ethics of, 349
Enterprise Resource Planning System (ERP), 106,
        134, 142
Equal Pay Act, 259*t*
ERG Theory, 44
ERISA. *See* Employee Retirement and Income Security Act
        of 1974
ERP. *See* Enterprise Resource Planning System
ESPs. *See* Employee suggestion programs
Ethical principles in quality, 115
Ethics
    ACHE Code of, 33, 33*t*
    behavior, 343
    biomedical concerns, 348
    case studies, 386–387, 468–470
    concepts of, 344–346
    of countries relying on IMGs, 240–241
    descriptive vs. normative, 343
    dilemmas, 336
    law and, 335–337, 337*t*
    managed care organizations and, 347–348

in marketing, 99 108, 346
source, 336
vs. law, 335–337, 337*t*
Execution, of strategic plan, 90–95
Executive orders, 339
Expectancy Theory, 46, 65
Expenditures, healthcare, 148–149, 148*t*, 149*f*
funding sources, 149, 149*f*
national, 148–149
Expense budget, 206
External auditors, 190
Extrinsic factor theories of motivation, 45
Extrinsic rewards, 41, 45, 47–51
Eye disease incidence, 317

F

Factoring receivables, 201
Fair Labor Standards Act, 259*t*
Fairness. *See* Justice
False Claims Act (FCA), 354–355, 366
False imprisonment, 341
Family Medical and Leave Act (FMLA), 259*t*
FCA. *See* False Claims Act
Federal Sentencing Guidelines, 363
Federal Trade Commission (FTC), 359
Federal Trade Commission Act, 359, 359*t*
Fee-for-service model
for health insurance coverage, 152
indemnity insurance and, 155
TRICARE plan option, 168–169, 172
Fee schedule, by CPT code, 192
Fidelity, 344
Fiduciary duty, 346
FIFO. *See* First-in, first-out
Finance, 187
Finance departments
accounting functions, 186
finance functions, 187
Finance staff, 208
Financial accounting, 187
Financial indicators, 84
Financial management
accounts receivable management, 201–202
analysis and decision making, 187
budget management, 205–208
case studies, 392–393, 405–407, 420, 474–476
charges, setting, 199
cost accounting, 196–198
allocation of costs, 196–197
break-even analysis, 198
classifying costs, 196–197, 197*t*

definition of, 186
functions of, 186–187
materials and inventory management, 202–205
objectives for, 186–187
purposes/function of, 187
responsibility for, 189–190
working capital management, 199–200
Find, in FOCUS-PDCA framework, 124
First-in, first-out (FIFO), 203, 204*t*
Fishbone diagram, 128, 129*f*
Fixed assets, 207
Flexible health benefits, 272
Flexible spending accounts, 272
Flexner, Abraham, 292
Flexner Report, 292
Flowcharting, 126, 128, 128*f*
FMLA. *See* Family Medical and Leave Act
FOCUS-PDCA framework, 123–124
Followership, 19–20
Foreign educated nurses, 233
Foreign Medical Graduates. *See* International
Medical Graduates
Forming, of teams, 298
For-profit healthcare organizations
financial goals of, 188
tax status, 187–188, 189*t*
vs. not-for-profit, 187–188, 189*t*
Fraud
adoption of corporate compliance plan and,
363–365
antitrust issues, 359
in billing for services, 365
case studies, 377–378, 471–473
Criminal-Disclosure Provision of Social Security Act and,
356–357
criminal disclosure provisions of laws, 358*t*
definition of, 354
EMTALA and, 357–358, 358*t*
enforcement tools, Balanced Budget Act and, 361
forms of, 354
Operation Restore Trust and, 353, 355
patient referral kickbacks (*See* Referrals, patient)
prevention, 354, 356
safe harbor regulations, 361–362
Free-rider syndrome, 306
Frequency chart, 128
Frustration-regression principle, 44
FTC. *See* Federal Trade Commission
Functions of management, 4–5
Fundraising systems, 134
Future service volumes, 260–261

G

GAAP. *See* Generally Accepted Accounting Principles
Gainsharing, 270
Generally Accepted Accounting Principles (GAAP), 190
Generational issues, 51–53
Geographic mapping, 126
Global leader, 23*t*
GME. *See* Graduate Medical Education
Goal-sharing programs, 270
Governance, 29–31, 30*t*, 188–190
Graduate Medical Education (GME), 215
"Granny-cams", 235
The Great Man Theory, 20, 23*t*
Green Belts, 125
Group model health maintenance organizations, 156
Guidelines for Teamwork, 306–307, 306*f*

H

Hallmarks of the Professional Nursing Practice
      Environment, 231
Hart-Scott-Rodino Antitrust Improvements
      Act of 1976, 359
HCPCS. *See* Healthcare Common Procedure
      Coding System
Headhunter, 263–264
Health care, demand for, 254
Healthcare Common Procedure Coding System
      (HCPCS), 194
Healthcare financial management. *See* Financial
      management
Healthcare Financial Management Association (HFMA), 35*t*
Healthcare financing, 148–149
Healthcare industry, employment statistics, 2
Health Care Fraud Prevention and Enforcement Action
      Team, 354, 356
Healthcare managers. *See* Managers
Healthcare marketing, 95–109. *See also* Marketing
      history of, 98–100
      process, 100–105
Healthcare occupations employment, projected
      growth in, 255, 255*t*
Healthcare organizations
      cultural competence of, 323
      EMTALA liability issues for, 357
      financial risk, control of, 190–195
      for-profit
            financial goals of, 188
            tax status, 187–188, 189*t*
            vs. not-for-profit, 187–188, 189*t*
      governing bodies, 189–190

performance, employees as drivers of, 256–257
      sensemaking in, 68–69
      tax status, 187–188, 189*t*
Healthcare professionals, 213–241
      advanced practice nurses, 237–239
      allied health professionals, 239–241
      categories of, 213–214
      case studies, 384–385, 388–389, 390–391, 394–395,
            452–453
      diversity competence of, 318–319, 322, 324–325
      home health aides, 236
      midlevel practitioners, 236–239
      nurses (*See* Nurses)
      nurse's aides, 234–236
      physician assistants, 239
      physicians (*See* Physicians)
      respiratory therapists, 241
      supply of, 254
      teams of (*See* Teams)
Healthcare provider, legal responsibilities of, 345–346
Healthcare reform, 13, 36, 41, 129, 349
      individual mandate, 177
      legislation, 151
      fraud and, 354
      managed care and, 348
      tort reform, 340
Healthcare Service Organizations (HSOs), 253–256
Healthcare spending, national, 148–149,
            148*t*, 149*f*
Healthcare Information and Management Systems Society
            (HIMSS), 136
Health disparities, 176–177, 315–330
      addressing, 320–329, 329, 330*f,*
      causes of, 317
      definition, 316
      elimination of, 329
      initiatives, 329
      strategies to address, 318–319
Health inequality, 316
Health inequity, 316
Health information technology (HIT). *See* Information
            technology
Health Information Technology for Economic and Clinical
            Health Act (HITECH), 140–141
Health insurance, 147–180
      access to care restrictions, 154
      access to, 317
      benefits, types of, 153–154
      case study, 444–446
      catastrophic coverage 154, 156–157

characteristics of, 152–155
coordination of benefits, 154
cost of, 174–175, 175*t*
cost sharing, 150, 152–153
coverage, 150, 174, 174*f*
as employee benefit, 271
expansion of public sector coverage, 151
forms of payment, 152
group policies, 150
history of, 150–152
intent of, 150
moral hazard, 154
plan characteristics, comparison of, 158*t*
policy limitations, 152
premiums, 174–175
private, 149, 152, 155–157, 158*t*, 174*f*
provider choice, 154
reimbursements 190–195
Health Insurance Portability and Accountability Act
      (HIPAA)
   Anti-Kickback Act and, 361
   challenges of, 140
   confidentiality of patient information and, 140, 142, 347
   enactment of, 82, 259*t*
   Notice of Privacy Practice (NOPP), 140
   pre-existing conditions and, 159
   privacy, 140
   respect for persons and, 344
   security of data, 139–140
   training/employee orientation and, 266
Health maintenance organizations (HMOs)
   characteristics of, 158*t*
   closed-panel, 155
   enrollment, 157*t*
   forms of, 155–156
   group model, 156
   Independent Practice Association, 156
   negotiation case study, 405–407
   open-panel, 155
   premiums, 175*t*
   staff model, 156
   TRICARE plan option, 168–169
Health policy, 329
Health Savings Accounts (HSAs), 156–157
Healthy People 2010, 316
Heart disease incidence, 317
Herzberg's Two Factor Theory, 44
Heuristics, 63–64, 71
HFMA. *See* Healthcare Financial Management Association
HHAs. *See* Home health agencies

HHRGs. *See* Home Health Resource Groups
Hierarchy of needs, 22, 43
High-deductible health plan, 156–157, 157*t*, 158*t*, 175*t*
HIMSS. *See* Healthcare Information and Management
      Systems Society
HIPAA. *See* Health Insurance Portability and
      Accountability Act
HIT (health information technology). *See* Information
      technology
HITECH. *See* Health Information Technology for
      Economic and Clinical Health Act
HIV and AIDS incidence, 317
Holidays, as a benefits, 271
Home health agencies (HHAs), 354
Home health aides, 236
Home Health Resource Groups, 160, 195
Hospital Outpatient Prospective Payment System (OPPS),
      160, 195
Hospitals
   accreditation of, 134
   alignment with physicians, 293–294
   case study, 408–411
   compliance with EMTALA, 358
   departments, involved in accounts receivable
      management, 201, 201*t*
   EMR adoption in, 138–139
   Medicaid/Medicare reimbursements, 193–194
   Patient Advocate Office, 348
Hospital-surgical health insurance policies, 153
Hourly rated positions, 269
HRIS. *See* Human resources information system
HSAs. *See* Health Savings Accounts
HSOs. *See* Healthcare Service Organizations
Human resources information system (HRIS), 258, 261, 269
Human resources management, 251–283. *See also*
      Employees
   administrative view of, 252
   case studies, 381–383, 384–385, 388–389, 394–395,
      408–413, 414–417, 427–432, 441–443, 457
   definition, 252
   diversity policies, 324–325
   environmental forces and, 253–256, 254*t*, 255*t*,
   examples of, 252–253
   functions of, 257–266
   leadership development, 281–282
   legislation and, 258, 259*t*
   pay equity, 269
   recruitment, 261–266
      advertising methods for, 263
   responsibilities for, 257–258, 257*t*, 263, 263*t*

Human resources management, 251–283. *See also*
   Employees (*cont.*)
   retention of employees (*See* Retention, employee)
   staffing projections, 260–261
   strategic perspective of, 252
   and unions, 279–281

I

ICD-9. *See* International Classification of Disease
ICU. *See* Intensive care unit, nurse residency programs
IDI. *See* Intercultural Development Inventory
IMGs. *See* International Medical Graduates
Immigration Reform and Control Act, 259*t*
Implementation, of strategic plan, 88–89, 89*f*
Improve, in DMAIC, 125
Incentive compensation plans, 269–270
Indemnity plans, characteristics of, 155, 157*t*, 158*t*
Independent auditor, 190
Independent Practice Association (IPA)
   description of, 156
   negotiation case study, 405–407
Indirect costs, 191, 196, 197*t*
Individual mandate, 151, 161, 178
Infant mortality, 316, 317
Infliction of mental distress, 340
Information and communication, for internal control,
   363, 364*t*
Information technology (IT), 133–143
   adoption of, 136–139, 137*f*
   applications, 134–136, 135*t*
   case studies, 379–380, 454–456
   challenges, 139–141
   financial incentives for adoption, 141
   financial resources, 139
   health manager role in, 142
   historical overview, 133–134
   interoperability and, 137
   professionals, 136–137, 142
Informed consent, 347, 348, 358
Injury or damages, in tort, 340
Inspirational leadership, 24
Institute of Medicine (IOM),
   Crossing the Quality Chasm, 113, 115
   definition of healthcare quality, 115
Institute for Diversity in Health Management, 320
Integrated delivery systems, 155
Integrated health information system, 141–142
Intensive care unit (ICU), nurse residency programs, 228
Intentional torts, 340, 341
Intercultural Development Inventory (IDI), 325–326

Interdisciplinary health teams. *See* Teams
Internal Assessment, 83–85, 256
Internal auditor, 190
Internal control, 363
International Classification of Disease (ICD-9), 193
International Medical Graduates (IMGs),
   221–223
Interoperability, as information technology challenge,
   134–139
Interpretive justice, 330
Interviewing, 231, 264–265
Intrinsic factor theories of motivation, 45–46
Intrinsic rewards, 40, 45–46, 48–51
Invasion of privacy, 341
Inventory, performance, evaluation of, 203
Inventory management, 202–206, 205*t*
IOM. *See* Institute of Medicine
IPA. *See* Independent Practice Association
Ishikawa diagram, 128
IT. *See* Information technology

J

JCAHO. *See* The Joint Commission
JIT. *See* Just-in-time inventory method
Job analysis, 258–260
Job application, 264
Job burnout, of physicians, 225
Job descriptions, 261, 262*f*
Job fairs, 264
Job pricing, 269
Job satisfaction
   organizational climate and, 229–231
   physicians and, 225
Johnson, President Lyndon B., 151
The Joint Commission
   communication standards, 230
   diversity standards, 322
   health information and, 134,
   leadership standards, 32
   licensure standards, 260
   quality standards, 11, 114
   retention of nursing staff and, 228
   safety standards, 11, 114
Judgment, systematic errors of, 63–64
Judicial authority, 338
Juran, Joseph M., 117–118, 124
"Juran Trilogy", 118
Justice, 344, 345
Just-in-time inventory method (JIT), 203
J-Visa, 223

K

Kennedy, President John F., 151
Kerr-Mills Act, 151
Kickbacks, for referrals, 360–361

L

Labor relations, 279–281
Laboratory tracking system, 135*t*
Last-in, first-out (LIFO), 203, 204*t*
Latinos, 317
Law, 335–348
    biomedical concerns, 348
    case studies, 396–397, 414–417, 468–470
    concepts, torts, 337–341
    constitution, 338
    creation of, 336
    definition, 338
    ethics and, 336–337, 337*t*
    as leadership barrier, 31, 31*t*
    legal concepts, 337–343
    managed care organizations and, 347–348
    patient rights and, 345–347
    provider responsibilities and, 345–347
Leader-Member Exchange Theory, 21, 23*t*
Leaders
    competencies of, 19, 19*t*
    focus of, 18–19, 18*f*
    professional associations for, 33, 33*t*
    of teams, 303, 304
    transformational, 21
Leadership
    authentic, 23–24
    barriers/challenges of, 31–32, 31*t*
    case studies, 408–413, 447–451
    competencies, 19, 19*t*, 27, 28*t*
    Contingency Theory of, 21, 23*t*
    in Continuous Quality Improvement, 119, 199*f*,
        123, 125
    development, 12, 33–36, 281–282, 304
    diversity, 24
    domains, 27, 28*t*
    emotional intelligence and, 23, 23*t*
    ethical responsibility of, 32–33, 33*t*
    followership and, 19–20
    future concerns and, 33–36
    governance and, 29–31, 30*t*, 188–190
    history, in United States, 20–22
    inspirational, 24
    models, 20–25
    in organizational diversity, 324
    Path-Goal Theory of, 21
    protocols, 27–29, 29*t*
    servant, 24–25
    situational approach, 21, 23*t*
    spirituality, 25, 25*t*
    strategy execution and, 90–92
    style approach, 20, 23*t*
    styles, 26, 26*t*
    of teams, 303
    theories, in United States, 20–22, 23*t*
    vs. management, 17–19, 18f, 19*t*
Learning organizations, 70
Legislation. *See also* specific legislation
    human resource management and, 258, 259*t*
    major healthcare-related, 159–162
    regulatory issues, in setting charges and
        prices, 199
Licensed Practical Nurses (LPNs), 234
Licensed Vocational Nurses (LVNs), 234
Licensure
    of nurses, 227, 232
    of physicians, 216–217
Life expectancy, 316
Life insurance benefits, 271
Lifetime limit, on health insurance benefits, 153, 162
LIFO. *See* Last-in, first-out
Liquidity, 200
Locke's Goal Setting Theory, 46
Long-term capital assets, budgeting for, 207
Long-term care facilities
    EMR adoption in, 139
Long-term care insurance, 162
Loss leaders, 196
LPNs. *See* Licensed Practical Nurses
LVNs. *See* Licensed Vocational Nurses

M

Major medical health insurance policies, 153
Malcolm Baldrige National Quality Award, 34,
        118–120, 119*f*
Malfeasance, 340
Malpractice, 341–342, 349
Managed care health plans, 155–157, 157*t*, 158*t*, 175*t*
Managed care organizations (MCOs)
    case study, 405–407
    formulary, 348
    goals of, 347
    legal/ethical concerns, 347–348
    prospective reimbursements, 191–192
    rationing of care, 347

Management, healthcare
  competencies, 1–5, 8, 9–13, 19
  definition of, 4
  domains, 3
  functions, 4–5, 9–13
  health policy, 13
  hierarchy, 6–8
  history of, 293
  learning and, 68–69
  methods, for teams, 305–307
  models, 6–8
  motivation of workforce, 39–42
  of patient safety, 69
  organizational behavior field (*See* Organizational
      behavior)
  skills, 5
  succession planning, 12, 35–36
  talent, 9–10
  of teams, 5–6, 8–9 , 305–307, 306*f*
  vs. leadership, 17–19, 18*f*, 19*t*
Management education, healthcare, humor strategies
      case study, 458–461
Management Information System (MIS) case studies,
      379–380, 454–456
Management theories of motivation, 46
Managerial accounting, 186
Managers
  budgeting importance for, 206
  competencies of, 1–5, 8, 19, 19*t*, 27, 28*t*, 142, 318–319
  compliance and internal controls, 363
  conflict of interest and, 226–227
  culture of safety and, 229–231
  diversity, 324–325
  ethical responsibility, 32–33, 33*t*, 349
  financial, 189–191
  in financial analysis/decision making, 190
  fraud and abuse, 357
  in information technology, 142
  in labor relations, 279–281
  in legal issues, 345, 349
  liability for fraud and abuse, 357
  in quality improvement, 125
  roles and responsibilities, 1–3, 9–13, 142
  role in
    performance appraisal, 275–279
    recruitment and retention, 225, 232, 235, 256
  strategic planning, 92
  training and continuing education, 230–231
    staff member questions for, 231
    teamwork and, 293–294, 300–301

Mapping processes, for data collection, 126, 128
Market Assessment, 79*f*, 80–83
Market research, 100
Market segmentation, 103–105, 104*t*
Marketing. *See also* Healthcare marketing
  buyer behavior, 105–107, 107*t*
  case study, 398–400
  concepts, 97–98
  consumer buyer behavior in, 106–107, 107*t*
  definition, 96
  ethical concerns, 108, 346
  four P's, 101*f*, 107
  history in health care, 98–100
  mix, 101*f*, 107
  non-profit vs. for-profit, 98
  organizational buyer behavior in, 105–106
  orientation vs. production and sales, 97, 97*f*
  plan, 108
  process, 100
  segmentation strategies, 103–105, 104*t*
  social responsibility, 108
  systems, 134
Maslow's hierarchy of need, 22, 43–44
Master Black Belts, 125
Master's of Science in Nursing (MSN), 227
Materials management, 202–203, 204*t*–205*t*
Matrix management model, 6–8
MBTI. *See* Myers-Briggs Type Indicator
MCAT. *See* Medical College Admission Test
McClelland's Acquired Needs Theory, 44–45
McGregor's Theory X and Theory Y, 46, 62–63
MCOs. *See* Managed care organizations
Measure, in DMAIC, 125
Measurement, in quality improvement, 120–122
Measurement reliability, 120–121
Medicaid
  Balanced Budget Act of 1997 and, 160–161
  benefits, 165
  cost containment, 160, 167–168
  eligibility requirements, 165–166
  establishment of, 159
  expenditures, 166–167, 167*f*
  financing of, 166
  fraud and abuse regarding claims, 354–356, 357
  historical development of, 151
  insureds, 174*f*
  integrity program, 168
  patient referrals Anti-Kickback Act and, 361
  provider services, 165
  recipients, 166

reimbursements, 193–194
requirements for HSOs, 255
services, mandatory, 165
vs. VA programs, 171*t*–172*t*
Medical College Admission Test (MCAT), 214
Medical education system, reorganization of, 292
Medical errors, 113–114, 115–117
Medical Group Management Association
    (MGMA), 35*t*
Medical malpractice, 341–342
Medical Screening Exam (MSE), 357, 358
Medical staff office, 219
Medically indigent, 165
Medicare
    Balanced Budget Act of 1997 and, 160–161
    cost containment efforts, 160–162, 165
    enrollees, growth in, 163–164
    establishment of, 159
    expenditures, 164, 164*f*
    financing of, 163, 163*f*
    fraud and abuse regarding claims, 354–356, 357
    historical development of, 151, 159–162
    insureds, 174*f*
    managed care and, 161
    Part A, 159, 162
    Part B, 159, 162–163
    Part C, 161, 163
    Part D, 161, 163
    patient referrals Anti-Kickback Act and, 361–362
    reimbursements, 193–195
    requirements for HSOs, 255
    vs. VA programs, 171*t*–172*t*
Medicare and Medicaid Anti-Kickback Act.
    See Anti-Kickback statutes
Medicare Prescription Drug Improvement and
    Modernization Act, 156, 161
Medication errors
    Computerized Provider Order Entry and,
        135*t*, 137*f*
MediGap policies, 154
Mental distress, 340
Mental health incidence, 317
Mental Health Parity Act, 159
Mental models, 68
Mentoring of employees, 12
Mergers, hospital
    patient-focused care model for, 296–297
MGMA. *See* Medical Group Management Association
Midlevel practitioners, 221, 236–239
Midwives, nurse, 238–239

Military health care system
    description of, 168–173
    insureds, 174*f*
Minority ethnic populations, in United States, 316–318,
    319–320, 319*f*
Minority Health and Health Disparities Research and
    Education Act, 320
MIS. *See* Management Information System
Misfeasance, 340
Mission, Vision, and Values (MVV) statements, 83–84
Misuse of resources, 115–117
Monitoring for internal control, 363
Moral hazard, 154
Morbidity rates, 316
Mortality rates, 317
Motivation
    case studies, 401–402, 403–404, 424–426
    compensation and, 270
    definition of, 40
    emotional intelligence and, 22, 23*t*
    of employees, 40–42
    employee satisfaction and, 48–50
    of generations, 51–53
    rewards for, 40–41, 47–50
    strategies for, 50–51
    theories, 42–47, 65
    vs. engagement, 40
MMA. *See* Medicare Prescription Drug, Improvement and
    Modernization Act of 2003
MSE. *See* Medical Screening Exam
MSN. *See* Master's of Science in Nursing
Multicultural organization, 320–329
Multilingual services, 320–322, 321*t*, 327–328
MVV. *See* Mission, Vision, and Values statements
Myers-Briggs Type Indicator (MBTI), 301–302

N

NAHSE. *See* National Association of Health Services Executives
National Association of Health Services Executives
    (NAHSE), 35*t*, 323–324
National Center on Cultural Competence, 318
National Center on Minority Health and Health
    Disparities, 320
National Commission for the Protection of Human Subjects
    of Biomedical and Behavioral Research, 344
National Committee for Quality Assurance (NCQA),
    standards, 11, 322
National Council Licensure Examination (NCLEX), 227
National Council Licensure Examination-Practical Nurse
    (NCLEX-PN), 234

National Forum for Latino Healthcare Executives (NFLHE), 35*t*
National health spending, 148–149
National Institute on Minority Health and Disparities, 322
National Labor Relations Act, 259*t*, 279
National Labor Relations Board (NLRB), 279–280
National Practitioner Data Bank (NPDB), 220–221
National Residency Matching Program (NRMP), 215
National Standards on Culturally and Linguistically Appropriate Services (CLAS), 320–322, 321*t*
Native Americans, 316, 317
NCLEX. *See* National Council Licensure Examination
NCLEX-PN. *See* National Council Licensure Examination-Practical Nurse
NCQA. *See* National Committee for Quality Assurance
Needs-based motivation theories, 43–45
Negligence, 340
Negotiations case study, 405–407
Net working capital, 199
Network model HMO, 156
Never events, 11
NFLHE. *See* National Forum for Latino Healthcare Executives
Nightingale, Florence, 292
NLRB. *See* National Labor Relations Board
Non-criteria-based capital budgeting, 208
Nonfeasance, 340
Nonmaleficence, 344–345
NOPP. *See* Health Insurance Portability and Accountability Act, Notice of Privacy Practice (NOPP)
Norming, of teams, 298
Not covered or uncompensated care, 177, 195
Not-for-profit healthcare organizations
    business-oriented, tax status, 187–188, 189*t*
    charity care, 195
    financial goals of, 188
    government-owned, tax status, 188, 189*t*
    tax status, 187–188, 189*t*
    vs. for-profit organizations, 187–188, 189*t*
NPDB. *See* National Practitioner Data Bank
NPs. *See* Nurse practitioners
NRMP. *See* National Residency Matching Program
NRPs. *See* Nurse residency programs
Nurse practitioners (NPs), 237
Nurse residency programs (NRPs), 228
Nurses
    advanced practice or APNs, 237–239
    foreign educated, 233
    Licensed Practical or LPNs, 234
    Licensed Vocational or LVNs, 234
    Midlevel practitioners, 239–239
    Registered (*See* Registered nurses)
Nurses' aides, 234–236
    training, 235
    turnover, 235
Nursing/clinical documentation system, 135*t*
Nursing education, outside the U.S., 233
Nursing profession, development of, 292
Nursing school curriculum, 226–227
Nursing specialties, 231–232
Nursing staff
    patient-to-nurse ratios, 229
    retention, strategies for, 228–229
    shortages, 227, 233
    turnover, 228–229, 235, 291, 295–296

O
OBRA. *See* Omnibus Reconciliation Act
Obstetricians
    Occupational safety and health, 273
Occupational Safety and Health Act, 259*t*
Office of Inspector General (OIG), 354, 362
Office of Minority Health, 318, 320, 321*t*
OIG. *See* Office of Inspector General
Omnibus Reconciliation Act (OBRA), 160, 166, 193
Open-panel health maintenance organizations, 155
Operating budget, 206
Operation Restore Trust (ORT), 353, 355
Opportunity costs, 296
OPPS. *See* Outpatient Prospective Payment System
Organization chart, example of, 7*t*
Organizational
    dashboard or scorecard, 89, 90*f*
    diversity as a business strategy, 325
    ethical responsibility
        to employees, 346
        to patients, 345–347
    governance, 188–198
    hierarchy, 8–9
    level management, 9
    performance, 10–11, 251–252, 255–256, 256–257
    performance measurement, 11
    policies/procedures, 225–226
    volume forecast, 84
Organizational buyer behavior, 105–106
Organizational behavior, 57–73
    definition of, 58
    influence of thinking on, 60–61
    as interdisciplinary field, 58
    issues in health organizations, 59–60

Organizational culture, diversity in, 324–325

Organize, in FOCUS-PDCA framework, 124

Orientation, employee, 265–266

ORT. *See* Operation Restore Trust

Ouchi's Theory Z, 46

Out-of-pocket expenditures, for healthcare, 149, 150, 152, 153

Outcomes, as elements in quality, 114

Outpatient Prospective Payment System (OPPS), 160, 195

Overuse of resources, 115–117

P

Pacesetting style of leadership, 26, 26*t*

PACs. *See* Picture Archive Communication Systems

Paid-time-off (PTO), 271

Pareto chart, 128

Participative style of leadership, 26, 26*t*

PAs. *See* Physician assistants

PAS. *See* Physician-Assisted Suicide

Path-Goal Theory of Leadership, 21, 23*t*

Patient accounts. *See* Accounts receivable

Patient Advocate Office, 348

Patient care delivery, appropriate, 202

Patient-centered care, 322

Patient-centered care model

    collaborative practice, 229

    multilingual services, 327–328

    team communication and, 304–305

Patient consent, 343, 347

Patient dumping, 357

Patient-focused care model, teams in, 296–297

Patient "handoff" protocols, 216

Patient information, privacy of, 139–140, 143

Patient mix, 208

Patient Protection and Affordable Care Act, 13, 36, 348, 349

    funding for fraud and abuse, 354

    impact on financial management, 209

    individual mandate, 151, 161, 177

    legislation, 151, 161–162, 165, 159*t*

    reimbursement of Medicare and Medicaid, 193

    tort reform, 340

    uninsured and, 178

Patient responsibility, 345–347

Patient rights, legal aspects of, 345–347

Patient safety, 229–231

Patient self-determination, 345, 346–347

Patient-to-nurse ratios, 229

Patient transfer requirements under EMTALA, 358

Pay-for-performance (PFP) programs, 191, 269–270

PCPs. *See* Primary care physicians

PDCA (Plan-Do-Check-Act) cycle model, 117, 123–124

Precedent, 338

Perception

    definition of, 63

    sensemaking and, 68–69

    systematic errors of, 63–64

Per diagnosis payments, 192

Per diem payments, 191

Performance improvement, 113–129 (*See also* Continuous Quality Improvement)

Performance appraisal systems, 274–279, 276*f*, 277*f*

Performing, of teams, 298

Personnel. *See* Employees and Human Resources

PFP programs. *See* Pay-for-performance programs

Pharmacy tracking system, 135*t*

PHI. *See* Protected Health Information

Physician assistants (PAs), 214, 239, 224, 239

Physician-Assisted Suicide, 349

Physician practice

    EMR adoption in, 139

Physicians

    and advanced Practice Nurses, 237

    alignment with hospitals, 293–294

    board certified, 217

    board eligible, 217–218

    cognitive biases of, 63–64

    competencies, 217–218

    credential verification, 220–221

    credentialing of, 217–218

    criminal background checks, 217

    educational requirements, 215–216

    failure to embrace teamwork, 293

    gap between educational and employment placements, 220

    International Medical Graduates (IMGs), 221–223

    licensure requirements, 216–217

    number of, 214

    as patient advocates, 346, 348

    premedical programs for, 214

    primary care, 222–223

    privileges, 218–219

    problem behaviors, 230, 293

    referrals, Stark laws I and II, 360–362

    reimbursements to, 194

    relationship with nurses, 229–230

    residency training programs for, 215–216

    resistance to acknowledge nurses as professionals, 230

    review of credentials, 218–221

    supply of, 221–223

Physician Self-Referral laws, 360–362, 360*t*

Picture Archive Communication Systems (PACs), 82, 135*t*

Pillars of excellence, 10
Plan-Do-Check-Act (PDCA) cycle model, 117, 123–124
Planning, in FOCUS-PDCA framework, 124
Point-of-service plans (POSs), 149, 156, 157*t*, 158*t*, 175*t*
Population projections, 319–320, 319*f*
Position descriptions, 261, 262*f*
POSs. *See* Point-of-service plans
PPOs. *See* Preferred Provider Organizations
PPS. *See* Prospective payment system
Preauthorization, 155
Preconceptions, 63–64
Preemption, 338
Pre-existing condition, 154, 159, 162
Preferred Provider Organizations (PPOs)
    characteristics of, 156, 157*t*, 158*t*
    enrollment, 158*t*
    TRICARE Extra, 168–169
Pregnancy Discrimination Act, 259*t*
Prejudices, 334
Prepayment, of health insurance coverage, 152, 155
Prices
    determinants of, 199
    published, 198–199
    setting, 198–199
    vs. charges, 198–199
Pricing tactics, 199
Primary care physicians (PCPs)
    employment of, 223–224
    IMGs, 222
    turnover of, 224–225
PRIME, 168–169, 169*t*
Privacy, of healthcare data, 139–140
Privileged health information, 140, 142, 143
Probationary period, 277–278
Problems
    in healthcare management, tame vs. wicked, 299–300
    identification, 124
    problem solving, 70–73
    in teams, 307
Process elements, in quality, 114
Process variation, 116, 117–118, 120–121, 125
Professional associations, 34–35, 35*t*
Professional charges, 198–199
Professional development, 12, 33–36
Professionalism, 28–29
Profitability, improvement of, 202
Proposal reviewers, for capital budget, 208
Prospective payment system (PPS), 77, 160
Prospective reimbursements, 191–192, 194–195
Protected Health Information (PHI), privacy rule, 140, 143

Provider's Guide to Quality and Culture, 323
Psychiatric health aides, 234–236
PTO. *See* Paid-time-off

Q
Quality, healthcare, 114–115
    components of, 114
    CQI (*See* Continuous quality improvement)
    definition of, 114–115
    fundamental questions, 115
    importance of, 115–117
    problems misuse, overuse and underuse, 115–117
    systems perspective, 118–120
Quality improvement
    case studies, 418–419, 421–423, 462–467
    key concepts, 120–122
    measurement, 120–121
    models
        CQI, 122–123 (*See also* Continuous quality improvement)
        Six Sigma, 124–125
    process variation, 121–122
    statistical process control, 121–122
    system thinking and, 118–120
    teams, 125, 291
    tools, 125–128, 127*f*, 128*f*, 129*f*
Qui tam provision, 355

R
RAC. *See* Recovery Audit Contractors
Racial groups
    uninsured population and, 175–176, 176*f*
    in U.S. population, 316–318, 319–320, 319*f*
Radiology tracking system, 135*t*
Rate setting, 198–199
Rationing, 347
RBRVS. *See* Resource-Based Relative Value System
Recovery Audit Contractors (RAC), 354, 355–356
Recruiters, 263–264
Recruitment, 256, 261–265, 263*t*
    advertising methods for, 263–264
    responsibilities for, 261, 263, 263*t*
Referrals, patient
    Anti-Kickback statutes, 360–362
    safe harbor regulations, 360–361
    Stark Laws I and II, 360, 360*t*
Registered nurses (RNs), 226–233
    board certification, 231–232
    burnout, 246
    continuing education for, 232
    criminal background checks, 227

educational requirements for, 226–227
foreign educated, 233
job dissatisfaction, 228–229, 231
job satisfaction, organizational climate and, 229–231
licensure, 227
new, concerns of, 229–231
number of, 214,
relationship with physicians, 228–229
specialties for, 232
turnover, 228–229
unionization, 279
Regulations. *See* Rules and regulations
Rehabilitation Act, 259*t*
Reimbursement,
based on performance, 191
concerns about, 253–254, 254*t*
of physicians, 194
prospective, 191–192
of providers, 190–195
retrospective, 191
by uninsured individuals, 195
Relator (whistle blower), 266, 355
Reliability, 121
Residency training programs, for physicians, 215–216
Resource-Based Relative Value System (RBRVS), 160, 194
Resource allocation
in marketing, 103–104
in strategic planning, 78, 87
Resources
allocation, 348
allocation of, strategic planning and, 78
misuse of, 115, 116
overuse of, 115, 116
underuse of, 115, 116
Resource Utilization Groups (RUGs), 160, 192, 194
Respect for persons, 345
Respectful guardianship, 344
Respiratory therapists (RTs), 241
Respondeat superior, 340
Retention, employee, 256
benefits and, 270–273
compensation for, 268–270
Employee Assistance Programs and, 273–274
employee suggestion programs and, 282
labor relations management and, 279–281
nurses, 228–229
Retirement benefits, 272
Retrospective reimbursements, 191

Revenue budget, 207
Rewards
definition of, 40–41
for desired behavior, 50
extrinsic, 41, 47, 49
intrinsic, 40, 45–46, 48–49
tailored, 49–51
Risk assessment, for internal control, 363
Risk sharing, 150
Roe v. Wade, 349
RTs. *See* Respiratory therapists
RUGs. *See* Resource Utilization Groups
Rules and regulations, 339

S
Safe harbor laws, 360, 361–362
Sarbanes-Oxley, 30
Schemas, 66–67
Schiavo, Terri, 336
Scientific Management Theory, 46
Security, of healthcare data, 139–140
Segmentation in marketing, 103–105, 104*t*
Selection of quality improvement plan, in FOCUS-PDCA framework, 124
Self-Actualized Leadership Theory, 22, 23*t*
Self-awareness, 22, 23*t*
Self-funded health plan, 159
Self management, 8, 22
Self-regulation, 22, 23*t*
Sensemaking, 68–69, 73
Sentinel events, 229, 230
Servant leadership, 24–25
Service connected conditions, veterans and, 170, 170*t*
Service line
approach, to teamwork, 209, 291, 294, 295
management model, 6–8
Services, upcoding, 354
Sexual harassment case study, 414–417
Sherman Antitrust Act, 359, 359*t*
Shewhart, Walter A., 117
Shewhart cycle, 117–118
Shortages, of healthcare personnel, 222–223, 241, 254, 254*t*
Sick leave benefits, 271
Simplifications, cognitive, 66–67
Situational approach to leadership, 21, 23*t*
Six Sigma, 124–125
Skill sets, 5
Skinner's Reinforcement Theory, 45
Social awareness, 303–304
Social facility, 303–304

Social health insurance. *See* Medicaid; Medicare
Social insurance
    evolution, 159–162
    Medicaid, 165–168, 167*f*
    Medicare, 162–165, 163*f*, 164*f*
    TRICARE, 168–169, 169*t*
Social intelligence, 303–304
Socialized medicine, 151
Social loafer syndrome, 306
Social marketing, 97–98
Social Security Act (SSA), Amendments of 1965, 159
Social Security Act (SSA), Criminal-Disclosure Provision of,
        356–367
Social skills, 22, 23*t*
SPC. *See* Statistical process control
"Special cause" variation, 117, 121–123
Specific identification, for valuing inventory, 203
Spina Bifida Healthcare Program, for Vietnam veterans,
        172–173
Spirituality leadership, 25, 25*t*
SSA. *See* Social Security Act
Staffing needs, 260–261
Staff model health maintenance organizations (HMOs), 156
Staff training, cultural competency and, 326–327
Standard of care, 340
Stark Laws I and II, 360, 360*t*, 361, 362
State Boards of Physician Quality Assurance (BPQA), 216
Statements of Antitrust Enforcement Policy In
        Health Care, 359
Statistical process control (SPC), 120–122
Statistics budget, 207
Statutes, 339
Storming, of teams, 298
Strategic marketing
    components, 100–101, 101*f*
    defined, 95–96
    management of, 102–105
    process, 100–103, 102*f*
Strategic planning, 77–91
    case studies, 408, 439–440
    Continuous Quality Improvement, 119, 119*f*
    definition of, 77
    diversity initiatives, 324
    execution, 79*f*, 90–92
    financial forecasts, 84–85
    in health care, history of, 77–78
    healthcare manager role in, 92
    implementation of plan, 79*f*, 88–89
    importance of, 78
    market assessment, 80–86

    mission, vision, and values (MVV), 83–84
    monitoring and control, 89–90, 90*f*
    organizational assessment, 84–86
    participants, 91–92
    process, 78–83, 79*f*
    in quality improvement, 119, 119*f*
    supporting plans for, 88–89
    SWOT Analysis, 80–83
    workforce cultural competence strategy, 325
Strategy
    execution, 79*f*, 90–92
    identification and selection, 79, 86–88, *t*87
    purpose of, 78
    resource allocation and, 78
    rollout of plan, 79*f*, 88–89
    tactical plans, 79, 88–89, 88*t*, 89*f*
Strict liability, 361
Strengths, Weaknesses, Opportunities, Threats.
        See SWOT Analysis
Stroke incidence, 317
Structural elements in quality, 114
Structured interviews, 265
Style approach to leadership, 20–23*t*
Succession planning, 12, 35–36, 281–282
Suicide incidence, 317
Supply chain management, 202
Surrogate decision makers, 345, 348
SWOT Analysis,
    components, 79–83, 79*f*, 80*f*, 86
    in marketing management, 102
    purpose, 79
Systems perspective, of healthcare quality, 114, 119,
        125, 129
Systems thinking, 70, 78
    in health information systems, 139–141
    in quality improvement, 118–120

T
Tame problems, 299
Task forces, 292
Tax Equity and Fiscal Responsibility Act (TEFRA),
        160, 193
Tax Relief and Healthcare Act of 2006, 354
Tax status, of healthcare organization, 187–188, 189*t*
Teams
    benefits of, 294–296
    communication in, 304–305, 305–306
    composition of, 301
    conflict resolution in, 306–307
    convening, 301

definition of, 290–305
diversity of, 304
effectiveness of, 295, 305–306
interdisciplinary, 290, 293
leadership of, 23*t*, 305–307
management of, 6, 8–9, 294, 305–307
members
    personalities of, 301–302
    selection of, 300–302
with minimal interpersonal conflict, 305
in patient-focused care model, 304–305
of physicians and nurses, 229–231
purpose of, 317
in quality improvement, 125
stages of, 298
trust building for, 294
Teamwork, 289–308
case study, 392–393, 424–426, 433–436, 437–438,
    452–453, 454–456
challenges for healthcare organizations, 292–294
costs of, 296, 298
in FOCUS-PDCA framework, 124, 125
Guidelines for Teamwork, 306, 306*f*
problems, 299–300
real-world focus of, 299–300
requirements for, 290
service line approach, 209, 291, 294, 295
TEFRA. *See* Tax Equity and Fiscal Responsibility Act
Termination, employee, 278–279
Theory X and Theory Y, 46, 62–63
Theory Z, 46, 62–63
Thinking
    in communication, 71–72
    influence on organizational behavior, 60–69
    mental models and, 58
    in problem solving, 70–73
    schemas and, 66–67
    sensemaking and, 68–69
Third-party mediation, for teams, 307
Third-party payers
    policies, in setting charges and prices,
        192–195, 198
    reimbursement by, 190–195
    relationships/contracts with, 193–195
    relationships with, 193–195
360-degree performance appraisal systems, 278
Tobert's Action Inquiry, 72
To Err is Human (Institute of Medicine report), 113
Tort law, 340–342
    vs.contract law, 342, 343*t*

Torts
    assault and battery, 340
    defamation, 341
    definition, 339
    false imprisonment, 341
    intentional, 340, 341
    invasion of privacy, 341
    malpractice, 341–342
    negligence, 339
Total Quality Management (TQM), 21–22, 117–118. *See
    also* Continuous quality improvement
TQM. *See* Total Quality Management
Training, employee, 267–268, 364*t*
Transformational leader, 21, 23*t*
Treasurer, 190
TRICARE plan, 168—169, 169*t*
Trust building, for teams, 294
Truth-telling, 344
Turnover
    costs of, 224, 228, 296
    healthcare workers, 254
    nurses, 228–229, 231
    physicians, 224–225
    staff, 254

U

Uncompensated care, 177, 195
Underserved
    health problems of, 316–317
    populations, 315–320
Understand, in FOCUS-PDCA framework, 124
Underuse of resources, 115–117
Uninsured individuals, provider reimbursements, 195
Uninsured population
    addressing problem of, 177
    by age group, 176–177, 176*f*
    characteristics of, 175–177, 176*f*
    myths about, 177, 178*t*
    by racial group, 176, 176*f*
Unions, 279–281
Unit management, 8–11
Upcoding, 354
U.S. Constitution, 338, 341
U.S. population, racial groups in, 319–320, 319*f*

V

Vacation benefits, 271
Validity, 121
Values statement, 83
Valuing inventory, methods for, 203

Variation in medical practice, 116
Veteran Integrated Service Networks (VISN), 170
Veterans Health Administration (VHA)
    CHAMPVA program, 168, 172
    enrollment categories170, 170*t*
    financing for, 173
    performance, vs. non VA programs, 171, 171*t*–172*t*
    population demographics, 173*f*
    problems of, 169–170
    Veteran Integrated Service Networks, 170
    Vietnam Veterans and, 172–173
    Vietnam Veterans, healthcare programs for, 172–173
VHA. *See* Veterans Health Administration (VHA)
Vision statement, 83
VISN. *See* Veteran Integrated Service Networks
Voting, in teams, 307
Vroom's Expectancy Theory, 46, 65
Vulnerable population groups, culturally-sensitive care and, 329

W

Weighted average, for valuing inventory, 203, 205*t*
Welfare magnets, 165
Whistleblower Protection Act, 259*t*, 266

Whistle blower (relator), 355
Wicked problems, 299–300
Wickline v. California, 348
Worker Adjustment and Retraining Notification
    Act, 259*t*
Worker's compensation coverage, 273
Workflow diagrams, 126, 127*f*
Workforce issues, 251–282
    diversity strategies, 323–325
    planning/recruitment, 257–266, 257*t*,
        262*f*, 263*t*
    retention, 257–258, 257*t*, 266–282,
        276*f*, 277*f*
    retirement, 255
    supply, 254
Work-hour rules, residents, 215–216
Working capital
    definition of, 199
    management
        problems/concerns for, 200
        purposes of, 200
    sources of, 199
Worklife analysis, 235–236